W9-CAR-506

# COMPILER CONSTRUCTION FOR DIGITAL COMPUTERS

# COMPILER CONSTRUCTION FOR DIGITAL COMPUTERS

**David Gries**
**Cornell University**

**John Wiley & Sons, Inc.**
**New York • London • Sydney • Toronto**

Library of Congress Catalogue Card Number: 74-152496

ISBN 0-471-32776-X

Printed in the United States of America.

19 18 17 16 15 14 13 12

**To My Wife**

# Preface

Compilers and interpreters are a necessary part of any computer system -- without them, we would all be programming in assembly language or even machine language! This has made compiler construction an important, practical area of research in computer science. The object of this book is to present in a coherent fashion the major techniques used in compiler writing, in order to make it easier for the novice to enter the field and for the expert to reference the literature.

This book is oriented towards so-called syntax-directed methods of compiling. In fact, over one third of the book is devoted to the subject of formal language theory and automatic syntax recognition. I feel very strongly that anybody involved in compiler writing should have a basic knowledge of the subject. This does not mean that every compiler should be written using automatic syntax methods. There are many programming languages where these methods are not suitable. But a basic knowledge of formal language theory will give the compiler writer more insight into what is happening inside his compiler, and should help him design and program more systematically and efficiently.

Syntax analysis, however, is only a small part of compiler construction, and I have included chapters on all the major topics -- symbol table organization, error recovery, code generation, code optimization, and so forth. Several topics (e.g. conversion of constants, incremental compilers) have been omitted in order to keep the size of the book reasonable.

The book is meant to serve two needs; it can be used as a self-study and reference book for the professional programmer interested in or involved in compiler construction, and as a text in a one-semester course in compiler writing. In fact, the book covers all the topics (and more) listed for the course I5 (Compiler Construction) recommended by the ACM curriculum committee in the March 1968 issue of the *Communications of the ACM*.

The reader should have at least one year of experience programming in a high-level language (eg. FORTRAN, ALGOL, PL/I), and in an assembly language, and should be able to read and understand ALGOL programs. In some parts, elementary Boolean matrix theory is assumed (with a short introduction).

It is assumed the reader knows what a set is, what the union of two sets is, and so on. Beyond this, the reader should have the mathematical experience of, say, a sophomore or junior math major.

The need for experience with a high-level language is obvious; the book is about translating programs written in such languages. Experience with an assembly language is similarly necessary. Assembly language experience is more important, however, for the maturity and understanding of how computers work that it provides. Actually, we will have little to do with any specific assembly language. The few IBM 360 assembly language programs scattered throughout the book can be skipped over without loss of understanding.

A compiler is just a program written in some language. Hence, examples of parts of compilers must be given in some programming language, and I have chosen an ALGOL-like language for its readability. The examples are usually very short, so that they can be followed easily. Where too much detail will cause us to lose sight of the problem at hand, I have taken the liberty to write English instead of ALGOL. I have checked these program segments quite carefully by hand, but the reader is warned that they have not all been debugged on a computer!

A brief description of the bastard ALGOL used appears in the appendix. This description is short and relies heavily on a knowledge of ALGOL. Should the reader not be familiar with ALGOL and syntax descriptions of languages, it is suggested that he wait until after studying chapter 2 to read the appendix.

There is more material than can usually be covered in a one-semester course. The following minimum set is suggested:

Chapter 1. Introduction
Chapter 2. Grammars and languages; omit section 7
Chapter 3. Scanners; omit sections 4,5,6
Chapter 4. Top-down parsing; especially section 3
Chapter 5. Simple precedence grammars
Chapter 8. Runtime storage organization; omit sections 6 and 9
Chapter 9. Organizing symbol tables
Chapter 10. The data in the symbol table; omit section 2
Chapter 11. Internal forms of the source program; omit sections 4,5
Chapter 12. Introduction to semantic routines
Chapter 13. Semantic routines for ALGOL-like constructs; omit section 6
Chapter 14. Allocation of storage to runtime variables; omit section 3
Chapter 16. Interpreters
Chapter 22. Hints to the compiler writer

You will notice that I emphasize the simple precedence technique for syntax analysis. This is not because it is the best (it is probably the worst), but it is the easiest to teach. Should more time be available, the instructor is encouraged to add his favorite bottom-up syntax method: operator precedence (section 6.1), higher order precedence (section 6.2), transition matrices (section 6.4), production language (chapter 7), or any other not covered.

The order of presentation may also be changed. In fact, when teaching a course, it is best to break up the study of syntax theory with some practical material. Chapter 8 on runtime storage administration is independent, while chapters 9, 10, 11, and 16 on symbol tables, internal source program forms, and interpreters can be studied in that order at any time.

Chapter 21 deserves special mention. It is a collection of assorted facts and opinions that a compiler writer should be familiar with. They don't belong anywhere else, or are two important to be buried in some other chapter. The reader should browse through this chapter from time to time and read the sections of current interest.

A compiler-writing course should be a laboratory course. Students should write and debug a compiler or interpreter for some simple language, in groups of one to three people. Only then will they really understand what goes into a compiler. An interpreter is best, since the students don't have to worry about messy machine language details; the ideas are important, not the details. Following this line, the whole project should be programmed in a high-level language. My experience is that PL/I or an ALGOL-like language is better than FORTRAN. Compilers in FORTRAN tend to be larger and much more difficult to read. A translator writing system should be used if available.

To produce some variability and creativity, start with a basic, simple language containing integer variables, assignment statements, expressions, labels and branches, conditional statements, and finally simple read and write statements. Then let each group extend it by adding one or two features. Examples are arrays, records (structures), different data types, block structure, procedures, macros, and iterative statements.

The compiler can be written and checked out in stages as the course progresses. First the scanner, then the syntax analyzer, then the symbol table routines, and finally the semantic routines. The interpreter itself can be designed and implemented as soon as the chapters dealing with it have been covered. In this way, the work is spread out evenly throughout the semester, and is not bunched up at the end.

Most references to publications are given in a section at the end of each chapter, although some occur within other sections. The appearance of a name of a person is automatically a reference to a publication listed in the bibliography. This bibliography is in alphabetical order by author, and within each author it is arranged chronologically. If a person has more than one publication the reference will appear in the form <name>(<year>), where the year refers to the year of publication. An example is Gries(68). Should an author have more than one publication in one year, the first listed in that year is referenced by (<year>a), the second by (<year>b), and so on. Thus Floyd(64b) refers to Floyd's paper on the syntax of programming languages.

Except for headings and some figures, these notes were produced on the IBM 360/65, using a program called FORMAT written by Gerald M. Berns(69). The author is also indebted to John Ehrman, who made several important changes and additions to the program. The use of FORMAT made it easier to edit the original material and distribute it to students at various stages. However, it forced me to deviate somewhat from conventional notation. The two main changes are the following. The printer chain which printed the book has no subscripts and no superscripts (except for $^0$ through $^9$). Exponentiation is therefore written using the operator !. That is, c!b means c to the bth power. The lack of subscripts forced me to write a sequence of n symbols as S[1], S[2], ..., S[n]. Where its meaning is obvious, we write this simply as S1, S2, ..., Sn.

Sections of this book originated as lecture notes in compiler writing courses at Stanford and Cornell, and I have had the opportunity to use the notes in revised form in short courses at the Michigan Summer School at Ann Arbor, Cornell, and the 1970 International Seminar in Advanced Programming Systems in Israel. I am indebted to the students in these courses for their critical comments on these notes. I have had helpful advice from a number of people; among them are Richard Conway, Jerry Feldman, John Reynolds, Bob Rosin, and Alan Shaw. My sincere appreciation goes to Steve Brown, who read the manuscript carefully and thoroughly, found many mistakes, and gave valuable comments and criticisms. Finally, I would like to thank my wife, who showed amazing patience and understanding while I was writing this book.

# Table of Contents

# COMPILER CONSTRUCTION FOR DIGITAL COMPUTERS

# Chapter 1.
# Introduction

## 1.1 COMPILERS, ASSEMBLERS, INTERPRETERS

A _translator_ is a program which translates a _source program_ into an equivalent _object program_. The source program is written in a _source language_, the object program is a member of the _object language_. The execution of the translator itself occurs at _translation time_.

If the source language is a high-level language like FORTRAN, ALGOL, or COBOL, and if the object language is the assembly language or machine language of some computer, the translator is called a _compiler_. Machine language is sometimes called _code_; hence the object program is sometimes called the _object code_. The translation of the source program into the object program occurs at _compile-time_; the actual execution of the object program at _runtime_.

An _assembler_ is a program which translates a source program written in assembly language into the machine language of a computer. Assembly language is quite close to machine language; indeed, most assembly language statements are just symbolic representations of machine language statements. Moreover, assembler statements usually have a fixed format, which makes it easier to analyze them. There are usually no nested statements, blocks, and so forth.

An _interpreter_ for a source language accepts a source program written in that language as input and executes it. The difference between a compiler and an interpreter is that the interpreter does not produce an object program to be executed; it executes the source program itself.

A pure interpreter will analyze a source program statement _each_ time it is to be executed in order to discover how to perform the execution. This of course is very inefficient and is not used very often. The usual method is to program the interpreter in two phases. The first analyzes the complete source program, much the way a compiler does, and translates it into an internal form. The second phase then interprets or executes this internal form of the source program. The internal form is designed to minimize the time needed to "decode" or analyze each statement in order to execute it.

As explained earlier, a compiler is itself just a program written in some language -- its input is a source program and its output is an equivalent object program. Historically, compilers were written in the assembly language of the computer at hand. In many cases this was the only language available! The trend is, however, to write compilers in high-level languages, because of the reduced amount of programming time and debugging time, and the readability of the compiler when finished. We also find many languages designed expressly for compiler writing. These so-called "compiler-compilers" are a subset of the "translator writing systems" (TWS); we discuss these briefly in chapter 20.

This book serves to introduce you to compiler construction. The problems of interpreters will also be discussed; this will add comparatively little to the book since most techniques used in compiler construction are also used in writing interpreters. We will not discuss assemblers, but anyone who understands compiler construction should have no trouble understanding what an assembler does and how it performs its job.

You will not find a complete compiler anywhere in this book. The idea is not to see how I write one particular compiler, but to learn how to write your own. You will of course find examples and discussions of many (but of course not all - I do not even presume to say most) of the techniques and methods used in compiler construction. Examples will be programmed in a bastard ALGOL language, a brief description of which appears in the appendix. If you are using this book as a text in a course, hopefully you will write your own compiler or interpreter in ALGOL, FORTRAN, PL/1 or other high-level language; this is the best way to learn about compiler construction.

## 1.2 A BRIEF LOOK AT THE COMPILATION PROCESS

A compiler must perform an analysis of the source program and then a synthesis of the object program. First decompose the source program into its basic parts; then build equivalent object program parts from them. In order to do this, the compiler builds several tables during the analysis phase which are used during both analysis and synthesis. Figure 1.1 shows the whole process in more detail; dotted arrows represent flow of information, while solid arrows indicate program flow. Let us briefly describe the different parts of a compiler.

### Tables of Information

As a program is analyzed, information is obtained from declarations, procedure headings, for-loops, and so forth, and saved for later use. This information is detected at a local level and collected so that we have access to it from all parts of the compiler. For example, it is necessary to know with each use of an identifier how that identifier was declared and used elsewhere. Exactly what must be saved depends of course upon the source language, the object language, and how sophisticated the compiler is. But every compiler uses a symbol table (sometimes called an identifier list or name table) in one form or another. This is a table of the identifiers used in the source program, together with their attributes. The attributes are the type of the identifier, its object program address, and any other information about it which is needed to generate code.

What other information must be collected? We will most likely need a table of constants used in the source program. This table will include the constant itself and the object program address assigned to it. We may also need a table of for-loops showing the nesting structure and the loop variables, information about FORTRAN-like EQUIVALENCE statements, and a list of the object program sizes of each procedure being compiled. When designing a compiler, one cannot determine the form and content of the information to be collected until the object code for each source program statement and the synthesis part of the compiler have been thought out in some detail. Much depends on how much code optimization is going to be performed.

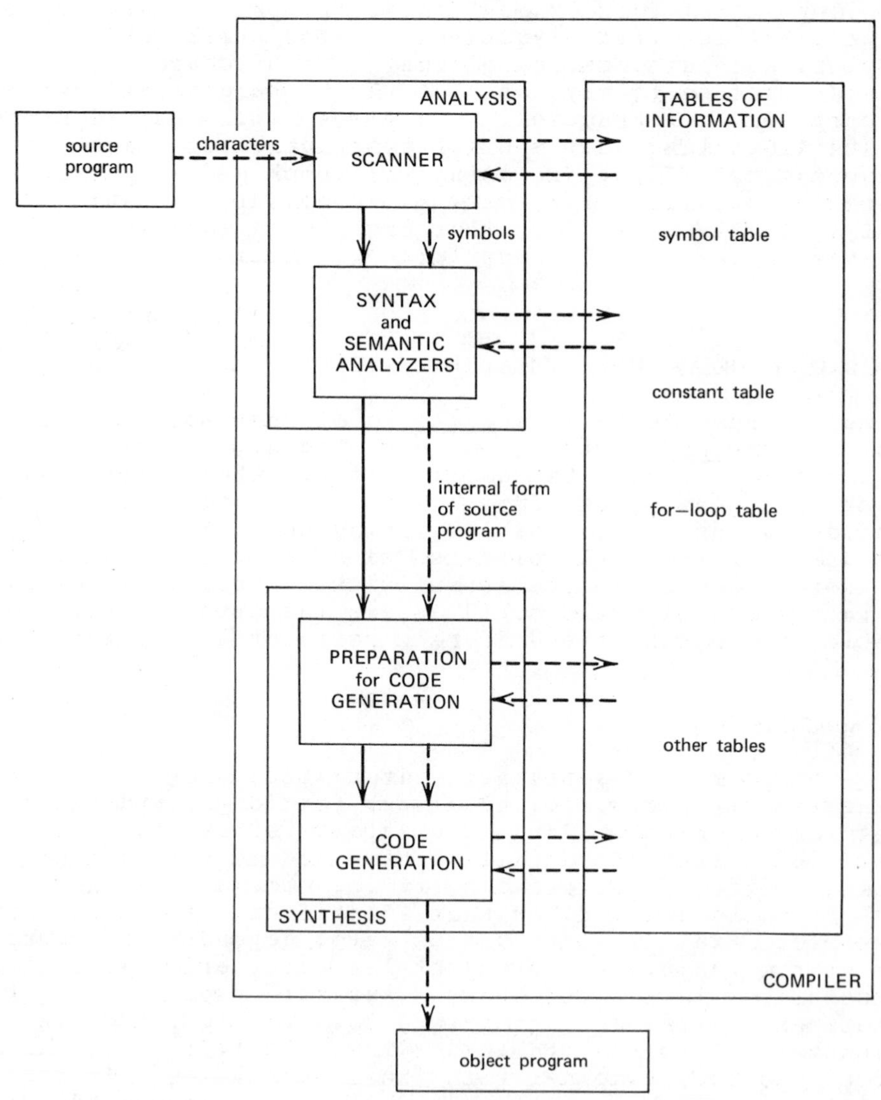


**FIGURE 1.1. Logical Parts of a Compiler.**

**The Scanner**

The scanner -- the simplest part of the compiler -- is sometimes called a _lexical analyzer_. It scans the characters of the source program from left to right and builds the actual _symbols_ of the program -- integers, identifiers, reserved words, two-character symbols like ** and //, and so forth. (In the literature, the terms _token_ and _atom_ are sometimes used for _symbol_.) These symbols are then passed on to the actual analyzer. Comments can be deleted. The scanner may also put the identifiers into the symbol table and perform other simple tasks that can be done without really analyzing the source program. It can do most of the macro processing for macros which allow only a textual substitution.

The symbols are usually passed by the scanner to the analyzer itself in an internal form. Each delimiter (reserved word, operator or punctuation mark) will be represented by an integer. An identifier or constant can be represented by a pair of numbers. The first, different from any integer representing a delimiter, will indicate "identifier" or "constant"; the second will give the address or index of the identifier or constant in some table. This allows the rest of the compiler to operate in an efficient manner with fixed-length symbols rather than variable length strings of characters.

**The Syntax and Semantic Analyzers**

These analyzers do the actual hard work of disassembling the source program into its constituent parts, building the internal form of the program and putting information into the symbol table and other tables. A complete syntax and semantic check of the program is also performed.

The standard analyzers are controlled by the syntax of the program. In fact the trend has been to separate the syntax from semantics as much as possible. When the syntax analyzer (parser) recognizes a source language construct it calls a so-called _semantic procedure_ or _semantic routine_ which takes the construct, checks it for semantic correctness, and stores necessary information about it into the symbol table or the internal form of the program. For example, when a simple declaration is recognized, a semantic routine will check the declared identifiers to make sure they have not been declared twice and will add them to the symbol table with the declared attributes. When an assignment statement of the form

<variable> := <expression>

is recognized, a semantic routine will check the <variable> and <expression> for type compatibility and will then put the assignment statement into the internal program.

### The Internal Source Program

The internal representation of the source program depends largely on how it is to be manipulated later. It may be a tree representing the syntax of the source program. It may be the source program in something called Polish notation. Another form used is a list of (operator, operand, operand, result) quadruples, in the order in which they are to be executed. For example, the assignment statement "A = B + C * D" would appear as

```
*, C, D, T1
+, B, T1,T2
=, T2, A,
```

where T1 and T2 are temporary variables created by the compiler. The operands in the above example would not be the symbolic names themselves, but pointers to (or indexes to) the symbol table elements which describe the operands.

### Preparation for Code Generation

Before code can be generated, it is generally necessary to manipulate and change the internal program in some way. Runtime storage must be allocated to variables. In FORTRAN, COMMON and EQUIVALENCE statements must be processed. One important point included here is the <u>optimization</u> of the program in order to reduce the execution time of the object program.

### Code Generation

This is the actual translation of the internal source program into assembly language or machine language. This is perhaps the messiest and most detailed part, but the easiest to understand. Assuming we have an internal form of quadruples as outlined above, we generate code for each quadruple in order. For the three quadruples listed above we could generate, on the IBM 360, the assembly language

```
     L     5,C     Put C in register 5
     M     4,D     The result of the mult. is in regs. 4,5
     A     5,B     Now add B to the result of the mult.
     ST    5,A     Store the result
```

In an interpreter, this part of the compiler would be replaced by the program which actually executes (or interprets) the internal source program. The internal form for the source program in this case would not be too much different.

Figure 1.1 represents a logical connection of the compiler parts rather than a time connection. All four of the logically successive processes -- scanning, analysis, preparation for code generation and code generation -- can be performed in the order given by Figure 1.1, or they could be performed in a parallel, interlocked manner. One criterion for this is the amount of available memory. It is often advantageous or even necessary to have several passes (core loads). Hopefully in these cases the "other information" can be kept in memory to save I/O time. Other criteria are the goals of the project. How fast should the compiler itself be? How fast should the object program be? How much debugging facilities should the object program provide? Another factor is the number of people on the project. The more people, the more passes there are likely to be, so that each can be responsible for a distinct and separate part.

It is also true that not all the parts need be used. In a one-pass compiler, the internal form of the program is not necessary, while the preparation and code generation parts are fused with the semantic routines of the semantic analyzer. A typical one-pass scheme is given in Figure 1.2. The syntax analyzer calls the scanner when it needs a new symbol and calls a procedure when a construct is recognized. This procedure does semantic checking, storage allocation, and code generation for the construct before returning to the parser.

Not all languages are structured so that they can be translated by a one-pass compiler.

One may well ask where the main difficulties lie in implementing a compiler. The scanner is almost trivial and is well understood. Syntax analyzers are also fairly well understood for the simple formal languages we deal with. In fact, this part can be largely automated. (Since syntax has been formalized, much of the research in compiler writing has dealt with it instead of semantics.) The hardest and "dirtiest" parts are semantic analysis, program preparation and code generation. All three are interdependent and must be designed together to a large extent, and the design can change radically from one object program language and machine to another.

With this brief introduction we are ready to begin with our first subject - formal language theory and its application to compiler construction. If you wish (it is not necessary), glance over the next section which gives some examples of existing compilers in order to reinforce the material presented here.

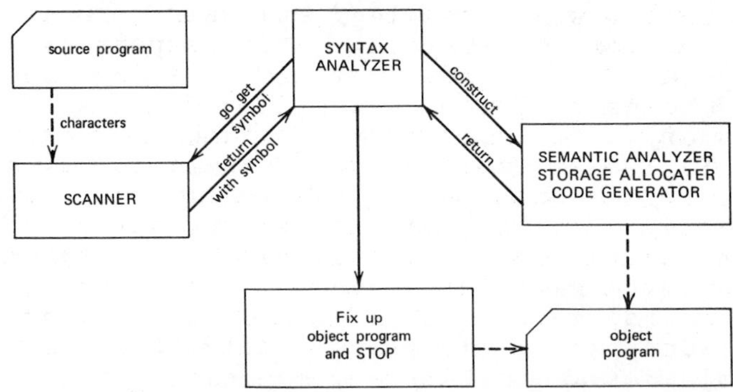


**FIGURE 1.2. A One-Pass Compiler.**

## 1.3 SOME EXAMPLES OF COMPILER STRUCTURE

We present four examples of existing compilers. We have chosen two ALGOL compilers to illustrate how radically the computer for which the compiler is constructed can affect the design. Secondly, we describe two different FORTRAN compilers for the same computer, to show how the goals of the compiler can affect the design.

### ALCOR Illinois 7090 Compiler (see Gries (65))

This is a four-pass compiler for the IBM 7090-7040 computers; the source language is ALGCL 60 with the exception of <u>own</u>. The compiler does a good job of optimizing the evaluation of subscripts within for-loops (a FORTRAN compiler described later does a more complete job of code optimization). Output is 7090 machine language in the form of a binary deck to be loaded by the system loader.

| Pass | Task |
|---|---|
| 1 | Scanner and partial syntax analysis to produce a block-structured symbol table of all identifiers. Each symbol of the program is replaced by a fixed-length integer. |
| 2 | Complete syntax and semantic analysis. Preparation for optimization of subscripted variables. Runtime storage allocation (this is actually synthesis). |
| 3 | Optimization of subscripted variables, and code generation. |
| 4 | Generation of the binary deck from the output of pass 3, and output of any error messages. |

**Gier ALGOL Compiler (see Naur (63b))**

This compiler is written for a machine with a memory of only 1024 42-bit words and a drum of 128000 words. In spite of the size of the computer the compiler still translates essentially full ALGOL. One can see why the compiler must be split into the nine passes (coreloads) given below. Passes 1 and 2 are lexical analysis, pass 3 is a syntax analysis, passes 4,5 and 6 form the semantic analysis (but note that part of the synthesis -- allocation of runtime storage -- is also done here). Passes 7 and 8 represent synthesis. Pass 9 is peculiar to this compiler and is necessary in order to create an efficient object program.

| Pass | Task |
|---|---|
| 1 | Scanner, which changes delimiters (all symbols except constants and identifiers) into an internal form. |
| 2 | Replacement of each identifier in the source program by a fixed-length integer. |
| 3 | Syntax analysis. Extra delimiters are inserted and others are changed in order to facilitate further processing. |
| 4 | Symbol table construction. For each block, the identifiers declared or specified in the block are stored in the table, together with their attributes. |
| 5 | Allocation of runtime storage to variables. In addition each identifier in the source program (represented by an integer) is replaced by four bytes which give the type and kind, block number, runtime address, and number of parameters or subscripts (where applicable) of the identifier. |
| 6 | Check of types and kinds of all identifiers and other operands. Conversion of the source program to Polish notation. |
| 7 | Code generation. |
| 8 | Final addressing of some instructions. Segmentation into drum tracks. Production of final code. |
| 9 | Rearrangement of the program segments on the tracks on the drum. |

**/360 WATFOR (see Cress et al.)**

WATFOR is a submonitor and compiler implemented on the IBM 360 for batch processing FORTRAN IV programs. Its purpose is to provide fast turn-around for normal, small to medium size FORTRAN programs with relatively little execution -- the type of programs one finds in an educational environment. To this end, the whole system resides in core, and the only input/output is the source program itself and the output it produces. The system needs a minimum of 128000 bytes (32000 words).

The compiler does no code optimization and produces a relatively inefficient object program in absolute machine language, which the system executes immediately. This is where some of the time-saving arises -- no expensive linkage editing and loading is necessary.

The compiler is essentially a one-pass compiler. The scanner translates one FORTRAN statement at a time into an internal form, determines the type of statement, and calls the appropriate semantic routine (a procedure) to process it. This routine analyzes the the syntax and semantics of the statement and generates object code for it immediately. The analysis and synthesis are performed together. In FORTRAN, runtime storage cannot be completely allocated until all COMMON and EQUIVALENCE statements have been processed. Hence the addresses in the object code are not runtime storage addresses, but pointers to the entries for the corresponding variables and temporaries in the compiler's symbol table. When the main pass is finished, a second, small pass is invoked which allocates storage to all runtime variables and then replaces each of the symbol table pointers in the object code by the appropriate runtime address.

**IBM 360 FORTRAN IV H Compiler (see IBM(a))**

The object of this compiler is to produce as efficient an object program as possible; it does an excellent job at this. Because of the code optimization, the compiler itself is very slow. The compiler has the following passes.

| Pass | Task |
|---|---|
| 1 | Scanner and syntax analysis, producing the internal source program in the form of (operator - operand) pairs and a symbol table. |
| 2 | (Actually three separate passes)<br>a) Process COMMON and EQUIVALENCE statements;<br>b) Change the internal source program into quadruples (operator, operand, operand, result);<br>c) Allocate runtime storage. |
| 3 | Code optimization<br>a) Remove redundant operations, move operations to outer loops where possible, etc.;<br>b) Runtime register assignment;<br>c) Optimization of branches. |
| 4 | Final code generation. |

# Chapter 2.
# Grammars and Languages

For the reader with no knowledge of formal language theory, this may be the hardest chapter in the book. Over 40 terms which we often use informally, like "phrase," "sentence," "language," and "ambiguity," are given precise meanings. Section 2.11 contains a list of them in order of definition. When you finish the chapter, be sure to check this list and restudy any of the definitions which are not at your fingertips. A complete understanding of the contents of this chapter will greatly simplify your reading of the rest of the book and make it more enjoyable.

## 2.1 DISCUSSION OF GRAMMARS

Consider the sentence "The big elephant ate the peanut". Our knowledge of English tells us this is a sentence of the language, and this might be shown by diagramming the sentence as in Figure 2.1.

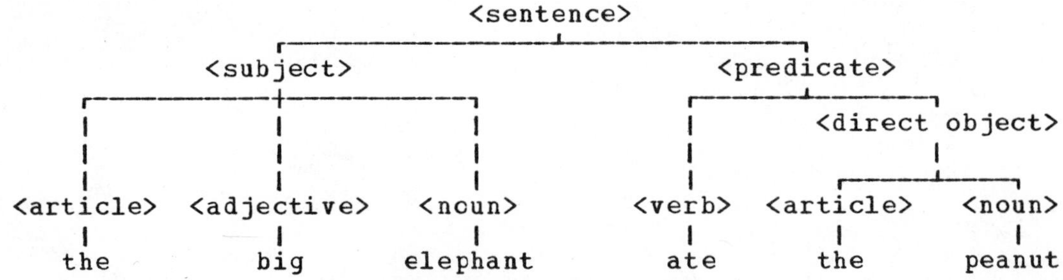


**FIGURE 2.1. A Syntax Tree.**

A sentence diagram like that of Figure 2.1 is called a <u>syntax tree</u>. It describes the syntax, or structure, of the sentence by breaking it into its constituent parts. Thus we see that the <sentence> is composed of a <subject> followed by a <predicate>, the <subject> is composed of an <article> followed by an <adjective> followed by a <noun>, and so on.

To describe this structure we have used new symbols -- the "syntactic entities" or "syntactic classes" like <sentence>. These symbols are enclosed in angular brackets "<" and ">" in order to distinguish them from the basic words of the language.

We know that the sentence "The big elephant ate the peanut" is a sentence, either intuitively or by applying <u>ad hoc</u> rules taught in grammar school; indeed, each of us could produce an informal syntax tree for any simple English sentence. However in order to mechanically decompose sentences we must give formal, precise rules which indicate their structure. For this purpose we will design a <u>metalanguage</u> -- a language in which we can describe other languages. In French courses, English is often used to describe the French language to the students. Hence English is being used as a metalanguage. In English classes, English is used as a metalanguage to describe itself.

We are at this point mainly interested in describing the *syntax* (structure) of programming languages, and not their *semantics* (meaning); diagrams such as Figure 2.1 convey no meaning. Such a syntactic description we call a *grammar*.

The metalanguage we will use was first proposed by Noam Chomsky(56) in an attempt to describe natural languages. The particular notation we use is due to John Backus(59). As Chomsky mentions, the metalanguage is only useful for describing small subsets consisting of simple sentences, and the linguists have turned to more powerful metalanguages. Even for the description of the structure of fairly simple formal languages such as ALGOL or FORTRAN it is not entirely sufficient. However, we use it since it is the best compromise between power and practicability of use.

Consider again the sentence "The big elephant ate the peanut". As we mentioned, Figure 2.1 indicates that the <sentence> is composed of a <subject> followed by a <predicate>. If we abbreviate "may be composed of" by the symbol ::= , our grammar might contain rules like

```
<sentence>        ::= <subject> <predicate>
<subject>         ::= <article> <adjective> <noun>
<article>         ::= the
<adjective>       ::= big
<predicate>       ::= <verb> <direct object>
<verb>            ::= ate
<direct object>   ::= <article> <noun>
<noun>            ::= peanut
<noun>            ::= elephant
```

Note that the grammar can contain more than one rule describing how a particular syntactic entity may be formed. For instance, from Figure 2.1 we have two rules to show what a <noun> may be composed of.

Once we have a set of rules, they can be used to *derive* or *produce* a sentence by the following scheme. (For this reason the rules are often called *productions.*) We begin with the syntactic entity <sentence>, find a rule with <sentence> to the left of ::=, and rewrite it as the string to the right of ::=,

```
<sentence> => <subject> <predicate>
```

Thus we are replacing a syntactic identity by one of the strings of which it may be composed. Repeat the process. Take one of the syntactic entities in the string <subject> <predicate>, say <subject>; find a rule with <subject> to the left of ::=, and replace <subject> in the string by the corresponding string to the right of ::=. This yields

<subject><predicate> => <article><adjective><noun><predicate>

The symbol => means that one symbol to the left of => is replaced, using a rule of the grammar, to yield the string to the right of =>. A complete derivation of the sentence "the big elephant ate the peanut" would be

```
<sentence> => <subject> <predicate>
           => <article> <adjective> <noun> <predicate>
           => the <adjective> <noun> <predicate>
           => the big <noun> <predicate>
           => the big elephant <predicate>
           => the big elephant <verb> <direct object>
           => the big elephant ate <direct object>
           => the big elephant ate <article> <noun>
           => the big elephant ate the <noun>
           => the big elephant ate the peanut
```

We abbreviate this derivation of a sentence by using a new symbol =>+

```
<sentence>  =>+ the big elephant ate the peanut
```

At each step one can replace <u>any</u> syntactic entity. In the above derivation we have always replaced the leftmost one. Note also that a rule such as <sentence> ::= <subject> <predicate> may be used to describe many different sentences; one just needs to have different ways of forming <subject>s and <predicate>s. From the seven rules

```
<sentence>    ::= <subject> <predicate>
<subject>     ::= We
<subject>     ::= He
<subject>     ::= I
<predicate>   ::= ran
<predicate>   ::= sat
<predicate>   ::= ate
```

we can form a total of nine sentences!

```
We ran    He ran    I ran
We ate    He ate    I ate
We sat    He sat    I sat
```

One purpose of a grammar is to describe <u>all</u> sentences of a language with a reasonable number of rules. This is significant if we realize that a language usually has an infinite number of sentences.

With this introduction, we are almost ready to describe the formal notions of grammars and languages, but in the next section we must first define some terms that we have been using informally.

**EXERCISES FOR 2.1**

1. Look up the words "language", "meta", "metalanguage", "syntax" and "semantics" in a good dictionary.

2. Draw syntax trees for the sentences "John ate the big peanut", "John ate the big brown peanut", "John ate the big brown roasted peanut," and "John ate the salted big brown roasted peanut". In English, any word can be modified by any number of adjectives. Now try to give only two rules for a new syntactic class, say <noun phrase>, from which a <noun> preceded by any number of adjectives (including none) can be derived.

## 2.2 SYMBOLS AND STRINGS

We informally define a language to be a subset of the set of all sequences of "words" or symbols from some basic vocabulary. Again, we attach no meaning to these sequences. For example, English consists of sentences which are sequences of words (if, he, is, etc.) and punctuation marks (eg. commas, periods, parentheses). The programming language ALGOL consists of programs -- sequences of symbols like <u>if</u>, <u>begin</u>, <u>end</u>, punctuation marks, letters, and digits. The language of even integers consists of sequences of digits 0, 1, ..., 9, the last one of which must be 0,2,4,6,or 8.

An <u>alphabet</u> is a nonempty finite set of elements. We call elements of an alphabet <u>symbols</u>. Any finite sequence of symbols from an alphabet A is called a <u>string</u>. Some strings "over the alphabet" A = {a,b,c} are a, b, c, ab, and aaca. We also allow the <u>empty string</u> $\varepsilon$ -- the string with no symbols in it. The order of the symbols in a string is important; the string ab is not the same as ba, and abca is different from aabc. The <u>length</u> of a string x, written |x| , is the number of symbols in it. Thus

$$|\varepsilon| = 0, \ |a| = 1, \ |abb| = 3.$$

Capital letters M, N, S, T, U,... are used as variables or names of symbols of an alphabet, while small letters t, u, v, w,... name strings of symbols. Thus we might write

$$x = STV,$$

which means "x is the string consisting of the symbols S, T and V, in that order". Since this book is being written using a computer which does not have subscripts on the printer chain, we use ALGOL-like brackets to indicate them. Thus x[1], ..., x[n] represents n strings x sub 1 to x sub n. Where no confusion can arise, we will leave off the brackets: x[1] is equivalent to x1, x[2] to x2, x[i] to xi and x[j] to xj.

When x and y are strings, their catenation xy is the string obtained by writing the symbols in y after those in x. For example, if x = XY, y = YZ, then xy = XYYZ and yx = YZXY. Following this convention, since $\mathcal{E}$ is the string containing no symbols, for any string x we may write

$$\mathcal{E}x = x\mathcal{E} = x.$$

If z = xy is a string, then x is a head and y a tail of z. Finally, x is a proper head if y is not empty (y is not $\mathcal{E}$), while y is a proper tail if x is not empty. Thus, if x = abc then the heads of x are $\mathcal{E}$, a, ab and abc, while all are proper except abc.

Sets of strings over an alphabet are usually denoted by capital letters A, B,... The product AB of two sets of strings A and B is defined by

$$AB = \{xy \mid x \text{ in } A \text{ and } y \text{ in } B\}$$

which we read as "the set of strings xy such that x is in A and y in B." For example if A = {a,b} and B = {c,d}, then AB is the set AB ={ac,ad,bc,bd}. Since $\mathcal{E}$x = x$\mathcal{E}$ = x for any string x, we have

$$\{\mathcal{E}\}A = A\{\mathcal{E}\} = A.$$

Note here the use of braces around the symbol $\mathcal{E}$. The product is defined for sets, and $\mathcal{E}$ is not a set but a symbol. {$\mathcal{E}$} is a set consisting of the empty symbol $\mathcal{E}$.

We can now define powers of strings. If x is a string then $x^0$ is the empty string $\mathcal{E}$, $x^1 = x$, $x^2 = xx$, $x^3 = xxx$, and in general, x!n is defined as

$$\underbrace{xx\ldots xx}_{n \text{ times}}$$

Note the use of the exclamation point when the power is a variable. Only digits appear as superscripts on the print chain being used, so we resort to the new notation. For n > 0 we have x!n = xx!(n-1) = (x!(n-1))x, where the parentheses are used as metasymbols to make things clearer.

We can also define powers of an alpabet A:

$$A^0 = \{\mathcal{E}\},\ A^1 = A,\ A!n = AA!(n-1) \text{ for } n > 0.$$

Using this, we define the two last operations in this section -- the closure A* of a set A and the positive closure A+ of a set A:

$$A+ = A^1 \text{ union } A^2 \text{ union } \ldots \text{ union } A!n \text{ union } \ldots$$

$$A* = A^0 \text{ union } A+.$$

Thus if A = {a,b}, A* includes the strings

ε,a,b,aa,ab,ba,bb,aaa,aab,...

Note that A+ = AA* = (A*)A.

Examples:

Let z = abb. Then |z| = 3.
Heads of z are ε, a, ab, abb. Proper heads of z are ε, a, ab.
Tails of z are ε, b, bb, abb. Proper tails of z are ε, b, bb.
Let x = a, z = abb.
Then zx = abba xz = aabb
$z^0$ = ε, $z^1$ = abb, $z^2$ = abbabb $z^3$ = abbabbabb.
$|z^0|$ = 0, $|z^1|$ = 3, $|z^2|$ = 6, $|z^3|$ = 9.
Let S = {a,b,c}.
Then S+ = {a,b,c,aa,ab,ac,ba,bb,bc,ca,cb,cc,aaa,...}.
S* = {ε,a,b,c,aa,ab,ac,...}.

It is sometimes convenient (and usually clearer) to write

x... for xy

when we are not really interested in the latter part of the string, y. Thus three dots "..." means any possible string -- including the empty string. The most frequent uses are:

| <u>notation</u> | <u>meaning</u> |
|---|---|
| z = x... | x is a head of the string z. We don't care what the tail is. |
| z = ...x | x is a tail of z. We don't care what the head is. |
| z = ...x... | x appears somewhere in the string z. |
| z = S... | the symbol S is the first symbol in the string z. |
| z = ...S | the symbol S is the last symbol in z. |
| z = ...S... | the symbol S appears somewhere in the string z. |

**EXERCISES FOR 2.2**

1. Define "string" and "catenation."

2. Let A = {$}. Let z = $. Write down the following strings and their lengths. z, zz, $z^2$, $z^5$, $z^0$. What is A*?

3. Let A = {0,1,2}. Let x = 01, y = 2 and z = 011. Write down the following strings, and their lengths, heads, and tails. xy, yz, xyz, $x^4$, $(x^3)(y^2)$, $(xy)^2$, $(yxx)^3$.

4. Let A = {0,1,2}. Write 7 of the shortest strings of the set A+ and of the set A* .

## 2.3 FORMAL DEFINITION OF GRAMMAR AND LANGUAGE

We are now in a position to formalize the notion of rules, or productions as they are sometimes called, and to abstractly define a grammar and language using these rules.

(2.3.1) DEFINITION. A _production_ or _rewriting rule_ is an ordered pair (U,x), usually written

U ::= x

where U is a symbol and x is a nonempty finite string of symbols. U is the _left part_ and x the _right part_ of the production. We will use the shorter term _rule_ for production. ▪

(2.3.2) DEFINITION. A _grammar_ G[Z] is a finite nonempty set of rules. Z is a symbol which must appear as the left part of at least one rule. It is called the _distinguished symbol_. All the symbols used in left parts and right parts form the _vocabulary_ V. ▪

Where it is obvious from the context (or if we don't care) what the distinguished symbol Z is, we write G instead of G[Z].

(2.3.3) EXAMPLE. Let the grammar G1[<number>] be the following 13 rules.

```
(1) <number> ::= <no>              (08) <digit> ::= 4
(2) <no>     ::= <no> <digit>      (09) <digit> ::= 5
(3) <no>     ::= <digit>           (10) <digit> ::= 6
(4) <digit>  ::= 0                 (11) <digit> ::= 7
(5) <digit>  ::= 1                 (12) <digit> ::= 8
(6) <digit>  ::= 2                 (13) <digit> ::= 9
(7) <digit>  ::= 3
```

V = {0, 1, 2, 3, 4, 5, 6, 7, 8, 9, <digit>, <no>, <number>}. ▪

(2.3.4) DEFINITION. Given a grammar G, those symbols appearing as a left part of a rule are called _nonterminals_ or _syntactic entities_. They form the set of nonterminals VN. Those symbols not in VN are called _terminal symbols_. They form the set VT. ▪

Thus we have V = VN union VT. We will usually use angular

brackets "<" and ">" to distinguish nonterminals from terminals. In grammar G1 of example 2.3.3 the terminal symbols are 0,1,2,3,4,5,6,7,8 and 9. The nonterminals are <number>, <no>, and <digit>.

When we need to distinguish between different occurrences of the same nonterminal, we use superscripts. Thus we may write <no$^1$> ::= <no$^2$> <digit>, instead of <no> ::= <no> <digit>.

As an abbreviation for a set of rules U ::= x, U ::= y, ..., U ::= z with identical left parts, we write

```
U ::= x | y | ... | z .
```

For example, grammar G1 could be written as

```
<number>      ::= <no>
<no>          ::= <no> <digit> | <digit>
<digit>       ::= 0 | 1 | 2 | 3 | 4 | 5 | 6 | 7 | 8 | 9
```

This particular notation is called BNF, which is an abbreviation for *Backus-Normal Form* or *Backus-Naur Form*. It was first developed by Backus(59) for describing ALGOL in the ALGOL 60 report (see Naur(63a)). Naur was the editor of the report. There are several other notations used to describe formal languages which we will discuss later.

Now that we have a grammar, how do we indicate the language corresponding to the grammar? What are the sentences of the language? To do this we must define the symbols => and =>+ used intuitively in Section 2.1 to derive sentences. Informally, v => w if we can derive w from v by replacing a nonterminal in v by the corresponding right part of a rule.

(2.3.5) DEFINITION. Let G be a grammar. We say that the string v *directly produces* the string w, written

v => w,

if we can write

v = xUy , w = xuy

for some strings x and y, where U ::= u is a rule of G. We also say that w is a *direct derivation* of v, or that w *directly reduces* to v. ∎

The strings x and y of course may be empty. Therefore for any rule U ::= u of the grammar G we have U => u. The following table gives some examples of direct derivations, using the grammar G1 of example 2.3.3 and the notation used in the above definition.

| v | w | rule used | x | y |
|---|---|---|---|---|
| <number> | => <no> | 1 | & | & |
| <no> | => <no> <digit> | 2 | & | & |
| <no> <digit> | => <digit> <digit> | 3 | & | <digit> |
| <digit> <digit> | => 2 <digit> | 6 | & | <digit> |
| 2 <digit> | => 22 | 6 | 2 | & |

**FIGURE 2.2. Examples of Direct Derivations.**

(2.3.6) DEFINITION. v *produces* w, or w *reduces* to v, written v =>+ w, if there exists a sequence of direct derivations

v = u0 => u1 => u2 => ... => u[n] = w

where n > 0. The sequence is called a *derivation* of *length* n. The string w is also said to be a *word* for v. Finally we write v =>* w if v =>+ w or v = w. ■

Let us give an example of a derivation. Take a look at the first line of Figure 2.2. From it we see that <number> =>+ <no>; the length of the derivation is 1. Along with line 2 of the table this indicates that <number> =>+ <no> <digit>; the length of the derivation is 2. If we continue down the lines of Figure 2.2. we see that

<number> => <no> => <no> <digit> => <digit> <digit>
=> 2 <digit> => 22

Thus <number> =>+ 22 and the length of the derivation is 5.

Note that as long as there is a nonterminal in a string, one can derive a new string from it. However, if there is no nonterminal, then the derivation must terminate. Hence the term "terminal symbol" for a symbol not appearing in a left part of some rule.

What would be considered the *language* described by the grammar G[<number>]? The next definition says that this particular language is the set of sequences of one or more digits.

(2.3.7) DEFINITION. Let G[Z] be a grammar. A string x is called a *sentential form* if x is derivable from the distinguished symbol Z -- if Z =>* x. A *sentence* is a sentential form consisting only of terminal symbols. The *language* I(G[Z]) is the set of sentences:

L(G) = {x | Z =>* x and x in VT+} ■

Thus the language is just a subset of the set of all *terminal* strings -- strings over VT. The structure of a sentence is given by the grammar. Several different grammars can however generate the same language. We will often say "a sentence of the grammar" for "a sentence of the language defined by the grammar".

(2.3.8) EXAMPLE. We write a grammar for a language containing variations on our friend "the big elephant ate the peanut". The grammar G2[<sentence>] is

```
<sentence>       ::= <subject> <predicate>
<subject>        ::= <article> <adjective> <noun> | <pronoun>
<predicate>      ::= <verb> <direct object>
<direct object>::= <article> <noun>
<pronoun>        ::= he
<article>        ::= the
<adjective>      ::= big
<verb>           ::= ate
<noun>           ::= elephant | peanut
```

The set of terminals is {he, the, big, ate, elephant, peanut}. The language L(G2) is the set of sequences of those terminals which are derivable from (are words for) the distinguished symbol <sentence>. Some of the sentences are

he ate the peanut
he ate the elephant
the big elephant ate the elephant ▪

The following definition is important. The reader should not proceed further until he is sure he understands it.

(2.3.9) DEFINITION. Let G[Z] be a grammar. Let w = xuy be a sentential form. Then u is called a *phrase* of the sentential form w for a nonterminal U if

Z =>* xUy and U =>+ u.

Secondly, u is called a *simple phrase* if Z =>* xUy and U => u. ▪

One must be careful with the term *phrase*. The fact that U =>+ u does not necessarily mean that u is a phrase of a sentential form xuy; we must also have Z =>* xUy. To illustrate this, consider the sentential form <no> 1 of grammar G1 (example 2.3.3). Does the existence of the rule <number> ::= <no> mean that <no> is a phrase? Emphatically no, because we cannot generate <number> 1 from the distinguished symbol <number>.

What are the phrases of <no> 1? We have

<number> => <no> => <no> <digit> => <no> 1.

Thus

(1) <number> =>* <no> and <no> =>+ <no> 1;
(2) <number> =>* <no> <digit> and <digit> =>+ 1;

The phrases are <no> 1 and 1. The only simple phrase is 1.

We will have to talk frequently about the *leftmost* simple phrase of a sentential form. We therefore give it a name:

(2.3.10) DEFINITION. A *handle* of any sentential form is a leftmost simple phrase. ▪

The grammar G1 of example 2.3.3 describes an infinite language. That is, there are an infinite number of sentences in it. This is because the rule <no> ::= <no> <digit> contains <no> both in the left and right parts. In a sense, <no> is used to define itself. In general, if U =>+ ...U... we say that the grammar is *recursive in U*. If U =>+ U... it is *left recursive*; if U =>+ ...U it is *right recursive*. A rule is called left (right) recursive if it has the form U ::= U... (U ::= ...U). If a language is infinite, a grammar defining it must be recursive.

## EXERCISES FOR 2.3

1. Let G[<id>] be the rules

<id> ::= a | b | c | <id> a | <id> c | <id> 0 | <id> 1

Write down VT and VN. Give derivations where possible for the strings a, ab0, a0c01, 0a, 11, aaa.

2. What are the sentences of the language L(G1) where G1 is given in example 2.3.3?

3. Write a grammar whose language is the set of even integers.

4. Write a grammar whose language is the set of even integers, this time with no leading zeros allowed.

5. Let G be the rules <A> ::= b <A> | cc. Prove that cc, bcc, bbcc, bbbcc,..., are in L(G).

6. Construct a grammar for the language

{a(b!n)a | n = 0,1,2,3,...}.

7. Construct a grammar for the language

{(a!n)(b!n) | n = 1,2,3,...}.

8. The following grammar G3[<exp>] is often used for arithmetic expressions using binary operators (i stands for "identifier"):

```
<exp>       ::= <term> | <exp> + <term> | <exp> - <term>
<term>      ::= <factor> | <term> * <factor>
                | <term> / <factor>
<factor>    ::= ( <exp> ) | i
```

Give derivations for the following arithmetic expressions: i, (i), i*i, i*i+i, i*(i+i).

9. List all the phrases and simple phrases of the sentential form <exp> + <term> * <factor> of grammar G3 (exercise 8).

## 2.4 SYNTAX TREES AND AMBIGUITY

<u>Syntax trees</u> are an aid to understanding the syntax of sentences. Figure 2.1 is an illustration of what we mean by a syntax tree. Let us illustrate how to draw a tree for the following derivation of the sentence 22 of the grammar G1 (example 2.3.3):

```
(2.4.1) <number>  => <no> => <no> <digit>
                  => <digit> <digit> => 2 <digit> => 22
```

We start with the distinguished symbol <number> and draw a <u>branch</u> downward from it to indicate the first direct derivation, as in Figure 2.3a. A branch is the set of lines together with the <u>nodes</u> (the symbols) below these lines. The nodes of the branch form the string which replaced the name of the branch in the first direct derivation <number> => <no> .

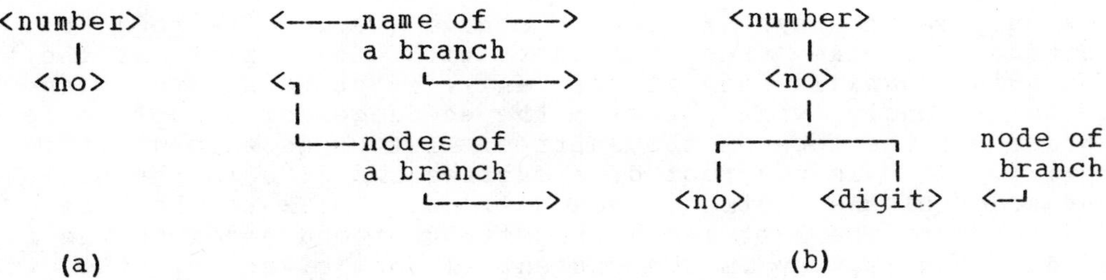


**FIGURE 2.3. Syntax Trees for Two Derivations.**

To indicate the second derivation, from the node representing the symbol being replaced, we draw a branch whose nodes form the replacing string (Figure 2.3b). Continuing in this manner would yield, in order, the three syntax diagrams of Figure 2.4.

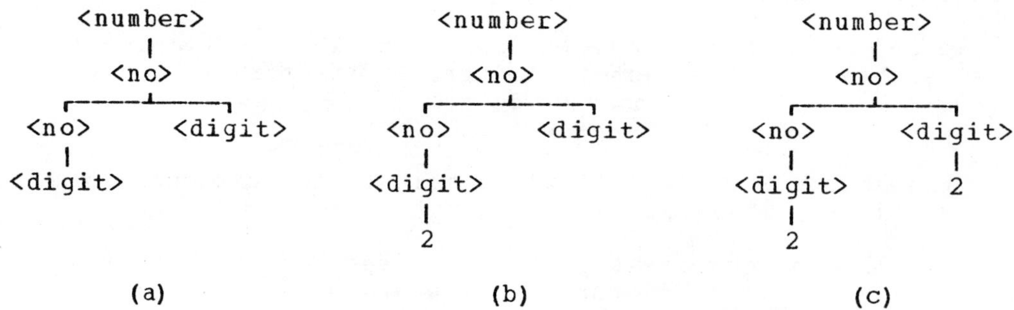


**FIGURE 2.4. Syntax Trees for Derivation (2.4.1).**

The *end nodes* of a syntax tree are those nodes which have no branches emanating downward from them. Reading from left to right, these end nodes form the string derived by the derivation which the tree represents. Thus, after the third direct derivation in (2.4.1), the string of end nodes is <digit> <digit> (see Figure 2.4a).

An *end branch* is a branch, all of whose nodes are end nodes. In Figure 2.3b there is one end branch; its nodes are <no> and <digit>. In Figure 2.4c there are two end branches, with nodes 2 and 2 respectively.

The following terminology is often used when discussing trees. Let N be a node of a tree. N's *sons* are the nodes of the branch N names; N is their *father*. The sons are *brothers*, the youngest being the leftmost one. In Figure 2.4b, the only son of <number> is <no>. This same <no> has two sons: <no> and <digit>. The father of the node 2 is <digit>.

A *subtree* of a syntax tree is a node (called the *root* of the subtree) of the tree together with that part of the tree emanating downward from it (if any). Subtrees are connected quite strongly with phrases; the end nodes of a subtree form a phrase for the root of the subtree. Let us go through this in detail. If U is the root of a subtree and if u is the string of end nodes of the subtree, then $U \Rightarrow^{+} u$. Let x be the string of end nodes to the left and y the string of end nodes to the right of u. That is, xuy is the sentential form given by the tree. Then $Z \Rightarrow^{*} xUy$ and this means that u is a phrase for U in xuy.

**Constructing a Derivation from a Tree**

One can reconstruct a derivation from a syntax tree by reversing the process. From Figure 2.4c, the end nodes indicate that the final string is 22. The rightmost end branch indicates a direct derivation in the sequence:

2 <digit> => 22.

To arrive at the syntax tree for 2 <digit>, we prune the branch from the tree -- delete it. For instance, pruning this branch (in Figure 2.4c) gives us Figure 2.4b. This process is often called a direct reduction.

Observing Figure 2.4b, we see that the last derivation here must have been <digit> <digit> => 2 <digit>. This gives us so far

<digit> <digit> => 2 <digit> => 22.

We continue in this manner, always reconstructing a last direct derivation indicated by an end branch of the syntax tree, and then pruning that branch.

Let us summarize by making the following statements about syntax trees:

- For each syntax tree there exists at least one derivation.
- For each derivation there is a corresponding syntax tree (but several derivations may have the same tree).
- A branch of the tree indicates a direct derivation in which the name of the branch was replaced by the nodes of the branch. Thus a rule exists in the grammar whose left part is the name of the branch and whose right part is the string of branch nodes.
- The end nodes of the tree form the derived sentential form.
- Let U be the root of a subtree for a sentential form w = xuy where u forms the string of end nodes of that subtree. Then u is a phrase for U of the sentential form w. It is a simple phrase if the subtree is a single branch.

Besides derivation (2.4.1), there is another derivation of the sentence 22 of G1:

```
(2.4.2) <number>  => <no> => <no> <digit>
                  => <digit> <digit> => <digit> 2 => 2 2
```

Its syntax tree is the same as that of derivation (2.4.1). In fact there is even a third derivation of 22:

```
(2.4.3) <number>  => <no> => <no> <digit>
                  => <no> 2 => <digit> 2 => 22
```

Note that these derivaticns differ only in the <u>order</u> in which the rules were used in the derivation, and that the syntax tree does not specify the exact order in which the derivations occur. This difference of order in derivations is of no practical importance to us at this point, and we consider derivations which yield the same tree as equivalent.

### Ambiguity

Of much more importance is the uniqueness of the syntax tree. Consider a grammar containing, among others, the rules

```
<sentence>        ::= <subject> <predicate>
<sentence>        ::= <predicate> <direct object>
<subject>         ::= <noun>
<direct object> ::= <ncun>
<predicate>       ::= <verb>
<noun>            ::= time | flies
<verb>            ::= time | flies
```

From these rules we could generate the sentence "time flies" in two different ways, with different syntax trees (Figure 2.5).

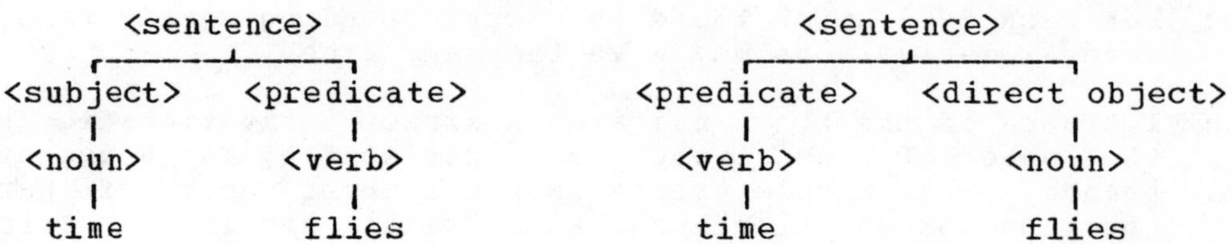


**FIGURE 2.5. Syntax Trees for an Ambiguous Sentence.**

Each way the sentence makes sense in English -- either "time flies by very quickly", or "go find out how fast flies fly". The problem is that, out of context, we cannot tell what the sentence means because we cannot "parse" it correctly; we cannot unambiguously break it up into its constituent parts. If a compiler is to be able to translate all valid source programs, it is reasonable to require that the language be unambiguously defined. We therefore introduce the following

(2.4.4) DEFINITION. A sentence of a grammar is <u>ambiguous</u> if there exists two syntax trees for it. A grammar is <u>ambiguous</u> if it contains an ambiguous sentence; else it is <u>unambiguous</u>. ▪

Note that we call the grammar ambiguous, and not the language itself. By changing an ambiguous grammar -- without of course changing the sentences of it -- we may sometimes arrive at an unambiguous grammar for the same set of sentences. There are however languages for which no unambiguous grammar exists; such languages are called inherently ambiguous. (See section 2.10).

Remember also that we are at this point only concerned with syntax. A sentence may be unambiguous according to the definition above, but we might still not know what it means because of ambiguities in the meaning of the words.

Unfortunately, it has been proven that the property of ambiguity is undecidable. This means that no algorithm exists (or can be written) which will accept any BNF grammar and determine with certainty and in a finite amount of time whether it is ambiguous or not. What we can do is to develop (Chapters 5, 6) fairly simple but nontrivial conditions which, if satisfied by a grammar, assure us that the grammar is unambiguous. These are sufficient conditions for unambiguity, but in no sense of the word are they necessary.

### An Unambiguous Grammar for Arithmetic Expressions

If a sentential form is ambiguous, then it has more than one syntax tree and therefore, in general, more than one handle. Let us illustrate this with an example which at the same time will provide us with a useable grammar for arithmetic expressions. Consider the following grammar for expressions using the single operand i (for identifier), parentheses and the binary operators + and *:

(2.4.5) <E> ::= <E> + <E> | <E> * <E> | ( <E> ) | i

The sentential form <E>+<E>*<E> has two syntax trees (Figure 2.6) and two handles -- <E>+<E> and <E>*<E>. If we want to parse this sentential form which handle should we reduce? There is an ambiguity in the grammar and either one would do. Thus we cannot tell whether to perform the multiplication before or after the addition.

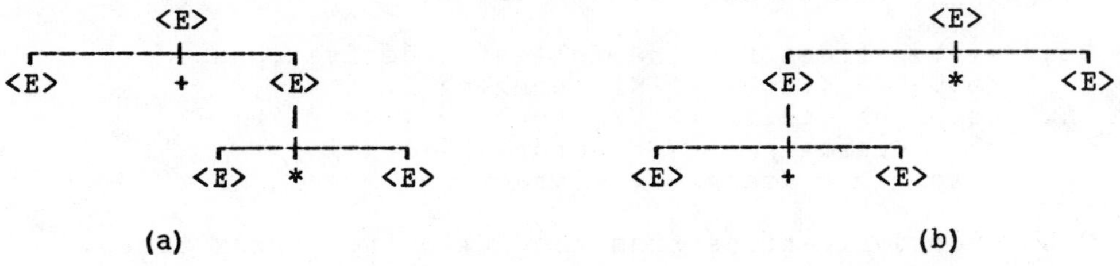


FIGURE 2.6. Two Syntax Trees for <E> + <E> * <E>.

Consider now the grammar G3[<exp>] of exercise 2.3.8:

```
(2.4.6) <exp>      ::= <term> | <exp> + <term> | <exp> - <term>
        <term>     ::= <factor> | <term> * <factor>
                     | <term> / <factor>
        <factor>   ::= ( <exp> ) | i
```

The only tree for the expression i+i*i is shown below, and thus according to this grammar the sentence is unambiguous. In fact, all sentences of G3 are unambiguous. Now let us determine whether, according to G3, the multiplication or the addition should be performed first in i+i*i. The operands of + according to the tree below are the <exp> from which i is generated, and the <term> from which i*i is generated. We interpret this to mean that the multiplication i*i must be performed first in order to produce the <term> for the addition; hence the multiplication has precedence over the addition.

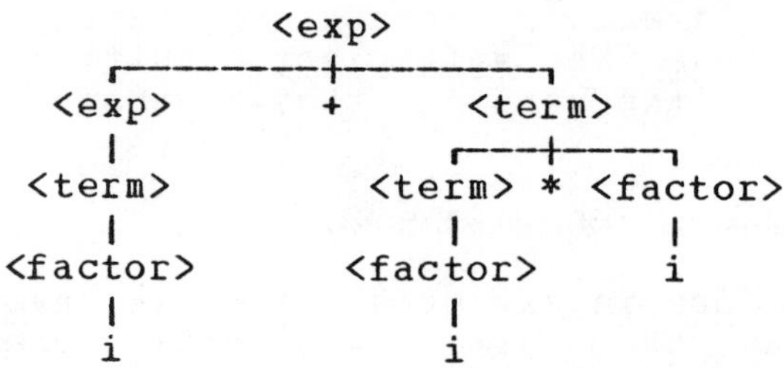


Grammar G3 is preferable to grammar (2.4.5) for two reasons: it is unambiguous and indicates that multiplication has precedence over addition.

## EXERCISES FOR 2.4

1. Draw syntax trees for the following derivations.
   a. <number> => <no> => <no> <digit> => <no> 3
      => <no> <digit> 3 => <no> 2 3 => <digit> 2 3 => 1 2 3.
   b. <number> => <no> => <no> <digit> => <no> 3
      => <no> <digit> 3 => <digit> <digit> 3
      => 1 <digit> 3 => 1 2 3.
   
   Do they have the same syntax trees?

2. Draw syntax trees for the following derivations.
   a. <exp> => <term> => <factor> => i.
   b. <exp> => <term> => <factor> => ( <exp> )
      => ( <term> ) => ( <factor> ) => ( i ).
   c. <exp> => + <term> => + <factor> => + i.

3. Construct derivations from the following syntax trees.

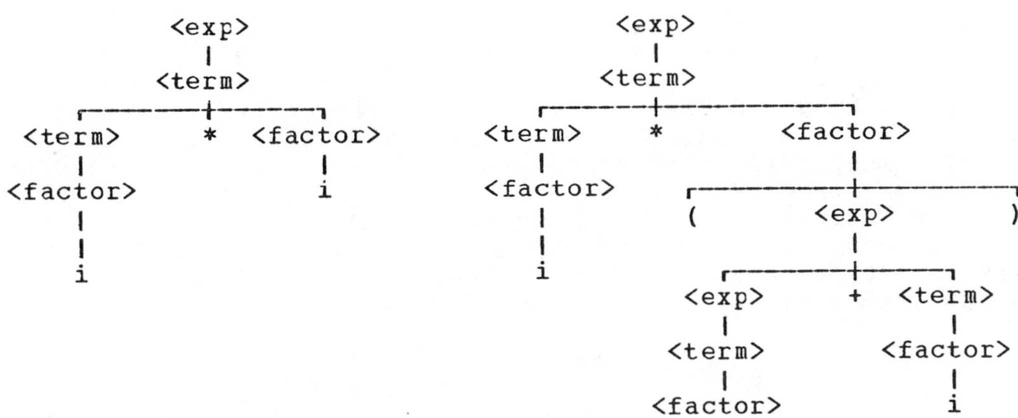


4. Show that the following grammar G[<exp>] is ambiguous by constructing two syntax trees for each of the sentences i+i*i and i+i+i.

```
<exp>          ::= i | ( <exp> ) | <exp> <op> <exp>
<op>           ::= + | - | * | /
```

5. Show that the sentences i+i*i and i+i+i of grammar G3 (2.4.6) are unambiguous. In the sentence i+i*i which operator has precedence? Which has precedence in the sentence i*i*i?

## 2.5 THE PARSING PROBLEM

A *parse* of a sentential form is the construction of a derivation and possibly a syntax tree for it. A parsing program, or parser, is also called a *recognizer*, since it recognizes only sentences of the grammar in question. This of course is our problem at this point -- we want to recognize programs of a programming language.

All the parsing algorithms we describe are called *left-to-right* parsing algorithms, because they examine and process the leftmost symbols of the string in question first, and proceed further to the right only when necessary. We could similarly define right-to-left parsers, but left-to-right is more natural. Statements in programs are executed in a left-to-right manner; we read from left to right.

Parsing algorithms are further classified into the two categories *top-down* and *bottom-up*. The terms refer to the way in which the syntax trees are built. A top-down parser builds the tree starting from the root -- the distinguished symbol -- and works downward to the end nodes. Consider the sentence 35 of the following grammar for integers (sequences of one or more digits):

```
(2.5.1) N    ::= D | N D
        D    ::= 0 | 1 | 2 | 3 | 4 | 5 | 6 | 7 | 8 | 9
```

The first step would be to construct the direct derivation N => N D, as indicated in the first tree of Figure 2.7. At each succesive step, the leftmost nonterminal V of the current sentential form xVy is replaced by the right part u of a rule V::=u to arrive at the next sentential form. This is shown for the sentence 35 by the five trees of Figure 2.7. The trick is, of course, to arrive at the sentential form which was the original string.

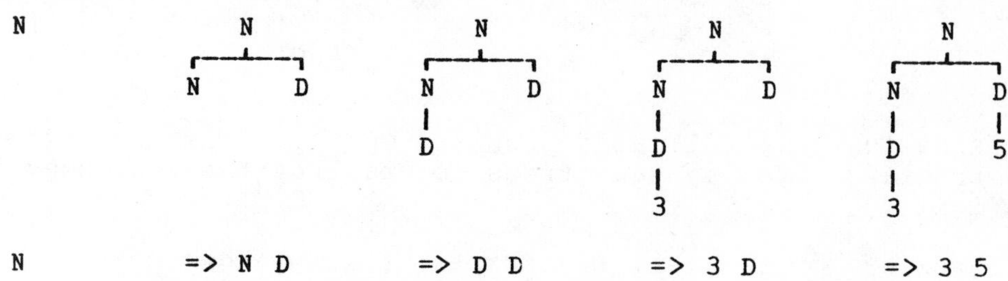


**FIGURE 2.7. Top-Down Parse and the Derivation It Constructs.**

The bottom-up technique is to start at the string itself and try to reduce it to the distinguished symbol. The first step in parsing 35 is to reduce the 3 to D, yielding the sentential form D5. Thus we have constructed the direct derivation D5=>35, as shown in the rightmost partial syntax tree of Figure 2.8. The next step is to reduce the D to N, as illustrated by the second tree from the right. This proceeds until the first tree is formed. We have arranged the trees below from right to left because this illustrates more clearly the derivation constructed, which now reads as usual from left to right. Note that the derivations produced by the two different parses are different, but that the same syntax tree is produced.

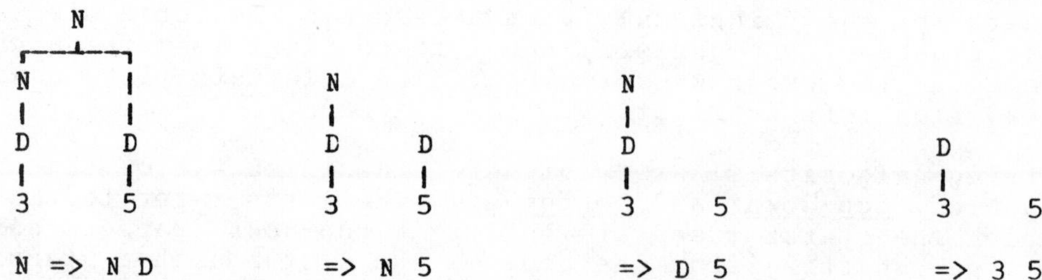


**FIGURE 2.8. Bottom-Up Parse and the Derivation it Constructs.**

Since we will refer often to the type of derivation produced by a left-right bottom-up parse, we coin a term for it. Note that in such a parse, at each step a handle (leftmost simple phrase) of the current sentential form is reduced, and thus *the string to the right of this handle always contains only terminals*.

(2.5.2) DEFINITION. A direct derivation xUy => xuy is *canonical*, written xUy ‡> xuy, if y contains only terminals. A derivation w =>+v is *canonical*, written w ‡>+ v, if every direct derivation in it is canonical. ■

Every sentence has a canonical derivation, but not every sentential form. Consider for example a sentential form 3D of grammar (2.5.1). Its only derivation is

<number> => N D => D D => 3 D,

and the second and third direct derivations are not canonical. This does not bother us, since we are interested mainly in parsing programs, which are sentences of a programming language. A sentential form which has a canonical derivation is called a *canonical* sentential form.

We have of course overlooked the main problems in parsing:

1. In a top-down parse, suppose the leftmost nonterminal to be replaced is V and suppose there are n rules

   V ::= x1 | x2 | ... | xn.

   How do we know which string xi to replace V by?
2. In a bottom-up parse, the handle is to be reduced at each step. How do we find the handle and what do we reduce it to?

These questions are not always easy to answer -- exercise 2 should point this up clearly. Chapter 4 is devoted to solving the problem for the top-down method, while chapters 5 and 6 discuss various techniques for solving the bottom-up problem.

One solution is to just pick at random one of the possible alternatives, hoping it is the correct one. If a mistake is later detected, then we must backtrack to the point of error and try another alternative. This is called *backup*. Obviously it can be very time consuming.

The other solution is to look at the context around the substring currently being processed. We do this ourselves when we evaluate an expression like A+B*C. We ask ourselves whether A+B should be evaluated first, and answer the question by noting that the * following A+B indicates that we should not.

One of the first parsing algorithms actually used in writing a compiler was described in Irons(61a). Ingerman's(66) syntax-oriented translator is also based on this algorithm. The method is neither top-down nor bottom-up, but a mixture of both. We shall not discuss it further.

### EXERCISES FOR 2.5

1. Find the canonical parse of the sentences 561, 0 and 0012 of the grammar G1 (example 2.3.3).

2. Parse the sentences (, )(*, i(, (+(, (+(i(, and (+)(i(*i( of the grammar

```
<goal>     ::= V1
V1         ::= V2 | V1 i V2
V2         ::= V3 | V2 + V3 | i V3
V3         ::= ) V1 * | (
```

3. What is the language of the grammar V ::= aaV | bc?

## 2.6 SOME RELATIONS CONCERNING A GRAMMAR

### Relations

The symbols => and =>+ defined in section 2.3 are examples of relations between strings. In general, a (binary) relation on a set is any property that either holds or does not hold for any two ordered symbols of the set.

Another example of a relation is the LESS THAN (<) relation defined on the set of integers: i < j if and only if j-i is a positive nonzero integer. One non-mathematical relation is the relation CHILD OF defined on the set of people; person A is either the child of person B or he is not.

We have been using the infix notation for relations -- if the relation holds between members c and d of a set we write c R d. (Note also that the order of the two objects is important; d R c doesn't follow automatically from c R d.) We can also consider a relation to be the set of ordered pairs for which the relation holds: (c,d) in R if and only if c R d.

We say that a relation P *contains* another relation R if (c,d) in R implies (c,d) in P.

The *transpose* of a relation R, written TRANSPOSE(R), is defined by

c TRANSPOSE(R) d   if and only if   d R c.

The transpose of the GREATER THAN relation is the LESS THAN relation. The transpose of the CHILD OF relation would be the PARENT OF relation.

A relation R is called _reflexive_ if c R c holds for all elements c of the set. For example, the relation LESS THAN OR EQUAL (≤) is reflexive ( $i \le i$ for all real numbers i) while the relation LESS THAN is not.

A relation is called _transitive_ if a R c follows from a R b and b R c. The LESS THAN relation over the integers is transitive. The CHILD OF relation is not transitive -- if John is a child of Jack and Jack is a child of Jill, usually John is not also a child of Jill.

Given any relation R we will want to define a new relation called its _transitive closure_ R+. It is called this because it is also contained in any transitive relation which contains R. In other words, suppose P is transitive and contains R: (c,d) in R implies (c,d) in P. Then P also contains R+.

First, given two relations R and P defined over the same set, we define a new relation called the _product_ of R and P by

c RP d if and only if there is an e such that c R e and e P d.

This operation is associative -- R(PQ) = (RP)Q for any relations R, P and Q.

As an example, consider the relations R and P over the integers defined by

a R b if and only if b = a+1
a P b if and only if b = a+2

Then a RP b if and only if there is a c such that a R c and c P b -- if and only if b = a+3.

Using the product, we next define powers of a relation R by

$R^1 = R$, $R^2 = RR$, R!n = R!(n-1)R = R(R!(n-1)) for n>1

We define $R^0$ to be the _identity_ relation

a $R^0$ b if and only if a = b.

Finally, the _transitive closure_ R+ of a relation R is defined as

(2.6.1) A R+ b if and only if a R!n b for some n > 0.

Obviously, if a R b then a R+ b. We leave it as an exercise to show that R+ is actually transitive. It is clear why we pick the notation R+ for the transitive closure; when we consider relations as sets of ordered pairs, we have

$$R+ = R^1 \text{ union } R^2 \text{ union } R^3 \text{ union } \ldots$$

We define the reflexive transitive closure R* of a relation R as

a R* b   if and only if   a = b or a R+ b.

Thus $R* = R^0$ union $R^1$ union $R^2$ ....

### Relations Concerning Grammars

Why all this interest in relations? First of all, it should now be obvious that the symbol =>+ (cf. (2.3.6)) is just the transitive closure of the relation => defined in (2.3.5)! Secondly, there are several important sets of symbols related to a grammar which we will have to construct later. These sets are easily definable in terms of quite simple relations and their transitive closure. In Section 2.7 we will give one simple algorithm which will let us compute all of the sets from the simple relations. The only requirement will be that the relations be defined over a finite set of elements. Before doing this let us take a look at the sets we will need.

Given a grammar and a nonterminal U, we will need to know the set of head symbols of derivatives of U. Thus if U =>+ Sx, Sx is a derivative of U and S is in this set. Let us call this set head(U). It is formally defined by

(2.6.2.)   head(U) := {S | U =>+ S...}

(Remember that the three dots "..." represent a (perhaps empty) string which at this point does not interest us.) For most purposes this definition might suffice. Note however that it is in terms of the relation =>+ on the infinite set V* of strings over the vocabulary V (even though the set head(U) is finite) and we might have trouble constructing it. We therefore redefine head(U) in terms of another relation on a finite set as follows. Define the relation FIRST over the finite vocabulary V of the grammar by

(2.6.3) U FIRST S if and only if there is a rule U ::= S...

We then have by the definition of transitive closure,

(2.6.4) U FIRST+ S if and only if there is a chain of (at least one) rules U ::= S1..., S1 ::= S2..., ..., Sn ::= S...

This obviously implies that

U FIRST+ S if and only if U =>+ S...

Note now that our relation FIRST+, when thought of as a set, completely defines the set head(U) of (2.6.2) for all symbols U of the vocabulary V:    head(U) = {S | (U,S) in FIRST+}.

(2.6.5) EXAMPLE. To illustrate both the relations FIRST and FIRST+, we list some rules and to the right of each rule the relation FIRST derived from it.

| | Rule | Relation |
|---|---|---|
| | A ::= Af | A FIRST A |
| | A ::= B | A FIRST B |
| | B ::= DdC | B FIRST D |
| (2.6.6) | B ::= De | B FIRST D |
| | C ::= e | C FIRST e |
| | D ::= Bf | D FIRST B |

We then have the following pairs in FIRST+:

(A,A) (A,B) (A,D) (B,B) (B,D) (D,B) (D,D) (C,e)

The head symbols of derivatives of A are thus A, B and D; those of B are B and D; that of C is e. ▪

There are three other sets we wish to define here. All of them can be defined in the manner in which we defined FIRST+. The first is the set of symbols which _end_ a derivative of some symbol U. This is defined for all symbols U by the relation LAST+ -- the transitive closure of LAST:

(2.6.7) U LAST S if and only if there is a rule U ::= ...S.

The second is the set of symbols within a word for a nonterminal U. It is defined by the relation WITHIN+ -- the transitive closure of the relation WITHIN:

(2.6.8) U WITHIN S if and only if there is a rule U ::= ...S....

The last one we wish to define is the set of _symbols_ S which are derivatives of a nonterminal U. This is defined by the relation SYMB+ -- the transitive closure of the relation SYMB defined by

(2.6.9) U SYMB S if and only if there is a rule U ::= S.

## EXERCISES FOR 2.6

1. Are the following relations reflexive? What is the transitive and reflexive transitive closure of each? a) IS SMALLER THAN (on the set of people). b) > (GREATER THAN) on the set of real numbers. c) The relation R defined by a R b if and only if a = -b (on the set of real numbers).

2. Calculate the sets FIRST+, LAST+, WITHIN+ and SYMB+ for the grammar G1 of example 2.3.3.

3. Prove that the product operation on relations is associative.

4. Show that R+ is transitive for any relation R.

5. Let P be any transitive relation such that if c R b then c P b. Prove that if c R+ b then c P b. (Thus R+ is the smallest transitive relation containing R).

6. What is the product of the FATHER relation with itself?

## 2.7 CONSTRUCTING THE TRANSITIVE CLOSURE OF RELATIONS

We have just defined four important sets in terms of the transitive closure of four very simple relations. Let us now turn to the problem of constructing the transitive closure of relations over finite sets.

Suppose for some relation R on a set A and some element U we wish to construct the set

B = {S | U R+ S}

where R+ is the transitive closure of R. If the set A is infinite, this may be difficult to do, if not impossible, even if B itself is finite. This is because there is no bound on the number n such that a R!n b for two elements a,b such that a R+ b. But if A is finite we can bound the length of the chain needed, as the following theorem shows.

(2.7.1) THEOREM. Let A be an alphabet of n symbols and let R be any relation on A. If for two symbols S1 and b we have S1 R+ b, then there exists a positive integer k ≤ n such that S1 R!k b.

Proof. Since S1 R+ b, there exists an integer p > 0 such that S1 R!p b. This means there exist symbols S2, S3,...,Sp in A such that

S1 R S2, S2 R S3, ..., S[p-1] R Sp and Sp R b

(by definition of R!p). Suppose that the smallest such p is greater than n. Then, for this smallest p, for two integers i and j with i < j ≤ p we must have Si = Sj, since A has only n symbols. But then the relations

S1 R S2, ..., S[i-1] R Si,
Sj R S[j+1], ..., S[p-1] R Sp, Sp R b

show that S1 R!k b where k = p-(j-i), in contradiction to the fact that p was the smallest. Thus our hypothesis that p > n is false and the theorem is proved. ■

**Boolean Matrices and Relations**

We will want to represent relations over an alphabet in a computer. The best representation for our purposes is a <u>Boolean matrix</u> B. This is a matrix whose elements B[i,j] may take only the values 1 or 0 (true or false). "Addition" of n by n Boolean matrices consists of "or-ing" the matrices elementwise; the element D[i,j] of the matrix

$$D = B + C$$

is defined as

D[i,j]:= B[i,j] + C[i,j]:= if B[i,j] = 1 then 1 else C[i,j]

"Multiplication" of n by n Boolean matrices is as in numerical matrix multiplication except that multiplication is replaced by "and" and addition by "or". Thus, if B and C are n by n matrices and D = BC, the element D[i,j] is defined by

D[i,j] := B[i,1]*C[1,j] + B[i,2]*C[2,j] + ... + B[i,n]*C[n,j]

where * is defined by

a*b := if a = 0 then 0 else b.

For example, if

$$B = \begin{bmatrix} 0 & 0 \\ 1 & 1 \end{bmatrix} \quad \text{and} \quad C = \begin{bmatrix} 1 & 0 \\ 1 & 0 \end{bmatrix}$$

then

$$D1 = B+C = \begin{bmatrix} 1 & 0 \\ 1 & 1 \end{bmatrix} \quad \text{and} \quad D2 = BC = \begin{bmatrix} 0 & 0 \\ 1 & 0 \end{bmatrix}$$

Please note the different meaning we have given to + and * in this context.

Boolean matrix addition is obviously associative (A+(B+C) = (A+B)+C) and commutative (A+B = B+A), while Boolean matrix multiplication is only associative (A(BC) = (AB)C). The two operations also satisfy the distributive law (A(B+C) = AB + AC).

Suppose we have a relation R defined on a set S of n symbols S1, ..., Sn. We construct an n by n Boolean matrix B to represent this relation by putting 1 in B[i,j] if and only if Si R Sj. For example, take the relation FIRST defined over the set {A,B,C,D,e,f} in (2.6.6). The matrix B for it is given in Figure 2.9.

| | S1=A | S2=B | S3=C | S4=D | S5=e | S6=d | S7=f |
|---|---|---|---|---|---|---|---|
| S1=A | 1 | 1 | 0 | 0 | 0 | 0 | 0 |
| S2=B | 0 | 0 | 0 | 1 | 0 | 0 | 0 |
| S3=C | 0 | 0 | 0 | 0 | 1 | 0 | 0 |
| S4=D | 0 | 1 | 0 | 0 | 0 | 0 | 0 |
| S5=e | 0 | 0 | 0 | 0 | 0 | 0 | 0 |
| S6=d | 0 | 0 | 0 | 0 | 0 | 0 | 0 |
| S7=f | 0 | 0 | 0 | 0 | 0 | 0 | 0 |

**FIGURE 2.9. Matrix for the Relation First.**

We can make the following obvious assertion.

(2.7.2) The transpose of a relation R is given by the transpose of the Boolean matrix representing R.

Let us discuss the product D = BC of two matrices B and C which represent two relations P and Q on an alphabet S. If D[i,j] = 1 then, from the definition of D[i,j], for some k we must have

B[i,k] = 1 and C[k,j] = 1.

Thus Si P Sk and Sk Q Sj, which means that (Si, Sj) is in the product PQ of the two relations P and Q.

Conversely, if (Si, Sj) is in PQ, then there exists a k such that Si P Sk and Sk Q Sj, and D[i,j] must be 1. This means that the matrix D represents the relation PQ. We have therefore proved the following

(2.7.3) THEOREM. The product of two relations over the same alphabet is given by the product of the Boolean matrices representing those relations. ∎

Since in general R!n is defined recursively by (R)(R!(n-1)) for n > 1, it follows by induction on n that the matrix B!n = BBB...B (n times) represents the relation R!n. From the definition of R+, theorem 2.7.1, and and theorem 2.7.3 we immediately derive the following theorem:

(2.7.4) THEOREM. Let B be an n by n Boolean matrix representing a relation R over an alphabet S of n symbols. Then the matrix B+ defined by

B+ = B + BB + BBB + ... + B!n

represents the transitive closure R+ of R. ∎

As an example, Figure 2.10 shows the matrices B, $B^2$, ..., $B^7$ and B+ for B of Figure 2.9 (the relation FIRST of grammar (2.6.6)). From B+ we have, again, the following pairs in FIRST+:

(A,A) (A,B) (A,D) (B,B) (B,D) (D,B) (D,D) (C,e)

$$B = \begin{bmatrix} 1 & 1 & 0 & 0 & 0 & 0 & 0 \\ 0 & 0 & 0 & 1 & 0 & 0 & 0 \\ 0 & 0 & 0 & 0 & 1 & 0 & 0 \\ 0 & 1 & 0 & 0 & 0 & 0 & 0 \\ 0 & 0 & 0 & 0 & 0 & 0 & 0 \\ 0 & 0 & 0 & 0 & 0 & 0 & 0 \\ 0 & 0 & 0 & 0 & 0 & 0 & 0 \end{bmatrix} \qquad B^2 = B^4 = B^6 = \begin{bmatrix} 1 & 1 & 0 & 1 & 0 & 0 & 0 \\ 0 & 1 & 0 & 0 & 0 & 0 & 0 \\ 0 & 0 & 0 & 0 & 0 & 0 & 0 \\ 0 & 0 & 0 & 1 & 0 & 0 & 0 \\ 0 & 0 & 0 & 0 & 0 & 0 & 0 \\ 0 & 0 & 0 & 0 & 0 & 0 & 0 \\ 0 & 0 & 0 & 0 & 0 & 0 & 0 \end{bmatrix}$$

$$B^3 = B^5 = B^7 = \begin{bmatrix} 1 & 1 & 0 & 1 & 0 & 0 & 0 \\ 0 & 0 & 0 & 1 & 0 & 0 & 0 \\ 0 & 0 & 0 & 0 & 0 & 0 & 0 \\ 0 & 1 & 0 & 0 & 0 & 0 & 0 \\ 0 & 0 & 0 & 0 & 0 & 0 & 0 \\ 0 & 0 & 0 & 0 & 0 & 0 & 0 \\ 0 & 0 & 0 & 0 & 0 & 0 & 0 \end{bmatrix} \qquad B+ = \begin{bmatrix} 1 & 1 & 0 & 1 & 0 & 0 & 0 \\ 0 & 1 & 0 & 1 & 0 & 0 & 0 \\ 0 & 0 & 0 & 0 & 1 & 0 & 0 \\ 0 & 1 & 0 & 1 & 0 & 0 & 0 \\ 0 & 0 & 0 & 0 & 0 & 0 & 0 \\ 0 & 0 & 0 & 0 & 0 & 0 & 0 \\ 0 & 0 & 0 & 0 & 0 & 0 & 0 \end{bmatrix}$$

**FIGURE 2.10. Calculation of B+ from B.**

The use of relations and Boolean matrix theory has provided us with a single algorithm for calculating a number of different important sets. These sets will be used later for constructing parsing algorithms. Surprisingly, the concepts used are simple and easy to understand.

### EXERCISES FOR 2.7

1. Warshall(62) developed the following efficient algorithm for calculating the matrix B+ = B + BB + ... + B!n from the matrix B. Prove that his algorithm works.

    1. Set a new matrix A = B.
    2. Set i := 1.
    3. For all j, if A[j,i] = 1 then for k = 1,...,n, set A[j,k] := A[j,k] + A[i,k].
    4. Add 1 to i.
    5. If i ≤ n then go to step 3; otherwise stop.

## 2.8 PRACTICAL RESTRICTIONS ON GRAMMARS

In this section we wish to discuss grammars in order to arrive at some practical restrictions on them. These conditions do not actually restrict the set of languages which can be described by a grammar. Algorithms are outlined which check a grammar for these conditions. This section should also give the reader more familiarity with manipulating grammars before we get into the problem of parsing.

A rule like U ::= U is obviously unnecessary in a grammar; moreover it makes the grammar ambiguous. For the rest of the book we therefore assume that

(2.8.1) no grammar contains a rule U ::= U.

Grammars can also contain superfluous rules which may not be used in deriving even one sentence. For example, in the following grammar G4[Z], the nonterminal <d> cannot be used in the derivation of a sentence, since it appears in no right part.

```
Z       ::= <b> e
<a>     ::= <a> e | e
<b>     ::= <c> e | <a> f
<c>     ::= <c> f
<d>     ::= f
```

Parsing sentences of grammars is easier if the grammar contains no superfluous rules. We can also reasonably assert that a grammar of a programming language which contains superfluous rules must have some mistake in it. An algorithm which checks a grammar for superfluous rules can therefore be an aid to the language designer.

A nonterminal U must satisfy two conditions in order to appear somewhere in the derivation of a sentence. First of all U must appear in some sentential form:

(2.8.2) Z =>* xUy for some strings x and y

where Z is the distinguished symbol of the grammar. Secondly we must be able to derive a string t of terminal symbols from U:

(2.8.3) U =>+ t for some t in VT+.

Clearly, if a nonterminal U does not satisfy both of these conditions, rules containing U as the left side may not be used in any derivation. On the other hand, if all nonterminals satisfy these conditions then the grammar contains no superfluous rules. For if U ::= u is any rule, we have first of all Z =>* xUy => xuy. Secondly, since we can derive a string of terminal symbols from each nonterminal in the string xuy, we have

xuy =>* t for some t in VT+.

Putting these together gives Z =>+ t, where the rule U ::= u has been used in the derivation.

In grammar G4 above, <c> does not satisfy condition (2.8.3) since, if it is replaced in a direct derivation, it must be replaced by <c> f. This obviously cannot lead to a terminal string. If we discarded all rules which could not be used in generating at least one sentence, we would be left with the rules

Z ::= <b> e, <a> ::= <a> e, <a> ::= e, and <b> ::= <a> f.

(2.8.4) DEFINITION. A grammar G is called _reduced_ if each nonterminal U satisfies (2.8.2) and (2.8.3). ■

We assume throughout the rest of the book that all grammars are reduced.

Note that a nonterminal U satisfies condition (2.8.2) if and only if Z WITHIN+ U where the relation WITHIN was defined in (2.6.8). Thus we can use the results of the last section to test a grammar for condition (2.8.2).

Figure 2.11 contains a flow chart of an algorithm which checks the nonterminals of a set of rules for condition 2.8.3. It begins by "marking" in some manner those nonterminals for which a rule U ::= t with t in VT+ exists (first execution of box P1). Such nonterminals obviously satisfy (2.8.3). The algorithm then checks all unmarked nonterminals U to see if there exists a rule U ::= x where x consists only of terminal symbols or previously marked symbols (second execution of box P1). These clearly also satisfy (2.8.3). This process continues until either all nonterminals are marked or no nonterminals become marked during an execution of box P1. When finished, unmarked nonterminals do not satisfy condition (2.8.3).

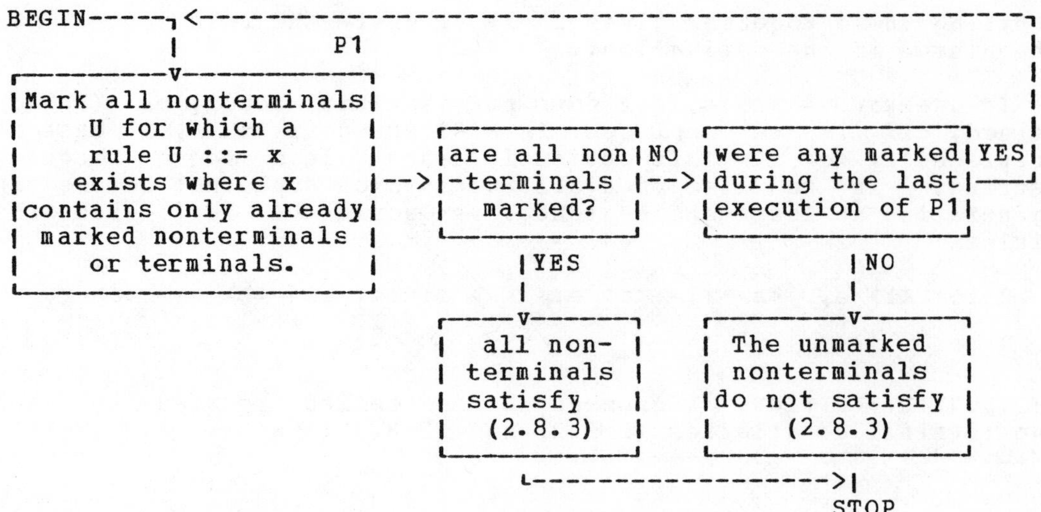


Details of box P1. i is a counter for the nonterminals. Assume rules are {Ui::=xi | i=1,...,n}.

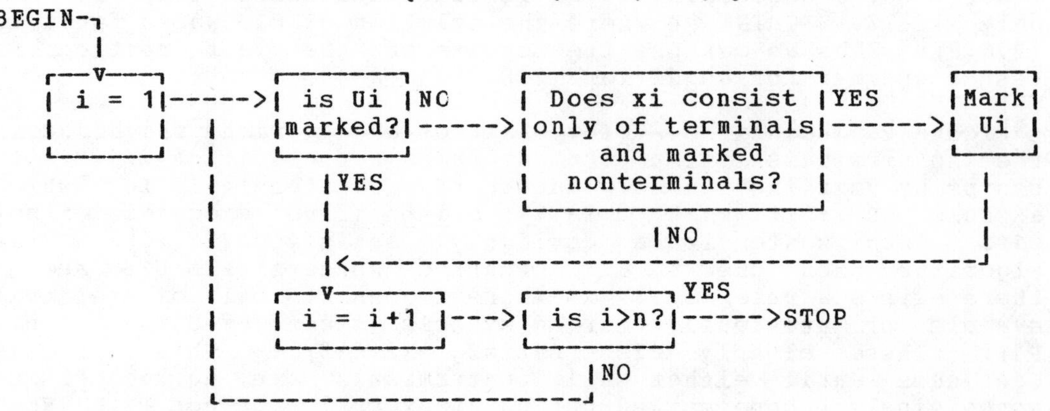


**FIGURE 2.11. Algorithm for Testing for (2.8.3).**

## EXERCISES FOR 2.8

1. Consider the following grammar.

```
Z      ::= E + T
E      ::= E | S + F | T
F      ::= F | FP | P
P      ::= G
G      ::= G | GG | F
T      ::= T * i | i
Q      ::= E | E + F | T | S
S      ::= i
```

Perform the following operations on the grammar.

A. a) Calculate the relation WITHIN+.
   b) Delete all rules containing (in the left or right part) a nonterminal which does not satisfy (2.8.2).

B. a) Perform the algorithm in Figure 2.11.
   b) Delete all rules containing a nonterminal which does not satisfy (2.8.3).
   c) Make a list of symbols which were nonterminal previous to step B but which are now terminals.
   d) Delete all rules containing symbols listed in step c).
   e) Repeat steps c and d until no rules are deleted.

C. Repeat steps A and B until no rules are deleted.

D. Change the grammar resulting from step C to satisfy (2.8.1). Write down the language L(G).

## 2.9 OTHER SYNTAX NOTATIONS

Several other notations are used in the literature for defining the syntax of various languages. We would like to review them briefly here. They have the same power as BNF -- what can be expressed in any of these notations can also be expressed in BNF. In many respects they are more readable than pure BNF, and we shall use them frequently throughout the book.

### Braces

In BNF, the only way to indicate a list of an arbitrary number of elements is through recursion. Thus we write

(2.9.1) <id list> ::= <identifier> | <id list> , <identifier>

and

(2.9.2) <integer> ::= <digit> | <integer> <digit>

Assuming that braces { and } are metasymbols used to bracket a string x to mean zero or more occurrences of x, we can rewrite (2.9.1) and (2.9.2) as

(2.9.3) <id list> ::= <identifer> {, <identifier>}.
<integer> ::= <digit> {<digit>}.

The two notations are assumed to be structurally equivalent. Sometimes a subscript and/or superscript is used after the braces to indicate the minimum and maximum number of times the string can be repeated. For example, FORTRAN identifiers having a maximum of six alphanumeric characters can be described by

```
                                              5
(2.9.4) <FORTRAN id> ::= <letter> {<an>}
                                              0

          <an>       ::= <letter> | <digit>
```

While we can represent this in BNF, it is awkward:

```
<FORTRAN id> ::= <letter> | <letter> <an list>
<an list>    ::= <an> | <an><an> | <an><an><an>
               | <an><an><an><an>
               | <an><an><an><an><an>
```

In order to get a one-dimensional representation (without subscripts or superscripts), we adopt the convention that the minimum number of times the string inside the braces may appear is 0, and we put the maximum number directly behind the closing braces -- with no blanks between. Hence we can write (2.9.4) as

```
<FORTRAN id> ::= <letter> {<an>}5
```

Note that this is different from

```
<FORTRAN id> ::= <letter> {<an>} 5
```

because of the space between the brace and the 5 in the latter.

The use of braces also allows us to use the metasymbol | inside braces to indicate a choice. { x | y | z } means a sequence of zero or more strings, each of which is an x, y, or z. We can use this to rewrite the syntax for a FORTRAN identifier as

```
<FORTRAN id> ::= <letter> {<letter> | <digit>}5
```

#### Brackets

Brackets [ and ] are often used to indicate an optional string. They are therefore equivalent to using braces followed directly by a 1. Suppose we wanted to describe a simple ALGOL-like loop statement where either the initial value or the step value (or both) could be omitted. We could do this by

```
<for loop>   ::= FOR <variable> [ := <expression> ]
                 [ STEP <expression> ]
                 UNTIL <expression> DO <statement>
```

#### Parentheses as Metasymbols

In right parts of rules, the catenation operator has precedence over alternation. Thus A B | C means either AB or C. When necessary, we use parentheses to override the normal precedence just as we do in conventional arithmetic expressions. Thus A ( B | C ) means either AB or AC. Parentheses as metasymbols will be useful in factoring within right parts, as we shall see in a moment. However, this does present problems when we want to use parentheses as terminal symbols of the language being defined. Henceforth we shall use the parentheses as normal terminal symbols, unless explicitly stated otherwise.

### Factoring

If we use parentheses as metasymbols, we can write the rules

```
U ::= xy | xw | ... | xz
```

as

```
U ::= x (y | w | ... | z)
```

where we have factored out the common head x of all the alternates. Parentheses can be nested to any level, just as in arithmetic expressions. For example, suppose y = y1y2 and w = y1y3. Then the above rules could be rewritten as

```
U ::= x (y1 (y2 | y3) | ... | z) .
```

As we shall see later, such factoring makes parsing easier at times.

If we consider the rules E ::= T | E+T to mean at least one T, followed by zero or more occurrences of +T, we can rewrite them as

```
E ::= T {+ T} .
```

Moreover, E ::= T | E + T | E - T can be written as

```
E ::= T {(+ | -) T}
```

Such a transformation which gets rid of the left recursion in a rule will be useful in top-down parsing.

### Metasymbols as Terminals

From time to time we must describe a language containing a terminal which is also a metasymbol, like ::=, |, or {. In this case we use quote marks around it to distinguish it from the metasymbol. For example a BNF rule can be partially described by

```
<rule> ::= <left part> '::=' <right part>
```

This of course makes the quote symbol a metasymbol. It must be represented as a terminal symbol within quotes by two quotes. Hence <quote> ::= '''' describes the nonterminal <quote>; the only string derivable from it is the string consisting of a single quote '.

## 2.10 SURVEY OF FORMAL LANGUAGE THEORY AND REFERENCE

Formal language theory has advanced rapidly since Chomsky(56) first described a formal language. The majority of the papers published are not concerned directly with our problem of parsing sentences of a programming language; rather they deal with the mathematical theory of languages and grammars. Different classes of languages with certain properties are defined. These languages are characterized in terms of grammars which generate only languages in the class and in terms of automata (machines) which recognize only languages in the class. Some typical questions asked are: If L1 and L2 are two languages of a class T, is the union (intersection) of the two languages also in T? Is a grammar ambiguous? Can we give an algorithm which, for any grammar of a class T will tell us whether that grammar is ambiguous or not? Are two grammars equivalent in some sense? Hopcroft and Ullman(69) is a good text on the subject. Ginsburg(66) contains more material but is more concise and harder to read. Two periodicals which contain many articles on the subject are _Information and Control_ and _Journal of the ACM_.

Chomsky(56) defined four basic classes of languages in terms of grammars, which are 4-tuples (V, T, P, Z) where

1. V is an alphabet;
2. T in V is an alphabet of terminal symbols;
3. P is a finite set of rewriting rules; and
4. Z, the distinguished symbol, is a member of V-T.

The language of a grammar is the set of terminal strings which can be generated from Z. The difference in the four types of grammars is in the form of the rewriting rules allowed in P. First of all, we say that G is a (Chomsky) _type 0_ or a _phrase-structure grammar_ if the rules in P have the form

(2.10.1) u ::= v  with u in V+ and V in V*.

That is, the left part u can also be a sequence of symbols and the right part can be empty. Comparatively little work has been done with phrase-structure grammars. We get the more interesting class of _type 1, context sensitive_ or _context dependent_ languages, if we restrict the rewriting rules to the form

(2.10.2) xUy ::= xuy  with U in V-T, x, y in V*, and u in V+.

The term context sensitive refers to the fact that we are allowed to rewrite U as u only in the context x...y. A further restriction yields a class of grammars which is quite similar to the class we are using; a grammar is called _context free_ if all the rules have the form

(2.10.3) U ::= u with U in V-T and u in V*.

This class is called context free because U can be rewritten as u regardless of the context in which it appears. In a context free grammar a rule may have the form U ::= ε where ε is the empty string. We do not allow this in our grammars because it unnecessarily complicates our terminology and our proofs. Given a context free grammar G one can construct an _ε-free grammar_ G1 (our kind) such that L(G1) = L(G) - {ε}. Moreover, if G is unambiguous, so is G1, so that we really don't have a restriction.

If we restrict the rules once more to the form

(2.10.4) U ::= N or U ::= WN, with N in T and U and W in V-T,

we have a _type 3_, or _regular grammar_. Regular grammars play a fundamental role in both language theory and automata theory. The set of strings generated by a regular grammar is also "accepted" by a machine called a _finite state automaton_ (which we will define in the next chapter), and vice versa. Thus we have a characterization of this class of grammars in terms of automata. Regular languages (those generated by a regular grammar) are also called regular sets. It is known that if L1 and L2 are regular sets, then so are L1 union L2, L1 intersection L2, L1-L2, L1.L2 = {xy | x in L1 and y in L2}, and L1* = {ε} union I1 union $L1^2$ union $L1^3$ union ...

The four classes of grammars we have defined are increasingly restricted. That is, there are phrase structure languages which are not context sensitive, context sensitive languages which are not context free, and context free languages which are not regular. Most of the work done in formal language theory deals with context free or regular languages, or subsets of them, so let us now restrict ourselves to these.

One of the basic questions that arises is whether a grammar is ambiguous or not. Unfortunately (or fortunately, depending on how you look at it) it has been proven that this question is _undecidable_ for context free grammars. This means that you cannot give an effective algorithm (write a program) which, given any grammar will always decide in a finite amount of time whether it is ambiguous or not. It turns out that many of the interesting questions concerning context free languages (e.g. are two languages equal, are two languages disjoint?) are undecidable. When this happens, one looks for interesting subclasses of languages where the property in question is decidable. Most proofs of undecidability theorems in formal language theory depend either directly or indirectly on a single theorem by Post(46).

It has been proven that the problem of deciding whether an arbitrary context free grammar is ambiguous or not is undecidable. The next question one might ask is whether there exists an unambiguous grammar for an arbitrary context free language. The answer is no. There are languages for which _no_ unambiguous grammar exists; this was first shown by Parikh(61).

Such languages are called <u>inherently</u> <u>ambiguous</u>. An example of one is

$$\{(a!i)(b!i)(c!j) \mid i,j \geq 1\} \text{ union } \{(a!i)(b!j)(c!j) \mid i,j \geq 1\}.$$

There is much literature which <u>is</u> concerned with our problem of parsing sentences of a language. We will be discussing solutions to the problem in the next few chapters.

## 2.11 REVIEW

This chapter forms the basic material for the next five chapters. It should be well understood before the reader proceeds. In order to help the reader review the material, we give below a list of definitions with page numbers, in the order presented.

# Chapter 3.
# The Scanner

## 3.1 INTRODUCTION

The scanner is that part of the compiler which reads in the original source program characters and constructs the source program words or symbols (identifiers, reserved words, integers, and single and double character delimiters like *, +, **, /*). The terms _token_ and _atom_ are sometimes used for _symbol_. In its pure form, the scanner performs a simple _lexical_ analysis of the source program, as opposed to a syntactic analysis, and is therefore sometimes called a _lexical analyzer_.

One may justly ask why the lexical analysis cannot be incorporated into the syntactic analysis. After all, we can use BNF to describe the syntax of symbols. For example, FORTRAN identifiers can be described by

(3.1.1) <identifier> ::= letter {letter | digit}5

There are several good reasons for separating lexical from syntactical analysis:

1. A large portion of compile-time is spent in scanning characters. Separation allows us to concentrate solely on reducing this time. One way is to program part or all of the scanner in assembly language, and this is easier if the separation is made. (For example, on the IBM 360, one can execute a _single_ TRT instruction to sequence through 1 to 256 characters looking for a non-blank character.) Of course, we don't recommend using assembly language unless the compiler is really going to be used often.

2. The syntax of symbols can be described by very simple grammars. If we separate scanning from syntax recognition, we can develop efficient parsing techniques which are particularly well suited for these grammars. Moreover, we can then develop automatic methods for constructing scanners which use these efficient techniques.

3. Since the scanner returns a symbol instead of a character, the syntax analyzer actually gets more information about what to do at each step. Moreover, some of the context checks necessary in order parse symbols are easier to perform in an ad hoc manner than in a formal syntax analyzer. For example, it is easy to recognize what is meant by the FORTRAN statement DO10I=... by determining whether a , or ( occurs first after the equal sign.

4. Development of high-level languages requires attention to both lexical and syntactic properties. Separation of the two allows us to investigate them independently.

5. Often one has two different hardware representations for the same language. For example, in some ALGOL implementations, reserved words are surrounded by quote characters, and blanks have essentially no meaning -- they are completely

ignored. In other implementations, reserved words cannot be used as identifiers, and adjacent reserved words and/or identifiers must be separated by at least one blank. The hardware representation on paper tape, cards, and on-line typewriters may be totally different.

Separation allows us to write one syntactic analyzer and several scanners (which are simpler and easier to write) -- one for each source program representation and/or input device. Each scanner translates the symbols into the same internal form used by the syntactic analyzer.

A scanner may be programmed as a separate pass which performs a complete lexical analysis of the source program and which gives to the syntax analyzer a table containing the source program in an internal symbol form. Alternatively, it can be a subroutine SCAN called by the syntax analyzer whenever the syntax analyzer needs a new symbol (Figure 3.1). When called, SCAN recognizes the next source program symbol and passes it to the syntax analyzer. This alternative is generally better, because the whole internal source program need not be constructed and kept in memory. We will assume that the scanner is to be implemented in this manner in the rest of this chapter.

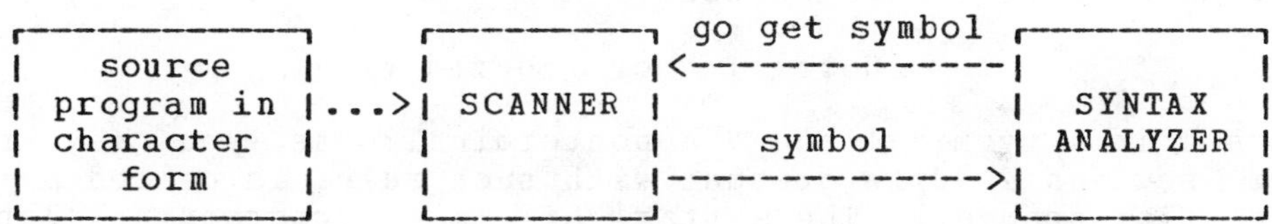


**FIGURE 3.1. Scanner as Subroutine of the Syntax Analyzer.**

Throughout this chapter, we shall assume that the source program is written in a free field format and that it is just a continuous stream of characters. Changes and additions for handling fixed field representations and cases where the end of a card means the end of a statement (e.g. FORTRAN) will be discussed at the end of section 3.3.

The difference between symbols and higher constructs is vague at times. For example, we can consider both integers and real numbers of the form

<integer> . <integer>

as symbols, or we can consider an integer to be a symbol and a real number to be a high-level construct. We will make arbitrary choices in such cases, mainly in the interest of simplicity of presentation.

### Using Regular Grammars

Most symbols in programming languages fall into one of the following classes:

> identifiers
> reserved words (which are a subset of the identifiers)
> integers
> single character delimiters (+, -, (, ), /, etc.)
> double character delimiters (//, /*, **, :=, etc.)

These symbols can be described by the following simple rules:

```
<identifier>     ::= letter | <identifer> letter
                   | <identifer> digit
<integer>        ::= digit | <integer> digit
<delimiter>      ::= + | - | ( | ) | / | ...
<delimiter>      ::= <SIASH> / | <SLASH> *
                   | <AST> * | <COLON> =
<SLASH>          ::= /
<AST>            ::= *
<COLCN>          ::= :
```

Of course the rules could be simpler, but we have written them so that each rule has the form

```
U ::= T    or    U ::= VT
```

where T is a terminal and V a nonterminal. As you may recall from section 2.10, a grammar with such rules is called a <u>type 3</u> or <u>regular</u> grammar. The syntax of most programming language symbols can be specified in such a form, so that it would be advantageous to find an efficient way of parsing sentences of a regular grammar. Let us therefore begin by designing an efficient parsing scheme.

## 3.2 REGULAR EXPRESSIONS AND FINITE-STATE AUTOMATA

This section contains some results which we will not formally prove. We are interested mainly in how to program scanners, and for this the proofs are not really necessary. See the books referenced in section 3.6 for detailed proofs.

### Stage Diagrams

Consider the regular grammar G[Z]

```
Z ::= U 0 | V 1
U ::= Z 1 | 1
V ::= Z 0 | 0
```

A brief investigation shows that the language consists of sequences of pairs of 01 or 10. That is,

$$L(G) = \{B!n \mid n > 0\} \text{ where } B = \{01, 10\}.$$

We draw a <u>state diagram</u> to help us recognize sentences of G as in Figure 3.2a. In the diagram, each nonterminal of G is represented by a node or <u>state</u>, and in addition we have a <u>start state</u> S (assuming there is no nonterminal S in the grammar). For each rule Q ::= T in G there is a directed arc labeled T from the start state S to the state Q. For each rule Q ::= RT in G there is an arc labeled T from state R to state Q.

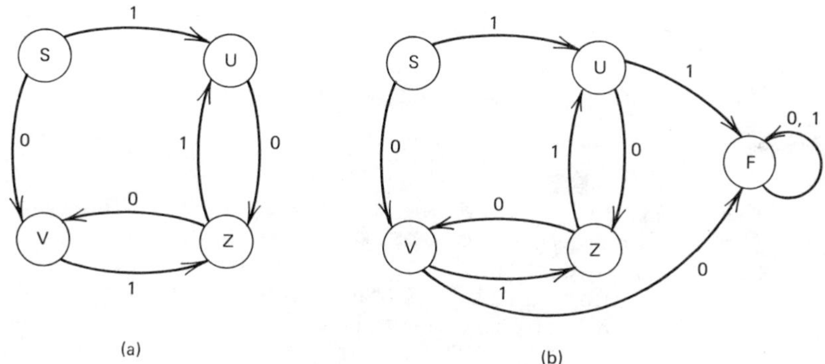


**FIGURE 3.2. State Diagrams.**

We use the state diagram to parse or recognize a string x as follows.

1. Begin in the start state S -- it is the initial "current" state. Starting with the leftmost character of x we iterate step 2 until the right end of x is reached.
2. Scan the next character of x. Proceed along an arc labeled with that character emanating from the current state to the next current state.

If at any iteration of step 2 there is no such arc, x is not a sentence and we stop. If we reach the end of x, then x is a sentence if and only if the last current state is Z.

The reader will recognize this to be a bottom-up parse. At each step (except the first), the handle is the name of the current state followed by the incoming symbol. The symbol to which it is reduced is the name of the next state. As an example, we show a parse of the sentence 101001. Each line of Figure 3.3a shows the state of the parse at the beginning of step 2.

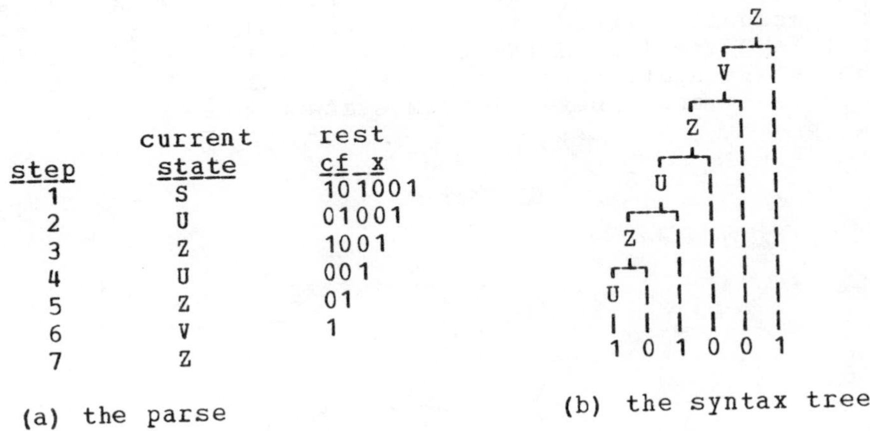

| step | current state | rest of x |
|---|---|---|
| 1 | S | 101001 |
| 2 | U | 01001 |
| 3 | Z | 1001 |
| 4 | U | 001 |
| 5 | Z | 01 |
| 6 | V | 1 |
| 7 | Z | |



(a) the parse (b) the syntax tree

**FIGURE 3.3. Parse and Syntax Tree for 101001.**

Parsing is so simple here because of the simple nature of the rules. Since a nonterminal occurs only as the first symbol of a right part, the first step always reduces the first symbol of the sentence to a nonterminal. Each successive step reduces the first two symbols UT of the sentential form UTt to a nonterminal V, using a rule V ::= UT. While performing this reduction, the name of the current state is U and the name of the next state is V. Since each right part is unique, the symbol to reduce to is unique. Syntax trees for sentences of regular grammars always have the shape given by the tree of Figure 3.3b.

In order to dispense with testing at each step whether there is an arc with the correct label, we can add one more state named F (for FAILURE), and add any necessary arcs from all states to F. We then also add an arc labeled with all possible characters leading from F back to F. This would change the diagram of Figure 3.2a to that of Figure 3.2b.

### Determining Finite Automata

In order to be able to manipulate state diagrams easily we want to formalize the idea a bit more, in terms of the states; the input characters; the start state S; a "mapping" M which, given a current state Q and an input character T, tells us what the next current state is; and the final states corresponding to Z in the above example.

(3.2.1) DEFINITION. A (deterministic) <u>finite state automaton</u> (fa) is a 5-tuple (K, VT, M, S, Z) where

1. K is an alphabet of elements, called <u>states</u>;
2. VT is an alphabet called the <u>input alphabet</u> (the characters which can appear in a string or sentence);
3. M is a <u>mapping</u> (or function) from K x VT into K (if M(Q,T) = R, then when in state Q with incoming character T, we switch to state R).
4. S (which must be in K) is the <u>start</u> state; and
5. Z is a nonempty set of <u>final</u> states, all of which must be in K. ■

We can also formally define what we mean by running the fa (or state diagram) with an input string t. We do this by extending the mapping which tells us how to switch states depending on the input character. We define

M(Q,ε) = Q    for all states Q;
M(Q,Tt) = M( M(Q,T), t)    for each t in VT* and T in VT.

The first line means that if the input character is the empty symbol, we stay in the same state. The second indicates that when in state Q, with input string Tt, we apply the mapping M to get to state P = M(Q,T) with input string t, and then apply the mapping M(P,t). Finally, a string t is <u>accepted</u> by an fa if M(S,t) = P where P is a state in the set of final states Z.

This type of automaton is called deterministic because at each step the next input character determines uniquely the next current state.

(3.2.2) EXAMPLE. The fa corresponding to the state diagram in Figure 3.2b is ({S,Z,U,V,F}, {0,1}, M, S, {Z}) where

M(S,0) = V    M(S,1) = U
M(V,0) = F    M(V,1) = Z
M(U,0) = Z    M(U,1) = F
M(Z,0) = V    M(Z,1) = U
M(F,0) = F    M(F,1) = F ■

Let us stop for a moment and review what we have done. We started with a regular grammar whose right parts were unique. From it we were able to construct a state diagram. This diagram was really an informal representation of an fa. It is easy to see that if a sentence x belongs to the grammar G, then it is also accepted by the fa for G. It is a little bit harder to show that for any fa there exists a grammar G whose sentences are just those strings accepted by the fa. We won't go through a proof here since we won't use the result.

### Representation Within a Computer

An fa with states S1,...,Sn and input characters T1,...,Tm can be represented by an n by m matrix B. The element B[i,j] contains the number k of the state Sk such that M[Si,Tj] = Sk. We can adopt the convention that S1 is the start state, and can have a list of the final states in a vector. Such a matrix is sometimes called a <u>transition matrix</u>, since it indicates how we switch from one state to another.

Another representation is a list structure. Each state with k arcs emanating from it is represented by 2*k+2 words. The first contains the name of the state, the second the value k. Each of the following pairs of words contains a terminal symbol from the input alphabet and a pointer to the beginning of the representation for the state to transfer to.

### Nondeterministic FA

We run into trouble when constructing an fa if G contains two rules

V ::= UT   and   W ::= UT

with the same right parts. For then there will be <u>two</u> arcs labeled T emanating from U in the state diagram, and the mapping M will not be single valued! An fa constructed from such a diagram is called a nondeterministic fa and is defined as follows:

(3.2.3) DEFINITION. A <u>nondeterministic fa</u>, or <u>nfa</u>, is a 5-tuple (K,VT,M,S,Z) where

1. K is an alphabet of states;
2. VT is the input alphabet;
3. M is a mapping of K x VT into <u>subsets</u> of K;
4. S in K is the set of start states; and
5. Z is the set of final states (which are all in K). ■

Again, the important difference here is that the mapping M yields a (possibly empty) set of states instead of a single state. The second difference is that several states may be start states. We extend the mapping M to K x VT* as before by defining

$$M(Q,\varepsilon) = \{Q\}$$

and

M(Q,Tt) is the union of the sets M(P,t) for P in M(Q,T)

for each T in VT and t in VT+. We extend it further by defining M({P1,P2,...,Pn},t) as the union of the sets M(Pi,t) for i=1,,n.

A string t is <u>accepted</u> by the automaton if there is a state P in both M(S,t) and Z, the set of final states.

As an example, consider the regular grammar G[Z]:

```
Z ::= U 1 | V 0 | Z 0 | Z 1
U ::= Q 1 | 1
V ::= Q 0 | 0
Q ::= Q 0 | Q 1 | 0 | 1
```

A brief investigation shows that the language L(G) is the set of all sequences of 0's and 1's containing at least two consecutive 0's or two consecutive 1's. (To see this, start generating sentences from Z). Figure 3.4a gives the corresponding state diagram and Figure 3.4b the nfa. The FAILURE state here is the subset ∅ containing no symbols.

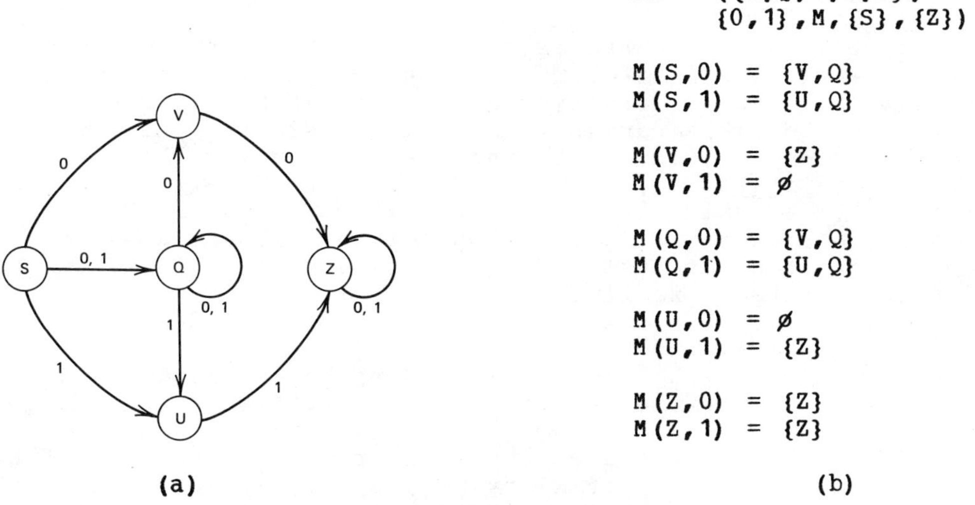


```
FA = ({S,Q,V,U,Z},
      {0,1},M,{S},{Z})

M(S,0) = {V,Q}
M(S,1) = {U,Q}

M(V,0) = {Z}
M(V,1) = ∅

M(Q,0) = {V,Q}
M(Q,1) = {U,Q}

M(U,0) = ∅
M(U,1) = {Z}

M(Z,0) = {Z}
M(Z,1) = {Z}
```

(b)

**FIGURE 3.4. State Diagram and its NFA.**

The problem here is that at each step there may be more than one arc labeled with the next input character, so that we don't know which path to take. At each step we know what the handle of the current sentential form is, but we don't know what to reduce it to. Let us show the acceptance of the string 01001 for the above machine, at each step picking the right path. To begin with, we are in state S. Upon reading the initial 0 we switch to either state V or Q; we choose Q. Since the next character is 1, the third state is either U or Q; we again choose Q. The following chart shows the complete parse.

| step | current state | rest of input string | possible successors | our choice |
|---|---|---|---|---|
| 1 | S | 01001 | V, Q | Q |
| 2 | Q | 1001 | U, Q | Q |
| 3 | Q | 001 | V, Q | V |
| 4 | V | 01 | Z | Z |
| 5 | Z | 1 | Z | Z |

Note, now, that from any regular grammar G we can construct a state diagram and then an nfa. The state diagram may have any number of start states. It is fairly obvious that any sentence of G is accepted by the nfa; running the nfa is just a different way of saying we are performing a bottom-up parse. As in the deterministic case, for any nfa we can find a regular grammar G whose sentences are just those strings accepted by the nfa. This we will not prove.

### Creating an FA from an NFA

The problem with the nfa is that at each step we don't know which arc to take if more than one exists with the same label. We now show how to construct an fa from an nfa which in a sense tries all possible parses in parallel, deleting those which come to a dead end. That is, if the nfa has for example the choices of three states X, Y, and Z, then the fa will have a single state [X,Y,Z] which represents the three of them. Note that the possible states at each step of the nfa are a subset of the complete set of states of the nfa, and that the number of different subsets is finite.

(3.2.4) THEOREM. Let F = (K,VT,M,S,Z) be an nfa accepting a set of strings L. Define the fa F' = (K',VT,M',S',Z') as follows:

1. The alphabet of states consists of all the subsets of K. We denote an element of K' by [S1,S2,...,Si] where S1,S2,...,Si are states of K. (We assume always that the states S1,S2,...,Si are in some canonical order, so that for example, the state of K' for the subset {S1,S2} = {S2,S1} is [S1,S2].)
2. The set of input characters VT are the same for F and F'.
3. We define the mapping M' by

   M'([S1,S2,...,Si],T) = [R1,R2,...,Rj]

   where

   M({S1,S2,...,Si},T) = {R1,R2,...,Rj}

4. Let S = {S1,...,Sn}. Then S' = [S1,...,Sn].
6. Let Z be {Sj,Sk,...,Sl}. Then Z' = [Sk,Sj,...Sl].

Then the set of strings accepted by F' is the same as that for F. The proof is left to the reader. ■

(3.2.5) EXAMPLE. The diagram below on the left is a state diagram for an nfa, with start states S and P and one final state Z. The diagram on the right is the corresponding fa; the start state is [S,P], while the set of final states is {[Z], [S,Z], [P,Z], [S,P,Z]}. Note that the states [S] and [P,Z] can be deleted, since there is no way of reaching them. We have in no sense produced a minimal fa -- one with the fewest number of states possible. There exists an algorithm for constructing a minimal fa; see the texts referenced in section 3.6. ▪

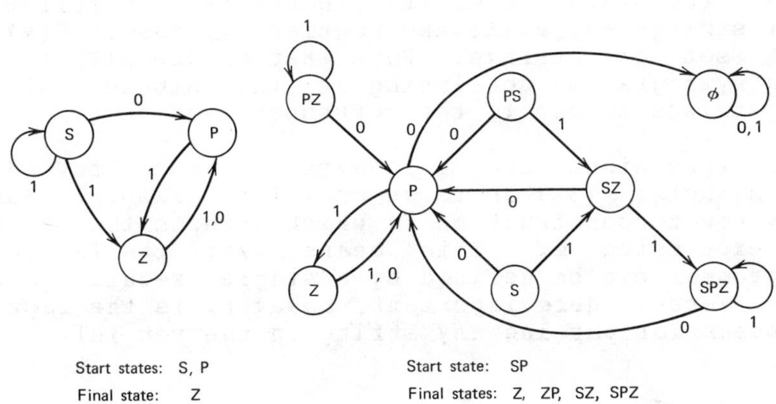


Start states: S, P
Final state: Z

Start state: SP
Final states: Z, ZP, SZ, SPZ

**Regular Expressions**

THE REST OF THIS SECTION NEED ONLY BE READ IN ORDER TO UNDERSTAND SECTION 3.5 ON THE AED RWORD SYSTEM.

In section 2.9 we discussed the use of symbols and the metasymbols |, (, ), {, and } within a sequence of right parts for the rules for a single nonterminal. There is a close connection between such right parts and regular expressions. Let S = {S1,...,Sn}. Then

1. ∅, ε, S1, ..., Sn are regular expressions over the set S.
2. if $e^1$ and $e^2$ are regular expressions over S, then so are

$$(e^1), \quad \{e^1\}, \quad \{e^1\}n, \quad e^1\, e^2, \quad \text{and } e^1 \mid e^2$$

ε represents the empty symbol and ∅ the empty set. The regular expression {e}n for some integer n is equivalent to the expression

$$\varepsilon \mid e \mid (e)(e) \mid \ldots \mid (e)\ldots(e)$$

where in the last alternate (e) is repeated n times. Hence we shall not need to discuss it further.

The value of a regular expression e, written |e|, is a set over S, and is defined as follows:

1. |ø| = ø, the empty set
2. |ε| = {ε} (the set consisting of the empty symbol)
3. |Si| = {Si} for i = 1,...,n
4. |(e)| = |e|
5. $|e^1\ e^2| = |e^1|\ |e^2| = \{xy \mid x \text{ in } |e^1| \text{ and } y \text{ in } |e^2|\}$
6. $|e^1|e^2| = |e^1|$ union $|e^2|$
7. |{e}| = closure of |e| = |e|*

With the exception of the symbol ø, the meaning of a regular expression is similar to that for the set of right parts of rules for a nonterminal. For example, we write E ::= 0 {+1} to mean that the syntactic entity E generates a 0 followed by any number of strings +1, while the regular expression 0{+1} defines the same set of strings. Note that the regular set ø can be described by a grammar consisting of the single rule V::=V, since no strings belong to the corresponding language.

Regular expressions are a convenient tool for describing lexical symbols; (3.1.1) is an excellent example. Moreover we will show how to construct an fa which accepts the set |e| for a regular expression e. This means that the language of any regular grammar can be defined by a single regular expression, and vice versa. More important, however, is the fact that the fa is a means for parsing any string in the set |e|.

### Constructing an FA for a Regular Expression

We create an fa for a regular expression e in four steps:

1. Construct a transition system (to be defined) for e;
2. Construct a state diagram from the transition system;
3. Construct an nfa from the state diagram, and
4. Construct an fa from the nfa.

Steps 3 and 4 have already been described, so we need only explain steps 1 and 2. The use of the transition system simplifies the process of combining diagrams representing several regular expressions.

(3.2.6) DEFINITION. A <u>transition system</u> is a state diagram with a unique start state S and a unique final state Z. S has no arcs leading to it while Z has no arcs leading from it. In addition, an arc may be labeled with the empty symbol ε. ■

Figure 3.5b is a transition system. It accepts the same set as does the corresponding state diagram of Figure 3.5a. The general idea of "running" a transition system is the same as that for running a state diagram; we need only explain the meaning of an arc labeled ε, which we do as follows. If the current state is A and an arc labeled ε leads to a state B, then we consider the current state to be either A or B. That is, the next state can be a successor of either A or B.

(3.2.7) THEOREM. There exists a transition system for any state diagram.

Construction. Let S be the state diagram, with start states S1, S2, ..., Sn and final states Z1, Z2,..., Zm. Add a new state S, the new unique start state, with arcs labeled ε leading to S1, S2, ..., Sn. Add a new state Z, the final state, with arcs labeled ε leading to it from Z1, Z2, ..., Zm. Figure 3.5b is the transition diagram corresponding to the state diagram of Figure 3.5a. ∎

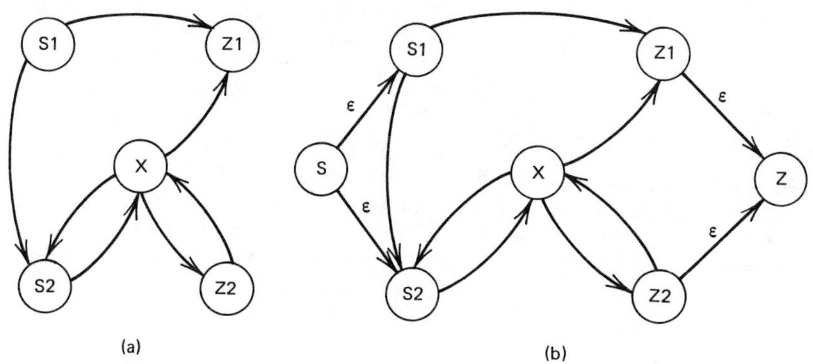


**FIGURE 3.5. State Diagram and Equivalent Transition System.**

(3.2.8) THEOREM. For each regular expression e there exists a transition system which accepts |e|.

Construction. The transition systems for ∅, ε, and Si are, respectively,

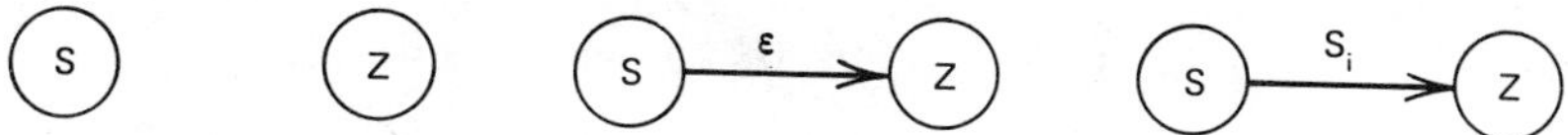


The transition system for (e) is the same as that for e. Suppose we have transition systems for $e^1$ and $e^2$, and let them be represented by

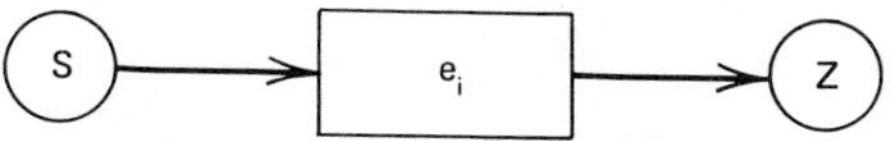

where S is the start state and Z the final state. Then the transition systems for $e^1 \mid e^2$ and $e^1 e^2$ are, respectively,

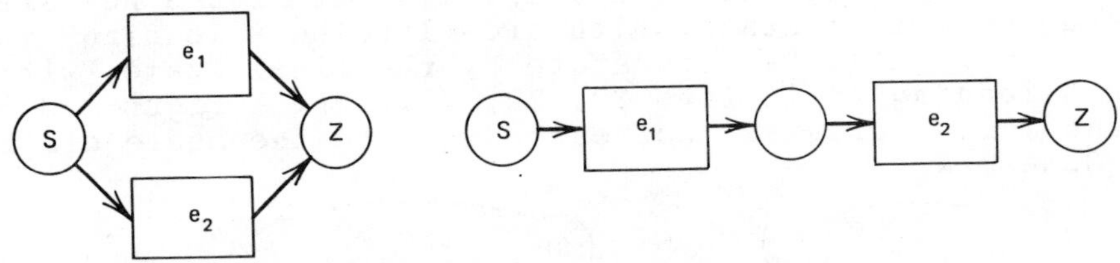


In the first diagram above, the final state of $e^1$ has been identified with the start state of $e^2$; in the second, the start states are identified and the final states are identified. The diagram below is for the regular expression $\{e^1\}$. We leave it to the reader to satisfy himself that the transition systems constructed are indeed the desired ones. ■

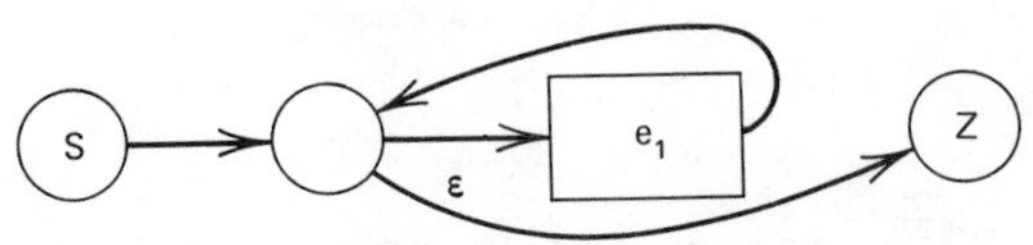


The last step is to construct a state diagram from a transition system. We must get rid of the arcs labeled ε. The following algorithm deletes at least one such arc without changing the set of strings accepted by the system (it may increase the number of start or final states). If we repeat the algorithm enough times, then, all arcs labeled ε will be deleted.

1. Find a state with an arc labeled ε leading from it. Follow that arc to the next state, and continue along arcs labeled ε in this manner until a situation

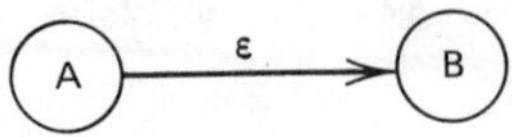


is found where B has no arc labeled ε leading from it. If no such situation exists, then execute step 3; otherwise execute step 2.

2. If there is a sequence of arcs labeled ε leading from a start state to A (and thus to B), make B a start state. If B is a final state make A a final state. Delete the arc labeled ε from A to B. For each arc labeled Si leading from B to a state C, add an arc labeled Si leading from A to C. This is illustrated in Figure 3.6.
3. If no situation as illustrated in step 1 exists, there must be a sequence of states A1, A2, ..., An, A1, such that an arc labeled ε leads from each Ai to A[i+1], for i = 1, ..., n-1, and in addition, an arc labeled ε from An to A1. (The proof is left to the reader.) Identify all these states; that is, make a single state out of all of them. Delete the arcs labeled ε just mentioned. If any of the states Ai was a start (final) state, make the new state a start (final) state. This is illustrated in Figure 3.7.

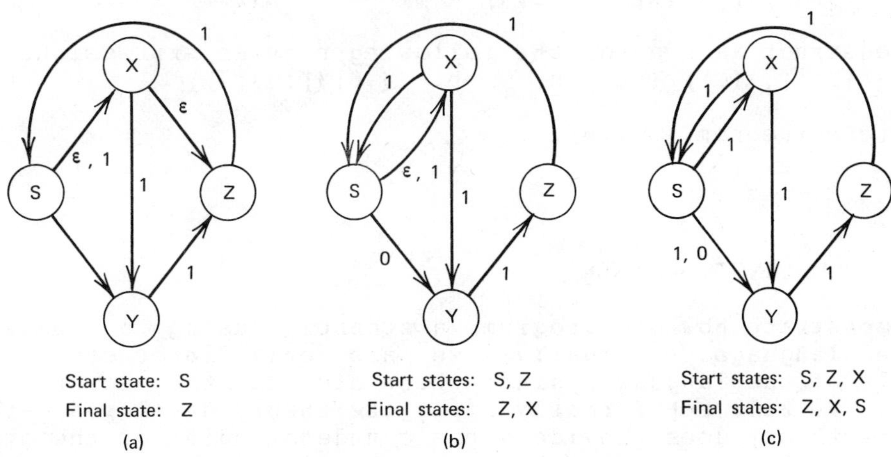


**FIGURE 3.6. Deleting Arcs Labeled ε (Step 2).**

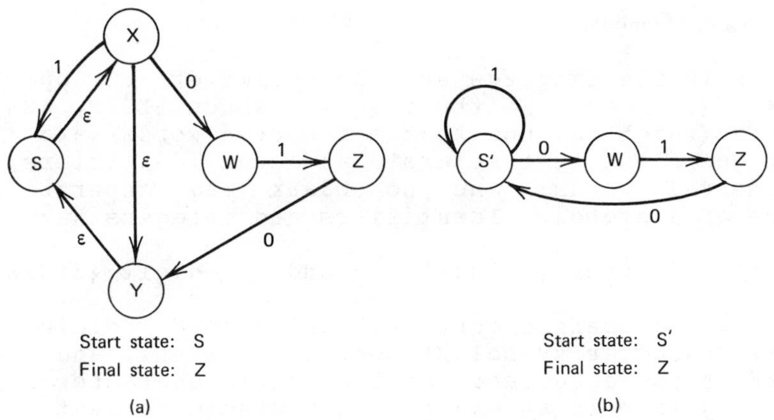


**FIGURE 3.7. Deleting Arcs Labeled ε (Step 3).**

## EXERCISES FOR 3.2

1. Construct an automaton for the following grammar G[Z]. Is it deterministic? What is the corresponding language?

Z ::= A 0     A ::= A 0 | Z 1 | 0

2. Construct an fa which accepts all strings in {0,1} such that every 1 has a 0 immediately to its right. Construct a regular grammar for the same language.

3. Construct an fa for the nfa of Figure 3.4.

4. Construct an fa from the nfa ({X,Y,Z}, {0,1}, M, {X}, {Z}) where

M(X,0) = {Z}     M(Y,0) = {X,Y}     M(Z,0) = {X,Z}
M(X,1) = {X}     M(Y,1) = ∅     M(Z,1) = {Y}

5. Construct an nfa for the following regular expressions:
a. ((A|B) |{A|C}) | D E M     b. {{0|1}|(1 1)}

6. Prove theorem (3.2.4).

## 3.3 PROGRAMMING A SCANNER

We demonstrate how one programs a scanner, using a small and simple language. Actually, we are only interested in the symbols of the language, since these are what the scanner must build. We will not formally apply the theory developed earlier, but the theory does provide a basic understanding of the problem and will guide us very much in our thinking.

### The Source Language Symbols

The symbols in the language are the delimiters or operators /, +, -, *, (, ) and //, the reserved words BEGIN, ABS and END, identifiers (which may not be the reserved words) and integers. At least one blank must separate adjacent identifiers, integers and/or reserved words; and no blank may separate adjacent characters of a symbol. Identifiers and integers have the forms

letter {letter | digit}     and     digit {digit}

In addition, the scanner must recognize and delete comments. The double character symbol /* begins a comment, and the comment ends at the first occurrence of the double character symbol */. The following line is an example of a single comment:

/* This is * / / a single comment */

### The Output of the Scanner

A scanner builds an internal representation of each symbol. In most cases this is a fixed length integer (a byte, halfword, word, etc.). The rest of the compiler can process these integers much more efficiently than the variable length strings which are the actual symbols.

We include in this internal representation a number meaning "identifier" and another for "integer". That is, all identifiers have the same internal number to represent them. This is natural, because the term "identifier" is a terminal symbol to the syntax analyzer, and which identifier it happens to be is of no consequence. However, the identifier itself is needed by the semantic analyzer, so it must be stored somewhere. The solution is to output two values; the first is the internal representation and the second is the actual symbol itself or a pointer to it. (It is sometimes easier if the scanner keeps a table of all different symbols and returns a fixed integer as the second value -- the index of the entry in the table).

Let us for the rest of this chapter settle on the following internal representations of the symbols. Note that we assign a mnemonic name to each, which we shall use throughout. (In the programming language in which the scanner is being written we assume $ is a letter and can be used in identifiers.) The name could be associated with the number either through a macro definition or through the use of a variable initialized with the number. This technique is invaluable in programming. It makes programs more readable and facilitates changes.

| internal repr. | symbol | mnemonic name | internal repr. | symbol | mnemonic name |
|---|---|---|---|---|---|
| 0 | undefined | $UND | 6 | / | $SLASH |
| 1 | identifier | $ID | 7 | + | $PLUS |
| 2 | integer | $INT | 8 | - | $MINUS |
| 3 | BEGIN | $BEGIN | 9 | * | $STAR |
| 4 | ABS | $ABS | 10 | ( | $LPAR |
| 5 | END | $END | 11 | ) | $RPAR |
| | | | 12 | // | $SLSL |

**FIGURE 3.8. Internal Representation of Symbols.**

As an example, consider the program segment

```
BEGIN A + / BC// /* COMMENT ++*/ END 11
```

The scanner would pass the following to the calling routine.

| step | output | meaning |
|---|---|---|
| 1 | 3, 'BEGIN' | BEGIN |
| 2 | 1, 'A' | identifier A |
| 3 | 7, '+' | + |
| 4 | 6, '/' | / |
| 5 | 1, 'BC' | identifier BC |
| 6 | 12, '//' | // |
| 7 | 5, 'END' | END |
| 8 | 2, '11' | integer 11 |

### The State Diagram

As a start at implementing the scanner, we draw a state diagram showing how a symbol is parsed (Figure 3.9). There are several points to be discussed here. The label D is an abbreviation for the labels 0,1,2,...,9. That is, D represents the class of digits. This is done to keep the diagram simple. Similarly, the label L represents the class of letters A,B,...,Z and DELIM represents the class of single character delimiters +, -, *, (, and ). Note that / is not in the class since it must be handled in a special manner.

Several of the arcs have no labels on them. These are the arcs to be taken if the character scanned is one that does not explicitly appear on an arc. For example, when in state INT, as long as we scan a digit we stay in state INT. If a non-digit is scanned we proceed along the arc to OUT.

The arcs to OUT and ERROR are an additional feature to the state diagram. All we mean here is that we have detected the end of a symbol and want to leave the scanner. One of the problems here is that when going to OUT we may or may not have scanned the character following the symbol recognized. We have if we go to OUT from INT or ID, but we haven't if we have just recognized a delimiter (DELIM). When the next symbol is desired, we will have to know whether its first character has been scanned or not. This can be done through some switch. We will subsequently adopt the alternate convention that the next character will <u>always</u> be scanned before we leave the scanner.

One more point. We have written a deterministic rather than a nondeterministic diagram. Thus, we have taken care of the problems of determining whether / begins a $SLASH, $SLSL or a comment by always going to the common state SLA.

This informal state diagram has helped us figure out how to parse the symbols. Now let us see how to add "semantics" -- how to add information to tell us what to do with a symbol as it is being parsed.

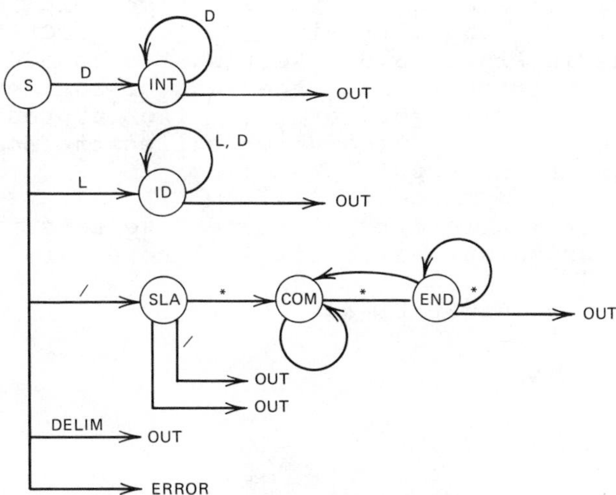


**FIGURE 3.9. State Diagram Scanning Symbols.**

### Global Variables and Routines Needed

The scanner will need the following variables and routines:

1. CHARACTER CHAR. CHAR is a global variable which will always hold the character of the source program being scanned.
2. INTEGER CLASS. CLASS contains an integer representing the class of the character in CHAR. We will use D (digit) = 1, L (letter) = 2, the class containing the character / = 3, and the class DELIM = 4.
3. STRING A. A is a location which will contain the string of characters making up the symbol.
4. GETCHAR is a procedure whose purpose is to scan the next source program character, put it in CHAR, and put its class in variable CLASS. GETCHAR will take care of reading and printing the next source program line when necessary, and any other similar details. It is a good idea to use a separate routine for this purpose, rather than have several copies of the statements necessary to scan the next character.
5. GETNONBLANK is a routine which tests CHAR to see whether it is the blank character and if so, repeatedly calls GETCHAR until a nonblank character appears.

### Adding Semantics to the State Diagram

Now that we have a general outline of parsing the symbols, we add statements which take care of building the symbols. This is done in Figure 3.10. The diagram is essentially the same as that of Figure 3.9, but in addition we have put commands to be executed underneath each arc. We have also explicitly put in the command GC, an abbreviation for GETCHAR. This was implicitly done in Figure 3.9. We also had to add a bit of a flow chart upon recognizing the end of an identifier to see whether it is a reserved word or not. The expression OUT(C,D) means to return to the routine which called the scanner with the two values C and D as output.

Under the first arc leading to state S we have put the command INIT which means do any initialization necessary. In our case, we execute

```
GETNONBLANK;    A := '';
```

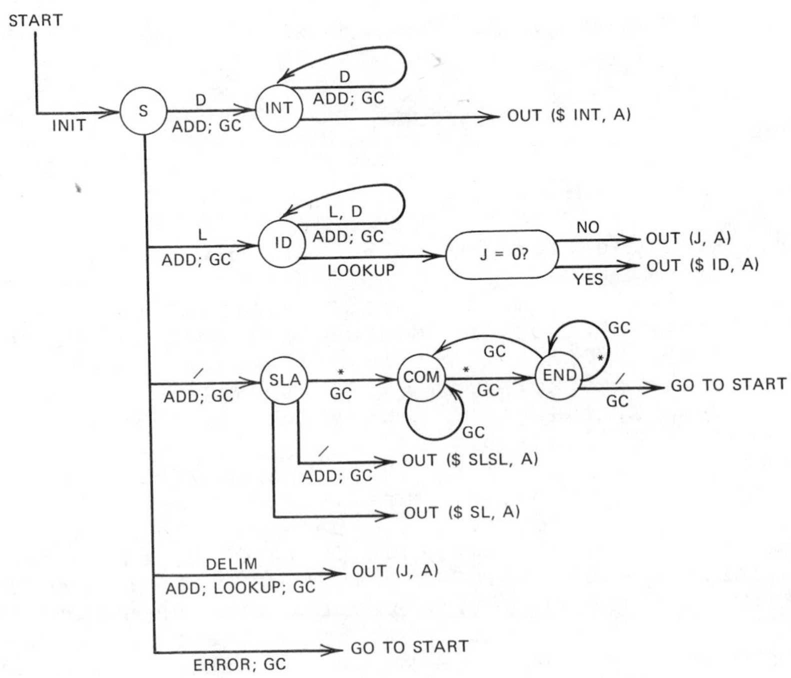


**FIGURE 3.10. State Diagram with Semantics.**

This makes sure we have a nonblank character in CHAR and initializes the location A which will contain the symbol. The command ADD means to add the character in CHAR onto the symbol in A, by A := A CAT CHAR; The LOOKUP command looks in the table of reserved words for the symbol in A. If found, its index is put into the global variable J; otherwise 0 is put there.

Notice that when a comment or an error is detected, we don't return but continue again to scan the following symbol.

Let us step through the parse of the symbol //. We begin by executing the initalization (INIT). We are then in state S. Checking CHAR, which is /, sends us along the arc to state SLA. While going there we add / to A (the ADD command) and call GETCHAR to scan the next character. In state SLA we check the new character in CHAR and take the arc labeled /. While traversing the arc, we catenate the character in CHAR onto the string in A and scan the next character (GC). We end by returning with the pair ($SLSL,0). Note that the character <u>following</u> the symbol is in CHAR upon exit.

The reader is encouraged to step through the parse of the following symbols +, 235, BEGIM, BEGIN, /*COMMENT*/, and /.

### The Program

The ALGOL-like procedure below was programmed directly from the state diagram of Figure 3.10. The procedure has two parameters -- the first is the internal representation of the symbol that is built, the second is the string of characters making up the symbol. Alternatively, SYN and SEM could be global locations -- global to the scanner and all places which call the scanner. This is in general more efficient and is to be recommended.

The procedure uses a CASE statement based on the class number of the character in CHAR to determine which arc to take from the initial state S.

### Discussion

There are several points we want to discuss here. First of all, note that the scanner always builds the longest symbol possible. Thus ABC12 is a single identifier, not an identifier followed by an integer. This works out well in most cases, but not all. The famous example is the FORTRAN statement DO10I = 1,20 where DO10I is not an identifier but is the keyword DO followed by the statement number 10 followed by the identifier I. Obviously, our method won't work perfectly on FORTRAN. It is usually fairly easy to design a small program segment to look ahead in the source program and make a decision in such cases.

PROCEDURE SCAN( INTEGER SYN; STRING SEM)

```
START:GETNONBLANK; A := '';    |This line is INITialization.
CASE CLASS OF                  |CASE statement is used to move
BEGIN                          |along an arc from state S to
                               |INT, ID, SLA, etc.
  BEGIN WHILE CLASS = 1 DO     |CLASS = 1 means digit. This is
       BEGIN A:=A CAT CHAR;    |state INT. Just scan characters
             GETCHAR;          |and add them to A until a non-
       END;  SYN := $INT;      |digit is found. Then fix param-
  END;                         |eter SYN.
                               |
  BEGIN WHILE CLASS ≤  2 DC    |This is state ID - came here
       BEGIN A:=A CAT CHAR;    |because CHAR was a letter. Scan
             GETCHAR;          |the characters until one
       END;  SYN := $ID;       |which is not L or D is found.
                               |
      LOOKUP(A);               |See if it's a reserved word.
      IF J≠0 THEN SYN := J;    |If so, fix SYN.
  END;                         |
                               |
  BEGIN A := CHAR; GETCHAR;    |This is state SLA.
   IF CHAR = '*' THEN          |If next character is * we have
    BEGIN B: GETCHAR;          |a comment. Scan until another
   C:IF CHAR≠'*' THEN GOTO B;  |* is found.
     GETCHAR;                  |The next character may be the /
     IF CHAR≠'/' THEN GOTO C;  |to end the comment.
     GETCHAR; GO TO START      |Have /, so it's ended. Scan and
    END;                       |go to get a new symbol.
   IF CHAR = '/' THEN          |
    BEGIN A := A CAT CHAR;     |This is the arc labeled / out
          GETCHAR; SYN:=$SLSL; |of state SLA
    END                        |
   ELSE SYN := $SLASH          |This is the unlabeled arc from
  END;                         |state SLA
                               |
  BEGIN LOOKUP(A);             |Look up the delimiter's number
        SYN := J; GETCHAR;     |and assign it to SYN.
  END;                         |
                               |
  BEGIN ERROR; GETCHAR;        |Have a character which is not
        GO TO START;           |allowed. Skip it and continue.
  END                          |
END;   SEM ::= A;              |End of case statement,  scanner
```

FORTRAN also has fixed fields -- the label field is columns 1-5, the statement field is columns 7-72. The modifications necessary for fixed field source language representations are simple and we won't go into it here.

FORTRAN and many other languages allow only one statement per card. The scanner in FORTRAN must also watch out for continuation cards, which are indicated by a nonblank character in column 6. The problem is most easily solved in the GETCHAR routine. When GETCHAR reaches the end of a card it reads in the next and checks column 6. If nonblank it continues by passing the characters in columns 7, 8,...; if blank, then it passes a special "end of card" character to the scanner, which passes it on to the syntax analyzer as a special internal symbol. It is good to isolate these problems and solve them in the most logical place, rather than make provisions all over the program for them.

In some source language representations blanks are completely ignored (except in strings). This can be accomplished by having the GETCHAR routine just skip over "ignore" characters. Another alternative is to have an arc emanating from each state (labeled with the blank character) and going directly back to that state. This may be a better solution if the GETCHAR routine is to be used by several different scanners, which is our next topic.

Some programming languages can be divided into several parts, each of which has entirely different rules for forming symbols. This is so for the normal FORTRAN statements as opposed to the FORMAT statement. In ALGOL, blanks within strings have meaning, while outside of strings they are completely ignored. Some languages allow you to intersperse statements with assembly language statements.

In such cases, it is advantageous to have a different scanner for each different part of the language, and to have statements (procedure calls) which switch from one to the other. This is a rather simple thing to accomplish and needs no further discussion.

The simplest and most efficient way for the GETCHAR routine to compute the CLASS of a character is through a vector C. Using the EBCDIC (ASCII, or BCD) representation of the character as an integer i, the element C(i) will contain the class number for character i. This is of course assuming that each character is put in only one class. Instructions like the IBM 360 TRT instruction can be used to scan ahead to the first nonblank character and put its class in a register.

## EXERCISES FOR 3.3

1. Write procedures GETCHAR and GETNONBLANK in bastard ALGOL.

2. Program and debug the complete scanner in some high-level language.

## 3.4 A CONSTRUCTOR FOR COMPILER SCANNERS

The overall structure of symbols in most programming languages is sufficiently similar that we can write one general scanning algorithm for all the languages. The scanning algorithm will use several tables, and it is just these tables which will vary depending on the language. We can then program a constructor which accepts a description of the symbols of a programming language and which produces the necessary tables for that language (Figure 3.11). Once the constructor has built the tables, we can throw it away. Thus, in the figure we can delete everything to the left of the double line.

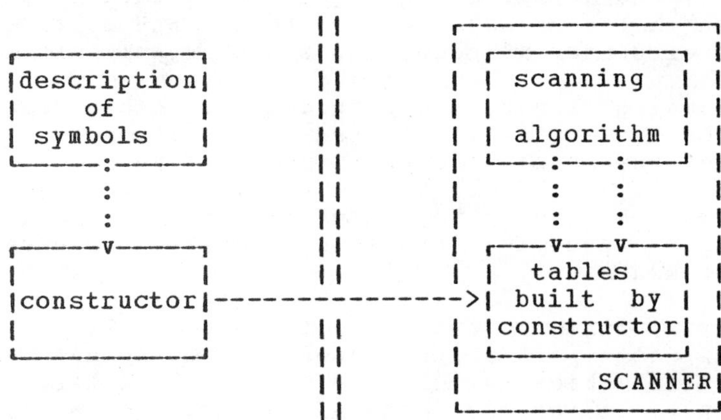


**FIGURE 3.11. Constructor and Scanner.**

We begin by describing the general structure of symbols (3.4.1). Next (3.4.2) we draw a state diagram for the scanning algorithm. We also describe the tables needed by the scanning algorithm. We finally show what the input will look like to the constructor.

### 3.4.1 Structure of Symbols

We shall need to parse the following types of symbols.

1. Identifiers or reserved words of the form

   <beginning character> {<other characters>}

   In general, the beginning character must be a letter, while the others can be letters or digits. Some languages allow $, _, - and other characters in identifiers. In addition, there is sometimes a maximum number of characters allowed.
2. Integers of the form <digit> {<digit>}. In general the digits are 0,1,...,9, but they could be 0,1,...,7 for octal,

or 0,1,...,9,A,...,F for hexadecimal.
3. Single character delimiters like /, -, +.
4. Double character delimiters like //, /*.
5. "Keywords" like 'BEGIN' in ALGOL, .EQ. and .AND. in some FORTRAN IV implementations. In some implementations they cannot be used as identifiers; this makes scanning and parsing much easier.

Other than this we have only to specify what meaning blanks and similar characters have. Are they completely ignored, or do they terminate other symbols, or are they normal characters? We shall not implement comments in the scanner since we will allow a user to switch back and forth between scanners. Thus, when he detects a symbol beginning a comment he can switch to a different scanner to process it.

### 3.4.2 The Scanning Algorithm

#### Classes of Characters

An investigation of the types of symbols to be parsed indicates the need for the following classes of characters:

1. DIGIT -- those characters which can appear in a symbol called "integer".
2. IDBEG -- those characters which can appear as the first character of an "identifier".
3. IDCHAR -- those characters which can appear as the second, third, fourth, ..., character of an "identifier".
4. IGNORE -- those characters which are to be completely ignored or deleted by the scanner (like a blank in some ALGOL implementations).
5. INVTERMIN -- those characters which signal the end of any symbol being formed, but which are otherwise ignored and are to be deleted (like a blank in some ALGOL implementations).
6. DELIM -- those characters which are themselves symbols -- like +, -, :, /, ( and ). They may of course be used later to form double character delimiters and to quote keywords.

Most of these classes must be disjoint -- no character may appear in two of them. The only overlap allowed is with the classes DIGIT and IDCHAR. In our implementation, for efficiency purposes, we will actually break up the DELIMiters into four classes as follows.

6. Those delimiters which do not begin a double-character symbol or a keyword.
7. Those delimiters which begin at least one keyword but no double-character symbol.
8. Those delimiters which begin at least one double-character symbol but no keyword.
9. Those delimiters which begin both a keyword and a double-character symbol.

### The State Diagram

Using these classes we can now draw a state diagram as in Figure 3.12. There is one additional feature needed which we haven't had to use before -- backup. Suppose we have the input characters .ED. where "." begins at least one keyword. Is this the single symbol .ED. or the three symbols ., ED, and . ? We don't know until we have looked up .ED. in the list of symbols. If .ED. is not a symbol, we ask the GETCHAR routine to "take back" the characters so we can start again. This is accomplished by marking the beginning character position in some manner (MARK) and then, when necessary, asking the GETCHAR routine to BACKUP to begin again at the last-marked character. Note that we back up over ignored characters too; it is not just a matter of copying those "good" characters which have to be rescanned. This is because recognition of a symbol may at any time cause a switch to another scanner, thus changing the meaning of characters.

Because of the restricted nature of backup here, we need only keep track of the last marked character, and that one only for a limited amount of time. As soon as we output a symbol we need no longer remember the mark.

### The Tables for the Scanning Algorithm

The particular representation of the necessary information may very well depend upon the machine and language in which the scanning algorithm is implemented. Nevertheless, we can give some general guidelines here.

First of all, one needs a table of all the symbols in the language, together with their internal representation. This includes all the delimiters, reserved words and keywords. It is used by the LOOKUP command to find the internal representation of a symbol. Since this occurs very often, it should probably be hash-coded (see Chapter 9).

The second table needed is used in order to find the CLASS of a character when we are in state S. The best type of table is a vector V where the EBCDIC representation of the character is used as the index: for a character C, V(C) contains the class. Note here that whether a character is in class IDCHAR or not plays no role here; we are interested only in the classes IGnore, INVtermin, DIGIT, IDBEG, and the DELIM classes.

We need a third table, used when in states ID and KY2 to distinguish between classes IG, IDCHAR and all others.

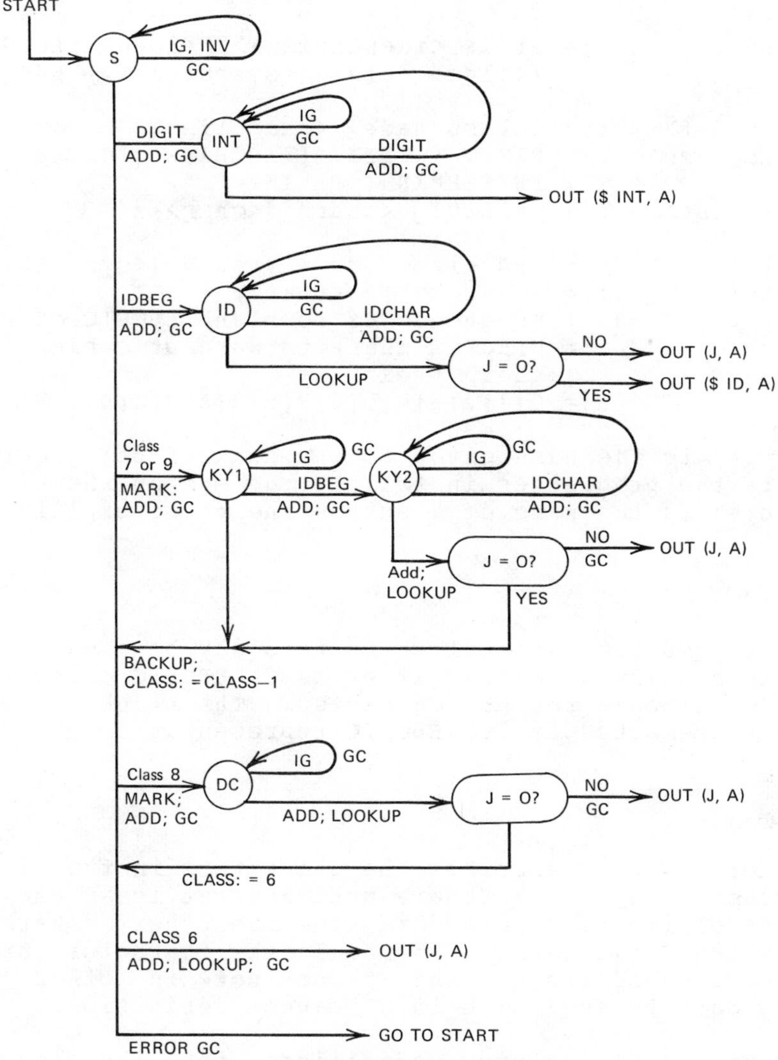


**FIGURE 3.12. Scanning Algorithm.**

### 3.4.3 Input to the Constructor of the Tables

We need only give the constructor the characters in each class and all the reserved words together with their internal representation. The job of the constructor itself is to read in the scanner definition and to build the internal tables used by the scanning algorithm. The syntax for a scanner definition is as follows:

```
<scanner>      ::= BEGIN <identifier¹> [<identifier²>]
                   {<class def>} {<symbol def>} END

<class def>    ::= <class name> <char list>
<class name>   ::= DIGIT | IDBEG | IDCHAR | IGNORE
                 | INVTERMIN | DELIM
<char list>    ::= [ALLBUT] <char> {<char>}

<symbol def>   ::= RES <integer> <symbol> {<symbol>}
<symbol>       ::= <char> {"|" <char>}
                 | "sequence of nonblank EBCDIC characters"
<char>         ::= "EBCDIC character except a blank"
                 | <hex> <hex>
<hex>          ::= 0|1|2|3|4|5|6|7|8|9|A|B|C|D|E|F
```

<identifier$^1$> is the name given to the scanner being defined and is used by the programmer in telling the system when to use it. <identifier$^2$> is the name of a subroutine to be explained later.

### Characters (⟨char⟩)

So that all possible internal characters may be used, we allow the user to specify a <char> either as an EBCDIC character or as the hexadecimal code for the character. The blank (space) must always be represented by its EBCDIC representation: X'40'.

### Class Definitions

A <class definition> describes the characters in the class given by the class name. Each <char> must have at least one blank on either side of it, to separate it from the other <char>s. The use of ALLBUT indicates that all the characters are in the class, except those listed and those not in other classes. ALLBUT may only be used once in a scanner definition.

As an example, the class definitions for the language in section 3.3 would be

```
DIGIT        0 1 2 3 4 5 6 7 8 9
IDBEG        A B C D E F G H I J K L M
             N O P Q R S T U V W X Y Z
IDCHAR       A B C D E F G H I J K L M
             N O P Q R S T U V W X Y Z
             0 1 2 3 4 5 6 7 8 9
INVTERMIN    40
DELIM        * / + 0 ( )
```

Suppose we wished to define a scanner for comments, to be used when the symbol beginning the comment is recognized by a different scanner. Thus we need only scan until the end symbol is detected. Suppose it is ; . The class definitions would be

```
IGNORE ALLBUT ;          DELIM ;
```

### Symbol Definitions

A symbol definition has the form

```
RES <integer> <symbol> {<symbol>} .
```

The <integer> is the internal representation of the first <symbol> in the list; each successive <symbol> is assigned the next highest integer. Several symbol definitions may occur. At least one blank must separate RES from <integer>, <integer> from the first <symbol>, and each adjacent pair of <symbol>s. Different symbols may be given the same internal represenation.

A <symbol> can be a sequence of non-blank EBCDIC characters (except "RES", "|", and "END") or any two hexadecimal digits. In order to use these as symbols, we use "|" for catenation and use a sequence of two <hex>s to mean an internal representation. For example, we can define the symbol " RES" by 40 | R | E | S and the symbol "'" as 7D.

In addition, each symbol must have one of the following formats:

```
      DELIM [DELIM]
      DIGIT {DIGIT}
      IDBEG {IDCHAR}
DELIM IDBEG {IDCHAR} DELIM
```

We show below the symbol definitions for the simple language discussed in section 3.3:

```
RES 3   BEGIN ABS E | N | D
RES 6   / + - * ( )
RES 12  //
```

### The Subroutine Call

In order to make the whole system more flexible, we allow the user to specify the name of a subroutine to call (<identifier$^2$>) whenever a new source program line is read. The purpose is to allow him to take a look at the line and make any changes necessary. This could be used to change a fixed field format into free field by inserting some internal symbols, to check for a continuation card or perhaps to check for a comment card. Of course, this routine should not do too much processing; this would defeat the whole purpose of the system -- a fast, automatic scanner.

The routine itself has two string parameters -- the first is the input line, the second is the name of a variable to hold the actual line the scanner is to process. If used, the routine must move the string to be scanned to the variable designated by the second parameter.

Let us give an example of the preprocessing routine for FORTRAN. If the card is not a comment or continuation card, we output first of all the internal character X'03'. This will be defined as a delimiter and used to terminate the statement on the last card. We will then change column 6 to the character X'04', which will terminate the label field. Comments (C in column 1) we will delete ourselves, thus saving scanning it. For continuation cards we just use columns 7 through 72.

```
PROCEDURE FORT(STRING IN,OUT);   |Procedure to preprocess a
BEGIN                            |FORTRAN card.
IF SUBSTR(IN,0,1)='C' THEN       |If we have a comment on card
  OUT := X'03'                   |then just end the last card.
ELSE IF SUBSTR(IN,5,1) ≠ ' '     |If it's a continuation card
     THEN OUT:=SUBSTR(IN,6,66)   |then only columns 7-72. Else we
     ELSE BEGIN OUT := X'03'     |end the last statement,
          CAT SUBSTR(IN,0,72);   |tell it to process cols 1-72,
       SUBSTR(OUT,5,1):=X'04';   |and put in label terminator.
          END                    |
END                              |
```

### EXERCISES FOR 3.4

1. Program and debug the general scanning algorithm in some convenient language.

## 3.5 THE AED RWORD SYSTEM

The last section discussed a scanner and constructor for scanning symbols with four restricted formats

```
            DIGIT {DIGIT}
            IDBEG {IDCHAR}
            DELIM [DELIM]
      DELIM IDBEG {IDCHAR} DELIM
```

The syntax of symbols was restricted so that the scanning algorithm was simple and could be implemented efficiently and quickly.

The AED RWORD (Read a WORD) system (see Johnson et al(69)), an integral part of the AED-1 system for generating compilers, interpreters, operating systems, etc., takes a different approach. The system constructs a scanner as the preceding one does, but it is much more general. Any number of classes of characters can be defined, and one can specify any structure for symbols in terms of these classes, as long as they can be parsed by an fa. In addition, a user routine can be called whenever a symbol of a certain type is built, and not only when each new card is read in. This generality allows it to be used for many other functions besides scanners for compilers.

This is not to say that, because of the generality, it must be inefficient. According to Johnson, one scanner constructed by RWORD on the IBM 7094 processed 3000 characters per second, while a carefully hand-coded analyzer for the same job processed at a rate of 8000 characters per second. New techniques for handling frequent and common symbols (like identifiers) are being added to reduce the time further.

Let us begin our discussion of RWORD by looking at the input to the constructor. Please note that, in the interests of uniformity of presentation, we have made some purely notational changes to the RWORD system.

### Syntax for the Scanner Definition

A scanner definition has the form

```
BEGIN {<character class description>} END
BEGIN {<symbol description>} END
FINI
```

The form is much the same as that of the system described in the previous section 3.4. It is in the character class and symbol descriptions that the generality enters.

### Character Class Descriptions

One can describe a class in two ways. The first allows only EBCDIC characters to be put into classes; the second is used when it is desired to give the actual internal representation of a character. Two examples of the first kind are

```
LET = /ABCDEFGHIJKLMNOPQRSTUVWXYZ/
```

and

```
PUNCTUATION = A.,;+-=()$/A
```

The first example says that the class LET consists of all the letters; the second puts the characters . , ; + - = ( ) $ and / into the class PUNCTUATION.

In each example, the first nonblank character following the = sign acts as a delimiter of the class characters. Every character following (including a blank) up till the next occurrence of the first character is in the class. In the first example above, the delimiter is /; in the second it is A. Of course, the delimiter itself may not be in the class. This is a clever technique.

An example of the second method of describing a class is

XX = $21,22,25$

This indicates that the class XX consists of those characters whose internal representations are 21, 22, and 25. The use of the delimiter $ always means that the internal representations of the characters are given. Thus the dollar sign cannot be used as a delimiter when using the first form.

A class name can be any sequence cf letters except BEGIN, END and FINI. Of interest is the class of characters with the special class name IGNORE, which consists of all characters which are to be completely skipped or ignored by the scanner if they appear in the input; this corresponds to the IGnore class of the last section.

### The Symbol Descriptions

Each description of a class of symbols has the form

<identifier> ( <integer> ) = <regular expression> $

where the regular expression is as defined in section 3.2. The variables of the expression can be

1. Any EBCDIC character except |, (, ), ', $ and a blank
2. The null string &
3. The name of a class of characters
4. An apostrophe ' followed by any EBCDIC character except a blank. (This is an escape mechanism to allow one to use the characters not allowed by 1. The character used is the one following the apostrophe.)

We give three examples:

PUNCT(5) = PUNCTUATION $
BEG(3) = '' B E G I N '' $
ID(1) = LET { LET | DIG }5 $

The first says that symbols in PUNCT, which all have the internal representation 5, are those characters in the class PUNCTUATION. The second indicates that the symbol 'BEGIN' has internal representation 3, while the third indicates that symbols consisting a letter followed by 0 to 5 letters or digits have internal representation 1. Any symbol which is put in the special class IGNORE is never passed on to the user, but is completely ignored. Since no internal representation is necessary, the definition for this class has the form

IGNORE = <regular expression> $

Note carefully the difference in the class of characters IGNORE and the class of symbols IGNORE. Suppose we have the input

```
BEGIN IGNORE / /   LET /AB/ END
BEGIN ID(1) = LET {LET}$ END FINI
```

Then the input string "AB A" will be parsed as the single identifier ABA, because blanks are ignored. Suppose on the other hand we have

```
BEGIN SPACE  / /   LET /AB/ END
BEGIN IGNORE = SPACE$   ID(1) = LET {LET}$ END FINI
```

Then "AB A" will be parsed as the two identifiers AB and A, since the blank is a symbol which will be actually constructed but not passed on to the user.

The last feature to be discussed is the invoking of a subroutine when a symbol is constructed during scanning. If we declare a symbol class using the format

<identifier> ( <integer> , <sub name> ) = <regular expression> $

then whenever a symbol in the class <name> is constructed, the subroutine <sub name> is called. This routine may do any processing whatsoever. For example, the routine connected with identifiers would look up the identifier to see whether it is a reserved word or not; this is not done automatically as in the previously described system.

In many cases it will be possible to parse the input string in several different ways. RWORD always attempts to match the longest string of characters as a symbol in the conventional manner. X123 would be an identifier and not the identifier X followed by the integer 123. There are cases where RWORD cannot resolve an ambiguity. When this happens it prints a message and stops.

### Examples of Scanner Definitions

The first example illustrates how the scanner of section 3.3 would be defined:

```
BEGIN  SPACE / /
       LET /ABCDEFGHIJKLMNOPQRSTUVWXYZ/
       DIG /0123456789/
END
BEGIN  ID(1,CHECKRES) = LET { LET | DIG } $
       INT(2) = DIG { DIG } $
       SSL(6) = / $  SPLUS(7) = + $  SMINUS(8) = - $
       SSTAR(9) = * $  SLPAR(10) = ( $  SRPAR(11) = ) $
       SSLSL(12),COMMENT) = /* $
       IGNORE = SPACE $
END    FINI
```

It is assumed that CHECKRES will check the identifier to see whether it is a reserved word ABS, BEGIN or END, and take some appropriate action. The procedure COMMENT will execute calls on SCAN using a different scanner (given below) to skip over the comment, and then return. As an alternative, we could have defined the character class PUNC = A/+-*()A and then the symbol class PUNCT(6) = PUNC$. All the delimiters would then have had the same internal representation, and the user would have to decide which one it was.

The scanner for comments would be

```
BEGIN  IGNCHAR = $00,01,02,03,...,A0,A1,...,FF$ END
BEGIN  IGNORE = IGNCHAR $
       NOEND(1) = * | / $
       TERMIN(2) = */ $
END    FINI
```

### The Constructor

The RWORD system is interesting in that it directly applies the formal language theory developed in Section 3.5. We won't go through all the details of the constructor. In a sense, the constructor is just a compiler, translating the input which defines character and symbol classes into a program which will recognize symbols.

The constructor operates in two stages called RWORD PART I and RWORD PART II. The general flow chart of RWORD PART I is given in Figure 3.13. The first phase stores the character classes internally; and then parses the regular expressions for each symbol class, producing one nfa for each one. The second phase collects all these nfa's and constructs a single <u>deterministic</u> fa from them. The deterministic fa is outputted in the form of a program, written in a language called AED-0, which consists of tables and calls (with appropriate arguments) on subroutines. There is one call for each state of the fa; the arguments essentially describe the mapping from this state to others based on the input string characters.

This program, when compiled, linked with subroutines, and executed, would scan and parse symbols of the defined language. It would be inefficient, due to the numerous subroutine calls at each step and the size of the tables. This program is therefore put through RWORD Part II for more processing.

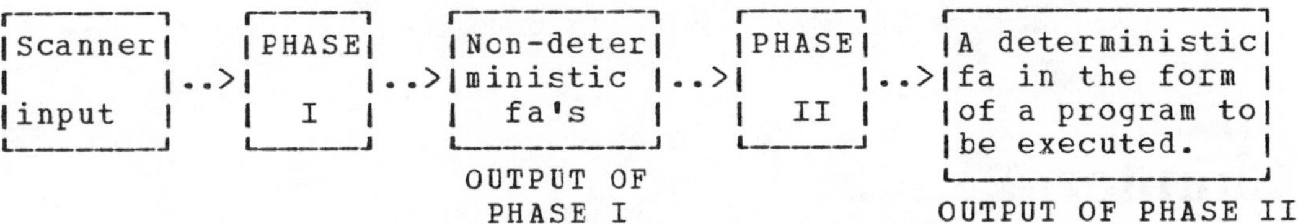


**FIGURE 3.13. RWORD System Part I.**

Briefly, RWORD PART II is needed in order to produce an efficient scanner, with respect to both time and space. Certain optimizations are performed which we won't go into here. In addition, several scanners may be linked together (because they will be used in the same job), to produce one large integrated scanner. The output of RWORD PART II is the tables in assembly language macro call form. That is, the output must then be assembled using a library of previously written macro definitions. This allows some degree of machine independence, since the macro definitions could be rewritten at any time to produce tables for another machine.

## 3.6 HISTORICAL REFERENCES

The notion of a finite state device is attributed to McCulloch and Pitts(43). The formalism we use is similar to that suggested by Moore(56). Regular expressions and their connection to automata were described by Kleene(56). We have of course barely scratched the surface of the theory of automata, and the reader is referred to texts by Gill(62), Ginsburg(62), and Hopcroft and Ullman(69).

The constructor discussed in section 3.4 is a development of the one used in Feldman's(66) FSL, a compiler implementation system. The AED RWORD System, in operation since 1966 (see Johnson et al(69)), is the first to apply the formal theory of fa's to lexical analysis.

# Chapter 4.
# Top-down Recognizers

We begin our discussion of parsing methods for context-free grammars by introducing top-down, predictive, or goal oriented recognizers as they are sometimes called. They are called this because of the way in which they work and build the syntax tree. Section 4.1 discusses the method in all its generality, coming up with a scheme which is inherently slow because of the amount of backup that may be necessary. A second algorithm is then given which reduces the amount of backup for certain grammars. In section 4.2 we talk about the problems with top-down methods and see how we can rearrange rules and use other notations to get around the difficulties. The representation of grammars in a computer is also discussed. Finally, section 4.3 talks about programming the top-down method by using recursive procedures.

## 4.1 TOP-DOWN WITH BACKUP

The top-down parsing algorithm builds the syntax tree, starting with the root node and working down to the sentence, as illustrated in Figure 2.7 of section 2.5. As shown by that example, the basic idea is simple and straightforward. Complications arise mainly because of the bookkeeping necessary to perform backup in a manner which assures us that all possible trees are attempted. To keep these complications to a minimum, we describe the algorithm in terms of men whose job it is to build the tree. At any point of the parse, one man stands on each node of the partial tree formed so far. The men whose nodes are terminals stand on the symbols of the sentence.

One man is assigned the goal of parsing the sentence x. He begins by noting that he must find a derivation Z =>+ x where Z is the distinguished symbol, and therefore the first direct derivation must be Z => y where Z ::= y is a rule. Let the rules for Z be

```
Z ::= X1X2...Xm  |  Y1Y2...Yn  | ... |  Z1Z2...Zl
```

The man tries first of all to use the rule Z ::= X1X2...Xm. If he cannot build the tree using it, he then tries the second rule Z ::= Y1Y2...Ym. If this one doesn't work, he tries the next one, and so on.

How does he see whether the direct derivation Z => X1X2...Xn is the correct one? Note that if it is, for some strings xi we have x = x1x2...xn where Xi =>* xi for i = 1,...,n. The man first of all adopts a son M1 whose job it is to find a derivation X1 =>* x1 for any x1 such that x = x1... If M1 can find this derivation, he (and any of his sons, grandsons, etc.) step on or cover the string x1 in the sentence x, and M1 reports success to his father. His father then adopts a second son M2 to find a derivation X2 =>* x2 where x = x1x2..., and awaits his report. And so on. As long as son M[i-1] reports success, he adopts a new son Mi to find a derivation Xi =>* xi. If son Mn reports success, the parse has been found.

What if son Mi cannot find a derivation Xi =>* xi? Mi then reports his failure to his father, who gets rid of him (disowns him), and tells Mi's older brother M[i-1] the following: "You already found a derivation, but it is the wrong one. Find another one for me." If M[i-1] find another derivation, he again reports success and everything proceeds as before. If M[i-1] reports failure, then he gets disowned, and his older brother M[i-2] is asked to try again. If in this process, M1 is disowned, then the direct derivation Z => X1X2...Xn is the wrong one, and the original man tries the next one Z => Y1Y2...Ym.

How does each son Mi work? Suppose his goal Xi is a terminal. The input string has the form x = x1x2...x[i-1]T... where the symbols in x1, x2, ..., x[i-1] are already being stepped on by other people. Mi sees whether the next uncovered symbol T is the same as his goal Xi. If so, he steps on the symbol and reports success. If not, he reports failure.

If Mi's goal Xi is a nonterminal, he works exactly as his father did. He begins testing right parts of rules for that nonterminal by adopting and disowning sons when necessary. If all his sons report success, Mi reports success to his father. If his father asks him to find another derivation and his goal is a terminal, Mi reports failure, since no other such derivation exists. Otherwise, Mi asks his youngest son to find another derivation and acts on his report as before. If his sons all report failure, Mi reports failure to his father.

You can see why this method is called predictive, or goal-oriented. It is also called top-down because of the way the syntax tree is being built. One starts with the distinguished symbol and reaches down to the sentence (Figure 4.1).

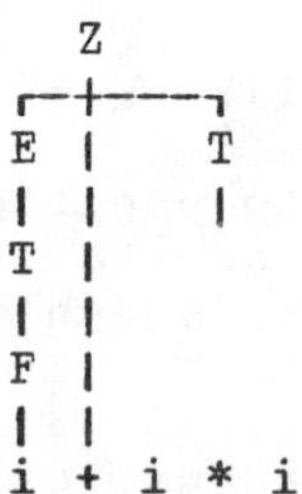


**FIGURE 4.1. Partial Top-Down Parse of i+i*i.**

The nice thing about this method (or its presentation) is that each man must only keep track of his own GOAL, his father, his sons, and where he is stationed in the grammar and the input string. Hence no one need know exactly what is going on everywhere else. This is what we strive for in programming, in general; Each program segment or subroutine need only worry about its own inputs and outputs, and nothing else.

To simulate adopting and disowning men in a program, we use a LIFO (last-in-first-out) <u>stack</u>, or <u>pushdown</u> <u>store</u> as it is sometimes called. The stack is the basic mechanism used in almost all types of recognizers. Indeed, whenever one talks about recursion one talks about stacks. A stack is a storage device into which one stores data. However, data can only be entered at the "top", thus "pushing down" the data already in it. Accordingly, one can only reference or change the top (or the top few) elements. When no longer needed, the top elements are deleted, thus "popping" up the ones below. One example of a stack from everyday life is a coin holder, shown at the right. If a coin is pushed in the ones already in are pushed down; only the top coin is accessible.

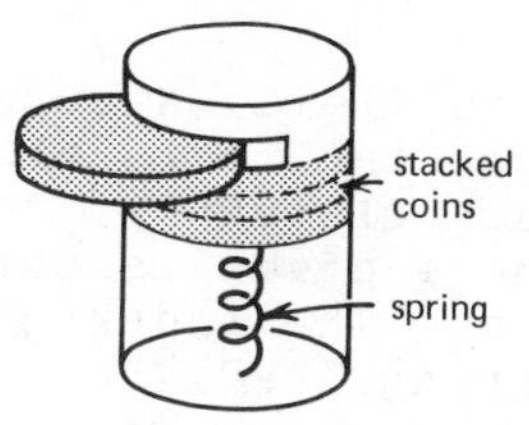


The usual method of implementing a stack is to use an array S, say, and a counter v. If v=0 the stack is empty. If v=n where n>0, then the stack contains S(1), S(2), ..., S(n) where S(n) is the top stack element.

We can make the algorithm more explicit by writing it in bastard ALGOL. First of all, we assume the grammar is listed in a one dimensional array GRAMMAR with each set of rules U ::= x | y | ... | z inserted as Ux|y|...|z|$. That is, each symbol uses one location, each right part for U is followed by "|" and the last right part for U is followed by "|$". Thus the grammar

```
         Z     ::= E #
(4.1.1)  E     ::= T + E | T
         T     ::= F * T | F
         F     ::= ( E ) | i
```

would look like

(4.1.2) ZE#|$ET+E|T|$TF*T|F|$F(E)|i|$.

Each element of the stack represents one man and has the five components

(GOAL, i, FAT, SON, BRO)

with the following meaning:

1. GOAL is the symbol which the man is to try for. That is, he must find a head of the currently uncovered part of the sentence which reduces to GOAL, and cover it. This GOAL is given to him by his father.
2. i is an index in GRAMMAR pointing to the symbol in a right part of a rule for GOAL which the man is currently working on.

3. FAT is his father's name (his father's stack element number).
4. SON is the name of his most recently adopted son.
5. BRO is the name of his elder brother.

For each field, a zero indicates the absence of a value. Within the program, v is the number of men working (the current number of stack elements), c is the name (number of the stack element) of the man who is currently working. Everybody else is waiting for him. The index j refers to the leftmost uncovered symbol of the string INPUT(1),...,INPUT(n).

In the program, GOAL, i, FAT, SON and BRO, unless otherwise specified, refer to those components of the man who is currently working (his name is c). <u>This is an important point to remember when reading the program</u>. For example, we should write S(c).GOAL instead of GOAL, to refer to the GOAL field of S(c). We have made this abbreviation to avoid cluttering up the program.

We mentioned earlier that each man must keep track of his sons. One method is to keep the names of all his sons in his stack element, but this would require a variable number of fields there. Our solution is to use the SON field to point to the <u>last</u> (youngest) son. This son's BRO field then points to his older brother, and so on.

To illustrate this, consider the syntax tree of Figure 4.2a for the sentence i+i*i of grammar (4.1.1). The stack at the end of the parsing algorithm is given in Figure 4.2b. Now man 2 (S(2)) has the goal E; he is supposed to use rule E::=T+E, according to the syntax tree. Thus he should have three sons to find the T, +, and E. S(2).SON = 7, so his youngest son is man 7, who's goal is E. His next youngest son is S(7).BRO, which is 6; this man's goal is +. His oldest son's name is in the BRO field of man 6, and is thus 3.

You see, we do have a list of each man's sons, but this list is "threaded" throughout the stack. The use of such threaded lists is common in programming, and the reader who doesn't understand completely would do well to study the example until he feels at ease with it. It should be clear that the final stack is just an internal form of the syntax tree.

Note the use of the delimiter # at the end of each sentence, according to grammar (4.1.1). This makes sure that the whole sentence is parsed, and not just some head of it.

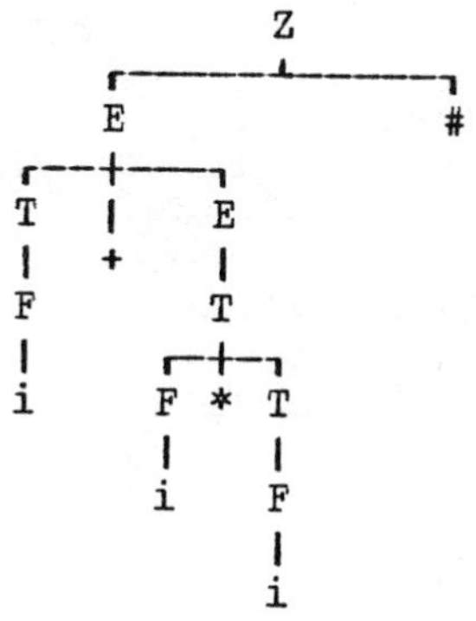

```
              Z
     ┌────────┴────────┐
     E                 #
 ┌───┼───┐
 T   |   E
 |   +   |
 F       T
 |     ┌─┼─┐
 i     F * T
       |   |
       i   F
           |
           i
```

(a) SYNTAX TREE

| STACK | GOAL | i | FAT | SON | BRO |
|---|---|---|---|---|---|
| 1 | Z | 4 | 0 | 15 | 0 |
| 2 | E | 10 | 1 | 7 | 0 |
| 3 | T | 20 | 2 | 4 | 0 |
| 4 | F | 28 | 3 | 5 | 0 |
| 5 | i | 0 | 4 | 0 | 0 |
| 6 | + | 0 | 2 | 0 | 3 |
| 7 | E | 12 | 2 | 8 | 6 |
| 8 | T | 18 | 7 | 12 | 0 |
| 9 | F | 28 | 8 | 10 | 0 |
| 10 | i | 0 | 9 | 0 | 0 |
| 11 | * | 0 | 8 | 0 | 9 |
| 12 | T | 20 | 8 | 13 | 11 |
| 13 | F | 28 | 12 | 14 | 0 |
| 14 | i | 0 | 13 | 0 | 0 |
| 15 | # | 0 | 1 | 0 | 2 |

(b) STACK AFTER PARSE

GRAMMAR = ZE#|$ET+E|T|$TF*T|F|$F(E)|i|$

**FIGURE 4.2. Stack After a Top-Down Parse of i+i*i.**

The top-dcwn parsing algorithm follows. It has been divided into six sections in order to separate the different functions. We have made liberal use of English where unimportant details would have made the algorithm seem less clear.

INITIALIZE

```
┌─────────────────────────────────────────────────────────────────┐
|S(1):=(Z,0,0,0,0); c:=1;        |Adopt the head man.  His goal   |
|v:=1; j:=1; GO TO NEW MAN       |is Z, the distinguished symbol. |
└─────────────────────────────────────────────────────────────────┘
```

NEW MAN

```
┌──────────────────────────────────────────────────────────────────┐
|IF GOAL is terminal THEN        |A new man looks for his goal.    |
|   IF INPUT(j) = GOAL THEN      |It's terminal. If GOAL matches   |
|    BEGIN j:=j+1; GOTO SUCCESS|the sentence symbol, he covers     |
|    END                         |it and reports his success.      |
|   ELSE GO TO FAILURE;          |Didn't match - report failure.   |
|                                |                                 |
|i:= index in GRAMMAR of the     |The new man's goal is a non-     |
|     first right part for GCAL;|terminal. Get set to look at      |
|GO TO LOOP                      |right parts of rules for         |
|                                |GOAL.                            |
└──────────────────────────────────────────────────────────────────┘
```

LOOP

```
IF GRAMMAR(i) = "|"                |Looking at a right part.
THEN IF FAT ≠ 0                    |We reached end of right part,so
     THEN GO TO SUCCESS            |we report success. If no father
     ELSE STOP--HAVE SENTENCE;     |we stop with a sentence.
IF GRAMMAR(i) = "$"                |
THEN IF FAT ≠ 0                    |No more right parts to try, so
     THEN GO TO FAILURE            |report failure  or stop without
     ELSE STOP-NOT A SENTENCE;     |a sentence if no father.
                                   |
v:=v+1;                            |GRAMMAR(i) is another GOAL to
S(v):=(GRAMMAR(i),0,c,0,SON);      |try. Adopt a son. You are his
                                   |father, and his older brother
                                   |is your current youngest son.
SON:=v; c:=v;                      |Switch your attention to new
GO TO NEW MAN                      |son and await his report.
```

SUCCESS

```
c:=FAT;                            |Report success to your father
i:=i+1; GO TO LOOP;                |who goes on to his next step.
```

FAILURE

```
c:=FAT;                            |Report failure to your father.
v:=v-1;                            |He disowns you and asks your
SON := S(SON).BRO;                 |older brother to try again.
GO TO TRY AGAIN                    |
```

TRY AGAIN

```
IF SON = 0 THEN                    |Do you have a son who can try
 BEGIN WHILE GRAMMAR(i) ≠ "|"      |again? No. So skip over this
       DO i:=i+1;                  |right part--it's not the one we
       i:=i+1; GO TO LOOP          |want--and go test the next one.
 END;                              |
i:=i-1; c:=SON;                    |You have a son. Ask him to
IF GOAL is nonterminal             |try again. His GOAL is non-
THEN GO TO TRY AGAIN;              |terminal, so he goes to try
                                   |again for a SUCCESS.
j:=j-1;                            |His GOAL is terminal--he can't
GO TO FAILURE                      |try again. So he uncovers his
                                   |symbol and reports the failure.
```

While it may look good, this algorithm has a serious flaw which will be explained in the next section. First let us modify the algorithm so that it doesn't back up so much. Note that when somebody reports failure, we disown him and tell his older brother to "try again" -- to find a different substring which reduces to his goal. In doing so, we show what little confidence we have in our son. If we check carefully before adopting, and bring him up right, we should have more confidence in him. We should assume that he will do the job correctly the first time. Therefore there should be no reason to ask him to try again. When somebody fails we should just assume that we are on the wrong track and try a completely different alternative (right side of a rule).

In order to do this, we have to order the rules for each nonterminal so that the correct one is found the first time. With most of the programming languages, this can usually be done, but there is no automatic way of doing it. One aid here is to put the longest alternative first. Grammar (4.1.1) is already in this form. Thus, if a man has the goal E, he first tries for T+E. If T matches but + doesn't, he doesn't ask again for his first son to find another T, but disowns all his sons and skips to the next rule E ::= T.

With this change we don't need the BRO component of the stack, but we will have to keep better tabs on what part of the string is covered or uncovered. Our stack element looks like

(GOAL, i, FAT, SON, j)

where GOAL, i, FAT and SON are as before, but j contains the index in INPUT where we ourselves are currently looking or waiting for a report. While we are at it, since the whole problem is simpler, we can check the terminals in the right parts ourselves, thereby saving the cost of adopting a son to do the job.

Note again, that this new algorithm only works correctly if the rules are ordered so that the correct rules are tried first.

INITIALIZE

| | |
|---|---|
| S(1):=(Z,0,0,0,1); c:=1;<br>v:=1; GO TO NEW MAN | Appoint a new man with the goal Z, beginning at first symbol. |

NEW MAN

| | |
|---|---|
| i:= index in grammar of the first right part for GOAL;<br>GO TO LOOP | A son is adopted only for nonterminals. He finds his rules and goes to work. |

LOOP

```
|IF GRAMMAR(i) = "|"              |Looking at right part.           |
|THEN IF FAT ≠ 0                  |We reached the end of it, so we|
|     THEN GO TO SUCCESS          |report success, or stop with     |
|     ELSE STOP--HAVE SENTENCE;   |sentence if no father.           |
|IF GRAMMAR(i) = "$"              |                                 |
|THEN IF FAT ≠ 0                  |No more right parts to try, so   |
|     THEN GO TO FAILURE          |report failure or stop if you    |
|     ELSE STOP-NOT A SENTENCE;   |have no father. Not a sentence.|
|IF GRAMMAR(i) is terminal        |                                 |
|THEN IF INPUT(j) = GRAMMAR(i)    |If the terminal matches we       |
|     THEN BEGIN j:=j+1;i:=i+1;   |cover the terminal and go on     |
|                GO TO LCOP       |to next symbol.                  |
|          END                    |                                 |
|     ELSE GO TO TRY ALTERNATE;   |Terminal doesn't match so we     |
|                                 |try another right part.          |
|v:=v+1;                          |Adopt a new son for GOAL which   |
|S(v):=(GRAMMAR(i),0,c,0,j);      |is nonterminal. His father is    |
|SON:=v; c:=v;                    |you. Switch your attention to    |
|GO TO NEW MAN                    |him and await his report.        |
```

SUCCESS

```
|c:=FAT; j:= S(SCN).j;            |Report to father and tell him    |
|i:=i+1; j:= j+1;                 |what you covered. He then        |
|GO TO LOCP                       |proceeds on his own.             |
```

FAILURE

```
|c:=FAT;                          |Report failure to your father.   |
|v:=c; SON:=0;                    |He disowns you and all the rest|
|                                 |of his sons, and then tries      |
|GO TO TRY ALTERNATE              |another alternative.             |
```

TRY ALTERNATE

```
|IF FAT ≠ 0                       |Find out from your father        |
|THEN j:=S(FAT).j ELSE j := 1;    |where to begin covering again.   |
|WHILE GRAMMAR(i) ≠ "|"           |Find the beginning of next       |
|DO i:=i+1;                       |alternate, if any, and           |
|i:=i+1; GO TO LCOP               |begin again.                     |
```

## 4.2 TOP-DOWN PROBLEMS AND THEIR SOLUTION

### Direct Left Recursion

There is a basic flaw in the algorithms of section 4.1. -- the use of a GOAL which is left recursive. If our own GOAL is X and the first rule for X is X ::= X..., then we immediately adopt a son to try for an X. He also immediately adopts <u>his</u> son to try for an X. So everybody passes the buck to his son, and all the people in China would not be enough to solve the problem.

This is the reason grammar (4.1.1) has its rules written in right recursive fashion, instead of the more conventional left recursive way. A better way to get rid of direct left recursion is to write the rules using the iterative and optional notation discussed in section 2.9. We write the rules

```
(4.2.1)      E ::= E + T | T    as    E ::= T {+ T}
```

and

```
        T ::= T * F | T / F | F    as    T ::= F {* F | / F}
```

We now give two rules for transforming rules involving direct left recursion into equivalent ones using iteration.

(4.2.2) Factoring. Whenever rules U ::= xy | xw | ... | xz exist, replace them by U ::= x(y | w | ... | z), where the parentheses are meta symbols.

This factoring could also be applied in a more general fashion, as in arithmetic expressions. For example, if in (4.2.2) y = y1y2 and w = y1w2, we could replace U ::= x(y|w|...|z) by

```
                    U ::= x( y1(y2|w2) | ... | z).
```

Note that if the original rules are U ::= x | xy, we transform them into U ::= x(y|ε) where ε is the empty string. Whenever we do this, ε is always placed as the <u>last</u> alternative, since we adopt the convention that it always matches when it is the goal.

The use of factoring not only aids us in deleting direct recursion, but it also reduces the size of the grammar and permits more efficient parsing. This we will see later.

Once (4.2.2) has been applied there can exist at most one direct left recursive right part for a nonterminal. If there is one, we do the following:

(4.2.3) Let U ::= x | y | ... | z | Uv be the rules with the left recursive right part last. These rules indicate that a member of the syntactic clas U is an x, y, or z, followed by zero or more v's. Transform these rules into U ::= (x | y | ... | z) {v}.

We used step (4.2.3) to make the transformation in (4.2.1), deleting the unnecessary parentheses around the T. As another example we transform A ::= BC | BCD | Axz | Axy:

Rule (4.2.2) yields A ::= BC(D|ε) | Ax(z|y); (4.2.3) yields A ::= (BC(D|ε)){x(z|y)}. We can delete one unnecessary pair of parentheses, yielding A ::= BC(D|ε){x(z|y)}.

With these changes, of course, we have to change our top-down parsing algorithm. It must now be able to handle alternates not only for a right part, but for a substring of a right part; it must be able to handle the empty string ε; and it must be able to handle iteration. We leave these changes to the reader.

The use of iteration instead of recursion does change the structure of our trees somewhat. Thus Figure 4.3a would look like Figure 4.3b. We agree that these two trees are to be treated as equivalent; the plus operators are to be evaluated from left to right.

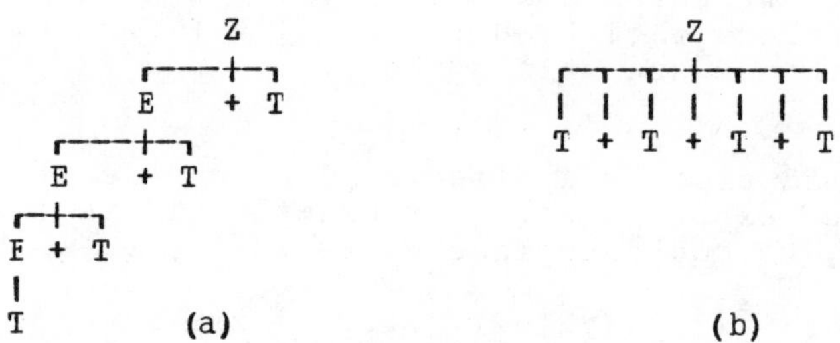


**FIGURE 4.3. Trees Using Recursion and Interation.**

### General Left Recursion

We have not solved the whole problem of left recursion; direct left recursion is out, but left recursion in general is not. Thus, the rules

U ::= Vx     and     V ::= Uy | v

yield U =>+ Uyx. There is no simple way of getting rid of this, but we can check for it. Take the original grammar and delete all direct left recursive rules. Then a symbol U of the resulting grammar is left recursive if and only if U FIRST+ U. This we know how to check.

### Representing the Grammar in Core

One of the problems with top-down methods is the representation of the grammar in the computer. One representation, of course, is the one used in section 4.1. This is obviously a bad representation because of the work necessary to find the rules for any nonterminal. We discuss another representation below. Before we do, we should just mention that it is a fairly simple exercise to write a constructor to accept a grammar, do any of the transformations we just talked about, check for left recursive rules, and generate the tables for the grammar in one of the forms we will describe; we again leave this to the reader.

We use a list structure to represent the grammar, called a syntax graph. Each node represents a symbol S in a right part, and consists of the four components NAME, DEFINITION (DEF), ALTERNATE (ALT) and SUCCESSOR (SUC), where

1. NAME is the symbol S itself, in some internal form.
2. DEFINITION is 0 if S is terminal; otherwise it points to the node for the first symbol in the first right part for S.
3. ALTERNATE points at the first symbol of the next alternate right part following the one in which the node is; (0 if none). This is only for the first symbol in a right part.
4. SUCCESSOR points to the next symbol in the right part (0 if none).

In addition, each nonterminal is represented by a node with one component, which points to the first symbol in its first right part. As an example, Figure 4.4 is the syntax graph for the grammar (4.2.4). The components of each node are in the following positions:

```
┌─────────────────┐
│      NAME       │
├─────┬─────┬─────┤
│ DEF │ ALT │ SUC │
└─────┴─────┴─────┘
```

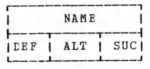

```
(4.2.4) E ::= E <aop> T | T            <aop> ::= + | -
        T ::= T <mop> F | F            <mop> ::= * | /
        F ::= ( E ) | i
```

The syntax graph is a good notation on which to perform transformations (4.2.2) and (4.2.3). Figure 4.5 shows the modified syntax graph for grammar (4.2.4). We have some extra symbols in a node to indicate the iteration. An ST in a node indicates that that symbol begins a string enclosed in braces, while an asterisk indicates the symbol ends such a string.

Be careful here. Depending on the way the analyzer works, for a right part like {{X Y} Z}, we might have to put $ST^2$ in X's node to indicate that X starts two nested iterations.

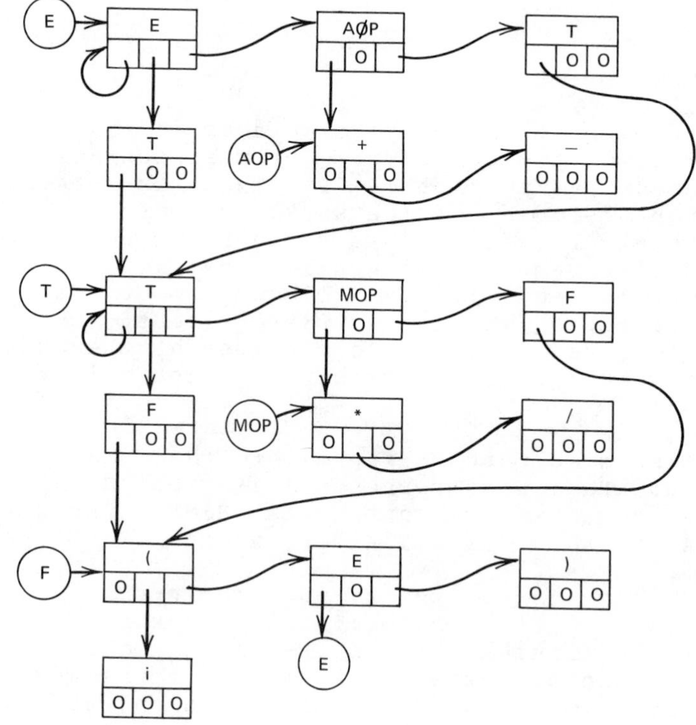


**FIGURE 4.4. Syntax Graph for Grammar (4.2.4).**

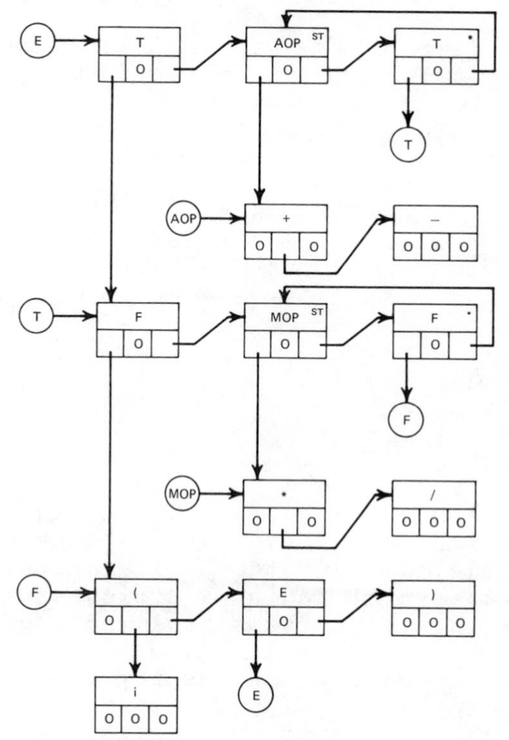


**FIGURE 4.5. Modified Syntax Graph.**

We could also identify nodes of the graph which have identical components. For example, in Figure 4.4 the two nodes with name F are the same. While the algorithm still works when we do this, we begin to lose sight of the original grammar, and for semantic reasons (which will become clear much later), this is not a good idea.

If one is programming in a language which doesn't allow pointer variables, then one dimensional arrays can be used; pointers will be represented by indexes (subscripts) into the arrays.

### Parsing Without Backup

The syntax analyzer of a compiler should never back up. We want to be sure that every goal predicted is a correct one. This is because we will associate semantics with syntax and, as we predict and find goals, we will process the symbols in question semantically. Some examples of "processes" are (1) when processing declarations, putting the identifiers into a symbol table; (2) when processing arithmetic expressions, checking operands for type compatibility.

If we have to back up because we predicted the wrong goal, then we have to undo any semantic processing we performed while trying to find that goal. This is not the easiest thing to do, so we try to parse without backup.

The usual context one uses in a compiler to prohibit backup is the next "uncovered" symbol of the source program. We then require from the grammar that, whenever we have alternates x | y | ... | z, that the sets of symbols which can begin a word for x, y, ..., z be pairwise disjoint. That is, if x =>* Au and y =>* Bv, then A ≠ B. This requirement lets us determine quite simply which of the alternates x, y or ... z is our goal. Note that factoring is actually a help here. If we have U ::= xy | xz, then transforming it to U ::= x(y|z) aids in making the sets of first symbols for alternates disjoint.

We shall not pursue this technique any further here, although we shall see it in use in the next section.

## 4.3 RECURSIVE DESCENT

In some compilers, the syntax analyzer has one recursive procedure for each nonterminal U, which parses phrases for U. The procedure is told where in the program to begin looking for a phrase for U; hence it is goal oriented or predictive. We predict we can find such a phrase. The procedure finds it phrase by comparing the program at the point indicated with right parts of rules for U, calling other procedures to recognize subgoals when necessary.

Actually, the tree is formed during the parse exactly the way it is in the parsing algorithm of section 4.1 (without backup); only the notation for expressing the parse is different.

In order to illustrate the technique we write procedures for the nonterminals of the following grammar.

```
        <state>    ::= <var> := <expr>
                     | IF <expr> THEN <state>
                     | IF <expr> THEN <state> ELSE <state>
(4.3.1) <var>      ::= i | i ( <expr> )
        <expr>     ::= <term> | <expr> + <term>
        <term>     ::= <factor> | <term> * <factor>
        <factor>   ::= <var> | ( <expr> )
```

We rewrite this grammar for our purposes as

```
        <state>    ::= <var> := <expr>
                     | IF <expr> THEN <state> [ELSE <state>]
(4.3.2) <var>      ::= i [ ( <expr> ) ]
        <expr>     ::= <term> {+ <term>}
        <term>     ::= <factor> {* <factor>}
        <factor>   ::= <var> | ( <expr> )
```

We assume that we can parse without backup. The only context used to eliminate backup is the single symbol following the partial phrase already parsed. We write the routines in bastard ALGOL, with the following conventions:

1. A global variable NXTSYMB always contains the next symbol of the source program to be processed. When calling a procedure to find a new goal, the first symbol it should check is already in NXTSYMB.
2. Likewise, before returning from a procedure to report success, the symbol _following_ the substring parsed is put into NXTSYMB.
3. The procedure SCAN scans the next source program symbol and puts it in NXTSYMB.
4. A routine ERROR is called when an error is detected. It will print the message and return. Upon return we will just continue as if no error had occurred (see discussion following the procedures).
5. To begin parsing a statement, we call SCAN to put the first symbol into NXTSYMB and call the procedure STATE.

```
PROCEDURE STATE;                      |Routine for <state>. We usually
  IF NXTSYMB = "IF"                   |assume we can tell the kind of
  THEN                                |statement from the first symbol
   BEGIN SCAN; EXPR;                  |Get first symbol of expression
     IF NXTSYMB ≠ "THEN"              |and call the expression proc.
     THEN ERROR                       |Must be followed by "THEN" and
     ELSE                             |a statement.
      BEGIN SCAN; STATE;              |We call ourselves recursively.
       IF NXTSYMB="ELSE" THEN         |Parse the "ELSE" statement
        BEGIN SCAN; STATE END         |if it appears.
      END                             |
   END                                |
  ELSE                                |It's not an IF-statement. Must
   BEGIN VAR;                         |be an assignment. Go parse the
     IF NXTSYMB ≠ ":="                |variable, check for := and then
     THEN ERROR                       |parse the expression.
     ELSE BEGIN SCAN;EXPR END         |
   END;                               |End of procedure for <state>
```

```
 PROCEDURE VAR;                       |Routine for <var>.
   IF NXTSYMB ≠ "i" THEN ERROR        |It must begin with an i.
   ELSE BEGIN SCAN;                   |Get the symbol after i.  If and
         IF NXTSYMB = "(" THEN        |only if it is an open paren, we
          BEGIN SCAN; EXPR;           |go to parse the expression
           IF NXTSYMB ≠ ")"           |and check to make sure it is
           THEN ERROR                 |followed by a closing paren.
           ELSE SCAN                  |Make sure NXTSYMB contains the
          END                         |symbol following the construct
        END;                          |recognized.
```

```
PROCEDURE EXPR;                       |Routine for <expr>.
  BEGIN TERM;                         |It must start off with a term.
        WHILE NXTSYMB = "+" DO        |After that we just keep looking
         BEGIN SCAN; TERM END         |for any number of "+ <term>"s.
  END;                                |Stop when next symbol is not +.
```

```
PROCEDURE TERM;                       |Routine for <term>.
  BEGIN FACTOR;                       |This routine is similar to the
        WHILE NXTSYMB = "*" DO        |one for <expr> and needs no
         BEGIN SCAN;FACTOR END        |explanation.
  END;                                |
```

```
PROCEDURE FACTOR;                 |Routine for <factor>,
  IF NXTSYMB = "(" THEN           |Look at first symbol, see which
   BEGIN SCAN; EXPR;              |alternate to use. It's a
         IF NXTSYMB ≠ ")"         |parenthesized expression. Check
         THEN ERROR;              |for closing parenthesis and
         ELSE SCAN                |scan the next symbol.
   END                            |
  ELSE VAR;                       |It's just a variable.
```

One strange thing about these procedures is that they don't need any local variables. In fact, the only variable used is NXTSYMB. In essence, we are just using the normal stack mechanism which links procedures at runtime to simulate the stack used in section 4.1.

The advantages of this method are fairly clear. One can rearrange rules as one programs to fit the needs of the procedures. It is assumed that the compiler writer knows the source language well, so he can rearrange things so that no backup is necessary. The method is also very flexible for semantic processing. One can insert code for it anywhere within a procedure, and not just at the end when the phrase has been detected. We will see this in more detail when we talk about semantics.

The prime disadvantage is that it requires more work than in a partially automatic system: more programming and more debugging. Still, it is a reasonable method, and many compilers use it.

Most compilers, when an error is found, will just fail all the way up to the statement level. At this level, the source program is skipped until a BEGIN, END or semicolon is detected and one can start anew. This, of course, is not very sophisticated. We will deal with this topic in chapter 15.

A little thought should convince the reader that a program could be written which would accept a suitable grammar and produce the recursive subroutines (written in some language) for that grammar. Some restrictions would of course have to be placed on the grammar.

### EXERCISE FOR 4.3

1. Execute the procedures presented above (by hand) in order to parse the following statements: (a) i:=i (b) i:=i(i) (c) IF i THEN i:=i. Begin by executing the statements SCAN; STATE.

## 4.4 HISTORICAL REFERENCES

One of the first papers to discuss a fixed parsing algorithm with tables which describe the language was by Irons(61a). His method is not a pure top-down parse as we have described it, but is a mixture of top-down and bottom-up -- the other method we will describe. Kuno and Oettinger used the top-down technique for research in natural languages. The particular algorithm given in section 4.1 was taken from Floyd's(64b) survey article. The way of introducing the idea of top-down parsing in terms of men was also borrowed from this paper. A tutorial on the subject of using predictive methods in compiling was given at the SJCC by Cheatham and Sattley(64). Grau(61) also describes a compiler using recursive procedures.

Techniques for prohibiting backup are described by Unger(68), while Lewis and Stearns(68) and Rosenkrantz and Stearns(69) investigate the LL(k) grammars and languages -- those which can be parsed top-down without backup by examining at each step all the symbols processed so far and k symbols more to the right.

Reynolds'(65) symbolic processing language COGENT uses a top-down scheme which parses alternates in parallel, deleting them when they reach a complete failure. Thus, ambiguous languages can be handled; all the parses of an ambiguous sentence are produced. Top-down analysis is a favorite of the META compiler writing systems (see Schorre(64)) and is used in the oldest compiler-compiler -- that of Brooker et al(63). Rosen(64) contains a description of it. Among the compilers using recursive descent are the Burroughs extended ALGOL compiler and the SHARE 7090 ALGOL compiler.

# Chapter 5.
# Simple Precedence Grammars

## 5.1 PRECEDENCE RELATIONS AND THEIR USE

This chapter describes a technique for parsing using the bottom-up method. Recall that this method parses by repeatedly finding the handle (leftmost simple phrase) u of the current sentential form and reducing it to a nonterminal U, using a rule U::=u. The problem with any bottom-up method is to find the handle, and then to know what nonterminal to reduce it to. In this chapter we solve this problem for a certain class of grammars called (simple) <u>precedence grammars</u>. This does not, of course, solve the problem for <u>all</u> grammars. Since we are going left-right bottom-up, all our sentential forms will be canonical, and all derivation produced will be canonical. Within this chapter, "sentential form" means "canonical sentential form."

Given a sentential form x, how can we find its handle? We would like to proceed from left to right, looking at just two adjacent symbols at a time, and be able to tell when we find the <u>tail</u> of the handle. Then we would like to go back towards the left end of the sentential form and find the head of the handle, again using only two symbols at a time to make the decision. Thus we are faced with the following problem. Given a string ...RS..., is R always the tail of the handle, or can both RS appear together in the handle, or what? We would like to examine the grammar before we do any parsing, and decide about each pair of symbols R and S.

Consider, then, two symbols R and S in the vocabulary V of a grammar G. Suppose there is a (canonical) sentential form ...RS... At some point of a canonical parse either R or S (or both) must be in a handle. The following three possibilities arise.

1. R is part of a handle but S is not (Figure 5.1a). In this case we write R ⋗ S and say that R is greater than S, or that R <u>has precedence</u> over S, because it must be reduced first. Note that R must be the tail symbol of some rule U ::= ...R. Note that since the handle is to the left of S, S must be terminal.

2. R and S are both in a handle (Figure 5.1b). We say that R ≐ S. They have the same precedence and must be reduced at the same time. Obviously there must be a rule U ::= ...RS... in the grammar.

3. S is part of a handle but R is not (Figure 5.1c). We say that R ⋖ S or that R is less than S. S must be the head of some rule U ::= S...

If there is no (canonical) sentential form ...RS... then we say that no relation exists between the ordered pair (R,S). Note that the three new precedence relations ⋖, ≐ and ⋗ are not symmetric. For example, S ⋖ R does not follow from R ⋖ S.

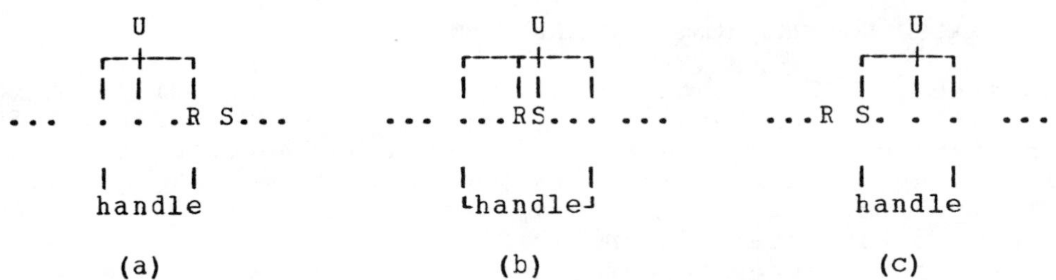


**FIGURE 5.1. Illustration of Precedence Relations.**

As an example, consider the following grammar G5[Z]:

```
            Z ::= b M b
(5.1.1)     M ::= ( L | a
            L ::= M a )
```

The language L(G5) includes the strings bab, b(aa)b, b((aa)a)b and b(((aa)a)a)b. Each column of the table below shows a sentential form, a syntax tree for it, the handle of the tree and the relations that can be derived from the tree.

```
Sentential        b a b           b ( L b            b ( M a ) b
form:
Syntax              Z                Z                     Z
tree:           ┌───┼───┐        ┌───┼───┐          ┌────────┼────────┐
                b   M   b        b   M   b          b        M        b
                    │                │                       │
                    a              ┌─┴─┐                   ┌─┴─┐
                                   (   L                   (   L
                                                             ┌─┼─┐
                                                             M a )

Handle:             a               ( L                  M ) a

Relations         b ⋖ a            b ⋖ (                 ( ⋖ M
given by          a ⋗ b            ( ≐ L                 M ≐ a
tree:                              L ⋗ b                 a ≐ )
                                                         ) ⋗ b
```

Figure 5.2 gives the <u>precedence matrix</u> for grammar G5 -- a matrix which shows all the precedence relations. Element B[i,j] of the matrix contains the relations for the symbol pair (Si,Sj). A blank matrix element indicates that no precedence relation exists between the two symbols.

At first sight it may seem difficult to find all the relations for the symbols of a grammar. It seems as though we have to look at enough syntax trees until we find <u>all</u> the relations. How can we be sure we have found all of them? We will redefine the relations in the next section in such a way that for any grammar they can be constructed quite easily.

|   | Z | b | M | L | a | ( | ) |
|---|---|---|---|---|---|---|---|
| Z |   |   |   |   |   |   |   |
| b |   |   | ≐ |   | ⋖ | ⋖ |   |
| M |   | ≐ |   |   | ≐ |   |   |
| L |   | ⋗ |   |   | ⋗ |   |   |
| a |   | ⋗ |   |   | ⋗ |   | ≐ |
| ( |   |   | ⋖ | ≐ | ⋖ | ⋖ |   |
| ) |   | ⋗ |   |   | ⋗ |   |   |

**FIGURE 5.2. Precedence Matrix for Grammar G5.**

How dc these relations help us parse sentences? If more than one relation exists between any pair of symbols (R,S), then the relations don't help us at all. However if <u>at most one relation</u> holds between any pair, then the relations will indicate to us the handle for any sentential form. In this case we can say that the handle of any sentential form S1...Sn is the leftmost substring Sj...Si such that

```
         S[j-1] ⋖ Sj
(5.1.2)  Sj ≐ S[j+1] ≐ S[j+2] ≐ ...  ≐ Si
         Si ⋗ S[i+1].
```

(We have to change this assertion a bit to take care of the case that the symbol Sj (Si) of the handle is the first (last) symbol of the sentential form; we will do this later.) It is quite obvious from the definition of the relations that a handle Sj...Si satisfies (5.1.2). It is not so obvious that the leftmost substring satisfying (5.1.2) is the handle. We prove this assertion in the next section. Let us take it for granted

```
                                        Reduce      Direct Derivation
Step  Sentential Form       Handle    Handle to       constructed

  1   b  (  a  a  )  b        a           M         b(Ma)b => b(aa)b
        ⋖  ⋖  ⋗  ≐  ⋗

  2   b  (  M  a  )  b      M a )         L         b(Lb => b(Ma)b
        ⋖  ⋖  ≐  ≐  ⋗

  3   b  (  L  b             ( L          M         bMb => b(Lb
        ⋖  ≐  ⋗

  4   b  M  b               b M b         Z         Z => bMb
        ≐  ≐

Derivaticn Constructed: Z => bMb => b(Lb => b(Ma)b => b(aa)b
```

**FIGURE 5.3. Parse of the Sentential Form b(aa)b.**

for now and end this section with an example -- the canonical parse of the sentence b(aa)b of grammar G5 using the precedence matrix of Figure 5.2. Figure 5.3 illustrates the parse. Each step shows the sentential form, along with the relations which exist between the symbols according to Figure 5.2.

### EXERCISES FOR 5.1

1. Determine all precedence relations from the following syntax trees. (After you finish determining the relations from the handle, prune that handle from the tree to arrive at another tree. Then determine the relations from the new tree.)

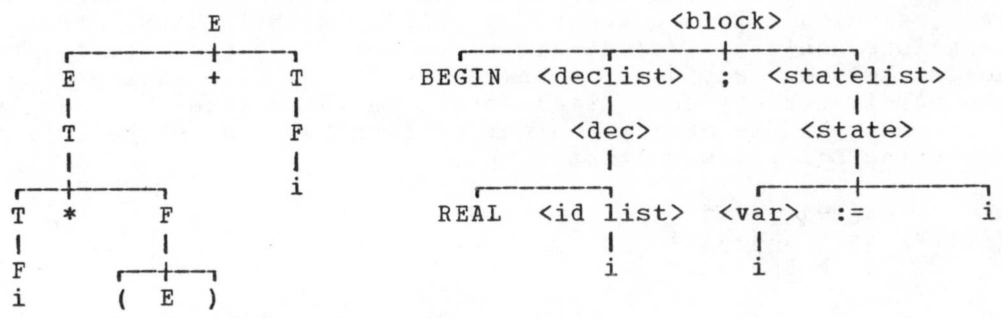


2. Parse the following sentences of grammar G5, using the precedence matrix of Figure 5.2 to find the handles: bab, b(aa)b, b(((aa)a)a)b.

3. Try to find all the precedence relations for grammar (4.1.1).

## 5.2 DEFINITION AND CONSTRUCTION OF THE RELATIONS

In section 5.1 we defined the three precedence relations in terms of the syntax trees of sentential forms. We wish now to redefine them with respect to the rules of the grammars only, so that we can see how to construct the relations and prove the assertion of the last section. These definitions look rather formidable, but are necessary in order to prove our points.

(5.2.1) DEFINITION. Given a grammar G we define the <u>precedence relations</u> between symbols of the vocabulary V as follows:

1. R $\doteq$ S if and only if there is a rule U ::= ...RS... in G.
2. R $\lessdot$ S if and only if there is a rule U ::= ...RV... such that the relation V FIRST+ S holds (see (2.6.4)).
3. R $\gtrdot$ S if and only if S is terminal and there is a rule U ::= ...VW... such that V LAST+ R and W FIRST* S hold (see (2.6.7) and (2.6.4)). ■

We will at times also need the following two relations

R $\lessdot$= S  if and only if  R $\doteq$ S or R $\lessdot$ S.
R $\gtrdot$= S  if and only if  R $\doteq$ S or R $\gtrdot$ S.

We have to prove that these relations defined in such a strange way are equivalent to the more lucid ones described in section 5.1. We will show this for $\doteq$ and $\gtrdot$ and leave the proof for $\lessdot$ to the reader (exercise 1).

(5.2.2) THEOREM. R $\doteq$ S if and only if the substring RS appears in a handle of some sentential form.

Proof. Suppose R $\doteq$ S. We must construct a syntax tree with RS in the handle. By definition, there exists a rule U ::= uRSv for some u and v. Since every rule can be used in the derivation of at least one sentence (we assume the grammar is reduced), we have Z =>* xUy for some x and y, where Z is the distinguished symbol. We construct the desired syntax tree in three steps:

1. Construct the tree for the derivation of xUy.
2. Make reductions (prune handles) of the tree constructed in step 1 until U becomes part of the handle. This can be done since every symbol is part of the handle at some point.
3. Add one more branch to the tree of (2) for the rule U ::= uRSv. Since U was in the handle, the new handle must be uRSv, and the tree has been constructed.

Conversely, if RS is part of a handle, by definition of handle there must be a rule U ::= ...RS... ∎

(5.2.3) THEOREM. R $\gtrdot$ S if and only if there exists a canonical sentential form ...RS... where R is the tail symbol of a handle.

Proof. Suppose that R $\gtrdot$ S. We will show how to construct a syntax tree with the required attribute. First, since R $\gtrdot$ S we have a rule U ::= uVWv where V LAST+ R and W FIRST* S. What does this mean? Since the grammar is reduced we know that Z =>* xUy => xuVWvy (Z is the distinguished symbol). Secondly, V LAST+ R means that V =>+ ...R, and this yields

(5.2.4) Z =>+ xuVWvy =>+ xu...RWvy.

We construct the desired tree as follows:

1. Draw the syntax tree for the derivation (5.2.4).
2. Make a sequence of reductions of the handle until R becomes part of the handle. Note that since V =>+ ...R, R must be the tail symbol of the handle.

3. We know that W =>* S..., since by definition W FIRST* S. Add to the syntax tree of step 2 the branches for this derivation. Obviously, the handle does not change here, since it contains R and branches are added to the right of R. Thus R is the tail of the handle and is followed by S.

Conversely, suppose that we have a tree where R is the tail of the handle and is followed by S. First, make a sequence of reductions of the canonical parse until S is in the handle. This yields a tree for a sentential form ...VS... for some V such that V =>+ ...R. Two cases arise:

1. If both V and S are in the handle we are finished, because a rule U ::= ...VS... must exist and we have U ::= ...VW... where V =>+ ...R and W = S.
2. If S is the head of the handle, make a series of reductions until we have a sentential form ...VW... for some W where V is finally in the handle. Note then that W =>+ S... Moreover, W must also be in the handle, for if V were the tail symbol of the handle it would also be a tail symbol of the handle of the string from the first step, in contradiction to the fact that S was in the handle.

Thus a rule U ::= ...VW... exists where V =>+ ...R and W =>+ S... and the theorem is proved. ∎

(5.2.5) THEOREM. R ⋖ S if and only if there exists a sentential form ...RS... with S as the head of the handle.

Proof. We leave the proof to the reader (exercise 1). ∎

We see that the formal definitions (5.2.1) are equivalent to those given informally in terms of syntax trees in section 5.1. It is important for the reader to study the definition given in terms of syntax trees. Without a complete understanding, there is no reason for progressing further. We are now ready to define a simple precedence grammar.

(5.2.6) DEFINITION. A grammar G is called a (simple) <u>precedence grammar</u> or a <u>(1,1) precedence grammar</u> if

1. at most one relation holds between any two symbols of the vocabulary; and
2. no two productions have the same right part. ∎

The (1,1) refers to the fact that we use one symbol on each side of a possible handle to help us decide if it is a handle or not.

That is, if a symbol R is in the handle we look only at the next symbol S to tell us whether R is the tail of the handle or not; and similarly when looking for the head. If G is a precedence grammar, the relations tell us how to find <u>the</u> handle of any sentential form, while the second condition above assures us that we can reduce the handle to only one nonterminal. We prove this in the following theorem. Before we get to the theorem there is one more problem we must discuss. We want to show that the handle is the leftmost string Sj...Si satisfying (5.2.9) below. However, we must take care of the case where the first symbol S1 in the sentential form is in the handle, for then there is no symbol S0 such that S0 $\lessdot$ S1. Let us solve this problem by assuming the following:

(5.2.7) Each sentential form is enclosed between the symbols # and # (assuming that # is not a symbol of the grammar). Moreover, we agree that # $\lessdot$ S and S $\gtrdot$ # for any symbol S of the grammar. ■

With this assumption, let us go on to our theorem.

(5.2.8) THEOREM. A precedence grammar is unambiguous. Moreover the unique handle of any sentential form S1...Sn is the leftmost substring Sj...Si such that

(5.2.9) S[j-1] $\lessdot$ Sj $\doteq$ S[j+1] $\doteq$ ... $\doteq$ Si $\gtrdot$ S[i+1].

Proof. We first show that the handle x of any sentential form is unique. We take as obvious the fact that if Sk...Sp is a handle, then

S[k-1] $\lessdot$ Sk $\doteq$ ... $\doteq$ Sp $\gtrdot$ S[p+1]

This arises from the definition of $\lessdot$, $\doteq$ and $\gtrdot$. Suppose there is a syntax tree which does not have the leftmost substring Sj...Si satisfying (5.2.9) as the handle. Then any number of pruning steps will never make it a handle, since if at any time it forms the leftmost complete branch, it does so now also.

During the canonical parse, each symbol S[j-1],Sj,...,S[i+1], must at some time appear as part of a handle. Let St be the first which does. Since the handle cannot be Sj...Si, one of the following must hold:

1. t = j-1, in which case S[j-1] $\doteq$ Sj or S[j-1] $\gtrdot$ Sj;
2. t = i+1, in which case Si $\doteq$ S[i+1] or Si $\lessdot$ S[i+1];
3. j ≤ t ≤ i
   a) S[j-1] is in the handle, in which case S[j-1] $\doteq$ Sj;
   b) S[i+1] is in the handle, in which case Si $\doteq$ S[i+1];
   c) For some k, j < k ≤ t, Sk is the head of the handle, in which case S[k-1] $\lessdot$ Sk.
   d) For some k, t ≤ k < i, Sk is the tail of the handle, in which case Sk $\gtrdot$ S[k+1].

In each case, we see that another relation exists between two of the symbols S[j-1],...,S[i+1], violating the precedence grammar definition. Hence Sj...Si must be the unique handle.

Thus, at each step of a parse of any sentential form x the handle is uniquely determined. Since the handle may be the right part of only one rule (condition 2 of (5.2.6)), there is only one symbol to which the handle can be reduced; hence at each step the direct reduction to make is unique. This means that the syntax tree is unique for any sentence and therefore the grammar is unambiguous. ▪

We see that sentences of precedence grammars are easy to parse, once the relations have been determined. This is perhaps the simplest class of nontrivial grammars which can be used practically. The relations themselves are fairly easy to understand when viewed as described in section 5.1, even if the actual definitions look rather messy. We will turn later on to other classes of grammars which are harder to define but which are more practical. For the moment, though, let us play with precedence grammars some more and give algorithms for constructing the relations and for the actual recognizer, or parser, of sentences of a precedence grammar.

### Constructing the Precedence Relations

The construction of the simple precedence relation $\doteq$ needs practically no explanation. One must only sequence through the right parts of the rules and set R $\doteq$ S for each R and S such that ...RS... is a right side.

The relations $\lessdot$ and $\gtrdot$ require more work, but are still quite simple to calculate; we must only apply the Boolean matrix theory of section 2.7.

(5.2.10) THEOREM. The relation $\lessdot$ is equal to the product of the relations $\doteq$ and FIRST+. That is,

$$\lessdot \; = \; (\doteq)(\text{FIRST+})$$

Proof. This follows directly from the definition of the product of relations and definition (5.2.1) of $\lessdot$. ▪

(5.2.11) THEOREM. Let I be the identity relation. We have R $\gtrdot$ S if and only if S is terminal and

$$R \; (\text{TRANSPOSE}(\text{LAST+}))(\doteq)(\text{I+FIRST+}) \; S$$

Proof. The proof is left to the reader (exercise 4). ▪

Theorem (5.2.10) indicates that we can construct the relation $\lessdot$ by (1) constructing the Boolean matrix F for the relation FIRST; (2) constructing the matrix F+ using, say, Warshall's algorithm; (3) constructing the matrix EQ for the relation $\doteq$; and (4) multiplying EQ by F+. The process for calculating the relation $\gtrdot$ is almost as simple.

**EXERCISES FOR 5.2**

1. Prove that R $\lessdot$ S if and only if there is a sentential form ...RS... where S is the head of the handle.

2. Show that the following grammar is not a precedence grammar: Z ::= b E b, E ::= E + T | T.

3. Show that the following grammar is not a precedence grammar: Z ::= b E1 b, E1 ::= E | E + T | T | i, T ::= i | ( E1 ).

4. Prove theorem (5.2.11).

5. Construct the relations for grammar (5.1.1), using theorems (5.2.10) and (5.2.11).

6. Write and debug a program in some high level language for constructing and printing out the relations. The input to the program is the grammar in some suitable form.

## 5.3 THE PARSING ALGORITHM

When actually using the precedence relations to recognize sentences we want a compact way of representing them. The usual technique is to have a matrix P with the values

P[i,j] = 0 if no relation exists between Si and Sj.<br>
P[i,j] = 1 if Si $\lessdot$ Sj<br>
P[i,j] = 2 if Si $\doteq$ Sj<br>
P[i,j] = 3 if Si $\gtrdot$ Sj

We can do this for a precedence grammar because we know that at most one relation exists between any two symbols.

The rules themselves must be in a table, structured in such a way that given a right side, we can find it in the rules and find the corresponding left side.

The parsing algorithm works as follows. The symbols of the input string are processed from left to right and stored on a stack S, until the precedence relation $\gtrdot$ exists between the symbol at the top of the stack and the next incoming symbol. This means that the top stack symbol is the tail of the handle, and therefore the whole handle is in the stack. This handle is then found in the list of rules and replaced, in the stack, by the corresponding nonterminal to which it should be reduced. The process repeats, until the stack contains Z (Z is the distinguished symbol) and the next input symbol is #.

Figure 5.4 gives a flow chart for the recognizer using the following notation:

1. S is a stack used to hold the symbols; its counter is i.
2. j is an index used to refer to the top few stack elements.
3. The sentence to be parsed is T1T2...Tn. We start with the sentence delimiter # in the stack, and assume that it has also been appended to the sentence as T[n+1].
4. Q and R are symbol-valued variables used to hold certain symbols as the parse progresses.

Note that if the string T1...Tn is not actually a sentence, then the algorithm will stop and indicate this. Comments about the numbered boxes of the flow chart follow.

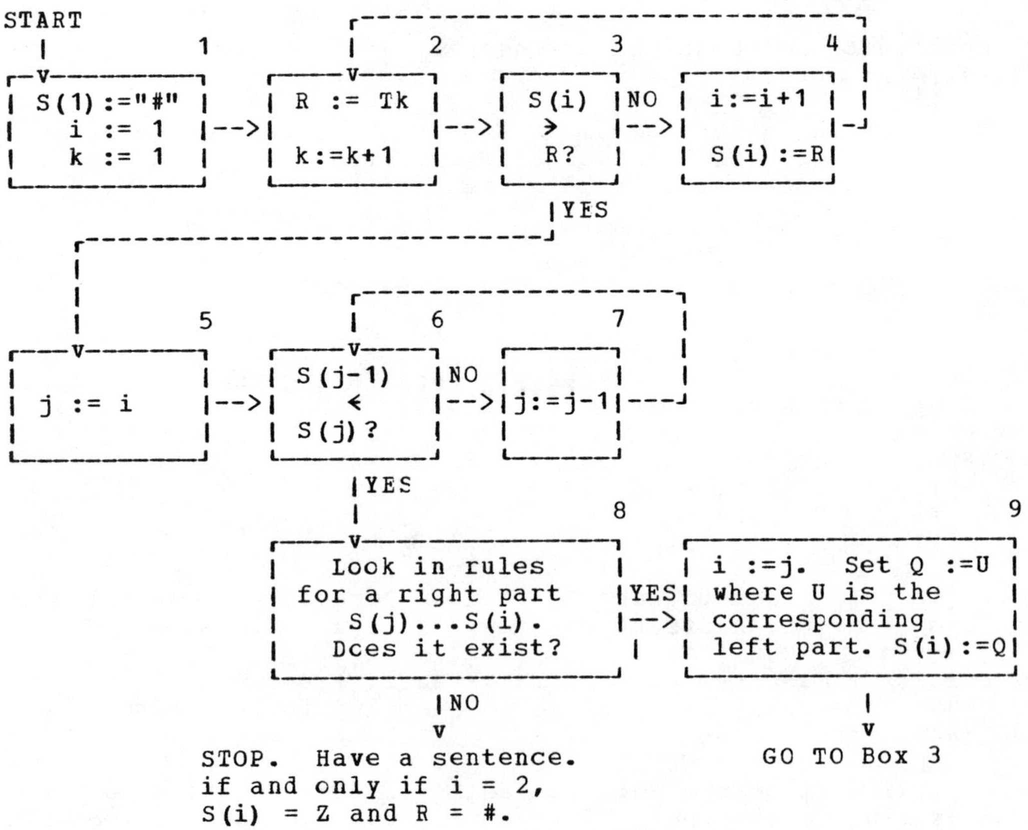


**FIGURE 5.4. Simple Precedence Recognizer.**

Box 1. Initialize the stack S to hold the sentence delimiter. Set the sentence index to point to the first symbol.

Box 2. "Scan" the next symbol -- put it in R and increment k.

Box 3. If (S(i),R) is not in ⋗ the handle is not completely in the stack, so stack R and go scan the next symbol.

Boxes 5 - 7. S(i) ⋗ R. Thus the handle should be in the stack. These boxes look for the head of the handle.

Boxes 8 - 9. Check the string S(j)...S(i). If it is not the right part of a rule, we are finished. The string was a sentence if and only if i = 2 and S(i) = Z, the distinguished symbol. If it is the right part of a rule, we delete the handle from the stack (box 9), push the symbol to which it is reduced onto the stack, and return to box 3 to look for the next handle.

One nice thing about this and similar recognizers is that the complete string of input symbols need not be in memory at the same time (unless we have a very perverse grammar). The symbols are read one at a time from the input medium and stacked, but as the handle is reduced they disappear. Only if the handle is at the right end of the string need the whole string be stored, and our programming language grammars are not structured this way.

Using this flow chart, we again parse the sentence b(aa)b of grammar (5.1.1). Figure 5.5 gives this parse, showing at each step the contents of the stack S, the scanned symbol R, the relation between the top stack symbol S[i] and R, and that part of the sentential form that has not yet been scanned, all before execution of box 3.

| Step | S1S2... | Relation | R | Tk... |
|---|---|---|---|---|
| 0 | # | ⋖ | b | ( a a ) b # |
| 1 | # b | ⋖ | ( | a a ) b # |
| 2 | # b ( | ⋖ | a | a ) b # |
| 3 | # b ( a | ⋗ | a | ) b # |
| 4 | # b ( M | ≐ | a | ) b # |
| 5 | # b ( M a | ≐ | ) | b # |
| 6 | # b ( M a ) | ⋗ | b | # |
| 7 | # b ( L | ⋗ | b | # |
| 8 | # b M | ≐ | b | # |
| 9 | # b M b | ⋗ | # | |
| 10 | # Z | | # | |

**FIGURE 5.5. Parse of b(aa)b.**

### EXERCISES FOR 5.3

1. Use the algorithm of Figure 5.3 and the precedence matrix of G5 (example 5.1.1) to try to parse the following strings (not all are sentences): #aa#, #((aa)a)#, #()#, #((((aa)a)a)a)#.

2. Program and debug the parsing algorithm of Figure 5.4. To do this you must determine the form of the precedence matrix (it should be the output of the program of exercise 5.2.6). Secondly, the input to the parser could be the output of some scanner, say one programmed in exercise 3.3.2. In any case, the internal representation used for each symbol should be the row or column number for it in the precedence matrix.

## 5.4 PRECEDENCE FUNCTIONS

A precedence matrix can take up much memory. If the language has 160 symbols we need a 160 by 160 matrix of at least 2-bit elements. In many cases, however, the information in the matrix can be represented by two functions f and g such that

$$
\begin{aligned}
&R \doteq S \text{ implies } f(R) = g(S)\\
(5.4.1)\qquad &R \lessdot S \text{ implies } f(R) < g(S)\\
&R \gtrdot S \text{ implies } f(R) > g(S)
\end{aligned}
$$

for all symbols of the grammar. This is called a <u>linearization</u> of the matrix. We can thus cut down on the storage necessary from n*n locations to 2*n locations. Functions f and g for the precedence matrix of Figure 5.2 are

(5.4.2)

| | Z | b | M | L | a | ( | ) |
|---|---|---|---|---|---|---|---|
| f | 1 | 4 | 7 | 8 | 9 | 2 | 8 |
| g | 1 | 7 | 4 | 2 | 7 | 5 | 9 |

It should be noted that the functions are not unique -- there are an infinite number of such functions f and g if any exist at all. There are also many precedence matrices for which no functions exist. Even the following 2 by 2 precedence matrix for symbols S1 and S2 can not be linearized:

$$
\begin{bmatrix} \doteq & \gtrdot \\ \doteq & \doteq \end{bmatrix}
$$

Why not? If functions do exist, then from (5.4.1) we must have

$$
\begin{aligned}
&f(S1) > g(S2),\ g(S2) = f(S2),\\
&f(S2) = g(S1),\ g(S1) = f(S1),
\end{aligned}
$$

and this leads to the contradiction f(S1) > f(S1).

We construct precedence functions (if they exist) as follows:

(5.4.3) THEOREM. To construct the precedence functions perform the following steps:

1. Draw a directed graph with 2*n nodes, labeled f1, ..., fn and g1, ..., gn. Draw a directed arc from fi to gj if Si >= Sj. Draw a directed arc from gj to fi if Si <= Sj.
2. Assign a number to each node equal to the number of nodes accessible from that node (counting itself). The number assigned to fi is f(Si); the number assigned to gj is g(Sj).
3. Test the constructed functions f and g for inconsistencies with the original relations (with (5.4.1)). If no inconsistencies exist f and g are valid functions. If one exists, then <u>no</u> precedence functions can exist.

Proof. We must show that Si ≐ Sj implies f(Sj) = g(Sj), Si ⋖ Sj implies f(Si) < g(Sj), and Si ⋗ Sj implies f(Si) > g(Sj). The first follows immediately from the construction, for if Si ≐ Sj there is an arc from fi to gj and one from gj to fi. Hence, any node reached from one can be reached from the other.

The other two conditions are symmetric, and we shall prove only that Si ⋗ Sj implies f(Si) > g(Sj). Since Si ⋗ Sj, there is an arc from fi to gj. Hence any node accessible from gj is also accessible from fi, and f(Si) ≥ g(Sj). We need only show that if equality exists (if f(Si) = g(Sj)), then no precedence functions exist at all.

Suppose f(Si) = g(Sj). Then there must be a path

fi to gj, gj to fk, fk to gl, ..., gm to fi

Hence

Si ⋗ Sj, Sk <= Sj, Sk >= Sl, ..., Si <= Sm

This sequence shows that for <u>any</u> functions f and g we must have f(Si) > f(Si), and this is a contradiction. ∎

A directed graph describes a relation R over the set of nodes; x R y if and only if there is an arc from node x to node y. Hence we can represent the original graph of the construction by a 2*n by 2*n Boolean matrix B, as follows:

```
(5.4.4) B :=      ┌          ┐
                  | 0    GE  |
                  | LET  0   |
                  └          ┘
```

where GE is the n*n matrix for the relation >= and LET is the transpose of the matrix for the relation <=. Thus, for i,j = 1,...,n we have

```
        B[i,j]      = B[n+i,n+j] = 0;
(5.4.5) B[i,n+j]    = 1 if and only if Si >= Sj
                      (in the upper right quarter);
        B[n+j,i]    = 1 if and only if Si <= Sj
                      (in the lower left quarter).
```

Rows 1,...n correspond to f1,...fn, while rows n+1,...,2*n correspond to g1,...,gn. We leave it to the reader to prove the following theorem:

(5.4.6) THEOREM. The following construction yields the precedence functions if they exist:

1. Construct the matrix B cf (5.4.4);
2. Construct the reflexive transitive closure B* of B.
3. Let f(Sj) := number of k such that B*[j,k] = 1.
   Let g(Sj) := number of k such that B*[n+j,k] = 1. ∎

As an example, for the precedence matrix of Figure 5.2 we have

$$GE = \begin{bmatrix} 0&0&0&0&0&0&0 \\ 0&0&1&0&0&0&0 \\ 0&1&0&0&1&0&0 \\ 0&1&0&0&1&0&0 \\ 0&1&0&0&1&0&1 \\ 0&0&0&1&0&0&0 \\ 0&1&0&0&1&0&0 \end{bmatrix} \qquad LET = \begin{bmatrix} 0&0&0&0&0&0&0 \\ 0&0&1&0&0&0&0 \\ 0&1&0&0&0&1&0 \\ 0&0&0&0&0&1&0 \\ 0&1&1&0&0&1&0 \\ 0&1&0&0&0&1&0 \\ 0&0&0&0&1&0&0 \end{bmatrix}$$

Thus

$$B = \begin{bmatrix} 0&0&0&0&0&0&0&0&0&0&0&0&0&0 \\ 0&0&0&0&0&0&0&0&0&1&0&0&0&0 \\ 0&0&0&0&0&0&0&0&1&0&0&1&0&0 \\ 0&0&0&0&0&0&0&0&1&0&0&1&0&0 \\ 0&0&0&0&0&0&0&0&1&0&0&1&0&1 \\ 0&0&0&0&0&0&0&0&0&0&1&0&0&0 \\ 0&0&0&0&0&0&0&0&1&0&0&1&0&0 \\ 0&0&0&0&0&0&0&0&0&0&0&0&0&0 \\ 0&0&1&0&0&0&0&0&0&0&0&0&0&0 \\ 0&1&0&0&0&1&0&0&0&0&0&0&0&0 \\ 0&0&0&0&0&1&0&0&0&0&0&0&0&0 \\ 0&1&1&0&0&1&0&0&0&0&0&0&0&0 \\ 0&1&0&0&0&1&0&0&0&0&0&0&0&0 \\ 0&0&0&0&1&0&0&0&0&0&0&0&0&0 \end{bmatrix} \quad B^* = \begin{bmatrix} 1&0&0&0&0&0&0&0&0&0&0&0&0&0 \\ 0&1&0&0&0&1&0&0&0&1&1&0&0&0 \\ 0&1&1&0&0&1&0&0&1&1&1&1&0&0 \\ 0&1&1&1&0&1&0&0&1&1&1&1&0&0 \\ 0&1&1&0&1&1&0&0&1&1&1&1&0&1 \\ 0&0&0&0&0&1&0&0&0&0&1&0&0&0 \\ 0&1&1&0&0&1&1&0&1&1&1&1&0&0 \\ 0&0&0&0&0&0&0&1&0&0&0&0&0&0 \\ 0&1&1&0&0&1&0&0&1&1&1&1&0&0 \\ 0&1&0&0&0&1&0&0&0&1&1&0&0&0 \\ 0&0&0&0&0&1&0&0&0&0&1&0&0&0 \\ 0&1&1&0&0&1&0&0&1&1&1&1&0&0 \\ 0&1&0&0&0&1&0&0&0&1&1&0&1&0 \\ 0&1&1&0&1&1&0&0&1&1&1&1&0&1 \end{bmatrix}$$

Counting the number of 1's in each row i of B* gives us the f(Si) for i = 1,...,n; and counting the number of 1's in each row n+j, j = 1,...,n, gives us the g(Sj) of (5.4.2).

When a compiler discovers an error in a program it should try to recover and continue the process of syntax analysis in order to find more errors. It is thus sometimes important to find an error as soon as possible in order to be able to recover. The use of functions may prolong detection of errors. Information is lost by the linearization because you no longer know if a relation actually exists between two symbols. To illustrate this, let us try to parse the string ba)))))b according to G5 using first the full matrix and secondly the functions:

1) Parsing using the matrix

| Step | S1S2 ... | Relation | R Tk ... |
|---|---|---|---|
| 0 | # | $\lessdot$ | b a ) ) ) ) ) b # |
| 1 | # b | $\lessdot$ | a ) ) ) ) ) b # |
| 2 | # b a | $\doteq$ | ) ) ) ) ) b # |
| 3 | # b a ) | none | ) ) ) ) b # |

2) Parsing using the functions f and g

| Step | S1S2 ... | f Rel g | R Tk ... |
|---|---|---|---|
| 0 | # | 1 < 7 | b a ) ) ) ) ) b # |
| 1 | # b | 4 < 7 | a ) ) ) ) ) b # |
| 2 | # b a | 9 = 9 | ) ) ) ) ) b # |
| 3 | # b a ) | 8 < 9 | ) ) ) ) b # |
| 4 | # b a ) ) | 8 < 9 | ) ) ) b # |
| 5 | # b a ) ) ) | 8 < 9 | ) ) b # |
| 6 | # b a ) ) ) ) | 8 < 9 | ) b # |
| 7 | # b a ) ) ) ) ) | 8 > 7 | b # |

With the use of the functions four more steps were executed before an error was detected.

**EXERCISES FOR 5.4**

1. Construct the precedence functions f and g for the following matrix

$$\begin{bmatrix} \gtrdot & & \gtrdot & \gtrdot \\ \gtrdot & & \gtrdot & \\ \lessdot & \doteq & \lessdot & \\ \doteq & & \doteq & \end{bmatrix}$$

2. Prove theorem 5.4.6.

3. Change the program of exercise 5.2.6 to output the precedence functions also.

4. Change the parsing algorithm of exercise 5.3.2 to use functions instead of the precedence relations.

## 5.5 DIFFICULTIES WITH CONSTRUCTING PRECEDENCE GRAMMARS

We have presented this technique first because it is the simplest and illustrates most of the syntax techniques we will be using. Theoretically, it seems like a sound, efficient technique. Practically, though, it is not always good. In fact, almost any other technique will work better than this one. Very often more than one relation may hold between two symbols. All we can do then is to manipulate and change the grammar to alleviate the conflict. This may change the whole structure of the language, besides making the grammar unreadable.

One problem may arise from left recursion. Suppose there exists a rule U ::= U... If another rule V ::= ...SU... exists, we have both S $\doteq$ U and S $\lessdot$ U. This conflict can sometimes be avoided by introducing another nonterminal W and an intermediate reduction; we change

```
V ::= ...SU...
```

to

```
V ::= ...SW..., W ::= U
```

where W is a new symbol, yielding S $\doteq$ W and S $\lessdot$ U. This is sometimes called <u>stratification</u> or <u>separation</u>. This is however rather artificial, and we will derive other recognizer techniques where such conflicts do not occur so often. The same problem arises with the relations $\gtrdot$ and $\doteq$ when right recursion exists. Stratification does not always work, since it often introduces other conflicts. If both R $\lessdot$ S and R $\gtrdot$ S occur, there is not much help, and it would be better to use another technique.

To illustrate stratification, we take our usual grammar for arithmetic expressions:

```
        E       ::= E + T | T
(5.5.1) T       ::= T * F | F
        F       ::= ( E ) | i
```

From the first rule we have + $\doteq$ T and since T is left recursive we have also + $\lessdot$ T. We have a similar problem with ( and E. We can change the grammar, without really damaging the sentence structure and without changing the language, to

```
E       ::= E1
E1      ::= E1 + T1 | T1
T1      ::= T
T       ::= T * F | F
F       ::= ( E ) | i
```

We have, then, the following relations FIRST+ and LAST+:

| U | S such that (U,S) in FIRST+ | S such that (U,S) in LAST+ |
|---|---|---|
| E | E1, T, T1, F, (, i | E1, T1, T, F, ), i |
| E1 | E1, T, T1, F, (, i | T1, T, F, ), i |
| T1 | T, F, (, i | T, F, ), i |
| T | T, F, (, i | F, ), i |
| F | (, i | ), i |

This gives the precedence matrix and functions

| | E | E1 | T1 | T | F | i | ( | + | * | ) | f | g |
|---|---|---|---|---|---|---|---|---|---|---|---|---|
| E | | | | | | | | | | ≐ | 2 | 2 |
| E1 | | | | | | | | ≐ | | > | 4 | 3 |
| T1 | | | | | | | | > | | > | 5 | 4 |
| T | | | | | | | | > | ≐ | > | 6 | 5 |
| F | | | | | | | | > | > | > | 7 | 6 |
| i | | | | | | | | > | > | > | 7 | 7 |
| ( | ≐ | < | < | < | < | < | < | | | | 2 | 7 |
| + | | | ≐ | < | < | < | < | | | | 4 | 4 |
| * | | | | | ≐ | < | < | | | | 6 | 6 |
| ) | | | | | | | | > | > | > | 7 | 2 |

This may not seem like much of a change, but if the grammar has 100 rules and some 100 odd symbols (this happens for languages like ALGOL) it takes an experienced person a long time to manipulate the grammar into a precedence grammar.

The reader might ask at this point why the other techniques we will introduce are better. Note that the precedence technique uses very little of the context around a possible handle to make a decision. In fact, for each decision it only uses two adjacent symbols. If we use different symbols, or more symbols, the chances are we won't have as many conflicts. Thus, instead of looking only at Si and S[i+1] in order to detect the tail of the handle we lock at

S[i-1], Si, and S[i+1]     or     Si, S[i+1], and S[i+2].

To illustrate this, suppose we have the sentential form E+T*F of grammar (5.5.1). We have the conflict + < T and + ≐ T, and thus we do not know frcm just the two symbols + and T whether T is the head of the handle or not -- whether or not we should perform the addition. But intuitively we know from the two symbols + and *, or frcm the three symbols +T* that the addition cannot be performed and thus that + is not in the handle.

## EXERCISES FOR 5.5

1. Change the following grammar into a precedence grammar without changing the language. Find all relations.

```
<declaration> ::= <type> <id list>
<type>        ::= REAL | INTEGER | BOOLEAN
<id list>     ::= i | <id list> , i
```

2. Change the following grammar into a precedence grammar without changing the language. Find all relations.

```
P             ::= <be>
<be>          ::= b := <be> | <ae> = <ae>
<ae>          ::= a := <ae> | <at>
<at>          ::= <at> - <ap> | <ap>
<ap>          ::= a | ( <ae> ) | @ ( <be> )
```

(<be> stands for Boolean expression, <ae> for arithmetic expression, <at> for arithmetic term, and <ap> for arithmetic primary. "b" ("a") is a Boolean (arithmetic) identifier. (To evaluate a Boolean expression b := <be> one evaluates <be> and assigns it to b. The value of the expression is then the value of b. Similarly for the arithmetic expression a := <ae>. The value of(<be>) is 1 if <be> is true, 0 otherwise.)

## 5.6 HISTORICAL REFERENCES

Floyd(63) first formalized the idea of precedence relations and precedence functions. We will discuss Floyd's particular formalization in the next chapter. The present form of the relations was published by Wirth and Weber(66). The particular method of calculating the relations appeared in Martin(68). The method used to calculate the precedence functions is due to Bell(69). The ALGOL W compiler (see Bauer, Becker and Graham(68)) uses an automatically constructed precedence matrix. There have been several papers extending simple precedence. See the references at the end of chapter 6.

# Chapter 6.
# Other Bottom-Up Recognizers

Chapter 5 discussed the simple precedence technique for bottom-up parsing. In this chapter we discuss several other bottom-up parsing algorithms. All of them operate in the same manner, in that they iterate the following steps until the sentence has been reduced to the distinguished symbol.

1. Find the handle x (or some variation of it);
2. Find a rule U ::= x with x as the right part;
3. Reduce x to U, creating one branch of the syntax tree.

The recognizers differ in two ways; in the number and position of the symbols used to determine the handle, and in the way the rules and tables are structured in the recognizer itself. Each of the recognizers is implemented in the following steps:

1. Program the recognizer in a general manner which uses tables. The tables describe the grammar.
2. Program a <u>constructor</u> which, given a grammar, checks it for suitability and builds the necessary tables for the recognizer.
3. To implement the recognizer for a given grammar, run the constructor with the grammar as data and merge the output with the recognizer.

One then has the recognizer for sentences of that grammar. It can be used as often as desired, without having to run the constructor each time. In the case of simple precedence, the recognizer is the flow chart of Figure 5.4; the tables are the precedence matrix and the rules.

Some of the bottom-up techniques are formalizations of techniques used in earlier compilers; the requirements for the grammars were determined largely by the way the intuitively-built recognizers worked. This is so for operator precedence and transition matrices. Others, like (m,n) bounded context and LR(k), were first derived theoretically and have not yet been used practically.

Each of the following sections is devoted to a particular type recognizer. We will keep the discussion of each complete, but short. Proofs are left to the reader as exercises. Remember that all of these techniques are similar in that they solve the problem of finding the handle and the symbol to which it should be reduced by looking at the context in which the handle occurs.

## 6.1 OPERATOR PRECEDENCE

### Operator Grammars

Anybody asked to evaluate the expression 2+3*5 will arrive at the answer 17. When asked why he performed the multiplication first, he will reply that multiplication is always done before addition, that the operator * <u>has precedence</u> over the operator +. The important point here is that the operands 2, 3 and 5 play no role in determining which operation to perform first; just the operators are involved. Recall that the simple precedence technique defined precedences between *all* symbols -- operators and operands -- and that this caused some difficulties. The operator precedence technique formalizes the notion of precedences between operators only, the operators being just the terminal symbols of the grammar.

Let us begin by illustrating briefly how this technique has been used in an ad hoc fashion in a number of compilers, usually for arithmetic expressions. The syntax analyzer uses two stacks instead of one, an *operator* stack OPTOR and an *operand* stack OPAND. OPTOR holds binary and unary operators, parentheses, and the delimiter # which begins and ends each expression. OPAND holds identifiers and other operands as they get produced. Along with these stacks, we have two integer vectors f and g similar to the simple precedence functions of section 5.4.

A step of the general parsing algorithm is performed as follows, where S1 is the symbol at the top of the operator stack and S2 is the incoming symbol:

1. If S1 is an identifier, put it on the operand stack and skip the rest of these steps 2 and 3.
2. If $f(S1) \le g(S2)$, then push S2 onto the operator stack and scan the next input symbol.
3. If $f(S1) > g(S2)$, then call a (semantic) routine determined by S1. This routine will do semantic processing, will delete S1 and perhaps other symbols from the operator stack, will delete its associated operands from OPAND, and will push onto OPAND something which describes the result of the operator S1. This corresponds to the reduction of the handle of the sentential form.

To illustrate this for parsing arithmetic expressions, we will show the parse of #A+B+C#; as we do this we will begin filling in the vectors f and g with the proper values. The parse begins with # in stack OPTOR and stack OPAND empty. The first step pushes identifier A into OPAND. The second should push + into OPTOR (we cannot reduce or process + until we know what both its operands are). In order to have this performed, we need $f(\#) < g(+)$, so let us assign $f(\#) = 1$ and $g(+) = 4$ (say).

The third step pushes B into OPAND, yielding

```
        | + |            | B |
 OPTOR: | # |     OPAND: | A |   rest of         f(#)=1
        L___|            L___|   string: +C#        g(+)=4
```

Note now, that + is at the top of OPTOR and its operands A and B are at the top of OPAND. We now want to process + semantically, perhaps producing an internal form of the operation like (+ A, B, T1), and then do the following: delete + from OPTOR, delete A and B from OPAND, and push onto OPAND the name of the temporary T1 which represents the result of A+B. This yields

```
OPTOR:| # |        OPAND:| T1|   rest of       f(#)=1
      └───┘              └───┘   string: +C#   f(+)=5  g(+)=4
```

To do this, we need f(+) > g(+), and so we have set f(+) to 5 above. Note that the process corresponds to a reduction using a rule E::=E+T.

The next step pushes C onto OPAND, yielding

```
      | + |              | C |
OPTOR:| # |        OPAND:| T1|   rest of       f(#)=1
      └───┘              └───┘   string: #     f(+)=5  g(+)=4
```

Now note again that + is in OPTOR and its operands are at the top of OPAND, so that we again want to process or reduce the + operation. To do this we need f(+) > g(#). After this step, we end up with

```
OPTOR:| # |        OPAND:| T2|   rest of       f(#)=1  g(#)=1
      └───┘              └───┘   string: #     f(+)=4  g(+)=5
```

Thus one figures out the f and g functions, by seeing for each pair (top element in OPTOR, incoming symbol) what one wants to have performed and fixing the functions accordingly. Note that from #A+B*C# we want f(+) < g(*) so that when + is in OPTOR and * is the incoming symbol we will stack * also. We might do this by setting g(*) = 6. A more systematic way of finding the functions would be to first figure out all the relations desired, and then use either the graph method or the Boolean matrix method of section 5.4.

In order to test for errors and to detect whether minus is binary or unary, we have to check carefully whether an operand actually follows each operator or parenthesis or not. To do this we keep a single bit in each element of OPTOR, initially set to zero. Whenever an operand is pushed into OPAND, this bit of the top symbol in OPTOR is set to 1 to indicate it is followed by an operand.

This method is also known by the term <u>double priority</u>, since two functions are used to determine which operator has precedence, or priority. One might think that only a single function h could be used; if h(S1) > h(S2) then perform a stack reduction, otherwise stack S2. The conventional uses of parentheses in expressions makes this impossible. From #(A)*B# we would want h()) > h(*), while from #(A*B)# we would want h(*) > h()), and this is impossible.

Note that when a "reduction" is made in OPTOR, the top symbol determines in some fashion the subroutine to be executed. One representation of a symbol S in OPTOR is

| f(S) | address of subroutine to execute |
|---|---|

One reason people still program compilers in assembly languages is that many such efficient representations cannot be used in the normal high-level programming language.

We have barely outlined the process above, to indicate what the normal compiler writer goes through. Let us now discuss in more detail the formalization of this techniqe. In it, we will use a single stack instead of two, although the reader will realize later that whether one uses one or two is just a matter of taste.

We restrict the grammars somewhat so that an unlimited number of operands (nonterminals) cannot appear between operators in a sentential form. In other words, operations must be in infix form.

(6.1.1) DEFINITION. A grammar G is called an *operator grammar* (OG) if no rule has the form U ::= ...VW... where V and W are nonterminals. ■

Thus, in an OG no right part contains two adjacent nonterminals. This has implications on the sentential forms; we can prove (exercise 1) that no sentential form of an OG contains two adjacent nonterminals. Most grammars we work with can be made into OGs without much trouble.

We will use the words *operator* and *terminal* interchangeably. The same goes for *operand* and *nonterminal*. Figure 6.1 indicates the operands and operators of a few rules.

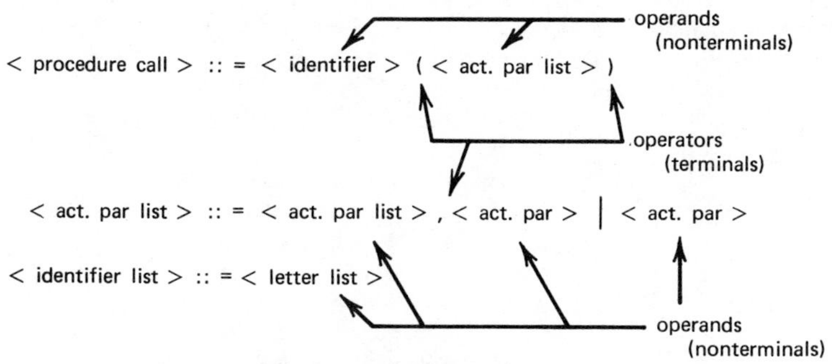


**FIGURE 6.1. Operators and Operands.**

### Operator Precedence Grammars

The following relations are quite similar to the simple precedence relations. The only difference, again, is that we define the relations for operators only.

(6.1.2) DEFINITION. Let G be an OG and let R and S be any two operators (terminals). Then

1. R $\doteq$ S if and only if there is a rule U ::= ...RS...
   or U ::= ...RVS...
2. R $\lessdot$ S if and only if there is a rule U ::= ...RW...
   where W =>+ S... or W =>+ VS...
3. R $\gtrdot$ S if and only if there is a rule U ::= ...WS...
   where W =>+ ...R or W =>+ ...RV

for some nonterminals V and W. ■

(6.1.3) DEFINITION. An OG is called an <u>operator precedence grammar</u> (OPG) if at most one of the relations $\lessdot$, $\gtrdot$, and $\doteq$ holds between any two terminals. ■

(6.1.4) EXAMPLE. Consider again the grammar G[E]:

```
E ::= E + T | T
T ::= T * F | F
F ::= ( E ) | i
```

From the last line we have ( $\doteq$ ). This is the only $\doteq$ relation, since no other right part has two terminals in it. Since E => E+T => T+T => T*F+T => F*F+T => i*F+T, we have from the rule F::=(E): ( $\lessdot$ +, ( $\lessdot$ * and ( $\lessdot$ i. The same rule and sequence of direct derivations also shows us that + $\gtrdot$ ). The complete operator precedence matrix is given in Figure 6.2. Since at most one relation holds between two terminals, we have an OPG. ■

| | + | * | ( | ) | i |
|---|---|---|---|---|---|
| + | $\gtrdot$ | $\lessdot$ | $\lessdot$ | $\gtrdot$ | $\lessdot$ |
| * | $\gtrdot$ | $\gtrdot$ | $\lessdot$ | $\gtrdot$ | $\lessdot$ |
| ( | $\lessdot$ | $\lessdot$ | $\lessdot$ | $\doteq$ | $\lessdot$ |
| ) | $\gtrdot$ | $\gtrdot$ | | $\gtrdot$ | |
| i | $\gtrdot$ | $\gtrdot$ | | $\gtrdot$ | |

**FIGURE 6.2. Precedence Matrix for Grammar (6.1.4).**

### Constructing the Relations

The construction of the relation $\doteq$ needs no detailed explanation; one must just search the right parts of rules looking for the pattern RVS or RS. To construct the relation $\lessdot$, for each W we must find some way of finding the set of terminals S such that W =>+ S... or W =>+ VS... with V a nonterminal. (A similar statement can be made about the construction of the relation $\gtrdot$). To do this, define two new relations as follows:

(6.1.5) DEFINITION. Let G be an OG. Let S be a terminal. Then

```
 U FIRSTTERM S if and only if there is a rule U ::= S...
               or U ::= VS...
 U LASTTERM  S if and only if there is a rule U ::= ...S
               or U ::= ...SV
```

where V is any nonterminal. ■

"FIRSTTERM" ("LASTTERM") stands for the first (last) terminal in the right part of the rule. These relations are obviously easy to construct from the rules. We can now use the relations $\doteq$ (the <u>simple</u> precedence relation), FIRST, FIRSTTERM, LAST and LASTTERM, all of which we know how to construct as Boolean matrices, to construct the relations $\lessdot$ and $\gtrdot$:

(6.1.6) THEOREM. $\lessdot$ is the product of the three relations $\doteq$, FIRST* and FIRSTTERM: $\lessdot$ = ($\doteq$)(FIRST*)(FIRSTTERM). Similarly, $\gtrdot$ = TRANSPOSE((LAST*)(LASTTERM))($\doteq$). ■

(We leave the simple proof to the reader in exercise 3). We have therefore a simple means of calculating the relations $\lessdot$ (and $\gtrdot$ also). Just construct the Boolean matrices for three relations from the rules, take the <u>reflexive</u> transitive closure of one of them, and multiply the three matrices together.

### Prime Phrases—Their Detection and Reduction

The relations cannot be used to find handles consisting of a single nonterminal because, to the relations, the nonterminals are invisible. For example, consider the sentential form F+T of the arithmetic grammar of example (6.1.4). The handle is F, but the relations we have are # $\lessdot$ + and + $\gtrdot$ # (assuming, again, that we have delimited the sentential form by # and have agreed that # $\lessdot$ S and S $\gtrdot$ # for all terminals S). The operator precedence technique will therefore not be able to construct the canonical parse as we have defined it, but will calculate a parse which is somewhat similar to it. The parse is still bottom-up, but not strictly left to right. At each step it will recognize and reduce something which we shall call the leftmost _prime phrase_.

(6.1.7) DEFINITION. Let G be a grammar with distinguished symbol Z. A _prime phrase_ (of a sentential form) is a phrase which contains at least one terminal but no prime phrase other than itself. ▪

Consider the sentential form (delimited by #) #T+T*F+i# of the grammar of (6.1.4). The phrases of it are T+T*F+i, T+T*F, i, the leftmost T, and T*F (this we see by looking at the only syntax tree for the sentential form, Figure 6.3). Which of these are prime phrases? A prime phrase cannot contain another phrase with a terminal in it, so this leaves out T+T*F+i, which contains i. Similarly T+T*F contains the phrase T*F. The other possibilities are T, T*F and i. T cannot be a prime phrase since it does not contain a terminal symbol (note that T is the handle of the sentential form but is not a prime phrase). The prime phrases are therefore T*F and i.

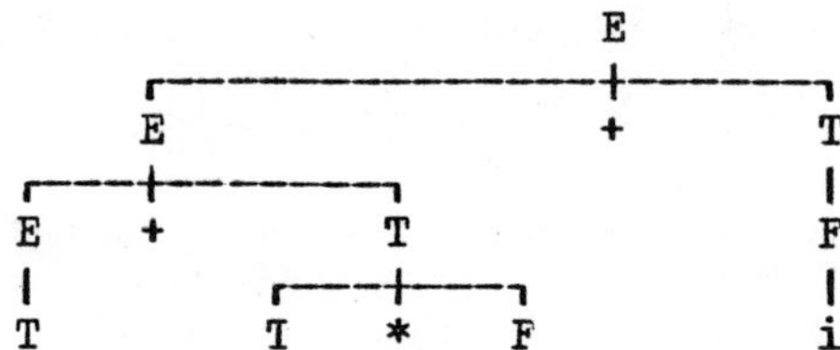


**FIGURE 6.3. Syntax Tree for T+T*F+i.**

Let us for the moment write a general sentential form, enclosed between delimiters # and #, as

#N1T1N2T2...NnTnN[n+1]#

where the Ni are nonterminals which may or may not be present and the Ti are terminals. In other words, the sentential form consists of n terminals with no more than one nonterminal between each adjacent terminal pair. Remember that any sentential form of an OG has this form. Exercises 6-8 are devoted to proving the following theorem:

(6.1.8) THEOREM. The leftmost prime phrase of a sentential form of an OPG is the leftmost substring NjTj...NiTiN[i+1] such that

(6.1.9) T[j-1] $\lessdot$ Tj, Tj $\doteq$ T[j+1], ... T[i-1] $\doteq$ Ti, Ti $\gtrdot$ T[i+1] ■

This theorem looks monotonously similar to the corresponding one for simple precedence; the main difference here is the exclusion of nonterminals from the relations. Note that a nonterminal appearing to the left of Tj or to the right of Ti <u>always</u> belongs to the prime phrase.

To illustrate the theorem, we show below the parse of the sentential form T+T*F+i, using the precedence matrix of Figure 6.2. The reader should study it carefully, along with the syntax tree of Figure 6.3. The table gives the symbol to which each prime phrase should be reduced, although we have not yet explained how to determine it. This will be discussed subsequently.

| <u>step</u> | <u>sentential form</u> | <u>relations</u> | <u>prime phrase</u> | <u>reduce to</u> |
|---|---|---|---|---|
| 1 | #T+T*F+i# | # $\lessdot$ + $\lessdot$ * $\gtrdot$ + | T*F | T |
| 2 | #T+T+i# | # $\lessdot$ + $\gtrdot$ + | T+T | E |
| 3 | #E+i# | # $\lessdot$ + $\lessdot$ i $\gtrdot$ # | i | F |
| 4 | #E+F# | # $\lessdot$ + $\gtrdot$ # | E+F | E |

The above parse indicates the nonterminal to which each prime phrase is to be reduced. Note, however, that the nonterminals are not used at all in finding the leftmost prime phrase to be reduced. Hence it makes absolutely no difference whether the correct nonterminal is placed on the stack or not. In fact, the nonterminals could be completely omitted!

In a compiler, much semantic information is usually connected with each nonterminal or operand -- its type, its address, whether it is a formal parameter or not. As described briefly in chapter 1, we will have semantic routines which process prime phrases. These routines will be interested only in the semantic information associated with the symbols, and not the symbols themselves. For example, the semantic routine which reduces T*F does not care whether it is T*F or F*T or F*F. It only uses the semantics of each nonterminal involved -- its type, address, and so forth. Hence the actual nonterminal names are not that important to the semantic routines. We should remember from section 2.4 that the nonterminals T and F were used in this grammar only to make the grammar unambiguous and to give precedence to operators; not for semantic reasons.

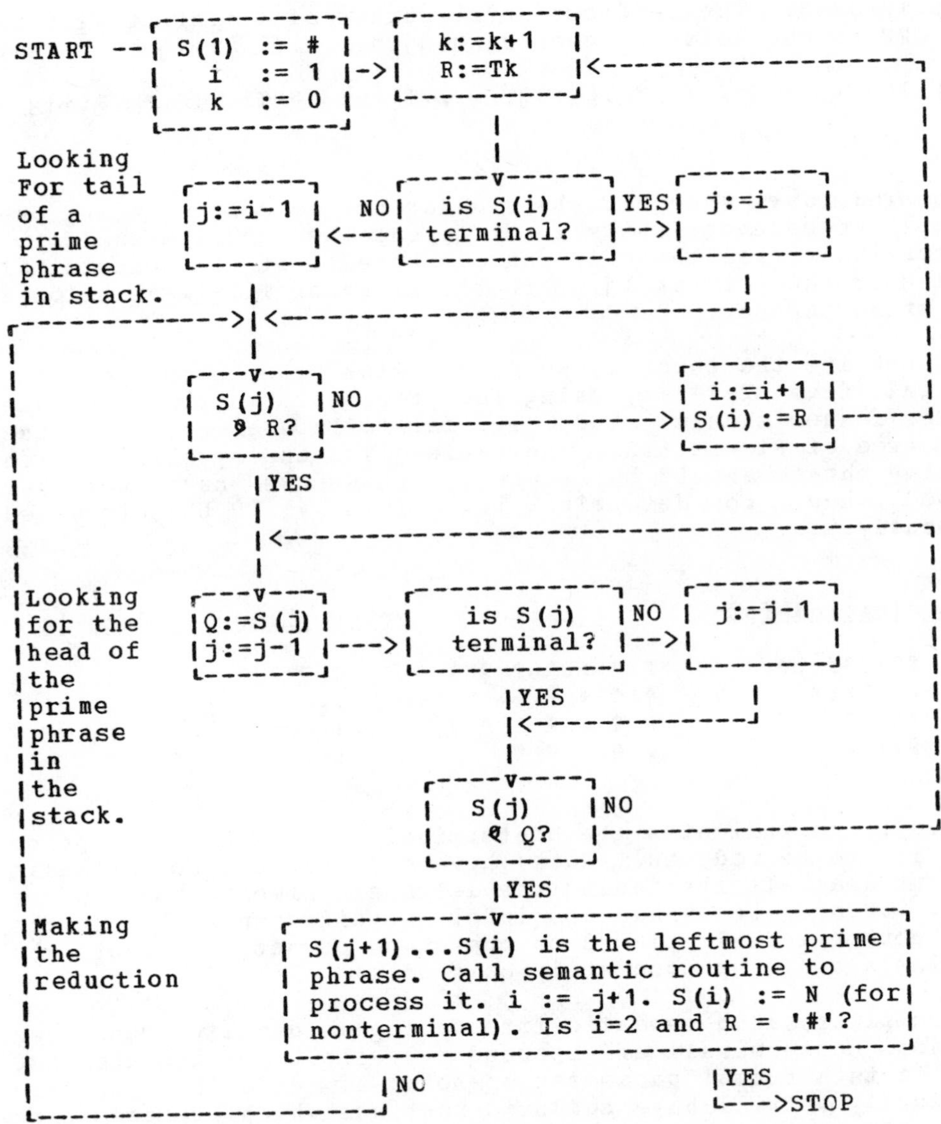


**FIGURE 6.4. Operator Precedence Recognizer.**

Please note that if we required a formal parsing algorithm, we <u>would</u> have to specify the nonterminal to which the prime phrase is to be reduced. We do not, however, want to be formal -- just practical. Note that we haven't said that the syntax tree for every sentential form is unique. It may not be. But we can say that its <u>structure</u>, disregarding the names on nodes representing nonterminals, is unique. This is obvious since the leftmost phrase is unique at each stage of the parse.

We are of course putting more burden on semantic routines. They must do more checking of operands than when simple precedence is used. But we do gain something, because the recognizer is more efficient. Note that space is saved since the precedence matrix is smaller; it need only contain rows and columns for terminals. Moreover, the recognizer does not explicitly make any reductions like E => T or T => F, since T and F are not prime phrases. This is good, because there is no semantics involved in such reductions.

Figure 6.4 gives the flow chart of the OPG recognizer which uses as usual a stack S with counter i, an input string T1...Tn with counter k, an integer variable j, and two symbol-valued variables R and Q.

We can build precedence functions from the operator precedence relations, and use them as we used them in sections 5.4. We are then doing formally what we explained in an ad hoc fashion at the start of this section.

As an example, we parse the sentence i*(i+i) of the grammar in example (6.1.4):

| Step | S(1)... | Relation | R | T(k)... |
|---|---|---|---|---|
| 0 | # | ⋖ | i | *(i+i)# |
| 1 | #i | ⋗ | * | (i+i)# |
| 2 | #N | ⋖ | * | (i+i)# |
| 3 | #N* | ⋖ | ( | i+i)# |
| 4 | #N*( | ⋖ | i | +i)# |
| 5 | #N*(i | ⋗ | + | i)# |
| 6 | #N*(N | ⋖ | + | i)# |
| 7 | #N*(N+ | ⋖ | i | )# |
| 8 | #N*(N+i | ⋗ | ) | # |
| 9 | #N*(N+N | ⋗ | ) | # |
| 10 | #N*(N | ≐ | ) | # |
| 11 | #N*(N) | ⋗ | # | |
| 12 | #N*N | ⋗ | # | |
| 13 | #N | STOP ■ | | |

**EXERCISES FOR 6.1**

1. Prove that in an OG no sentential form contains two adjacent nonterminals. Hint: Prove by induction on the number of direct derivations in the derivation of sentential forms.

2. Let G be a grammar. Prove that if a right part contains two adjacent nonterminals then at least one sentential form contains two adjacent nonterminals. Hint: Remember that all the grammars are reduced (cf. definition 2.8.4).

3. Prove Theorem (6.1.6).

4. Build the Boolean matrices for the relations ≐, ±, FIRST FIRSTTERM, LAST and LASTTERM for the grammar of example (6.1.4).

Next calculate FIRST* and LAST* from FIRST and LAST. Finally, calculate the relations ⋖, and ⋗ using theorem 6.1.6.

5. List the phrases and prime phrases of the following sentential forms of the grammar of example (6.1.4): E, T, i, T*F, F*F, i*F, F*i, F+F+F.

6. Prove that if T is in a phrase of a sentential form, then so is any nonterminal U which directly precedes (follows) T. Hint: if not, create a sentential form with two adjacent nonterminals.

7. Prove that any prime phrase satisfies (6.1.9) (assuming that the sentential form is delimited by the symbol # and that # ⋖ S, S ⋗ # for any terminal S).

8. Prove that any substring NiTi...NjTjN[j+1] of a sentential form that satisfies (6.1.9) is a prime phrase. Hint: use the proof of Theorem (5.2.8) as an example.

9. Parse the sentences i, i+i, i*i+i, i*(i*i) and i*(i+i*i)+((i+i)*i) of grammar (6.1.4) using the matrix of Figure 6.2 and the recognizer in Figure 6.4.

## 6.2 HIGHER ORDER PRECEDENCE

### (1,2) (2,1) Precedence

This technique extends simple precedence in two steps to arrive at a more practical recognizer -- one which can be used for more grammars. First of all, the problems of finding the tail and the head of the handle are separated. When looking for the tail, we look for the relation ⋗. It doesn't really matter if both R ⋖ S and R ≐ S hold, since we just want to know whether R is the tail or not. Hence we use only the relations ⋗ and ⋖=. Similarly, when looking for the head, we use only the relations ⋖ and ⋗=.

The second step is to use three symbols instead of two to detect the head and tail of the handle. We define the following relations.

(6.2.1) DEFINITION. Let G be a grammar. Let R, S and T be three symbols. We define

RS °> T if there is a canonical sentential form ...RST... with S as the tail of a handle.
RS °<=T if there is a canonical sentential form ...RST... with T in a handle.
R °< ST if there is a canonical sentential form with S as the head of a handle.
R °>=ST if there is a canonical sentential form with R in a handle ∎

The terminology (1,2)(2,1) precedence refers to the number of symbols used to detect the head and tail of the handle. To detect the tail, we test three symbols R, S, and T for the relation RS °> T or RS °<= T; thus the term (2,1). Once the tail symbol has been detected we step to the left of it to find the head by testing for the relations R °< ST or R °>= ST. Thus the term (1,2).

Fewer conflicts exist than in the simple precedence case. In grammar (6.2.2) for expressions we have + ≐ T and + ⋖ T. This is now resolved by using the symbol following the T -- we have + °>= T+ and + °< T*.

(6.2.2) E ::= T | E + T    T ::= F | T * F    F ::= i | ( E )

The relations given in (6.2.1) can be redefined in terms of derivations as follows (Z is the distinguished symbol. A substring in brackets may or may not be present.)

```
RS °> T  if there is a derivation Z ‡>* ...[R]UTx ‡> ...RSTx
RS °<=T  if there is a derivation Z ‡>* ...[R][S]Ux ‡>
         ...RST...x
R °< ST  if there is a derivation Z ‡>* xRU[T]... ‡> xRST...
R °>=ST  if there is a derivation Z ‡>* xU[S][T]... ‡>
         xRST...
```

See exercises 1-5 for definitions leading to algorithms for calculating the relations from the grammar. Let us now give <u>some</u> of the precedence relations for grammar (6.2.2):

```
+T °> )      (( °<= T      ( °< E+      ( °>= E)
(F °> )      (( °<= F      ( °< F+      T °>= +T
+F °> )      (( °<= (      ( °< i+      F °>= +F
*F °> )      (( °<= i      ( °< T*      i °>= +F
(i °> )      (E °<= )      ( °< F*      T °>= *F
+i °> )      (E °<= +      ( °< i*      F °>= *F
E) °> )      (E °<= )      + °< (E      i °>= *F
+T °> +      +T °<= *      + °< T*      + °>= T+
```

We can now define a (1,2)(2,1) precedence grammar:

(6.2.3) DEFINITION. A <u>(1,2)(2,1) precedence grammar</u> G is a grammar satisfying the following conditions:

1. all right parts of rules are unique;
2. for any symbols R, S and T both RS °> T and RS °<= T do not hold;
3. for any symbols R, S and T both R °< ST and R °>= ST do not hold. ■

We can prove (exercise 6) that a (1,2)(2,1) precedence grammar is unambiguous and that the handle of any canonical sentential form S1S2...Sn is the leftmost sequence Sj...Si satisfying

```
S[j-1] °< SjS[j+1],
Sj °>= S[j+1]S[j+2], ..., S[i-1] °>= SiS[i+1],
S[i-1]Si °> S[i+1].
```

As in simple precedence grammars, we have to be careful with the beginning and end of the string being parsed. Since our relations are defined for three symbols, we will need to put two symbols ## at the beginning and end of each string to be parsed and agree that, for any symbols S1 and S2 of the grammar,

(6.2.4) S1S2 °> #, #S1 °> #, # °< S1S2, # °< S1 #

The recognizer for (1,2)(2,1) precedence grammars is quite similar to the one for simple precedence grammars and has the same flow chart form as Figure 5.4. Box 1 has to be changed somewhat to account for the different sentence delimiters we just described. Box 3 will test for S(i-1)S(i) °> R using, say, a three dimensional matrix PT holding the relations °> and °<=, while box 6 is changed to test for S(j-1) °< S(j)S(j+1) using a three-dimensional matrix PH containing the relations °< and °>=. (Note that in box 3 we assume that S(i+1) is contained in the variable R).

Most of our formal language grammars are close to (1,2)(2,1) precedence and require few changes to bring them into line. Practically, however, the technique is unusable, since it requires two three-dimensional matrices. For a grammar with 100 symbols we need two 100*100*100 matrices! Since the matrices are usually sparse, memory may be conserved by keeping a list of only those triples R, S and T for which a relation holds, but even this list itself may be prohibitively large. The rest of this section is devoted to showing how we can manipulate the grammar and algorithm to make it practical. We will not show all the techniques developed by Mckeeman et al(70), but enough to show the possibilities that arise.

### Making (1,2) (2,1) Precedence Practical

Step 1. Eliminate the matrix PH containing °< and °>=. The matrix PH is used to find the head of the handle, once the tail has been found. For most handles we don't need this matrix because we can just match the top stack symbols with the right parts of rules. The only time we have a problem is if one right part is a proper tail of another; if U ::= ux and V ::= x are two rules and the stack contains ux, which reduction should we perform? The following theorem answers this for right parts of length 2 or greater (the proof is left to the reader).

(6.2.5) THEOREM. Let G be a (1,2)(2,1) precedence grammar. Let Si be the tail symbol of the handle which contains at least two symbols. Then the complete handle is the *longest* substring Sj...Si which is a right part of a rule. ∎

Hence we only have to consider the case of two rules U ::= uX and U ::= X. For each such case we can keep a list of those triples (R,X,T) for which R °< XT. During the parse, when RX °> T occurs, we check the list for the pair (R,X,T). If it appears, then use the rule U ::= X; otherwise use the unique rule with the longest right part which matches the top of the stack.

We have thus eliminated the matrix PH; in its place we just check all right parts for the longest match, taking into account of course, the problem just discussed.

*Step 2. Delete the unnecessary part of the matrix PT.* The matrix PT is used to detect the tail of the handle. Since we are performing a canonical parse of a sentence, the symbol to the right of any handle is a terminal. We can therefore delete all columns from the matrix PT which represent nonterminal symbols. This is approximately half the matrix.

*Step 3. Use simple precedence relations where possible.* The (2,1) relations °> and °<= require too much storage, while the (1,1) relations ⋗ and <= are not adequate or flexible enough for our programming languages. We compromise by using the simple precedence relations when possible and switching to (2,1) relations when conflicts arise. To implement this we use a two-dimensional matrix P containing the values 0 (no relation), 1 (<=), 2 (⋗) and 3 (both <= and ⋗). For P[i,j] = 3 we include a list TQ of quadruples (Sk, Si, Sj, q), where q = 1 if SkSi °> Sj and q = 2 if SkSi °<= Sj.

### The Revised (1,2) (2,1) Parsing Algorithm

Figure 6.6 gives the revised recognizer, using the following variables and tables. Tables P, TQ, TH and PROD would be built by the constructor.

1. S is a stack, its counter is i.
2. T1...Tn is the input string; k is used to index the symbols.
3. P is a two dimensional n by m matrix where n is the number of symbols and m the number of terminal symbols.
   P[i,j] = 0 if no relation holds between Si and Sj.
   P[i,j] = 1 if Si <= Sj,
   P[i,j] = 2 if Si ⋗ Sj.
   P[i,j] = 3 if Si <= Sj *and* Si ⋗ Sj.

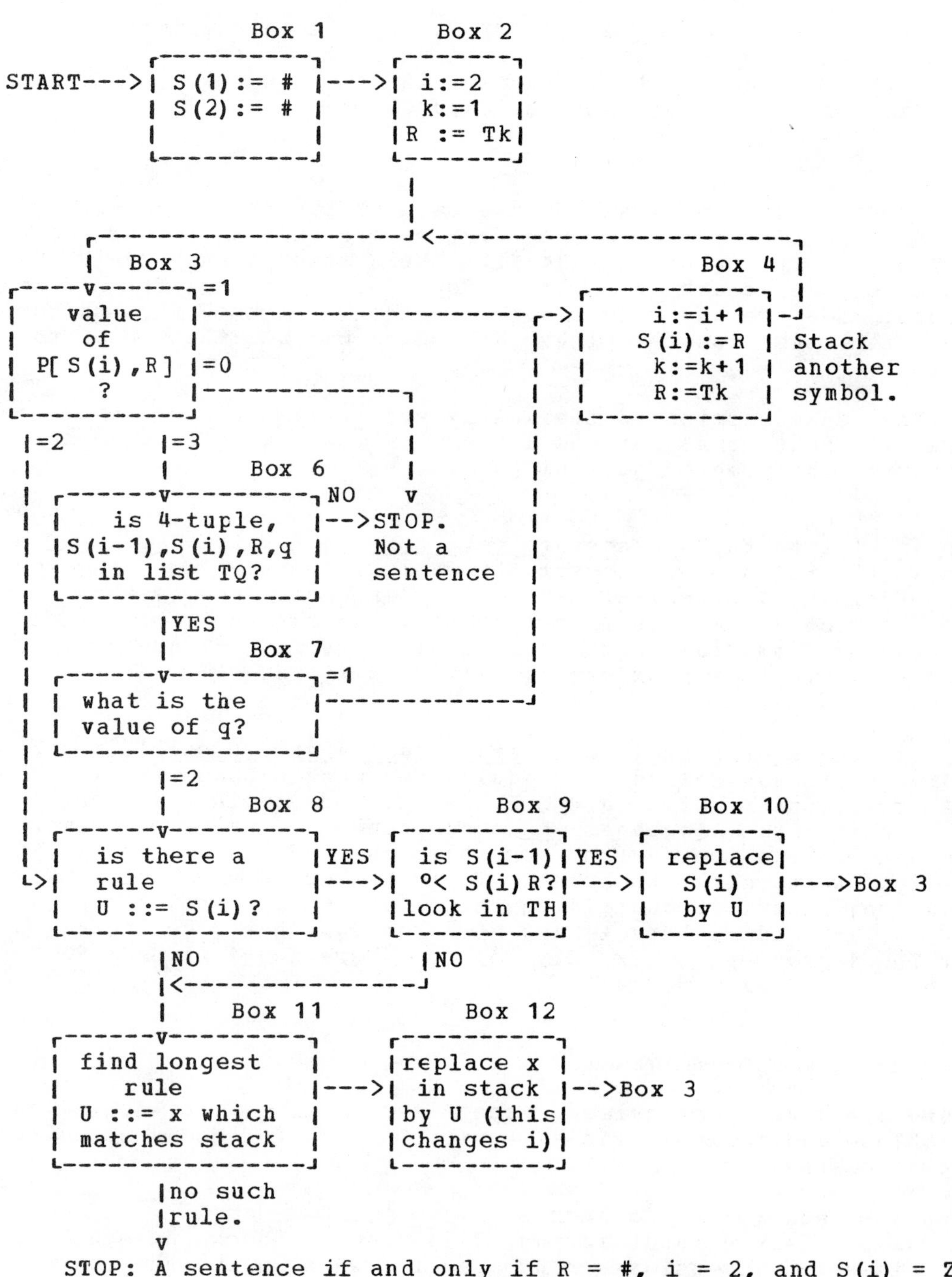


**FIGURE 6.6. (1,2) (2,1) Precedence Recognizer.**

4. TQ is a list of quadruples (R,S,T,q) where R and S are symbols, T is a terminal symbol and q is 1 or 2.
   (R,S,T,1) is in the list if S <= T, S > T and RS °<= T.
   (R,S,T,2) is in the list if S <= T, S > T and RS °> T.
5. PROD is a list of rules. For fast access, it should be sorted by the tail symbcl of the right part.
6. TH is a list of triples used for deciding whether to use a rule whose right part is a single symbol. Thus (R,X,T) is in the list if T is terminal, if there exists a rule U ::= X and at least cne other rule V ::= ...X, and if R °< XT.

As an example, Figure 6.5 contains the tables needed for the grammar (6.2.2).

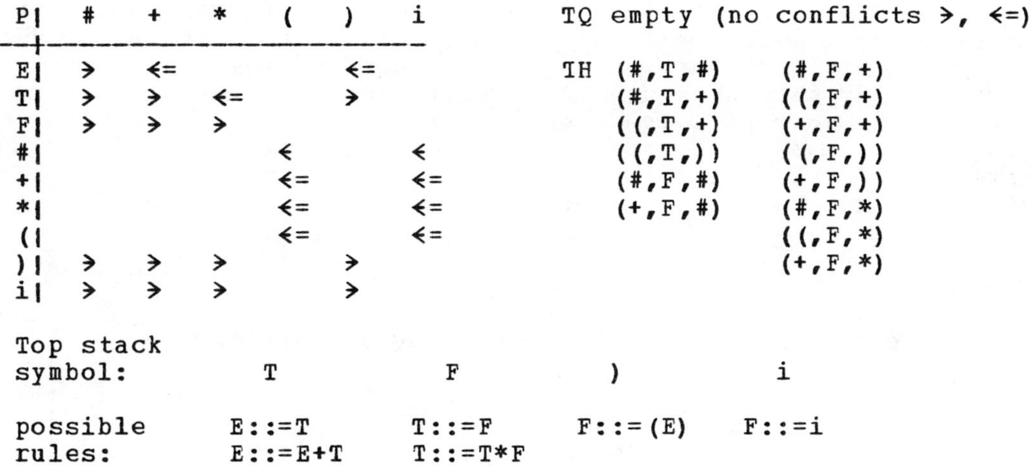

| P | # | + | * | ( | ) | i |
|---|---|---|---|---|---|---|
| E | > | <= | | | <= | |
| T | > | > | <= | | > | |
| F | > | > | > | | | |
| # | | | | < | | < |
| + | | | | <= | | <= |
| * | | | | <= | | <= |
| ( | | | | <= | | <= |
| ) | > | > | > | | > | |
| i | > | > | > | | > | |

TQ empty (no conflicts >, <=)

TH (#,T,#) (#,T,+) ((,T,+) ((,T,)) (#,F,#) (+,F,#) (#,F,+) ((,F,+) (+,F,+) ((,F,)) (+,F,)) (#,F,*) ((,F,*) (+,F,*)

| Top stack symbol: | T | F | ) | i |
|---|---|---|---|---|
| possible rules: | E::=T | T::=F | F::=(E) | F::=i |
| | E::=E+T | T::=T*F | | |

**FIGURE 6.5. (1,2) (2,1) Tables for Grammar (6.2.2).**

### (m,n) Precedence

One might think that if (1,1) precedence doesn't work for a particular grammar, and if (1,2)(2,1) precedence also isn't sufficient, that one could look at even more context in order to get unique relations. This is true for many grammars, and we wish to outline the method here. It should be noted, however, that the scheme we will outline is not practical due to the size of the precedence matrices that will be necessary. One could come up with all sorts of tricks like in the (1,2)(2,1) precedence case, but it is not really worth it.

We define (m,n) precedence relaticns for a grammar in terms of syntax trees as follows: Let m > 0 and n > 0 be two integers. Let x and y be arbitrary strings with |x| = m and |y| = n. Then x ⋖ y  if there is a canonical sentential form ...xy... where the head symbol of y is the head of the handle.

x ≐ y  if there is a canonical sentential form ...xy... where the head symbol of y and the tail symbol of x are in the handle.

x ⋗ y  if there is a canonical sentential form ...xy... where the tail symbol of x is the tail of the handle.

An (m,n) precedence grammar is then a grammar which satisfies the following conditions:

1. All right parts of rules are unique; and
2. For any pair of strings x and y with |x| = m and |y| = n at most one of the three (m,n) precedence relations holds.

Simple precedence is the same as (1,1) precedence. We could also show that an (m,n) precedence grammar is unambiguous, that the handle of a canonical sentential form is uniquely determined by the relations, and so forth. We leave this to the reader. The difficult part, of course, is to define the relations in such a way that they can be constructed. One way to construct the relations is to look at enough syntax trees, constructing relations from each one, until one is sure that all relations have been found. This is actually the method used by McKeeman et al(70) in the (1,2)(2,1) precedence case.

### EXERCISES FOR 6.2

Some of the exercises use the following definitions:

S is an <u>allowed predecessor</u> of U, written U AP S, if there is a rule U1 ::= ...SV... and V FIRST* U.

S is an <u>allowed successor</u> of U, written U AS S, if there is a rule U1 ::= ...VW... such that V LAST* U and W FIRST* S.

1. Prove that the relation AP is defined by AP := (≐)(FIRST*).

2. Show that RS °> T if and only if one of the following holds:
   a) there is a rule U ::= VW... where U AP R, V SS+ S and W FIRST* T;
   b) there is a rule U ::= ...VW... where V ‡>+ ...RS and W FIRST* T;
   c) there is a rule U ::= ...RVW... where V SS+ S and W FIRST* T.

3. Show that RS °<= T if and only if one of the following holds:
   a) there is a rule U ::= SW... where U AP R and W FIRST* T;
   b) there is a rule U ::= ...RSW... where W FIRST* T.

4. Show that R °< ST if and only if one of the following holds:
   a) there is a rule U ::= ...RW where W SS+ S and U AS T;
   b) there is a rule U ::= ...RW... where W ǂ>+ ST...
   c) there is a rule U ::= ...RWV... where W SS+ S and V FIRST* T.

5. Show that R °>= ST if and only if one of the following holds:
   a) there is a rule U ::= ...RS where U AS T;
   b) there is a rule U ::= ...RSV... where V FIRST* T.

6. Prove that, with assumption (6.2.4), in a (1,2)(2,1) precedence grammar, the handle of any canonical sentential form S1...Sn is the leftmost sequence of nodes Sj...Si satisfying S[j-1] °< SjS[j+1], SkS[k+1] °<= S[k+2] for k = j,...,i-2, S[i-1]Si °> S[i+1].

7. Prove Theorem (6.2.5).

8. Use the program of Figure 6.6 and the tables of Figure 6.5 to parse the following sentences of grammar (6.2.2): i+i+i, i*i+i, i+i*i, (i+i)*i. Try to parse the non-sentences ii, i+*i.

9. Construct all the necessary tables for the following grammar. This grammar is the same as (6.2.2) except that the operators are evaluated from right to left instead of left to right: E ::= T | T + E, T ::= F | F + T, F ::= ( E ) | i.

10. Parse the following sentences using the grammar and tables from exercise 9: i+i+i, i*i+i.

11. Explain why the grammar A ::= ( B ) | d B e, B ::= c | c B is not a simple precedence grammar, even though the following grammar for the same language _is_ a simple precedence grammar: A ::= ( B ) | d B e, B ::= c | B c.

## 6.3 BOUNDED CONTEXT

One of the problems with the simple precedence technique is that two or more rules with identical right parts are not allowed. Consider for example the grammar

(6.3.1) Z ::= a U a | b V b   U ::= c   V ::= c

This is not a simple precedence grammar, but we can easily tell by looking at the context around c in a sentence whether c should be reduced to U or V. In the sentence aca, c would be reduced to U, while in bcb it would be reduced to V. The bounded context schemes allow us to use the actual symbols (instead of just precedences between symbols) on either side of a detected handle to aid in telling us what the handle should be reduced to. Note that the changes to the (1,2)(2,1) precedence technique allowed us to do this a bit also.

### Definition of (1,1) Bounded Context

Suppose that we have Z ⫢>+ xTURy where U := u is a rule of the grammar. Then, when parsing the canonical sentential form, if xTu appears in the stack with R the incoming symbol, we should reduce u to U. We would like to be able to tell just from TuR that u is a simple phrase for U of <u>any</u> canonical sentential form ...TuR... That is, we want to use just the context T...R around a possible handle to tell whether it is the handle and secondly to tell what it should be reduced to. If we have Z ⫢>+ ...TuR... what other possibilities arise for the handle?

First of all, since the reduction we are performing is canonical, if ...Tu appears on the stack, we know that the handle cannot be completely to the left of the tail symbol of u. This is because of the nature of our parsing; as soon as the tail symbol of the handle is pushed onto the stack, we reduce it. Now we can list the following possibilities for the handle:

```
        1.  ...Tu
        2.  u; but it would be reduced to V where V ≠ U
        3.  u2, where u = u1u2
(6.3.2) 4.  ...TuR...
        5.  uR...
        6.  u2R...
        7.  completely to the right of u
```

For each of these cases we can show what canonical derivations would produce such handles:

```
        1.  Z ⫢>+ ...VR...      where V ::= ...Tu
        2.  Z ⫢>+ ...TVR...     where V ::= u and V ≠ U
        3.  Z ⫢>+ ...Tu1VR...   where V ::= u2 and u = u1u2
(6.3.3) 4.  Z ⫢>+ ...V...       where V ::= ...TuR...
        5.  Z ⫢>+ ...TV...      where V ::= uR...
        6.  Z ⫢>+ ...Tu1V...    where V ::= u2R... and u = u1u2
        7.  Z ⫢>+ ...TuV...     where V...  =>+ R...
```

If none of these seven cases arises, then we know that the only action possible in the case ...TuR... is to reduce u to U.

(6.3.4) DEFINITION. A rule U ::= u is a (left-to-right) <u>(1,1) bounded context rule</u> if for every possible pair of symbols T and R such that Z ⫢>+ ...TUR... none of the seven cases (6.3.3) arise. ∎

(6.3.5) DEFINITION. A grammar G is a (left-to-right) <u>(1,1) bounded context grammar</u> if every one of its rules is (left-to-right) (1,1) bounded context. ∎

We put in the extra term "left-to-right" because we could also have defined (1,1) bounded context for parsing from right to left. We could even define it in such a way that we could parse in either direction or from the middle. That is, any simple phrase could be detected, not just the handle.

The following grammar is not (1,1) bounded context, because the rules U ::= c and V ::= c are not (1,1) bounded context; in the string abc#, from the context bc# we cannot tell whether the rule U::=c or V::=c should be used to reduce the rightmost c.

```
Z ::= a b U | c b V        U ::= c        V ::= c
```

### The (1,1) Bounded Context Recognizer

The recognizer will use a single table, each row of which has three columns. The first column contains <u>stack contents</u>, each of which has the form Tu where T is any symbol or the delimiter # (which we put at each end of a sentence to be parsed) and u is the right part of the rule. The second column contains corresponding <u>right contexts</u>, each of which is a single terminal or the delimiter #. The third column contains a rule number. This table is used by the recognizer as follows. At each step, the recognizer searches the rows of the table for one whose first column matches the top of the stack and whose second column matches the last scanned symbol of the sentence. If such a row is found, then a reduction is to be performed; the handle in the stack is replaced using the rule determined by the third column. If no such row is found then no reduction can take place, so the last scanned symbol is pushed onto the stack and the next symbol of the sentence is scanned.

The table contains all possible configurations (Tu, R, i) where in the context TuR, u should be reduced using rule i. If at most one row can match at any time, then each reduction can be performed knowing only the context T...R, and the grammar is (1,1) bounded context. Figure 6.7 illustrates the table for the following grammar:

```
(6.3.6) (1) Z ::= V        (4) V ::= b U        (7) W ::= 0 W 1
        (2) Z ::= a W      (5) U ::= U 0        (8) W ::= 0 1
        (3) V ::= V 1      (6) U ::= 0
```

The language of the grammar is the union of the two sets {a(0!n)(1!n)|n > 0} and {b(0!n)(1!m)|n>0,m≥0}. In looking at the table, note that <u>all</u> possible stack combinations Tu and incoming symbol R that indicate a reduction have been listed.

The recognizer itself is in Figure 6.8. It uses, as usual, a stack with counter i, The sentence to be parsed is T1...Tn. We append the symbol T[n+1] = #, our sentence delimiter, and start with # in the stack. The counter k is used for scanning the sentence.

| Stack content | Right context | Rule number |
|---|---|---|
| a 0 1 | # | 8 |
| 0 0 1 | 1 | 8 |
| 0 0 W 1 | 1 | 7 |
| a 0 W 1 | # | 7 |
| # a W | # | 2 |
| b 0 | 0 | 6 |
| b 0 | 1 | 6 |
| b U 0 | 0 | 5 |
| b U 0 | 1 | 5 |
| # b U | 1 | 4 |
| # V 1 | 1 | 3 |
| # V 1 | # | 3 |
| # V | # | 1 |
| (If stack contains this | and scanned symbol R is this, then | use this rule to reduce.) |

**FIGURE 6.7. Bounded Context Table for Grammar 6.3.6.**

1. Set i := 1, k := 1 and S(1) := #.
2. If the top stack symbols match a stack content of the table and if Tk matches the corresponding right context, then let j be the row which matched, and go to step 3; otherwise go to step 4.
3. Stack contains Tu where Tu is given by column 1 (stack content) of row j. Reduce u to U, using the rule determined by the third column of row j. Go to step 2.
4. If Tk is equal to "#" then go to step 6.
5. i := i+1; S(i) := Tk; k := k+1; go to step 2.
6. Stop. Have a sentence if and only if i := 2 and S(i) = Z.

**FIGURE 6.8. (1,1) Bounded Context Recognizer.**

### Definition of (m, n) Bounded Context

Just as we extended (1,1) precedence to (m,n) precedence, so we can extend (1,1) bounded context to (m,n) bounded context. No compiler actually uses (m,n) bounded context, although some may at some point. We therefore only outline the basic points here. We include this method because the grammars accepted by all other recognizers we have discussed or will discuss are (m,n) bounded context for some m and n.

(6.3.7) DEFINITION. Consider a rule U ::= u. Suppose for every pair of strings v, w with |v| = m, |w| = n, and Z ‡>* xvUwy for some x and y, that u is the handle of every canonical sentential form ...vuw..., and that u should be reduced to a unique symbol U. Then the rule is <u>(m,n)</u> <u>bounded</u> <u>context</u>. ▪

What this means is the following. Suppose U::=u is a bounded context rule and suppose further that we know a derivation Z ‡>* xvUwy ‡> xvuwy exists. Then <u>whenever</u> the left-to-right bottom-up parser has ...vu on the stack and w... as the rest of the input string, the u can be reduced to U. Note that we haven't listed the cases which should not happen, as we did in (6.3.3) in the (1,1) bounded context case; we leave this to the reader.

(6.3.8) DEFINITION. A grammar is <u>(m,n)</u> <u>bounded</u> <u>context</u>, if every rule is (m,n) bounded context. ▪

### The (m,n) Bounded Context Recognizer and Constructor

As in the (1,1) bounded context case, we use a table of three columns. The first contains the <u>stack</u> <u>contents</u> tu. The second contains the corresponding <u>right</u> <u>contexts</u> v, while the third contains the number of the rule to use to reduce ...tuv... to ...tUv... The recognizer itself is essentially the same, except that now more symbols must be compared at each step.

The constructor of the tables is a fairly complex algorithm, as you might imagine. The first step is to build a (1,1) bounded context table. That is, for every canonical derivation Z ‡>* ...VUW... ‡> ...VuW..., a row is added to the table (if not already there) with first column Vu, second column W, and third column the number of the rule U::=u. (The reader is reminded that every such derivation cannot be examined; there are an infinite number of them. But the grammar can be examined in such a way which indicates for each rule U::=u and symbols V and W whether such a derivation exists.)

Once the table is built, the rows are examined for a pair of the form

| | | |
|---|---|---|
| V1u1 | W | n |
| V2u2 | W | m |

where V2u2 is a tail of V1u1 (not necessarily proper). If none exist, the grammar is (1,1) bounded context, and the table has been constructed. It is (1,1) bounded context because, at each step, at most one row can match the stack.

Suppose however that two (or more) such rows do exist. Then when V1u1 is in the stack and W is the incoming symbol either row can be used to make a reduction. The table must be altered to add more context -- either to the right of W or to the left of V2u2. Suppose for example that we want to add context on the left, and suppose all canonical derivations involving ...V2u2W... using rule m have the form Z =>* ...XV2UW... => ...XV2u2W... or Z =>* ...YV2UW... => ...YV2u2W... Then we can change the above rows to

| V1u1 | W | n |
|---|---|---|
| XV2u2 | W | m |
| YV2u2 | W | m |

This may or may not get rid of the ambiquity. If not, context must be added again, either on the left or the right. Note that at each step, only those rows involved in a conflict must be examined and changed. The others are all right. One of the problems is to know on which side to extend the context. There is no hard and fast rule to indicate this. Another problem is that we don't know whether the grammar is bounded context or not until we actually arrive at a table which has no conflicts.

### 6.4 TRANSITION MATRICES

One of the problems with most of the methods discussed is that one must always search the rules or tables in order to find the reduction to make. Of course, one can structure the table in such a way as to minimize search time. The technique we discuss here uses a large matrix, sometimes called a decision table or transition matrix, in order to minimize this search time. We assume first of all that we have an operator grammar (OG), since this formalization corresponds to the intuitive use of transition matrices. We will illustrate the technique using the following OG:

```
         <prog>  ::= <state>
         <state> ::= IF <expr> THEN <state>
(6.4.1)  <state> ::= <var> := <expr>
         <expr>  ::= <expr> + <var> | <var>
         <var>   ::= i
```

We make up a transition matrix M whose rows represent heads (which end in a terminal symbol) of right sides of rules which may appear in the stack, and whose columns represent the terminal symbols, including the sentence delimiter # (Figure 6.9a). The elements of the matrix will be numbers or addresses of subroutines.

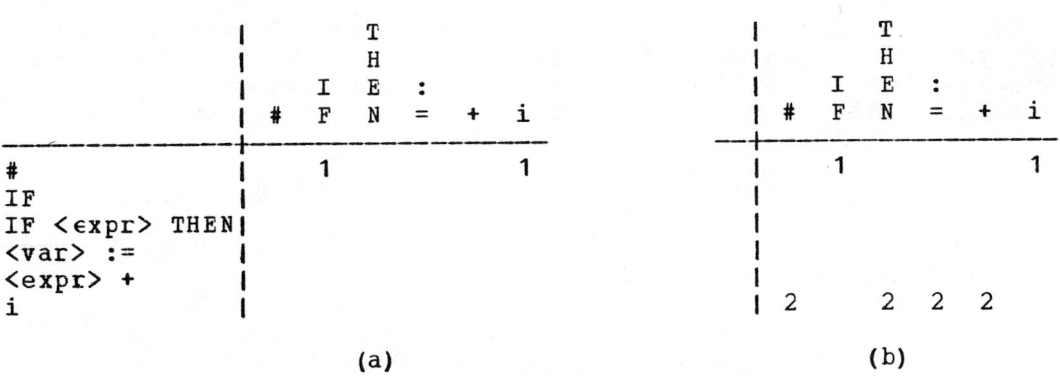

|  | # | IF | THEN | := | + | i |
|---|---|---|---|---|---|---|
| # |  | 1 |  |  |  | 1 |
| IF |  |  |  |  |  |  |
| IF <expr> THEN |  |  |  |  |  |  |
| <var> := |  |  |  |  |  |  |
| <expr> + |  |  |  |  |  |  |
| i |  |  |  |  |  |  |

(a)

|  | # | IF | THEN | := | + | i |
|---|---|---|---|---|---|---|
|  |  | 1 |  |  |  | 1 |
|  |  |  |  |  |  |  |
|  |  |  |  |  |  |  |
|  |  |  |  |  |  |  |
|  |  |  |  |  |  |  |
|  | 2 |  | 2 | 2 | 2 |  |

(b)

**FIGURE 6.9. Partially Filled Transition Matrices.**

The recognizer uses the typical stack S and incoming symbol variable R. We structure the stack a little differently, though. Instead of just symbols, we let strings of symbols appear in a stack element. Strings appearing here will be heads (which end in a terminal symbol) of right parts of rules. For example, if the conventional stack at some point contained

# IF <expr> THEN IF <expr> THEN <var> :=

the stack would look like

```
|                |
|    <var> :=    |
|IF <expr> THEN|
|IF <expr> THEN|
|       #        |
|________________|
```

Note that all we are doing is keeping together those symbols which we know must be reduced at the same time. One final point: we need a third variable U. It is either empty or contains the symbol to which the last prime phrase has been reduced. Thus, if the partial string parsed so far is

# IF <expr> THEN IF <expr> THEN <var> := <expr>

then the stack would be as above and <expr> would be in U.

The recognizer uses the matrix as follows. At each step, the top stack element corresponds to some row of the matrix, since both represent the head (ending in a terminal symbol) of some right part. The incoming terminal symbol R determines a column of the matrix. These two together determine an element of the matrix which is the number of a subroutine to execute. This subroutine will perform the necessary reduction or will stack R and scan the next source symbol.

For example, when we start out we have # in the stack and U empty. The incoming symbol, according to grammar (6.4.1), must be either IF or i. Since these begin right parts, we want to stack them and go on. The first subroutine (see Figure 6.9a) is then

```
1:  IF U ≠ '' THEN ERROR; i := i+1; S(i) = R; SCAN.
```

where SCAN means to put the next symbol of the input string into R. The check on U being empty will become clearer in a moment.

Suppose i is at the top of the stack. What can be a valid symbol in R? i can be followed by the symbols #, THEN, := or +. What we want to do in all these cases is to change i to <var>, making a reduction ...<var>... => ...i.... Subroutine 2 (see Figure 6.9b) to do this is

```
2:  IF U ≠ '' THEN ERROR; i := i-1; U := '<var>'.
```

Each matrix element, then, is a number of a subroutine which either stacks the incoming symbol or makes a reduction. The stacking is a little bit more involved because of the way each stack element looks. The complete matrix and subroutines for grammar 6.4.1 are in Figure 6.10. It is suggested that the reader perform a parse of the following sentence using them: # IF i + i THEN i := i #.

### Advantages and Disadvantages of Transition Matrices

This technique was used in a number of early ALGOL compilers, where the matrices were all constructed by hand in much the same manner as we have done. Each element of the matrix was filled in by determining from the language what the incoming symbol could be and what corresponding action should be performed. The use of the matrix allowed the compiler writer to concentrate on one particular construct at a time and thus helped break the project up into a number of little ones. The technique is very fast, because no searching is required at all; each subroutine knows exactly what it has to do. Another nice point is that error recovery can be incorporated very easily. Each zero in the matrix corresponds to a syntax error and, since over half the elements are usually zero, one can write many routines to handle these errors and have several ways of recovering. With all the other techniques no good error recovery has been devised, because one cannot really break it up easily into subcases. The one disadvantage with this technique is the space used. One typical ALGOL compiler on the IBM 7090 had a 100 by 45 matrix with roughly 250 subroutines.

| | # | IF | THEN | := | + | i |
|---|---|---|---|---|---|---|
| # | 5 | 1 | 0 | 6 | 0 | 1 |
| IF | 0 | 0 | 9 | 0 | 3 | 1 |
| IF <expr> THEN | 7 | 1 | 0 | 6 | 0 | 1 |
| <var> := | 8 | 0 | 0 | 0 | 3 | 1 |
| <expr> + | 4 | 0 | 4 | 0 | 4 | 1 |
| i | 2 | 0 | 2 | 2 | 2 | 0 |

```
1: IF U ≠ '' THEN ERROR;
   i:=i+1; S(i):=R; SCAN.

2: IF U ≠ '' THEN ERROR;
   i:=i-1; U:='<var>'.

3: IF U ≠ '<expr>' OR
      U ≠ '<var>'THEN ERROR;
   i:=i+1; S(i):='<expr> +';
   U := ''; SCAN.

4: IF U ≠ '<var>' THEN ERROR;
   i:=i-1; U:='<expr>'.

5: IF U ≠ '<prog>' OR
      U ≠ '<state>' THEN ERROR;
   STOP.

6: IF U ≠ '<var>' THEN ERROR;
   U:= ''; i:=i+1;
   S(i):='<var>:='; SCAN.

7: IF U ≠ '<state>'
   THEN ERROR;
   i:=i-1; U:='<state>'.

8: IF U ≠ '<var>' OR
      U ≠ '<expr>'
   THEN ERROR;
   i:=i-1; U:='<state>'.

9: IF U ≠ '<var>' OR
      U ≠ '<expr>'
   THEN ERROR;
   S(i):='IF <expr> THEN';
   U := ''; SCAN.

0: ERROR; STOP.
```

**FIGURE 6.10. Matrix and Subroutines for Grammar (6.4.1).**

### Constructing the Augmented Operator Grammar

We have so far discussed how a transition matrix works in an intuitive manner. We now outline the construction of a matrix itself. All proofs are left to the reader as exercises. Remember that the formal approach parallels closely the intuitive one.

We start with an OG, as in the operator precedence case. We further assume that a derivation of one nonterminal from another is unique. That is, if Ui =>+ Uj, there is only one such derivation.

The first step is to transform the grammar into an equivalent one in which each rule has at most three symbols in its right part. To do this we introduce new nonterminals, which we shall call *starred nonterminals* (SNTS); these are assumed to be distinguishable from the original unstarred nonterminals (UNTS). We distinguish by underlining the SNTS. Furthermore, each SNTS is constructed so that it represents the head (ending in a terminal) of a right part of a rule of the original OG, and thus corresponds exactly to a row of the transition matrix described earlier. This new grammar we call an *augmented operator grammar* (AOG). It is not necessarily also an OG.

The construction is as follows: Execute step 1 repeatedly until no longer applicable; then do the same for step 2. Finally, alternately repeat steps 3a and 3b until no longer applicable. In the steps, T is a terminal symbol, U is a nonterminal, and $\underline{U}$ is a SNTS.

1. If there is a rule U1::=Ty1 (y1 may be empty), and if k-1 SNTS $\underline{U}$1,...$\underline{U}$[k-1] have been introduced so far, create a new SNTS $\underline{U}$k, replace each rule Ui::=Tyi ( each rule which begins with the same T) by the rule Ui::=$\underline{U}$kyi and add the rule $\underline{U}$k::=T.

2. If there is a rule U1::=UTy1 and if k-1 SNTS have been created so far, create a new SNTS $\underline{U}$k, replace each rule Ui::=UTyi (each one which begins with the same symbols UT) by Ui::=$\underline{U}$kyi, and add the rule $\underline{U}$k::=UT.

3. (a) If there is a rule U1::=$\underline{U}$Ty1, and if k-1 SNTS have been created so far, create another SNTS $\underline{U}$k, replace each rule Ui::=$\underline{U}$Tyi by Ui::=$\underline{U}$kyi, and add the new rule $\underline{U}$k::=$\underline{U}$T.
   (b) If there is a rule U1::=$\underline{U}$UTy1, and if k-1 SNTS have been created so far, create a new SNTS $\underline{U}$k, replace each rule Ui::=$\underline{U}$UTyi by Ui::=$\underline{U}$kyi, and insert the new rule $\underline{U}$k::=$\underline{U}$UT.

By noticing the form of the rules after each step, the reader should prove the following lemma (exercise 1).

(6.4.2) LEMMA. In an AOG each rule has one of the seven forms

U1 ::= U2, U1 ::= $\underline{U}$, U1 ::= $\underline{U}$U2
$\underline{U}$ ::= T, $\underline{U}$ ::= UT, $\underline{U}$2 ::= $\underline{U}$1T, $\underline{U}$2 ::= $\underline{U}$1UT ▪

Secondly, the reader should perform the construction for grammar (6.4.1) (exercise 2). Thirdly, the reader should prove the following two lemmas and theorem.

(6.4.3) LEMMA. For each rule U::=y of the OG where y is not a nonterminal, there exists a unique set of rules $\underline{U}$1::=y0, $\underline{U}$2::=$\underline{U}$1y1, ..., $\underline{U}$n::=$\underline{U}$[n-1]y[n-1], U::=$\underline{U}$nyn of the AOG such that y = y0y1...yn. ▪

(6.4.4) LEMMA. For each different syntax tree of a sentential form s of the OG we can construct a different syntax tree for s according to the AOG, by the following: replace each branch corresponding to the application of a rule U1::=y by the set of branches corresponding to applications of the rules described in lemma (6.4.3). ▪

(6.4.5) THEOREM. If an AOG is unambiguous, so is the corresponding OG. ■

As an illustration of the construction of lemma (6.4.4), we replace the branch of a tree in Figure 6.11a by the subtree in Figure 6.11b. The underlying grammar is (6.4.1). In the figure, <if> and <if-then> are the SNTS. The reader should satisfy himself that a bottom-up parse according to the AOG is essentially the same as a parse according to the OG; only some extra intermediate reductions have been introduced.

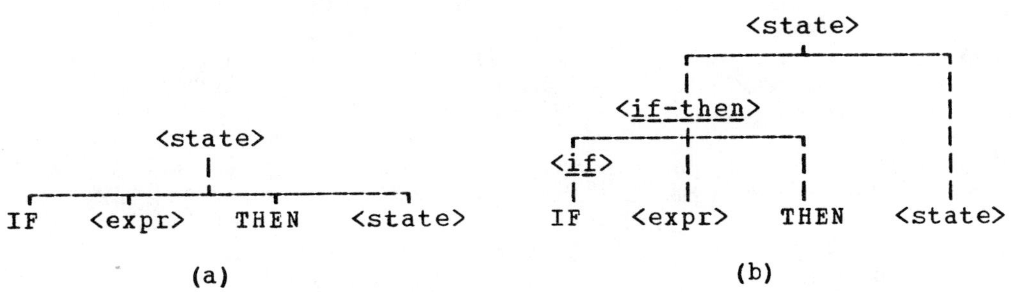


**FIGURE 6.11. OG and Corresponding AOG Branches.**

### Parsing in an AOG

The bottom-up parser recognizes at each step the leftmost <u>AOG prime phrase</u>, where an AOG prime phrase is defined to be a phrase which contains no other AOG prime phrase but at least one terminal or SNTS. The reader should contrast this with definition (6.1.7). We can alternatively say that y is an AOG prime phrase of a sentential form xyz if there exists a sentential form xVz (where V is a SNTS or UNTS) such that V::=y; or V::=y1, y1 =>* y, and all the direct derivations in the sequence y1 =>* y are applications of rules Ui::=Uj for UNTS Ui and Uj.

From lemma (6.4.2) we see that an AOG prime phrase must have one of the six forms

(6.4.6) <u>U</u> <u>U</u>T T <u>U</u>U UT <u>U</u>UT

The reader should now prove (exercise 6) the following:

(6.4.7) THEOREM. Each reduction of a parse of a sentence of the AOG, which reduces the leftmost AOG prime phrase, has one of the following six forms:

$$\underline{uU}t \Rightarrow \underline{u}Ut \qquad \underline{uU}1t \Rightarrow \underline{uU}2Tt \qquad \underline{uU}1t \Rightarrow \underline{u}Tt$$
$$\underline{uU}1t \Rightarrow \underline{uU}U2t \qquad \underline{uU}1t \Rightarrow \underline{uU}2UTt \qquad \underline{uU}t \Rightarrow \underline{u}UTt$$

where $\underline{u}$ is a (possibly empty) string of SNTS, t is a string of terminals, U, U1, U2 are UNTS, and $\underline{U}$, $\underline{U}1$, $\underline{U}2$ are SNTS. Hence any sentential form of the parse has the form $\underline{u}$t or $\underline{u}$Ut. ∎

The parsing algorithm uses a stack S, to hold the substring $\underline{u}$ of the sentential form $\underline{u}$(U)t. A variable U will hold the symbol U if present; otherwise it will be empty. The matrix consists of one row for each SNTS and one column for each terminal. Note that, since each SNTS corresponds to a row, each SNTS can be represented in the stack by its row number.

At each step of the parse, the top stack symbol (an SNTS) and the next incoming symbol determine an element of the matrix. This is the number of a subroutine to execute. The subroutine checks the variable U and takes the appropriate action, performing one of the six possible reductions. In a moment we shall give sufficient conditions which, if satisfied, allow the reduction to be performed at each step to be determined solely by the top stack symbol, the incoming terminal, and variable U.

### Sufficient Conditions for an Unambiguous AOG

We now state some conditions for an AOG to be unambiguous. Furthermore, these conditions will allow us to detect at each step of a parse the leftmost AOG prime phrase and the symbol to which it is to be reduced. We know that each sentential form has the form $\underline{u}$[U]t (where the brackets indicate that the symbol U may or may not be present). The conditions will let us determine just from the tail symbol of $\underline{u}$, the head symbol of t, and the variable U, what reduction to make, if any.

(6.4.8) DEFINITION. AP(S) is the set of allowed predecessors of the symbol S: AP(S) := {S1 | ...S1S... is a sentential form} ∎

Condition 1. For each pair $\underline{U}$, T where $\underline{U}$ is a SNTS and T is a terminal, at most one of the following three statements holds:

(6.4.9) there is a rule U::=$\underline{U}$ with U in AP(T)
(6.4.10) there is a rule $\underline{U}$1::=$\underline{U}$T
(6.4.11) there is a rule $\underline{U}$1::=T with $\underline{U}$ in AP($\underline{U}$1)

Furthermore, if (6.4.9) holds, there is only one such UNTS U. ▪

Condition 2. For each triple $\underline{U}$, U, T where $\underline{U}$ is a SNTS, U a UNTS and T a terminal, at most one of the following statements holds:

(6.4.12) there is a rule U1::=$\underline{U}$U2 with U1 in AP(T) and U2 =>* U
(6.4.13) there is a rule $\underline{U}$1::=$\underline{U}$U2T with U2 =>* U
(6.4.14) there is a rule $\underline{U}$1::=U2T with $\underline{U}$ in AP($\underline{U}$1) and U2 =>* U

Furthermore, if (6.4.12) holds both U1 and U2 are unique, while if (6.4.13) or (6.4.14) holds, U2 is unique. ▪

We leave the proof of the following theorem to the reader (exercise 7):

(6.4.15) THEOREM. An AOG which satisfies conditions 1 and 2 is unambiguous. ▪

## EXERCISES FOR 6.4

1. Prove lemma (6.4.2).

2. Construct the AOG for grammar (6.4.1). As a start, the first step replaces the second rule by the two rules $\underline{U}$1::=IF and <state>::=$\underline{U}$1 <expr> THEN <state>, and replaces the last rule by $\underline{U}$2::=i, <var>::=$\underline{U}$2.

3. Prove lemma (6.4.3). (The lemma follows easily from the construction.)

4. Prove lemma (6.4.4).

5. Prove theorem (6.4.5). Hint: Show that if a syntax tree of a sentential form of the AOG is unique, then so must be the corresponding tree in the OG.

6. Prove theorem (6.4.7). Hint: Note the six possible forms of an AOG prime phrase and the corresponding reductions for them.

7. Prove theorem (6.4.15).

## 6.5 HISTORICAL REFERENCES

Floyd(63) formalized the idea of operator precedence, a technique which was used in an intuitive manner in earlier compilers. For references see Allard et al(64), Galler and Perlis(67) and Gries(65). Wirth and Weber's simple precedence is used in the ALGOL W compiler (see Bauer, Becker, and Graham(68)). Wirth and Weber also introduced (m,n) precedence, but their definitions are wrong. The (1,2)(2,1) precedence extension is McKeeman's(66). It has been further refined and is used in the XPL compiler writing system by McKeeman et al(70). Colmeraur(70) has defined a precedence technique which includes both operator precedence and simple precedence as subcases. Briefly, the compiler writer can choose his operators. (There are a few restrictions for it to work, one being that all terminals be operators.) If he chooses just the terminals, he gets the operator precedence technique; if he chooses all symbols as operators, he gets simple precedence.

Several other people have attempted to extend simple precedence to make it more usable. Ichbiah and Morse(70), for example, define "weak precedence" relations in order to use pattern matching to find the head of the handle in the stack instead of the relations. This follows closely what we did in the (1,2)(2,1) precedence case. Zimmer(70) relaxes the condition about unique right parts and allows context checks to determine which rule to use to make a reduction. This begins to approach (1,1) bounded context.

Bounded context of degree (1,1) has its roots in Paul(62) and was first published by Eickel et al(63). Floyd(64) and Irons(64) both extended it to (m,n) bounded context, but their definitions are not the same. We have followed Floyd's formalization. The latter two papers were presented at the Working Conference on Mechanical Language Structures, held in August 1963. The February 1964 issue of CACM is the proceedings for this conference, and is worth reading. The first paper which actually showed how to construct tables for a (m,n) left to right bounded context recognizer was Eickel(64). The paper is not only hard to read bu also hard to obtain. Loeckx(69) introduced a new algorithm for constructing the tables which is easier to follow.

The end result of all this left-to-right bottom-up recognizing is Knuth's(66) LR(k) grammars and languages. Knuth shows how to construct a recognizer for an LR(k) grammar, which is allowed to look at <u>all</u> the symbols in the stack and the k symbols to the right in order to determine the reduction to be made. Actually, the stack need not really be searched at each step. Along with each stack symbol is kept a "state" which provides enough information about the rest of the stack to make the decision.

It should be mentioned that LR(k), or at least a slight restriction of it due to DeRemer(70), may be efficient enough to use practically in compilers. Horning(70) indicates that a good implementation of it may be faster and may take up less space than an equivalent (1,2)(2,1) parser.

Transition matrices, first described by Samelson and Bauer(60), were used in a number of ALGOL compilers written by the ALCOR group (see Gries(65)). The NELIAC people (see Halstead) also use transition matrices, but without a stack, under the name CO-NO tables (Current Operator and Next Operator). The technique was formalized by Gries(68).

At this point we should mention other formalizations of the syntax recognition process, although not all we will mention are bottom-up. Lynch(68) defined ICOR grammars and gave a parsing algorithm for them. Domolki's algorithm is described in Hext and Roberts(70). Gilbert adds to a context sensitive grammar a <u>selection function</u>, which indicates (based on the current sentential form) which rule to use in making a reduction. Thus the grammar is a synthetic rather than an analytic grammar; it can be used, without having to be processed by a constructor, as a parsing algorithm.

Tixier(67) considers each set of rules for a nonterminal to be a regular expression defining the set of strings for that nonterminal. One can construct an fa to recognize strings for each one. The problem is first of all to know when to switch from one fa to another, and second of all to know which fa to switch to. For example, if we have V ::= Ax | By, do we switch to the fa to recognize a string from the set A or to the fa for B? Tixier puts certain restriction on the grammars accepted by his constructor in order to solve these problems with limited context.

All the recognizers described so far have no output. That is, they recognize sentences of a grammar but don't really translate them into another form. This is handled by so-called semantic routines to be introduced in Chapter 12. Lewis and Stearns(68) define syntax oriented transducers, which not only recognize but also translate the sentence into some other form. The formal model is not yet general enough to be really useful in compiler construction.

Stearns and Lewis(68), and independently Whitney, extend context free grammars to allow access to a table of some sort at each step of a parse. The purpose is to formalize the notion of looking up identifiers in a table, and checking and changing their attributes. Hence more of the definition of a language can be formalized, making it easier to produce compilers.

# Chapter 7.
# Production Language

Production language (PL) is a programming language for writing syntax recognizers. A program consists mainly of a sequence of *productions*. The use of this word here is unfortunate, since it conflicts with the usual meaning of the word as a rewriting rule of a grammar. These new productions would better be called *reductions*, since they are (usually, but not always) used to reduce a sentence to the distinguished symbol of the grammar. Rather than coin a new term, we will stick to the word *production* which has been used consistently in the literature.

PL is usually imbedded in a translator writing system (a system designed for implementing programs like assemblers or compilers), and a PL program is preceded by a scanner definition much like that described in section 3.4. Thus a PL program will work with the internal representation of source language symbols -- reserved words, identifiers, and the like -- and not the actual characters.

Notation for PL changes from one implementation to the next. The reader should therefore not assume that the one presented here is the only one, or the best one. We are interested mainly in what a PL program can do, and not in how one punches it on cards.

## 7.1 THE LANGUAGE

### Productions

A PL program automatically uses a LIFO stack, which we call SYN, just like all the other recognizers we have discussed. The stack can contain source language symbols or entities similar to nonterminals. The program itself consists primarily of a sequence of productions, each of which has the form

```
[<label> :]   <symbol> {<symbol>}   [-> {<symbol>} ]   {<action>}
              └────left part────┘   └─right part──┘
```

The <symbol>s are source language symbols, or identifiers (possibly enclosed in angular brackets < and >) called nonterminals, while the <label> is any conventional identifier. As noted above, those <symbol>s directly following the <label>, if present, form the *left part* of the production, while the *right part* consists of the arrow -> and any following <symbol>s.

A production indicates a pattern matching and a stack transformation, as follows. During the execution of a PL program there is always a *current* production. When a production becomes current, the <symbol>s in its left part are compared with the <symbol>s at the top of the LIFO stack SYN. If they do not all match, then the next production in the sequence becomes current and the comparison is again made. This continues until a match occurs. When it does, the matched <symbol>s on the stack are replaced by the <symbol>s in the right part of the production. (If the right part is completely missing, no change occurs in the stack.) The <action>s, if present, are then executed, in order. Among other things, these <action>s may cause source program symbols to be scanned and stacked, and may indicate the next current production.

(7.1.1) EXAMPLE. Suppose the production

```
COND:  IF <E> THEN  ->  <ICL>   SCAN  GO THENPART
```

is the current production. If the top, second, and third stack elements are THEN, <E>, and IF respectively, then the following happens:

1. The top three stack elements are deleted from SYN;
2. The symbol <ICL> is pushed onto the stack;
3. The two <action>s are executed:
   a) SCAN - the next source language symbol is scanned and pushed onto the stack, and
   b) GO THENPART - the production labeled THENPART becomes the current production.

Putting this in terms of rewriting rules, we have reduced IF <E> THEN to <ICL> using the rule <ICL> ::= IF <E> THEN .■

The program of Figure 7.1 contains more examples of productions, which we shall look at later. It is a recognizer for arithmetic expressions with the syntax of (7.1.2).

### Metasymbols

The metasymbol ANY is used often in productions as a <symbol>. Its meaning is different from the usual nonterminal; when it appears in a left part it always matches the corresponding stack symbol.

There must be at least as many ANYs in the left part as there are in the right part. Remembering that any <symbol> in the right part is put on the stack, we attach the following meaning to ANY in this position: counting from right to left, the ith ANY in the right part is the symbol currently on the stack which matched the ith ANY in the left part. Two examples will make this clear.

Suppose the current production is

```
T * F ANY  ->  T ANY  GO IE
```

and that the stack contains T * F +. Then the stack contents match the symbols in the left part. The ANY in the right part is the symbol + which matched ANY in the left part, and the stack will be changed to T +. Production LE then becomes the current production.

If the stack contains W X Y Z and the current production is ANY Y ANY -> ANY U ANY V, then the stack will be changed to W X U Z V.

Two other metasymbols are I, which matches any identifier detected by the scanner, and N, which matches any integer.

### Actions

After a left part has matched the stack symbols and the stack transformation has been made, the <action>s are executed. Two of the more important ones -- SCAN and GO -- we have already seen. Execution of the <action> SCAN causes the scanner to be called. It scans the next source symbol, pushes it on the top of the syntax stack, and returns. Execution of the <action> GO <label> causes the production labeled <label> to become current and stack comparison to begin.

The <action>s CALL, RETURN, and EXEC will be explained later at the proper time. The other conventional <action>s are

ERROR <integer> and HALT <integer> .

The first causes the message "ERROR <integer>", where <integer> is an integer, to be printed on the standard output medium. The second causes the message "HALT <integer>" to be printed, after which the syntax recognition stops.

### An Example

Figure 7.1 presents productions which recognize sentences of grammar (7.1.2). In the program, we assume again that the scanner recognizes identifiers I and integers N. When the program begins, we assume the system has put the delimiter # into the stack and that # also appears at the end of the sentence.

```
        Z ::= E
(7.1.2) E ::= T  |  E + T  |  E - T
        T ::= F  |  T * F
        F ::= I  |  N  |  ( E )
        I ::= letter {letter | digit}
        N ::= digit  {digit}
```

```
|ST: #                        SCAN          |Put 1st symbol in stack|
|LF: I          -> F          SCAN   GO LT  |These check 1st symbol |
|    N          -> F          SCAN   GO LT  |of an F (I,N or () and |
|    (                        SCAN   GO LF  |proceed accordingly.   |
|    ANY                      HALT 2        |Error - stop.          |
|LT: T * F ANY -> T ANY       GO LT1        |Reduction T ::= T*F.   |
|    F ANY      -> T ANY                    |Reduction T ::= F.     |
|LT1:T *                      SCAN   GO LF  |Check for *.  If there,|
|                                           |get following F.       |
|LE: E + T ANY -> E ANY       GO LE1        |These three prod.  make|
|    E - T ANY -> E ANY       GO LE1        |reductions E ::= E+T,  |
|    T ANY      -> E ANY                    |E ::= E-T and E ::= T. |
|LE1:E +                      SCAN   GO LF  |Now see what to do     |
|    E -                      SCAN   GO LF  |with the E.            |
|    ( E )      -> F          SCAN   GO LT  |Reduction F ::= (E).   |
|    # E #      -> # Z #      HALT 0        |Reduction Z ::= E, stop|
|    ANY                      HALT 3        |Error - stop.          |
```

**FIGURE 7.1. PL Program for Grammar 7.1.2.**

Before we actually parse a sentence using Figure 7.1, let us discuss it a bit. Production LF+2 illustrates a production with no right part. Thus the stack is not changed after a match occurs here. Note also that production LT+1 has no actions at all. If a production has no GO action, then, when all actions have been executed, the next production becomes the current one (LT1 in this case).

The productions have been written as follows. Production ST always matches, and then scans the first symbol of the sentence. Productions LF through LF+2 check for a symbol which begins a factor F; if not present, production LF+3 signals the error. If the factor is I or N, the reduction is made to F, the next symbol is scanned, and production LT becomes current. If the factor begins with a parenthesis, production LF+2 scans the first symbol of the expression inside the parentheses and transfers to LF again.

The order of the productions LT and LT+1 is important. Here we always have F ANY on the stack, so production LT+1 will always change the F to a T (rewriting rule T::=F). Before we do it, however, we must check to see whether the rule T ::= T*F is applicable. Once one of these reductions is made, we see whether a * is in the stack. If so, we prepare for a later reduction T ::= T*F by scanning the next symbol and going back to LF to find the phrase for F. If * is not there, we test for reductions to E and make the proper one. Here also the order of the productions LE to LE+2 is important.

The last production to be executed is LE1+3, which checks for the ending delimiter # and reduces the E to Z.

Figure 7.2 shows the parse of the sentence (A+B)*C. Each line indicates the first current production following the last match, the contents of the stack at that point, the production which produces the next match, and finally the next current production.

| current production | stack contents | match at production | next production |
|---|---|---|---|
| ST | # | ST | LF |
| LF | # ( | LF+2 | LF |
| LF | # ( I | LF | LT |
| LT | # ( F + | LT+1 | LT1 |
| LT1 | # ( T + | LE+2 | LE1 |
| LE1 | # ( E + | LE1 | LF |
| LF | # ( E + I | LF | LT |
| LT | # ( E + F ) | LT+1 | LT1 |
| LT1 | # ( E + T ) | LE | LE1 |
| LE1 | # ( E ) | LE1+2 | LT |
| LT | # F * | LT+1 | LT1 |
| LT1 | # T * | LT1 | LF |
| LF | # T * I | LF | LT |
| LT | # T * F # | LT | LT1 |
| LT1 | # T # | LE+2 | LE1 |
| LE1 | # E # | LE1+3 | HALT 0 |
| | # Z # | | |

**FIGURE 7.2. Parse of (A+B) *C According to Figure 7.1.**

### Class Names

Productions LE and LE+1 of Figure 7.1 are the same except that one contains + and the other - . In order to abbreviate this, we precede all productions by the declaration

```
CLASS PM + - ;
```

and replace the two productions by the single production

```
LE: E PM T ANY  ->  E ANY    GO LE1
```

In general, a declaration

```
CLASS <class name> <symbol> {<symbol>} ;
```

associates the <symbol>s with the <class name>, which can be any conventional identifier. When used in a left part, a class name matches any symbol with which it has been associated in a declaration.

If a <class name> appears in the right part of a production, there must be at least as many occurrences of that <class name> in the left part as there are in the right part. The meaning of a <class name> in a right part is similar to the meaning of ANY. Counting from the right, the ith occurrence of the class name in the right part is the symbol currently on the stack which matched the ith occurrence in the left part. For example, using the above declaration, if the stack contains + - A + and if the current production is

```
PM A PM  ->  B C PM PM
```

the stack is changed to + B C - + . Note that the above production is equivalent to the four productions

```
+ A +   ->   B C + +
+ A -   ->   B C + -
- A +   ->   B C - +
- A -   ->   B C - -
```

In section 7.3 we will discuss the advantages of associating so-called semantic routine numbers with the symbols in a class. To associate the routine number 20 with + and 2 with -, we rewrite the above declaration of PM as

```
CLASSNO   PM   + 20   - 2 ;
```

One can use such a class name exactly as before; its additional use will be explained in section 7.3. The format of this new declaration is

```
CLASSNO <class name> <symbol> <integer> {<symbol> <integer>}
```

The use of class names adds no real power to PL; what one can do with class names one can also do without. Class names do, however, make programming in PL much simpler and also help to reduce the size of programs.

### Conflicts Between Source Language and PL Symbols

If -> is a source language symbol, what would the production

```
(7.1.3)   ANY   ->   ANY   ->   B
```

mean? It is, of course, ambiguous. In order to resolve the ambiguity (and others that might arise), we adopt the convention that any source language symbol which contains one of the characters : -> $ ; or #, or which is one of the PL symbols CLASS, CLASSNO, I, N, ANY, CALL, ERROR, EXEC, and GO, must be preceded by a dollar sign "$". The dollar sign is thus an escape symbol which indicates that the following characters (up to the next blank character) make up one source language symbol.

Using this notation, we write down three different possible interpretations of production (7.1.3):

```
ANY  ->  ANY $-> B
ANY $->  ANY $-> B
ANY $->  ANY  -> B
```

As another example, the production IABE: I $: $$ -> <label> will match a stack with "$" in the first (top) element, ":" in the second and an identifier in the third element, and will replace these three by the single element <label>.

### Syntax Summary

A PL program has the syntax

```
<program>     ::= {<declaration>} {<production>}
<declaration> ::= CIASS <class name> <symbol> {<symbol>}
                | CIASSNO <class name> <symbol> <integer>
                  {<symbol> <integer>}
<production>  ::= [<label> :] <left part> [<right part>]
                  {<action>}
<left part>   ::= <symbol> {<symbol>}
<right part>  ::= -> {<symbol>}
```

where

1. Each <label> and <class name> is a unique, conventional identifier which is not a source symbol or PL symbol.
2. Each <symbol> is
   a) one of the metasymbols I, N or ANY; or
   b) a unique, conventional identifier, possibly enclosed in angular brackets < and >, which is not a PL symbol or source language symbol; or
   c) a source symbol not containing : -> $ ; or #, and which is not a PL symbol; or
   d) any sequence of nonblank characters preceded by $.
3. An <integer> is a nonempty sequence of digits 0 through 9;
4. The PI symbols are ANY, CALL, CIASS, CLASSNO, EXEC, GO, I, and N.
5. The <action>s and their meaning are as follows:
   a) CALL <label>. Execute the productions starting at the one labeled <label>, and continue until the action RETURN is executed. Then continue with the next action or production. Thus this is just a subroutine call; it is illustrated in section 7.2.
   b) ERROR <integer>. Print "ERROR <integer>."
   c) EXEC <integer>. Execute the semantic routine labeled <integer>. When done, continue with the next action. (This will be explained in section 7.3).
   d) EXEC <class name>. The <class name> must appear in the left part of the production. Its declaration must associate semantic routines with the symbols. The semantic routine associated with the symbol on the stack

which matched the <class name> in the left part is executed. This action will be explained in section 7.3.

e) GO <label>. Make the production labeled <label> the current one and begin matching again. Any other actions following this one will never be executed.

f) HALT <integer>. Print the message "HALT <integer>" and stop executing the PI program.

g) RETURN. Return to the point following the last CALL executed (see action a).

h) SCAN. Call the scanner to build the next source symbol and push that symbol on the stack. If no more symbols exist, the delimiter # is stacked.

### EXERCISES FOR 7.1

1. Parse the following sentences of grammar (7.1.2) by executing (by hand) the PL program of Figure 7.1. Assume the scanner parses identifiers and integers: (a) A*B (b) (A) (c) A+B+1 (d) A*B*1 (e) A+(B+1) (f) A*(B+1).

2. Rewrite the following six productions, using <class name>s to reduce the number cf productions to two:

```
X Y  -> Y,     X Z  -> Z,     X ANY  -> Y,
W Y  -> Y,     W Z  -> Z,     W ANY  -> W
```

3. What is wrong with each of the following productions?

```
a)  E + T  ->  ANY
b)  L: L1:  E + T  ->  E   SCAN GO Y
c)  L:  I:  ->  <label>   SCAN GO STATE
```

4. Write a PL program to recognize sentences of the following grammar G[z]: Z ::= + | Z + | Z -.

## 7.2 USING PL

Because PL is a programming language and not a mechanical constructor of a recognizer like most of the other parsers we have studied, it is more flexible. One need not follow the formal grammar exactly in parsing, but can attempt to program efficiently. One also has more flexibility in fitting the syntax to semantics. This latter problem is discussed in chapters 12 and 13. In this section we want to give a few hints on programming in PL. First of all, we show how an (m,n) bounded context recognizer can be programmed in PL. Secondly, we show hcw tc program the method of recursive descent discussed in section 4.3. Finally, we turn to a simple example to illustrate a few programming techniques.

### Bottom-Up Parsing in PL

This part requires a knowledge of section 6.3. Figure 6.7 of chapter 6 illustrates a table for a (1,1) bounded context bottom-up recognizer for grammar (6.3.6). Each of the lines indicates a pattern match and a stack transformation. For example, the first line says that if "a 0 1" is on the stack and if "#" is the incoming symbol, then change the stack to "a W".

Aside from the notation, the main difference between a PL program and this table is that the table is not an algorithm, or program; the table is just data for the algorithm in Figure 6.8. A PL production indicates what to do after its transformation is made; a line in Figure 6.7 does not.

We can construct a PL program which is essentially the same recognizer by combining the table of Figure 6.7 with the algorithm of Figure 6.8. We have done this in Figure 7.3. In the program, the right context R always appears at the top of the stack, since this is the only way PL allows us to refer to the source symbols.

Figure 7.3 begins as usual with the production which scans the first symbol of the sentence. Productions L through M then perform step 2 of the algorithm in Figure 6.8. Each production corresponds to one line of Figure 6.7. If one production matches, then the stack transformation is made as given in step 3 of Figure 6.8, and the program transfers back to production L to compare again. If no production matches, then productions N through N+2 perform steps 4 through 6 of Figure 6.8; stop with "HALT 0" printed out if the input was actually a sentence, stop with "HALT 2" printed if it was not a sentence, or scan the next symbol and go to L to begin matching again.

Of course, the PL program in Figure 7.3 is not very efficient. The productions can be reordered and more labels used to reduce the number of comparisons at each step. For example, the only one applicable after the transformation in production L is production L+4.

However we have illustrated how any table for a (1,1) bounded context grammar could be translated -- even mechanically. In fact the process could be easily modified to translate a table for an (m,n) bounded context grammar into PL. We would just have to take care of the added context on each side of a possible handle. Since a grammar accepted by any of the bottom-up techniques described is also (m,n) bounded context for some m and n, we can also write a PL program to perform bottom-up recognition for that grammar.

```
S:             #         SCAN
L:  a  0  1  #   ->  a  W  #  GO  L
       0  0  1  1   ->  0  W  1  GO  L
   0  0  W  1  1   ->  0  W  1  GO  L
   a  0  W  1  #   ->  a  W  #  GO  L
       #  a  W  #   ->  #  Z  #  GO  L
          b  0  0   ->  b  U  0  GO  L
          b  0  1   ->  b  U  1  GO  L
       b  U  0  0   ->  b  U  0  GO  L
       b  U  0  1   ->  b  U  1  GO  L
       #  b  U  1   ->  #  V  1  GO  L
       #  V  1  1   ->  #  V  1  GO  L
       #  V  1  #   ->  #  V  #  GO  L
M:        #  V  #   ->  #  Z  #  GO  L
N:        #  Z  #              HALT 0
                #              HALT 2
              ANY        SCAN  GO  L
```

**FIGURE 7.3. Bottom-Up Parser in PL.**

### Top-Down Without Backup in PL

This part requires a knowledge of section 4.3. The two actions CALL and RETURN allow us to use a group of productions much like a procedure is used in ALGOL or FORTRAN. This allows us to program a top-down parse in PL using the method of recursive descent of section 4.3. In fact, since PL is designed for symbol manipulation, recursive descent is much easier to program here.

Figure 7.4 illustrates a PL program for recognizing sentences of grammar (4.3.2). The figure contains a set of productions for each rule of the grammar. The first production performs the initialization; stack the first symbol of the sentence and call the productions for <state>. If the program halts with "HALT 2" printed out, the input was not a sentence.

The productions follow the same conventions as those of the recursive subroutines. When a set of productions is called, the first symbol of the phrase to be detected is in the stack, and, upon return, the symbol following that phrase is on the stack. If the reader will compare each set of productions to the corresponding procedure in section 4.3, he will find they are remarkably similar; only the notation has changed.

```
S:  #                                      SCAN  CALL STATE
S0:  # <state> #                           HALT 0
     ANY                                   HALT 2

STATE:IF                                   SCAN  CALL EXPR  GO ST1
     ANY                                   CALL VAR SCAN CALL EXPR
 <var> $:= <expr> ANY ->  <state> ANY      RETURN
ST1: IF <expr> THEN   ->                   SCAN CALL STATE GO ST2
     ANY                                   HALT 2
ST2: <state> ELSE     ->                   SCAN  CALL STATE
     <state> ANY                           RETURN
     ANY                                   HALT 2

VAR: I                                     SCAN
     I (                                   SCAN CALL EXPR GO VAR1
     I ANY            ->  <var>            RETURN
VAR1:I ( <expr> )     ->  <var>            SCAN  RETURN
     ANY                                   HALT 2

EXPR:ANY                                   CALL TERM
     <term> +         ->                   SCAN  GO EXPR
     <term> ANY       ->  <expr> ANY       RETURN
     ANY                                   HALT 2

TERM:ANY                                   CALL FACTOR
     <factor> *       ->                   SCAN  GO TERM
     <factor> ANY     ->  <term> ANY       RETURN
     ANY                                   HALT 2

FACTOR:(                                   SCAN CALL EXPR GO FAC1
     ANY                                   CALL VAR
     <var> ANY        ->  <factor> ANY     RETURN
FAC1:( <expr> )       ->  <factor>         SCAN  RETURN
     ANY                                   HALT 2
```

**FIGURE 7.4. A Top-Down Parser in PL.**

### Programming in PL

While one can program either a pure bottom-up or a pure top-down recognizer (without backup) in PL, neither will be the most efficient program possible. As we saw, the bottom-up recognizer was inefficient because so many productions had to be compared at each step (this may be true even if the productions are rearranged and the GO actions changed to reduce the number of comparisons). On the other hand, a pure top-down recognizer will execute many CALLS and RETURNS, and these are slower than pure jumps.

The best solution is usually a mixture of the two. Write a subroutine (i.e. a set of productions used as a subroutine) for the major units of the source language. For example, for ALGOL, write one for statements, one for declarations and one for expressions. (Note that such a separation allows several people to program part of the program almost completely independently.) Each of these may call other subroutines in several places. The statement subroutine calls the expression subroutine and, in fact, calls itself whenever a substatement is to be parsed.

Within each subroutine, a bottom-up approach tends to be easier to write, as illustrated (Figure 7.1) and discussed earlier. The idea is to use context and jumps to limit the number of productions compared at each step.

Within subroutines corresponding to a set of rewriting rules all of which have the same left part, one usually begins with a few productions which test the first symbol to determine which alternative to try, branching to a subset of the productions to parse that alternative. A subroutine for <statement> is a good example of this. Consider the partial grammmar

```
<statement> ::= IF <expr> THEN <statement>
              | <var> := <expr>
              | FOR <var> := <for list element>
                DO <statement
              | READ ( <var> )
```

The PL program for this would be as given below. Note that <var> is considered a major syntactic entity and is recognized by a subroutine. This is because it is used in so many different places. If we used a normal GO VAR, then, after recognizing <var>, we would need a long sequence of productions to figure out, depending on the context, where to return to.

```
STATEMENT:IF      SCAN CALL EXPR GO CONDL
          FOR     SCAN CALL VAR GO FORL
          READ    SCAN GO READL
          ANY     CALL VAR GO ASSL
CONDL:(productions to recognize cond.state)
FORL: (productions to recognize FOR loop)
READL:(productions to recognize READ)
ASSL: (productions to recognize assignment)
```

Again, much programming effort and execution time can be saved by using class names. Look at the difference in

```
REAL      ->  EXEC 1 SCAN GO IDLIST
INTEGER   ->  EXEC 2 SCAN GO IDLIST
BOOLEAN   ->  EXEC 3 SCAN GO IDLIST
STRING    ->  EXEC 4 SCAN GO IDLIST
COMPLEX   ->  EXEC 5 SCAN GO IDLIST
```

```
and            CLASSNO      TYPE  REAL 1  INTEGER 2
                            BCOLEAN 3  STRING 4  COMPLEX 5;
               TYPE   ->    EXEC TYPE SCAN GO IDLIST
```

The latter is easier to write and much easier to read.

**EXERCISES FOR 7.2.**

1. Make the PL program of Figure 7.3 more efficient by reordering productions and changing the GO actions.

2. Write a PL program tc recognize sentences of the following grammar using (1) a top-down approach, and (2) the bottom-up method. Z ::= b M b | M c, M ::= ( L a, L ::= M a )

## 7.3 CALLING SEMANTIC ROUTINES

We explain here the use cf the EXEC actions. What we discuss may not be too clear at this point, since we have not yet discussed semantic routines. The reader should reread this section after studying chapters 12 and 13.

In any PL implementaticn there are actually at least two stacks which work in parallel. Cne, the syntax stack SYN, we have already discussed. The second, called the semantic stack SEM, holds the "meaning" of the symbols in the first stack. That is, SEM(i) holds the "meaning" or "semantics" of the symbol in SYN(i). Just what this meaning is will become clear in chapters 12 and 13.

The original semantics of most terminal symbols is undefined. That is, when the scanner pushes a symbol onto SYN, the corresponding location in SEM does not receive a new value. This is not so, however, for the terminals I and N. When the scanner scans an identifier (integer) and puts I (N) on the syntax stack SYN, it also puts that identifier (integer) on SEM. (This may be alternatively a pointer to the identifier or integer, but this is irrelevant to this discussion.) Thus the semantics of I (N) is the identifier (integer) to which the I (N) refers.

In any implementation of PL there is also an associated semantic language, in which the semantic routines are programmed. This may be assembly language, FORTRAN, PL/1, ALGOL -- it doesn't really matter. By a semantic routine we just mean a set of statements in the semantic language which is identifiable in some way. Each may be a separate procedure, each may be a single substatement of a large case statement, or the semantic language may provide a special "semantic label" to identify the beginning of a semantic routine.

Within the semantic language one also has access to the semantic stack SEM. When an action EXEC 5 (say) within a PL production is executed, semantic routine number 5 of the semantic program is executed. It does its calculations using the top elements of SEM and the variables declared in the semantic language, and then returns.

For example, suppose the production

```
I  ->  F   EXEC 5  SCAN  GO LT
```

is current and suppose the stacks look like

```
        ┌─────┐   ┌─────────────┐
        │  I  │   │     AB      │
        ├─────┤   ├─────────────┤
        │  *  │   │meaning of * │
SYN     ├─────┤   ├─────────────┤    SEM
        │  T  │   │meaning of T │
        ├─────┤   ├─────────────┤
        :  :  :   :      :      :
        └─────┘   └─────────────┘
```

The left part therefore matches the stack, and the top element in SYN is changed from I to F. Routine 5 is then called. It can take the identifier AB on the top of SEM, look it up in a symbol table, and put into the top element of SEM the entry number 3 (say) of the identifier AB in the table, yielding

```
        ┌─────┐   ┌─────────────┐
        │  F  │   │     3       │
        ├─────┤   ├─────────────┤
        │  *  │   │meaning of * │
SYN     ├─────┤   ├─────────────┤    SEM
        │  T  │   │meaning of T │
        ├─────┤   ├─────────────┤
        :  :  :   :      :      :
        └─────┘   └─────────────┘
```

Semantic routine 5 then returns, the next symbol is scanned, and production LT becomes current.

The only other point to discuss here is the use of the action EXEC <class name>. Remember that the class name must also appear in the left part of the production. To execute the action, the semantic routine associated by the declaration of <class name> with the symbol currently on the stack which matched the <class name> in the left part of the production, is executed. This is easier to illustrate than to say: Consider the declaration

```
CLASSNO OPER  * 1  + 2  - 3  / 4;
```

and current production E OPER E -> E EXEC OPER. If the stack contains E - E then routine 3 will be executed.

## 7.4 HISTORICAL REFERENCES

Production language has its origin in Floyd(61b). The language introduced in his paper is intended for symbol manipulation and is much like PL except for notation. The language was further developed by Evans(64). PL is used as the syntax method in FSL, a translator writing system (TWS) designed and implemented by Feldman(66). It is also being used in several other TWS efforts. Several constructors (one by Earley) have been designed which, given a suitable grammar, produce a PL program which is a syntax recognizer for it. Ichbiah and Morse(70) describe an algorithm generating "optimal" productions from precedence grammars. Their technique does not make use of the semantic actions CALL and RETURN.

# Chapter 8.
# Runtime Storage Organization

This chapter illustrates runtime organizations for parts of three well-known high-level languages. In doing so we will describe solutions for many of the concepts appearing in programming languages. We can indicate simple organizations for languages like FORTRAN, more complicated ones for ALGOL-like languages, and the most complicated ones made necessary by languages like PL/I with structures, pointer variables, and ALLOCATE and FREE statements.

We cannot of course give all the details for all these languages. Our purpose is to give the basic details of storage administration and to give some general viewpoints. The reader should be able to design his own runtime administration routines for any language after digesting the material given here. One thing should be made clear by reading this chapter. There are many points which escape one's attention unless one knows the source language thoroughly.

Some languages require dynamic storage allocation schemes, where blocks of core are allocated, then released, and then reallocated for another purpose, in a random fashion. A complete discussion of such schemes falls outside the scope of this book. We do present one storage allocation method in section 8.10 for the sake of completeness, but the reader is encouraged to study these techniques in Knuth(68). For the moment, then, let us assume the existence of two routines

GETAREA(ADDRESS,SIZE) and FREE(ADDRESS,SIZE).

The first of these assigns a sequence of SIZE locations to the calling program, beginning at the output parameter ADDRESS. FREEAREA releases the SIZE locations beginning at address ADDRESS.

In some systems, storage is allocated, but never explicitly released. When no more storage is available, the system invokes a <u>garbage collector</u>, which finds those locations which are not actually being used and frees them. It may also be necessary to compact the used space -- move all the data being used into contiguous locations -- so that a large block of contiguous locations is then free, instead of many small ones. We discuss this problem briefly in section 8.10; for the moment, let us also assume the existence of a routine FREEGARBAGE to perform this.

The chapter is structured as follows. Section 8.1 introduces the concept of a <u>data area</u> in an attempt to unify the whole presentation. Section 8.2 discusses templates, while sections 8.3 through 8.6 are devoted to the problems arising with implementing data structures, in increasing order of complexity. Section 8.7 discusses procedure calls and formal-actual parameter correspondence. We then turn to problems associated with FORTRAN and ALGOL. We end the chapter with section 8.10 on dynamic storage allocation and garbage collection.

## 8.1 DATA AREAS AND DISPLAYS

A data area is a set of contiguous locations -- a block of core storage -- set aside for data which logically belong together in some way. Often (but not always) all the locations in a data area have the same *scope* in the source program; they can be referred to by the same sets of statements (i.e., the scope can be a block or procedure body). The term *activation record* has been used by Wegner(68) for a similar concept; we prefer the shorter term, data area.

The variables declared in the FORTRAN COMMON statement would be allocated storage in a single data area, the blank COMMON data area. In ALGOL, the runtime locations for simple variables declared in the main program, together with the locations for temporary values needed in it, could form a data area.

At compile-time, the runtime location of any variable can be represented by an ordered pair (data area number, offset) where the data area number is some unique number assigned to the data area and the offset is the address of the variable relative to the beginning of the data area. (Thus the first location of data area 3 is represented by (3,0), the second by (3,1), etc.) Of course, when we generate code to reference a variable, this must be translated into the actual address of the variable. This is usually done by putting the *base address* (machine address of the first location) of the data area in a register and referencing the variable by the offset plus the contents of the register. The pair (data area number, offset) has then been translated into the pair (base address, offset).

Data areas fall into two classes -- *static* and *dynamic*. A static data area has a fixed set of locations allocated to it before runtime. These locations remain allocated to it throughout runtime. Hence a variable in a static data area can be referenced by its absolute address instead of by a pair (base address, offset).

A dynamic data area is not always present at runtime. It comes and goes, and each time it goes all values in it are lost. An example of this is a data area which holds the variables of an ALGOL procedure. When the procedure is called, it invokes GETAREA to allocate storage for its fixed length data area. Just before returning to the calling program, it calls FREEAREA to release the space. Note that the same memory locations may not be given to the procedure for its data area. However, GETAREA always returns the base address of the data area allocated, and the procedure always stores it in the same location BA (say). Thus the address of any variable in the data area is always CONTENTS(BA)+OFFSET. If a procedure is called recursively, then several copies of the data area for it are in core, one for each call of the procedure. This is what we want; each time the procedure is called it should have a new area to play in. Such a data area does not belong to the procedure itself, but to an *execution* of the procedure.

```
BEGIN  PROCEDURE A;
         BEGIN PROCEDURE B; BEGIN ... END;
                PROCEDURE C; BEGIN ... END;
         END;

       PROCEDURE D; BEGIN ... END;
  :
END;
```

**FIGURE 8.1. An ALGOL Program Procedure Structure.**

At any point of execution it may be possible to reference variables in several data areas. For example, consider an ALGOL program with the procedure structure of Figure 8.1. If a different data area exists for the main program and for each of the procedures, then, when executing procedure B we can reference data areas for procedures A, B, and the main program. To put some order in the way we reference them, we collect the addresses of these referencable data areas in a DISPLAY. For this particular example, when executing procedure B the DISPLAY would be

```
           ┌──────────────────────────────────────┐
           |address of data area for main program|
           ├──────────────────────────────────────┤
DISPLAY    |address of data area for procedure A |
           ├──────────────────────────────────────┤
           |address of data area for procedure B |
           └──────────────────────────────────────┘
```

Thus when we create (get storage for) data areas we have a fixed place for storing their addresses. Some questions we have to answer are: where does the DISPLAY itself go? In what order do we put the addresses into the DISPLAY? These will be answered when we discuss implementations of particular languages.

In general, several DISPLAYs must be available during runtime, for use in executing different parts of the program. Suppose, in the above example, that procedure B calls procedure D. At this point we must construct a DISPLAY containing only the addresses of the data areas for D and the main program, for use in D. We must still keep the previous DISPLAY intact; it will be used again when D finishes and returns to B. At any point of execution the active DISPLAY is the one being used currently to reference data areas.

### EXERCISES FOR 8.1

1. What should the current DISPLAY look like when executing procedure C of Figure 8.1? When executing procedure A? What should the DISPLAY look like when executing procedure D of Figure 8.5 (page 194)? When executing procedure B?

## 8.2 TEMPLATES

If a compiler knows all the attributes of variables at compile-time then it can generate all the necessary code to reference them based on these attributes. But in many instances this information may be dynamically specified at runtime. For example, in ALGOL the lower and upper bounds of the array dimensions are not known. Also, in some languages actual parameters do not have to correspond exactly in type with formal parameters. In such cases the compiler cannot generate simple, efficient code because it must allow for each set of attributes possible.

To solve this problem the compiler allocates space not only for the variable but also for a <u>template</u> for it, which describes the attributes determined at runtime. (Webster's Seventh Collegiate defines a template as a gauge, pattern, or mold used as a guide to the form of a piece being made.) This template is then filled and changed as the attributes become known and changed at runtime.

To take a simple example, if a formal parameter is a simple variable and the corresponding actual parameter type may vary, the actual parameter passed to the procedure might look like

| Template 0=REAL, 1=INTEGER, 2=BOOLEAN, etc |
|---|
| Address of value (or value itself) |

When the formal parameter is referred to in the procedure, the procedure must interrogate or interpret this template and then perform any necessary type conversion. It may of course call another routine to perform this.

In many cases the compiler cannot allocate space for the value of such a variable because the space attributes are not known. Such is the case for arrays in ALGOL. All the compiler can do is allocate space for the fixed-length template in the data area with which the variable is associated. At runtime, when the space attributes become known, GETAREA is called to allocate the space, and the address of this storage is put in the template. The value is then always referenced through this template.

Structures or records may also require templates, in fact much more complicated ones, which specify how the components and subcomponents are related. We discuss this in section 8.6.

The more attributes one allows to change at runtime, the more must be done at runtime. The reason one can compile more efficient programs for FORTRAN than for ALGOL or PL/I is that practically all attributes are known at compile time and no templates and their interpretations are required.

## 8.3 STORAGE FOR ELEMENTARY DATA TYPES

Data types of the source program have to be mapped into equivalent data types of the machine. For some types, there is a one-to-one correspondence (integers, reals, etc.); for others, several machine words may be needed. We briefly mention the following:

1. Integer variables are usually contained in one word or location of a data area; the value is stored in the standard internal integer form of the machine.

2. Real variables are usually contained in one word. If more precision is desired than is possible with one word, the machine's "double-word" floating point format can be used. On machines without a floating point format, two words may be used -- one for the exponent and one for the (normalized) mantissa. Floating point operations must then be carried out by subroutines.

3. Boolean or logical variables can be contained in one word, with zero representing FALSE and non-zero or 1 representing TRUE. The particular representation for TRUE and FALSE is determined by the instructions on the machine that can be used for the logical operations. One could also use a single bit for each Boolean variable and pack as many Boolean variables or constants into one word as possible.

4. A <u>pointer</u> is the address of (a reference to) another value. In certain instances it may be necessary to implement a pointer as two consecutive locations; one points to (or is) the template of the current value being pointed at, while the other points to the actual value. This is necessary if at compile-time it is not possible to determine with each use of a pointer the type of value referenced.

## 8.4 STORAGE FOR ARRAYS

We assume that each element of an array or vector occupies one location in memory. The generalization to more than one is left to the reader.

### Vectors

The elements of vectors (one-dimensional arrays) are usually allocated contiguous locations in a data area and are placed in descending or ascending order. The order depends on the machine and its instruction repertoire. For example, on the IBM 7090 the contents of an index register are <u>subtracted</u> from the basic address to get an effective address; therefore array elements are usually stored in descending order.

We assume that the more conventional ascending order is used. Thus the elements of the array defined by ARRAY A[1:10] are in the order A[1], A[2], ..., A[10].

### Matrices

There are several ways of storing two-dimensional arrays. The usual way is to store them in a data area by row (in row major order); that is, in the order (for an array declared by ARRAY A[1:M,1:N])

A[1,1],A[1,2],...,A[1,N],A[2,1],...,A[2,N],...,A[M,1],...,A[M,N]

A look at the ordering involved indicates that the element A[i,j] is located at the address ADDRESS(A[1,1]) + (i-1)*N + (j-1), which we write as

(8.4.1)          (ADDRESS(A[1,1]) - N-1) + (i*N+j) .

The first quantity is a constant and need be calculated only once. Thus to find A[i,j] requires a multiplication and two additions. IBM FORTRAN IV requires arrays to be in column major order.

A second method is to allocate a separate data area for each row and to have a vector of pointers to these data areas. The elements of each row are in contiguous locations in ascending order. Thus the declaration ARRAY A[1:M,1:N] yields

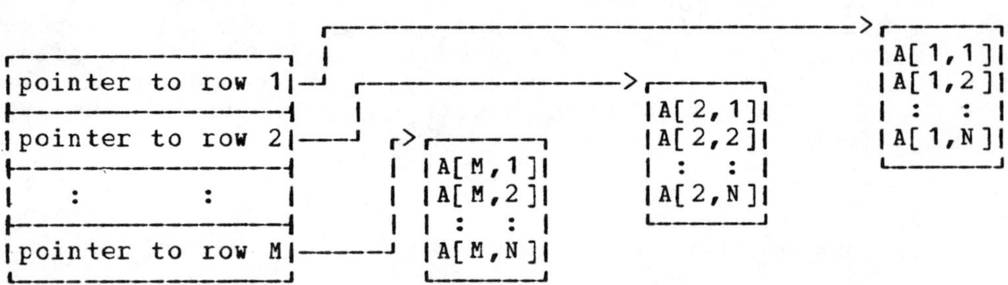


The vector of pointers to the rows is stored in the data area with which the array is associated while the array itself is stored in a separate data area. The address of an array element A[i,j] is CONTENTS(address of vector + i-1) + (j-1).

No multiplications are required, which is one reason for using such a method. Another reason is that not all the rows need be in core at the same time. The pointer to a row can contain some value which causes a hardware or software interrupt in case the row is not in memory. When an interrupt occurs the row needed is brought into core, replacing another row. This method is used in the Burroughs extended ALGOL compiler on the B5500. It does require more space if all the rows are in core, for the vector of row pointers.

A third method is used when matrices are known to be sparse (most elements are 0). A hash addressing scheme based on the values i and j of the array element A[i,j] can be used, which hashes to a relatively small table of array elements (see chapter 9 for *hashing*). Only the non-zero elements are recorded in the table.

### Multi-Dimensional Arrays

We consider storage allocation and referencing of multi-dimensional arrays with, say, the following ALGOL declaration:

```
ARRAY A[L1:U1,L2:U2,...,Ln:Un]
```

The one method we consider is a generalization of the first method presented for the two-dimensional case; it also applies to the one dimensional case.

The subarrays A[i,*,...,*] are in the order A[L1,*,...,*], A[L1+1,*,...,*], and so on up to A[U1,*,...,*]. Within each subarray A[i,*,...,*] are the sub-subarrays A[i,L2,*,...,*], A[i,L2+1,*,...,*], ..., and A[i,U2,*,...,*]. This repeats for each dimension. Thus as we ascend through the array elements the *last* subscripts change most rapidly:

```
┌──────────────────────────────────────────────────────┐ ┌──────────┐     ┌────────┐
| subarray A[L1]                                       | |A[L1+1]   |     |A[U1]   |
| ┌──────────┐ ┌──────────────┐      ┌────────────┐    | |          |     |        |
| |A[L1,L2]  | |A[L1,L2+1]    |      |A[L1,U2]    |    | |          |     |        |
| |          | |              |...   |            |    | |          | ... |        |
| └──────────┘ └──────────────┘      └────────────┘    | |          |     |        |
└──────────────────────────────────────────────────────┘ └──────────┘     └────────┘
```

The problem is how to reference an element A[i,j,k,...,l,m]. Let us write

```
d1 = U1-L1+1, d2 = U2-L2+1, ... , dn = Un-Ln+1.
```

That is, di is the number of different subscript values in the ith dimension. Following the 2-dimensional case, we find the beginning of the subarray A[i,*,...,*] by

```
BASELOC + (i-L1)*d2*d3*...*dn
```

where BASELOC is the address of the first element A[L1,L2,...Ln] and d2*d3*...*dn is the size of each subarray A[i,*,...,*]. The beginning of the sub-subarray A[i,j,*,...,*] is then found by adding

```
(j-L2)*d3*...*dn
```

to this value. Continuing in this manner we end up with

```
(8.4.2)    BASELOC + (i-L1)*d2*d3*...*dn + (j-L2)*d3*...*dn
           + (k-L3)*d4*...*dn + ...  + (l-L[n-1])*dn + m-Ln.
```

Factoring yields

```
(8.4.3)     CONSPART + VARPART
```

where

```
(8.4.4)     CONSPART = BASELOC
               -((...((L1*d2+L2)*d3+L3)*d4+...+L[n-1])*dn+Ln)
```

and

```
(8.4.5)     VARPART = (...((i*d2)+j)*d3+...+l)*dn+m.
```

The value CONSPART need only be calculated once and saved, since it depends only on the lower and upper bounds and where the array is placed in storage. VARPART depends on the subscripts i,j,...,m and the number of subscript values in each dimension d2,d3,...,dn. The calculation looks rather formidable, but it has been put in this form because it can actually be calculated easily by executing the following statements:

```
    VARPART := first subscript (i)
    VARPART := VARPART*d2 + second subscript (j)
    VARPART := VARPART*d3 + third subscript (k)
            :               :
    VARPART := VARPART*dn + nth subscript (m)
```

Thus there is method to all this madness; it is quite easy to program or generate code for the calculation of the address of a subscripted variable using the above scheme. In fact, it is just as easy to generate code for any multi-dimensional array reference as it is to generate code for a 2 or 3 dimensional array, due to the iterative nature of the calculation.

In some cases, where code optimization is to be performed, it is better to use (8.4.2) (separated into a constant and variable part, of course) where the di have not been factored, since it separates the calculation into several independent parts. We will see this in chapter 18.

### Dope Vectors

In FORTRAN the upper and lower bounds of arrays are known at compile time. The compiler can therefore allocate storage for the arrays and generate the code for referencing the array elements using the upper and lower bounds and the values d1,d2,...,dn as constants. In ALGOL and PL/I this is not possible since the bounds can be computed at runtime. Thus at runtime we need a template for the array giving the necessary information. For arrays this template is called a <u>dope vector</u> or an <u>information vector</u>. The dope vector will have a fixed size known at compile time, so space can be allocated to it at compile time in the data area with which the array is associated. Storage for the array itself can not be allocated until runtime, when the block in which the array is declared is entered. When it is entered, the bounds of the array are evaluated and an array allocation routine is called. This routine calculates the number of locations needed, calls GETAREA to allocate a data area of that size, and fills in the dope vector with all the necessary information. A flow chart of the array allocation routine appears in Figure 8.3.

What information goes into the dope vector? For the n-dimensional scheme proposed above, we need the values d2,...,dn, and CONSPART. This is the bare minimum. If subscripts are to be checked for validity before array referencing we should also include the upper and lower bounds themselves. Figure 8.2 indicates the information that might be required.

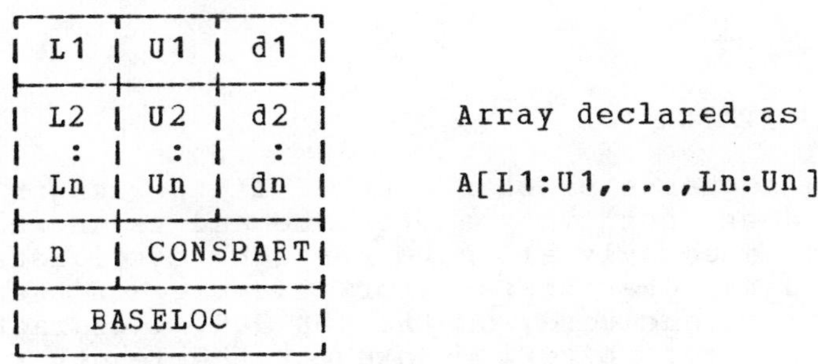


**FIGURE 8.2. Dope Vector for Array.**

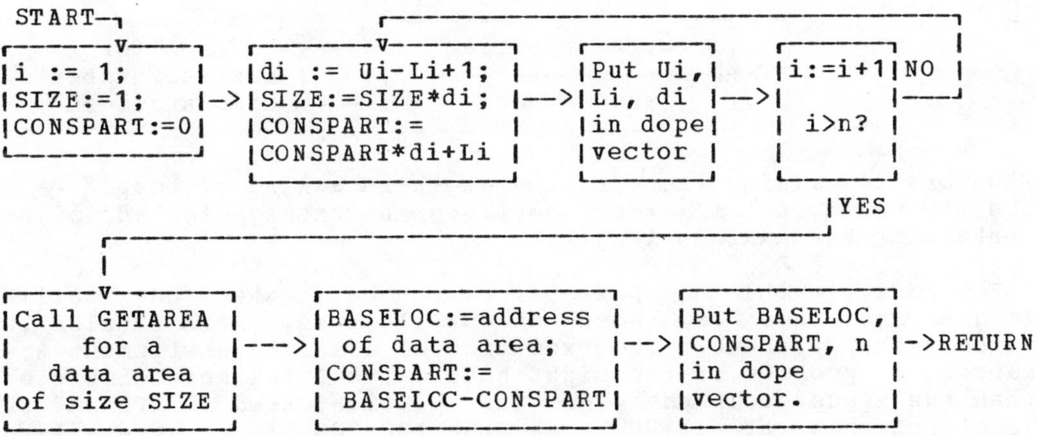


**FIGURE 8.3. Array Allocation Routine.**

### EXERCISES FOR 8.4

1. Separate (8.4.2) into a constant part and a variable part which depends on the subscripts, but do not factor out the di. Suppose this new formula is to be used to reference array elements. What values should be in the dope vector to make the calculation efficient? Redo the array allocation routine flowchart to store these values in the dope vector.

2. Program and debug the array allocation routine in some language. Write a dummy procedure GETAREA to check it out.

3. Suppose arrays are to be stored in column major order. Redo the evaluation of an array element A[i,j,...,m]. Redesign the array allocation routine and the dope vector format.

## 8.5 STORAGE FOR STRINGS

A string is a sequence of characters. If the length (number of characters) does not vary at runtime and is known at compile-time, then one need only allocate enough contiguous words to allow that many characters (for example, on the IBM 7090, 6 characters fit in one word, on the IBM 360, 4 characters fit in one word (one per byte). However the length is not always known. If the maximum length is known, then one can allocate enough words for that length and precede these words by a word containing the current number of characters:

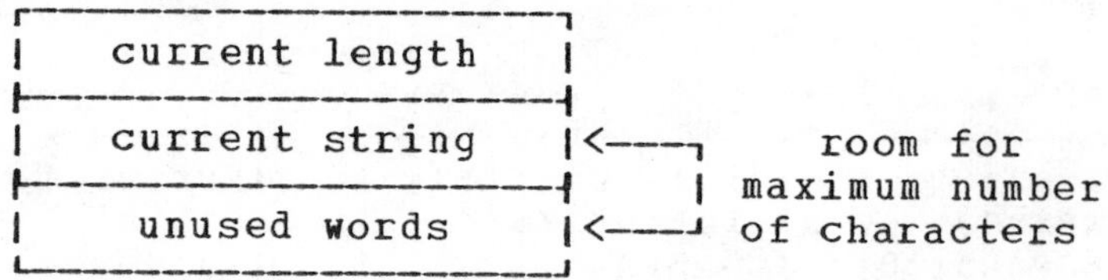


The word containing the current length is a kind of template for the value. It is also sometimes necessary to add a word containing the maximum length.

The most flexible and powerful case occurs when the maximum length need not be known at compile time. This is also the hardest to implement. The execution of a string assignment A:=B causes a problem if the right hand value B has more characters than the space occupied by A. One solution, used in XPL and SPL (see McKeeman et al(70)) on the IBM 360, is to have a large string space static data area available to hold all strings. Each string variable has a template consisting of two contiguous words containing the current length of the string and a pointer to the string itself in the string space. This type of template we call a string pointer. If we execute the assignments S1 := 'AB', S2 := 'QED', and S3 := 'F' we would have

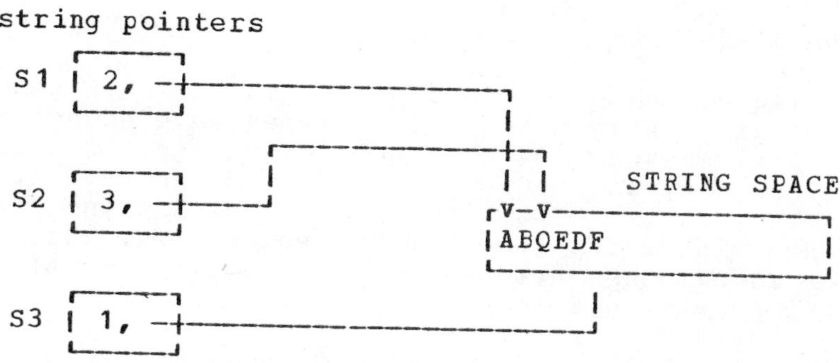


Execution of a statement like S1 := S2 does not change the string, but only the string pointer. Statements like S3 := SUBSTR(S2,1,1) can be executed similarly. For example, executing these two would change the above diagram to

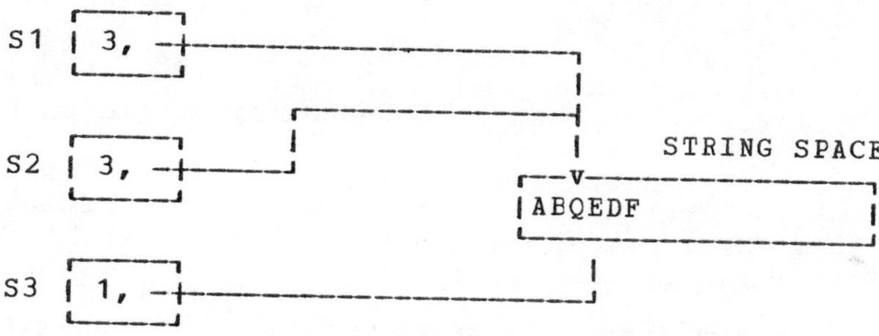


Note that all three string pointers are pointing to parts of the same string. Since only string pointers are changed and not the string itself, simple assignment statements are executed efficiently. Concatenation of strings (S1 := S2 CAT S3, say) is slow because the whole string must be made up in a free place. Executing this statement would yield

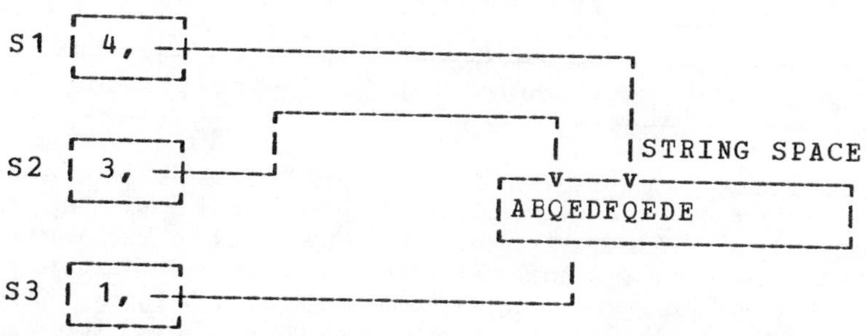


At some point the string space is going to be filled up. But much of it will be garbage -- just characters which are no longer pointed at by any string pointer. The characters AB in the above area are garbage. When this happens, FREEGARBAGE is called to find the garbage, throw it out, and compact the useful information into the beginning of the string space.

## 8.6 STORAGE FOR STRUCTURES

A number of alternatives for defining new data types as a composition of previously defined data types have been designed. We call values with such a type <u>structured values</u>. COBOL, PL/I, ALGOL W, ALGOL 68, and SNOBOL all have some sort of structure definition. They vary in their flexibility of use and thus in the efficiency with which they can be implemented. We describe three of them and discuss briefly how they could be implemented. There are four points to discuss:

How to allocate space for a structured value;
How to construct structured values;
How to reference a component of a structured value; and
How to release the space.

### Hoare Records (Wirth and Hoare (66))

A definition of a new data type has the form

```
RECORD <identifier> (<component>,<component>, ...,<component>)
```

where each component has the form <simple type> <identifier>, and <simple type> is one of the basic types in the language -- REAL, INTEGER, POINTER, etc. (ALGOL W uses the term REFERENCE instead of POINTER). For example,

```
RECORD COMPLEX ( INTEGER REALPART, INTEGER IMAGPART )
```

defines the new type COMPLEX to consist of two INTEGER components named REALPART and IMAGPART. At compile-time all attributes of all components are known, including, for pointers, what data type the pointer can point to. No template for the structure itself or for the components is needed at runtime and efficient code can be generated. Any structured value with n components can be in storage in the form

| component 1 | component 2 | ... | component n |
|---|---|---|---|

Since all attributes are known at compile-time the amount of storage needed for each component is also known and thus the compiler knows the offset of each component with respect to the beginning of the value. For purposes of garbage collection, it is best to assign a unique number to each data type (including programmer defined ones) and to have a template for each pointer. The template is the number describing the type of value which is currently being pointed at.

Space for pointers and their templates can be allocated by the compiler in the data area with which they are associated; they have a fixed length and cause no trouble. A separate static data area can be used to hold current structured values, with a special GETAREA routine allocating the space. ALGOL W has no explicit statements for releasing space, so that when no more space exists, FREEGARBAGE is called by the system. Note that it must know where all pointers are, including those which are components of structured values, in order to be able to find the garbage.

One constructs a new value of type COMPLEX with components S1 and S2 by executing a statement

```
P := COMPLEX (S1, S2)
```

where P has been declared a pointer to values of type COMPLEX. At runtime this is executed by calling GETAREA for the correct amount of storage and by storing the calculated values S1 and S2 into it, and the address of the new value in P.

Structured values are referenced only through declared pointers. If one executes

```
P1 := P; P := COMPLEX (S3,S4)
```

the first value assigned to P is not lost because P1 contains a pointer to it. Note that just after execution of P1:=P, both P1 and P point to the same value.

A component is referenced by

<name of component> ("pointer to structured value")

Thus, executing IMAGPART(P) := IMAGPART(P)+1 adds 1 to the second component of the structured value pointed at by P. Efficient code can be generated for this. For example, the instructions for the above statement on the IBM 360 might be

```
    L      1,P        |Put the value of P in register 1.
    L      2,4(1)     |Put IMAGPART in register 2. Note that
                      |the offset 4 is known at compile-time.
    A      2,=F'1'    |Add 1 to register 2.
    ST     2,4(1)     |Store the result in IMAGPART.
```

### PL/I Structures

PL/I structures are more complicated than Hoare records in that components may themselves have subcomponents. An example is

```
DECLARE 1 PERSON,
          2 NAME CHARACTER(20),
          2 FATHER POINTER,
          2 MOTHER POINTER,
          2 CHILDREN,
            3 OLDEST1 POINTER,
            3 OLDEST2 POINTER,
            3 OLDEST3 POINTER,
          2 AGE FIXED;
```

The structure is a tree whose nodes are associated with names and whose end nodes have data values. The root PERSON has level 1, and nodes which can be reached by a path of length i-1 from the root are on level i.

If the ability to have subcomponents were the only difference between Hoare records and PL/I structures there would essentially be no difference at runtime; one could still allocate all components and subcomponents so that each would have a fixed offset from the beginning of the structure and this offset would be known at compile-time. However PL/I has two more extensions.

As a space saver, the CELL attribute for a component indicates that all of its subcomponents are to occupy the same space. Only one alternate may contain a value at any given time. Assignment to a subcomponent causes the previously referenced subcomponent to lose its value. For example,

```
DECLARE 1 DATE CELL,  2 A FLOAT,  2 B FIXED;
```

causes both components A and B to use the same storage. This produces complications at compile-time but does not really change much of the runtime code, unless the object program must check at each subcomponent reference to make sure the value for the subcomponent referenced is actually present.

The second extension does require more runtime administration. In PL/I the root node of the structure tree, or *any* of the subcomponents may be dimensioned. For instance, we could rewrite the first DECLARE statement as

```
DECLARE 1 PERSON,
          2 NAME CHARACTERS (20),
          2 FATHER POINTER,
          2 MOTHER POINTER,
          2 CHILDREN(3) POINTER,
          2 AGE FIXED;
```

to get essentially the same effect; one component, CHILDREN, consists of three pointers (they are referenced differently). As another example, consider the structure definition

```
DECLARE 1 A, 2 B(2), 3 X(M,N),  3 Y(M,N), 3 Z,
             2 C LIKE B,
             2 N(2);
```

It yields the structure

```
         ┌───────
         |
         |       ┌─────
         |       | X(1,1), X(1,2), ..., X(1,N), ..., X(M,N)
         | B(1)  | Y(1,1), Y(1,2), ..., Y(1,N), ..., Y(M,N)
         |       | Z
         |       └─────
         |
         |       ┌─────
A        | B(2)  |  (like B(1))
         |       └─────
         |
         |       ┌─────
         | C(1)  |  (like B(1))
         |       └─────
         |
         |       ┌─────
         | C(2)  |  (like B(1))
         |       └─────
         |
         | N(1)
         | N(2)
         └───────
```

Since the expressions which specify the subscript ranges are to be evaluated at runtime, we must, as in the case of arrays, use templates, or dope vectors, for them. In the preceding DECLARE statement, we need dope vectors for all components except A itself and Z.

PL/I has three different methods of storage allocation -- STATIC, AUTOMATIC, and CONTROLLED. There is no difference in the storage allocation method for structured values and other values, as there is in ALGOL W. We should mention that PL/I requires the programmer to free the space allocated to CONTROLLED values. No garbage collection is performed for them.

A component is referenced by the sequence of names of nodes which lead to it, separated by periods. Thus, in the first example in this section, one references the component OLDEST1 by PERSON.CHILDREN.OLDEST1.

When components are dimensioned, the subscript desired must appear. In the last example, to reference component X(1,2) of C(1) write A.C(1).X(1,2). Certain other variations are possible. The more dimensions that appear in a structure definition, the more work must be done at compile-time to create, reference and delete values of that structure type.

**Standish Data Structures (Standish (68))**

We are progressing from the simple to the complicated -- from the data structures which can be implemented efficiently to those which cannot, but which are richer and more powerful. In his thesis, Standish presents a notation for structures embedded in ALGOL 60 which allows the structures themselves to be variable at runtime. Not only the dimensions of the components, but the number of components and their types as well can change dynamically. In general, nothing is known at compile-time and everything must be done at runtime in terms of templates which themselves will be constructed at runtime. For example, execution of the TEMPLATE PROCEDURE

```
TEMPLATE PROCEDURE SEQ (n,t); INTEGER n; TEMPLATE t;
          SEQ := n*[t];
```

produces a template describing a structure consisting of n components of type t. (Standish uses the term DESCRIPTOR for TEMPLATE.) Executing

```
D1 ::= SEQ(2,REAL); D2 ::= SEQ(k,D1)
```

puts in the TEMPLATE variable D1 a template of a structured value having two REAL components, and puts in D2 a template of a structured value consisting of k components, each of type D1. There are many other ways of constructing templates at runtime, besides methods for allocating storage for structured values and constructing the values. We shall not go into that here; the only point we want to make here is that at runtime we must keep a template for every structured value. In fact, this template is much like the set of symbol table elements used by a compiler to help compile, say, PL/I structures! As we shall see in chapter 10, such descriptions of structures are best implemented as a tree where each node must specify at least

1. Whether it is an end node or not;
2. If an end node, what its type is;
3. If an end node, a pointer to the value if it has one.
4. If not an end node, pointers to nodes for subcomponents.
5. Its dimensions.

Whenever a component of a value is referenced, the template must be interpreted. Starting from the root node, the path to the referenced node is found, the type of that node is checked, and finally the value is used or changed.

## 8.7 ACTUAL-FORMAL PARAMETER CORRESPONDENCE

We discuss the various types of formal parameters and their correspondence to actual parameters, and show how each of them can be implemented. By a formal parameter we mean an identifier in a procedure which is replaced by another identifier or an expression when the procedure is called. In a FORTRAN subroutine beginning with

```
SUBROUTINE A(X,Y)
```

X and Y are the formal parameters. An equivalent ALGOL procedure begins with PROCEDURE A(X,Y). When a procedure is called, say by A(B,C*D), the formal parameters are connected in some way to the <u>actual parameters</u> B and C*D.

When a procedure in any language is called, a list of addresses of the arguments is passed to it. The procedure copies these addresses into its own data area and uses them to make the actual-formal parameter correspondence. Besides the actual parameters, there are often several implicit parameters which the programmer is not aware of. One of course is the return address. (We could also include all the index registers to be saved in this list; this is however machine dependent, and we will not discuss such features further.) We will see which other language-dependent parameters are needed as we investigate the different types of parameters in the different languages.

The following sort of list is therefore passed to the called procedure:

```
          implicit parameter 1
                 :        :
          implicit parameter m
     address of actual parameter 1
                 :        :
     address of actual parameter n
```

Please note that all parameters may not actually be passed in such a list; we present it this way for convenience. For example, the return address is usually passed in a register of some sort.

What do the addresses in the list represent? That depends on the language and the type of the parameter, and we discuss this below. The types of parameters we look at are listed below. Exercises 2 and 3 are designed to convince the reader that the first five, in the proper context, are all different.

1. Call by reference
2. Call by value
3. Call by result
4. Dummy arguments
5. Call by name
6. Array names as actual parameters
7. Procedure names as actual parameters

### Call by Reference

This is the easiest type of parameter to implement. At runtime, prior to the call, the actual parameter is processed; if it is not a variable or constant it is evaluated and stored in a temporary location. The address (of the variable, constant or temporary location) is then calculated and this address is passed to the called procedure. The called procedure uses it to reference the location(s) containing the value. For example, suppose we call a procedure P defined by

(8.7.1) PROCEDURE P(X); BEGIN ... X:=X+5; ... END

with the call P(A[I]) where A is an array. Before the procedure is called, the address of A[I] is calculated and put in the list to be passed to the procedure. Execution of the statement X:=X+5 within the procedure causes 5 to be added to this element A[I]. The code for this statement would be something like

1. load register 1 (say) with the actual parameter address
2. load register 2 (say) with the value in 0(1)
3. add 5 to register 2
4. store register 2 in location 0(1)

where 0(1) means the location at address 0+CONTENTS(register 1).

### Call by Value

The <u>called</u> procedure in this type of correspondence has a location allocated in its data area for a value of the type of the formal parameter. As in the call by reference, the address of the actual parameter is calculated prior to the call and passed in the parameter list to the called procedure. However, before actually beginning execution, the procedure takes the value at the address and puts it in its own location. This location is used, then, as the location of the value, just like any local variable of the procedure. Thus there is <u>absolutely no way</u> for the procedure to change the value of the actual parameter.

To look at it another way, a VALUE parameter is a variable local to the procedure which, upon entry, is initialized to the value of the corresponding actual parameter.

Suppose the parameter X of the procedure (8.7.1) is called by VALUE. Then the corresponding object program would be something like

```
            ┌  ...
initialize  │ load register 1 with actual parameter address
procedure:  │ load register 2 with the value in 0(1)
            │ store register in X (in the data area of this
            │ procedure)
            └  ...
            ┌  ...
   body:    │ load register with X; add 5; store in X
            └  ...
```

### Call by Result

In ALGOL W (see Bauer et al(68)), for any formal parameter X declared to be a RESULT parameter, the following happens:

1. A location in the procedure data area is set aside for the parameter X. This location is used by the procedure as a local location for the variable X.
2. As with a VALUE parameter, upon calling the procedure, the actual parameter address is evaluated and passed.
3. When the procedure is finished, the final value of X is stored at the address described in step 2.

In other words, a RESULT parameter is a variable local to the procedure whose value, upon exit, is stored in the corresponding actual parameter (which must of course be a variable). The RESULT concept was designed to complement the ALGOL call by name (to be discussed later), since the latter is quite inefficient and more powerful than need be in most cases.

A parameter X in ALGOL W may be declared both as VALUE and as RESULT, in which case the local variable X is initialized upon entry to the procedure and the final value of X is stored back into the actual parameter. In FORTRAN II all arguments are called by reference; in FORTRAN IV, the normal parameter is called by VALUE RESULT, but the programmer may specify that it should be called by reference.

### Dummy Arguments

In FORTRAN II, a call P(3) of the procedure P of (8.7.1) results in an undetected error. Because FORTRAN passes the address of the location containing the constant 3, execution of the statement X=X+5 changes the constant itself to 8! This value 8 is used thereafter whenever 3 is supposed to be referenced. PL/I solves this problem by handling the following actual parameters differently:

1. Constants,
2. Expressions which are not also variables, and
3. Variables whose data attributes are different from those specified for the corresponding formal parameter;

For such an actual parameter, a temporary variable is allocated for it by the *calling* procedure. The actual parameter is evaluated and stored in the temporary variable, and the address of this variable is passed in the parameter list. Thus, in the above example, the constant 3 would *not* be changed.

Such a temporary variable is called a *dummy argument*. Aside from the fact that the temporary variable is allocated by the calling procedure, a PL/I dummy argument is similar to a call by VALUE in ALGOL.

There is, however, another difference to the programmer. In ALGOL, the *formal* parameter is declared VALUE. In PL/I the *calling* procedure has the choice of using an actual parameter as VALUE or as a FORTRAN-like call by reference. For example, if one writes P(J), the actual parameter J is a call by reference; if one writes P((J)) it is a call by VALUE, or dummy argument.

### Call by Name

According to the ALGOL report, the use of a call by name parameter implies a *textual* substitution of the formal parameter name by the actual parameter. Thus, if the procedure

```
PROCEDURE R(X,I);    BEGIN I:=2; X:=5; I:=3; X:=1 END
```

is called by

```
(8.7.2) R(B[J*2],J)
```

this would result in changing the body to

```
BEGIN J:=2; B[J*2]:=5; J:=3; B[J*2]:=1 END
```

just before executing it. It cannot of course be implemented efficiently by such a textual substitution, and we must devise an equivalent way of doing it. Note that the actual parameter corresponding to X *changes* whenever the value of J changes, so we cannot just evaluate the address of the actual parameter initially and use it; we must recompute it *every* time we reference the formal parameter within the procedure.

The usual way of implementing call by name parameters is to have a separate routine or procedure in the object code for each such parameter. The term *thunk* was coined by Ingerman(61a) for this routine and the term has stuck. When called, the thunk evaluates the actual parameter (if it is not a variable) and returns the *address* of the value. For each reference to a formal parameter in the body of the procedure, a call of this thunk appears, followed by a reference to the value using the address returned by the thunk.

We illustrate below the object code for the call (8.7.2). It should be mentioned that several other implicit parameters are necessary in order for thunks to work properly; these will be described in section 8.9.

```
      Jump to L
  A1: ┌───────────────────┐
      │thunk to evaluate  │
      │address of B[J*2]  │
      └───────────────────┘
  A2: ┌───────────────────┐
      │thunk to evaluate  │   Parameter list for the call at L
      │address of J       │
      └───────────────────┘   ┌─────────────────────────────┐
                              │RET(return address)          │
  L: call R with this list->  │A1 (address of first thunk)  │
  RET:                        │A2 (address of second thunk) │
                              └─────────────────────────────┘
```

The difference between a call by reference and a call by name is the following: the address of an actual parameter called by reference is evaluated only once, before the procedure is actually called, while for a call by name, the address is evaluated <u>each</u> time the formal parameter is referenced in the procedure body.

### Array Name as Actual Parameters

In this case both actual and formal parameters must be arrays to make sense. The address of the first array element (for languages which do not require dope vectors) or the address of the dope vector is passed to the procedure, and is used by the procedure to reference array elements.

### Procedure Names as Actual Parameters

The address passed is the address of the first instruction of the procedure appearing as the actual parameter. If this name is itself a formal parameter, then the address was passed to the calling procedure when <u>it</u> was called.

This is all the information needed for FORTRAN calls. More is needed for ALGOL and PL/I calls, but we defer the discussion to section 8.9 on ALGOL runtime storage administration.

### EXERCISES FOR 8.7

1. Write a procedure EXCHANGE(X,Y) in a high-level language to exchange the values of the actual parameters for X and Y (which must be variables). What type of parameters must X and Y be? Can you write such a procedure in ALGOL? Hint: Consider two calls EXCHANGE(A[I],I) and EXCHANGE(I,A[I]).

2. Consider the following ALGOL-like program:

```
BEGIN INTEGER I; INTEGER ARRAY B[1,2];
      PROCEDURE Q(X); INTEGER X;
      BEGIN I:=1; X:=X+2; B[I]:=10;
            I:=2; X:=X+2
      END;
   B[1]:=1; B[2]:=1; I:=1; Q(B[I])
END
```

Execute the program 5 times (and indicate what the resulting values in B[1] and B[2] are), considering the formal parameter X to be (1) called by reference, (2) called by VALUE, (3) called by VALUE RESULT, (4) called by RESULT, and (5) called by name. Hint: one of the calls results in an undefined value; in all others the results are different!

3. Execute the program in exercise 2, assuming that X is a PL/I type argument. Then change the procedure call from Q(B[I]) to Q((B[I])) and execute again. Do the final values in I, B[1], and B[2] differ?

## 8.8 STORAGE ADMINISTRATION FOR FORTRAN

FORTRAN does not allow nested subroutines, recursive subroutines or dynamic arrays. Since there are no nested subroutines, the only variables one can reference are those local to a routine (in its data area) and those in COMMON. A COMMON area is STATIC, and is allocated a fixed set of locations before runtime; therefore references to variables in COMMON can be absolute references to machine locations.

What about references to local variables? The lack of recursive subroutines means that each subroutine must be executed to completion before it may be called again. Therefore its data area can also be STATIC. Thus, _all_ references to FORTRAN variables may be to absolute machine locations.

Since dynamic array allocation is not allowed (all bounds given in a DIMENSION statement must be constants), no runtime storage administration is needed. Arrays can be allocated storage by the compiler in the fixed length data area.

This all implies that no real DISPLAYs are needed. Remember, DISPLAYs are necessary to keep track of the data areas which can be referenced at any point of the program. But we just saw that all references in FORTRAN are absolute.

Figure 8.4 illustrates a typical FORTRAN STATIC data area. The implicit parameters include the return address and any imposed by the machine design (registers, accumulators, etc). A subroutine call consists of the following operations:

1. evalute addresses of actual parameters and store them in the parameter list (in the calling subroutine's data area).
2. put the address of the parameter list in some agreed upon global location (e.g. a register).
3. put the return address in the list and jump.

Before executing its body, the subroutine must

1. move implicit parameters to its data area, and
2. move actual parameter addresses to its data area.

The procedure return consists of reloading the implicit parameters saved and jumping to the return address.

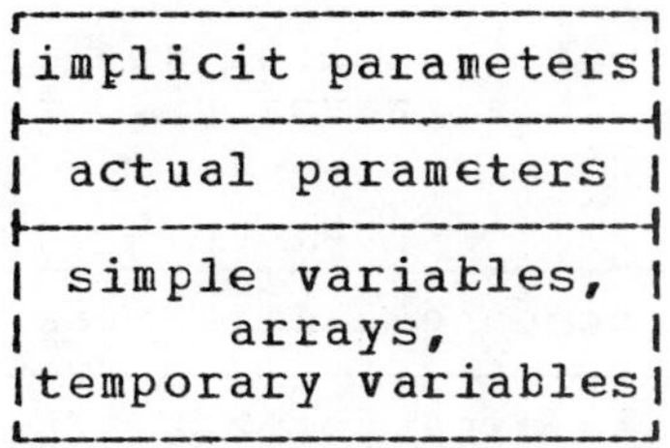


**FIGURE 8.4. Typical FORTRAN Subroutine Data Area.**

## 8.9 STORAGE ADMINISTRATION FOR ALGOL

ALGOL has a block and procedure structure which requires some runtime storage administration. However, it can be implemented by a fairly simple scheme. ALGOL does not allow pointer variables, which are one of the main causes of increased storage allocation complexity. Furthermore, the nested block and procedure structure allow us to use a simple mechanism for storage allocation, our old friend the stack.

Briefly, a large table of contiguous locations is used as a stack which is initially empty. One dynamic data area is associated with each execution of a procedure for its fixed-length variables and dope vectors, etc. (We consider the main program as a procedure without parameters called by the system.) When a procedure is invoked, it takes enough storage for its data area from the current top of the stack; when it returns to the point of call it "pops" the stack, freeing all the locations it used. Blocks, since they are nested within each other and within procedures, work the same way. Enter a block, get storage for the data area to contain the elements of each array from the top of the stack; leave a block, pop the locations used from the stack. Since the scheme is so simple, we won't actually need routines GETAREA and FREEAREA; the allocation and freeing can be done by a few instructions, without having to jump to a subroutine.

We do have to make sure that procedure linkages and global variable references work correctly; this is what we will discuss in this section. The particular method we describe is perhaps more complicated than others found in the literature. The reason is that we want to make block entries and exits as efficient as possible. The exercises at the end of the section outline other schemes.

To illustrate the stack concept as used here, suppose we have the program with structure of Figure 8.5. Storage is first allocated for the main program data area. Suppose the procedure call for C at label L1 is executed. The data area for C is then allocated, followed by the data area for array G. Following the procedure call of A at label L2 we allocate storage for the procedure A data area. This leaves us, at label L3, with the following:

```
|---------------------------|
| Procedure A data area     |  top of stack
|---------------------------|
| data area for array G     |
|---------------------------|
| Procedure C data area     |
|---------------------------|
| main program data area    |  bottom of stack
|---------------------------|
```

```
   BEGIN ...
     PROCEDURE A(X,Y);  PROCEDURE X; INTEGER Y;
        BEGIN  PROCEDURE B(Z);  PROCEDURE Z;
                  BEGIN  ARRAY F[1:10];
L4:                         Z(F[1]+Y);
                  END;
L3:            B(X);
        END;
     PROCEDURE C;
        BEGIN  ARRAY G[1:10];
               PROCEDURE D(W); INTEGER W;
                  BEGIN
L5:                     G[1] := W;
                  END;
L2:       A(D,1);
        END;
L1: C;
   END;
```

**FIGURE 8.5. Nested and Parallel Procedure Structure.**

In this section, we will cover the following points, in order:

(8.9.1)
1. Relation between the active DISPLAY and data area;
2. Format of procedure data areas;
3. Block entry, array declarations, and block exit;
4. Call of a procedure which is not a formal parameter;
5. Procedure initialization and exit;
6. Thunks and how to call them;
7. Call of a procedure which is a formal parameter;
8. Actual parameters which are procedure names;
9. Jumps.

### Relation Between the Active Display and Data Area

In an ALGOL implementation there is a dynamic data area for each execution of a procedure (we call the main program a procedure also). At any time, several procedures may be in the process of being executed, but only one will be actually <u>active</u>; the others will be waiting for it to finish and return. The DISPLAY and data area associated with the active procedure are also called <u>active</u>. If the active procedure has level of nesting i, then it can reference variables in procedures on levels 1,2,...,i-1 and in the main program, besides its own. The active DISPLAY will therefore have the form given in Figure 8.6.

| address of main program data area (level 0) |
|---|
| address of data area for procedure on level 1 |
| : |
| address of data area for procedure on level i |

**FIGURE 8.6. Active Display When in a Procedure on Level i.**

Where should the DISPLAYs themselves go? One often-used convention is to keep a separate stack for them. We will adopt a second alternative; since there is a DISPLAY associated with each data area, we put the DISPLAY in the first few locations of that data area. Thus, the address of the active DISPLAY is always the address of the active data area, and vice versa. We furthermore assume that a global location (e.g. an index register), called ACTIVEAREA, always contains the address of the active DISPLAY (and data area), for the procedure currently being executed.

All references to data from within the active procedure are made using ACTIVEAREA and the DISPLAY referenced by it.

### Procedure Data Areas

Each procedure data area has a fixed length known at compile-time. We give below a list of the data in each area, in order of appearance. Several parts of the list will not make any sense at this point, and we will discuss them at the proper time.

1. The DISPLAY for the procedure.
2. A location named STACKTOP. It contains the address of the top stack location just after this procedure data area has been allocated, and is thus the address of the last location in this data area.
3. Four implicit parameters to the procedure:
   a) The return address;
   b) The actual parameter DISPLAY address;
   c) The global DISPLAY address;
   d) The top stack location address at the point of call.
4. The actual parameters themselves (or their addresses).
5. For each block in the procedure:
   a) A location STACKTOP which will contain the address of the top of the stack while in the block;
   b) Locations for simple variables;
   c) Locations for dope vectors for arrays declared in the block;
   d) Locations for temporary results needed in the block.

The order of the locations for simple variables, dope vectors and temporary locations within a block is not important. The easiest way is to allocate in the order of the declarations within the block. Since the variables in parallel blocks cannot be referenced at the same time, parallel blocks can also use the same locations, but this is not necessary. Consider the procedure of Figure 8.7, with the blocks inside it numbered at the right. The data area for it is given below. The variables in block 2 share locations with those in block 3 and 4.

<table>
<tr><td colspan="2">DISPLAY (addresses of main program and A data area)</td></tr>
<tr><td colspan="2">A's STACKTOP location (address of last word in A's data area)</td></tr>
<tr><td colspan="2">implicit parameters</td></tr>
<tr><td colspan="2">actual parameters X and Y</td></tr>
<tr><td colspan="2">block 1 STACKTOP, variable Z, B's dope vector</td></tr>
<tr><td rowspan="2">block 2 STACKTOP,<br>variables D and E</td><td>block 3 STACKTOP, A's dope vector</td></tr>
<tr><td>block 4 STACKTOP, variable E</td></tr>
</table>

```
PROCEDURE A( X, Y);  INTEGER X, Y;
L1: BEGIN  REAL Z; ARRAY B[X:Y];                    ┐ 1
       L2: BEGIN REAL D,E;                      ┐ 2 |
       L3:  :                                   |   |
            END;                                ┘   |
                                                    |
       L4: BEGIN ARRAY A[1:X];                  ┐ 3 |
             L5: BEGIN REAL E;              ┐ 4 |   |
             L6:  :                         |   |   |
                  END;                      ┘   |   |
       L7: END;                                 ┘   |
L8: END;                                            ┘
```

**FIGURE 8.7. Block Structured ALGOL Program.**

**Addressing a Variable**

Suppose a reference to a variable or formal parameter occurs in a procedure on level i. If the reference is to a local variable or parameter declared in the procedure, its runtime address is

(offset in data area) + ACTIVEAREA

If the variable or parameter is declared in a surrounding procedure on level k, its address is

(offset in data area) + CONTENTS(ACTIVEAREA + k)

We can often use this level number k instead of the data area number in the description of each identifier. Procedures on the same level will have the same number, but they will never be processed at the same time by the compiler.

### Block Entry, Array Declarations, and Block Exit

Each block has a set of locations set aside for it, for simple variables, dope vectors and temporary locations used within the block. Storage for arrays must be allocated when the block is entered and freed when the block is left. The particular scheme in mind has been designed to minimize the work for block entry and exit. Indeed, block entry consists of two instructions, while block exit needs absolutely no instructions!

As mentioned earlier, storage for arrays will be allocated at the top of the runtime stack. We make the following rule: when a block is being executed, location STACKTOP for that block contains the address of the top stack location for that block. This means that

(8.9.2) The top of the runtime stack is always defined by the location STACKTOP of the active block -- the block currently being executed.

Recall that each procedure data area has a location STACKTOP which contains the top of the stack after the data area has been allocated. This can be considered to be a STACKTOP location for a fictitious block surrounding the procedure body.

When entering a block, in order to follow rule (8.9.2) we need to copy the STACKTOP location from the surrounding block (the fictitious block if entering the main block of the procedure) into the STACKTOP location of the block being entered. Block entrance is therefore very efficient.

The next step is to allocate storage to arrays declared in the block. For each array, the following happens:

1. Evaluate the lower and upper bounds;
2. Call the array allocation routine. Parameters:
   a) The lower and upper bounds;
   b) The address of the dope vector;
   c) The address of the STACKTOP location for the block.

The array allocation routine calculates and initializes all the information in the dope vector. It then pushes the correct number of locations onto the stack, using the third parameter to indicate the current top of the stack. Finally, it puts into this third parameter the new top stack location address.

One may well ask why a separate STACKTOP location is needed for each block. The reason comes out when one considers block exits. If just one global STACKTOP location were present, then every time a block exit occurred this location would have to be changed to pop the locations used for arrays declared in that block. This causes trouble with jumps across multiple block boundaries, and so forth. With the system we are using this is not necessary, because of (8.9.2); nothing need be done for a normal block exit.

Let us give an example of this block structure mechanism. Figure 8.8a shows the contents of the stack when procedure A of Figure 8.7 has been called and initialized, but before the actual execution has begun (at label L1). Figure 8.8b then indicates the stack contents after the main block is entered but before any array allocation. Both STACKTOPs point to the top of the stack. Next (Figure 8.8c) the array is allocated, and thus the STACKTOP location for block b1 is changed to point to the last location of the stack, which is the last location in array B. Note that the procedure STACKTOP remains where it was. When block 2 is entered (Figure 8.8d), the STACKTOP for block 1 is copied into the STACKTOP for block 2. No arrays are declared, so nothing else need be done.

Now let us leave block 2. We revert back to Figure 8.8c, since the variables in block 2 are no longer active. Note that no code is actually executed for this block exit. The values D, E, and b2 STACKTOP are still in the data area, but they won't be referenced anymore.

Upon entrance to block 3, we copy the STACKTOP location and allocate storage to array A, yielding Figure 8.8e. Three STACKTOPS are now valid, indicating the top of the stack in block 3 (the active one), in block 1, and in block 0 -- the procedure itself. Upon entrance to block 4 we again copy a STACKTOP, yielding Figure 8.8f. We then exit several blocks; leaving block 4 yields Figure 8.8e, leaving block 3 yields Figure 8.8c, and leaving block 1 yields 8.8a.

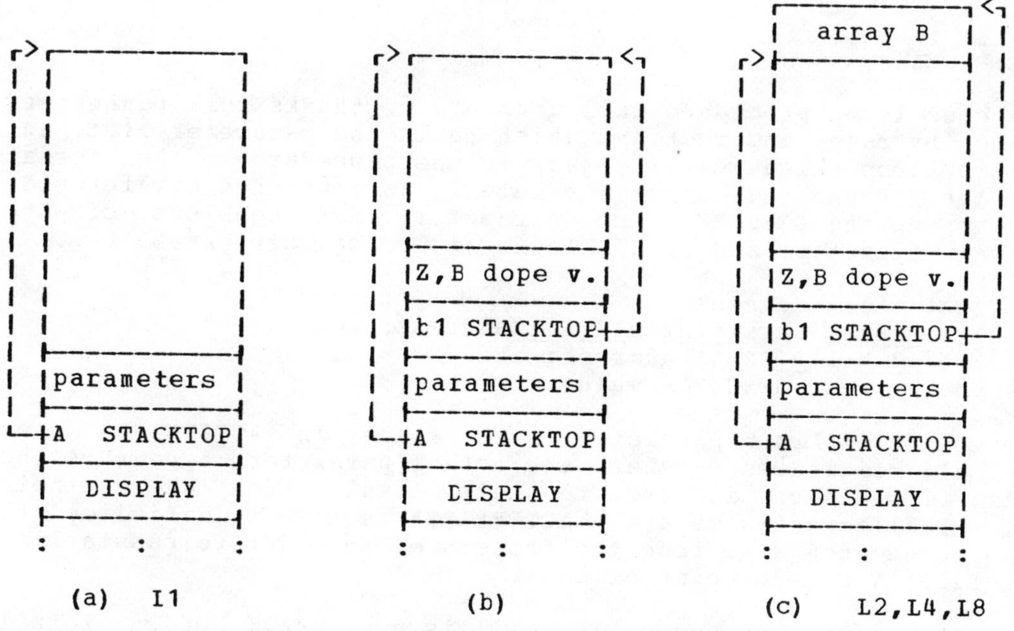


**FIGURE 8.8. Block Structure Mechanism.**

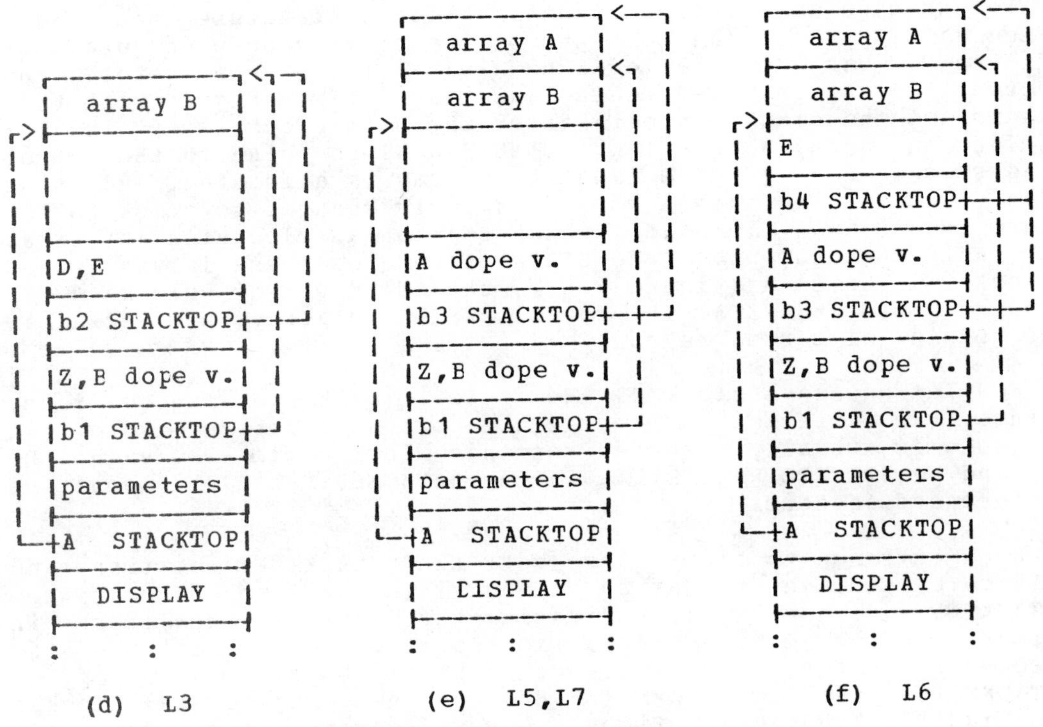


**FIGURE 8.8. Block Structure Mechanism (continued).**

### Procedure Call

The code for a procedure call consists of thunks for parameters called by name, instructions which build the parameter list, and instructions which actually jump to the procedure. The format of the thunks we leave for later. As mentioned earlier when discussing the DISPLAY, the parameter list consists of the actual parameters and the following four implicit parameters:

1. The return address;
2. The <u>actual parameter DISPLAY</u> address;
3. The <u>global DISPLAY</u> address; and
4. The current STACKTOP value.

The second implicit parameter is the value in ACTIVEAREA when the call originates -- where the actual parameters appear in the call. It is saved and used to help thunks know where their referencable variables are. ACTIVEAREA is also reinitialized to this value upon exit from the procedure, in order to reestablish the DISPLAY at the point of call.

At this point, we assume the call is not a call of a formal parameter procedure. With this restriction, the second and third parameters are the same. The third parameter, the global DISPLAY address, is used in establishing the DISPLAY for the called procedure, which we now explain.

Suppose we call a procedure A from a procedure B (or the main program). Then two cases arise. First of all, procedure A may be declared inside procedure B (Figure 8.9a). Suppose that B is on level i. Then procedure A is on level i+1. It can reference any variable which is global to B and any variable declared in a block of B which surrounds the declaration of A. Thus, the first i+1 locations of the DISPLAY for the procedure A are the same as those for procedure B. In building A's DISPLAY, A need therefore only copy these i+1 locations beginning at the address given by this third parameter, the global DISPLAY address.

In the second case (Figure 8.9b), A is declared outside B but it must be referencable from B; hence A is declared in a surrounding block. If A has level i+1, then it and B can both reference variables in the procedures on level 0,1,...,i. As in the first case, A need only copy the first i+1 locations beginning at the global DISPLAY address.

```
PROCEDURE B;
  BEGIN PROCEDURE A;
          BEGIN ... END;
L1: A;
  END;
```

(a)

```
PROCEDURE A;
  BEGIN ... END;
PROCEDURE B;
  BEGIN ... L1: A; ... END;
    :
```

(b)

**FIGURE 8.9. Procedure B Calling Procedure A.**

The fourth implicit parameter, the current STACKTOP value, is the address of the currently last location in the runtime stack. This is used by the called procedure in order to know where it should get its storage. Assuming the call does not originate in a thunk, this is the value in the STACKTOP location for the block in which the call occurs.

### Procedure Initialization and Exit

When a procedure is called, it must get storage for its data area, initialize its DISPLAY, and move implicit and actual parameters into its data area. More explicitly, the steps for a procedure with level of nesting i+1 are:

1. Push the locations for the procedure's data area onto the stack (the fourth implicit parameter indicates the current stack top). Store the address of the data area into location i+1 of the data area (into the DISPLAY) and into

the global location ACTIVEAREA. Store the address of the new stack top into STACKTOP for the procedure.

2. Move the four implicit parameters into this data area.
3. Copy the first i+1 addresses from the address specified by the third implicit parameter into locations 0,1,...,i of this new data area.
4. Move the actual parameters, as follows:
   a) Array names: copy the dope vector;
   b) Procedure names: copy the actual parameter address (how it is used will be explained later);
   c) Call by name parameters: copy the address of the thunk;
   d) Call by VALUE parameters: move the value at the actual parameter address into the new data area.

A procedure exit must restore the environment as it was at the calling point, and then return. (In addition, if the procedure is a function, the value of the function must be communicated through a register. The environment restoration is easy; just put into the global location ACTIVEAREA the second implicit parameter to the procedure. Note again that one need not do anything to indicate where the top of the stack is. You might think this necessary since the procedure data area is no longer used, but the STACKTOP location defining the top of the stack is (because of rule (8.9.2)) defined by the currently active block, and this is being changed.

### Thunks and How to Call Them

As described in section 8.7, a thunk is a routine which calculates and returns the address of an actual parameter corresponding to a formal parameter called by name. Since the actual parameter is an expression, it contains no declaration or blocks. Therefore it can use locations in the block in which the call appears for its temporary results. There are special considerations one must give to function calls appearing within a thunk (within an actual parameter expression), and we will discuss them here. But first let us discuss a call of a thunk and the thunk itself.

For each reference to a formal parameter X called by name, a call of the thunk is generated, with the following parameter list:

1. The return address;
2. The current value in ACTIVEAREA;
3. The value of the second implicit parameter of the procedure of which X is a formal parameter
4. The current address of the top stack element.

As you can see, this looks much like a call of a procedure without parameters. The second parameter is not really used by the thunk; it is just saved and then restored upon return. The third parameter is used by the thunk to initialize its environment. If you glance at the parameter list for a normal procedure call, you will note that this third parameter is the address of the DISPLAY of the procedure in which the call originated. The thunk uses the fourth parameter as an implicit parameter to any function it calls, in order to tell that function where the top of the stack is.

The thunk itself does the following:

1. Put parameter 3 into ACTIVEAREA;
2. Save all four parameters in temporary locations (in the data area referred to by ACTIVEAREA);
3. Calculate the address of the actual parameter (this is the body of the thunk).
4. Put the second implicit parameter of the call to the thunk into ACTIVEAREA;
5. Put the address calculated in step 3 into a special register and jump to the return address.

The address in the special register is then used by the procedure which called the thunk to reference the actual parameter.

Function calls within a thunk are executed as usual, except for the fourth implicit parameter. This is supposed to be the address of the current top stack location and, if not in a thunk, is the value in the STACKTOP location of the block in which the function call occurs. When the function call appears in a thunk, however, the current top stack location is given by the STACKTOP location of the block in which the call of the thunk appears. This is the fourth implicit parameter to the thunk.

#### Procedure Names as Actual Parameters

These present problems only for the strangest cases which rarely occur in real-life programs. Nevertheless one must still be able to handle them. Consider the program of Figure 8.5 (page 194). It consists of two parallel sets of nested procedures. Let us execute it carefully. First, at label L1, C is called. Inside C, at label L2, procedure A is called, with procedure D as an actual parameter. Procedure A now calls B (at L3), with its formal parameter X, a procedure, as the actual parameter. Finally, at label L4, the formal parameter Z is called. Since B's formal parameter Z is X which in turn is D, procedure D is invoked. Now D needs to know two things.

1. The address of the DISPLAY active at label L4, so that it can give it to the thunk for the actual parameter of the call at L4. We call this the _actual parameter DISPLAY_ address.
2. The address of the DISPLAY of the procedure where D was referenced, which is C, so that D can reference global variables. We call this the _global DISPLAY_ address.

These are the second and third parameters to D, respectively. In the case of a normal procedure call, both of these are the same -- the value in ACTIVEAREA at the point of call.

When a procedure name occurs as an actual parameter, the address passed in the parameter list is the address of two locations containing the following:

| address of the procedure |
|---|
| ACTIVEAREA at the point of call |

The value in the second location is used as the third implicit parameter, the global DISPLAY address, of a call to the corresponding formal parameter procedure. An actual parameter which itself is a formal parameter procedure, is represented by the actual parameter address passed to <u>it</u>.

To illustrate this, we give below the parameter lists for the calls at L1, L2, L3, and L4 of the program of Figure 8.5 (page 194). Note that at L2, the address DAC describes the actual parameter D. This address is copied into the list for the call at L3. It is used by procedure B at the call at L4 to give the global DISPLAY address for that call.

```
L1: procedure called is C        L2: procedure called is A
1.  return address               1.  return address
2.  main data area address       2.  C data area address
3.  main data area address       3.  C data area address
4.  STACKTOP at the call         4.  STACKTOP at the call
                                 5.  address DAC (see below)
                                 6.  address of thunk for "1"

L3: procedure called is B        L4: procedure called is Z (D)
1.  return address               1.  return address
2.  A data area address          2.  B data area address
3.  A data area address          3.  C data area address
4.  STACKTOP at the call         4.  STACKTOP at the call
5.  address DAC (see below)      5.  address of thunk for "F[1]+Y"
```

DAC

| address of procedure D |
|---|
| C data area address |

### Jumps

A jump GOTO L which doesn't jump out of a procedure requires nothing more than the branch instruction. Suppose, however, that L appears in a surrounding procedure on level i. Then the address of the data area for that procedure must be put into ACTIVEAREA before the branch. Since this address is in the active DISPLAY, this can be accomplished by

```
ACTIVEAREA := CONTENTS(ACTIVEAREA+i)
```

Suppose that L is a formal parameter. The corresponding address in the parameter list is the address of a thunk, and this thunk is called, as usual. A thunk for an actual parameter which is a label (or any designational expression) does not return; instead, after initialization, it jumps to the label.

Note again, that with this particular scheme we need never worry about releasing storage when leaving a procedure or block; the top of the stack is always given by the STACKTOP location in the active block.

### EXERCISES FOR 8.9

1. Discuss the possibility of treating each actual parameter called by name as a function (POINTER procedure) without parameters, declared in the block in which the call occurs. It returns the address of the actual parameter value. The actual and formal parameters are then procedure names, and a reference in the procedure body to the formal parameter is a function call. How does this approach compare with ours? Are all implicit parameters still needed?

2. Suppose that a more general storage allocation scheme is used. GETAREA(ADDRESS,SIZE) must be called to allocate a data area of size SIZE, and FREEAREA(ADDRESS,SIZE) must be called to release the data area of size SIZE beginning at location ADDRESS. No STACKTOP locations are needed, because GETAREA and FREEAREA do all the necessary bookkeeping; hence only three implicit procedure parameters are needed. Describe in detail block entry, block exit, procedure entry, procedure exit, and jumps. Be careful with block exit, procedure exit and expecially jumps across block and/or procedure boundaries; it may be necessary to release several data areas.

3. Give some restrictions on the order in which data areas for arrays and procedures may be released (in exercise 2) so that GETAREA and FREEAREA may still use a stack mechanism for storage allocation.

4. Design another ALGOL storage administration scheme which allocates one data area to an execution of each <u>block</u> and procedure. The DISPLAY for each data area must now hold the addresses of surrounding block and procedure data areas.

5. Design a storage administration scheme which uses a single GLOBAL DISPLAY which, at all times, contains the addresss of referencable data areas. (Decide yourself whether data areas are assigned only to procedures, or to both blocks and procedures; each is okay). Care must be taken when calling procedures; it may be necessary to save part of the global DISPLAY in the procedure data area, to be restored upon return. Calls of thunks are also more trouble.

## 8.10 DYNAMIC STORAGE ALLOCATION

As we have seen, at runtime some languages require a dynamic storage allocation scheme, where blocks of core are reserved, used, and then released for further use. In the ALGOL implementation described in section 8.9, the allocation mechanism was a single stack. In other applications a stack cannot be used because allocation and releasing of storage is not performed in any standard or predetermined order. We have seen two examples in this chapter: allocation of storage to strings in XPL (section 8.5) and allocation of storage to structures in ALGOL W (section 8.6). Another example is PL/I, where the programmer himself can determine through the use of ALLOCATE and FREE statements when storage should be reserved and released.

There are two main methods for general storage allocation. In both, a GETAREA(ADDRESS,SIZE) routine of some kind is called to allocate an area of SIZE locations; the routine stores into ADDRESS the address of the area. In the first method, storage must be explicitly released by calling a routine FREEAREA (ADDRESS,SIZE). In the second method, no storage is explicitly released. Instead, when GETAREA can find no area of the size needed, it calls a FREEGARBAGE routine to find those areas of core which are not being used by the program and return them to the system. In addition, it may <u>compact</u> the used areas -- move them together, so that the free locations are again all in one block.

Let us begin by describing one way of implementing the first method.

### The Boundary Tag Method of Storage Allocation

Storage allocation proceeds as follows. When a program begins execution, one large block of locations is used as free storage. As the program executes, GETAREA may be called several times. Each time it allocates the neccessary locations from the beginning of the free storage block, leaving it in the following form:

```
|USED|USED| ...|USED|                    FREE                       |
```

Note that the USED areas need not be the same size. At some point, FREEAREA will be called to free one of the used areas. In general, it will not be the last one allocated. After several calls on GETAREA and FREEAREA, the block might look like

```
|USED| ...|USED|FREE|USED| ...|USED|FREE|FREE|USED| FREE |
```

where, again, not all areas are the same size. The system must keep track of all the free areas, so that they can be used again. Moreover, adjacent free areas should be collapsed into one free area, so that storage does not get fragmented into areas too small to use. In the above diagram, two free areas could be collapsed.

The particular method we describe is Knuth's(68) boundary tag method. It requires two locations reserved for system use at the boundaries of each area (one in the beginning and one at the end). This is a small price to pay, since the situations in which the method would be used would require rather large areas, like procedure data areas and storage for arrays. The advantage of this technique is that essentially a fixed amount of time is neccessary to free an area and to collapse it with adjacent free areas, if possible. In other methods, a list of some sort must be searched to perform this.

The format of each used and free area is given below. The first word contains a TAG field which indicates whether the area is free or not, while the SIZE field gives the number of words in the area. Free areas are linked together in a doubly linked list. The FLINK (Forward link) field points to the next area on the list, while the BLINK (Backward link) field points to the previous one.

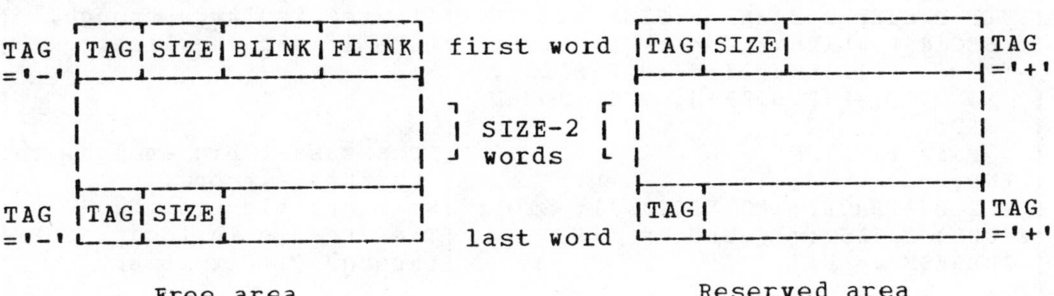


Free area

Reserved area

In addition, a single variable FREE has the form

```
        TAG SIZE BLINK                      FLINK
       ┌───┬────┬───────────────────────┬─────────────────────────┐
  FREE | + | 0  |to last area in list   |to first area in list    |
       └───┴────┴───────────────────────┴─────────────────────────┘
```

The BLINK field of the first area on the list points at location FREE, as does the FLINK field of the last area. Finally, we assume that the block of storage used for allocation is preceded and followed by a word containing '+' in its TAG field, to indicate it is reserved. Such a convention simplifies the process of collapsing adjacent areas.

We are now ready to give the GETAREA routine. The routine uses the "first-fit" method; it sequences through the list of free areas and chooses the first one that is large enough. While a "best-fit" method would appear at first sight to be better, this is not always so (see Knuth(68)), and in addition would clearly take more time. In the routine, if SIZE words are needed, and a block of up to SIZE+10 words is discovered, it is not broken up into two areas, with one being left on the free list. This might cause the system to become fragmented into many very small, unusable areas. The number 10 was picked rather arbitrarily.

```
GETAREA(ADDRESS,SIZE);
┌────────────────────────────────────────────────────────────────────┐
|BEGIN POINTER P,Q,Q1; INTEGER S,S1;|P points to current area.      |
| P := FREE.FLINK;                  |S is minimum size needed.      |
| S := SIZE+2; S1 := SIZE+10;       |Any area less than S1 is       |
|                                   |not split into two areas.      |
| WHILE P ≠ ADDRESS(FREE) DO        |Look at areas, in order.       |
| BEGIN IF P.SIZE ≥ S1 THEN         |                               |
|  BEGIN S1 := P.SIZE-S; Q := P+S;  |Split a large area into        |
|   Q1 := Q+S1-1;                   |two, with sizes S and S1.      |
|   CONTENTS(Q) := CONTENTS(P);     |Move the whole word at P       |
|   Q.SIZE:=Q1.SIZE:=S1; Q.TAG:='-';|to word pointed at by Q.       |
|   P.FLINK.BLINK:=P.BLINK.FLINK:=Q;|Put upper area in list.        |
|   Q:=Q-1; P.SIZE := S; GOTO FOUND;|Fix the SIZE of the lower      |
|  END;                             |area and jump out.             |
|  IF P.SIZE ≥ S AND P.SIZE ≤S1 THEN|If area is large enough,       |
|  BEGIN P.BLINK.FLINK := P.FLINK;  |take it off the list.          |
|        P.FLINK.BLINK := P.BLINK;  |                               |
|        Q:=P+P.SIZE-1; GOTO FOUND  |                               |
|  END;                             |                               |
|   P := P.FLINK                    |Area wasn't big enough, so     |
| END;                              |try the next one.              |
| WRITE('ERROR.  NO BLOCK.'); STOP; |No block big enough.           |
|FOUND: P.TAG := Q.TAG := '+';      |The area is in location P      |
| ADDRESS := P+1;                   |through Q. Fix it up.          |
|END                                |                               |
└────────────────────────────────────────────────────────────────────┘
```

The FREEAREA routine frees an area and collapses it, if possible, with adjacent free areas. Note that the parameter SIZE is not used with this particular method, since the needed information resides in the area.

```
 PROCEDURE FREEAREA(ADDRESS,SIZE)
r-------------------------------------------------------------------1
|BEGIN POINTER L,M,U,Q;                |Set up pointer M to this   |
| M:=ADDRESS-1; U:=M+M.SIZE; L:=M-1;|area, U to the upper, and |
|                                      |L to end of lower area.    |
| IF U.TAG = '-' THEN                  |If upper area is free,     |
|  BEGIN M.SIZE := M.SIZE+U.SIZE;      |then append it to middle   |
|        U.BLINK.FLINK := U.FLINK;     |area and delete it from    |
|        U.FLINK.BLINK := U.BLINK;     |the list.                  |
|  END;                                |                           |
| Q := M+M.SIZE-1;                     |Q points to the end of M.  |
| IF L.TAG = '-' THEN                  |If the lower area is free,|
|  BEGIN L := M-L.SIZE;                |then just add this area to|
|        L.SIZE := L.SIZE+M.SIZE;      |it;                        |
|        Q.SIZE :=L.SIZE; Q.TAG:='-'|                           |
|  END                                 |                           |
| ELSE BEGIN Q.SIZE := M.SIZE;         |otherwise, add the area to|
|            M.TAG := Q.TAG := '-';    |the beginning of the free  |
|            M.FLINK := FREE.FLINK;    |list.                      |
|            M.BLINK:=ADDRESS(FREE);|                           |
|            FREE.FLINK.BLINK := M;    |                           |
|            FREE.FLINK := M           |                           |
|END   END                             |                           |
L-------------------------------------------------------------------J
```

### Garbage Collection

In the second method of storage allocation, when GETAREA can not find a suitable area, it calls a FREEGARBAGE routine, whose purpose is to find those areas not being used and put them on some sort of a free area list. In order to do this, FREEAREA must be able to determine the following:

1. The location of every declared pointer variable;
2. Exactly what each of the pointers point at -- the length of the value, and whether it contains any pointers;
3. For each pointer in a value referred to by another pointer, the length and location of pointers in it.

As one might imagine, this is a rather tall order, and it requires a disciplined use of pointers. For this reason, garbage collection is usually used where the system has some assurance that pointers are used correctly and where the number of different formats for values is small. LISP is a good example of such a system. Another is the XPL string manipulation scheme, which has the advantage that values referenced by string pointers are only strings of characters; so that a value pointed at never contains another pointer.

A further problem is the difficulty of determining exactly which areas are free at any stage. An illustration in ALGOL W will show this nicely. Suppose we have the following:

```
RECORD LISTOFREAL( REAL A; POINTER NEXT);
P := LISTOFREAL( 2.0, LISTOFREAL( 3.0, 0));
```

To execute the last statement, space is first allocated to a LISTOFREAL value and this space is initialized to (3.0,0). Next, space is allocated to a second LISTOFREAL value, which is initialized with the value (2.0,Q) where Q is a pointer to the first value (3.0,0). Suppose now, that space doesn't exist for the second value. Then FREEGARBAGE is called. Note, however, that the address Q has never been stored in a pointer variable, so that the locations containing (3.0,0) appear to be unused!

This is not to say that such situations cannot be corrected, but they do crop up unexpectedly if one is not careful.

Garbage collection usually proceeds in two phases. The first phase marks all used values in some manner. The usual method is to have an extra bit in each value solely for marking, but this is rather annoying in some cases. An alternative method is to collect all the mark bits in a table, with a suitable correspondence between locations and mark bits. However, this requires a special table for the mark bits, and presumably very little free storage exists when the garbage collector is called!

In the second phase, we sequence through storage, putting unmarked areas on a list of free areas and, at the same time turning off all marked bits. The latter step is done so that the next time the garbage collector is called, they are initialized correctly.

A third phase is sometimes used to compact the areas, so that all free locations form one large block. This requires the garbage collection routine to change pointer values when the data is moved.

The reader is referred to chapter 2 of Knuth(68) for actual garbage collection algorithms.

#### Two-Level Allocation Systems

Some systems have two levels of allocation; large blocks of core are reserved and freed using one method, while each large block may be subdivided using a second method. ALGOL W uses this technique. Each different type of structure is assigned a unique integer, and one template for each type is kept in a table. This template contains the number of locations used by a value and the locations of any pointers in the value. An actual structured value then contains one extra byte (on the IBM 360); seven of the bits give the integer for the structure type, while the last bit is used for garbage collection marking.

Each different structured type is allocated another large block of core whenever necessary. In it are kept all values with that structure type, with free values being linked together in a free list. This allows the actual allocation of storage to a value to be performed efficiently, by taking the next free value on the free list for that type. This is so easy because all the free areas on a list have the same number of locations.

If no free areas exist on the list for a structured type, the system asks for another large block. If no more large blocks exist, garbage collection is performed, with unused values being returned to the free list for each type, and empty large blocks being returned to the main storage allocation routine.

## 9.11 HISTORICAL REFERENCES

Two short surveys of ways for referencing and storing arrays are Hellerman(62) and Gower(62). Actually, these methods have been independently discovered and rediscovered by many programmers, and it is hard to attribute them to any one person. Knuth(68) presents several other methods for storing arrays, most notably for triangular and sparse matrices.

For discussions of implementations of various types of structures, see Wirth and Hoare(66); Standish(68); Bauer, Becker and Graham(68); and the IBM PL/I programming logic manual. Hoare(68) gives a more complete discussion of structures and their implementation.

The January 1961 issue of CACM is worth reading for its historical value with respect to ALGOL implementation, although many of the techniques described are outmoded. Randell and Russell(64) describe the ALGOL implementation technique in which one data area is allocated to each execution of a block, with a global DISPLAY being used. The particular techniques described in detail in section 8.9 were used in the ALCOR ILLINOIS 7090 compiler (see Gries, Paul, and Wiehle(65)).

As mentioned several times, chapter 2 of Knuth(68) contains an excellent description of storage allocation techniques, with many more appearing as exercises. He also presents an analysis of the efficiency of several methods. Ross(67b) discusses the AED free storage package, a good example of a two-level storage allocation scheme in a general system.

# Chapter 9.
# Organizing Symbol Tables

Checking for semantic correctness and generating code requires knowledge of the attributes of the identifiers used in the source program. These attributes are found in declarations and in the way the identifiers are used in the program, and are collected and stored in a <u>symbol</u> <u>table</u> or <u>identifier</u> <u>list</u>. This chapter discusses ways of organizing, building, and searching symbol tables. While we are interested in the basic problem of general table organization, we direct our attention mainly to our specific problem of symbol tables.

## 9.1 INTRODUCTION TO TABLE ORGANIZATION

Tables of all types have the general form

```
                    Argument   Value
                  ┌───────────┬────────┐
         entry 1  │           │        │
                  ├───────────┼────────┤
         entry 2  │           │        │
                  ├───────────┼────────┤
                  │           │        │
                  :───────────:────────:
         entry N  │           │        │
                  └───────────┴────────┘
```

where the left side is a list of arguments and the right side the corresponding values. Each entry usually occupies more than one word, or location, in a computer. If an entry occupies k words and space is required for N entries, then k*N words of storage are needed. There are two ways of implementing this:

1. Put each entry into k consecutive words and have a table with k*N words.
2. Have k tables, say T1, T2,..., Tk, each with N words. The total ith entry is then found in the words T1[i],...,Tk[i].

The only difference between these two methods is one of programming convenience.

In our particular case the arguments of the table are symbols or identifiers and the values their attributes. Since the number of characters in identifiers is variable, one often stores a pointer to the identifier into the argument instead of the identifier itself. This keeps the size of the argument fixed. The identifiers are then stored in a special string list. The number of characters in each identifier can be stored as part of the argument or in the identifier list just before the identifier. Figure 9.1 illustrates these two different techniques with a table containing entries for the identifiers I, MAX, and J.

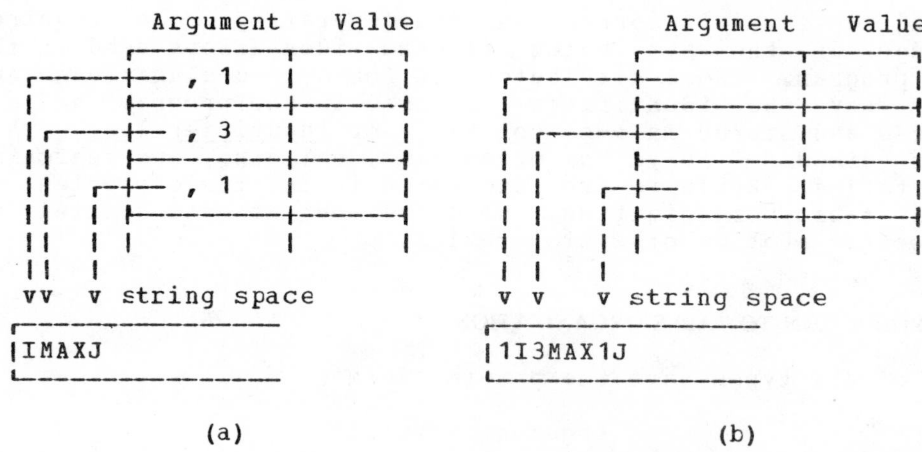


**FIGURE 9.1. Two Ways of Storing Arguments.**

When a compiler begins translating a source program, the symbol table is empty or contains just a few entries for reserved words and the standard functions. As compilation progresses, an entry is added only once for each new identifier, but the table is searched once for <u>every</u> occurrence of an identifier. Since much of compile time is spent in this process it is important that we investigate table organizations which provide for efficient searching.

We will want to compare different methods with respect to the search time. We will do this in terms of the expected number E of comparisons of arguments necessary in order to find a particular symbol. This expected number often depends on the <u>load factor lf</u> of the table at any point -- the current number of entries n divided by the maximum number N of entries possible

$$lf = n/N.$$

We will give equations for the expected number of comparisons but will not derive them -- the actual analysis can be found in the literature referenced in section 9.6.

### 9.2 UNSORTED AND SORTED TABLES

The easiest way to organize a table is to add entries for arguments in the order in which they arrive, without any attempt at ordering. A search requires a comparison with each entry of the table until a match is found. For a table containing n entries, on the average n/2 comparisons would be performed. If n is large (20 or more), this is inefficient.

Searching can be accomplished more efficiently if the table entries are sorted according to some natural ordering of the arguments. In our case where the arguments are strings of characters, the most natural is the ordering induced by the internal representation of the strings of characters. This is usually the same as the alphabetic ordering. Thus the strings A, AB, ABC, AC, BB would be in ascending order. An effective method of searching an ordered list of n entries is the so-called <u>binary</u> <u>search</u> or <u>logarithmic</u> <u>search</u> method. The symbol S to be found is compared with the argument of the middle entry (n+1)/2. If this entry is not the desired one, we have only to look either in the block of entries numbered 1 to (n+1)/2-1 <u>or</u> in the block of entries (n+1)/2+1 to n, depending upon whether S was less than or greater than the compared entry. We then iterate the process using the smaller block. Since at each stage the number of entries which may contain S is cut in half, the maximum number of comparisons is 1 + log(base 2) n.

If n = 2 we need at most 2 comparisons; if n = 4, 3; if n = 8, 4. If n = 128, the binary search method requires at most 8 comparisons while the unsorted method requires <u>on</u> <u>the</u> <u>average</u> 64 comparisons. A binary search program follows.

```
PROCEDURE binsearch(T,n,ARG,k);       |Look in array T for a
 STRING ARRAY T; STRING ARG;          |string equal to ARG. If
 INTEGER n,k;                         |found, put index of entry
BEGIN INTEGER i, j;                   |in k; otherwise put 0. n>0.
 i := 1; j := n;                      |First block is whole array.
LOOP: k := (i+j)//2;                  |k points to middle entry of
 IF ARG ≠ T[k] THEN                   |block. See if it's entry k.
  BEGIN IF ARG < T[k]                 |See whether in upper or
        THEN j:=k-1 ELSE i:=k+1;      |lower half. Then check to
        IF j ≥ i THEN GOTO LOOP;      |make sure there is a block.
        k :=0;                        |No more block to try, so
  END                                 |argument isn't in.
END                                   |
```

To use the binary search method the entries must be sorted. One way of doing this is the sort-by-insertion method. This is used because the table is searched often before it is completed and must therefore be sorted at all stages. In this method an entry for a symbol S is inserted as follows.

1. Use the procedure binsearch to find a k such that Sk < S < S[k+1].
2. Move entry n to position n+1; entry n-1 to position n, ..., entry k+1 to position k+2.
3. Put S into entry k+1 (which was vacated by step 2).

If the table will be completely full before any searching is to be performed, then the sorting can wait until all the entries have been collected. We will not discuss sorting here; references can be found in section 9.6.

### 9.3 Hash Addressing

This is a method for converting symbols to indexes of entries in the table (the entries are numbered 0,1,2,...,N-1 where the table has N entries). The index is obtained by "hashing" the symbol -- by performing some simple arithmetic or logical operation on the symbol (and possibly its length). One simple hash function is the internal representation of the first character of the symbol. Thus, if the binary representation of A is 11000001, the symbol ABE hashes to 11000001 (C1 in hexadecimal). The first entry we look at in searching for one with argument ABE is entry 11000001. Figure 9.2 illustrates this for identifiers ABE, B and I.

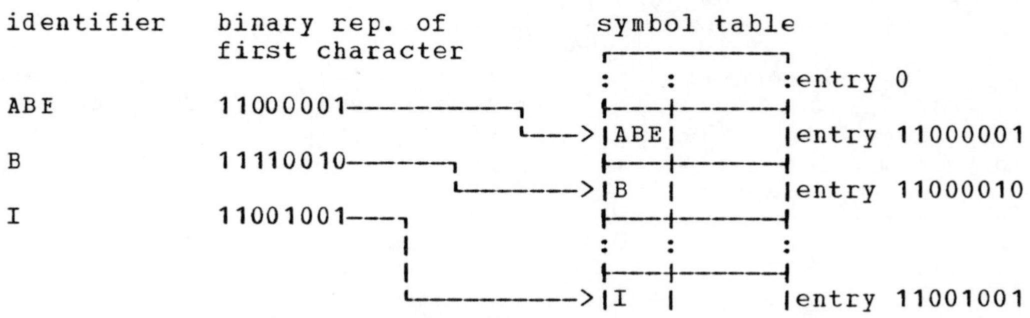


**FIGURE 9.2. Hash Addressing.**

As long as two symbols do not hash to the same index the cost of a search is just the cost of doing the hashing. Thus we have a tremendous saving over the time for searching an unordered table of n items (on the average, n/2 comparisons) or even over the time for searching an ordered table. Trouble occurs, however, if two symbols hash to the same index. This is called a <u>collision</u>. Obviously only one symbol can be placed at that entry, so we must find another spot for the second. A good hash function spreads the calculated addresses uniformly across the available addresses so that collisions do not occur too often. The hash function described above is obviously bad, since all identifiers beginning with same letter hash to the same address. We shall look at different hash functions in a moment; first let us discuss two methods of solving the collision problem -- <u>rehashing</u> and <u>chaining</u>.

We assume that the table entries are all one word long. The hash function h therefore creates integers 0,1,2,...,N-1 for a table with N entries. If the table entries are k words long, we need only multiply the hashed value h by k in order to get the correct number to add to the base address of the table.

### 9.3.1 Rehashing

Suppose we hash a symbol S and find that a different symbol already occupies the entry h. A collision has occurred. We then compare S against an entry h+p1 (modulo the table size N) for some integer p1. If a collision occurs again we compare with an entry h+p2 (modulo N) for some integer p2. This continues until some entry h+pi (modulo N) is empty, contains S, or is again entry h (pi = 0). In the latter case we stop the program because the table is full.

Thus, if i collisions have occurred, comparison i+1 will be at the entry hi = h+pi (modulo N). The values pi should be chosen so that the expected number E of comparisons is low and so that as many entries as possible are covered. In the ideal case, the pi should cover the range of integers 0,1,...,N-1. We will discuss four possible methods of defining the pi.

Rehashing is usually asssociated with the term <u>scatter storage</u>, since the filled entries are scattered throughout the table. Note that all table entries must be initialized with some value which cannot appear as a symbol, in order to distinguish empty entries from filled entries. Also, the table must initially allow for the maximum number of entries -- there is no easy way to allow the table to expand when the initial part gets full without recomputing the hash addresses of all symbols entered and moving them to the corresponding new entries.

#### Linear Rehash

The oldest known method of rehashing (and probably the least efficient) is to take p1 = 1, p2 = 2, p3 = 3, and so on. Thus succeeding entries are compared. Suppose for example, that the symbols S1 and S2 were hashed and entered at entries 2 and 4 respectively (Figure 9.3a).

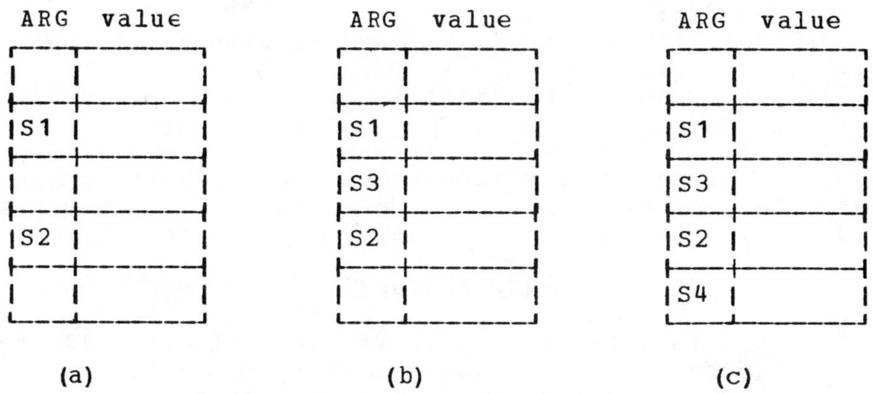


**FIGURE 9.3. Linear Rehash Illustration.**

Suppose now that symbol S3 also hashes to entry 2. Because of the collision it will be stored in entry 3 (Figure 9.3b). Finally, suppose the next symbol S4 also hashes to entry 2. There will be three collisions -- with S1, S3 and S2 in that order -- before S4 is finally stored at the 5th entry (Figure 9.3c).

The reason for the poor efficiency with this method is fairly clear with this example; after a few collisions have been resolved in this way, the entries tend to cluster together, giving long chains of filled entries. An approximation to the average number E of comparisons necessary to search for an item is

$$E = (1 - lf/2)(1-lf)$$

where lf is the load factor. Thus, if the table is 10 percent full we would expect 1.06 comparisons; if half full, 1.5 comparisons; and if 90 percent full, 5.5 comparisons. Note that E does not depend on how big the table is, but only on how full it is.

While we can find better values p1, p2, ... this method is still much faster than the binary tree search. Suppose a table of 1024 entries is half-filled. Thus 512 entries are filled. In the binary tree search we expect 9 to 10 comparisons while here we expect only 1.5. The search time for sorted or unsorted tables depends not on the maximum size of the table, but on the current number of entries.

### Random Rehash

This method eliminates the clustering problem in linear rehashing by picking the integers pi in a pseudorandom fashion. The following method works well when the table size is a power of two (N = 2**k for some k) (see Morris):

1. Initialize an integer R to 1 when the routine is called.
2. To calculate each pi, do the following:
   a) Set R = R*5;
   b) Mask out all but the low-order k+2 bits of R and place the result in R;
   c) Take the value in R, shift it right 2 bits, and call the result pi.

The important property of this method which prevents clustering is that the numbers p[i+k]-pi are all different. A good approximation to the expected number of comparisons E is

$$E = -(1/lf)\ \log(1-lf)$$

where lf is the load factor. Thus if the table is 10 percent full one expects 1.05 comparisons; if half full, 1.39 comparisons, and if 90 percent full 2.56 comparisons.

### Add-the-Hash Rehash

Take pi = ih, where h is the original hash index. Thus we try at entries h, 2h, 3h, 4h, ..., (all modulo the table size). This works well if the table size N is a prime number, since all sequences cover the whole range 1,...,N-1 of indices possible. The new hash index is very simple to compute. However, we must take as h's the integers 1,2,3,...,N-1 instead of 0,1,...,N-1 so that h is never 0.

### Quadratic Rehash

This particular method uses pi = $ai^2$ + bi + c for some values a, b and c. Any values for a, b and c may be used. The main problem, however, is to make sure that enough table entries are covered by the pi. For example, if p1 = 5, p2 = 10, p3 = 5, p4 = 10, p5 = 5, p6 = 10, ..., then we can check at most three entries -- h, h+5 and h+10.

When the table size is a power of 2, it turns out that the number of entries is too few. When the table size is a prime, however, a quadratic search covers exactly half the table. This, of course, is not as good as the random rehash method, but both the number of collisions expected and the time required to calculate the pi are less.

The values a, b and c used may depend on the machine -- certain machine instructions may make it more efficient to use certain values for a, b and c. Let us go through an example of a quadratic rehash on the IBM 360, to indicate how one can choose the coefficients to construct an efficient program. We assume that a table of 787 entries starts at location HTBL.

We set c=0; thus if we assume the first entry tested is at h+p0, we have p0=0. Now p[i+1]-pi = 2ai+a+b. To get a coefficient of -1 for i, we take a=-1/2, yielding

$$p[i+1]-pi = -i-1/2+b.$$

Hence, when i is increased by 1, the increment is decreased by -1. If we start with -1/2+b in a register INC, to get to the next increment, we need only decrease INC by 1. We can also use INC to stop after half the table has been searched. We should stop after 393 tests, so that if we take b=392+1/2, we stop when INC=-1. The final equation is then

$$pi = -(1/2)i^2 + (392+1/2)i.$$

The reader should now note that since each table element is four bytes long, we should in general work in multiples of four. This the IBM 360 assembly language program below does. In order to clearly illustrate the rehashing, the program does not look for an entry equal to one to be inserted, but just for one equal to zero.

```
*        Registers used.     |
HASH     EQU  2              |Current hash h+pi. Initially h.
FR       EQU  3              |Contains -4 (4 bytes per entry).
INC      EQU  4              |Contains p[i+1]-pi.
KN       EQU  5              |Total nc. of bytes in table: 787*4.
ZO       EQU  6              |Contains 0.
INIT     L    HASH,H         |Get original hash value (0,4,8,...)
         LA   INC,1568       |Initial increment (b-1/2)*4)
         IA   KN,3148        |Table size = 787*4.
         SR   ZO,ZO          |Zero out fcr comparisons.
         B    CCMP           |Jump to try first comparison.
COLIS    BXLE INC,FR,FULI    |Take 4 from increment. If result is
*                            |-4, too many collisions, so go to
*                            |label FULL (not shown in program).
         BXH  HASH,INC,CCMP  |Add increment to hash value to get
*                            |h+pi. If result<KN (in register 5)
*                            |skip the next instruction.
         SR   HASH,KN        |Make it modulo the table size.
COMP     C    ZO,HTBL(HASH)  |Is entry 0? If not, jump to COLIS
         BNE  COLIS          |to fix INC and test next entry.
*When here, HTBL(HASH) contains 0.
```

### 9.3.2 Chaining

The chained hash addressing technique uses a <u>hash table</u> whose elements, called <u>buckets</u>, are initially 0; the symbol table itself which is initially empty; and a pointer POINTFREE which points to the current last entry in the symbol table. POINTFREE initially points to the location before the beginning of the table. The symbol table entries have an additional CHAIN field which may contain zero or the address of another symbol table entry. The initial conditions are thus

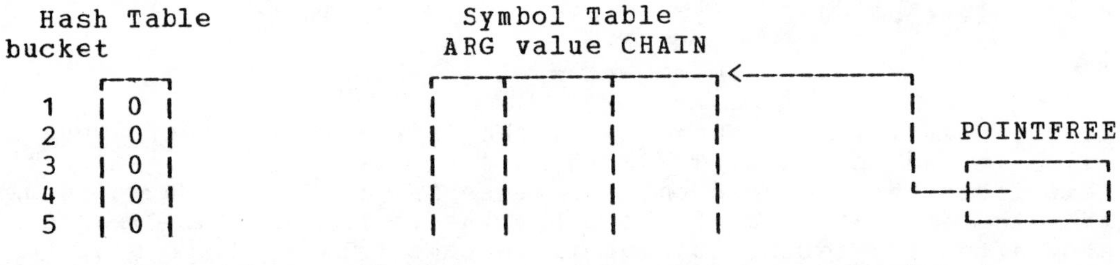

```
  Hash Table                 Symbol Table
 bucket                     ARG value CHAIN
                            ┌───┬────┬────┐<──────────┐
   1  | 0 |                 |   |    |    |           |
   2  | 0 |                 |   |    |    |           |  POINTFREE
   3  | 0 |                 |   |    |    |           |  ┌───────┐
   4  | 0 |                 |   |    |    |           └──┼──     |
   5  | 0 |                 |   |    |    |              └───────┘
```

Symbols hash to buckets of the hash table. Each bucket is zero or points to the symbol table entry for the first symbol which hashed to it. The chain field of each entry is used to chain entries whose symbols hash to the same bucket. Let us go through the process step by step. We start with the empty symbol table, as above. Suppose that a symbol, say S1, is to be entered into the symbol table. The hash function produces the address of a hash table entry, say bucket 4, which at this point is zero. We then do the following:

1. Add 1 to POINTFREE.
2. Insert the entry (S1, value, 0) into the symbol table entry pointed at by POINTFREE.
3. Put POINTFREE into bucket 4.

This yields

```
   Hash Table                    Symbol Table
      ┌───┐                   ┌──────────────────────┐
   1  | 0 |        ┌────────>|S1 |        |   0   |
   2  | 0 |        |          ├───┼────────┼───────┤<──────────┐    POINTFREE
   3  | 0 |        |          |   |        |       |           |   ┌─────────┐
   4  | ──┼────────┘          |   |        |       |           └───┼──       |
   5  | 0 |                   |   |        |       |               └─────────┘
```

As long as symbols are entered which hash to different buckets, they are inserted as above. Thus, if we enter symbols S2, S3 and S4 which hash to buckets 1, 3 and 6 respectively, the tables would look like

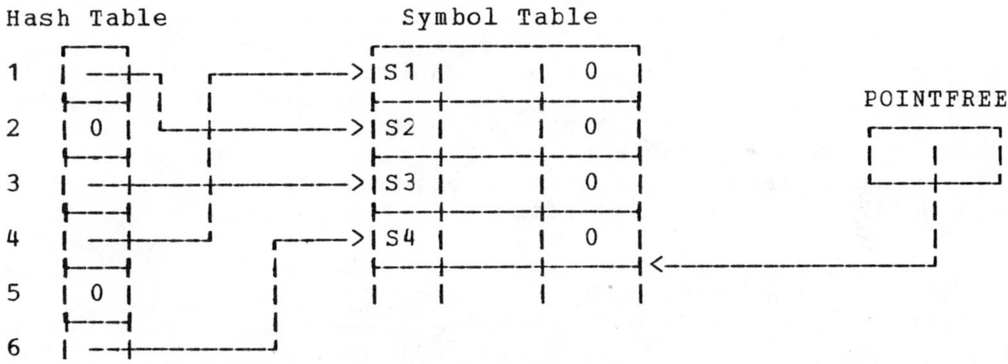


Eventually a symbol S5 will be entered which hashes to a bucket which has been used before. Here is where the CHAIN field comes into play. S5 will be entered into the symbol table and added to the end of the chain for that bucket. Thus, if S5 hashes to bucket 6, we have the following structure.

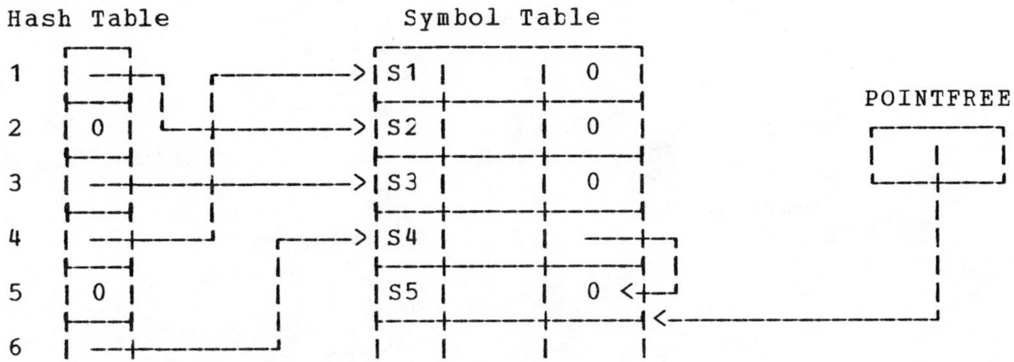

After insertion of symbols S6, S7, and S8 which hash, say, to buckets 4, 3, and 3 in that order, we would end up with the following structure.

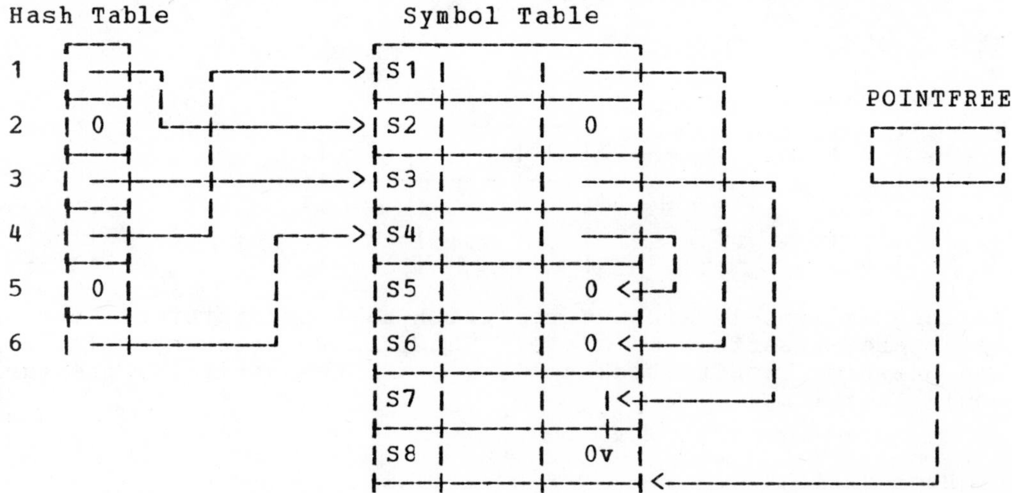


We can give the following flow chart for a procedure which searches the table for a symbol S and enters it if not there. In the flow chart, P1 and P2 are temporary pointer variables. HASH is the hash function which yields the address of a bucket of the hash table from its argument, the symbol S. When finished, P2 contains the address of the entry.

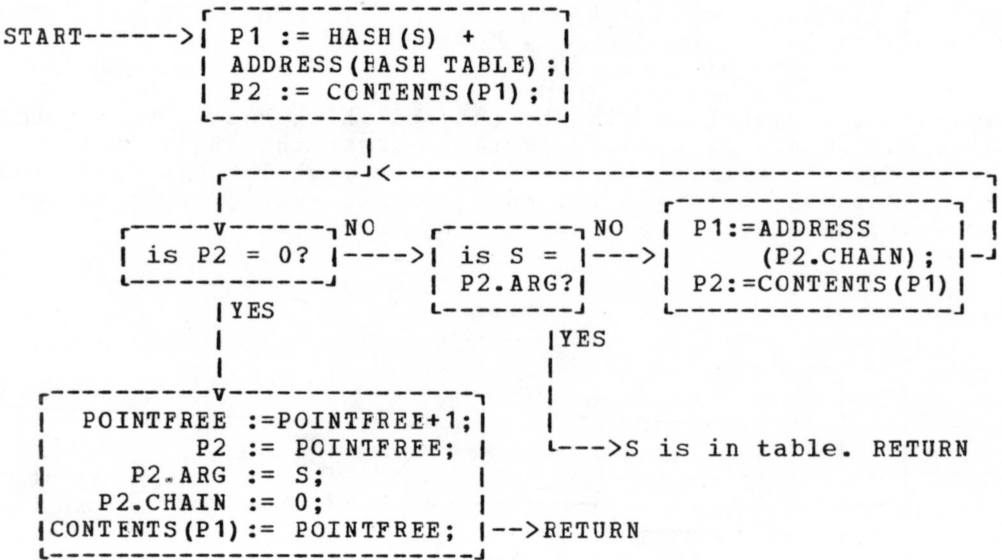

If the symbol table fills up, one can always add another block of entries for it (if the language or system permits dynamic storage allocation), since the hash function gives an index into the hash table and the symbol table entries are referenced only through pointers. Thus there is no maximum number of entries as in the rehash method. (There is, however, a maximum number of buckets). Note also that only the buckets need be initialized, not the entries themselves. One often uses anywhere from 100 to 300 buckets, but allows many more entries in the actual symbol table. Once all entries have been entered, the hash table can be thrown away and its space released for other purposes (we assume that all identifiers are replaced by the entry number in the symbol table or something similar.) Chaining does require one extra word for each entry; but this is worth it in many cases.

### 9.3.3 Hash Functions

If the argument S to be hashed is more than one computer word long, the first step of the hash function is to create a single computer word result S' from S. (For example, on the IBM 360, 4 characters fit into one word.) S' is usually computed by either adding all of the words of S together or using the EXCLUSIVE OR (EXOR) of all the words. (1 EXOR 1 = 0, 0 EXOR 0 = 0, 1 EXOR 0 = 1, 0 EXOR 1 = 1).

The second step is to compute the final index from S'. There are several ways of doing this:

1. Multiply S' by itself and use the middle n bits as the hash (if the table has 2**n entries). The middle n bits depend upon every bit of S', so this is a good method.
2. Use some logical operation, such as the EXCLUSIVE OR, on certain parts of S'.
3. If there are 2**n entries in the table, split S' up into n bit sections and add them together. Use the rightmost n bits of the result.
4. Divide S' by the size of the table and use the remainder as the hash index.

All of these methods have been in use with satisfactory results. Others could also be devised; one must only be sure that the hash function produces addresses which are random enough for the kinds of arguments that are likely to be used. In our case, if the table is going to be initialized with all the reserved words and standard identifiers of the language, it is a good idea to check the initialized table to see how many collisions actually occur. A hash function can be good enough statistically speaking, but it just might happen that 10 of the reserved words hash to the same address!

We should also mention that the leftmost two bits of the EBCDIC codes for all capital letters and numbers are the same (11) while the leftmost two bits of the ASCII codes for capital letters are all 10. So be careful with your hash function.

The PL/I F level compiler (see IBM(b)) uses the following hash function.

1. Add successive four-character sections of the identifier together into one 4-byte register.
2. Divide the result by 211 and get the remainder R.
3. Use 2*R as the index to a hash table of 211 buckets (each bucket is 2 bytes long).

Every identifier and constant in the source program is replaced by a reference to its symbol table entry. When no more entries are to be made, the hash table is discarded. Entries are variable length (minimum of 4 bytes plus the EBCDIC name).

## 9.4 TREE STRUCTURED SYMBOL TABLES

This method uses a binary tree -- a tree where each branch has only one or two nodes -- to order the entries. Each node of the tree represents a filled entry of the table, the root node being entry 1. Figure 9.4a shows the table with one entry for identifier G. Suppose now that the identifier D is to be entered. A branch is drawn for it to the left, since D < G, as in Figure 9.4b. Now let the identifier M be entered. Since G < M a branch is drawn for it to the right, from G (Figure 9.4c). Finally, let the identifier E be entered. E < G, so we travel down the left branch from G and hit D. D < E so we draw a branch from and to the right of D (Figure 9.4d). Figure 9.4e shows the tree after identifiers A, B and F have been added, in that order.

One can implement this by having two pointer fields with each entry, one for the low and one for the high branch. The number of comparisons required depends very much on the order in which the identifiers arrive. For example, if they arrive in the order A, B, C, D, E, F, to find F requires 6 comparisons. One can change the tree around at different stages to make a balanced tree out of it in order to minimize the largest search required. Binary trees as described here can easily be used to print out the list of identifiers in alphabetical order (see exercise 1).

The FORTRAN H compiler (see IBM(a)) has six such trees, one each for identifiers with 1, 2, 3, 4, 5, and 6 characters There is also one tree each for constants which take up 4, 8, and 16 bytes, a tree for statement numbers, and several others. All the entries are contained in the same table; each entry is 52 bytes (13 words).

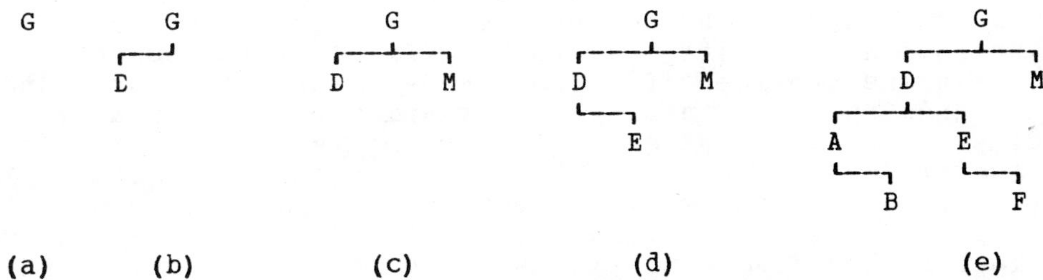


**FIGURE 9.4. Binary Tree Illustration.**

## EXERCISE FOR 9.4

1. Construct an algorithm for printing out the names of nodes of binary trees, in alphabetical order. Hint: you will need a stack to keep track of where you are in the tree at any point, and how you got there.

## 9.5 BLACK STRUCTURED SYMBOL TABLES

ALGOL-like languages have a nested block and procedure structure. The same identifier may be declared and used many times in different blocks and procedures, and each such declaration must have a unique symbol table entry associated with it. Given a use of an identifier, the problem is then to discover the correct symbol table entry for it.

Let us begin by numbering the blocks of a source program in the order in which they open (the order in which their <u>begins</u> appear). This is a natural ordering, since this is the order in which they will be encountered by a left-right parse.

```
BEGIN REAL a, b, c, d;                 ┌────────────────
        :                            1 │ a, b, c, d
      BEGIN REAL e,f;                  │    ┌───────────
        L1:                            │ 2  │ e, f, L1
      END;                             │    └───────────
      BEGIN REAL g, h;                 │    ┌───────────
            :                          │ 3  │ g, h, L2, L3
         L2:BEGIN REAL a;              │    │    ┌──
                  :                    │    │ 4  │ a
            END;                       │    │    └──
         L3:                           │    │
      END;                             │    └───────────
END;                                   └────────────────
```

**FIGURE 9.5. Block Structure.**

The rule for finding the correct declaration corresponding to the use of an identifier is to look first in the current block (the one where the identifier is used), then the surrounding block, and so on, until a declaration of that identifier is found. We can implement such a search by keeping all the symbol table entries for each block contiguous, and by using a *block list*. For the moment, we can assume the entries for each block are unordered. Entry i of the block list contains the number of the block surrounding block i (SURRNO), the number of entries in the symbol table for the block i (NOENT) and a pointer to these entries (POINT). Thus each block list entry is a 3-tuple

(SURRNO, NOENT, POINT).

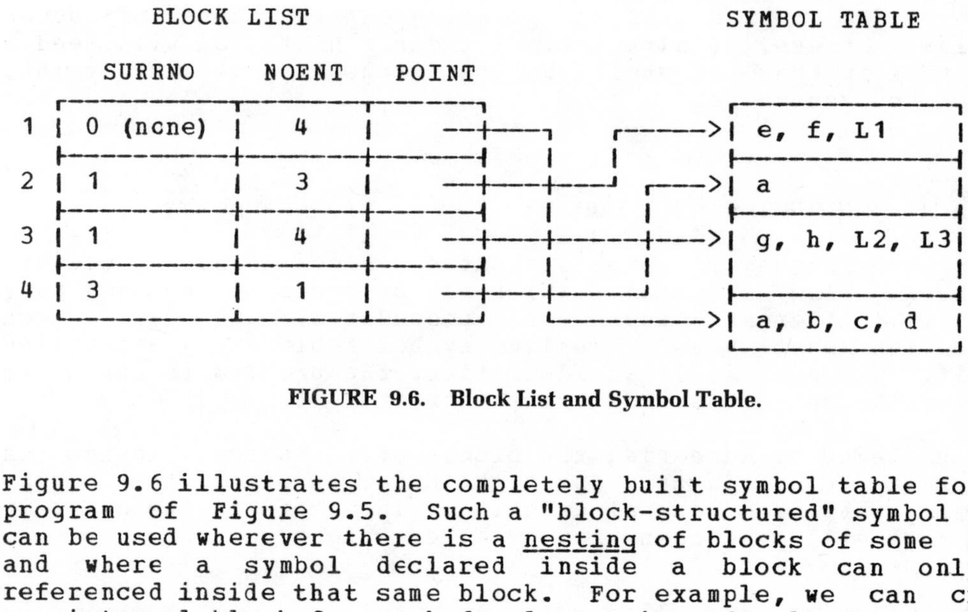

```
        BLOCK LIST                                         SYMBOL TABLE

     SURRNO       NOENT    POINT
  ┌────────────┬────────┬────────┐                      ┌──────────────┐
1 │ 0 (none)   │   4    │      ──┼────┐     ┌────────>│ e, f, L1     │
  ├────────────┼────────┼────────┤    │     │          ├──────────────┤
2 │ 1          │   3    │      ──┼────┼─────┘   ┌────>│ a            │
  ├────────────┼────────┼────────┤    │         │      ├──────────────┤
3 │ 1          │   4    │      ──┼────┼─────────┼────>│ g, h, L2, L3 │
  ├────────────┼────────┼────────┤    │         │      │              │
4 │ 3          │   1    │      ──┼────┼─────────┘      ├──────────────┤
  └────────────┴────────┴────────┘    └───────────────>│ a, b, c, d   │
                                                       └──────────────┘
```

**FIGURE 9.6. Block List and Symbol Table.**

Figure 9.6 illustrates the completely built symbol table for the program of Figure 9.5. Such a "block-structured" symbol table can be used wherever there is a *nesting* of blocks of some sort, and where a symbol declared inside a block can only be referenced inside that same block. For example, we can create an internal block for each for-loop, since for-loops are nested the same way as blocks. This will automatically detect jumps from outside into a for-loop, since the labels inside a for-loop will only be found by the search procedure if the use of the label is from within the for-loop block. An extra block can also be created for the formal parameters and procedure body of a procedure or function declaration, thus prohibiting the referencing of the formal parameters outside the procedure. (The procedure name itself, of course, does not belong to this internal block.)

### Opening and Closing Blocks

The blocks in the symbol table of Figure 9.6 are in the order 2, 4, 3, 1. This is actually the order in which the blocks were closed (the order in which their <u>end</u>s appeared in the program). This is necessitated by the fact that the entries for a block must be contiguous. To implement the process of building the tables we use the end (last few locations) of the symbol table as a stack. This stack S(N), S(N-1), ... will contain all entries for each block whose <u>begin</u> has been encountered (has been opened) during the parsing process, but whose <u>end</u> has not yet been parsed. After a complete block is processed its entries are moved to the beginning of the table. If we consider the syntax of a block as

```
(1) <blockbegin> ::= BEGIN
(2) <block> ::= <blockbegin> <declist> ; <statelist> END
```

we will "open" a block when the semantic routine for rule (1) is executed and "close" a block when the routine for rule (2) is executed. We present below the setup at three times during parsing of the program of Figure 9.5 -- at labels L1, L2, L3. The variables needed here are:

| | |
|---|---|
| S(1:N) | The symbol table with N elements. S(N), S(N-1), ... is used as a stack. All entries finally end up in S(1), S(2), ... |
| B(1:M) | The block list. Each entry has 3 integer fields SURRNO, NOENT, and POINT. |
| INTEGER CURRBL | current block number; initially 0. |
| INTEGER LASTBL | highest block number assigned; initially 0. |
| INTEGER TOPEL | index of top stack element; initially N+1. |
| INTEGER LASTEL | index of last permanent symbol table entry; initially 0. |

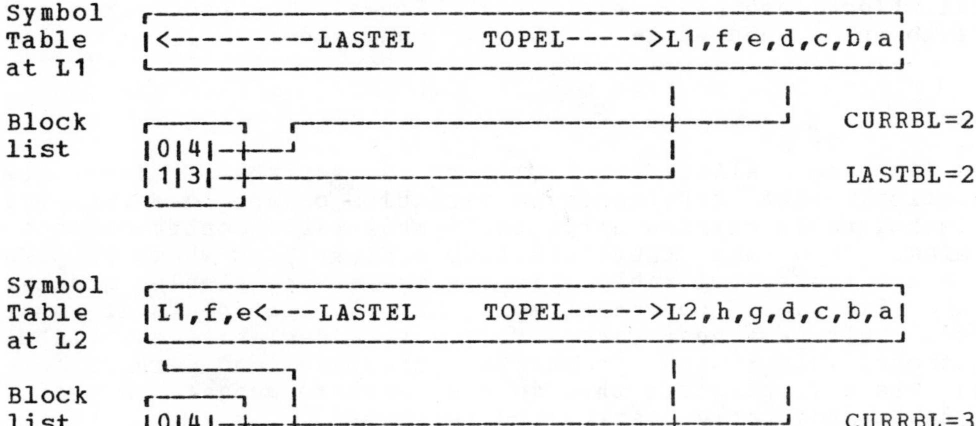

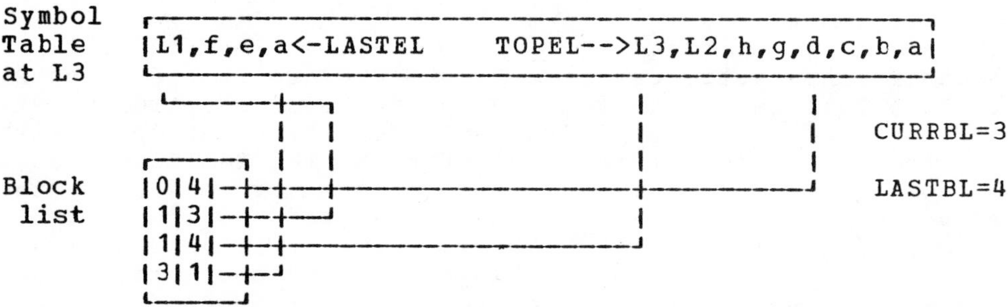


We can now give the program segments to open and close a block:

1. OPEN A BLOCK. Add an element to the block list and make it the current block: LASTBL := LASTBL+1; B(LASTBL) := (CURRBL,0,TOPEL); CURRBL := LASTBL.
2. CLOSE A BLOCK. Move the block's variable into permanent locations: B(CURRBL).POINT:=LASTEL+1;

```
FOR i := 1 STEP 1 UNTIL B(CURRBL).NOENT DO
 BEGIN LASTEL := LASTEL+1; S(LASTEL) := S(TOPEL);
       TOPEL := TOPEL+1
 END.
```

   Make the surrounding block current: CURRBL := B(CURRBL).SURRNO.

#### Entering and Searching

Entering an identifier into the current block is just a matter of adding it to the top block of the symbol table stack and increasing the identifier count for that block. There are two search procedures needed; one to look in the current block only (for example, at a declaration) and another to look in the current block and any surrounding ones. The procedures are simple to write, and we leave them to the reader.

#### Discussion

If the language allows the use of a variable before its declaration, then references to variables cannot be associated with symbol table entries until the symbol table construction is completed. One must therefore have a first pass whose purpose is to build the symbol table. It can use a very simple grammar for the language, so that most of the statements are just skipped. This pass must take into account declarations, label definitions, block and procedure structure, and perhaps for-loops. The next pass can then do the complete program analysis, using the symbol table constructed earlier.

Some languages do not allow the use of a variable before its definition. This restriction is usually put there only to make compiling easier. However, labels are almost always referred to before their definition, and it is not advisable to require the programmer to declare labels before their definition. Chapter 13 discusses ways of handling such labels in a one-pass compiler.

A pseudoblock surrounding the whole source program can be initialized before actual translation with the entries for standard functions and variables, so that these don't have to be treated separately.

In a one-pass compiler, as soon as a block has been closed its identifiers are no longer needed. One can therefore simply delete its entries from the symbol table stack instead of moving them to a permanent position. Such a table is then called a *stack symbol table*.

### Block Structure with Hash Addressing

When using hash addressing schemes one cannot easily order the symbol table by blocks. The first method of treating the block structure problem that comes to mind is to make the argument a combination of the block number concatenated with the identifier. Then any argument is unique. To find a use of an identifier B one would search first for the current block number concatenated with B, then the surrounding block number concatenated with B, and so on, until it was found.

Alternatively we can have a second pointer field associated with each entry -- it being used to chain entries for the same identifier, but in different blocks. Once the first entry has been found, we just have to search along the chain to find the correct entry. Unfortunately, the declarations in one block are not always completely scanned before a new block is opened (this happens, for example, with procedures). Thus the entry for identifier B in block 3, say, could be entered before the entry for identifier B in block 1. Hence we cannot be sure in what order the entries on the chain will appear. For efficient searching we may want to reorder the entries on the chain when one is inserted or when a block is closed.

## 9.6 HISTORICAL REFERENCES

See Flores(69) or Knuth(70) for a treatment of sorting and searching methods. Many introductory programming books also contain a section on the simpler sorting methods.

Hash addressing is another one of those programming techniques discovered by programmers through the years. Peterson(57) first published a paper on the subject; in it he discusses the linear rehash method. The random rehash technique (and its analysis) appears in a survey paper by Morris(68); it is a variant of a method due to Vyssotsky (see McIlroy(63)). The quadratic rehash method is due to Maurer(68). Recently, it has been extended in two directions. Radke(70) solves the problem of searching the other half of the table which is not searched by the quadratic rehash method. In the same issue of CACM, Bell(70) extends it by using the formula $pi=a(h)i^2+bi$ instead of $pi=ai^2+bi$. That is, the coefficient of $i^2$ is a function of the original hash address h. He shows analytically and empirically that this reduced the expected number of collisions.

Batson(65) describes the use of the linear rehash method in an ALGOL compiler.

Morris(68) also presents an analysis of the chaining method of solving the collision problem; the analysis for this first appeared in Johnson.

A more detailed discussion of binary trees appears in volume 1 of Knuth(68). The two methods discussed for organizing block structured symbol tables have been used in many compilers, and it is difficult to attribute them to anybody in particular.

# Chapter 10.
# The Data in the Symbol Table

## 10.1 THE DESCRIPTOR

All information about an identifier is stored in the "value" part of its symbol table element (see section 9.1). For _each_ occurrence of an identifier in a source program, the table will be searched for its symbol table element, the information gathered from the occurrence will be checked against the information already stored, and any new information will be inserted. Thus the symbol table is a very important part of the compiler; in a sense the whole translation revolves about it. It should be structured in a manner which allows efficient extraction and insertion of information. (At the same time, the elements should be as small as possible, in order to accomodate large programs with many identifiers. This is the usual time-space problem.) In general, the symbol table should be accessed and changed by as few routines as possible, so that necessary changes can be incorporated easily. A good idea is to agree as completely as possible on the format of the descriptor before any programming is done.

We use the term _descriptor_, for the "value" part of a symbol table element, since it describes the identifier. Another term for it is _semantic word_, introduced by Feldman(66).

The amount of information needed in the descriptor depends on what the identifier actually is -- simple variable, array, function, and so forth. Some implementations therefore allow a variable length descriptor. This is not possible with all table organizations. In order not to waste space, one can have the symbol table element size small, and just allocate two or three successive symbol table elements for identifiers which require more space. Another alternative is to use part of the descriptor as a pointer to a secondary table when necessary. This requires careful coding, since a field of the descriptor may have a different meaning depending on the type of entry.

For variables and procedures, the following information may be required in the descriptor:

Variables: Type (real, integer, string, complex, label, etc.);
Precision, scaling, length;
Form (simple variable, array, structure, etc.);
Runtime address;
If an array, how many dimensions? If dimensions are constant, what are they?
If a structure or component of one, the entry must be linked to other components in some manner;
Formal parameter or not; if so, the type of parameter correspondence;
Is it in a COMMON or EQUIVALENCE statement (FORTRAN)? If so, it must be linked to associated identifiers;
Was its declaration processed yet?
Is there a statement which will assign it a value?

Procedures: Is it external to the program?
Is it a function? What is its type?
Was its declaration processed yet?
Is it recursive?
What are the formal parameters? Their descriptors must be linked to the function name for purposes of comparing with actual parameters.

Perhaps the best way to indicate what goes into a descriptor is tc give examples from existing compilers. This we now do for two languages on different machines. Please note that we have changed the notation and format in the documents of these compilers slightly, and have deleted information irrelevant to the discussion. Thus these are not exact descriptions.

### The ALCOR Illinois 7090 Compiler (Gries, Paul, and Wiehle)

This is a four-pass ALGOL compiler for the IBM 7090. The first pass looks at declarations, labels, and the block, procedure, and for-loop structure to build a block-structured unordered symbol table with a block list. No attributes are filled in at this point. The second pass uses the transition matrix technique to parse the program and fill in the descriptor of each identifer. It allocates runtime storage and does some preliminary work for for-loop optimization. Pass three generates code, while pass four prints messages and puts the program in a loader-compatible form.

The IBM 7090 has 36-bit words, with addresses being 15 bits long. Bits 0-2, 3-17, 18-20, and 21-35 can be referenced separately by some instructions. Each descriptor in the ALCOR ILLINOIS 7090 compiler originally occupies two words, as given below. After pass 2 is finished the second word is discarded, leaving more room in memory for other purposes.

| 0-5 | 6-7 | 8 | 9-13 | 14-20 | 21-35 |
|---|---|---|---|---|---|
| type kind | formal parameter | declaration passed? | hierarchy no. | no. pars or subs. | object prog. address |

| 0-2 | 3-17 | 18-20 | 21-35 |
|---|---|---|---|
| use | entry number | | pointer used for loop testing |

| word | bits | meaning |
|---|---|---|
| 1 | 0-5 | This gives the type (2 bits) and kind (4 bits) of the variable. For instance,<br>0 0 0 0 0 0 = undefined (so far)<br>0 1 0 0 0 1 = integer simple variable<br>0 1 0 0 1 0 = integer array<br>1 0 0 0 0 1 = real simple variable<br>1 0 0 1 0 0 = real function<br>1 0 0 1 0 1 = real constant<br>0 0 1 1 1 1 = label |
| 1 | 6-7 | If the variable is a formal parameter, bit 6=1; if it is also called by VALUE, bit 7=1. |
| 1 | 8 | Initially 0. Set to 1 when pass 2 processes the declaration. |
| 1 | 9-13 | The hierarchy number (level of nesting) of the procedure in which it is declared. |
| 1 | 14-20 | If an array (procedure) name, the number of subscripts (parameters); otherwise 0. |
| 1 | 21-35 | The offset in the data area of the procedure in which it is declared. |
| 2 | 0-2 | This is used for a formal parameter called by name. It is initially 0. If the formal parameter is assigned a value within the procedure it is set to 1. If the corresponding actual parameter of a call is a constant, it is set to 2. Note that these two cases are incompatible, because you cannot assign a value to the constant. This is a way of detecting most of this type of errors. |
| 2 | 3-17 | The entry number of this entry in the table. |
| 2 | 21-35 | Used to test loops for optimization possibilities. See chapter 18. This is also used for error recovery purposes. See chapter 15. |

We said in chapter 8 that each runtime address is given by a pair (data area number, offset). The above scheme uses no data area number; instead, the hierarchy (level of nesting) is used. This can be used because those procedures which have the same hierarchy number are in parallel blocks; therefore the compiler never processes them at the same time. Note (see section 8.9) that if B, say, is declared in a procedure with hierarchy i, and is referenced in a procedure with hierarchy k ($i \leq k$), then location i of k's data area gives the address of i's data area, which is what we need to reference B. Thus the hierarchy number serves our needs.

**/360 WATFOR (Cress et al. (68))**

As mentioned in chapter 1, /360 WATFOR is essentially a one pass-compiler for FORTRAN IV on the IBM 360 computers.

The symbol table is made up of five different lists, one each for statement numbers; arithmetic constants; common block names, subroutine names, and variable names; and common block and subroutine names (thus entries appear for these on two lists). All entries in the lists are placed in the same table; the first two bytes of each entry are used to point to the next entry in the list of which it is a member. A search for a particular entry is therefore a linear search through a linked list.

The different types of entries have different lengths, ranging from 8 to 20 bytes. For example, the entries for variables are 16 bytes long, as follows (the first 2 bytes do not appear in the diagram).

```
Bytes  3-4  5-10        11-12       13-14      15-16
      ┌────┬──────────┬─────────┬─────────┬─────────────┐
      │ B2 │identifier│Dimension│COMMON   │EQUIVALENCE│
      └────┴──────────┴─────────┴─────────┴─────────────┘
```

The COMMON and EQUIVALENCE fields are used to link the entry with entries for associated COMMON and EQUIVALENCEd variables; chapter 14 explains this in detail. The dimension field is 0 if the variable is not dimensioned; otherwise it points to a separate entry containing all the dimension information: the upper bounds d1,...,dn and the total length d1*...*dn.

The two bytes labeled B2 contain the rest of the information, as shown in the diagram below. All fields are initially zero and, as information is extracted from the program, they are reset. For the single bit fields, a 1 indicates the information as shown in the diagram.

```
┌─────┬─────┬─────┬──┬──┬──┬──┬──┬──┬──┬──┬──┐
│ 0-1 │ 2-4 │ 5-6 │ 7│ 8│ 9│10│11│12│13│14│15│    B2
└──┬──┴──┬──┴──┬──┴─┬┴─┬┴─┬┴─┬┴─┬┴─┬┴─┬┴─┬┴─┬┘
   │     │     │    │  │  │  │  │  │  │  │  └─Equivalenced
   │     │     │    │  │  │  │  │  │  │  └─In COMMON
   │     │     │    │  │  │  │  │  │  └─Has an initial value
   │     │     │    │  │  │  │  │  └─ASSIGNed variable
   │     │     │    │  │  │  │  └─Currently a DO-parameter
   │     │     │    │  │  │  └─Formal parameter of a routine
   │     │     │    │  │  └─Use is established
   │     │     │    │  └─Type is established
   │     │     │    └─Optional length given by programmer
   │     │     └─Type(00=logical,01=integer,10=real,11=complex)
   │     └─Number of subscripts, if array
   └─10=simple variable, 11=array
```

## 10.2 DESCRIPTORS FOR COMPONENTS OF STRUCTURES

Symbol table entries for components of structures must be linked together in some way to represent the complete structure. There are many ways of doing this; we want a representation which will allow us to process references to structures and components efficiently. Examples of the structures we will deal with are

```
                   1 A                1 L
                     2 B                2 M
                       3 C                4 C
(10.2.1)               3 D      and       4 D
                     2 E                2 B
                     2 F                  5 C
                                          5 D
```

These are similar to COBOL or PL/I structures. The structure on the left has name A; it consists of three components: B, E, and F. E and F are <u>elementary</u> components, since they do not themselves contain subcomponents. Elementary components possess a type and can be assigned values, though we shall not discuss this since we are interested only in how the components are linked to each other. B is not elementary; it is the name of a <u>group</u> of (sub)components C and D. C and D are elementary. The structure names A and L are also group names.

The rules governing structures are as follows:

1. Each name is preceded by a positive integer called its <u>level number</u>.
2. The structure name is the first component in the description of a structure; its level number must be less than the level numbers of the other components.
3. Each group name is followed by its subcomponents. The subcomponents must all have the same level number, which must be greater than the level number of the group name.

We make no rules concerning the uniqueness of names at this point.

Each structure can be represented by a tree. The root node of the tree is the name of the structure. Each group name is the name of a branch whose nodes are the components in its group. The end nodes of the tree are the elementary components.

Components of a group (they all have the same level number) are often called <u>brothers</u>. the component naming the group is their <u>father</u>, while they are his <u>sons</u>. For example, in the above structure on the left, A's sons are B, E, and F; they are brothers. Component B has two sons C and D; their father is B.

A reference to a component has the form

An. ... .A1.A0

where $n \geq 0$ and where each name Ai must be the name of some component contained (but not necessarily directly) within a group named A[i+1], for i = 0,...,n-1. Only one component may satisfy this condition.

Note that the sequence An,...,A0 need not completely "qualify" A0. Assuming that the cnly structures defined are the two above, either A.B.C or A.C refers to component C of the group B in structure A, while M.D or L.M.D refers to component D of group M in structure L. L.C is ambiguous, since it could mean L.M.C or L.B.C. B.C is also ambiguous, since it could mean A.B.C or L.B.C.

If a single name appears as a reference, then that name must be uniquely defined. M refers uniquely to component M of structure L, while B is ambiguous.

Equivalent notations for a reference An. ... .A1.A0 are A0(A1(...(An)...)) and A0 CF A1 OF ... OF An. These notational differences do not substantially change the way structures are represented and processed.

### Representing Structures in the Symbol Table

We can represent a structure by having one entry per component. Besides the usual fields (which we won't discuss), each entry has three additional fields, FATHER, SON, and BROTHER. The FATHER field of an entry points to the entry for its father, the SON field points to its first son, while the BROTHER field points to its next brother in the sequence of brothers of a group of subcomponents. A field is 0 if the particular entry has no father, son, or next brother, respectively. Figure 10.1 illustrates the entries for the two structures given in (10.2.1). This information may be more (or less) than we need to reference the structure efficiently, and we shall see this as we progress.

Since several entries with the same name may exist, we also have a pointer field SAME, used to link them together. The first entry in the list with the same name has 0 in this field. This gives us the following five fields:

1. ID. The name of the component;
2. SAME. A pointer to the previous entry with the same name (0 if none);
3. FATHER. A pointer to the entry for the name of the group directly containing this component;
4. SON. A pointer to the entry for the first subcomponent of this one (this one must therefore be a group name, or this field contains 0);
5. BROTHER. A pointer to the next component in the group containing this one (0 if none).

| | ID | SAME | FATHER | SON | BROTHER |
|---|---|---|---|---|---|
| A1 | A | 0 | 0 | B1 | 0 |
| B1 | B | 0 | A1 | C1 | E1 |
| C1 | C | 0 | B1 | 0 | D1 |
| D1 | D | 0 | B1 | 0 | 0 |
| E1 | E | 0 | A1 | 0 | F1 |
| F1 | F | 0 | A1 | 0 | 0 |
| L1 | L | 0 | 0 | M1 | 0 |
| M1 | M | 0 | L1 | C2 | B2 |
| C2 | C | C1 | M1 | 0 | D2 |
| D2 | D | D1 | M1 | 0 | 0 |
| B2 | B | B1 | L1 | C3 | 0 |
| C3 | C | C2 | B2 | 0 | D3 |
| D3 | D | D2 | B2 | 0 | 0 |

**FIGURE 10.1. Structures in a Symbol Table.**

```
BEGIN POINTER P0, P, Q;                |P0 points to structure name
                                       |entry, Q to the component
                                       |being processed, and P to Q's
                                       |possible brother or father.
  ADDENTRY(P0,ID[1]); P := P0;         |Enter entry for 1st component.
  P0.LEV := LEVEL[1];                  |
  FOR i := 2 STEP 1 UNTIL n DO         |Loop through the components.
  BEGIN ADDENTRY(Q,ID[i]);             |Enter entry for ith component.
   Q.LEV := LEVEL[i];                  |
   TESTRELATION:                       |Case statement decides whether
   CASE SIGN(P.LEV-Q.LEV)+2 OF         |Q is P's brother, son, or if
   BEGIN                               |not directly related.
    BEGIN IF P.SON≠0 THEN STOP;        |SON. If P already has a son,
     Q.FATHER := P; P.SON := Q         |it's an error. Otherwise, fill
    END;                               |in father-son information.
    BEGIN Q.FATHER := P.FATHER;        |BROTHER. They have the same
     P.BROTHER := Q                    |father and Q is P's next
    END;                               |brother.
    BEGIN P := P.FATHER;               |NOT DIRECTLY RELATED. If P has
     IF P = 0 THEN ERROR;              |no father, it's an error. Else
     GOTO TESTRELATION;                |see whether Q is related to
    END;                               |P's father.
   END;                                |End of case statement. Next,
   P := Q;                             |fix P and repeat the process
  END;                                 |with next component.
 IF P0.SON ≠ 0 THEN ERROR;             |All done. Need only check that
END                                    |1st component has no brother.
```

**FIGURE 10.2. Program to Build the Table for a Structure.**

### Building the Symbol Table

The program in Figure 10.2 builds the symbol table for a structure represented by a sequence of pairs (level number, identifier). We assume these are in two arrays LEVEL and ID, and that n is an integer variable giving the number of pairs. We further assume the existence of a routine ADDENTRY(P,NAME), whose purpose is to enter a new entry for identifier NAME, initialize all components to 0, fill in the fields ID and SAME, and return with the address of the entry in the pointer P. Finally, we use one extra field LEV in each entry to hold the level number for the component. Once the table is built, this field isn't necessary and can be used for other purposes. The use of this extra LEV field can be omitted by complicating the program somewhat (see exercises 1 and 2).

### Processing a Reference An. . . . .Al.AO

There may be several entries for identifier A0; the problem is to find the one entry uniquely qualified by A1, A2, ..., An. Each of the entries A0 are tested. At each step i of a test of one of them, the father links beginning at the entry for A[i-1] are used to find the group name Ai. If in this manner a component for An is found, the A0 which began the test is the reference sought. Note that all A0 must be tested, in order to make sure the reference is unambiguous.

The program below assumes that the names Ai are in a STRING ARRAY A with lower bound 0; variable n indicates how many names are in the reference. When the program is finished, Q will contain the address of the component referenced, or will be 0 if none exists.

Find the component referenced by An. ... .A1.A0

```
BEGIN POINTER P, Q, S;          |P points to an entry for A0, Q
 INTEGER i;                     |will hold address of component
 P := "address of first entry   |referenced, S is a temporary,
   with name A[0]"; Q := 0;     |i counts from 0 (A0) to n (An)
 WHILE P ≠ 0 DO                 |Execute the loop once for each
 BEGIN S := P;                  |entry with name A0.
  FOR i := 1 STEP 1 UNTIL n DO  |Run up FATHER chain, looking
  BEGIN LOOP: S := S.FATHER;    |for A1, A2, ..., An.
    IF S = 0 THEN GOTO TRYNEWP; |Reached root of tree.
    IF S.ID ≠ A[i]              |If not the same, go try
    THEN GO TO LOOP;            |the next father.
  END;                          |
  IF Q ≠ 0 THEN ERROR;          |An entry is found. If Q isn't
  Q := P;                       |0, then it's ambiquous.
TRYNEWP: P := P.SAME;           |Put address of another entry
 END                            |with name A0 in P and try it.
END                             |
```

The program is in a sense a bottom-up search, which begins at each A0 and works its way up toward the root of the tree. Only the FATHER and SAME fields are used, so that the SON and BROTHER fields can be omitted if not used for another purpose (see exercise 3).

In some languages the structure name acts like a new data type, and variables with that type can be declared and created. In ALGOL W, for example, we can write

```
RECORD COMPLEX(REAL REALPART; REAL IMAGPART);
COMPLEX B
```

to create a variable B with two real components. In any reference An. ... .A1.A0 (eg. B.REALPART), An must be the name of (or a pointer to) a structured value, and the type of this structured value is known from An.

For such cases, then, a top-down search can be performed, which begins at the unique entry defined by An, and works its way down the tree to A[n-1], ..., A1, A0, using the SON and BROTHER fields. (We leave the construction of the program to do this to the reader.)

Although the tree to be searched is unique, there is no assurance that the top-down search will be faster than a bottom-up one. This is because at each level, all brothers must be tested. In the bottom-up search, only the father chain has to be processed; here all sons and brothers must be processed.

Note also that a bottom-up search could be speeded up even more by having another field in each entry, which points to the structure name itself.

### The Move Corresponding Verb

In COBOL one may write

```
MOVE CORRESPONDING A TO L
```

in order to move the values of all elementary components of A, which have corresponding names in L, to L. For example, assuming A and L are the structures listed at the beginning of this section, this statement is equivalent to

```
MOVE A.B.C TO L.B.C
MOVE A.B.D to L.B.D
```

while

```
MOVE CORRESPONDING A.B to L.M
```

is equivalent to

```
MOVE A.B.C TO L.M.C
MOVE A.B.D TO L.M.D
```

PL/I has a similar assignment "BY NAME" statement. The rules governing the execution of such a statement are as follows: A statement MOVE CORRESPCNDING X TO Y, where X and Y can themselves be qualified references, is an abbreviation for the sequence of all possible statements MOVE X1 TO Y1 such that

```
X1 = X.An. ... .A1.A0
Y1 = Y.An. ... .A1.A0
```

where X1 or Y1 (or both) are elementary components. Moreover, the chain of components An. ... .A1.A0 must be complete in each case; Ai must be the direct father of A[i-1] for i=1,...,n.

One way of transforming a MOVE CORRESPONDING statement into a sequence of simple MOVEs is as follows: at any step of the transformation we have a sequence of statements

```
MOVE CORRESPONDING X1 TO Y1
  :        :           :
MOVE CORRESPONDING Xn TO Yn
```

At first, n=1. Each Xi and Yi is of course represented by a pointer to its entry in the symbol table, and essentially we just need an array of pairs of pointers (Xi,Yi). The following process is iterated until no more statements exist in the sequence. The process partially transforms the first statement in the sequence and deletes it.

1. If either X1 or Y1 of the first statement in the sequence is an elementary component, then output the statement MOVE X1 TO Y1, and go to step 3.
2. For each son A of X1, if Y1 has a son with the same name A, then add the statement

   ```
   MOVE CORRESPONDING X1.A TO Y1.A
   ```

   to the sequence.
3. Delete the first statement (involving X1 and Y1) from the sequence.

While easy to understand, this transformation requires a table to hold the pairs (Xi,Yi). We present below another program which traverses the nodes of the subtrees of the structures for X and Y in another manner. The pointer P (Q) is used to travel around the subtree for X (Y).

The program is based on the assumption that no rules about uniqueness of names are in force. COBOL has a rule which states that any component of a structure must be uniqely referencable (see exercise 4). In such a case, once a pair (P,Q) is outputted, there is no need to see if any brother of Q has the same name as P. The program can therefore be modified to make it more efficient (see exercise 6).

MOVE CORRESPONDING processor

```
|BEGIN POINTER P, Q, P0;            |P (Q) traverses the subtree X |
| P:=P0:="address of entry for      |(Q). P0 always points to node |
|        X";                        |X.                            |
| Q:="address of entry for Y";      |                              |
|ELEM:                              |                              |
| IF P.SON=0 OR Q.SON=0 THEN        |If either P or Q is elementary|
|  BEGIN output(P,Q); GOTO NEXT;    |we output the pair and get    |
|  END;                             |next pair.                    |
| P := P.SON; Q := Q.SON;           |Traverse down the SON links.  |
|TESTEQ:                            |See if any brother of Q is the|
| IF P.ID = Q.ID THEN GOTO ELEM;    |same as P. If yes, go to ELEM.|
|NEXT:                              |                              |
| IF Q.BROTHER ≠ 0 THEN             |This tries Q's brother.       |
|  BEGIN Q := Q.BROTHER;            |                              |
|   GOTO TESTEQ                     |                              |
|  END;                             |                              |
|BROTHERP:                          |No brother of Q matches P, so |
| IF P.BROTHER ≠ 0 THEN             |try P's brother against Q and |
|  BEGIN P := P.BROTHER;            |his brothers.                 |
|   Q := Q.FATHER.SON;              |                              |
|   GO TO TESTEQ                    |                              |
|  END;                             |                              |
| P := P.FATHER; Q := Q.FATHER;     |P has no more brothers. Go    |
| IF P ≠ P0 THEN GOTO BROTHERP;     |back up father links. Stop if |
|END                                |we are back to P0.            |
```

**EXERCISES FOR 10.3**

1. Change the program which builds the symbol table so that it does not use a LEV field. Hint: LEV is used only when looking for the relationship between P and Q. The only level numbers needed at any point are for P and the components linked to P by the FATHER chain. Use a stack to hold them.

2. Change the program which builds the symbol table so that no LEV field is used, without using a stack to hold the level numbers. Hint: Again, level numbers are only needed for P and those on its FATHER chain. These components as yet have no brothers, so use the brother field to store the level numbers. Be sure to fix the brother field at the right time.

3. Change the program which builds the symbol table to eliminate the SON and BROTHER fields. Remember, you must check for mistakes like 1 A 3 B 2 C. This is now done by checking, when 2 C is processed, whether A already has a son. Another way is to use the level numbers themselves.

4. COBOL requires that all components of a structure be uniquely referencable. For example, in the structure

1 X 2 Y 3 Z 2 Z

component Z of X can never be referenced, because X.Z is ambiguous. Change the program which builds the symbol table to detect these errors.

5. Assuming that An of a reference An. ... .A1.A0 is always the name of a unique, known entry, construct a program to find the unique component referenced, using a top-down method.

6. Assuming the COBOL rule discussed in exercise 4, change the program which transforms a MOVE CORRESPONDING statement so that only those components P and Q which have a possibility of having the same name are checked.

# Chapter 11.
# Internal Forms of the Source Program

If space is a problem, or if the source language or the goals of the project are complicated enough, a compiler will first translate into an internal form which is easier to handle mechanically. In most internal forms, operators appear essentially in the order in which they are to be executed; this is a big help for subsequent analysis and code generation. Actually these internal forms could also be used for interpreting. That is, we could write a program which would execute the source program as it is represented in its internal form.

This chapter introduces several of the more frequently used internal forms. The ALGOL program segment of Figure 11.1 will be shown in each to provide examples. One should realize, of course, that the particular representation depends on the source language and the aims of the compiler. For example, in FORTRAN, DIMENSION statements need not be put into the internal source program, since all the information is put into symbol tables and no code need be generated. You will also note that the declaration INTEGER K of Figure 11.1 does not appear in any of the internal forms, since no code need be generated for it.

One must also determine hcw detailed the initial internal form should be. Should it include operations to convert values from one type to another, or will this be done later? As another example, a for-loop could appear in its equivalent form using just assignment, go to, and conditional statements, or it could appear on a much higher level to be translated at a later time. In general, the original form is more concise and smaller, while a more detailed, translated form allows more optimization to take place and in general makes things easier.

We begin our discussion with a section on operators and operands, and how they can be represented. In section 2 we describe our first internal form, Polish notation. We then discuss quadruples (section 3), triples, trees and indirect triples (section 4), and graph representations of the program (section 5).

The reader should realize that few compilers use one of these forms exclusively. Usually, a mixture of several of them is used, depending on the whims and prejudices of the compiler designer.

```
BEGIN INTEGER K;
      ARRAY A[1:I-J];
      K := 0;
L:    IF I > J
      THEN K := K + A[I-J]*6
      ELSE BEGIN I := I+1; I := I+1; GO TO L END
END
```

**FIGURE 11.1. An ALGOL Program Segment.**

## 11.1 OPERATORS AND OPERANDS

All internal forms have two things in common -- operators and operands. The differences are in how these operators and operands are connected. In our discussion, we use operators like +, -, /, *, BR (branch), and so forth. Internally, of course, each one will be represented by an integer. Thus we might use 4 for +, 5 for -, 6 for /, and so on.

It may be necessary to distinguish operators from operands, if the two can appear in almost any order. In this case, an operand occupies two locations; the first contains an integer different from any integer representing an operator, while the second contains the operand itself. (These two can sometimes be packed into one location.)

The types of operands we deal with are simple names (of variables, procedures, etc.), constants, temporary variables generated by the compiler itself, and subscripted variables. If all identifiers and constants are stored in the same table, then, except for subscripted variables, each operand can be represented by a pointer to the symbol table element which describes it. If the descriptions are in several tables, then it is necessary to have different integers for the different types of operands in the first location (see Figure 11.2).

The operand field can also specify indirect addressing, instead of having a separate operation for it. That is, an operand can indicate that the value referenced is the address of the value actually desired.

This can help us describe subscripted variables as follows. A sequence of operations describe the calculation of VARPART (see 8.4.5) for a subscripted variable A[i,j,...,k]. The next operation is a special operation SUBS (for subscript); its operands are the array name, VARPART, and a temporary T (say) into which the operation stores the final address of the array element. The reference to A[i,j,...,k] is then an indirect reference to T.

A second method for handling subscripted variables is to allow the specification of both the array name and the value of VARPART in an operand. Figure 11.2 illustrates this. The operand occupies more space now, but this internal representation can be more efficient when it comes to generating good object code; this will become clearer in later chapters.

Subsequently, we symbolically represent an operand which is a subscripted variable A[i,j,...,k] by A[T], where A is the array name and T is a variable which contains VARPART.

Other variations are possible, of course, as the reader will find out as he designs a compiler.

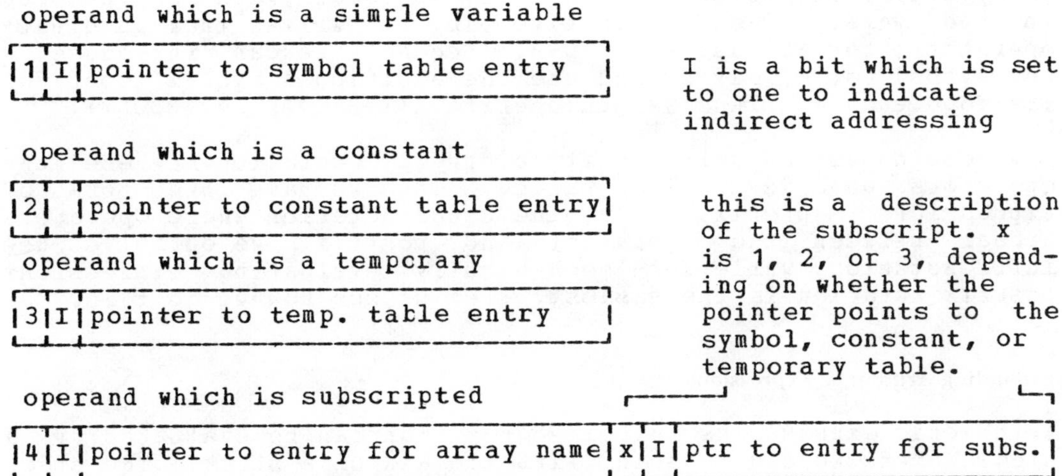


**FIGURE 11.2. Possible Operand Formats.**

## 11.2 POLISH NOTATION

### Arithmetic Expressions

Polish notation is used to represent arithmetic or logical expressions in a manner which specifies simply and exactly the order in which operators are to be evaluated. In addition, no parentheses are needed. In this notation, first employed by the Polish logician J. Lukasiewicz, the operators come immediately <u>after</u> the operands. It is therefore sometimes called <u>suffix notation</u> or <u>postfix notation</u>. As examples, A*B would be written as AB*; A*B+C as AB*C+; A*(B+C/D) as ABCD/+*; and A*B+C*D as AB*CD*+.

In chapter 12 we will explain how to mechanically convert arithmetic expressions in infix notation to Polish notation using syntax recognizers and semantic routines. Meanwhile, the following rules concerning Polish notation should help us do it by hand.

1. The identifiers appear in the same order in both infix and Polish notation.
2. In Polish notation, the operators appear in the order in which they are to be evaluated (from left to right).
3. The operators appear immediately <u>after</u> their operands. Thus, syntactically we might write
   <operand> ::= identifier | <operand> <operand> <operator>
   <operator>::= + | - | / | * | ...

Unary minus, and other similar unary operators, can be handled in two ways. One alternative is to write them as binary operators; for -B just write 0-B. Secondly we can introduce a new symbol for -, say @, and use the additional syntax <operand> ::= <operand> @. Thus we could write A+(-B+C*D) as AB@CD*++.

We could just as well specify a prefix notation, where the operators precede the operands. Thus we have three forms of expressions -- prefix, infix (the usual notation where operators appear between the operands) and postfix. We ourselves use infix notation, while for mechanically evaluating expressions postfix notation is the easiest. Let us see how we do this.

### Evaluating Arithmetic Expressions

Arithmetic expressions in Polish notation can be evaluated by a single left-to-right scan with the aid of a stack. The stack will hold all the operands which have been scanned or produced as the result of some operation, but not yet used. We begin with the leftmost symbol, process it, and go to the symbol on its right, process it, etc. The processing is as follows:

1. If the scanned symbol is an identifier or constant, push its value on the stack and scan the next symbol. This corresponds to using the rule <operand> ::= identifier.
2. If the scanned symbol is a binary operator, apply it to the two top stack operands, and replace them by the result. This is the semantic equivalent of using the rule <operand> ::= <operand> <operand> <operator>.
3. If the scanned symbol is a unary operator, apply it to the top stack operand and replace the operand by the result. This is the semantic equivalent of using a rule <operand> ::= <operand> <operator>.

We illustrate the algorithm for the expression AB@CD*++ (which is (A+(-B+C*D)) in infix notation) in Figure 11.3. (Values in the stack are separated by |).

### Extending Polish Notation to Other Operators

Polish notation can be extended quite simply. We must only follow the rule that operands be immediately followed by their operators. For example, an assignment statement with the usual syntax <var> := <expr> now has the syntax <var> <expr> :=. As a concrete illustration, the assignment statement A := B*C+D would look like ABC*D+:=. However, we must be careful when evaluating the := operator. After it has been evaluated, both the <var> and <expr> must be deleted from the stack, since there is no resulting value. In this respect it is different from the arithmetic binary operators. Secondly, we don't want the value of <var> on the stack, but its address, since the value of <expr> is to be stored into the <var>. We shall run across other operands which have similar problems.

```
step    string and        old stack              use    new stack
        scanned symbol    contents               rule   contents
           v
 1         AB@CD*++                               1     A
            v
 2         AB@CD*++       A                       1     A | B
             v
 3         AB@CD*++       A | B                   3     A | -B
              v
 4         AB@CD*++       A | -B                  1     A | -B | C
               v
 5         AB@CD*++       A | -B | C              1     A | -B | C | D
                v
 6         AB@CD*++       A | -B | C | D          2     A | -B | C*D
                 v
 7         AB@CD*++       A | -B | C*D            2     A | -B+C*D
                  v
 8         AB@CD*++       A | -B+C*D              2     A+(-B+C*D)
```

**FIGURE 11.3. Evaluating AB@CD*++.**

Let us describe how one would represent branches and conditional statements, array declarations and subscripting in Polish notation. This should be enough to illustrate how one goes about imbedding new operators in this form.

A jump GOTO A would be written as "A BRL", where the label A would be represented by the address of its symbol table entry and the operator BRL means branch to a label.

Conditional branches would have the syntax

<operand$^1$> <operand$^2$> BP

where the first operand is an arithmetic value and the second is the number or location of a symbol in the Polish string. If the first operand is positive, then the next symbol to scan is the one designated by the second operand; otherwise we proceed as usual. We also allow the operations BM, BZ, BMZ, BPZ for branch on minus, branch on zero, branch on minus or zero, and so forth.

A conditional statement

IF <expr> THEN <statement$^1$> ELSE <statement$^2$>

would have the form

<expr> <op$^1$> BZ <statement$^1$> <op$^2$> BR <statement$^2$>

where we assume that 0 = FALSE and ≠0 = TRUE for any expression. The other terms have the following meanings:

1. <op$^{1}$> is a constant which is the number of the symbol or location beginning <statement$^{2}$>.
2. BZ is an operator with two operands -- the <expr> and <op$^{1}$>. Its meaning is this: if (and only if) <expr> is zero then change the order in which the symbols are evaluated by beginning at the one numbered <op$^{1}$>.
3. <op$^{2}$> is the number of the symbol following <statement$^{2}$>.
4. BR (BRanch) is an operator with one operand -- <op$^{2}$>. Its meaning is to change the order in which the symbols are evaluated by beginning at the one numbered <op$^{2}$>.

Note that BZ is a binary operator which produces no result. When evaluating it, the stack contains <expr> <op$^{1}$> at the top. Part of the evaluation is therefore to delete these two stack elements. A similar statement can be said about the unconditional branch BR. Note also that we have two unconditional branch operators now. <label> BRL is used for source program goto statements and requires the address of the symbol table entry for the label; <op$^{2}$> BR is for internally generated branches.

It might be said that the operands of the conditional statement are <expr>, <statement$^{1}$> and <statement$^{2}$> and that therefore in Polish notation it should look like

<expr> <statement$^{1}$> <statement$^{2}$> IF.

Note, however, what would happen if we evaluated a Polish string with such a statement. When it came time to evaluate the operator IF, all three operands would have already been evaluated or executed. Remember, we evaluate from left to right except when the order is changed by a branch statement. What we had to do was structure the conditional statement so that when evaluated from left to right it would execute as desired.

An ALGOL declaration ARRAY A[L1:U1,...,Ln:Un] could be represented by L1 U1 ... Ln Un A ADEC, where ADEC is the only operator. It has a variable number of operands, depending on the number of subscripts. The operand A would, of course, be the address of the symbol table entry for A. The evaluation of ADEC includes looking at this entry to find out how many dimensions A has, and thus how many operands ADEC itself has.

Please note that the order of the identifiers has been changed. ADEC has a variable number of parameters, and with A as the last parameter, ADEC can determine from A's symbol table element how many parameters it has on any call. If instead we use A L1 U1 ... Ln Un ADEC, there is no way to detect the number of parameters, and the number of dimensions (say) must be inserted as an extra parameter just before the operator ADEC.

A subscripted variable A[<expr>, ..., <expr>] is similarly represented by <expr> ... <expr> A SUBS. Evaluation of SUBS causes the address of the array element to be evaluated, using the array symbol table element and the subscript expressions.

The operands are then deleted from the stack and a new one, specifying the type of the array element and its address, is pushed onto the stack.

Consider the program segment in Figure 11.1. In Polish notation this would be written as in Figure 11.4. In this figure, we have added two extra operators with no operands, one for opening a block (BLOCK) and one for closing a block (BLCKEND).

Note that we have used a SUBS operator to implement array subscripting; this is easier to use in Polish notation. In the next section we will see an example of the other way of describing subscripting.

```
(1)  BLOCK 1 I J - A ADEC K 0 :=
(11) I J - 29 BMZ
(16) K K I J - A SUBS 6 * + := 41 BR
(29) I I 1 + := I I 1 + := L BRL
(41) BLCKEND
```

**FIGURE 11.4. Polish Form of Figure 11.1.**

It may be helpful to see what this would really look like in a computer or in some high level language. Figure 11.5 shows this. One of the above symbols is placed on each line. Operators use only one location and are represented as follows: 6 = SUBS, 7 = :=, 8 = BMZ, 9 = BR, 10 = BRL, 11 = BLOCK, 12 = BLCKEND, 13 = ADEC, 14 = +, 15 = *, and 16 = -. If the symbol is a constant, two locations or words are used. The first contains "1" for "constant", the second contains the constant itself. Similarly, if the symbol is an identifier, the first word contains "2" for "identifier", while the second contains the index of the entry for that identifier in the symbol table. Please note also the change in numbering; the <u>words</u> are numbered, not the symbols.

### EXERCISES FOR 11.2

1. Put the following arithmetic expressions into Polish notation: 1+5*(6+8/4), -3+6*(-5+6), 25/(5/1+6-5).

2. Evaluate the Polish strings resulting from exercise 1, using the method described.

3. Put the following statements into Polish notation:
(1) FOR I := 1 STEP 1 UNTIL 10 DO A[I] := 1;
(2) CASE <expression> OF BEGIN S2; S2; ...; SN END;
(3) IF <expression> THEN S1;
(4) DO <statement no.> <var$^1$> = <var$^2$>,<var$^3$> (FORTRAN DO-LOOP).

| WORD NO. | ACTUAL WORDS | | SYMBOL |
|---|---|---|---|
| 1 | 11 | | BLOCK |
| 2 | 1 | 1 | 1 |
| 4 | 2 | 1 | I |
| 6 | 2 | 2 | J |
| 8 | 16 | | - |
| 9 | 2 | 3 | A |
| 11 | 13 | | ADEC |
| 12 | 2 | 4 | K |
| 14 | 1 | 0 | 0 |
| 16 | 7 | | := |
| 17 | 2 | 1 | I |
| 19 | 2 | 2 | J |
| 21 | 16 | | - |
| 22 | 1 | 45 | 45 |
| 24 | 8 | | BMZ |
| 25 | 2 | 4 | K |
| 27 | 2 | 4 | K |
| 29 | 2 | 1 | I |
| 31 | 2 | 2 | J |
| 33 | 16 | | - |
| 34 | 2 | 3 | A |

| WORD NO. | ACTUAL WORDS | | SYMBOL |
|---|---|---|---|
| 36 | 6 | | SUBS |
| 37 | 1 | 6 | 6 |
| 39 | 15 | | * |
| 40 | 14 | | + |
| 41 | 7 | | := |
| 42 | 1 | 64 | 64 |
| 44 | 9 | | BR |
| 45 | 2 | 1 | I |
| 47 | 2 | 1 | I |
| 49 | 1 | 1 | 1 |
| 51 | 14 | | + |
| 52 | 7 | | := |
| 53 | 2 | 1 | I |
| 55 | 2 | 1 | I |
| 57 | 1 | 1 | 1 |
| 59 | 14 | | + |
| 60 | 7 | | := |
| 61 | 1 | 5 | 5 |
| 63 | 10 | | BRL |
| 64 | 12 | | BLCKEND |

SYMBOL TABLE ENTRIES

| | | |
|---|---|---|
| 1 | I | |
| 2 | J | |
| 3 | A | |
| 4 | K | |
| 5 | L | 25 |

**FIGURE 11.5. Internal Representation of Figure 11.4.**

## 11.3 QUADRUPLES

### Quadruples for Arithmetic Expressions

A convenient form for a single binary operation is a quadruple

(<operator>, <operand$^1$>, <operand$^2$>, <result>)

where <operand$^1$> and <operand$^2$> specify the arguments and <result> the result. Thus we might represent A*B by

```
*, A,  B,  T
```

where T is some variable to which the result of A*B is assigned. In this manner we represent A*B+C*D by the sequence

```
*, A,  B,  T1
*, C,  D,  T2
+, T1, T2, T3
```

An important point to notice here is that the quadruples appear in the order in which they are to be executed, in contrast to the usual form A*B+C*D. Unary operators are written in this form with <operand$^2$> empty. Thus -A would be written "-,A,,T", which means "assign the value -A to T". In some instances we might want to use a different operator for unary minus as we did in Polish notation, in order to distinguish it from the binary minus.

### Extending Quadruples to Other Operators

The extension to other operators is fairly easy, and we will just give here a list cf operators we will need. In the following table, P, P1, P2 and P3 are operands in one of the forms given in Figure 11.2. Figure 11.6 illustrates the program segment of Figure 11.1 in quadruple form.

| | Operator | Operands | Meaning of quadruple |
|---|---|---|---|
| 1. | BR | i | Branch to quadruple i. |
| 2. | BZ[BP,BM] | i,P | Branch to quadruple i if the value described by P is zero [positive, minus]. |
| 3. | BG[BL,BE] | i,P1,P2 | Branch to quadruple i if the value described by P1 is greater [less, equal] than the value described by P2. |
| 4. | BRL | P | Branch to the quadruple described by the symbol table entry at P. |
| 5. | + [*,/,-] | P1,P2,P3 | Add [multiply, divide, subtract] the value described by P1 to that described by P2 and store the result in the place described by P3. |
| 6. | := | P1,,P3 | Store the value described by P1 in the location described by P3. |
| 7. | CVRI | P1,,P3 | Convert the value described by P1 from real to integer and store the result in the location described by P3. |
| 8. | CVIR | P1,,P3 | Convert from integer to real. |
| 9. | BLOCK | | Begin an ALGOL block. |
| 10. | BLCKEND | | End an ALGOL block. |
| 11. | BOUNDS | P1,P2 | P1 and P2 describe a pair of lower and upper bounds of an array. |
| 12. | ADEC | P1 | P1 is an ALGOL array being declared. If it has n dimensions, this quadruple is preceded by n BOUNDS operators which indicate the bounds of the n dimensions. |

To indicate how subscripting looks for two dimensional matrices, consider the statement C := [i,B[j]]. If d1 is a description of the number of subscripts in the second first dimension for A, we would have

```
*, i, d1, T1
+, T1, B[j], T2
:=, A[T2],, C
```

```
(1) BLOCK                  (10) +  K, T4, T5
(2) -  I, J, T1            (11) := T5, , K
(3) BOUNDS 1, T1           (12) BR 18
(4) ADEC A                 (13) +  I, 1, T6
(5) := 0, , K              (14) := T6, , I
(6) -  I, J, T2            (15) +  I, 1, T7
(7) BMZ 13, T2             (16) := T7, , I
(8) -  I, J, T3            (17) BRL L
(9) *  A[T3], 6, T4        (18) BLCKEND
```

**FIGURE 11.6. Quadruples for Figure 11.1.**

### EXERCISES FOR 11.3

1. Write the statements of exercise 11.2.3 in quadruple form.

2. Design quadruple notation for a procedure call A(X,Y,...,Z). The parameters may be array names, constants, variables, expressions, etc. Be careful. Remember that a parameter may itself contain a procedure (function) call.

## 11.4 TRIPLES, TREES, AND INDIRECT TRIPLES

### Triples

One of the drawbacks of quadruples is the number of temporary variables which must be described. The use of triples eliminates this problem. A triple has the form

<operator> <operand1> <operand2>

There is no field for the result. Instead, any later operand which is the result of this operation will refer directly to this operation. Thus, A+B*C would be represented by

```
(1) *  B, C
(2) +  A, (1)
```

In this notation, (1) refers to the result of triple 1; it is not the constant 1. We would express 1+B*C by

```
(1) *  B, C
(2) +  1, (1)
```

Of course, internally we must distinguish between this new type of operand -- a reference to another triple -- and other types, by a new integer in the first location of an operand.

Using the notation for operators as in the last section, we write the program segment of Figure 11.1 in Figure 11.7. Note that we need the same number of triples as quadruples to represent this program segment. However we no longer need all the temporary variables, and secondly, the triples take less space than quadruples. When the triples are processed, we will of course keep track of descriptions of operands which are results of other operations, but only those whose values are still being processed. For example, when we process triple (2) of Figure 11.7, we generate a description of its result. After triple (4) is processed, this description is no longer needed and can be discarded.

```
(1) BLOCK                     (10) +    K, (9)
(2) -    I, J                 (11) :=   (10), K
(3) BOUNDS 1, (2)             (12) BR   (18)
(4) ADEC A                    (13) +    I, 1
(5) :=   0, K                 (14) :=   (13), I
(6) -    I, J                 (15) +    I, 1
(7) BMZ  (13), (6)            (16) :=   (15), I
(8) -    I, J                 (17) BRL L
(9) *    A[(8)], 6            (18) BLCKEND
```

**FIGURE 11.7. Triples for Program Segment of Figure 11.1.**

**Trees**

Let us define <u>trees</u> for the usual arithmetic expressions as follows. The tree for simple variable or constant is that simple variable or constant. If $e^1$ and $e^2$ are expressions with trees $T^1$ and $T^2$, then the trees for $e^1+e^2$, $e^1-e^2$, $e^1*e^2$, $e^1/e^2$, and $-e^1$ are, respectively,

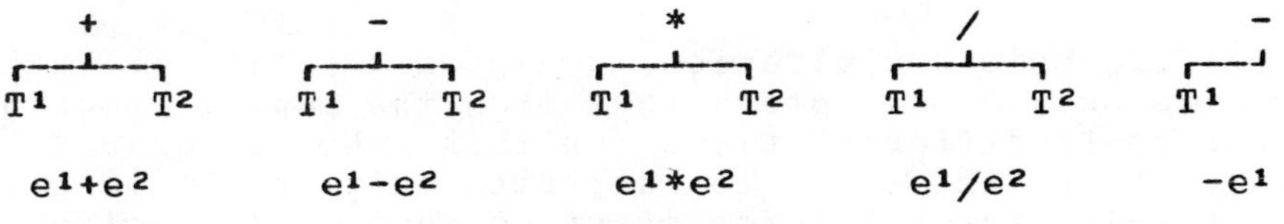

```
     +               -               *               /               -
 ┌───┴───┐       ┌───┴───┐       ┌───┴───┐       ┌───┴───┐       ┌───┘
 T¹      T²      T¹      T²      T¹      T²      T¹      T²      T¹

  e¹+e²           e¹-e²           e¹*e²           e¹/e²           -e¹
```

For example, the tree for A*B+C-D*E is given to the left below:

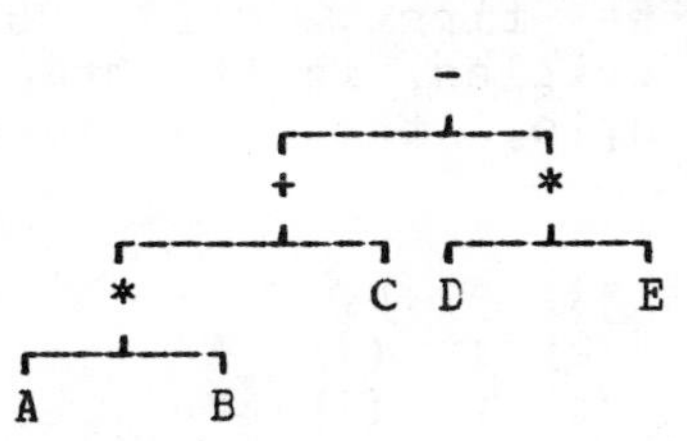

```
                 -
          ┌──────┴──────┐
          +             *
   ┌──────┴──────┐  ┌───┴───┐
   *             C  D       E
┌──┴──┐
A     B
```

```
(1) (* A, B)
(2) (+ (1), C)
(3) (* D, E)
(4) (- (2), (3))
```

Now, triples for any expression can also be thought of as a direct representation of the tree, as illustrated to the right of the tree above. The last triple 4 represents the root of the tree. Each triple i represents a subtree; the operator of the triple is the root of the subtree, while each operand is a variable name representing an end node or else is the number of a triple describing a sub-subtree.

How one generates code for triples depends on whether one thinks of the triples as just a sequence of operations to be executed in order, or a a tree. We will see this in chapter 17.

When it comes to statements, blocks, declarations, and so forth, triples don't form a complete tree in the same sense, because the links between the different statements and declarations are not explicitly given. For example, for a compound statement

```
BEGIN A := B; B := C; D := C; END
```

the tree and triples might look like

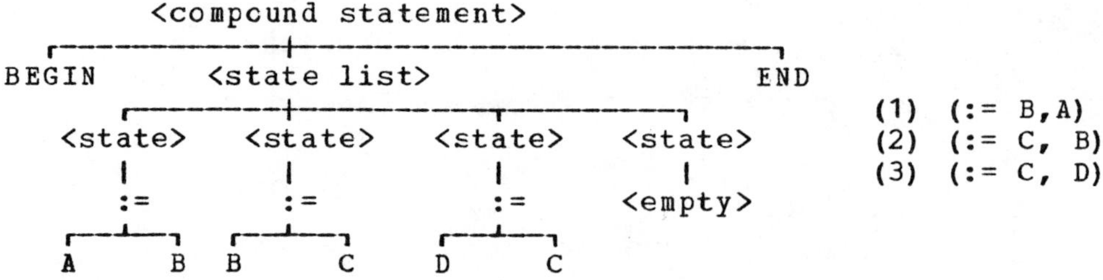


The tree has direct connections (pointers) to the statements, while these connections are implicitly implied in the triple form.

### Indirect Triples

When performing code optimization, (chapter 18), it is usually necessary to delete some operations from the source program and to move others to different places within the program. With quadruples, this is easy to do; with triples, it is harder, since the triples refer to each other so much. To solve this problem, we keep two tables. The second one, TRIPLE, contains the triples themselves, while the first, OPER, contains a sequence of references to the triples, in the order in which they are to be performed. For example, the statements A := B*C; B := B*C would appear as

```
1.  (1)                                (1) *  B, C
2.  (2)                                (2) := (1), A
3.  (1)                                (3) := (1), B
4.  (3)
OPER TABLE                             TRIPLE TABLE
```

We can now rearrange the operations in OPER without disturbing the triples and the references to them.

Note that those triples which are exactly the same need only appear in TRIPLE once. Two triples are the same if all three components are identical; the operands for two different variables B declared in separate blocks are of course different.

There are usually many identical triples in a source program, especially if subscripted variables occur, so that the number of triples is less than the number of operations in OPER. This means, of course, that when adding a triple to the table, the entire table must be searched to see whether it already exists, and this can be time consuming. A hash coding scheme could be used to great advantage here.

Figure 11.8 contains the program segment of Figure 11.1 in indirect triple form.

Care must be taken when an operand references a triple. The triple might be executed in several different places, and a reference to its result must be associated with the correct execution of that triple. For example, in Figure 11.8, the triple (+,I,1) is executed twice according to the OPER table, at operations 13 and 15. The second reference to triple 11 occurs at the evaluation of triple 12 at the operation number 15, and this must be associated with the result of evaluating triple 12 at operation number 14. This becomes more of a problem when the operations are moved around at code optimization time.

```
1.  (1)    10.  (8)         (1) BLOCK                (8)  +    K, (7)
2.  (2)    11.  (9)         (2) -    I, J            (9)  :=   (8), K
2.  (3)    12.  (10)        (3) BOUNDS 1, (2)       (10)  BR   18
4.  (4)    13.  (11)        (4) ADEC A              (11)  +    I, 1
5.  (5)    14.  (12)        (5) :=   0, K           (12)  :=   (11), I
6.  (2)    15.  (11)        (6) BMZ 13, (2)         (13)  BRL L
7.  (6)    16.  (12)        (7) *    A[ (2) ], 6    (14)  BLCKEND
8.  (2)    17.  (13)
9.  (7)    18.  (14)

       OPER                                  TRIPLE
```

**FIGURE 11.8. Indirect Triples for Figure 11.1.**

### 11.5 BLOCKS

When performing code optimization, it is often advantageous to break the program into "basic blocks" (not ALGOL-blocks), and to have a separate "program graph" which describes how these blocks are related. A basic block is a sequence of operations with one entrance and one exit, the first and last operations, respectively. Furthermore, these operations are to be executed in sequence -- no branches occur within the block. As an example, Figure 11.9a shows the blocks for the program segment of Figure 11.1, using quadruples (indirect triples could be used here also). Note that branches have block numbers instead of quadruple numbers for operands. The BMZ quadruple in block 2 has the following meaning: If T2 is minus or zero, go to block 4; otherwise go to block 3. In general, the last operation may jump to any number of blocks. Note also that if a block has only one succesor, we do not need to have an explicit branch to it at the end of that block; such a branch is implicitly given by the program graph.

```
1.  BLOCK                3.  -    I, J, T3
    -   I, J, T1             *    A[T3], 6, T4
    BOUNDS 1, T1             +    K, T4, T5
    ADEC A                   :=   T5,, K
    :=  0,, K
                         4.  +    I, 1, T6
                             :=   T6,, I
2.  -   I, J, T2             +    I, 1, T7
    BMZ 4, 3, T2             :=   T7,, I

                         5.  BLCKEND
```

(a) blocks

$$\begin{bmatrix} 0 & 1 & 0 & 0 & 0 \\ 0 & 0 & 1 & 1 & 0 \\ 0 & 0 & 0 & 0 & 1 \\ 0 & 1 & 0 & 0 & 0 \\ 0 & 0 & 0 & 0 & 0 \end{bmatrix}$$

(b) program graph

**FIGURE 11.9. Blocks and Program Graph for Figure 11.1.**

The program graph contains, for each basic block, a list of its immediate successors (those it branches to) and its immediate predecessors (those that branch to it). In Figure 11.9 this has been represented as a matrix M, where M[i,j] = 1 if and only if block j is a successor of block i. In practice, a list structure is a better way to represent it, because more information about each block may be needed, and because blocks may be created and destroyed as optimization progresses.

Representing a program in this manner allows us to optimize instructions within basic blocks, since they have a restricted format and meaning. We can also analyze the program graph to find loops and to move operations from one block to another. We discuss this in chapter 18.

Variations are possible. For example, if only the for-loops in the original source program are to be optimized, then the operations in them should be grouped into some kind of a block, in order to facilitate processing them.

### 11.6 HISTORICAL REFERENCES

Polish notation, quadruples, and triples have been used in many compilers as the internal form. The use of blocks and a program graph was designed to help in code optimization. Allen(69) uses such a scheme with indirect triples, while FORTRAN H on the IBM 360 uses the same sort of scheme but with quadruples (see Lowry and Medlock(69)).

Syntax trees in a list-structured form are used in several translator writing systems, most notably the Brooker and Morris compiler-compiler and Reynolds' COGENT. The ALGOL W compiler also uses them (see Bauer, Becker and Graham(68)).

# Chapter 12.
# Introduction to Semantic Routines

We discuss the idea of associating a <u>semantic</u> <u>routine</u> with each rule of a grammar. This routine does semantic processing when the rule it is associated with is involved in a syntactic reduction. Section 12.1 introduces the idea with the problem of converting arithmetic expressions from infix to Polish notation, assuming a bottom-up parse. In section 12.2 we explain how to generate quadruples from arithmetic expressions. This requires the addition of semantic information to the syntax tree. In section 12.3 we discuss how to represent this semantic information, and how the semantic routines could look in a compiler. Finally, in section 12.4 we take a look at semantic processing when using a top-down parse.

Our purpose in this chapter is to show how to translate arithmetic expressions with the following syntax to different forms; we are not interested in symbol tables, attributes, and so on.

```
          Z ::= E
(12.0.1)  E ::= T | E + T | E - T | - T
          T ::= F | T * F | T / F
          F ::= I | ( E )
```

## 12.1 TRANSFORMING INFIX TO POLISH NOTATION

We assume that the syntax recognizer is working in such a manner that, whenever the handle x of the sentential form is about to be reduced to a nonterminal U, the routine associated with the rule U ::= x is called. It processes the symbols in x semantically, and outputs the portion of the Polish string that directly concerns x. Note that we don't really care what recognizer is being used. All we expect at this point is that

(12.1.1) the handle is reduced at each reduction.

That is, the leftmost simple phrase is reduced (a slight modification must be made in the operator precedence case, but this does not concern us here.) Since the handle is being reduced, we can make the following important assumption:

(12.1.2) If any nonterminal V appears in the handle, the portion of the Polish string concerned with the substring which reduced to V has already been generated.

We assume that the Polish string being produced is stored in a one dimensional array P. An integer variable p, originally 1, contains the index of the array element which is to be filled next. Each array element can contain one symbol (an identifier or operator). We also assume that when a semantic routine is called it can reference the symbols of the handle which are in the syntax stack S(1)...S(i) used by the recognizer.

### The Semantic Routines

Consider the routine associated with the rule $E^1$ ::= $E^2$ + T. When it is invoked, we can assume that the Polish notation for both $E^2$ and T has been generated. In fact, the array P contains

... <code for $E^2$> <code for T>,

since $E^2$ is directly to the left of T. Note also that no other code has been generated to the right of T; only terminals are to the right of T in the source program since this is a left-to-right parse. All the routine must do, therefore, is to insert the plus sign into the Polish string. In doing so, it has translated from infix form $E^2$ + T to suffix form $E^2$ T +. The semantic routine is just P(p) := "+"; p := p+1.

Consider the semantic routine for F ::= I (I is any identifier). According to the rules given in Chapter 11 for Polish notation, identifiers precede their operators and, moreover, the identifiers appear in the same order in which they appear in infix form. All we have to do for this rule is to put the identifier in the output array P. The routine is therefore

P(p) := S(i); p := p+1

where S(i) is the top stack symbol.

The semantic routine for F ::= ( E ) does not have to do anything; in Polish notation parentheses do not appear, and any code for the operand E has been already generated.

The other routines can be constructed in the same manner; we give a list of them in Figure 12.1. When possible, the same routine should be used for several rules with similar meanings. For example, the semantic routines for rules 3, 4, 7, and 8 can be replaced by the single routine.

P(p) := S(i-1); p := p+1.

| Rule | Semantic Routine |
|---|---|
| (1) Z ::= E | nothing |
| (2) E ::= T | nothing |
| (3) E ::= E + T | P(p) := "+"; p := p+1 |
| (4) E ::= E - T | P(p) := "-"; p := p+1 |
| (5) E ::= - T | P(p) := "@"; p := p+1 |
| (6) T ::= F | nothing |
| (7) T ::= T * F | P(p) := "*"; p := p+1 |
| (8) T ::= T / F | P(p) := "/"; p := p+1 |
| (9) F ::= I | P(p) := S(i);p := p+1 |
| (10) F ::= ( E ) | nothing |

**FIGURE 12.1. Semantic Routines to Generate Polish Notation.**

### A Parse of a Sentence

Figure 12.2 illustrates a parse of the sentence A*(B+C). We have assumed a recognizer which uses a stack S, an incoming symbol R and the rest of the sentence Tk.... The figure shows each step of the parse -- either a reduction or the process of stacking R and scanning the next source symbol Tk. Just before a reduction takes place, the semantic routine is called. It may or may not produce part of the Polish string, which is given in the last column.

| Stack S | R | Tk... | Use rule number | Semantic Routine | Polish string produced so far |
|---|---|---|---|---|---|
| # | A | *(B+C)# | | | |
| #A | * | (B+C)# | 9 | 9 | A |
| #F | * | (B+C)# | 6 | 6 | A |
| #T | * | (B+C)# | | | A |
| #T* | ( | B+C)# | | | A |
| #T*( | B | +C)# | | | A |
| #T*(B | + | C)# | 9 | 9 | AB |
| #T*(F | + | C)# | 6 | 6 | AB |
| #T*(T | + | C)# | 2 | 2 | AB |
| #T*(E | + | C)# | | | AB |
| #T*(E+ | C | )# | | | AB |
| #T*(E+C | ) | # | 9 | 9 | ABC |
| #T*(E+F | ) | # | 6 | 6 | ABC |
| #T*(E+T | ) | # | 3 | 3 | ABC+ |
| #T*(E | ) | # | | | ABC+ |
| #T*(E) | # | | 10 | 10 | ABC+ |
| #T*F | # | | 7 | 7 | ABC+* |
| #T | # | | 2 | 2 | ABC+* |
| #E | # | | 1 | 1 | ABC+* |
| #Z | # | | STOP | | ABC+* |

**FIGURE 12.2. Parse of A* (B+C).**

### Discussion

The reader may feel we went through a lot of bother just to produce

ABC+* from A*(B+C).

After all, we had to invoke 12 semantic routines, many of which did not do anything! This is true in the sense that for the particular case of arithmetic expressions we could probably find and program a shorter method. However, we are looking at the <u>general</u> case of having to parse sentences of <u>any</u> suitable grammar and having to make some sense out of the sentence. We want some systematic way of doing it, so that we don't start completely from scratch every time a new language comes along.

We have separated the problem into two parts -- syntax and semantics. This has simplified the problem because first of all we know from the grammar how a sentence will be parsed -- we know in what order reductions will occur -- without having to program it each time. We use our constructor and recognizer which has been programmed once. Secondly, we can write one semantic routine for each production. This helps break the process into little independent pieces which can be done separately without having to think of everything at once.

Finally, slight changes in syntax or semantics require only slight changes in the corresponding rules or semantic routines. The different parts of analysis have been isolated so that the changes can be made easily.

### EXERCISES FOR 12.1

1. Parse the sentences A, A+B, (A+B), (((A))), ((A+B)*C+B)*C, using the semantic routines of Figure 12.1 and the grammar (12.0.1).

2. Add to grammar (12.0.1) the rule for an assignment statement S ::= I := E, and the rule for a read statement S ::= READ I. Determine the Polish notation for these statements and write semantic routines to translate them into the Polish form.

3. Parse the statements A:=A+B and READ C (see exercise 2).

4. Add rules to (12.0.1) for subscripted variables, and write the semantic routines for them.

## 12.2 TRANSFORMING INFIX TO QUADRUPLES

Let us try to parse the expression A*(B+C) and generate quadruples

```
+, B,  C,  T1
*, A,  T1, T2
```

making up the semantic routines as we go along. The logical place to produce the first quadruple is in the semantic routine for the rule E ::= E+T. Let us therefore execute the bottom-up parse until we arrive at an application of this rule. The sentential form produced at each step is given below with the handle underlined at each step, while Figure 12.3a gives the final partial syntax tree.

```
A*(B+C)        T*(T+C)
F*(B+C)        T*(E+C)
T*(B+C)        T*(E+F)
T*(F+C)        T*(E+T)
```

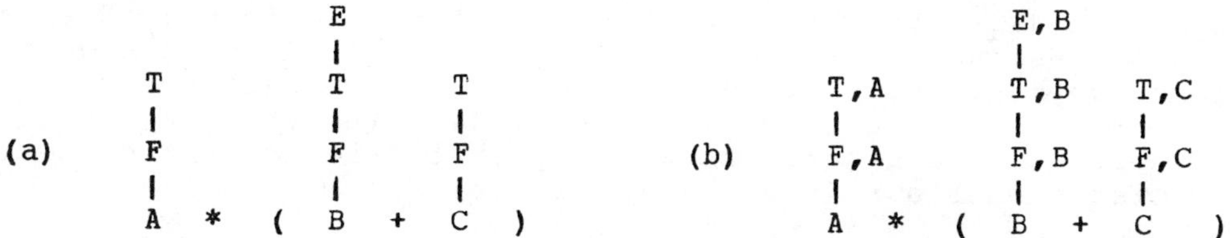


**FIGURE 12.3. Partial Syntax Trees without and with Semantics.**

The next step is to reduce E+T to E; at the same time the semantic routine should produce the quadruple. Unfortunately, we can't produce it, since the sentential form gives no information about the name of the operands E and T! This information was discarded when we made the reductions F ::= B and F ::= C.

The reason we had no trouble when producing Polish notation was that we put the names B and C into the output when making the reductions F ::= B and F ::= C. Obviously, when producing quadruples, we must save the names somewhere until they can be used, and this saving must be done in the routine for F ::= I.

Such information is almost always associated with a nonterminal. Thus, it seems reasonable to allow semantic information to be attached to nodes of the syntax tree as the parse progresses, as illustrated in Figure 12.3b. Note that this also allows us to represent identifiers more correctly than previously. Remember, the scanner recognizes identifiers and returns <u>two</u> arguments -- the symbol I (meaning identifier), and the identifier itself. I is the syntax symbol, while the identifier itself is associated with I, as illustrated in Figure 12.3b.

Below, we refer to the semantics associated with a nonterminal U in the tree by U.SEM. Secondly, we will need to generate names T1, T2, ..., to identify subexpressions. To do this, we use an identifier i which is initially 0. In our semantic language, "i:=i+1; U.SEM:=Ti" is used to generate a new identifier and associate it with U.

Finally, the procedure ENTER(W,X,Y,Z) is called to generate a quadruple in the output consisting of the four parameters.

Now let us parse the string A*(B+C) and figure out the semantic routines as we go along. The first handle is I (with associated semantics A); it should be reduced to F. The name A must be associated with the new nonterminal F, so the semantic routine for F ::= I is

F.SEM := I.SEM.

Figure 12.4a shows the part of the syntax tree formed after this step. The next handle is F, and it should be reduced to T. Again, we must associate with T the name currently associated with F, as in Figure 12.4b. After seeing these two cases we might be able to generalize and say that the semantic routine associated with a rule U ::= V will be

U.SEM := V.SEM.

This is indeed what we want for this simple grammar. Figures 12.4c through 12.4e illustrate a few of the partial trees occurring as the parse progresses. Figure 12.4e describes the tree at the point where the handle is E+T. Here, $E^2$+T should be reduced to $E^1$ using the rule $E^1$ ::= $E^2$+T. The semantic routine must first of all create a new identifier Ti and associate it with the new nonterminal $E^1$. Secondly, it must generate the quadruple for "+". The names of the operands are in $E^2$.SEM and T.SEM, while the resulting name is in $E^1$.SEM. Thus we execute the routine

```
i := i + 1; E¹.SEM := Ti;
ENTER("+",E².SEM,T.SEM,E¹.SEM)
```

yielding the syntax tree of Figure 12.4f.

We leave the rest of the parse to the reader, and hope he will follow through and design the rest of the routines. Compare the results with the routines given in Figure 12.5.

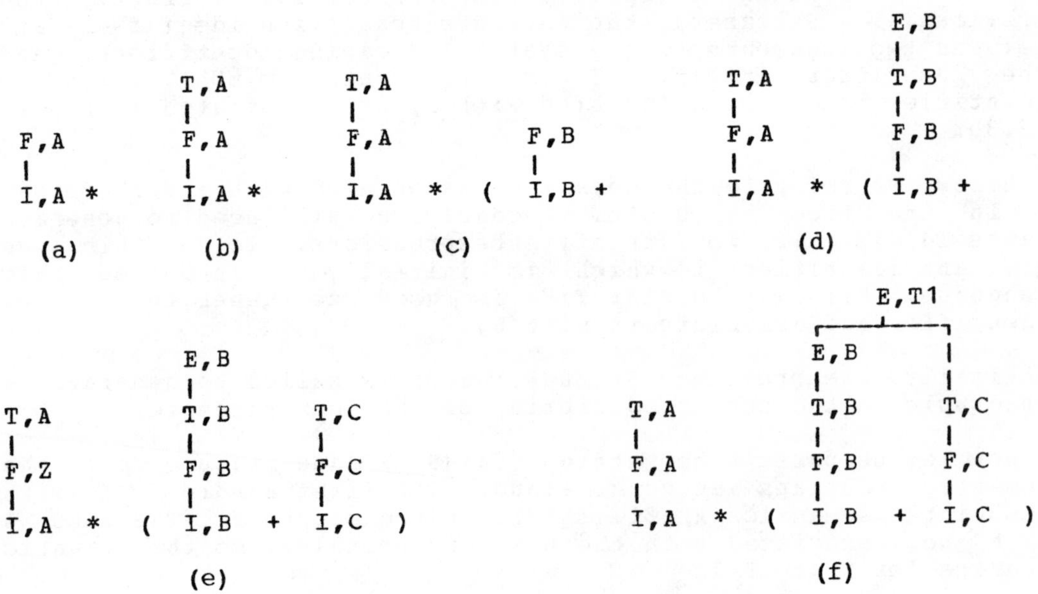


**FIGURE 12.4. Some Partial Trees with Semantics.**

```
Rule                        Semantic routine
(1) Z  ::= E                Z.SEM := E.SEM.
(2) E  ::= T                E.SEM := T.SEM.
(3) E¹ ::= E² + T           i := i+1; E¹.SEM := Ti;
                            ENTER("+", E².SEM, T.SEM, E¹.SEM).
(4) E¹ ::= E² - T           i := i+1; E¹.SEM := Ti;
                            ENTER("-", E².SEM, T.SEM, E¹.SEM).
(5) E  ::= - T              i := i+1; E.SEM := Ti;
                            ENTER("@", 0, T.SEM, E.SEM).
(6) T  ::= F                T.SEM := F.SEM.
(7) T¹ ::= T² * F           i := i+1; T¹.SEM := Ti.
                            ENTER("*", T².SEM, F.SEM, T¹.SEM).
(8) T¹ ::= T² / F           i := i+1; T¹.SEM := Ti;
                            ENTER("/", T².SEM, F.SEM, T¹.SEM).
(9) F  ::= I                F.SEM := I.SEM.
(10 F ::= ( E )             F.SEM := E.SEM.
```

**FIGURE 12.5. Semantic Routines to Generate Quadruples.**

### EXERCISES FOR 12.3

1. Parse the expressions A, (A+B), (((A))), and ((A+B)*C+B)*C using the routines of Figure 12.5.

2. Add the rules S ::= I := E and S ::= READ I to the grammar (12.0.1). Determine a form of the quadruples for these new statements, and write the semantic routines to produce them.

3. Parse the statements A:=A+B and READ C.

## 12.3 IMPLEMENTING SEMANTIC ROUTINES AND STACKS

In general, there may be several semantic attributes associated with a particular nonterminal. Note however, that when we make a reduction by applying a rule like $E^1$ ::= $E^2$+T, the information about $E^2$ and T is no longer needed. It is usually the case that we only need semantic information concerned with the nonterminals in the current sentential form, so let us determine a method of storing it. Since the current sentential form is in a stack S, we can easily have several semantic stacks S1, S2, ..., to hold the corresponding semantic information. These stacks work in parallel with the syntax stack S. A semantic routine can reference all the stacks S, S1, S2, .... For example, if S(i) contains the symbol E, then S1(i), S2(i), ... can be used to hold the type of E, its runtime location, and so on, as illustrated below. Actually, it doesn't matter whether one uses several stacks, or a single stack with separate fields to hold the syntax symbol and the semantic attributes.

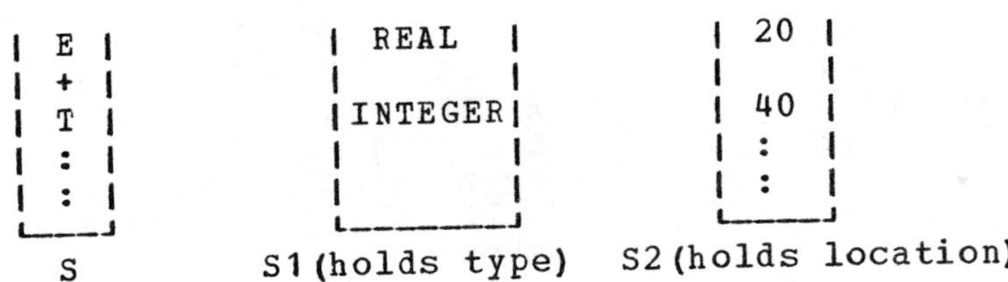


**Linking with Semantics**

One can program each separate semantic routine as a procedure in some language. However, the syntax recognizer must then know the name of each procedure, and this produces too many bookkeeping problems. A simpler method is to associate with each rule of the grammar a positive integer. Then, write one single procedure named SEMANTICS (say), which has as an argument the rule number. When making a reduction, the syntax recognizer calls SEMANTICS, with the number of the rule used in making the reduction as the argument. Figure 12.6 illustrates this for the routines used to generate Polish notation in section 11.2.

If the compiler is programmed in FORTRAN or ALGOL, a computed GO TO or switch designator can be used in place of the case statement.

The syntax and semantic stacks can be in COMMON, or can be global parameters if ALGOL is being used. Alternatively, they can be passed as arguments to the semantic routine.

```
PROCEDURE SEMANTICS(r);                    |The argument is the number
VALUE r; INTEGER r;                        |of the rule applied.
CASE r OF                                  |Pick out routine to execute
    ;                                      |rule 1
    ;                                      |rule 2
    BEGIN P(p):="+";   p:=p+1 END;         |rule 3
    BEGIN P(p):="-";   p:=p+1 END;         |rule 4
    BEGIN P(p):="@";   p:=p+1 END;         |rule 5
    ;                                      |rule 6
    BEGIN P(p):="*";   p:=p+1 END;         |rule 7
    BEGIN P(p):="/";   p:=p+1 END;         |rule 8
    BEGIN P(p):=S1(i);p:=p+1 END;          |rule 9
    ;                                      |rule 10
ENDCASE                                    |
```

**FIGURE 12.6. Semantic Procedure for Grammar 12.0.1.**

Perhaps the most efficient way (with respect to compile-time) is to have the syntax constructor build the syntax recognizer in the form of a program segment in the language that the compiler writer is programming. This segment would contain the necessary declarations for the stacks and other variables, the recognizer itself, and even the scanner. The compiler would include these cards as in Figure 12.7. Some conventions must be adhered to; the label SEM of the semantic routines, the label to return to when the semantic routine is finished, the name of the stacks, and so forth, must all be agreed upon. Note that no procedure is called for the semantic routine; everything is a simple jump. This method is used in Mckeeman's et al(70) XPL compiler writing system.

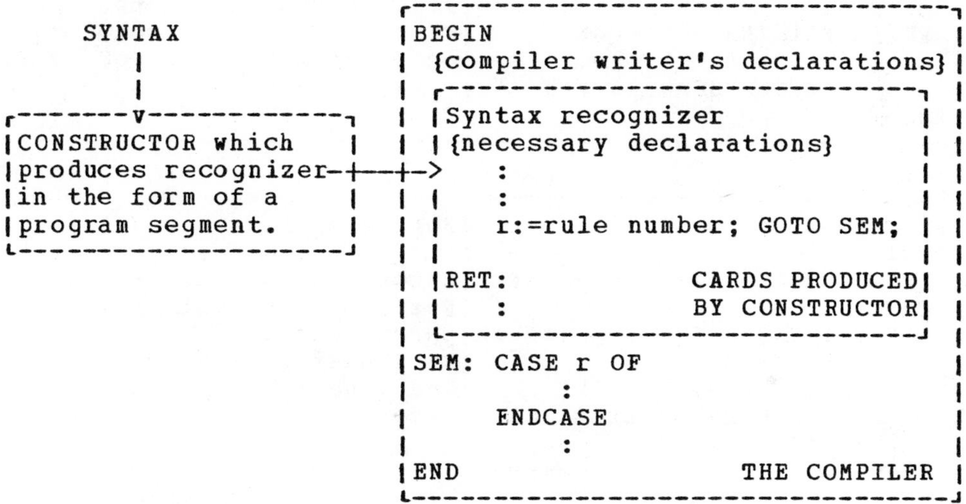


**FIGURE 12.7. Constructor Producing a Program Segment.**

## 12.4 SEMANTIC PROCESSING WITH TOP-DOWN PARSING

To implement recursive procedures for parsing and translating sentences of (12.0.1), we first rewrite the grammar as

```
Z ::= E
E ::= [-] T {(+ | -) T}
T ::= F {(* | /) F}
F ::= I | ( E )
```

We then write, as in section 4.3, the following four recursive procedures:

| PROCEDURE Z; E | For rule Z ::= E |
|---|---|

```
PROCEDURE E;                        |For rules E::=[-] T {(+ | -) T}
BEGIN                               |Begin by checking for the first
 IF NXTSYMB='-'THEN SCAN; T;        |unary minus. Then get the term.
WHILE NEXTSYMB = '+' OR             |Now, iteratively look for
       NXTSYMB = '-' DO             |occurrences of + T  or  - T.
         BEGIN SCAN; T END          |
END                                 |
```

```
PROCEDURE T;                        |For rules T::=F {(* | /) F}
BEGIN F;                            |First parse the Factor.
 WHILE NXTSYMB = '*' OR             |Then iteratively look for
       NXTSYMB = '/' DO             |occurrences of * F  or  / F.
         BEGIN SCAN; F END          |
END                                 |
```

```
PROCEDURE F;                        |For rules F::= I | ( E )
BEGIN                               |
 IF NXTSYMB = 'I' THEN SCAN         |Check for Identifier.
 ELSE                               |Not I, so it must start with a
  IF NXTSYMB ≠ '(' THEN ERROR       |parenthesis.
  ELSE BEGIN SCAN; E;               |An E must follow,
         IF NXTSYMB ≠ ')'           |and finally a closing
         THEN ERROR ELSE SCAN       |parenthesis.
END    END                          |
```

We now add statements to each of the procedures in order to process the symbols semantically. We will produce quadruples. We illustrate the process for procedures T and F, and leave the other two to the reader.

Note that we don't explicitly have a syntax tree or semantics stack. We could insert statements to build these but it isn't necessary. Instead, we use local variables in each procedure, and use formal parameters to pass semantic information.

The semantics of any nonterminal Z, E, T, or F is the name of a source program or temporary variable. When a phrase for a nonterminal is parsed, this name must be associated with it. Let us therefore have a STRING parameter X with each of these procedures. When a procedure is finished, it returns in X the name of the corresponding variable.

For example, we give below the altered procedure F(X). In it, we assume that when an identifier is scanned, the SCAN procedure puts 'I' into NXTSYMB and the identifier itself into NXTSEM. Note in the procedure the call on E(X), which returns in X the name of the variable for the phrase E. This same name is used as the name for F.

```
PROCEDURE F(X); STRING X;         |Return the semantics of F (the
BEGIN                             |name of the variable) in X.
 IF NXTSYMB = 'I' THEN            |If an identifier, its name has
  BEGIN X:=NXTSEM; SCAN END       |been put in NXTSEM by SCAN.
 ELSE                             |It is (E). Check for the paren.
  IF NXTSYMB ≠ '(' THEN ERROR     |and parse the E. The name
  ELSE BEGIN SCAN; E(X);          |associated with E is also the
         IF NXTSYMB ≠ ')'         |name to associate with F!
         THEN ERROR ELSE SCAN     |
END      END                      |
```

Now let us look at the procedure T, in which quadruples for * and / are generated. We first parse a Factor and put its name in local variable Y. Then we scan an operation * or / and its second operand and generate the quadruple for it. Note that after each quadruple generation, into Y is put the name of the variable holding its result. This process repeats as long as there are operations * or /.

```
PROCEDURE T(X); STRING X;         |Return in X the name of the
BEGIN STRING Y, Z, OP;            |variable for the phrase T.
 F(Y); OP := NXTSYMB;             |Parse first Factor, put its name
                                  |in local variable Y.
 WHILE OP='*' OR OP='/' DO        |For each operation, call F to
  BEGIN SCAN; F(Z); j:=j+1;       |parse the following Factor,
   ENTER(OP, Y, Z, Tj);           |generate a temporary name, and
   Y := Tj; OP := NXTSYMB;        |generate the quadruple. The name
  END;                            |of the result is Tj.
 X := Y                           |Put the result name Y into the
END                               |returned parameter X.
```

We said earlier that almost any parsing algorithm uses a stack. The stack here is not explicitly realized; it is implicitly realized in the stack mechanism used at runtime to store the procedure call information (see sections 8.8 and 8.9). Each procedure uses local variables to hold values, and please note that these variables are local to a particular execution of the procedure, which is what we want. Semantic information is passed as parameters of the procedures, instead of explicitly in a semantic stack.

Section 13.6 contains another example of the uses of top-down parsing in compiling.

## 12.5 HISTORICAL REFERENCES

The earliest technique for translating from infix expressions to another form was given by Rutishauser(52). His technique consisted of repeatedly scanning the whole expression, each time finding the innermost simple operation, generating an internal form for it, and replacing it by a single operand. The first FORTRAN compiler also made several scans over an expression to get it into an internal form (see Backus et al(57)). Samelson and Bauer(60) first described what could be called an (ad hoc) efficient bottom-up parsing algorithm (transition matrices) connected to routines which did semantic processing. They discuss translation for most of the ALGOL 60 constructs. Dijkstra(63) describes the use of the (ad hoc) operator precedence technique to translate expressions to Polish notation. Most of these historically interesting techniques are briefly described in Shaw(66).

The nice part about section 12.1 and 12.2 is that the methods described depend only on the fact that a bottom-up parsing algorithm is being used, not on which particular technique or implementation is begin used.

In early compilers, syntax and semantics were mixed together in an ad hoc manner. This is still the case in many existing compilers. The purpose of separating the two is to be able to formalize and automate the syntax process, and to be able to do things in a more systematic manner. The early syntax-directed compiler writing systems of Irons(61) and Brooker et al separated the two. The latter uses a top-down parsing scheme which actually builds the syntax tree. The programmer can then manipulate this tree in the semantic routines, called "FORMAT" routines in this system. The term "semantic" routine comes from Feldman(66); Wirth and Weber(66) call them "interpretation rules".

# Chapter 13.
# Semantic Routines for ALGOL-Like Constructs

We illustrate semantic routines to generate quadruples for variables, expressions, conditional statements, labels and branches, and for-loops. With this knowledge, the reader should have no difficulty with semantic routines for other constructs. In this chapter, we are not concerned with allocation of storage to runtime variables; this will be covered in chapter 14. We assume an ALGOL-like language without block structure, where all variables must be declared before they are used. Comments about handling FORTRAN and block structured languages will be made where relevant.

The semantic routines will generate quadruples, using the notation described in section 11.3. Please note however that operands will not be as described in Figure 11.2. To make up such operands would require too much detailed programming which would detract from our goal of a clear explanation. Instead, each operand will be a pointer to an entry in a single symbol table which will contain descriptions of all source program variables, temporaries, constants and so forth. We also assume a bottom-up parse, although the last section discusses a top-down parse for Boolean expressions.

The purpose of this section is not just to write a compiler, but to illustrate how one goes about writing one. The reader should try to understand <u>why</u> certain things are done in a particular way. It will be noted that we rearrange the syntax to fit the semantics, but we won't discuss the additional problem of making sure the new syntax is suitable for the type of recognizer being used.

Many of the techniques described in translating into quadruples will also be used in translating to other internal forms, and also in translating into machine language.

### 13.1 THE SEMANTIC ROUTINE NOTATION

We use a symbol table of all identifiers in a program, referenced through the following procedures LOOKUP, LOOKUPDEC and INSERT:

1. LOOKUP(NAME,P). Look in the symbol table for a valid entry with argument NAME (an identifier). Put the address of the entry in the variable P. If no entry exists, put 0 in P.
2. LOOKUPDEC(NAME,P). The same as LOOKUP, but it is used for a declaration. For a block structured language, the routine would look only at the identifiers in the current block.
3. INSERT(NAME,P). Put a new entry in the symbol table. The argument is NAME. Put the address of the entry in P.

These procedure calls could also be used for compiling FORTRAN or almost any language; the action of the particular procedures would just be different depending on how the symbol table was structured.

As for the attributes of the entries in the symbol table, we will be concerned only with the following five integer-valued components.

1. TYPE. Indicates the type -- 0 = UNDEFINED, 1 = REAL, 2 = INTEGER, 3 = BOOLEAN, 4 = LABEL.
2. TYPE1. 1 = simple variable, 2 = array name, 3 = subscripted variable.
3. TEMPORARY. 1 = temporary variable, 0 = no.
4. DECLARED. 0 = no, 1 = yes.
5. ADDRESS. The quadruple number of the label, or the address of some other symbol table entry.
6. NUMBER. The number of dimensions if an ARRAY.

It should be mentioned that UNDEFINED, REAL, INTEGER, BOOLEAN, and LABEL are considered to be integer valued variables in our compiler with the constant values described above. All operand descriptions are stored in the same table, so that an operand in the internal form can be just a pointer to the symbol table element describing it. This simplifies the presentation and allows us to concentrate our attention on other problems. Given a pointer P to a symbol table entry, we will refer to the attributes by P.TYPE, P.TYPE1, and so forth.

When a label is defined, component ADDRESS of its symbol table element contains the number of the quadruple it labels.

A subscripted variable is represented by an entry with TYPE1=3. In this case, TYPE is the type of the array element, NUMBER contains the address of the symbol table element describing the array, and ADDRESS is the address of the entry describing the VARPART for the subscripted variable.

**Referencing the Semantic Stacks**

When the handle x of the sentential form in question is about to be reduced to the nonterminal U (using the rule U ::= x), a routine is called to work on the semantics of the symbols. This involves

1. entering or checking information in the symbol table;
2. checking semantic information associated with x;
3. generating quadruples; and
4. associating semantic information with the nonterminal U.

As in chapter 12, a piece of information S associated with a symbol U will be referred to by U.S. For example, the symbol <expr> has associated with it a pointer ENTRY containing the address of the symbol table entry describing the expression. This is referred to by

<expr>.ENTRY.

Please remember that in any implementation, <expr> is likely to be somewhere on the syntax stack, while the value

<expr>.ENTRY would be in a corresponding semantic stack element. The following table gives an incomplete list of symbols we will be using, along with associated semantics.

1. I.NAME NAME is a string containing the actual characters of the identifier.
2. <variable>.ENTRY ENTRY contains a pointer to the symbol table entry for the variable.
3. <expr>.ENTRY Same as for <variable>.
4. <if clause>.JUMP The right side of the rule for <if clause> is IF <expression> THEN. When parsed, a BZ quadruple is generated but we don't know where to branch to yet. JUMP contains the number of the BZ quadruple so that the goal address can be filled in later.

**Subroutines and Variables Used**

The semantic routines are programmed in bastard ALGOL, using the following variables and routines:

1. ENTER(+, P1, P2, P3). Enter a quadruple whose components are the four arguments into the internal source program list.
2. ERROR(i) is a call on an error message routine to print out error message i and to stop the translation.
3. NEXTQUAD is an integer variable which always contains the number of the next quadruple to be generated. It is initially equal to 1.
4. QUAD(I,J) refers to the Jth component of the Ith quadruple which has been generated so far. It can be used to reference or to change that component.
5. GENERATETEMP(P) is a call on a routine which enters an element into the symbol table for a temporary variable and puts the address of the new symbol table element in pointer variable P.
6. CHECKTYPE(P,N) is a routine which checks the symbol table entry at pointer P to see if its type is N (e.g. CHECKTYPE(P,BOOLEAN)). If not, it prints an error message and stops translation.
7. CONVERTRI(P) routine checks the entry P for type INTEGER. If it is INTEGER, then it just returns. If it is REAL, then GENERATETEMP is called to get a new temporary variable which is given type INTEGER. A CVRI quadruple is generated to convert the input value to type INTEGER and store it into the new temporary. Finally the address of the new temporary symbol table entry replaces the argument of the procedure. If the type of P is not INTEGER or REAL, an error message is given.
8. CONVERTIR works the same way, except that it converts from INTEGER to REAL.
9. Variables will be used as compile-time temporaries when necessary (e.g. P, P1, P2); their types and usage will be clear from the context.

## 13.2 CONDITIONAL STATEMENTS

We start with routines for conditional statements because they are simple but still illustrate some of the problems involved. The usual definition of a conditional statement is

```
<statement1> ::= <if clause> <statement2> ELSE <statement3>
               | <if clause> <statement2>
<if clause>  ::= IF <expr> THEN
```

where the <expr> must have type BOOLEAN. Assuming 0 for FALSE and non-zero for TRUE, and assuming that the expression has been evaluated and assigned tc a temporary T, we should generate one of the following sequences:

```
(1)    Quads for T:=<expr>                 (1)    Quads for T:=<expr>
(p)    BZ q+1, T, 0                        (p)    BZ q, T, 0
       <statement2>          or                  <statement2>
(q)    BR r                                (q)
(q+1)  <statement3>
(r)
```

The quadruple BZ is generated by the routine for <if clause> ::= IF <expr> THEN. Of course, we don't know where to branch to, so we save the quadruple number as the semantics associated with <if clause> for later use. Note that we can assume that the code to evaluate the expression has been generated, no matter how complicated it is. Also, <expr> has associated with it in ENTRY the address of the symbol table entry describing it. The routine is:

```
 <if clause> ::= IF <expr> THEN
┌──────────────────────────────────────────────────────────────┐
|P := <expr>.ENTRY;             |Put into P the pointer to the  |
|CHECKTYPE(P,BOOLEAN);          |symbol table entry for <expr>. |
|<if clause>.JUMP:=NEXTQUAD;    |Save the address of the next   |
|                               |quadruple, which will be the   |
|                               |BZ over the THEN statement.    |
|ENTER( BZ, 0, P, 0);           |Generate the BZ quadruple.     |
└──────────────────────────────────────────────────────────────┘
```

Note the call on CHECKTYPE to make sure the expression is BOOLEAN.

This takes care of generating code to branch on FALSE. Let us now indicate the routine for the conditional statement without an ELSE. When <if clause> <statement$^{2}$> is to be reduced to <statement$^{1}$>, we can assume that all the quadruples for <statement$^{2}$> have been generated. They do, of course, follow the BZ, since no part of the <statement$^{2}$> was parsed until IF <expr> THEN was reduced. The only thing we have to do in this case is fill in the EZ over <statement$^{2}$>. If you recall, we saved its quadruple number in <if clause>.JUMP. The semantic routine is therefore

<statement$^{1}$> ::= <if clause> <statement$^{2}$>

| Semantic routine | Comment |
|---|---|
| `I := <if clause>.JUMP;` | Put the number of the next |
| `QUAD(I,2) := NEXTQUAD;` | quadruple into component 2 of |
| | the BZ quadruple (number I). |

When generating code for a conditional statement with an ELSE, using the above rules, we run into a problem. We must have the branch instruction between <statement$^{2}$> and <statement$^{3}$>. But, using the above syntax, both <statement$^{2}$> and <statement$^{3}$> have been parsed before we have a chance. To allow syntax to correspond with the desired semantics we change the syntax to

<statement$^{1}$> ::= <true part> <statement$^{3}$>
<true part> ::= <if clause> <statement$^{2}$> ELSE

This now allows us to write the following two semantic routines:

<true part> ::= <if clause> <statement$^{2}$> ELSE

| Semantic routine | Comment |
|---|---|
| `<true part>.JUMP:=NEXTQUAD;` | Save the address of the next |
| | quadruple so that we can fill |
| `ENTER( BR, 0, 0, 0);` | in the branch address later. |
| `I := <if clause>.JUMP;` | Fix up the BZ over |
| `QUAD(I,2) := NEXTQUAD;` | <statement$^{1}$> (as before). |

<statement$^{1}$> ::= <true part> <statement$^{3}$>

| Semantic routine | Comment |
|---|---|
| `I := <true part>.JUMP;` | Fill in the address of the |
| `QUAD(I,2) := NEXTQUAD;` | branch over <statement$^{2}$>. |

Again, this sequence of semantic routines illustrates two basic points. The first is that when a handle XY...Z is about to be reduced, all code for the nonterminals in the handle has been produced. If circumstances require extra code between these symbols, then we must change the syntax to fit the semantics.

The second point illustrated is the use of the semantics associated with a symbol in order to store information needed later. Note that we could have any number of nested conditional statements, yielding at some point of the parse any number of <if clause>s. Each has its associated JUMP component (address of the BZ), and the syntax mechanism -- the stack -- provides an automatic way to keep them separated.

We shall see these two points illustrated over and over again as we progress.

### EXERCISES FOR 13.2

1. The code produced for a statement like IF A ≤ B THEN <statement$^2$> is pretty bad. We subtract A from B and get the result TRUE or FALSE depending on whether the result is positive or not, then finally we BZ over the <statement$^2$>. Change the syntax of <if clause> to also recognize the special case IF <expr$^1$> ≤ <expr$^2$> THEN and in such a case to generate a single quadruple (BG, 0, <expr$^1$>, <expr$^2$>).

2. Change the syntax and semantics to also recognize IF <expr$^1$> ≥ <expr$^2$> and to generate (BG, 0, <expr$^2$>, <expr$^1$>).

## 13.3 LABELS AND BRANCHES

One definition of a label is through the syntax

<statement$^1$> ::= I : <statement$^2$>

where "I" is the nonterminal meaning identifier. A problem similar to that in conditional statements exists here, because the label I must be given the address of the beginning of the <statement$^2$>, and this is impossible because the code for <statement$^2$> has already been generated when we finally get to look at the identifier. We change the syntax to:

<statement$^1$> ::= <label definition> <statement$^2$>
<label definition> ::= I :

Remembering that labels can be referenced before their actual definitions, we write the following semantic routine.

<label definition> ::= I :

```
LOOKUPDEC(I.NAME,P);                 |Look up the identifier in the
IF P = 0 THEN                        |table. See if its there.
  BEGIN                              |It's not there yet so put it in
  INSERT(I.NAME,P);                  |and make it a label.
  P.TYPE:=LABEL                      |
  END                                |
ELSE BEGIN CHECKTYPE(P,LABEL);       |It's in; make sure its a label.
           IF P.DECLARED = 1         |If the declared bit is on this
           THEN ERROR(3)             |is a second declaration and we
     END;                            |print out error message 3.
P.DECLARED := 1;                     |Set the declared bit and
P.ADDRESS  := NEXTQUAD;              |fill in the address.
```

No additional semantics need be associated with the rule ,,,,, <statement$^1$> ::= <label definition> <statement$^2$>.

In FORTRAN, GO TO statements present no problem, since each statement number (label) must be unique. The semantic routine for branch GO TO I is

<statement> ::= GO TO I

```
LOOKUP(I.NAME, P);            |Look in the table for the
IF P = 0 THEN                 |identifier.
  BEGIN                       |It's not there, so insert
  INSERT(I.NAME, P);          |it into the symbol table
  P.TYPE := LABEL;            |with type LABEL and make it
  P.DECLARED := 0;            |undeclared.
  END                         |
ELSE CHECKTYPE(P,LABEL);      |It's in; check the type.
ENTER( BRL, P, 0, 0);         |Generate the branch.
```

#### Linking Branch Operations

It may be desirable to use BR instead of BRL operations for branches to labels. That is, we may want to put a quadruple number instead of the address of a symbol table entry in the operand field. Such a problem also occurs when we generate machine language for branches; the address of the instruction to branch to is put in the branch instruction.

However, a GO TO L may appear before the definition of label L, and therefore we can't fill in the quadruple number until the definition is parsed. Several such branches to the same label may occur, which complicates the problem.

A simple way to process forward references is to link the quadruples for the GO TO L statements together, and to keep the beginning of this linked list in the ADDRESS portion of the symbol table element for L. We illustrate this for the three references to L at quadruples 10, 20, and 40 in Figure 13.1. ,,, No separate stack or table is necessary to hold the links; we use the first operand field of a quadruple for this purpose.

When the definition of L is finally parsed, the semantic routine can then process this linked list to fill in the correct quadruple number in all the branch quadruples. Such a scheme is an extremely simple way of solving the forward reference problem, and it is also efficient. It can sometimes be used to process forward references to variables, procedures, etc., depending on the source language involved.

```
GO TO L;          (10) BR 0,0,0       NAME ADDRESS DECLARED
   :                  :               | L |  40   |   0   |
GO TO L;          (20) BR 10,0,0
   :                  :
GO TO L;          (40) BR 20,0,0      relevant symbol
source program    quadruples          table element fields
```

**FIGURE 13.1. Linking Forward References Together.**

### Forward References with Block Structure

We have a problem with forward references in block structured languages. When a label is referenced which is already defined in an outer block but not yet in the block in which the reference appears, will the label definition occur in this block or not? That is, when we parse the last statement of

BEGIN L: BEGIN GO TO L

does GO TO L refer to the previous label definition or to a label definition not yet parsed? One solution of course is to have a first pass look only at block structure, declarations, and label definitions in order to completely build the symbol table. The second pass then knows where each label is defined. If a one-pass compiler is desired, another solution is to require label declarations -- like LABEL L -- in the block in which the label is actually defined. This is a horrible solution from the programmers point of view and should rarely be used. It requires too much unnecessary programming effort. A third solution, which we outline briefly, requires more work from the compiler writer.

If a reference occurs to a label which is as yet undefined in the block, insert a symbol table entry for the label in that block. For each open block, and for each such label within the block, maintain a linked list of quadruples which reference the label, as described above. If and when the label is actually declared in the block, then all is well; the quadruples refer to the correct label. If the label is not declared in the block (we know this when the whole block is parsed), then we must delete this entry from the symbol table, add an entry for the label in the surrounding block (if not there), and add the list of references in the block being closed to the list of references to that label in the surrounding block.

Of course, we still have the problem of jumps out of blocks in case of implementations which require a call of a block exit routine. One can also link together the block exit instructions required for jumps to L, and fill in the correct parameters in the instructions when L's block number is finally determined.

### EXERCISES FOR 13.3

1. Change the semantic routines given for branches and labels to generate BR instructions instead of BRL instructions.

2. Design and write the semantic routines which implement the scheme to solve the forward reference problem in block structured languages.

### 13.4 VARIABLES AND EXPRESSIONS

The ALGOL-like rules we are concerned with are

```
<variable>  ::= I | I ( <expr list> )
<expr list> ::= <expr> | <expr list> , <expr>
```

The first, <variable> ::= I, requires no quadruples to be generated. We must only look up the identifier in the symbol table and associate its entry with <variable>. We thus have the semantic routine

```
 <variable> ::= I
+--------------------------------------------------------------------+
|LOOKUP( I.NAME, P);              |Look up the name associated       |
|IF P = 0 THEN ERROR(4);          |with the identifier. If P=0, it|
|                                 |was not found; give message.      |
|<variable>.ENTRY := P;           |Associate the address of the      |
|                                 |table entry with <variable>.      |
+--------------------------------------------------------------------+
```

If we were compiling FORTRAN, the fact that the identifier was not found would not be an error. What we would do is insert the identifier into the table using the INSERT procedure and make the TYPE attribute REAL or INTEGER depending on what the first character of the identifier was.

The use of a subscripted variable I ( <expr list> ) requires more effort on our part. We must actually produce quadruples to evaluate all the subscripts and to calculate the address of the array element referenced, using the scheme described in section 8.4. We also want to count the number of subscripts and make sure they check with the number declared.

We could use the syntax given above, but in order to use (8.4.5) to calculate VARPART, we change it to

```
<subs> ::= I ( <expr> | <subs> , <expr>
<variable> ::= <subs> )
```

The symbol table entry for an array identifier has TYPE1 = 2, while TYPE gives the type of each array element, and NUMBER the number of dimensions. To simplify matters, we assume that the symbol table also contains, in successive locations, the symbol table entries for d1, d2, d3, ..., dn (see 8.4.5). This wastes space, but is the simplest way to describe what is happening. The usual way of handling this is to have the runtime address of the dope vector in field ADDRESS, and to know from this address where d1, d2, etc. are in the dope vector.

Let us now turn to the routine for the rule <subs> ::= I ( <expr>. What we have to do is to look up the array identifier in the list, generate code for VARPART := <expr>, and associate the address of the symbol table entry for d1 with <subs>.

```
<subs>  ::= I ( <expr>
+--------------------------------------------------------------------+
|LOOKUP(I.NAME, P);              |Look up the identifier.            |
|IF P = 0 OR P.TYPE ≠ 2          |It must be declared and            |
|THEN ERRCR(5);                  |have type ARRAY.                   |
|                                |We have one subscript here         |
|<subs>.CCUNT = P.NUMBER-1;      |already. We'll use the COUNT to    |
|                                |check the number of dimensions.    |
|<subs>.ARR := P;                |Save address of array entry.       |
|<subs>.ENTRY := P+1;            |This puts the address of the d1    |
|                                |table entry into ENTRY.            |
|GENERATETEMP(P);                |Generate a table entry for a       |
|P.TYPE := INTEGER;              |temporary of type INTEGER for      |
|<subs>.ENTRY2 := P;             |VARPART; save its address.         |
|CONVERTRI(<expr>.ENTRY);        |Remember, this routine checks      |
|P := <expr>.ENTRY;              |the entry and generates a          |
|                                |conversion if necessary.           |
|ENTER(:=,P, ,<subs>.ENTRY2);    |Generate quadruple to store the    |
|                                |first subscript into VARPART.      |
+--------------------------------------------------------------------+
```

Let us list the semantic information associated with <subs>:

1. <subs>.ENTRY — Address of symbol table entry for di if code for the ith subscript has been processed.
2. <subs>.ENTRY2 — Address of the symbol table entry for VARPART.
3. <subs>.COUNT — (number of dimensions) - i, if code for the ith subscript has been generated.
4. <subs>.ARR — Pointer to the array name table element.

The next step is to program the routine for <subs$^{1}$> ::= <subs$^{2}$> , <expr>. Assuming that this is subscript i, we must generate code for VARPART := VARPART*di + <expr>.

```
<subs1> ::= <subs2> , <expr>
+--------------------------------------------------------------------+
|<subs1>.COUNT                   |Count the subscript.               |
|         := <subs2>.COUNT-1;    |                                   |
|<subs1>.ARR := <subs2>.ARR;     |Save the array element type.       |
|<subs1>.ENTRY                   |<subs1>.ENTRY now points at        |
|         := <subs2>.ENTRY+1;    |table entry for di.                |
|P1:=<subs2>.ENTRY2;             |Put the address of the VARPART     |
|<subs1>.ENTRY2 :=P1;            |table entry in P1 and ENTRY2.      |
|ENTER(*,P1,<subs1>.ENTRY,P1);   |Quadruple for                      |
|P:=<expr>.ENTRY;                | VARPART := VARPART*di.            |
|CONVERTRI(P);                   |Generate a quadruple to convert    |
|                                |the subscript to integer (only     |
|                                |if necessary, of course).          |
|ENTER(+, P1, P, P1);            |Quadruple for                      |
|                                | VARPART := VARPART + subscript    |
+--------------------------------------------------------------------+
```

Notice that it doesn't matter how complicated the subscript expression is. It could include references to other array elements, functions, or what have you, because when we get here, all we have is a pointer to a symbol table element describing the result. The final routine we have to program is for the rule <variable> ::= <subs> ). In the routine we can check the number of subscripts, and construct a table entry describing the array element.

```
 <variable> ::= <subs> )
┌─────────────────────────────────────────────────────────────────┐
|IF <subs>.COUNT ≠ 0              |COUNT now 0 means that the     |
|THEN ERROR(6);                   |number of subscripts was right.|
|GENERATETEMP(P)                  |Generate a temporary to        |
|P.TYPE1 := 3;                    |describe the array element.    |
|P.TYPE := <subs>.ARR.TYPE;       |Fill in the type,              |
|P.ADDRESS := <subs>.ENTRY2;      |Address of VARPART entry, and  |
|P.NUMBER := <subs>.ARR;          |Address of array ident. entry. |
└─────────────────────────────────────────────────────────────────┘
```

#### Arithmetic and Logical Operators

Binary operators are handled much like we discussed in chapter 12, and we really don't have to go into any detail here. For a rule like <expr$^1$> ::= <expr$^2$> + <term>, <expr$^2$> and <term> are checked for type compatibility and, if necessary, quadruples are generated to convert one or the other of the operands to a new type. A new temporary is generated to hold the result and the quadruple for the operator is generated. Unary operators are handled similarly.

#### EXERCISES FOR 13.4

1. Write the semantic routine for the rule <expr$^1$> ::= <expr$^2$> + <term>.

2. Write the semantic routine for <factor> ::= - <primary>.

### 13.5 FOR-LOOPS

We illustrate the semantic routines for the ALGOL for-loop defined by

<statement> ::= FOR <variable> := <for list> DO <statement>
<for list> ::= <expr$^1$> STEP <expr$^2$> UNTIL <expr$^3$>

where we assume that the step element <expr$^2$> is always positive. With this assumption, the for loop should be equivalent to

```
<variable> := <expr1>;
GO TO OVER;
AGAIN: <variable> := <variable> + <expr2>;
OVER:
IF <variable> ≤ <expr3>
THEN BEGIN <statement>; GO TO AGAIN END
```

Note that the for-loop variable is used in several places. As we parse the loop we must therefore keep a pointer to its symbol table entry in a convenient place. It should be fairly obvious by now that we have to change the rules somewhat, in order to generate the quadruples in the correct order. We use the rules

```
<for1> ::= FOR <variable> := <expr1>
<for2> ::= <for1> STEP <expr2>
<for3> ::= <for2> UNTIL <expr3>
<statement1> ::= <for3> DO <statement2>
```

We can now give the following semantic routines. In these routines, we have left out checks for types of operands and generation of quadruples for conversion, in order to make it easier to follow the logic.

```
<for1> ::= FOR <variable> := <expr1>
```

| Routine | Comment |
|---|---|
| LOOKUP(<variable>.NAME,P);<br>IF P = 0 THEN ERROR(7);<br>P1 := <expr1>.ENTRY;<br>ENTER( :=, P1,, P);<br><for1>.ENTRY := P;<br><for1>.JUMP := NEXTQUAD;<br><br>ENTER(BR, 0, 0, 0);<br><for1>.JUMP2 := NEXTQUAD; | Put symbol table address in P.<br><br>Generate code for initializing the loop variable.<br>Save the loop variable entry address and the address of the BR to OVER.<br>Generate BR to OVER.<br>We also need the address of the quadruple labeled AGAIN. |

```
<for2> ::= <for1> STEP <expr2>
```

| Routine | Comment |
|---|---|
| <for2>.JUMP2 := <for1>.JUMP2;<br><for2>.ENTRY := <for1>.ENTRY;<br>P := <expr2>.ENTRY;<br>ENTER(+, <for1>.ENTRY,<br>P, <for1>.ENTRY);<br>I := <for1>.JUMP;<br>QUAD(I,2) := NEXTQUAD; | Save the address of the label AGAIN and the loop variable.<br><br>Generate the quadruple to add the step value to the loop var.<br>Fill in the branch to OVER quadruple. |

```
<for3> ::= <for2> UNTIL <expr³>
┌─────────────────────────────────────────────────────────────────┐
|<for3>.JUMP2 := <for2>.JUMP2; |Save address of AGAIN.            |
|<for3>.JUMP  := NEXTQUAD;     |We're about to generate the       |
|                              |conditional branch for the IF     |
|                              |and have to save its address.     |
|ENTER(BG, 0, <for2>.ENTRY,    |This is the IF <identifier> ≤     |
|       <expr³>.ENTRY);        |<expr³>.                          |
└─────────────────────────────────────────────────────────────────┘

<statement¹> ::= <for3> DO <statement²>
┌─────────────────────────────────────────────────────────────────┐
|ENTER(BR, <for3>.JUMP2,0,0);  |This is the GO TO AGAIN - we      |
|                              |saved the quad. no. in JUMP2.     |
|I := <for3>.JUMP;             |Now fill in the address of the    |
|QUAD( I,2) := NEXTQUAD;       |BG <identifier>,<expr>            |
└─────────────────────────────────────────────────────────────────┘
```

**EXERCISES FOR 13.5**

1. Write the semantic routines for the same loop as discussed above, but do not assume that the step element is always positive.

2. Write semantic routines for the same for-loop but where the step value and end value <expr³> get evaluated only once.

3. Write semantic routines to generate quadruples for a WHILE statement with the syntax <statement> ::= WHILE <expr> DO <statement>.

4. Rewrite the semantic routines for the loop illustrated in the text, to generate better code in case the <variable> is an integer and all the expressions are constants. Assume a quadruple (TEST, <variable>, <constant¹>, <constant²>) which does the following: (1) Add <constant¹> to the <variable>; (2) If the result is greater than <constant²> execute the next quadruple; otherwise skip over the next quadruple.

## 13.6 OPTIMIZING BOOLEAN EXPRESSIONS

In this section we want to show two different methods of generating code for Boolean expressions with the syntax

```
           Z ::= E
(13.6.1)   E ::= T | E OR T
           T ::= F | T AND F
           F ::= I | ( E ) | NOT F
```

The identifiers are variables of type Boolean which take on the value TRUE or FALSE. The three operators OR, AND, and NOT are defined by the following tables:

```
     OR|TRUE FALSE       AND|TRUE  FALSE     NOT|TRUE  FALSE
     --|----------     -----|-----------     ---|-----------
 TRUE  |TRUE TRUE      TRUE |TRUE  FALSE        |FALSE TRUE
 FALSE |TRUE FALSE     FALSE|FALSE FALSE        |
```

From the syntax we see that AND has precedence over OR, and NOT has the highest precedence. Note that NOT NOT A is equivalent to A. The usual way of evaluating such expressions is the same way we evaluate arithmetic expressions; by evaluating the operators from left to right, taking into account their precedence and also the use of parentheses. The Polish notation for expression A AND (B OR NOT C) would be A B C NOT OR AND. One could easily program semantic routines to make the translation from infix to postfix form or quadruples this way. However, there is a more efficient way to evaluate such expressions.

### Optimal Evaluation of Boolean Expressions

Consider the expression A AND (B OR NOT C). If A is FALSE, there is no need to evaluate further; the result is FALSE. Similarly, if A is TRUE and B is TRUE the result is TRUE, and there is no need to evaluate NOT C. We want, then, to evaluate expressions from left to right, and stop as soon as we know what the result is. The above, by the way, is equivalent to

```
IF A
THEN IF B
     THEN TRUE ELSE NOT C
ELSE FALSE
```

and this is how we want to evaluate it. We can redefine the syntax and semantics of Boolean expressions by:

```
         Z ::= E
(13.6.2) E ::= T | T OR E
         T ::= F | F AND T
         F ::= I | ( E ) | NOT F
```

where

```
         c OR d    is defined by  IF c THEN TRUE ELSE d
(13.6.3) c AND d   is defined by  IF c THEN d ELSE FALSE
         NOT c     is defined by  IF c THEN FALSE ELSE TRUE
```

We want to generate quadruples using identifiers, the constants 0 and 1, and the two quadruples (:=,I,,T) and (B,I,i,j) where I is an identifier. The latter quadruple has the following meaning: if I is TRUE (1), then jump to quadruple i, otherwise jump to quadruple j.

Figure 13.2 shows some examples. One should notice a few things. First, the result will always be in a variable X. The first quadruple puts 1 in X; we are assuming the expression is TRUE. If it is, we branch to the quadruple following the last one listed; if FALSE, we branch to the last quadruple to put 0 in X.

Secondly, the identifiers appear in the same order in the quadruples as they did in the original expression. Finally, no operator appears for NOT. If A is represented by (B,A,i,j), then NOT A is represented by (B,A,j,i); we just switch the addresses to branch to for TRUE and FALSE.

It should be clear, once this section is understood, that we could just as well generate Polish notation or even machine language, and in a one-pass compiler. There would be more details to worry about, but the technique would be the same.

We are interested mainly in showing how to make sure that the branch addresses are filled in correctly, since this is the main problem. Hence we shall not worry about type checking, symbol table entries for identifiers, and so forth.

```
(1)  (:=, 1,, X)
(2)  (B, A, 5, 3)
(3)  (B, B, 5, 4)
(4)  (:=, 0,, X)
```

A OR B

```
(1)  (:=, 1,, X)
(2)  (B, A, 3, 5)
(3)  (B, B, 5, 4)
(4)  (:=, 0,, X)
```

NOT A OR B

```
(1)  (:=, 1,, X)
(2)  (B, A, 3, 4)
(3)  (B, B, 5, 4)
(4)  (:=, 0,, X)
```

A AND B

```
(1)  (:=, 1,, X)
(2)  (B, A, 6, 3)
(3)  (B, B, 6, 4)
(4)  (B, C, 5, 6)
(5)  (:=, 0,, X)
```

A OR B OR NOT C

```
(1)  (:=, 1,, X)
(2)  (B, A, 6, 3)
(3)  (B, B, 4, 6)
(4)  (B, C, 6, 5)
(5)  (:=, 0,, X)
```

A OR NOT B OR C

```
(1)  (:=, 1,, X)
(2)  (B, A, 3, 5)
(3)  (B, B, 6, 4)
(4)  (B, C, 6, 5)
(5)  (:=, 0,, X)
```

A AND (B OR C)

```
(1)  (:=, 1,, X)
(2)  (B, A, 4, 3)
(3)  (B, B, 6, 4)
(4)  (B, C, 5, 7)
(5)  (B, D, 7, 6)
(6)  (:=, 0,, X)
```

(A OR NOT B)
AND ( NOT C OR D)

```
(1)  (:=, 1,, X)
(2)  (B, A, 3, 4)
(3)  (B, B, 4, 7)
(4)  (B, C, 6, 5)
(5)  (B, D, 7, 6)
(6)  (:=, 0,, X)
```

(A AND NOT B)
OR (NOT C AND D)

```
(1)  (:=, 1,, X)
(2)  (B, A, 3, 6)
(3)  (B, B, 5, 4)
(4)  (B, C, 7, 5)
(5)  (B, D, 7, 6)
(6)  (:=, 0,, X)
```

(A AND (NOT (B OR
NOT C) OR D))

**FIGURE 13.2. Boolean Expressions in Quadruple Form.**

### 13.6.1 THE BOTTOM-UP METHOD

#### Rearranging the Productions

If we use the grammar (13.6.2), when the routine for, say, E ::= T OR E is called, the quadruples for both T and E have been generated. But we want to generate the code to look like

```
(1) (B, T, 3, 2)
(2) <quadruples for E>
```

That is, if T is TRUE, we want to jump over the evaluation of the E. In order to do this we have to break up our rules a bit, so that the T and E don't both appear in the same right part. We change the grammar to

```
         Z    ::= E
(13.6.3) E    ::= T | TOR E
         TOR  ::= T OR
         T    ::= F | FAND T
         FAND ::= F AND
         F    ::= I | ( E ) | NOT F
```

#### The Semantic Information

During the parse of a Boolean expression, whenever the handle is an identifier A (say), we generate the quadruple (B, A, 0, 0). What we don't know is the addresses to branch to when A is TRUE (1) or FALSE (0). We therefore associate with F (the rule is F ::= I) something which tells us that a branch to TRUE must be filled in (TCHAIN), and also that a branch to FALSE must be filled in (FCHAIN). In order to distinguish whether a number k refers to component 3 or 4 of that quadruple, we use k to refer to field 3 and -k to refer to field 4. Thus, after the first identifier in an expression is parsed, we have F.TCHAIN = 2, F.FCHAIN = -2, and the quadruples

```
(1) (:=, 1, , T)
(2) (B, A, 0, 0)
```

Consider any nonterminal E, TOR, T, FAND or F. Each can represent a quite complicated Boolean expression with many identifiers. In each, therefore, there may be a long list of branches on TRUE or FALSE in which we don't yet know where to branch. We will link all the branches on TRUE together, keeping the first one on the list associated with the nonterminal in TCHAIN. Likewise for FCHAIN. Thus, we are just constructing linked lists of forward references, in a manner similar to that presented in section 13.3.

Consider, for example, a subexpression (A OR B AND C). Suppose we have reduced it so far to F. The quadruples should look like

```
(1)   (:=, 1, , T)
(2)   (B, A, 0, 3)
(3)   (B, B, 4, 0)
(4)   (B, C, 0, 0)
```

where the zeros indicate we don't yet know where to branch. However if we use these fields to link up, we would have

```
F.TCHAIN = 4, F.FCHAIN = -4
```

and

```
(1)   (:=, 1,, T)
(2)   (B, A, 0, 3)
(3)   (B, B, 4, 0)
(4)   (B, C, 2, -3)
```

We use the following procedures MERGE and FILLIN in the semantic routines to help us manipulate such lists. The semantic routines themselves assume that the list of quadruples has been initialized to hold the first quadruple (:=, 1,, T). When first looking at these routines, start with those for the nonterminal F and work your way up; this makes it easier to understand the process.

```
PROCEDURE FILLIN(K);          FILLIN fills in the list beginning
VALUE K; INTEGER K;           at K with the number of the next
BEGIN INTEGER SAVE;           quadruple.
 WHILE K ≠ 0 DO               If K is 0, we're done.
  BEGIN I:=IF K > 0           Find out which field (3 or 4).
           THEN 3 ELSE 4;
   SAVE := ABS(K);            Get quad. number it references.
   K := QUAD(SAVE,I);         Get next entry on the chain.
   QUAD(SAVE,I):=NEXTQUAD     Fill in the field with the number
  END                         of the next quadruple.
END
```

```
PROCEDURE MERGE(K1, K2);      K1 and K2 are variables containing
INTEGER K1, K2;               the number beginning linked lists.
BEGIN INTEGER K;              Add list K2 to the end of list K1.
IF K1 = 0 THEN K1 := K2       If K1 is 0 just move K2 into K1.
ELSE
 BEGIN  K := K1;              Run down to the end of the K1 list.
  LOOP: I := IF K > 0
        THEN 3 ELSE 4;
  K := ABS(K);
  IF QUAD(K,I)≠ 0 THEN
   BEGIN K := QUAD(K,I);
         GO TO LOOP;
   END;
   QUAD(K,I) := K2;           Put list K2 on end of list K1.
 END; END
```

```
Z ::= E
┌─────────────────────────────────────────────────────────────┐
|FILLIN(E.FCHAIN);          |All done. Fill in all branches on |
|ENTER(:=, 0,, X);          |FALSE and generate the last quad. |
|FILLIN(E.TCHAIN)           |Fill in branches to TRUE.         |
└─────────────────────────────────────────────────────────────┘

E ::= T
┌─────────────────────────────────────────────────────────────┐
|E.TCHAIN := T.TCHAIN;      |The E and the T are the same seman-|
|E.FCHAIN := T.FCHAIN       |tically. Just copy the chains.    |
└─────────────────────────────────────────────────────────────┘

E¹ ::= TOR E²
┌─────────────────────────────────────────────────────────────┐
|E¹.FCHAIN := E².FCHAIN;    |The TOR FALSE branches were filled |
|E¹.TCHAIN := TOR.TCHAIN;   |earlier, so just copy those from E².|
|MERGE(E¹.TCHAIN,           |Merge the two lists of branches on |
|              E².TCHAIN)   |TRUE into a single list for E¹.   |
└─────────────────────────────────────────────────────────────┘

TOR ::= T OR
┌─────────────────────────────────────────────────────────────┐
|FILLIN(T.FCHAIN);          |Fix all the branches on FALSE in T |
|TOR.FCHAIN := 0;           |to go to next Polish string symbol.|
|TOR.TCHAIN := T.TCHAIN     |Save the list of branches on TRUE. |
└─────────────────────────────────────────────────────────────┘

FAND ::= F AND
┌─────────────────────────────────────────────────────────────┐
|FILLIN(F.TCHAIN);          |All the branches on TRUE in F go to|
|FAND.TCHAIN := 0;          |the next Polish string symbol. The |
|FAND.FCHAIN := F.FCHAIN    |branches on FALSE aren't known yet.|
└─────────────────────────────────────────────────────────────┘

T ::= F
┌─────────────────────────────────────────────────────────────┐
|T.TCHAIN := F.TCHAIN;      |NO COMMENT;                       |
|T.FCHAIN := F.FCHAIN       |                                  |
└─────────────────────────────────────────────────────────────┘

T¹ ::= FAND T²
┌─────────────────────────────────────────────────────────────┐
|T¹.TCHAIN := T².TCHAIN;    |The FAND branches on TRUE are     |
|T¹.FCHAIN := FAND.FCHAIN;  |already filled in, so just copy   |
|MERGE(T¹.FCHAIN,           |those for T². Merge the two lists of|
|              T².FCHAIN)   |branches on FALSE into a list for T¹|
└─────────────────────────────────────────────────────────────┘

F ::= ( E )
┌─────────────────────────────────────────────────────────────┐
|F.TCHAIN := E.TCHAIN;      |Any jumps on TRUE or FALSE are the |
|F.FCHAIN := E.FCHAIN       |same for F as they are for E.     |
└─────────────────────────────────────────────────────────────┘
```

$F^1$ ::= NOT $F^2$

```
┌─────────────────────────────────────────────────────────────┐
|F¹.TCHAIN := F².FCHAIN;  |Because of the NOT, F¹ is TRUE    |
|F¹.FCHAIN := F².TCHAIN   |where F² was FALSE. Switch chains. |
└─────────────────────────────────────────────────────────────┘
```

F ::= I

```
┌─────────────────────────────────────────────────────────────┐
|F.TCHAIN := NEXTQUAD;     |Fix the chains to point to next  |
|F.FCHAIN := -NEXTQUAD;    |quadruple, then generate the     |
|ENTER(B, I.SEM, 0, 0)     |quadruple.                       |
└─────────────────────────────────────────────────────────────┘
```

**EXERCISES FOR 13.6.1**

1. Parse the expressions given in Figure 13.2, using the above saemantic routines, to generate Polish notation.

2. Determine Polish notation for the same expressions, and change the semantic rcutines to generate it.

### 13.6.2 THE TOP-DOWN METHOD

As a means of comparison we show how the same thing could be done using recursive descent. Since we are going top-down and are writing our own syntax scheme, we have more flexibility. The procedures below are programmed in the manner described in section 12.4, and should need little discussion. They are programmed using the grammar (13.6.4) below, which uses iteration. Actually, it is easier to use grammar (13.6.2) which uses right recursion instead of iteration (see exercise 4).

The semantic information FCHAIN and TCHAIN is now passed as parameters to each routine.

```
          Z ::= E
(13.6.4)  E ::= T {OR T}
          T ::= F {AND F}
          F ::= I | NOT F | ( E )
```

```
┌─────────────────────────────────────────────────────────────┐
|PROCEDURE Z;                   |Procedure for Z ::= E.       |
| BEGIN INTEGER FCHAIN, TCHAIN; |                             |
|       ENTER(:=, 1,, X);       |Enter the first quadruple.   |
|       E(FCHAIN, TCHAIN);      |Parse E.                     |
|       FIILIN(FCHAIN);         |Upon return, fill in branches|
|       ENTER(:=, 0,, X);       |to FALSE and generate the quad.|
|       FILLIN(TCHAIN)          |to put 0 in T. Then fill in the|
| END                           |branches to TRUE.            |
└─────────────────────────────────────────────────────────────┘
```

```
PROCEDURE E(TCHAIN,FCHAIN);          Procedure for E::= T{OR T}
 INTEGER TCHAIN, FCHAIN;
 BEGIN INTEGER TC;
  TCHAIN:=0; FCHAIN:=0;              Start off with the lists empty.
 LOOP: T(TC, FCHAIN);                Parse a term.
       MERGE(TCHAIN, TC);            Add branches on TRUE to TCHAIN.
       IF NXTSYMB = "OR" THEN        If there is another OR we fill
        BEGIN FILLIN(FCHAIN);        in all branches to FALSE to
              FCHAIN := 0;           branch to the next symbol.
              SCAN; GO TO LOOP       Scan the next terminal and
 END    END                          go repeat the process.
```

```
PROCEDURE T(TCHAIN, FCHAIN);         Procedure for T::=F{AND F}.
 INTEGER TCHAIN, FCHAIN;
 BEGIN INTEGER FC;
  TCHAIN:=0; FCHAIN:=0;              Initialize lists to empty.
LOOP:  F(TCHAIN, FC);                Parse a factor.
  MERGE(FCHAIN, FC);                 Add new FALSE branches.
  IF NXTSYMB = "AND" THEN            Is there another AND?
   BEGIN FILLIN(TCHAIN);             Yes. Fill in branches to TRUE.
         TCHAIN := 0;
         SCAN; GO TO LOOP;           Go look for next factor.
   END
 END
```

```
PROCEDURE F(TCHAIN,FCHAIN);          Procedure for
 INTEGER TCHAIN, FCHAIN;             F ::= I | ( E ) | NOT F
BEGIN INTEGER K;
L:IF NXTSYMB = "(" THEN              If first symbol is a paren.,
  BEGIN SCAN;E(TCHAIN,FCHAIN);       go parse the expression and
        IF NXTSYMB = ")"             check for closing parenthesis.
        THEN SCAN ELSE ERROR;
        GO TO ENDF
  END;
 IF NXTSYMB = "NOT" THEN             If we have a NOT then parse the
  BEGIN SCAN;F(TCHAIN,FCHAIN);       following factor. Then switch
        K  := TCHAIN;                the chains (what was TRUE is
    TCHAIN := FCHAIN;                now FALSE, what was FALSE is
    FCHAIN := K; GOTO ENDF;          TRUE).
  END;
 IF NXTSYMB = "I" THEN
  BEGIN TCHAIN := NEXTQUAD;          We have an identifier. The
   FCHAIN := -NEXTQUAD;              branches are as indicated.
   ENTER(B, NXTSEM, 0, 0);           Generate the quadruple.
  END
 ELSE ERROR;
ENDF: END
```

**EXERCISES FOR 13.6.2**

1. Parse the expressions given in Figure 13.2 using the top-down routines.

2. Determine the form of the Boolean expressions in Polish notation, and change the procedures in this section to produce Polish notation.

3. Note that if an AND follows an identifier which is preceded by no NOTs, we can generate a quadruple (BZ,i,A,0) to branch to quadruple i on FALSE. Hence, when executing, the quadruple, if A is TRUE the program proceeds to the next quadruple. In Polish notation or machine language this gives us a more efficient program. A similar change can be made to handle identifiers followed by OR. Change the above procedures to generate this more efficient code.

4. Rewrite the above recursive procedures to follow grammar (13.6.2).

# Chapter 14.
# Allocation of Storage to Runtime Variables

Once the runtime storage allocation scheme and the formats of the runtime data areas have been designed (see Chapter 8), the implementation of storage assignment at compile-time is a fairly simple task. In section 14.1 we outline the general scheme, disregarding COMMON and equivalenced variables. We comment on when this storage assignment could take place. In section 14.2 we discuss allocating storage to temporary variables. Finally, in section 14.3 we treat the problem of assigning locations to COMMON and equivalenced variables.

Some computers have several fast registers which can be used to hold temporary results. While efficient use of these registers can be considered a storage allocation problem, we prefer to treat it with code optimzation in section 17.5.

## 14.1 ASSIGNING ADDRESSES TO VARIABLES

We assume the compiler generates one data area for each procedure being compiled. Into that data area goes all implicit parameters, actual parameters, programmer variables (or their templates) and temporary locations used in the procedure.

In FORTRAN, only one subroutine may be compiled at one time; thus only one data area need be maintained. The other extreme is ALGOL or PL/I, where any number of procedures may be compiled, each with its own data area.

In the general case, then, the compiler maintains a table D of all data areas needed by the object program. For each data area, its table element in D has a field indicating whether the area is static or dynamic, and a field LENGTH indicating the number of locations in the data area so far. LENGTH is initially 0.

The storage allocator assigns addresses to the variables in one procedure at a time. Its first task, for a procedure, is to assign the locations in the beginning of the data area for the DISPLAY (if used) and implicit parameters. LENGTH for the data area is set to the number of locations used by these standard, fixed length, entities.

The second task is to process the symbol table entries for the formal parameters and variables declared in the procedure, assigning addresses. For each symbol table entry, the following occurs:

1. Assign it the offset LENGTH of the data area; that is the address of the first free location in the data area.
2. Add to LENGTH the number of locations needed by the formal parameter or variable described by the symbol table entry.

This is a simple, straightforward process, and needs no further explanation. It does require that the number of locations needed for a variable be determined from its symbol table entry.

In some languages (e.g. FORTRAN IV) this information may not be known until the whole source program has been passed. Hence, a second pass is necessary after the usual analysis, to assign runtime addresses.

The FORTRAN IV WATFOR 360 compiler (see Cress et al), uses the following scheme. The first pass of the compiler, the main one, generates machine language directly from the source program. In the machine language code, a reference to a variable is represented by a pointer to the symbol table entry describing it. In a second, small pass, addresses are assigned to runtime variables and put into the symbol table entries. Then, the machine language code is scanned, and each address of a symbol table entry is replaced by the corresponding runtime address.

In languages which require declarations of variables before their use, storage assignment can be performed in the semantic routines for the declarations. Hence, one can have a true one-pass compiler.

#### Variables with Initial Values

So far, we have assumed that the actual runtime data area for a procedure is not needed at compile-time. This is usually true; we need only the counter LENGTH which tells us how big the data area is. Some languages allow variables to have initial values, which are determined at compile-time. The easiest way to implement this is to actually build a copy of the data area at runtime with the initial values inserted, and to include it as part of the object code. Another solution (which is not so good) is to generate a sequence of assignment statements which will be executed at the beginning of runtime, in order to assign the initial values.

#### Alignment Problems

The IBM 360 requires some values to be aligned on a doubleword, fullword, or halfword boundary. Suppose we allocate storage to variables B1, F1, H1, and D1, in that order (aligning when necessary), where they occupy 1, 4, 2, and 8 bytes respectively, and where their addresses must be a multiple of 1, 4, 2, and 8, respectively. Then storage will be allocated as follows:

| | | | |
|---|---|---|---|
| byte 0 | B1 | bytes 8-9 | H1 |
| bytes 1-3 | not used | bytes 10-15 | not used |
| bytes 4-7 | F1 | bytes 16-23 | D1 |

The problem is that there will be many bytes which are never used. A simple solution to this problem is to assign storage first to those variables which must be aligned on a doubleword boundary, then to those which must be aligned on a fullword, halfword, and byte boundary, in that order.

### Using Block Structure to Save Space

Suppose the runtime administration scheme for a block structured language assigns one data area to each procedure. In that data area are the locations for all variables in all blocks in that procedure. Thus, for the program in Figure 14.1, 7 locations would be needed.

We can, however, make use of the block structure to save space. For example, in Figure 14.1, A3 and A4 can be allocated the same location, as can A2 and A5; only 5 locations are needed.

```
BEGIN REAL A1,B1;
  BEGIN REAL A2,B2;
        BEGIN REAL A3; ... END;
        BEGIN REAL A4; ... END;
  END;
  BEGIN REAL A5; ... END;
END
```

| location | value |
|---|---|
| 0 | A1 |
| 1 | B1 |
| 2 | A2, A5 |
| 3 | B2 |
| 4 | A3, A4 |

**FIGURE 14.1. Block Structured Storage Allocation.**

We can implement this scheme by visualizing the runtime procedure data area as a stack. At runtime, when a block is entered, push locations for its fixed length variables onto the stack; when a block is left, pop those locations from the stack.

The compile-time algorithm which assigns addresses allocates storage for the blocks in order of their block begins. It uses two variables and a stack. Variable CURRENTLENGTH always contains the number of locations assigned so far for the open blocks still being processed, and LENGTH contains the maximum number of locations in the data area. Initially, both are 0. The stack S is used to hold the address of the first location assigned to each block which is still being processed. The algorithm is as follows:

1. BLOCK BEGIN: Push the value of CURRENTLENGTH onto S. This value will be restored when the block is ended, so that parallel blocks use the same space. Next, allocate storage to each variable K (say) declared in the block, as follows:
   Assign K the address CURRENTLENGTH;
   Add the number of locations needed by K to CURRENTLENGTH.
   Finally, assign storage to temporary variables needed in the block in a similar manner (see section 14.2)
2. BLOCK END: LENGTH := MAXIMUM(LENGTH, CURRENTLENGTH); Pop the top value in stack S and store it in CURRENTLENGTH.

To illustrate the algorithm, we show below how it processes the program in Figure 14.1. Each step shows the variables and stack before the step is executed.

| STEP | CURRENT LENGTH | LENGTH | STACK | ADDRESSES OF A1 | B1 | A2 | B2 | A3 | A4 | A5 | NEXTSTEP |
|---|---|---|---|---|---|---|---|---|---|---|---|
| 1 | 0 | 0 | | | | | | | | | BLOCK BEGIN 1 |
| 2 | 2 | 0 | 0 | 0 | 1 | | | | | | BLOCK BEGIN 2 |
| 3 | 4 | 0 | 0 2 | 0 | 1 | 2 | 3 | | | | BLOCK BEGIN 3 |
| 4 | 5 | 0 | 0 2 4 | 0 | 1 | 2 | 3 | 4 | | | BLOCK END 3 |
| 5 | 4 | 5 | 0 2 | 0 | 1 | 2 | 3 | 4 | | | BLOCK BEGIN 4 |
| 6 | 5 | 5 | 0 2 4 | 0 | 1 | 2 | 3 | 4 | 4 | | BLOCK END 4 |
| 7 | 4 | 5 | 0 2 | 0 | 1 | 2 | 3 | 4 | 4 | | BLOCK END 2 |
| 8 | 2 | 5 | 0 | 0 | 1 | 2 | 3 | 4 | 4 | | BLOCK BEGIN 5 |
| 9 | 3 | 5 | 0 2 | 0 | 1 | 2 | 3 | 4 | 4 | 2 | BLOCK END 5 |
| 10 | 2 | 5 | 0 | 0 | 1 | 2 | 3 | 4 | 4 | 2 | BLOCK END 1 |
| | 0 | 5 | | 0 | 1 | 2 | 3 | 4 | 4 | 2 | |

## 14.2 ALLOCATION STORAGE TO TEMPORARY VARIABLES

Temporary locations are needed mainly to hold partial results of expressions. Included here are temporaries to hold addresses of subscripted variables, actual parameter values, and parameter lists for calls to functions. Locations for temporaries are usually allocated in the data area of the procedure (or block) where the expression appears. We could assign a separate location to each temporary but this wastes space, so we want to design storage allocation algorithms which minimize the number of locations used. As a start, we consider only basic blocks -- sequences of instructions to be executed in order, with no branches into or out of the sequence.

Consider the sequence of quadruples for the statements E := A*B+C*D; F := A*B+1; G := C*D;:

```
          (1) *   A,B,T1          (6) +   T4,1,T5
          (2) *   C,D,T2          (7) :=  T5,,F
(14.2.1)  (3) +   T1,T2,T3        (8) *   C,D,T6
          (4) :=  T3,,E           (9) :=  T6,,G
          (5) *   A,B,T4
```

As far as storage allocation is concerned, this can be written in terms of ASSignments and REFerences to the temporaries T1, T2, ..., as

```
          (1) ASS T1         (7)   ASS T4
          (2) ASS T2         (8)   REF T4
(14.2.2)  (3) REF T2         (9)   ASS T5
          (4) REF T1         (10)  REF T5
          (5) ASS T3         (11)  ASS T6
          (6) REF T3         (12)  REF T6
```

The <u>range</u> of a temporary Ti is defined as the sequence of operations between its initial definition and its last reference. Obviously, temporary variables with disjoint ranges can be assigned the same location. In the above case, T1, T3, T4, T5, and T6 can all be assigned the same location.

A temporary storage allocation algorithm is often executed after the machine language code is generated; it processes the machine language instructions and not the internal form. This is because it is not necessary to allocate storage to all temporaries. For example, in the machine language code for (14.2.1), the value of T5 would probably be in an accumulator or fast register throughout its range, and no memory location would be needed. This is not known until code is generated.

We now illustrate temporary storage allocation as a separate pass in terms of a sequence of ASSignments and REFerences. The algorithm itself will be incorporated into the code generation phase or as a separate pass following code generation.

### Using a Runtime Stack for Temporaries

Suppose that runtime locations a, a+1, a+2, ... can be assigned to temporary variables. Let us first of all consider arithmetic expressions with simple variables and constants as operands. Secondly, assume that the expressions are evaluated strictly according to the following syntax rules:

```
E ::= E + T | E - T | T
T ::= T * F | T / F | F
F ::= ( E ) | I
```

When evaluating an expression E+T, first E is evaluated, then T, and finally E+T. This means that any temporaries used in evaluating E are no longer needed when the result E is formed, and similarly for T. Furthermore, once E+T is calculated, the temporaries holding E and T are no longer needed.

The important point to note here is that the ranges of two temporaries Ti and Tj are either disjoint, or one is nested in the other. For example, the sequence of ASSignments and REFerences to temporaries for the expression (A+B)*(C+(D*E)) is

```
(1) ASS T1        (T1 := A+B)
(2) ASS T2        (T2 := D*E)
(3) REF T2        (evaluating C+T2)
(4) ASS T3        (T3 := C+T2)
(5) REF T3        (evaluating T1*T3)
(6) REF T1        (evaluating T1*T3)
(7) ASS T4        (T4 := T1*T3)
```

(Actually, the references to T3 and T1 could be written as REF T1,T3 since they occur essentially at the same time.) Such a nesting of ranges of temporaries allows us to use the locations a, a+1, a+2,... as a runtime stack, as we did when evaluating expressions in Polish notation. This is implemented at compile-time as follows: maintain a location L, which is initially 0, to indicate how big the stack currently is. To allocate storage to temporaries, sequence through the operations. At each ASSignment to a temporary Tj which begins its range, assign it runtime location a+L and increase L by 1. At the last REFerence to a temporary Tj, decrease L by 1.

In the above example, this algorithm would assign a to T1, a+1 to T2, a+1 to T3, and a to T4; only two locations would be used.

Note that temporaries in expressions as defined above are ASSigned and REFerenced only once; hence their ranges are easily determined.

### A More General Allocation Scheme

If the internal source program is modified so that the ranges of two temporaries Ti and Tj may overlap, then the previous scheme is no longer applicable. For example, a code optimization pass could detect that, in (14.2.1), the expressions A*B and C*D need only be calculated once, and could therefore change (14.2.1) to

```
(1) *  A,B,T1        (5) +  T1,1,T5
(2) *  C,D,T2        (6) := T5,,F
(3) +  T1,T2,T3      (7) := T2,,G
(4) := T3,,E
```

Now, the ranges of T1 and T2 overlap:

```
          (1) ASS T1      (6)  REF T3
          (2) ASS T2      (7)  REF T1
(14.2.3)  (3) REF T2      (8)  ASS T5
          (4) REF T1      (9)  REF T5
          (5) ASS T3      (10) REF T2
```

We must therefore consider arbitrary sequences of operations ASS Ti and REF Ti. Dantzig and Reynolds(66) have proved that the following algorithm minimizes the number of locations used: Maintain a <u>compile-time</u> stack S, which originally contains the runtime addresses a+n, a+n-1, ..., a+1, a, with "a" at the top. To assign addresses, sequence through the operations. At each new assignment ASS Tj which begins Tj's range, take the address in the top location of the stack, assign it to Tj, and pop the top stack location. For the last reference REF Tj (which ends Tj's range), if storage has not been allocated to Tj this implies Tj is never assigned, and there must be an error. If storage has been allocated, then push the address assigned to Tj onto the stack S; the location is no longer needed.

We illustrate the algorithm below, using the sequence (14.2.3). The first column gives the stack contents, and the second the addresses assigned <u>before</u> the operation in column three is processed.

| stack | address of T1 | T2 | T3 | T5 | operation processed |
|---|---|---|---|---|---|
| a+3 a+2 a+1 a | 0 | 0 | 0 | 0 | (1) ASS T1 |
| a+3 a+2 a+1 | a | 0 | 0 | 0 | (2) ASS T2 |
| a+3 a+2 | a | a+1 | 0 | 0 | (3) REF T2 |
| a+3 a+2 | a | a+1 | 0 | 0 | (4) REF T1 |
| a+3 a+2 | a | a+1 | 0 | 0 | (5) ASS T3 |
| a+3 | a | a+1 | a+2 | 0 | (6) REF T3 |
| a+3 a+2 | a | a+1 | a+2 | 0 | (7) REF T1 |
| a+3 a+2 a | a | a+1 | a+2 | 0 | (8) ASS T5 |
| a+3 a+2 | a | a+1 | a+2 | a | (9) REF T5 |
| a+3 a+2 a | a | a+1 | a+2 | a | (10) REF T2 |
| a+3 a+2 a a+1 | a | a+1 | a+2 | a | |

Note that the addresses in the stack need not be sequential. In fact, they may be any set of addresses of locations which can be used for temporary storage.

The above algorithm assumes we know when the last REFerence to a temporary is being processed. This may require us to save more information in the description of each temporary; we will discuss this later. Actually, the original Dantzig and Reynolds(66) algorithm processed the operations in <u>reverse</u> order, under the assumption that only one ASSignment occurs to each temporary. Thus, when processing in reverse order, we assign a location when we process a REF Tj for the first time, and release the location when the single ASSign Tj is processed.

### Extending the Algorithm to Other Temporaries

Either storage allocation algorithm method extends easily to other temporaries besides those used in a basic block. For example, we make the range of a temporary T used to hold the step value of the expression B in a loop

```
FOR I := A STEP B UNTIL C DO <statement>
```

the complete sequence of code generated for the loop. This range then naturally includes the ranges of any temporaries needed in evaluating the <statement>.

For a conditional expression in the context (say)

```
... A + (IF B THEN C ELSE D) + ...
```

we could have the internal code

```
(1)    :              (5) := D,, T1
(2) BZ 5, B           (6) + A, T1, T2
(3) := C,, T1         (7)      :
(4) B  6
```

Hence the range of T1 could be taken to be quadruples 3 through 6 -- assign T1 an address just after the BZ operation is generated, and release the location when the value is referenced when adding A to T1.

When using a program graph and basic blocks as described in section 11.5, we can use the following rule for determining the range of a temporary used in several blocks (see section 18.3 for definitions of terms used here). The range of a temporary used in several blocks is the smallest region R which includes the blocks in which T is used with the following property: any path from a successor of R back into R and to a REFerence to T passes first through an ASSignment to T. In practice, such a region R may be impractical to find, so that information on the source program level will be used to find the range, as we did above.

### Indicating the Range in the Description of a Temporary

It may be necessary to keep information about the range in the symbol table entry of each temporary. We indicate three ways of doing this:

1. In the temporary variable description, keep a count of the number of times the temporary appears in the quadruples (this count is made up as the quadruples are generated and is maintained as code optimization occurs). When generating code for a quadruple, reduce by 1 the count field of each operand or result field which is a temporary. When the field is zero, the temporary is no longer needed and the space assigned to it is released.
2. In the temporary variable description, keep the number of the last quadruple in which the variable appears. After code is generated for that quadruple, the temporary is no longer needed.
3. As the quadruples are generated (and optimized), build a threaded list of all the references to each temporary, with the beginning and end of the list in the description of that temporary. For example, after generating quadruples for (14.2.3) we would have

```
(1) ASS T1(4)     (6)  REF T3(0)
(2) ASS T2(3)     (7)  REF T1(0)   Temporary:      T1 T2 T3 T5
(3) REF T2(10)    (8)  ASS T5(9)   First ASS at:   1  2  5  8
(4) REF T1(7)     (9)  REF T5(0)   Last REF at:    7  10 6  9
(5) ASS T3(6)     (10) REF T2(0)
```

   This requires an extra field in each operand in a quadruple, to hold the pointer to the next quadruple on the list.

   Such a threaded list for all variables (not just for temporaries) can be used to help optimize code (see the subsection LOOP OPTIMIZATION of section 18.4). It can also be used to help allocate registers in an efficient manner (see the subsection REGISTER ALLOCATION in section 18.4). Thirdly, we use it here to help allocate storage to temporaries, as follows: As we generate code, maintain in each temporary description the number of the next quadruple which references the temporary, for which code has not yet been generated. When this field is 0, the temporary is no longer needed.

#### EXERCISE FOR 14.2

1. Given a sequence of ranges (Fi,Li) for temporary variables, where Fi is the number of the first ASSignment and Li the number of the last REFerence to variable Ti, design an algorithm which assigns locations to the Ti. It should minimize the number of locations used. You may assume that if i < j then Fi < Fj. That is, temporary names are assigned in order of first assignment.

## 14.3 COMMON AND EQUIVALENCED VARIABLES

Before we discuss allocating storage to COMMON and equivalenced variables, we briefly review the FORTRAN statements connected with them. We are not concerned with their syntax and how to parse them, but with the meaning of these statements; we will not describe all possible syntactical variations.

It should be mentioned again that in FORTRAN, subroutines are not recursive and that the subscript ranges for all arrays are known at compile-time; hence the data area associated with a subroutine or main program can be STATIC and can contain all programmer variables, including arrays. Arrays are stored columnwise instead of rowwise. All bounds are known at compile-time, so no dope vectors are needed.

### COMMON Blocks

Suppose A appears in the FORTRAN statement

```
DIMENSION A(100)
```

and that C is a simple variable. Then the statement

```
COMMON /A1/ A,C,D(200)
```

specifies that the variables A(1), A(2), ..., A(100), C, D(1), D(2), ..., D(200) are to appear in that order in adjacent locations in a separate data area named A1, called the A1 "COMMON block." The characters "/A1/" can be omitted or replaced by the characters "//", in which case the data area is called the "blank" COMMON block. The appearance of the component D(200) in the COMMON statement specifies that D is an array of 200 variables; this eliminates the need for a separate DIMENSION statement for D.

If more than one COMMON statement for the same block appears in a program, then the variables listed in the first are followed by those listed in the second, and so on. Thus the three statements

```
COMMON /A1/ A,B
COMMON /A1/ X,Y
COMMON /A1/ E,D
```

are equivalent to the single statement COMMON /A1/ A,B,X,Y,E,D. The same identifier cannot appear more than once in the COMMON statements of a program, since this would mean it should occupy different places in memory at the same time.

### Equivalanced Variables

Suppose B and C are declared in a dimension statement

```
DIMENSION B(10,10),C(10,10)
```

Then the equivalence statement

```
EQUIVALENCE (A,B(1,1),C(11))
```

specifies that the variables A, B(1,1), and C(1,2) are to occupy the same location(s). C(11) refers here to the eleventh element of the array C. Since the FORTRAN convention is to store elements columnwise -- in the order C(1,1), C(2,1), ..., C(10,1), C(1,2), C(2,2), ..., C(10,2), ... -- this is C(1,2).

Equivalencing two elements of different arrays causes other array elements to use the same locations. Assuming that the array elements of B and C use one location each, for the above example B(2,1) and C(2,2) occupy the same location, as do B(3,1) and C(3,2), B(4,1) and C(4,2), and so forth.

A variable may be equivalenced to any number of other variables, as long as no conflicts arise. Consider the statement

```
EQUIVALENCE (A,B(1,1)),(A,C(1,2)),(B,C).
```

Since A is equivalenced to both B(1,1) and C(1,2), all three must occupy the same locations. The last equivalence of B to C (B(1,1) to C(1,1)) produces a conflict, since it equivalences C(1,1) to C(1,2), which is impossible.

A variable can be equivalenced to a COMMON variable. This forces the former variable (and any others to which it is equivalenced) into COMMON also. Such equivalencing cannot change the order of any of the variables already in COMMON, but it may increase the size of COMMON. Consider the statements

```
COMMON X,Y
DIMENSION C(5)
EQUIVALENCE (X,C)
```

Assuming that each variable occupies one location, the length of COMMON is 5, since C(1) through C(5) are in COMMON. Note that Y and C(2) occupy the same location.

A COMMON block cannot be extended on the other side; replacing the last EQUIVALENCE statement by EQUIVALENCE (X,C(2)) produces an error, because X <u>must</u> occupy the first location in the COMMON block.

### Compile-Time COMMON Block Table, and COMMON Chains

At compile-time we maintain a table COMB of the COMMON blocks used in the program being compiled. Each element of the list has the following format:

| NAME | DA | FP | LP | LENGTH |
|---|---|---|---|---|

NAME is the COMMON block name (blank if blank COMMON); DA is the data area number assigned to it; FP and LP are pointers to the symbol table entries for the first and last variables in the COMMON block; and LENGTH will be the total number of locations in the block.

A simple method of keeping track of the variables or arrays in a particular COMMON block is to chain their symbol table entries together, in order of occurrence in the COMMON statements, using an extra pointer field COMP (COMMON Pointer) in each entry. We will also chain equivalenced variables together, using a pointer field EQUIVP, so that the symbol table entry has the format shown in Figure 14.2. We have omitted from the figure those attribute fields which do not concern us at this point -- the type, kind, etc.

Note that both chains are circular; the last entry points back to the first. The pointers can therefore be used to indicate whether a variable is in COMMON (is equivalenced) yet, or not. Zero means no, non-zero means yes. Figure 14.3 illustrates the COMMON block list and COMMON chains after the following statements have been processed (but before storage has been allocated):

```
COMMON /A1/ A,B
COMMON /A2/ C,D
COMMON /A1/ E,F
```

| NAME | COMP | EQUIVP | DA | OFFSET |
|---|---|---|---|---|

```
NAME   - name of variable or array
COMP   - 0 if not yet in COMMON; else pointer to next  entry  in
         COMMON BLOCK (to first one if this is last one).
EQUIVP - 0 if not yet equivalenced; else pointer to  next  entry
         to which it is equivalenced (circular chain).
DA     - data area number (0 if not yet assigned).
OFFSET - offset in  data  area  or  equivalence  offset  (to  be
         described later).
```

**FIGURE 14.2. Relevant Fields of Symbol Table Entry.**

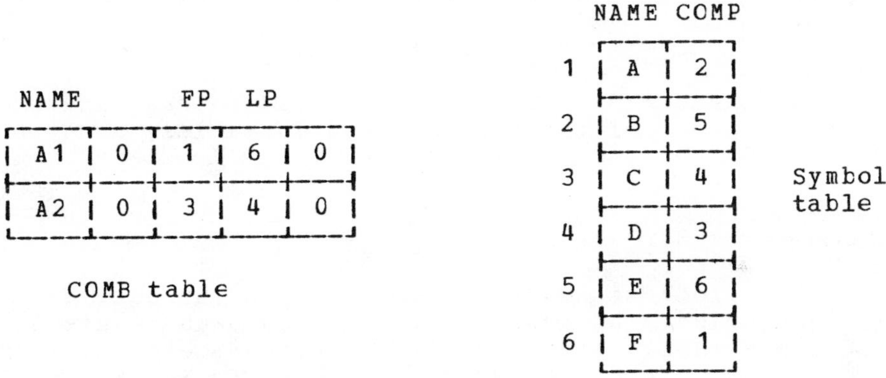

| NAME | | FP | LP | |
|---|---|---|---|---|
| A1 | 0 | 1 | 6 | 0 |
| A2 | 0 | 3 | 4 | 0 |

COMB table

| | NAME | COMP |
|---|---|---|
| 1 | A | 2 |
| 2 | B | 5 |
| 3 | C | 4 |
| 4 | D | 3 |
| 5 | E | 6 |
| 6 | F | 1 |

Symbol table

**FIGURE 14.3. COMMON Block and Chain Illustration.**

**Equivalence Chains**

Equivalenced variables are also chained together in a circular list, using the EQUIVP pointer field. The order of the variables in this list is not important, as it is in the case of COMMON variables, since all are assigned the same location anyway. We will make use of this fact to build the chain in the most convenient manner.

<u>All</u> the variables equivalenced together will appear on the same chain. This means we must merge chains together at times. Consider for example the statement EQUIVALENCE (A,B,C),(E,F,B). Just before processing the second occurrence of the identifier B, we have the two chains

```
┌───────────┐       ┌───────┐
└>A──>B──>C─┘  and  └─>E──>F─┘
```

When processing this second B, we note that B is already equivalenced, and merge the two chains into

```
┌──────────────────────┐
└─A──>B──>E──>F──>C─┘
```

The OFFSET field of the symbol table entry is used to indicate the position in memory of the first location of the variable relative to all the others. If all the equivalenced variables were simple variables this would not be necessary. But consider the statement

```
EQUIVALENCE (A,B(1),C(2))
```

and suppose that all array elements occupy one location. Then the symbol table entries for A and B have OFFSET = 0. The entry for C, however, has OFFSET = -1, since the array C must start one location <u>before</u> the variable A and the array B. If the additional statement

```
EQUIVALENCE (B(2),D)
```

follows, then, since B(1) has OFFSET 0, B(2) has address 1 relative to the rest of the equivalenced variables; hence D has OFFSET 1.

### Outline of the Implementation

There are two problems with FORTRAN which hinder us from actually assigning addresses to COMMON and equivalenced variables in one pass. First of all, a type statement for a variable A, say, (e.g. COMPLEX A) may follow a COMMON or EQUIVALENCE statement containing A. This means that the number of locations a variable uses is not always known as it is being processed in a COMMON or EQUIVALENCE statement. Secondly, a DIMENSION statement for an identifier may appear after its use in an EQUIVALENCE statement. Consider for example the statements

```
EQUIVALENCE (A,B(1,2))
DIMENSION B(10,10)
```

When first processing the EQUIVALENCE statement, the bounds for the array B are not known; hence we cannot calculate the position in the array of the element B(1,2) immediately.

This forces us to implement this part of the compiler in the four steps indicated below. The implementation could be made more efficient; we present the method in a less efficient manner in order to explain more easily the steps involved. Following this outline, we describe the four steps in more detail.

1. On the first pass through the source program, chain all COMMON variables (that is, their symbol table entries). Do not build equivalence chains, only because we have trouble describing the offsets of variables like B(1,2) whose array bounds are not known. Instead, just store the equivalence

statements in some internal form in a separate table for later processing. After the whole source program has been processed we assume the symbol table contains all necessary information about types, array bounds, etc. We then proceed to step 2.

2. Build the equivalence chains, filling in the OFFSET field at the same time.
3. Assign runtime addresses to COMMON variables and any variables equivalenced to them.
4. Assign runtime addresses to all other variables, including equivalenced variables.

### Step 1. Chaining Common Variables

Chaining the COMMON variables is a rather simple task which is performed when the COMMON statement is first processed. We consider a statement like

```
COMMON /A1/ A,B(100),C
```

with elements A, B(100) and C. Processing the statement consists of the following:

1. If no element in the block list exists for block A1, add one with NAME = A1, DA equal to the next available data area number, and FP = LP = LENGTH = 0. Let P be the pointer to the block list element for A1.
2. Process each of the elements in the list, in order, as follows:
   (a) Perform the normal symbol table processing for the element (look up in symbol table, and, if not there, add an entry for it; check type, dimensions, etc; if the element has the form <id>(<integer>,...,<integer>), process as an array declaration). Assign to a pointer variable PS the address of the symbol table entry.
   (b) If PS.COMP ≠ 0, it is already in COMMON. Give an error message and go on to the next element in the list.
   (c) Add symbol table entry PS to the chain, as follows:
   If P.FP=0 THEN P.FP:=PS ELSE P.LP.COMP:=PS;
   PS.COMP:=P.FP;
   (d) Fix the block list element: P.LP:=PS;

### Step 2. Chaining Equivalence Variables

This occurs after the source program has been processed once, and we assume that all type and dimension information has been stored into the symbol table. We use as input to this process the EQUIVALENCE statements in some internal form. For example, the identifiers can be represented by pointers to their symbol table entries.

This process is more difficult than the COMMON case, for two reasons: we have to merge chains together and we have to calculate offsets. However, we do not need an EQUIVALENCE table, similar to the COMMON block list COMB. Instead, we need only a pointer variable P which points to some element of the circular chain being currently built, and an integer variable BOFFSET which contains the current base offset, relative to which all element offsets are calculated. BOFFSET is initially 0 and changes only when lists are merged. To process a statement like

```
EQUIVALENCE (C,D,A(5),B(1,3))
```

we execute

```
P:=0; BOFFSET := 0;
```

and then perform the following actions for <u>each</u> of the elements in the equivalence list:

1. Let PS be the pointer to the symbol table entry for the equivalence element. Let L by the length (number of runtime locations) needed by it, or, if it is an array, needed by one array element. Calculate the OFFSET z for the element as follows:
   (a) If it has the form <id>, set z := BOFFSET.
   (b) If it has the form <id>(i), check that <id> is an array and that i falls in the subscript range. Set z := BOFFSET+L*(1-i).
   (c) If it has the form <id>(i1,...,in), check that <id> is an array with n dimensions, and that each subscript falls in its respective subscript range. Calculate the number j of the element <id>(i1,...,in) in the array (see section 8.4). Set z := BOFFSET+L*(1-j).
2. If PS is already equivalenced (if PS.EQUIV ≠ 0) go to step 4; otherwise step 3.
3. Add the new element PS into the chain, as follows:
   IF P = 0 THEN P := PS ELSE PS.EQUIVP := P.EQUIVP;
   P.EQUIVP := PS; PS.OFFSET := z. Skip step 4.
4. The same variable or array is equivalenced twice, so that two circular chains must be merged into one.
   (a) Recalculate the offsets in the chain being built to be relative to those of the old chain. While doing this, test for the chain linking into itself again:
   ```
   DIFF := z-PS.OFFSET; BOFFSET := BOFFSET-DIFF; Q := P;
   IF P=0 THEN BEGIN "New chain is still empty":
                    P := PS; GOTO step 4.(c)
                 END;
   LOOP: IF Q = PS THEN BEGIN IF DIFF ≠ 0
                                THEN give error message;
                           GOTO step 4.(c);
                           END;
         Q.OFFSET := Q.OFFSET-DIFF; Q1:=Q;
         Q := Q.EQUIVP; IF Q ≠ P THEN GO TO LOOP.
   ```
   (b) Now merge the two chains. Again, the order of the variables in the new chain doesn't matter:
   Q1.EQUIVP := PS.EQUIVP; PS.EQUIVP := P.
   (c) We are finished processing the element.

As an example, consider the statement

EQUIVALENCE (A,B(5),C(6)), (D,B(4),E), (F,C(2)).

Figure 14.4 shows how the symbol table elements are linked together after each of the equivalence elements is processed (assuming the variables have not appeared earlier in equivalence statements). The arrows represent the EQUIVP field, the numbers after each name the OFFSET field of the symbol table element. Note that the OFFSETs can be negative or positive.

```
STEP BOFFSET    P
                     ┌────┐
  1     0       A    └>A,0┘
                     ┌─────────────┐
  2     0       A    └>A,0──>B,-4┘
                     ┌─────────────────────┐
  3     0       A    └>A,0──>C,-5──>B,-4┘
                     ┌────┐ ┌─────────────────────┐
  4     0       D    └>D,0┘ └>A,0──>C,-5──>B,-4┘
                     ┌─────────────────────────────┐
  5    -1       D    └>D,-1──>A,0──>C,-5──>B,-4┘
                     ┌─────────────────────────────────────┐
  6    -1       D    └>D,-1──>E,-1──>A,0──>C,-5──>B,-4┘
                     ┌────┐ ┌─────────────────────────────────────┐
  7     0       F    └>F,0┘ └>D,-1──>E,-1──>A,0──>C,-5──>B,-4┘
                     ┌─────────────────────────────────────────────────┐
  8    -4       F    └>F,-4──>B,-4──>D,-1──>E,-1──>A,0──>C,-5┘
```

**FIGURE 14.4. Execution of Equivalence Chaining.**

**Step 3. Assigning Runtime Addresses in Common**

For each COMMON block we proceed down the chain of variables in the block, assigning addresses. We stop the process temporarily when one of the variables is equivalenced, in order to assign addresses to those on the equivalence chain. This may mean that a variable on a COMMON chain gets assigned an address before its normal processing; in this case we must check its address to make sure it coincides with the one it should have. Variable OFFS is used to hold the offset to be assigned to the next variable (initially 0). Pointer P contains the address of the COMMON block element in COMB being processed.

While assigning the addresses we must also determine the number of locations in COMMON and store it in the LENGTH component of the block list element.

In the algorithm below, the phrase "the length of the variable PS" appears. By this we mean the number of runtime storage locations needed by the runtime variable whose compile-time description is in the location pointed at by PS. If it is an array, this is the number needed for one array element times the number of elements.

See Figure 14.2 for a description of the relevant symbol table entry fields.

```
|PS := P.FP; IF PS = 0 THEN STOP;   |PS points to first entry on|
|OFFS := 0; P.LENGTH := 0;          |the COMMON chain.  OFFS is |
|                                   |the next offset to assign. |
|COMMONLOOP: L := length of the     |This loop processes one    |
|                variable PS.       |entry at a time.           |
|IF PS.DA = 0 THEN                  |If 0, not assigned yet.    |
|  BEGIN IF PS.EQUIVP = 0 THEN      |                           |
|      BEGIN                         |                           |
|      PS.DA := P.DA;                |Not equivalenced, so assign|
|      PS.OFFSET := OFFS             |it an address.             |
|      END                          |                           |
|     ELSE                          |Equivalenced.  Initialize  |
|      BEGIN AD:=OFFS-PS.OFFSET;     |for assigning addresses to |
|           Q := PS;                |those on the equiv. chain. |
|      EQUIVLOOP: Q.DA := P.DA;      |Assign address to entry.   |
|           Q.OFFSET:=Q.OFFSET+AD;  |                           |
|           IF Q.OFFSET < 0 THEN    |Extended COMMON on wrong   |
|              give error message;  |side.                      |
|           L1 := length of the     |L1 is number of locs needed|
|                 variable Q;       |by entry Q's variable.     |
|           P.LENGTH := MAXIMUM(    |See if COMMON has been     |
|            P.LENGTH,Q.OFFSET+L1); |extended.                  |
|           Q:=Q.EQUIVP; IF Q ≠ PS  |Get next                   |
|           THEN GOTO EQUIVLOOP;    |equivalenced entry.        |
|  END END                          |                           |
|ELSE BEGIN IF PS.DA ≠ P.DA OR      |Already assigned.          |
|              PS.OFFSET ≠ OFFS     |Make sure the old address  |
|           THEN give error mess.   |is same as the new.        |
|     END;                          |                           |
|OFFS := OFFS+L;                    |                           |
|PS:=PS.CCMP; IF PS ≠ P.FP THEN     |Proceed to next entry.     |
|                 GOTO COMMONLOOP;  |on COMMON chain.           |
|P.LENGTH:=MAXIMUM(P.LENGTH,OFFS);  |                           |
```

**Step 4. Assigning Other Runtime Addresses**

The final step is to sequence through the symbol table entries, assigning addresses to those variables not in COMMON. When an equivalenced variable is detected, two passes must be made over the circular chain to which it is attached. The first pass finds the minimum offset K of all the entries on the chain. The second assigns the addresses to the entries. If the beginning address to be assigned to a set of equivalenced variables is OFFS, then the address assigned to each entry is

OFFS-K+(OFFSET in the entry).

Thus the one with the minimum offset is assigned the address OFFS.

The algorithm is as follows:

```
1.  DA := data area number for the subprogram being compiled;
    OFFS := first free location to be assigned;
    PS := address of first symbol table entry;
2.  If PS.DA ≠ 0, PS has already been assigned an address.  Skip
    to step 4.
3.  If PS.EQUIVP ≠ 0, PS is equivalenced; execute step 3b only;
    otherwise execute step 3a only.
    (a)  Calculate the length L of the variable PS;
         PS.DA := DA; PS.OFFSET := OFFS; OFFS := OFFS+L.
    (b)  Assign addresses to all variables on the equivalence
         chain.
         b1.  Find minimum offset K: Q:=PS.EQUIVP; K:=PS.OFFSET;
              WHILE Q ≠ PS DO
               BEGIN K:=MINIMUM(K,PS.OFFSET); Q:=Q.EQUIVP END;
         b2.  Now assign addresses: K := OFFS-K;
               LOOP:Q.OFFSET := MOFFS+Q.OFFSET;
                Calculate length L of the variable Q;
                OFFS := MAXIMUM(OFFS,Q.OFFSET+L);
                Q := Q.EQUIVP; IF Q ≠ PS THEN GO TO LOOP.
4.  If there is another symbol table entry to process, put its
    address in PS and go to step 2.
```

# Chapter 15.
# Error Recovery

## 15.1 INTRODUCTION

A compiler should try to find as many errors as possible in a source program; programmers should be spared the bother of submitting a job three, four, or even more times before a program is finally compiled. Nevertheless, few compilers do a good job of it, and fewer papers have been written on the subject.

We use the term error recovery for the process of determining how to continue analyzing a source program when an error is found. In section 15.2 we discuss recovering from semantic errors; these concern mostly incorrect uses of identifiers and expressions. In section 15.3 the complementary problem of syntactic error recovery is treated, mainly from the point of view of automatic recovery in formal parsing algorithms. When designing error recovery procedures in an ad hoc syntax analyzer, for a particular error, keep in mind how an automatic recovery technique would react in the same situation. Even though they may not be directly applicable, knowledge of these more formal, automatic methods lends insight into how to attack the problem, and can help make the whole implementation more systematic.

The reader must realize that no good automatic error recovery scheme has been tested extensively and compared with a good, hand written one. We don't know just how good they are. On the other hand, they are certainly comparable to many of the intuitive recovery procedures found in compilers today.

Several compilers, most notably the compilers for CORC (see Conway and Maxwell(63), and Freeman(63)), CUPL, and PL/C (see Conway et al(70)), try to "correct" all errors, generate code, and actually execute the program. Every program goes into execution, no matter how many errors it has. This might seem like a waste of time, but since these compilers generate absolute code to be executed immediately; no expensive linkage editing and loading is required. The advantages to the programmer are obvious; fewer debugging runs because, no matter how many syntactic errors, he still has a chance to find a logical runtime error. One keypunch error doesn't stop a program from executing, and there is a good chance it will be corrected in the right manner.

Freeman(63) is the only publication which outlines error correction techniques in detail. It is difficult to draw any conclusions from it about general techniques for error correction; the paper describes only the correction in CORC, which is a rather simple language. The only technique which can be explained easily is spelling correction, which we will discuss in a moment.

I would venture to say that the general methods for error recovery discussed in sections 15.2 and 15.3 would suffice for error correction also. They must, of course, be made more exact. Error recovery requires only that we continue analyzing without too much possibility of generating several error messages for a single error. If we do happen to generate a few, it doesn't really matter. Error correction requires that we actually produce a correct program. For example, if we insert a new symbol table entry to replace one which was used incorrectly, we must be sure that all the attributes are filled in correctly. With error recovery, this may not be necessary.

The error correction procedure should perhaps delete a badly garbled statement and insert in its place an output statement which prints out that the statement was deleted. Also, when an error is corrected, the programmer must be told exactly how it is corrected, so that he can interpret his runtime results. This need not be done for normal error recovery.

### Spelling Correction

The latest paper on spelling correction in compilers is Morgan(70). The reader is referred to it for a more detailed discussion and for references to other papers on the subject.

There are several situations where a compiler can suspect an identifier to be misspelled. In such cases the compiler should compare the identifier with those in the symbol table and attempt to decide which symbol table identifier was misspelled. Let us look briefly at some of these situations.

1. During syntactic analysis, one often knows that the next symbol must be one of a subset of the reserved words. If an identifier appears instead, then it should be checked for a misspelling of one of the reserved words. One such case is in a language where every statement begins with a "keyword." Another case is when parsing a Boolean expression, and an operator like AND, OR, GE, or LE must appear.

One could also check for a "concatenation" error when a reserved word is expected. For example, if a BEGIN is expected and an identifier BEGINA appears, change this to BEGIN A.

2. During semantic analysis, suppose an identifier declared as a label is used in a context where only an array name may appear. Then the identifier may be misspelled and should be checked against the list of declared array names. Similar situations, where the context determines the type of identifier possible, occur frequently.

3. Often, because of a misspelling, an identifier appears only once or twice, with either no assignment to it or no reference to its value. These can be checked easily; just keep an assignment counter and a reference counter in each symbol table entry. After syntactic and semantic analysis, scan the symbol table entries; any one with one of the counters 0 is a candidate for spelling correction.

The next question we should ask is how to determine which symbol table identifier was misspelled. The first work on this in the context of compilers is in Freeman's(63) thesis on CORC. Freeman's technique estimates the "probability" that an identifier is a misspelling of another, based upon a complex scoring function. This function uses information like the number of letters which match, number of letters which match after one or two character transpositions, and the number which match after taking into account frequently occurring keypunch errors (like 0 for O, 1 for I).

Freeman's technique has been replaced by a more efficient (but less powerful) method, which is based on evidence that around 80 percent of all spelling errors in programs fall into one of the four classes

1. One letter wrong,
2. One letter missing,
3. An extra character inserted, and
4. Two adjacent characters transposed.

Hence, most spelling errors can be corrected just by checking for these types of errors; this is much faster than Freeman's technique. Morgan(70) gives a detailed flowchart for this. An outline of the spelling correction procedure is as follows:

1. From the symbol table select a subset containing all those of which the misspelled identifier might be a misspelling.
2. Test each identifier in the subset to see if it can be transformed into the misspelled identifier under one of the four transformations above.

The purpose of the first step is to limit the number of identifiers which have to be checked. The context in which the misspelled identifier is used (as described earlier) can be used for this. An obvious test is on the number of characters in the identifier; if the misspelled identifier has n characters, then it need only be checked against identifiers with n-1, n, or n+1 characters. It is not worthwhile to check for a misspelling when $n \leq 2$.

## 15.2 RECOVERING FROM SEMANTIC ERRORS

The purpose of this section is to describe a simple method of recovering from semantic errors -- those source program errors concerned with the incorrect use of identifiers and expressions. The main points of the section are:

1. Error recovery consists of replacing an incorrect identifier or expression by one that is "correct." This is done by inserting a new symbol table entry with attributes determined by the context in which the error occurred, and by changing the internal source program pointer to point at this new entry.

2. Extra error messages due to a wrong or incomplete recovery should be suppressed where possible.
3. All semantic error recovery should be localized in one place, preferably in the routine ERRMES (say) which prints out error messages (or which stores them in a table for later printout). This practice effectively separates the recovery from the rest of the compiler.

There are two main problems to be dealt with: (1) suppressing extra messages due to a single error, and (2) suppressing duplicate messages due to the same error occurring several times.

### Suppressing Extra Messages

In many cases where an identifier is used incorrectly, we can just print an error message and continue. For example, if a statement A := B is parsed and A is real and B Boolean, we can just print the message that A and B are not assignment compatible and continue, since no "semantics" need be associated with the nonterminal <assignment statement> and thus no extra messages will be printed.

On the other hand, consider a case, like a subscripted variable A[e1,...,en], where some "structure" is associated with the identifier A. Suppose A is not an array name, and that we print the error message and continue parsing the subscripts. When finished, the number of subscripts will be checked against the number of dimensions, supposedly in the symbol table entry for A. Since A is not an array name this is sure to produce a second error message.

A simple way to recover from such an error in order to suppress extra messages concerning the identifier is to replace it in the source program by a "correct" identifier. A new entry is inserted into the symbol table, with the attributes filled in as correctly as possible. The name associated with it is one that cannot appear in a source program, and we furthermore assume that the name is recognizable as a name inserted to correct an error. Let us call such an entry a CORRECTID entry, since it is inserted to correct a wrong identifier or expression.

Of course, all the attributes won't be known at the error point, so we may still get extra messages. For example, if A[e1,...,en] occurs, where A is not really an array name, at the time A[ is parsed we don't know how many subscripts A is supposed to have.

Let us assume the existence of a routine ERRMES which prints out error messages. In order to localize the suppression of extra messages, we perform this suppression in ERRMES, as follows:

> ERRMES is given as a parameter a pointer to the symbol table entry for the identifier which caused the error. ERRMES tests the entry's name to see if it is a CORRECTID entry -- one inserted to correct a previous error. If so, no message is printed.

It is also a good idea to have a single routine to build all new CORRECTID entries. Since the ERRMES routine is going to be called anyway, we can let _it_ handle this job also. The ERRMES routine will be described later.

### Suppressing Duplicate Messages

Duplicate error messages occur because the same identifier is used incorrectly several times. This may happen because a declaration couldn't be parsed correctly. It also happens in block structured languages where, because of a syntax error the complete block structure is wrong. For example, in the program

```
BEGIN REAL A; ...
      BEGIN BOCIEAN A ; ...
            BEGIM ... END;
            A := A AND B; C := A OR B;
END   END
```

the BEGIN on the third line is spelled wrong, so that the END closes the block beginning on line 2. Each reference to A on the fourth line then causes an error message "A is REAL, but should be BOOLEAN."

Duplicate messages can be suppressed easily. First of all, if an undeclared identifier is used, it should be inserted in the symbol table with the attributes that can be discovered from its use. Secondly, attached to the entry for an identifier, keep a list of elements describing the incorrect ways the identifier was used. When an identifier is used incorrectly, just sequence through this list; if it was used in the same way previously, don't print an error message. If not used previously in the same way, print a message and add this incorrect use to the list.

This procedure should also be performed in the error message routine ERRMESS, to be discussed in more detail later.

The programmer might want to know exactly where an identifier was used incorrectly, no matter how many messages it might give him. One can still reduce the output by keeping, with each element describing an incorrect use of an identifier, a list of card numbers where that incorrect use occurred. When analysis is complete, then print each message once, with a list of card numbers where the error occurred.

### The Routine ERRMES

This routine is called whenever a semantic error occurs. Its purpose is to print the message (suppressing it if possible) and then to correct the error. Parameters to the routine are:

1. NO: A number identifying the message to be printed.
2. ID: The identifier which caused the error (if applicable).
3. P: The variable containing (if applicable) the address of an entry describing the incorrect identifier. ERRMES will store into P the address of a CORRECTID entry which corrects the error.
4. T: A parameter which indicates the type that the identifier or expression should have (based on the context in which the error occurred).

Parameter T is used to fill in the attributes of the symbol table entry which corrects the error. Depending on the source language and the rest of the compiler, one may need more parameters to describe these attributes. We can now outline procedure ERRMES.

1. If error message NO is "undeclared identifier", execute step 2; otherwise go to step 3.
2. Insert a symbol table entry for ID, with type T. Insert its address in P. Print the message and return.
3. If P is the address of an entry inserted to correct a previous identifier (a CORRECTID entry), then return (this suppresses extra error messages).
4. If error message NO does not concern the wrong type of entry P, then print the message and return.
5. If P has already been used incorrectly in the same way, go to step 7. (Check this by searching the list of incorrect uses based on symbol table entry P).
6. Print the error message and, if P ≠ 0, add the incorrect use to the chain based on entry P.
7. If no CORRECTID entry exists with type T, build one and insert it in the symbol table. Change P to point to the CORRECTID entry with type T. Return.

## 15.3 RECOVERY FROM SYNTACTIC ERRORS

At any point of a parse of a source program, the program has the form

(15.3.1) xTt

where x represents the part already processed, T is the next symbol to be scanned, and t is the rest of the source program.

Suppose an error occurs. In the top-down method, this means that the partial tree built to cover x cannot be extended to cover T. In the bottom-up case, depending on the parsing method, there might be no precedence relation between a tail of x and T, or no tail of x forms a handle, or some similar situation.

At this point, we must determine how to change the program to "fix" the error. It can be changed most easily in the following ways (or perhaps combinations of them):

1. Delete T and try to parse again.
2. Insert a string of terminals q between x and T (yielding xqTt), and begin parsing using the head of qTt. This insertion should allow us to process all of qT before another error occurs.
3. Insert a string q between x and T (yielding xqTt), but begin parsing using T. (In a bottom-up parse, q would be put in the stack).
4. Delete some symbols from the tail of x.

Methods 3 and 4 are bad ways of recovering and should not be used, for the following reason. Since x has been processed, there may be semantic information associated with it. Adding q to x, or deleting part of x, means that we must change the semantic information accordingly, and this is not easy to do. If we don't change the stack by methods 3 and 4, we don't have to change any semantics. Methods 1 and 2 will be our main methods of recovering.

Note that we can perform the equivalent of 3 or 4 by inserting a string of terminals (method 2). For example, suppose we have

```
x = ... THEN <block begin>          Tt = ELSE ...
```

and we want to delete the <block begin>. Deleting it means we must do bookkeeping to fix the block structured symbol table, and so forth. Instead, let us insert the symbol END, yielding

```
x = ... THEN <block begin>          Tt = END ELSE ...
```

The normal compilation process will then handle all the bookkeeping as <block begin> END is processed and reduced.

It may seem plausible to add rules to the grammar to take care of errors. Thus, we might add a rule like

```
<assignment state> ::=  := E
```

to take care of the case when the variable to the left of := is missing. However, the grammar will quickly become large and unwieldy, and will be harder to change to a suitable form for a parsing algorithm. Production language is a good language to use from this standpoint; since you are actually programming, you can add any number of productions to take care of errors.

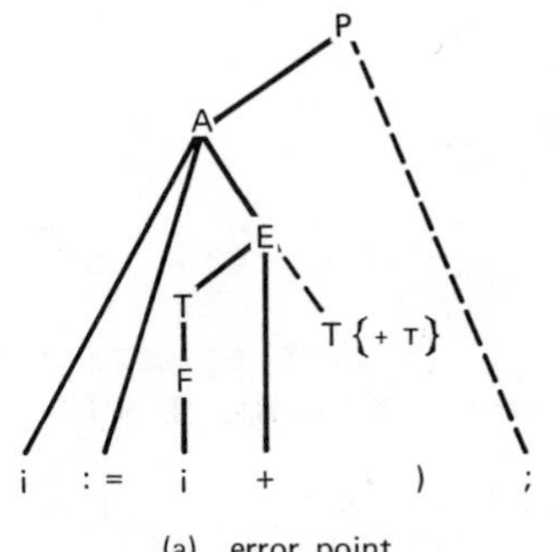


(a) error point

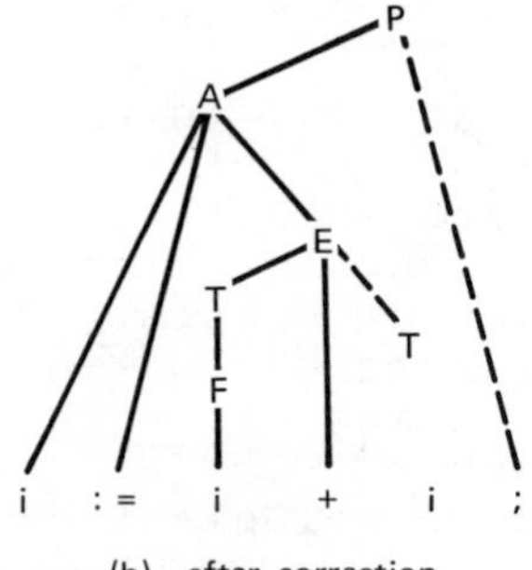


(b) after correction

**FIGURE 15.1. Top-Down Error Recovery.**

### Error Recovery in Top-Down Parsers

We will illustrate Irons'(61b) technique here, using the grammar

```
        P ::= A;
        A ::= i := E
(15.3.2) E ::= T {+ T}
        T ::= F {* F}
        F ::= i | ( E )
```

We assume a top-down parser which can work without backup. Either it performs alternate parses in parallel, dropping them as they reach dead ends, or it uses some context in order to be able to distinguish the correct rule to apply at each step.

At any step of a parse, one or more syntax trees have been constructed, with some incomplete branches. For example, in Figure 15.1a, the solid lines show a partially completed tree, while the dotted lines show how the branches named P and E might be completed.

An incomplete branch named U corresponds to an application of a rule

U ::= X1X2...X[i-1]Xi...Xn

where X1...X[i-1] is the completed part of the branch and Xi...Xn the <u>incomplete part</u> of the branch. In Figure 15.1a, the incomplete branch named P corresponds to an application of the rule P ::= A ;, and ";" is the incomplete part of the branch. The incomplete branch named E corresponds to an application of the rule E ::= T {+ T}. To complete the branch, we need a single T, followed by any number of "+T"s. The incomplete part is therefore T {+ T}.

As another example, consider a rule

U ::= (A | B C | D E) (F | G)

where the parentheses are metasymbols. Suppose that B is the complete part of the branch. Then the incomplete part is C (F | G), since either C F or C G will complete the right part.

These incomplete parts of branches play a large role in error recovery; they tell us, in effect, what can or should appear next in the source program.

Now let us suppose that an error occurs during a parse; no partially constructed syntax tree can be further built. The following error recovery is then performed:

1. A list L of the symbols in the incomplete parts of incomplete branches is constructed.
2. The head symbol T of Tt is repeatedly examined and discarded (yielding a new string Tt) until a T is found such that U =>* T... for some U in L (either U = T or U =>+ T...).
3. An incomplete branch which caused the symbol U of step 2 to be put in L is determined.
4. A terminal string q is determined such that, if inserted just before T, the continuation of the parse will cause T to be correctly linked to the incomplete branch of step 3. This is done by examining the incomplete branch of step 3 and all incomplete branches of the subtree determined by it. For each such incomplete branch, a string of terminals is generated which will complete it, and these strings are concatenated to form q.
5. The string q is inserted just before T and the parse is continued, beginning with the head symbol of q as the incoming symbol.

Consider, for example, the parse as indicated in Figure 15.1a. An error has occurred with ")" as the incoming symbol. We have L = {;, T, +}. Step 2 of error recovery consists of discarding the ")". The incomplete branch which caused ";" to be put in L is P ::= A;. We must therefore insert a string q to complete the branch E ::= T{+T}. The simplest string to insert is an identifier i (see Figure 15.1b).

Figure 15.2 illustrates how the scheme uses "global" context in determining how to recover. The error in Figure 15.2a seems to be the same as that in Figure 15.1a; "+" followed by ")". Now, however, L = {;,),+,T}, and this time the parenthesis is not discarded by step 2. The incomplete branch which caused ")" to be put in L is F ::= (E). To cause the ")" to be associated with this branch, we must insert a string to complete the branch E ::= T{+T}, and this again is i. (see Figure 15.2b).

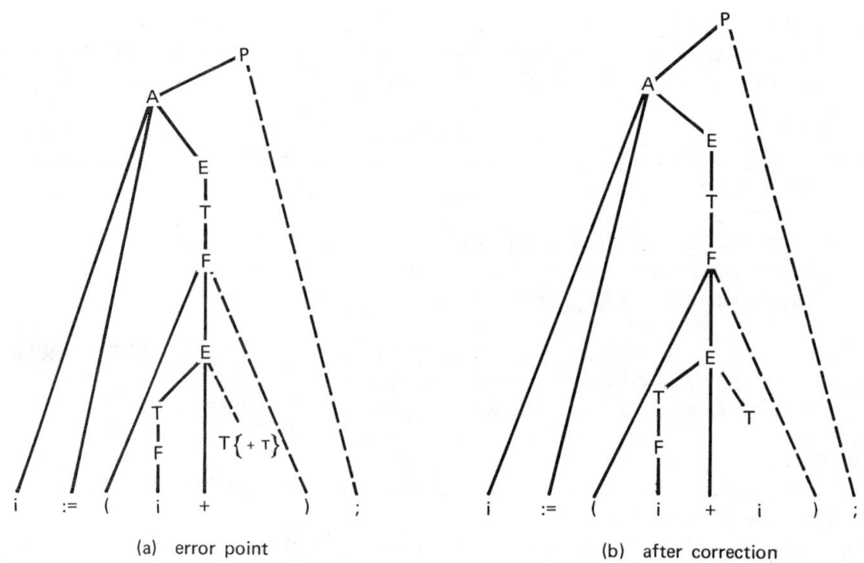


**FIGURE 15.2. Another Example of Top-Down Error Recovery.**

Note that the opening parenthesis could be much further away from the error point, but it would still be used in the error recovery decision. All the incomplete branches play a part in error recovery.

When using recursive descent (top-down using recursive procedures; see section 4.3), it would be nice to be able to use the top-down error recovery technique described earlier. However, the partially constructed syntax tree is not explicitly represented, so that this is not entirely possible. One method of recovering is the following:

If a recursive routine detects an error it prints an error message. Then, depending on the next source symbol T it can do one of two things: either insert something which will correct the error and continue, or return to the calling routine, with an error indication. For example, if the routine for

F ::= ( E ) | i

finds no "(" or "i", it can insert an "i" and continue. If it finds "( E", but no closing parenthesis, it can assume one is there and return.

What we are doing is essentially what the automatic error recovery method does. At each point of execution, each recursive procedure currently being executed represents an incomplete branch of the tree. The active procedure recovers as best as it can depending on the incoming source symbol and the incomplete branch which it represents. If it cannot, it reports failure to the routine which called it. This routine then tries to recover in the same way.

At some point this process should stop. "Important" routines, like the one for <statement> and <compound statement> should not return, but should skip source program symbols until they can recover -- until they reach an END, a semicolon, or recognizable beginning of a new statement.

### Error Recovery in Bottom-Up Parsers

The nice part about top-down error recovery is that the partially constructed tree conveys much usable information about what should appear next in the source program. This information is nct as readily available in the bottom-up method; all we have is xTt where x is that part of the sentential form already processed. Hence, we can't easily use such global context (like all incomplete branches), and we will have to rely on the local context immediately surrounding the error point.

The following method, used in the XPL compiler writing system (see McKeeman et al(70)), is similar to techniques used in many automatic bottom-up parsers. It is admittedly primitive.

The compiler writer is allowed to initialize an array STOPIT with "important" symbols, like ";" and END. When an error is detected, the following happens:

1. The symbols in Tt are examined and discarded until one is found which is in STOPIT.
2. We now have a new symbol T. Examine and discard tail symbols of x until the symbol T can legally follow what remains of x.

Note that the step violates our rule of keeping syntax and semantics separate (of not changing x). It would be better to insert a string of terminals which, when processed, would cause reductions to be made in the stack. This is harder to do.

A second method works well with the transition matrix technique (see section 6.4). This technique uses the top few symbols x1 of x = x2x1 which form the head of a right part of a rule, to pick out a row i of a matrix M; the incoming symbol T determines a column j. The element M(i,j) is the address of a subroutine which either stacks T and scans the next symbol, or performs a reduction. The nice part is that usually over half the matrix elements represent illegal pairs (x1,T), and hence one can detect many different error conditions.

The error recovery scheme we have in mind will use a constructor which, given the grammar, constructs the error recovery subroutines and fills in the matrix elements with their names. (If no such constructor is available, the compiler writer should figure out his own ad hoc error recovery, but keeping in mind the rules given below). Thus the error recovery routines will not have to figure out how to recover based on context; they recover based solely on x1 and T, in a predetermined fashion.

Remembering that we recover only by deleting T or inserting a terminal string q between x1 and T, the constructor could use the following rather natural methods for determining how to recover for a given (x1,T):

1. If there exists a rule U ::= x1zT... in the grammar, a terminal string q should be inserted such that z =>* q.
2. If there exists a rule U ::= x1V... such that V =>+ zT..., a terminal string q should be inserted such that z =>* t.
3. If there exists a rule U ::= ...VT... such that V =>+ ... Wz2 and W ::= x1z1 is a rule, a terminal string q should be inserted such that z = z1z2 =>* q.
4. If none of the above apply, T should be deleted.

Such rules are quite similar to those used by a top-down parser, but less context is used to make a decision. This means that the error recovery will not perform as well. We illustrate the determination of the string q in the table below. A conventional syntax for an ALGOL-like language is assumed. CS stands for <compound statement>, SL for <statement list>.

| case | x1 | T | rules | z | q |
|---|---|---|---|---|---|
| 1 | ( | ) | F ::= ( E ) | E | i |
| 2 | BEGIN | := | CS ::= BEGIN SL END<br>SL =>* i := E | i | i |
| 3 | E * | ) | F ::= ( E )<br>E =>* T<br>T ::= T * F | F | i |
| 4 | ARRAY | STEP | | (delete STEP) | |

In outlining this method, which has never been used or tested, we have left several important questions unanswered: if more than one rule applies, which should be applied? Which q such that z =>* q should be inserted? Are we sure that an insertion will not lead to an infinite sequence of other insertions? This technique has, however, been used successfully in an intuitive manner in the transition matrix of the ALCOR ILLINOIS 7090 compiler (see Gries et al(65)).

# Chapter 16.
# Interpreters

We use the term _interpreter_ for a program which performs two functions:

1. Translates a source program written in the source language (e.g. ALGOL) into an internal form; and
2. Executes (interprets, or simulates) the program in this internal form.

The first part of the interpreter is like the first part of a multi-pass compiler, and we will call it the "compiler". The internal form into which it translates should be designed to make the second part, the interpreter proper, as efficient as possible. Polish notation is often used here, and this is what we will describe. It will be interpreted as discussed in section 11.2, and the reader would do well to study this section again before proceeding. This chapter is limited to discussing more details about the actual implementation.

Although the term interpreter refers to the whole process (both parts above), we will subsequently use it to refer to the second part only, since this is where the internal form is being interpreted. This second part occurs at "interpretation time."

An interpreter is much slower in execution than an equivalent machine language program. Thus, it should not be used in a production environment, where most of the computer time is spent in execution. Interpretation lends itself to an educational environment, where most of the time is spent debugging source programs. As we shall see, it is easier to produce good runtime debugging facilities in an interpreter than in a compiler.

Interpreters could also be used for a source language where, at execution time, a good part of execution is spent in standard, system routines, and less time is spent actually executing object program instructions. This is the case, for example, in a matrix manipulation language, where most of the operations are calls on standard, preassembled system routines to perform matrix operations. Another case is symbol manipulation languages, like SNOBOL.

### The Overall Scheme

Internally, the Polish form of the source program is stored in an integer array P. During interpretation, an integer p, initially 1, contains the index in P of the symbol currently being processed. Thus, p is an "instruction counter". As described in section 11.2, to execute the Polish program we use a stack S with counter i. Initially, the stack is empty (i = 0).

The main part of the interpreter is a case statement, with one substatement for each of the possible different operators and types of operands in the Polish program. Thus, at each step

P(p) determines a substatement of the case statement, which is then executed. Figure 16.1 illustrates this for the representation of operators and operands given in section 11.2, which we list again here:

```
1  = constant                        11 = BLOCK (block begin)
2  = identifier                      12 = BLCKEND (block end)
6  = SUBS (subscript operator)       13 = ADEC (array declaration)
7  = := (assignment)                 14 = +
8  = BMZ (branch on minus, zero)     15 = *
9  = BR (branch)                     16 = -
10 = BRL (branch to label)
```

We have described most of the substatements in English; the purpose here is only to show the overall structure of the interpreter. Two other points are also illustrated by the figure. Substatement 8 deletes its two operands from the stack S. Each substatement must do this, and additionally push its result, if any, on S. Secondly, note that after a substatement is executed, the instruction counter is increased by one, so that the next symbol will be processed. Note the extra addition to p in substatements 1 and 2, since operands use two locations in our representation. Substatements for branches must change p themselves and jump directly to NEXT to process the next symbol, as does substatement 8 for BMZ.

```
NEXT:
CASE P(p) OF
   1:BEGIN p:=p+1; "Push P(p) onto stack S" END;
   2:BEGIN p:=p+1; "Push P(p) onto stack S" END;
   3: ;
   4: ;
   5: ;
   6:BEGIN "Perform subscripting"; END;
   7:BEGIN "Perform assignment"; END;
   8:BEGIN i:=i-2; IF S(i+1)≤0 THEN
                                 BEGIN p:=S(i+2);GOTO NEXT END;
   9:BEGIN i:=i-1; p:=S(i+1); GOTO NEXT END;
  10:BEGIN "Perform branch to label"; END;
  11:BEGIN "Perform block entry"; END;
  12:BEGIN "Perform block exit"; END;
  13:BEGIN "Perform array declaration"; END;
  14:BEGIN "Perform addition"; END;
  15:BEGIN "Perform multiplication"; END;
  16:BEGIN "Perform subtraction"; END;
ENDCASE;
p:=p+1; GOTO NEXT;
```

**FIGURE 16.1. General Structure of the Interpreter.**

### The VALUES on the Stack S

Let us for the moment assume that the only type of value in the source language is INTEGER. Problems with multiple types and conversions will be discussed later. We assume also that the symbol table can be used at interpretation time. The stack S may contain three possible kinds of values:

1. An integer value;
2. A pointer to a symbol table entry; and
3. The address of a variable.

Evaluation of an operation "A B +" leaves the first kind, an integer value, on the stack. The other two kinds arise, for example, when evaluating a subscripted variable which looks, in Polish notation, like

<expr> ... <expr> A SUBS

where A is a pointer to the symbol table entry for the array. On the stack, the <expr>s are represented by their integer values. The pointer A is needed so that the operator SUBS can determine the number of subscripts and evaluate the address of the subscripted variable. This address, the third kind of value, is placed on the stack as the result of a SUBS operation.

Each stack element needs two fields, which we call KIND and VALUE. S(i).KIND is 1, 2 or 3, depending on whether S(i).VALUE is an integer value, a symbol table entry address, or the address of a variable. Each operator, when executed, must check its operands on the stack and transform them to the correct KIND, before executing its operation.

For example, the operation * would perform the following steps (its operands are in S(i) and S(i-1)):

1. If S(i).KIND = 2, then put the value of the variable described by the symbol table entry at the address contained in S(i).VALUE, into S(i).VALUE. If S(i).KIND = 3, then put the value of the variable at address S(i).VALUE, into S(i).VALUE.
2. Perform the same operation as in (1), but on stack element S(i-1).
3. S(i-1).VALUE := S(i-1).VALUE*S(i).VALUE; S(i-1).KIND := 1. (Perform the multiplication and fix the kind.)
4. i := i-1. (Adjust the stack).

The above method obviously requires a lot of interpretation time; each operator must check its operands and fix the KIND of its result. If the <u>compiler</u> can determine the KIND of each operand of an operator, and also the KIND of its result, we can then design a more efficient implementation by letting the compiler insert conversion operators into the Polish notation. Hence, when an operator is ready to be executed, its operands will already have the correct KINDs.

Let us define the following three conversion operators:

1. CVPV. Convert the top stack operand from a pointer to a symbol table entry, to the value described by that entry.
2. CVPA. Convert the top stack operand from a pointer to a symbol table entry, to the runtime address of the value.
3. CVAV. Convert the top stack operand from a runtime address to the value at that address.

In addition, we split identifiers in the Polish notation into three categories. Remember that an identifier I was represented by a pair of locations

(1, pointer to its symbol table entry).

Instead, we now allow three possible numbers 2, 3 and 4 as the first location to tell us how to process the identifier, as follows:

2. Put the pointer to the symbol table entry on the stack. We represent this symbolically by P:I.
3. Put the address of the variable on the stack. We represent this by A:I.
4. Put the value of the variable described by the symbol table entry on the stack. We represent this by V:I.

For example, the statement C := B+A(I) ( C B I A SUBS + := in Polish form) would appear in this more explicit notation as:

```
A:C      We need C's address to store into
V:B      B'S value, for addition
V:I      I's value (the subscript)
P:A      Pointer to array A's symbol table entry
SUBS     This produces the address of A(I) on the stack.
CVAV     Get value of A(I) for addition
+        Add, leaving a value on stack
:=       Assign value to C.
```

In general, this second method is preferred: never put off to execution time what you can do at compile-time. Note that no KIND field is needed now, since each operator knows exactly what to expect.

### Conversion of Operands

Two similar philosophies exist with respect to conversion of operands from one type to another: we can have a field in each stack element to indicate the type of value and have each operator check this field, or we can describe the necessary conversions explicitly. Suppose the source language has types integer and real, and that I and J are integer variables and A and B real variables. If we represent a statement I := A*B+J as

I A B * J + :=

then we need a TYPE field to indicate the type of a stack element. (The two fields TYPE and KIND could be merged into a single field.) If the source language permits, a preferable representation is

I A B *R J CVIR +R CVRI :=I

Here, CVIR is a unary operator which converts the top stack operand from integer to real; CVRI similarly converts from real to integer. Note that we now need several Polish notation operators for some of the source program operators. In the above example, multiplication is represented by *R (multiply reals) and *I (multiply integers).

To make compilation simpler, we also need operands CVIR2 and CVRI2, which convert the second stack value instead of the first. Thus, I := J+A*B would be represented as

I J A B *R CVIR2 +R CVRI :=I

This is necessary because of the way the internal form would be generated; we don't know that J must be converted until after I J A B *R is generated.

The explicit method uses more space for the internal representation and uses almost twice as many operations as the implicit method (if the source language has two types). It also requires more work from the compiler. However, _if_ the type of each variable and partial result can be determined at compile-time, the explicit method is preferred, since execution is much faster.

Of course, in some languages the type of a variable may change at execution time (e.g. SNOBOL). In such cases, the implicit method must be used. In addition, the symbol table entry must be available to keep track of the current type of the variable. In this respect, the symbol table entry acts like a template for the variable.

In many cases, most of the types of variables can be determined from the context of the statement in which they are referenced. In such cases, it would be wise to use the explicit method as much as possible, switching to the implicit method only when necessary.

### Interpretation Time Storage Administration

The interpretation time storage administration differs little from that described in chapter 8, although it will be necessary to change some of the details to fit the language in which the interpreter is being written. For example, if ALGOL is being used for this purpose, and if the source language has types real and integer, it will be necessary to use two arrays to act as runtime stacks which hold the values of runtime variables. One will hold integers, the other reals. The address of any variable is then an index into one of these arrays. Everything must be done in terms of indexes into these two arrays, since ALGOL has no pointer variables. If the interpreter is being written in FORTRAN, then some bookkeeping can be saved by equivalencing the two arrays together, thus having only one.

If source language procedures are not recursive, then the current value of each simple variable can be stored in the symbol table entry for that variable. Thus it doesn't really need a runtime address.

### A Symbol Table Dump

One of the main advantages of an interpreter over a compiler is the ease of providing debugging facilities to the programmer. For example, it is fairly simple to implement an interpretation time procedure PRINTVALUE(P) which, given the address P of a symbol table entry, prints the associated source program identifier together with its current value. The current value is printed as an integer, decimal floating point number, etc., depending on the current type of the variable.

For source languages with no recursive procedures and therefore with a fairly simple runtime storage organization, PRINTVALUE can be used to give a symbol table dump. Whenever an interpretation time error occurs, just sequence through the symbol table, and call PRINTVALUE for each symbol table entry corresponding to a variable of the procedure which is currently being executed.

The important point here is that the dump is a symbolic one at the source program level; it is not a binary, octal, or hexadecimal dump of memory at the time the error occurred. Such a symbolic dump can (and should be) implemented in a conventional compiler also, but it is more difficult (see chapter 21).

For languages with block structure and recursive procedures, a symbolic dump of all variables and their current values can be achieved with a little bit more programming effort. In order to provide it, the block list which gives the block structure and indicates where the symbol table entries of each block are, must be available. Secondly, at any point of interpretation, we must be able to determine the current block. This may be done by inserting with each block-end operator (in the Polish string) its block number. Then, to find the block in which a symbol P(p) occurs, scan symbols P(p+1), P(p+2), ... until a block-end operator is found.

Thirdly, the procedure which performs the dump must be able to look in the runtime stack and determine where the data area of a procedure is. It needs this to find the implicit parameters of the procedure.

We outline the dump procedure here, assuming the dump is to occur at operation P(p). Details are left to the reader. The idea is to print out variables declared in the procedure currently being executed, then variables in the procedure which called this one, and so on, until the main program variables have been printed.

1. Beginning at P(p), search through P(p+1), P(p+2),..., looking for a block-end. When found, store the block number in variable B (say).
2. Using PRINTVALUE, print out all variables in block B.
3. Let B := number of the block surrounding block B.
4. If block B is a normal block, go to step 2; if a procedure block, go to step 5; if 0, stop (no more blocks).
5. Print out the VALUE formal parameters of the procedure B, if any.
6. Using the runtime stack, find out from where this procedure was called (look at the implicit parameters to the procedure). Change the stack as if a RETURN operator had been executed. Set instruction counter p to the return address. Go to step 1.

A number of compilers have used this scheme; problems associated with it in compilers are discussed briefly in chapter 21 (see also Bayer et al(68)). The SPL interpreter also uses it (see McKeeman et al(70).

### Other Debugging Facilities

Any interpretation time error message should contain the number of the source language line on which the error occurred. This can easily be accomplished by inserting line number operators (actually NO-OPS, or no operations) into the Polish string; each one is followed by the line number itself. These can be used similar to the way the block-end operator was used in the symbol table dump.

One could alternatively used statement numbers for this purpose, as the IBM F level PL/I compiler does.

The availability of the symbol table at interpretation time makes it easy to provide other debugging facilities. For example, one could allow a standard procedure call DUMP to provide a symbolic symbol table dump as described earlier, after which execution would resume. One could also allow a call PROCEDUREDUMP to "dump" only that part of the symbol table for the procedure currently being executed.

An important but easy to implement facility is a "trace". Execution of TRACE(A) would indicate that, from then on, every time A is assigned a value, the new value should be printed. NOTRACE(A) would turn the trace off.

To implement this, set aside a (1-bit) field in each symbol table entry, and have TRACE(A) (NOTRACE(A)) turn this bit on (off) in the symbol table entry for A. It is a simple matter in the substatement for the := operator to test this bit and call the PRINTVALUE routine if it is on.

Similarly, a LABEL trace could cause a message to be printed every time a label is explicitly branched to; this would be implemented in the substatement of the interpreter's case statement for the branch operation BRL. Another variation is the following: execution of LABEL(L,A,B,...,C) would cause the current values of A, B, ..., C to be printed every time label L is explicitly branched to.

The reader is invited to create his own debugging facilitites. Again the main advantage in an interpreter is the availability of the symbol table. Secondly, the code which implements a certain debugging feature can be limited to a few of the substatements for the Polish notation operators, and with little loss in interpretation time efficiency.

### Discussion

We have discussed mainly assignment statements and branches, in order to describe as briefly and clearly as possible what goes on in the interpreter. The reader should be able now to extend this to other types of operations. When doing so, make full use of the stack S to hold all temporary results. For example, when calling a procedure, all implicit and explicit parameters should be put on the stack just before calling; there is no need to have temporary storage elsewhere for this purpose. In fact, for an ALGOL-like language with block structure and recursive procedures, this stack could easily function as the runtime stack discussed in section 8.9.

For many source languages it is possible to omit the symbol table and references to it at interpretation time. After all, if this can be done when executing machine language object code, it can be done just as easily here. While this may free memory for other use, it defeats one of the advantages of interpreting over compiling: ease of providing good diagnostic facilities.

Don't assume that the methods discussed are the only ways of doing the job. You no doubt can find better ways of handling conversions and representing different values on the stack for your particular source language.

# Chapter 17.
# Code Generation

Section 1 discusses briefly the possible forms of the object code and the advantages of each. A description of the machine language which is used to discuss code generation throughout this chapter is given. In section 2 we illustrate how to generate machine language from the various forms of the internal source program. In this section, we restrict our attention to arithmetic expressions with simple variables, in order to describe as clearly as possible how code generation progresses, and the problems occurring with temporary variables. We assume that each operand in memory can be referenced absolutely (without using index registers).

Section 3 discusses in detail problems in generating machine language addresses of the operands of expressions, including subscripted variables and local and global variables in an ALGOL-like runtime environment.

In section 4 we extend code generation to other constructs. besides expressions. Most of the extensions are obvious, and we restrict ourselves to making comments about the more important and obscure points.

One of the problems with code generation for a complex high-level language is that the code generation routines become large and bulky. In section 5 we discuss various ways of compacting information about the code to be generated into tables which can be partially interpreted. Finally, in section 6 we describe the IBM 360 operating system object module format, so that the reader may learn as painlessly as possible how and why such object modules look the way they do.

## 17.1 INTRODUCTION

### Forms of Object Code

Code may be in one of three forms: absolute instructions, placed in fixed locations, which the compiler then executes immediately; an assembly language program which must then be assembled; or a machine language program placed on card images on secondary storage (a binary deck, or object module), which must be linked with other subprograms and then loaded, in order to be executed.

The first possibility is the most efficient from a time standpoint. Examples of compilers which do this are WATFOR, PUFFT (see Rosen et al(65)), and ALGOL W. A small 50 card program may only take a second or two to compile and begin executing on a large machine. The main disadvantage is that one cannot easily precompile several subprograms separately and then link them together to execute; all the subprograms must be compiled at the same time. What one gains in efficiency one loses in flexibility. Absolute code should be generated by a compiler in an environment where programs tend to be small, and where much debugging is done.

Producing assembly language is the easiest of the three alternatives, since one doesn't have to fool with generation of instructions as sequences of bits; one can produce card images with symbolic instructions on them. Calls on macros can be generated, whose definitions have been previously written in assembly language. For example, on some machines it takes three or four instructions to convert a floating point integer to fixed point. Instead of generating these three or four instructions, the compiler can generate a call on a macro FIX (say) and let the assembler produce the instructions later. This also helps to reduce the size of the compiler.

In spite of these advantages, generating assembly language is usually the worst alternative. It just adds one extra step to the process of translating a program, and this extra step often takes as long as the compilation itself!

Most commercial compilers produce an object module, or binary deck, of the object program. This is a sequence of card images containing the machine language instructions. See section 17.5 for details. Often, the object module may contain the symbolic names of other programs (subroutines) that it calls, and the names of entry points in itself which may be called by other programs. This object program is "linked" with these other programs and then loaded into some area of memory for execution.

This provides much more flexibility, and is standard procedure in many systems. It should be noted, however, that linking and loading is itself a time consuming process.

### The Machine Used to Describe Code Generation

We illustrate code generation into a machine language of a hypothetical machine with one accumulator (or acc) in which all arithmetic is done, and seven index registers. The machine is simple enough so that code generation can be described easily, yet complex enough to show most of the problems that arise.

The instructions, given below, are typical of those found on the average machine. Instructions exist to load the acc or a register from memory, to store the contents of the acc or a register into memory, to add (subtract, etc.) a number to the acc, and so on. The machine has both a fixed point and a floating point format for numbers. The exact formats are of no importance to us. A number in one of the index registers must be in fixed point format.

Within an instruction, a reference to a memory location uses an absolute integer k (the offset or displacement), two index registers, and a bit to indicate indirect addressing. Thus k(i,j) references the location whose address is

k + contents of register i + contents of register j

If i (or j) is zero, by "contents of register i" we mean 0. In other words k(0,0) references location k. We indicate that the indirect addressing bit is set to one by an asterisk: *k(i,j) refers to the location whose address is in location k(i,j). In the table of instructions in Figure 17.1, M represents a memory reference as we have just described it.

| instruction | meaning |
|---|---|
| LOAD M | Put the contents of location M in the acc |
| LREG i,M | Put the contents of location M in register i |
| STORE M | Put the contents of the acc in location M |
| SREG i,M | Put the contents of register i in location M |
| LACCR i | Put the contents of register i in the acc |
| LRACC i | Put the contents of the acc in register i |
| ADD (ADDF) M | Add the contents of location M to the acc |
| SUB (SUBF) M | Subtract the contents of location M from the acc |
| MULT(MULTF) M | Multiply the contents of the acc by the contents of location M |
| DIV (DIVF) M | Divide the contents of the acc by the contents of location M. For DIV, the result is truncated to an integer |
| FIX | Change the contents of the acc from floating point to fixed point |
| FLOAT | Change the contents of the acc from fixed point to floating point |
| ABS | Make the sign of the contents of the acc + |
| CHS | Change the sign of the contents of the acc |
| B M | Branch to the instruction in location M |
| BM M | Branch on acc negative to the instruction in location M (also BP, BZ, etc.) |

ADD, SUB, MULT, and DIV are for fixed point arithmetic
ADDF, SUBF, MULTF, and DIVF are for floating point arithmetic

**FIGURE 17.1. Symbolic Instructions in the Machine.**

## 17.2 GENERATING CODE FOR SIMPLE ARITHMETIC EXPRESSIONS

Code generation routines use a description (in the symbol table or other table) of each variable or temporary value, which gives its type, runtime address in some form, and other necessary information. However, our purpose in this section is just to outline the basic ideas of code generation and to show how things change depending on the format of the internal source program. To simplify, we assume in this section that each variable is represented by its symbolic name (and not by a pointer to its description), and that we will generate symbolic assembly language. A procedure GEN(X,Y), where X and Y are STRING variables, will be called to generate an assembly language instruction with operation X and operand Y (e.g. GEN('ADD','GAB')).

We deal only with arithmetic expressions using the operators +, -, *, and /, and unary minus, where all the operands have type integer and are simple variables. We illustrate code generation from quadruples, triples, trees, and Polish notation, using as an example the expression

(17.2.1) A*((A*B+C)-C*D)

### Generating Code from Quadruples

In quadruple notation, the operations appear in the order in which they are to be executed. Hence, we just sequence through them, generating code for each one in turn. The main problem will be to keep track of the contents of the acc, in which all arithmetic is done at runtime, in order to eliminate unnecessary LOAD and STORE instructions. To do this, we maintain a global STRING variable ACC. ACC is a <u>compile-time</u> variable which indicates the status of the <u>runtime</u> acc, just after the last instruction generated is executed at runtime. If ACC contains the string ' ', the acc is empty at runtime; if ACC is not blank, it contains the name of the variable or temporary value currently in the acc (after the last instruction generated has been executed at runtime).

A routine GETINACC(X,Y) will be called to generate instructions (if necessary) which load one of the runtime variables X and Y into the acc. GETINACC will be called, for example, when generating code for a multiplication X*Y, where either of the operands may be in the acc. Some operators (like X/Y) are not commutative on the machine, and require that the first operand be in the acc. In such cases, we use the convention that a call GETINACC(X,' ') must generate code to put X in the acc. Finally, note that GETINACC may have to generate instructions to save the contents of the acc, if the acc is not currently empty.

```
PROCEDURE GETINACC(X, Y);              |Generate code to put X or Y
 STRING X, Y;                          |in accumulator (X if Y =' ')
 BEGIN STRING T;                       |T is a temporary variable.
  IF ACC = ' ' THEN                    |If the accumulator is empty,
     BEGIN GEN('LOAD', X);             |generate a LOAD X and change
           ACC := X; RETURN            |the global variable ACC
     END;                              |accordingly.
  IF ACC = Y THEN                      |If Y is already in the acc,
     BEGIN T:=X; X:=Y; Y:=T END        |just exchange operands.
  ELSE IF ACC ≠ X THEN                 |If X is not in the acc, then
        BEGIN GEN('STORE',ACC);        |generate instructions to
         GEN('LOAD',X); ACC := X       |store the acc and load X.
 END;   END                            |
```

As mentioned before, we sequence through the quadruples, generating code for each in turn. Let us assume that a counter i is used to do the sequencing, and that the four fields of the ith quadruple are referenced using QD(i).OP, QD(i).OPER1, QD(i).OPER2, and QD(i).RESULT. The code generators invoked to generate code for each of the operators +, -, *, /, and unary minus are given below.

Note in the first code generator for the commutative operator +, that if the second operand is already in the acc, the GETINACC routine physically switches the two operands in the ith quadruple. In the last generator for unary minus, there is only one operand; hence the use of ' ' for the second argument of the GETINACC call.

Code generator for + quadruple

```
GETINACC(QD(i).OPER1,QD(i).OPER2); | Generate code to get an
                                   | operand in the acc.
GEN('ADD',QD(i).OPER2);            | Generate the ADD instr.
ACC := QD(i).RESULT                | Fix the acc status.
```

Code generator for * quadruple

```
GETINACC(QD(i).OPER1,QD(i).OPER2); | Get operand in acc.
GEN('MULT', QD(i).OPER2);          | Generate the multiply.
ACC := QD(i).RESULT                | Fix the acc status.
```

Code generator for - quadruple

```
GETINACC(QD(i).OPER1,' ');         | The first operand of SUB
                                   | must be in the acc.
GEN('SUB', QD(i).OPER2);           | Generate the SUB instr.
ACC := QD(i).RESULT                | Fix the acc status.
```

Code generator for / quadruple

```
GETINACC(QD(i).OPER1, ' ');        | The first operand must be
                                   | in the acc.
GEN('DIV', QD(i).OPER2);           | Generate the division.
ACC := QD(i).RESULT                | Fix the acc status.
```

Code generator for unary minus quadruple

```
GETINACC(QD(i).OPER1, ' ');        | There is only one operand.
GEN('CHS', ' ');                   | Generate the "change sign".
ACC := QD(i).RESULT                | Fix the acc status.
```

Column 1 of Figure 17.2 shows the quadruples for arithmetic expression (17.2.1); column 2 shows the corresponding code generated for each quadruple; while column 3 shows the contents of the global variable ACC just after that code has been generated. Note that even though we have a compile-time description of each temporary Ti, we don't have to assign a memory location to a temporary which remains in the acc during its range.

The code generators just designed may not work correctly for an expression from which common subexpressions have been removed. The reader is encouraged to find the mistake by executing them to generate code for the expression A*B+A*B, whose optimized quadruples are (* A,B,T1) (+ T1,T1,T2). We will remedy the situation in the next section.

| quadruples | instructions generated | ACC |
|---|---|---|
| (* A, B, T1) | LOAD A | |
| | MULT B | T1 |
| (+ T1, C, T2) | ADD C | T2 |
| (* C, D, T3) | STORE T2 | |
| | LOAD C | |
| | MULT D | T3 |
| (- T2, T3, T4) | STORE T3 | |
| | LOAD T2 | |
| | SUB T3 | T4 |
| (* A, T4, T5) | MULT T4 | T5 |

**FIGURE 17.2. Generation of Code from Quadruples.**

#### Generating Code from Triples

The main disadvantage with quadruples is that a description of each temporary value is maintained throughout compile-time. With triples, this is not necessary and, in addition, the internal source program is smaller, since triples require only three fields per entry.

We do need a description of each temporary when using triples, but it need only be maintained while code is being generated which can reference it. For example, when we generate code for the triple

(10) (* A, B)

we generate a description of its result. Then, after generating code for the last triple which references triple 10, we delete the description.

If the ranges of temporaries are pairwise disjoint or nested (see section 14.2), we can use a compile-time stack to hold descriptions of temporaries; otherwise a more complex scheme will be necessary to allocate and delete space for them. We illustrate code generation for the former case. In addition, we assume that each temporary value is referenced only once (as is the case for normal, unoptimized expressions).

During code generation, we keep a stack TRIP of the numbers of the triples for which code has been generated, but for which no code has been generated to reference the resulting value. A parallel stack TEMP contains the corresponding names Tk assigned to the resulting values. A counter j contains the number of elements currently in TRIP and TEMP.

Before generating code for a triple i, both operands must be checked, and if either is a reference to a previous triple, it must be replaced by the corresponding temporary name assigned to that triple. This is done by calling the procedure FIXTEMP(X,Y) given below. X is the operand field to be checked; Y will contain the name of the variable or temporary upon return.

After code has been generated for triple i, we must generate a name to describe the value resulting from executing that code. The name and triple number are pushed on the stacks TEMP and TRIP. Since the result of executing the code just generated is in the acc, we must also change the acc status indicator ACC. Procedure NEWTEMP performs these duties.

PROCEDURE FIXTEMP(X,Y)

```
IF X refers to triple k THEN           |If X is a reference to some
BEGIN FOR m:=j STEP -1 UNTIL 1 DO      |triple k, we look k up in
        IF TRIP(m)=k THEN GOTO F;      |stack TRIP and put the corr-
   F: Y := TEMP(m)                     |esponding TEMP name in Y.
END                                    |Otherwise, X is the name of
ELSE Y := X;                           |a variable, so put it in Y.
```

PROCEDURE NEWTEMP

```
T := name of a new temporary;          |Generate new temporary name.
j := j+1;                              |Push it, together with the
TEMP(j) := T; TRIP(j) := i;            |triple number i, on stack.
                                       |(i is a global variable).
ACC := T                               |Fix the acc status.
```

To generate code, we sequence through the triples, using a counter i. We assume that the ith triple is referenced by TR(i).OP, TR(i).OPER1, and TR(i).OPER2. The code generators for the different operators are similar to those used for quadruples. The differences are that more work must be performed to find the name corresponding to a triple number, to delete temporaries from the stack, and to generate and push on the stacks the name of the result of each triple.

Note that, because we assume the ranges of two temporaries are disjoint or nested, the name of a temporary is always in one of the two top stack elements when code is being generated to reference it. We can therefore find it just by looking at the two top stack elements, instead of searching the whole stack. This makes procedure FIXTEMP simpler.

Code generator for + triple (generator for * triple is similar)

```
FIXTEMP(TR(i).OPER1, T1);              |Get the names of operands
FIXTEMP(TR(i).OPER2, T2);              |into T1 and T2.
GETINACC(T1,T2); GEN('ADD', T2);       |Generate the instructions.
IF TR(i).OPER1 refers to a triple      |If an operand refers to a
THEN j := j-1;                         |triple, we can delete its
IF TR(i).OPER2 refers to a triple      |name from the stack; we
THEN j := j-1;                         |don't need it anymore.
NEWTEMP                                |Fix new temp and acc status.
```

Code generator for - triple (generator for / triple is similar)

```
FIXTEMP(TR(i).OPER1, T1);              |This is essentially the same
FIXTEMP(TR(i).OPER2, T2);              |as the segment for +.  The
GETINACC(T1,' '); GEN('SUB', T2);      |only difference is that,
IF TR(i).OPER1 refers to a triple      |since - is not commutative,
THEN j := j-1;                         |we must make sure that the
IF TR(i).OPER2 refers to a triple      |first operand is in the acc.
THEN j := j-1;                         |before generating the SUB.
NEWTEMP                                |
```

Code generator for unary minus

```
FIXTEMP(TR(i).OPER1, T1);              |Get operand name into T1.
GETINACC(T1,' '); GEN('CHS',' ');      |Generate the instructions.
IF TR(i).OPER1 refers to a triple      |If the operand is a temp.,
THEN j := j-1;                         |delete it from the stack.
NEWTEMP                                |Now fix acc status.
```

We illustrate in Figure 17.3 the generation of code from triples for expression (17.2.1). Column 1 contains the triples. For each triple, column 2 shows the effects of replacing operands which reference triples by the corresponding temporary name; column 4 shows the stacks TRIP and TEMP after processing the triple; and column 5 shows the acc status after processing the triple. Note that the code is the same as was generated for quadruples.

| triple | becomes | code | stack | ACC |
|---|---|---|---|---|
| (1) (* A, B) | (* A, B) | LOAD A | | |
| | | MULT B | 1,T1 | T1 |
| (2) (+ (1), C) | (+ T1, C) | ADD C | 2,T2 | T2 |
| (3) (* C, D) | (* C, D) | STORE T2 | | |
| | | LOAD C | 3,T3 | |
| | | MULT D | 2,T2 | T3 |
| (4) (- (2),(3)) | (- T2,T3) | STORE T3 | | |
| | | LOAD T2 | | |
| | | SUB T3 | 4,T4 | T4 |
| (5) (* A, (4)) | (* A, T4) | MULT A | 5,T5 | T5 |

**FIGURE 17.3. Code Generation from Triples.**

A few remarks are in order concerning the generation and deletion of descriptions (names) of temporary values. If the triples are not going to be processed once code has been generated, we can replace a triple by a description of its result. That is, once code is generated for triple i, we can put into one or more of the fields of TR(i) the name assigned to the result of triple i. We would therefore not need a stack, and we wouldn't have to delete descriptions.

If a temporary value may be referenced more than once, or if the ranges are not disjoint or nested, then we have to know just where each range ends. We need this not only in order to delete the description of a temporary, but also to know when the runtime value is being used, so that we can generate code to store it. We will talk about this in more detail later.

### Generating Code from a Tree

As explained in section 11.4, the sequence of n triples for a single arithmetic expression can be thought of as a tree, with TR(n) representing the root branch. Figure 17.4 gives the triples and corresponding tree for expression (17.2.1). We shall now generate code starting at the root node of the tree -- with the last triple instead of the first. This will allow us more flexibility in the order in which code is generated, and we will produce better code for (17.2.1) than we did before. We implement a single recursive procedure COMP(i), whose purpose is to compile code for the subtree whose root is TR(i). COMP(i)'s action depends on the operator TR(i).OP and its operands TR(i).OPER1 and TR(i).OPER2. The matrices on page 347 summarize the actions to be performed for the different operators. Consider the matrix for the + operator. If TR(i).OPER1 and TR(i).OPER2 are both variable names, we generate an instruction to load OPER1 into the acc and another one to add OPER2 to the acc.

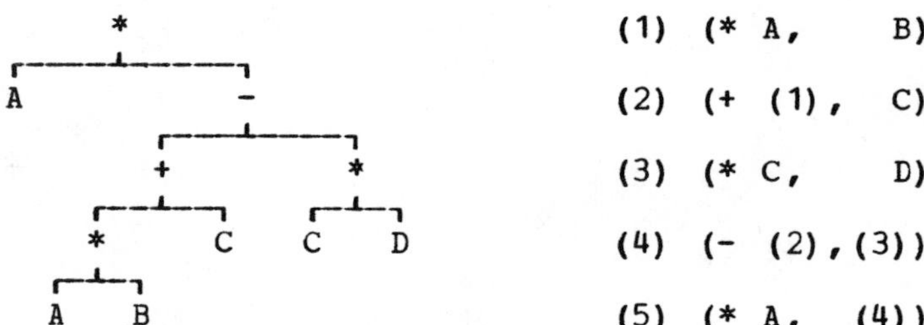


**FIGURE 17.4. Tree Representation of (17.2.1).**

If OPER1 is a variable and OPER2 is a subtree with an operator as its root, TR(i).OPER2 is the index of that root in the list of triples TR. We recursively call COMP to generate code for that subtree. Code will be generated to load the value of the corresponding expression into the acc. Upon return from COMP, we generate an ADD with OPER1 as the operand.

If both the operands are subtrees whose roots are operators, we call COMP to compile code for the first one. We then change the operand TR(i).OPER1 to indicate that that value is in the acc. Action REPEAT means to again use this matrix to determine what to do; we execute the actions specified by TR(i).OPER1 = ACC and TR(i).OPER2 = subtree. Here we generate a new temporary name, generate a STORE to save the contents of the acc, compile code for the second operand, and finally generate the ADD instruction.

In the table below we show the sequence of actions and the code generated for a call COMP(5) with the tree of Figure 17.4. Column 1 gives the node being processed and column 2 its current form. Columns 3, 4, and 5 give the actions executed before code is generated, the code that is generated, and the action performed after that code has been generated. Because we were able to generate code for the second operand first in the triple (- (2), (3)), we have saved a LOAD and a STORE operation.

| | triple | action | code | action |
|---|---|---|---|---|
| (5) | (* A,(4)) | COMP(4) | | |
| (4) | (- (2),(3)) | COMP(3) | | |
| (3) | (* C, D) | | LOAD C | |
| | | | MULT D | RETURN |
| (4) | (- (2),ACC) | | STORE T1 | COMP(2) |
| (2) | (+ (1),C) | COMP(1) | | |
| (1) | (* A, B) | | LOAD A | |
| | | | MULT B | RETURN |
| (2) | | | ADD C | RETURN |
| (4) | | | SUB T1 | RETURN |
| (5) | | | MULT A | RETURN |

Matrix for + (matrix for * is similar)

| OPER1 \ OPER2 | ACC | variable | integer (subtree) |
|---|---|---|---|
| ACC | not valid | GEN('ADD',<br>TR(i).OPER2) | T:=new temp. name<br>GEN('STORE', T)<br>COMP(TR(i).OPER2)<br>GEN('ADD', T) |
| variable | GEN('ADD',<br>TR(i).OPER1) | GEN('LOAD',<br>TR(i).OPER1)<br>GEN('ADD',<br>TR(i).OPER2) | COMP(TR(i).OPER2)<br>GEN('ADD',<br>TR(i).OPER1) |
| integer (sub-tree) | not valid | COMP(TR(i).OPER1)<br>GEN('ADD',<br>TR(i).OPER2) | COMP(TR(i).OPER1)<br>TR(i).OPER1:=ACC<br>REPEAT |

Matrix for - (matrix for / is similar)

| OPER1 \ OPER2 | ACC | variable | integer (subtree) |
|---|---|---|---|
| ACC | not valid | GEN('SUB',<br>TR(i).OPER2) | not valid |
| variable | T:=new temp. name<br>GEN('STORE', T)<br>TR(i).OPER2:=T<br>REPEAT | GEN('LOAD',<br>TR(i).OPER1)<br>GEN('SUB',<br>TR(i).OPER2) | COMP(TR(i).OPER2)<br>T:=new temp. name<br>GEN('STORE', T)<br>TR(i).OPER2:=T<br>REPEAT |
| integer (sub-tree) | T:=new temp. name<br>GEN('STORE', T)<br>COMP(TR(i).OPER1)<br>GEN('SUB', T) | COMP(TR(i).OPER1)<br>GEN('SUB',<br>TR(i).OPER2) | COMP(TR(i).OPER2)<br>TR(i).OPER2:=ACC<br>REPEAT |

Matrix for unary minus

| OPER1 | ACC | variable | integer (subtree) |
|---|---|---|---|
| | GEN('CHS', ' ') | GEN('LOAD',<br>TR(i).OPER1)<br>GEN('CHS', ' ') | COMP(TR(i).OPER1)<br>GEN('CHS', ' ') |

### Generating Code from Polish Notation

We discussed interpreting Polish notation in chapter 16. Generating code instead is performed in essentially the same manner. We sequence through the operators and operands from left to right. Instead of putting an operand value on the stack when it is scanned, we put its description there (its name in our simple scheme). Instead of executing a (binary) operation when it is scanned, we generate code to perform it, using the two top stack descriptions to describe the operands; when done, we replace these two descriptions by a description of the result.

Note that a binary operator always uses the two top stack operands, so that if any other stack element describes a value in the acc, an instruction must be generated to store the acc before the code for the binary operation is generated. This observation leads us to another way of keeping track of the contents of the acc.

No global variable ACC is used. Instead, a stack element can contain a name 'ACC' to indicate that the value is in the acc. When an operand name is scanned in the Polish string, we do the following:

1. If the second stack element (the one next to the top) is 'ACC', generate a new temporary name Ti, generate a STORE Ti instruction, and put the name Ti into that stack element.
2. Push the operand name onto the stack.

Thus, only the top two stack elements ever describe a value in the acc. A binary operator need never check to see whether it must dump the contents of the acc. A unary operator must check only the second element to see whether it must dump the contents of the acc.

### Generating Code in the Original Semantic Routines

If the semantic routines can generate quadruples or triples from which code is generated in the same order, then the semantic routines can just as well generate the code directly. That is, instead of

source program -> quadruples -> code

we have

source program -> code

This complicates the semantic routines much more, of course, but makes the whole compiler faster. We must know enough about the operands as the code is being generated; their descriptions must be fairly complete. This may place some restrictions on the source language, such as requiring a declaration of an identifier to appear before any reference to it.

### Producing Better Code

One of the problems with implementing a code generation system is that there are numerous tricks one feels one should play to save object code instructions here and there. These tricks depend on the particular machine language for which code is being generated, so that they are hard to standardize. Implementing them means that each program segment which generates code for a particular operator has to look for one, two, or more special cases and generate code differently for them. This tends to make the code generation system large and bulky. A few examples will suffice to illustrate the point.

A machine may have a MOVE instruction, which moves the contents of one memory location to another location. Thus, if code is to be generated for a quadruple (:= A,,B) and A is not in the acc, we should generate

```
     MOVE A,B          rather          LOAD  A
                        than           STORE B
```

Note, however, that if the following quadruple is, say, (+ A,C,T1), it would be better to generate the LOAD and STORE, since A must be in the acc anyway.

Some machines have "add immediate", and "load immediate" instructions, where the value to be added or loaded is the address portion of the instruction itself. Thus, for a quadruple (+ A, 3, T1) we should generate

```
     LOAD A            rather          LOAD A
     ADDI 3             than           ADD  L3
```

where L3 is a location containing the integer 3. Besides saving a location, this saves a memory reference each time the sequence is executed.

The machine may have an inverse divide INDIV (or subtract), where the denominator (or subtrahend) is in the acc. In such a case, we may save a LOAD and STORE instruction by generating

```
     INDIV A           rather          LOAD A
                        than           DIV  B
```

for a quadruple (/ A, B, T1) if B is already in the acc.

A LOADN (load negative) instruction can be used to advantage; for a quadruple (- A,, T1), if A is not in the acc, generate

```
     LOADN  A          instead         LOAD A
                         of            CHS
```

Some functions, like ABS and ENTIER in ALGOL, are often better performed inline instead of by a call of a subroutine.

## 17.3 ADDRESSING OPERANDS

The last section outlined the generation of code from the various forms of the internal source program. In order to keep things simple, each operand was represented by a symbolic name. In this section, we deal with the problem of determining how to produce the references to the operands in the machine language instructions. This can be a complex task for an ALGOL-like language, where several different data areas may be referenced at any point of execution, and where subscripted variables occur.

We illustrate the process for arithmetic expressions whose operands have type integer only, in order to keep our attention on the problem. The internal source program will be quadruples. The reader will notice that the general idea of code generation does not change; there are just more details to worry about.

We shall assume an ALGOL-like source language, with nested procedure declarations as discussed in section 8.9. At any point of code generation, we are generating code for one procedure body. At the corresponding runtime point, we assume that the address of that procedure's data area (DA) and DISPLAY (the active data area and DISPLAY) is in register 1 (see Figure 17.5). This is the only way register 1 will be used.

For generating code to reference subscripted variables, we shall assume a dope vector scheme, with (8.4.3) being used to reference a subscripted variable. We assume that the symbol table entry for an array name contains the address pair (data area, offset) of the dope vector, and that the first location of the dope vector contains CONSPART.

At this point, let us give an example of the type of code we want to generate. Consider the program segment of Figure 17.5. At runtime, when executing procedure Y, the address of the active data area (and DISPLAY, illustrated at the right), is in register 1. The code we want to generate for the expression B+P+C[M]+C[N] is given in Figure 17.6. The offset of each reference to a variable is given by the name of that variable, for readability purposes.

```
BEGIN INTEGER N, B;   PROCEDURE X;          ┌─────────────────────┐
   BEGIN INTEGER P;                         │address of main DA   │
      PROCEDURE Y;                          ├─────────────────────┤
        BEGIN INTEGER M;                    │address of X's DA    │
              INTEGER ARRAY C[1:10];        ├─────────────────────┤
                :                           │address of Y's DA    │
                                            ├─────────────────────┤
              ... B + P + C[M] + C[N] ...   │                     │
END END END                                 :                     :
```

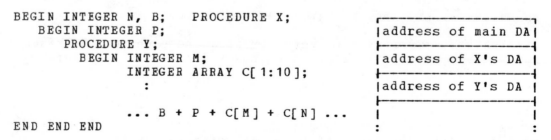

**FIGURE 17.5. Program Segment with Y's DISPLAY.**

```
        LREG   2,0(1)         |Get addresses of main and X DAs in
        LREG   3,1(1)         |registers 2,3 to reference B, P.
        LOAD   B(2)           |Load B, using register 2 which
                              |contains main's DA address.
        ADD    P(3)           |Add P, which is in X's DA.
        LREG   4,M(1)         |Get M in register 4.
        LREG   5,C(1)         |Get CONSPART for array C into reg 5
        ADD    0(5,4)         |Registers 4,5 give CONSPART + M,
                              |so we're adding C[M] to (B+P).
        LREG   6,N(2)         |N is in main program DA - use reg 2
        ADD    0(5,6)         |5 contains CONSPART for array C, 6
                              |contains N.  We add C[N] to rest.
```

**FIGURE 17.6. Code for B+P+C [M] + C [N].**

The first operands referenced are B and P, so the first two instructions load addresses of their data areas into registers 2 and 3. The next two instructions perform the addition B+P. Then, to reference C[M], we put M in register 4 and the value CONSPART for the array C in register 5. Instruction 7 adds C[M] to (B+P). Then, to reference the subscript N, we need the address of the main program data area, but this is already in register 2. Similarly, the value CONSPART for array C is already in register 5.

One of our main problems is to generate code which makes efficient use of the registers. You will notice that in the example we used the contents of registers 2 and 5 twice. Somehow we have to remember what is in each register.

Some compilers generate code assuming there are as many registers R1, ..., Rn as necessary to hold all the different values needed in a register. The next pass then scans the generated code and maps these n symbolic registers into the 7 real ones. As this mapping is made, LREG and SREG instructions are inserted into the code to take care of conflicting uses of the real registers. The object of course is to make the mapping in such a way as to minimize the number of extra LREGs and SREGs needed.

Our particular implementation will allocate the registers as code is being generated. In order to do this efficiently we maintain a set of register descriptions (to be described in detail later), much like the ACC description used in the last section.

Maintaining these register descriptions does take time and makes code generation more complex. If we are more interested in a fast, simple compiler than in good object code, we can forget about register descriptions completely. When beginning to generate code for <u>any</u> quadruple, just assume that the contents of the registers are undefined (except for register 1), and allocate registers 2, 3, ..., 7 as necessary. Had we done this when generating code for B+P+C[M]+C[N] in Figure 17.6, we would have generated two more LREG instructions.

This section may seem confused and complicated, because of the necessary detail. We give below a list of variables and procedures used in this section, together with brief descriptions. Don't study the list now; you'll only confuse yourself. Use it as a reference when reading the various parts of the section. Before we give the list, let us outline the points to be covered:

1. The format of the runtime variable descriptions in the quadruples.
2. The format of register and accumulator descriptions and how they are used. We call a description of a value in a register or the acc an <u>OPERAND</u>.
3. The format of runtime addresses which are put in the generated instructions to reference runtime values.
4. Procedures to generate code to load a value into a register and to build the address part of an instruction.
5. The main code generator for a + quadruple.

### List of Variables and Procedures Used

1. QD(i).OP, QD(i).OPER1, QD(i).OPER2, and QD(i).RESULT. The four fields of quadruple i. The last three are in a format similar to those of Figure 11.2.
2. INS1 and INS2. Two global locations, used to hold the machine language addresses of operands of binary and unary operations when generating code for a quadruple.
3. XRVALUE and XRSTATUS are two arrays used to describe the current contents of the acc and registers -- XRVALUE(0) describes the acc, XRVALUE(i) describes register i.
4. PROCEDURE FREEACC generates code (if necessary) to store the contents of the acc, and changes the acc description to "empty".
5. PROCEDURE FREEREG(I). If I ≠ 0, the procedure generates code (if necessary) to store register I, and changes its description to "empty". If I = 0, the procedure is allowed to choose which register it should empty, based on the current register descriptions. It returns the register number in the parameter I.
6. PROCEDURE GETINREG(OPERAND, I) generates code to load the OPERAND into some register and returns that register number in I. OPERAND may not describe a subscripted variable.
7. GETINACC(OP1, ADD1, OP2, ADD2), like its counterpart in the last section, generates code (if necessary) to load one of the operands OP1 and OP2 into the acc. OPi is an operand, ADDi its corresponding machine language address (in terms of an offset, one or two registers, and an indirect addressing bit). If OP2 is already in the acc, the two operands are exchanged.

8. PROCEDURE FIXAD(OPERAND, INSTR) puts into INSTR an address (offset, one or two registers and an indirect addressing bit) to reference the OPERAND. It returns 0(0,0) if the OPERAND is already in the acc, and j(0,0) if it is in register j.
9. PROCEDURE FIXADMEMORY(OPERAND, INSTR). This procedure is similar to FIXAD, and its design is left to the reader. The only difference is that it must return in INSTR an address which references memory. Hence, if the OPERAND is in the acc or a register and doesn't also exist in memory, then it must generate instructions to store the OPERAND in memory and return its address.

### Operands in Quadruples

Each operand and result field of a quadruple will be in a format similar to those described in Figure 11.2 of section 11.1. The particular format is not important here, just the information contained in the OPERAND. Note that subscripted variables have a more complex format than others; this will be necessary to generate the most efficient code for them.

The following parts of the description of an operand are important for code generation:

1. The type field (real, integer, Boolean, procedure, etc.). This indicates what format the corresponding runtime value has in memory. We are assuming that all operands are integers.
2. The address field, giving the data area number in which the variable has been allocated storage, and the offset of the variable within that data area. We assume it is easy to translate a data area number into the offset needed to reference the address of the data area in the active DISPLAY, and won't mention this problem again.

A description in the temporary table of a temporary value will contain fields which indicate the range of that value. Three methods for this were outlined in section 14.2. Our code generation scheme will allocate storage to temporaries as code is generated, and not in a subsequent, separate pass. Moreover, we will not allocate storage to a temporary which never needs to be stored (if it remains in the acc or a register throughout its range).

If the contents of the acc or a register must be stored at some point, a routine will allocate storage to that temporary, if necessary, and generate instructions to do the storing. After generating the code for a quadruple, we check each operand to see if it is a temporary whose range ends with this quadruple. If so, the location allocated to it is released (see section 14.2).

### Register and Accumulator Descriptions

An array XRVALUE contains descriptions of the runtime contents of the acc and registers, after the last instruction generated has been executed at runtime. XRVALUE(0) describes the acc, XRVALUE(i) describes register i for i = 1, ..., 7. XRVALUE(i) can contain:

1. An operand as in Figure 11.2. This indicates that that particular operand is in the acc or register.
2. An operand that indicates that the register contains the value CONSPART for the array described:

| 5 | 0 | pointer to symbol table entry for an array name |
|---|---|---|

3. An operand that indicates that the address of a data area is in the register:

| 6 | 0 | data area number |
|---|---|---|

Such a value just described which can appear in XRVALUE(i) we call a (description of a) OPERAND.

Besides knowing what is in a register, we need to know how important it is for that value to stay there. For example, register 1 should never be dumped, since it is the address of the active data area. We use a parallel array XRSTATUS, with the following possible values in XRSTATUS(i);

1. 0 Register i or the acc is empty.
2. 1 The value is also in memory. Thus, we don't need to store the register if we want to use it differently.
3. 2 The value does not appear in memory.
4. 3 Don't change the contents of this register at all.

When beginning to generate code for a procedure body, we set XRSTATUS(J) to 0 for J = 0, 2, ..., 7, and XRSTATUS(1) to 3. Finally, we set XRVALUE(1) to

| 6 | 0 | number of data area for that procedure |
|---|---|---|

These acc and register descriptions are updated each time code is generated for a quadruple. Two important procedures used in this connection are FREEACC and FREEREG(I). The first one checks the description XRVALUE(0) and XRSTATUS(0) of the acc, and generates instructions if necessary to save its contents, as follows:

1. If XRSTATUS(0) is 0, then return (the acc is empty).
2. If XRSTATUS(0) is 1, the acc contains a value which is also in memory. Set XRSTATUS(0) to 0 and return.
3. If XRSTATUS(0) is 2, the value is not in memory. Within our system, this should only occur if XRVALUE(0) describes a temporary value. Allocate storage to it in the active data area, say at offset k. Generate a "STORE k(1)" instruction. Set XRSTATUS(0) to 0. Return.
4. XRSTATUS(0) = 3 should never occur in our implementation.

FREEREG(I) performs a similar service; if I ≠ 0, code is generated (if necessary) to store register I and change its description to "empty". If I = 0, then the procedure can choose any register it wishes to free, and returns that register's number in the variable I. If the routine has its choice, it should of course give first preference to one which is currently empty, second preference to one whose value is already in memory (so that no instructions need be generated), and third preference to one with XRSTATUS(I) = 2. Once the register to free is determined, the steps to be executed are similar to those in FREEACC.

There is another restriction on the register which FREEREG can choose. However, we must wait till later for an explanation of this restriction.

### Forms of Addresses of Operands

When generating code for an operation like (+ A, B, T1), we have to know what address to use to reference A and B in memory.

The table below gives a list of the different operands possible in the internal source program. The second column outlines the instructions that might be generated to make the operand addressable, while the third gives the address and index register part of the instruction which finally references the operand. The indirect addressing bit may also be turned on if the operand specifies it. The first two entries are not really references to memory locations, but our way of indicating that an operand is in the acc or a register. We can do this since, in our runtime scheme, each memory reference uses at least one register.

| operand | instructions | INSTR |
|---|---|---|
| 1. in acc | | 0(0,0) |
| 2. in register j | | j(0,0) |
| 3. a location in the active DA, offset k | | k(1) |
| 4. a location in another DA, offset k | LREG m,DA address | k(m) |
| 5. subscripted variable in active DA. CONSPART has offset k | LREG j,subscript<br>LREG n,k(1) | 0(n,j) |
| 6. subscripted variable in other DA. CONSPART has offset k | LREG j,subscript<br>LREG m,DA address<br>LREG n,k(m) | 0(n,j) |

**The Procedure GETINREG (Operand, I)**

A look at the preceding table shows that we will have to generate instructions from time to time to load registers with subscripts, CONSPARTs of arrays, and data area addresses. The following procedure does this for the OPERAND, and puts into I the register number. The only restriction is that the OPERAND may not be a subscripted variable. The procedure uses local variables j, J, D, OP, and k, as indicated. The reader should relaize that there is nothing tricky about this routine (or almost all others described); it is just a case study of the OPERAND, with a lot of attention to detail.

1. If OPERAND is in register j, put j in I and return (check this by comparing OPERAND with XRVALUE(j) for j = 1,...,7).
2. If OPERAND is in the acc, perform this step: I:=0; call FREEREG(I); generate a "LRACC I" instruction. Copy XRSTATUS(0) and XRVALUE(0) into XRSTATUS(I) and XRVALUE(I). Return.
3. If OPERAND has the form (6,0,D), D is the number of a data area, and we want its address in a register. Perform the following: I:=0; call FREEREG(I). Let k be the offset in the active data area to reference data area D's address. Generate "LREG I,k(1)". Set XRSTATUS(I) to 1 and XRVALUE(I) to OPERAND. Return.
4. The OPERAND is a constant, temporary or identifier, with a description in some table. Let D be its data area number, k its offset. Make up an operand OP = (6,0,D) and call GETINREG(OP, J). (This gets the address of the data area into a register J. Note that this is a recursive call.) I:=0; call FREEREG(I); generate "LREG I,k(J) or "LREG I,*k(J)", depending upon whether the indirect addressing bit in OPERAND is off or on. Set XRSTATUS(I) to 1 and XRVALUE(I) to OPERAND. Return.

### The Procedure FIXAD (Operand, INSTR)

Given any OPERAND of some quadruple, this procedure makes up the address portion of an instruction which references it, and puts that address into INSTR. The result in INSTR may also take the form 0(0,0) or j(0,0) if the OPERAND is already in the acc or register j:

1. If OPERAND is in the acc, put the address (0,0) into INSTR and return.
2. If OPERAND is in register j, put the address j(0,0) in INSTR and return.
3. If OPERAND is subscripted, perform this step:
   a) Let SUBSCRIPT be that part of OPERAND which describes the subscript. Call GETINREG(SUBSCRIPT, I). Put the address 0(0,I) into INSTR.
   b) Let P be the pointer to the symbol table entry for the array name. Make up the operand OP:=(5,0,P). I:=0. Call GETINREG(OP, I) to generate instructions to put CONSPART into a register. "Or" the address 0(I,0) into INSTR.
   c) Turn on the indirect addressing bit in INSTR if OPERAND specifies it. Return.
4. OPERAND is a constant, temporary, or variable with a symbol table entry. The value is not in the acc or a register. Perform this step:
   a) Let D be the data area number of the operand address. Build an operand OP:= (6,0,D). Call GETINREG(OP, I).
   b) Let k be the offset in the data area of the OPERAND. Put the address k(I) into INSTR. Turn on the indirect addressing bit in INSTR if OPERAND specifies it. Return.

### Generating Code for Arithmetic Quadruples

We are finally ready to outline the procedure for generating code for the ith quadruple of the form (+ A, B, T1). Generating code for other quadruples is similar, and we leave the routine to the reader. The first task is to generate the addresses of the two operands and to put these addresses into two global locations INS1 and INS2. (The reason for having these two as global locations will be given later.) We then proceed to generate the instructions for the ADD. An outline of this code generator follows:

1. Set INS1 := 0; INS2 := 0 (initialize the operand addresses).
2. Call FIXAD(QD(i).OPER1, INS1). (This generates code, if necessary, to make OPERAND 1 addressable at runtime; its runtime address in the form k(i,j) is put into INS1).
3. Call FIXAD(QD(i).OPER2, INS2).
4. GETINACC(QD(i).OPER1, INS1, QD(i).OPER2, INS2). (The object is to generate instructions (if necessary) to get one of the operands into the acc. Each operand is given by two values -- the OPERAND description itself and the runtime address of

the operand. Upon return from the procedure, the first operand will be in the acc.)

5. Perform this step only if the second operand is in the acc or a register. We want to generate an ADD instruction, and this requires the operand to be in memory. If INS2 = 0(0,0) or j(0,0), we must redo the address computation, using a different procedure, to get a memory address: INS2 := 0; call FIXADMEMORY(QD(i).OPER2, INS2).
6. Generate an ADD instruction with the address INS2. Change the acc description to indicate that QD(i).RESULT is in it (set XRSTATUS(0) to 2).
7. If either of the operands QD(i).OPER1 and QD(i).OPER2 is a temporary whose range ends with quadruple i, perform the following: if it has been allocated storage, release that storage. If it is in a register, set the register description to "empty".
8. INS1 := 0; INS2 := 0.

The two locations INS1 and INS2 are global, and should be used in all the program segments which generate code for a binary or unary operator, for the following reason. Suppose we generate the address of the first operand, and that it uses registers 2 and 3. Then, when generating the address of the second operand, it is important that registers 2 and 3 remain untouched, since they contain values which are needed to reference the first operand. FREEREG must therefore leave the contents of these registers alone. The addition to FREEREG, mentioned earlier when describing that routine, is the following:

> if either INS1 or INS2 currently references a register j in the form j(0,0), k(j,m), or k(m,j), that register must not be freed.

#### Discussion

Although it may seem that we went into considerable detail, we have really only outlined the different procedures. Many details have been omitted. For example, we must try to implement the register descriptions so that the job of deciding which register a value is in (if any) can be performed as efficiently as possible. This might mean having a field in each symbol table entry, etc., which indicates whether or not the value is in a register. Or we might want to keep the registers on threaded lists, depending on their status (one list for empty registers, one for those with XRSTATUS(i)=1, etc.).

While the idea of code generation from quadruples is quite simple, to produce even locally efficient code can be quite complex. Each procedure consists of looking for several special subcases and proceeding with each one separately. Debugging may never be complete, because there is always that one last special case which was forgotten. Some of the cases we had to be careful of were (1) both operands of an addition being in the acc at the same time (arises from optimization of A*B+A*B), and (2) a value being in the acc and a register at the same time (arises from an addition M+A[M]).

It should be clear that even the process of generating operand addresses should be thought out clearly and simulated by hand for some time, before being implemented.

## 17.4 EXTENDING CODE GENERATION TO OTHER QUADRUPLE TYPES

We begin this section with a few more remarks about code generation for arithmetic expressions. We then turn to code generation for other types of quadruples. The idea is basically the same; we know what code we want to generate for each one, and it is simply a matter of designing the code generator to produce it. We will therefore discuss very briefly code generation for only a few of the quadruple operators, touching only on some of the points sometimes forgotten.

### Optimizing the Unary Minds and ABS Operators

A common local optimization technique is to attempt to delete these unary operators by propagating them as far out as possible. Thus, we can change the expression -C*(-(A+B)+D) to C*(A+B-D) in the three steps

-C*(-(A+B)+D) -> -C*(-((A+B)-D)) -> --C*(A+B-D) -> C*(A+B-D)

We have deleted two operations in the process.

We perform this at code generation time by keeping a 2-bit field in the description of each temporary, which indicates what operation must still be performed on that value: 0 = + (no operation), 1 = -, 2 = ABS, 3 = -ABS. The code generator for a quadruple (- A,,T) or (ABS A,,T) generates no code; instead, it just fills in the 2-bit sign field of T, depending on what A is, according to the following table:

| | | A: temporary with sign | | | | source program |
|---|---|---|---|---|---|---|
| | | + | - | ABS | -ABS | variable |
| Table of T's sign bits for (- A,,T) | T: | - | + | -ABS | ABS | + |
| Table of T's sign bits for (ABS A,,T) | T: | ABS | ABS | ABS | ABS | ABS |

In addition, some provision must be made for indicating in T's descriptor that its basic value is the same as A's, in case A is not in the acc or a register.

We now explain code generation for a quadruple (* T1,T2,T3) with sign bits in the operands. Assume T1 and T2 are temporaries; if source program variables, their signs are automatically +. We leave the extension to other binary operators +, -, and / to the reader.

The code generator for a quadruple (* T1,T2,T3) looks at the matrix of Figure 17.7 to determine the sign bits of T3. For a nonblank matrix element, the code generator need only generate a normal multiplication, and put that matrix element in as the sign field of T3. If a matrix element is blank, code should be generated to perform the specified ABS function on T1 (or T2), and to store the value in T1's (T2's) location (if it has one). The corresponding description should then be changed, and the code generator should begin again to generate code for the transformed quadruple.

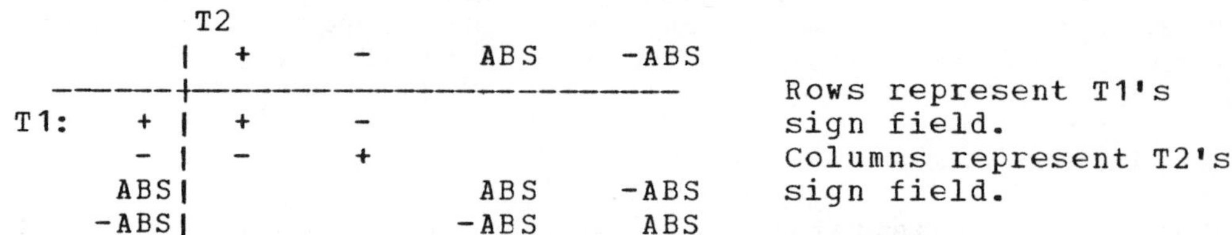

| T1: \ T2 | + | - | ABS | -ABS |
|---|---|---|---|---|
| + | + | - | | |
| - | - | + | | |
| ABS | | | ABS | -ABS |
| -ABS | | | -ABS | ABS |

Rows represent T1's sign field. Columns represent T2's sign field.

**FIGURE 17.7. Determining Sign Field for T3 in (*T1,T2,T3).**

It is not always the case that postponing a unary operation will lead to better code. If a temporary in a register with a sign field other than + must be stored, it may be better to perform the unary operation before storing.

For example, consider the quadruples in column 1 below for the expression ABS(A+B)+C*D. Column 2 illustrates the code generation which puts off the ABS operation as long as possible. Note that two more instructions are generated than in column 3, which generates the ABS sooner.

```
quadruples          postponed          normal
                    unary ops          generation
(+ A, B, T1)        LOAD  A            LOAD  A
                    ADD   B            ADD   B
(ABS T1,,T2)                           ABS
(* C, D, T3)        STORE T2           STORE T2
                    LOAD  C            LOAD  C
                    MULT  D            MULT  D
(+ T2,T3,T4)        STORE T3           ADD   T2
                    LOAD  T2
                    ABS
                    ADD   T3
```

### Generating Code for Mixed Expressions

Let us suppose that the original semantic routines which generated quadruples inserted conversion operators where necessary, so that the quadruples for K:=A*I+J would be as in the left column below (A is real, the others integer):

```
(CVIR I,,T1)                           (* A,I,T1)
(*R   A,T1,T2)                         (+ T1,J,T2)
(CVIR J,,T3)                           (:= T2,,J)
(+R   T2,T3,T4)
(CVRI T4,,T5)
(:=I  T5,,J)
```

The code generator for each different operator then knows exactly what type each operand and the result has. Thus the *R generator generates a MULTF, without checking the types of the operands and result, the *I generator a MULT, the CVIR generator a FLOAT, and so on. This means we have many different code generation segments, but each is fairly simple.

If on the other hand the quadruples look like the right hand column above, then the generator for each of the operators +, *, and so on, must check the types of the operand and result fields, generate conversions if necessary, and then determine which operation to generate. All we have done is to delay the conversion checking process from the original semantic routines to the code generators. It is probably best to do this earlier, in the original semantic routines, because the code generation segments are so involved already.

### Generating Code for a Quadruple (:=A,,B)

The code generated is a LOAD A and a STORE B. The acc description should be changed to indicate that B is in it (set XRSTATUS(0) to 1). This saves code, for instance, for the FORTRAN sequence

```
B = ...
IF (B) 2,3,2
```

B is known to be in the acc when we start to generate code for the IF statement, so code need not be generated to load it.

Be careful here and in similar situations. Suppose we have

```
B := ...  +B+ ...
```

so that the old value of B is in register 2 (say) just before executing the final assignment to B. After generating the assignment, the description of register 2 should be set to "empty", since the register contains the old value of B and not the new one.

Note that any quadruple like (+ A,B,T1) is also an assignment -- to T1. The difference is that we assume such a temporary is only assigned a value once, and therefore it can't be in a register at this point. A temporary which is assigned a value in more than one place must be treated a bit differently.

### Generating Code for Branches and Conditional Statements

Generating code for a branch (BRL L) or (BR k) presents no problem. If the label or quadruple branched to has not yet been processed, we maintain a threaded list of all branches to it, the way we did in section 13.3 when generating quadruples.

So far in this chapter, we have been generating code for basic blocks, or sequences of code with no branches into them or out of them. This allowed us to know exactly what was in each register. At any quadruple (or machine instruction) which is branched to, however, we don't know just before generating code for that quadruple, what is in the acc or registers. Hence, we should set all descriptions to "empty" (except those with XRSTATUS(J) = 3). Be careful when "emptying" the registers. If a description has XRSTATUS(j) = 2, this means the corresponding value is not in memory, and instructions should be generated to store the value.

One way of implementing this test for branched-to quadruples is have an extra field in each quadruple, indicating whether it is branched to or not. This field would be set by the pass which generates the quadruples.

Some register optimization can be performed with conditional statements (and similar constructs) where we know exactly how the branching occurs. For a statement

IF <E> THEN $S^1$ ELSE $S^2$

the contents of the acc and registers are the same at the beginning of the code for $S^1$ and $S^2$. Suppose we generate the quadruples

```
(1)    quads for T:=<E>                  (1)    quads for T:=<E>
(p)    (IFTEST q,T)                      (p)      (BZ q+1,T)
(p+1)  quads for S¹        instead       (p+1)  quads for S¹
(q)    (ELSE r)               of         (q)      (BR r)
(q+1)  quads for S²                      (q+1)  quads for S²
(r)    (ENDELSE q)                       (r)
```

for such a conditional statement (see section 13.2). Then, when generating code for it, we can tell where each of the different parts of the statement are, because of the new operators IFTEST, ELSE, and ENDELSE. In the code generator for the IFTEST quadruple, after generating a branch on T FALSE, we save the current register descriptions XRVALUE and XRSTATUS, and place a pointer P to them in one of the unused fields of the ELSE quadruple. Then, in the code generator for the ELSE quadruple, after generating code, we restore into the global arrays XRSTATUS and XRVALUE the register descriptions saved earlier in P. We are making use of our knowledge that the contents of registers are the same at the beginning of both $S^1$ and $S^2$.

We can also save the register descriptions $R^1$ and $R^2$ after generating the code for both $S^1$ and $S^2$, respectively, and use this information to determine the status of the registers after the complete conditional statement is executed, as follows: For each register i, if the description of register i in $R^1$ is the same as the description in $R^2$, then use it as its description for generating code for the next quadruple; if not, set i's description to "empty", since we don't know what is in it.

## 17.5 COMPACTING CODE GENERATION

The set of code generation routines is often very large and unwieldy. There are just too many program segments, one for each different quadruple operator. It is also true, however, that many of these segments are quite similar, and that there are only a few different operations being performed, like GETINACC, GETINREG, FREEACC, GEN, and so on. We should therefore be able to find ways of saving space. This section briefly describes some of them.

### Interpreting

One method of saving space is to design a small language in which the code generators for the different quadruples are to be written, and then to write a (pure) interpreter for that language. The language should have primitives for all the usual code generation operations (like GETINREG), plus the usual branch and conditional statements. The design of the language is facilitated by the fact that most of the code generators and procedures use global parameters, like the quadruples QD(i) and the locations INS1 and INS2 described in section 17.3.

To illustrate the idea, we indicate below how the program segment for the + quadruple on page 357 would look, both symbolically and internally. Each operation has an integer indicating it, plus several parameters. The operations are INITialize (1), call the FIXAD routine (2), generate code to get an OPERAND into the acc (3), generate an instruction (5), and so on. Note that we can represent the program segment in 20 words instead of, say 50 to 75 machine language instructions. We might also be able to pack one operation per word.

If the compiler is being written in assembly language or any language with good macro facilities, the internal tables of the program segment could be produced automatically from the symbolic form by having each symbolic instruction a macro call.

<u>Code generator for + quadruple</u>

| symbolic | internal | meaning |
|---|---|---|
| INIT | 1 | INS1 := 0; INS2 := 0. |
| FIXAD 1 | 2, 1 | Call the FIXAD routine to make the fist operand addressable. |
| FIXAD 2 | 2, 2 | Call the FIXAD routine to make the second operand addressable. |
| GETINACC 2 | 3, 2 | Call the GETINACC routine to get either of the operands into the acc. |
| CHECKREG 2 | 4, 2 | Make sure the second operand has a memory address in INS2. |
| GEN 'ADD' 2 | 5, 1, 2 | Generate an instruction. The operation is the 1st one in the table of instructions; the address portion is in INS2. |
| CHECKTEMP 1 | 6, 1 | Check operands; if temporaries |
| CHECKTEMP 2 | 6, 2 | whose ranges end, process them. |
| ENDSEG | 6 | Done. |

### Making More General Subroutines

The general plan for generating code for any of the arithmetic or logical operators is to (1) generate code to make the operands addressable, (2) generate code to perform any necessary type conversions, (3) generate code to load one of the operands into the acc, and finally (4) generate code for the operation.

It is often possible to write one, general, code generation procedure to handle all the arithmetic and logical operators. Parameters to it are the descriptions of the operands, the type the result should have, whether the operation is commutative, whether an inverse operation exists (like an inverse divide), and any others made necessary by the quirks of the particular computer. One important parameter is a sequence of skeleton instructions which is used by the procedure to generate the instructions for step (4) above.

The same idea is used in the IBM FORTRAN H compiler (although their code generation scheme is a bit different), which we now discuss.

### Bit Strips

The IBM FORTRAN H compiler (see Lowry and Medlock(69)) has a clever way of packing tables with information about how code is to be generated. To illustrate it, suppose that each register can also be used as an arithmetic unit (as on the IBM 360).

A previous pass has processed the quadruples to perform a quite complicated global register optimization. For each quadruple (say (+I T1,T2,T3)), we know which operands are already in registers, which operand values must remain in that register, and so on. For i = 1, 2, 3 a known register Ri has been assigned to hold the value of Ti, if necessary, and a register Bi is to hold the address of the data area in which Ti is. (Obviously, if in the active data area, Bi = 1). This information resides in the quadruple, along with the operands. Some of the registers may be the same. For example, if T1 need not stay in a register we have R3 = R1.

In addition, an 8-bit STATUS field exists along with the quadruple, with the following information (if the bit is 1, the information is true, otherwise the opposite holds).

Bit Meaning
1. Operand T1 is already in register R1.
2. The value of operand T1 must remain in register R1.
3. Operand T2 is already in register R2.
4. The value of T2 must remain in register R2.
5. The address of T1's data area is not yet in register B1.
6. The address of T2's data area is not yet in register B2.
7. The address of T3's data area is not yet in register B3.
8. T3 must be stored into memory after the operation.

The instructions which may be generated for the particular operation are kept in a table in skeleton form, in the order in which they may be generated, along with some bit sequences. This is illustrated for the +I operator in Figure 17.8. The process of generating code works as follows: A general routine is given the quadruple (with all its extra information) and the instruction table for the operator. It performs the following steps.

1. Use the first four bits of the 8 bit STATUS field to pick out a column of status bits -- 0000 picks out the first column, 0001 the second, and so on.
2. Replace the x's in the chosen column by the last four bits of the STATUS field. The last x is replaced by the bit 8, the second from last by bit 7, and so on.
3. Now sequence through the column of bits, in order; if a bit is 1, generate the corresponding instruction.

To see how this works, consider the 8 bit field 00000011, which says that both T1 and T2 are not in registers, neither operand must remain in its register, registers B1 and B2 are already loaded, B3 is not yet loaded, and the result must be stored. The first four bits pick out column 1, which is x010x010xx. Replacing the x's by the last four bits yields 0010001011. Hence, we generate, in order, the third, seventh, ninth, and tenth instructions:

```
LREG  R3,D(B1)     Load R3 with T1
ADD   R3,D(B2)     Add T2 to R3
LREG  B3,D(1)      Make T3 addressable
STORE R3,D(B3)     Store the result
```

The offsets D are determined from the operand descriptions; the register numbers are given in the quadruple.

The code generated can be made more efficient by adding extra instructions to the skeleton to take into account the commutativity of some operations and other such features.

```
     skeleton         |
    instructions      | status bits
----------------------+-----------------
                      | 0000000011111111
                      | 0000111100001111
                      | 0011001100110011
                      | 0101010101010101
----------------------+-----------------
  1 LREG   B1,D(1)    | xxxxxxxx00000000   ┐
  2 LREG   R1,D(B1)   | 0000111100000000   |fix T1
  3 LREG   R3,D(B1)   | 1111000000000000   |
  4 MREG   R3,R1      | 0000111100001111   ┘
  5 LREG   B2,D(1)    | xxxxxxxxxx00xx00   ┐
  6 LREG   R2,D(B2)   | 0100010001000100   |fix T2
  7 ADD    R3,D(B2)   | 1000101010001000   |and add
  8 ADDR   R3,R2      | 0111010101110111   ┘
  9 LREG   B3,D(1)    | xxxxxxxxxxxxxxxx   ┐Store result
 10 STORE  R3,D(B3)   | xxxxxxxxxxxxxxxx   ┘if necessary

MREG moves from one register to another,
ADDR adds one register to another.
```

**FIGURE 17.8. Bit Strips for +I.**

### 17.6 OBJECT MODULES

An object deck, or binary deck, is the object program on cards (or card images on secondary storage). If the program may be loaded anywhere in memory, the module is called "relocatable"; if it must be loaded into a specified set of memory locations, it is called "absolute". Before the object program is loaded, it can usually be linked automatically with any other required object modules, such as I/O subroutines, standard functions, and user subprograms which were compiled at a different time.

In relocatable form, each instruction or value which references a memory location within the program must be "relocatable" in some fashion, so that no matter where the program is loaded this memory reference can be changed accordingly. Machines like the IBM 360 make this relocation easier, since instructions must use base registers to reference memory. In some of the "time sharing" machines, this relocation is performed completely in the hardware, so that there is no difference between an absolute and relocatable module.

The relocatable object module format is almost as flexible to use as the symbolic assembly language format, but the extra assembly time is no longer needed. We should point out, however, that linking object modules and relocating is itself time-consuming; in an environment where execution times are usually small and most of the time is spent debugging, it is better to generate absolute code and execute it immediately.

In IBM OS/360 terminology, the linking of several object modules to form a <u>load module</u> is performed by a <u>linkage editor</u>. The final loading (with relocation) of the load module is done by a <u>loader</u>. (Actually, load modules themselves can be saved and later linked again with other object and load modules.) In simpler operating systems, these two steps may be carried out by a single program called a linking loader, or simply loader.

We will describe the basic format of the IBM OS/360 object modules. For more details than we can give, see IBM(d) and Ehrman(68). Software systems on other machines will use a similar -- perhaps more or less flexible -- format. The terminology is quite likely to be different.

In order to have a simple, understandable presentation, we restrict the format somewhat and omit some of the finer points. In the diagrams of cards in this section, any columns not described are blank. Columns 73-80 can be used for identification and numbering. Numbers are given in decimal for readability; they should be in hexadecimal characters.

The main points of interest are:

1. How does one specify which external subroutines are needed by this object program?
2. How does one specify "entry points" (instructions or data within this module which can be referenced by other subprograms)?
3. What makes the object program relocatable -- so that it can be placed anywhere in core?
4. Can we use the object module format to make compiling easier or faster?

### CSECTS

An object module consists mainly of <u>text</u> -- the machine language instructions and data which make up the object program. The module can contain one or more such subsections of text, called <u>control sections</u>, or <u>CSECTs</u>. Within a CSECT, the position of each byte of text (relative to the beginning of the CSECT) is fixed, and this order must be maintained when the CSECT is loaded into memory. The order of the CSECTs, however, is irrelevant, and a CSECT may be placed anywhere in memory.

The usual uses for a CSECT are

1. the instructions for the main program;
2. the instructions for a subroutine;
3. the data area for a main program or subroutine; and
4. the constants of a program.

However, one need not stick to these categories; any subsection of text may be put into a CSECT if it is convenient.

### Types of Object Module Cards

An object module consists of four parts, which must be in the order described in Figure 17.9. These parts are:

1. The ESD (external symbol dictionary). This defines and identifies (gives a unique name and number to) the following items:
   a) The CSECTs of the object program.
   b) the external references to CSECTs and other entry points which are used or called by this module but which are not included in it. These are linked to this module by the linkage editor.
   c) The entry points -- locations within this module which can be referenced by other modules. The occurrence of the name of an entry point as an external reference in another object module causes this module to be linked up to the other one. OS/360 refers to these as label definitions.
   d) blank and named COMMON areas (used mainly for FORTRAN).

2. The text, on "TXT" cards. This gives the actual machine language instructions and data of the object program.

3. The RLD (relocation dictionary). This describes the addresses appearing in the text which are to be relocated.

4. END card. This ends the object module.

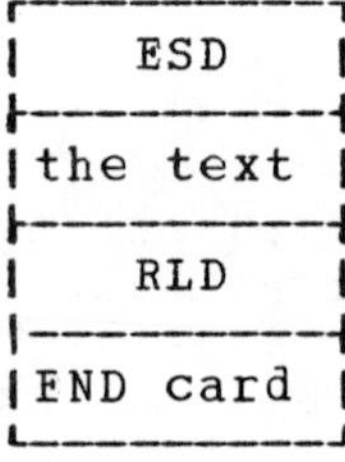


**FIGURE 17.9. Format of an Object Module.**

### The External Symbol Dictionary

Each ESD card describes one ESD "item" -- a CSECT, external reference, entry pcint, or COMMON area -- as illustrated in Figure 17.10. Columns 17-24 contain the symbolic name of the routine or area as specified by the programmer (or by the system, fcr routines internal to it -- I/O, standard functions, etc.). The name is blank for blank COMMON.

Each item (except an entry point) also has a unique 16 bit ESD number, called an ESDID (ESD identifier). The ESDID, assigned by whoever actually built the module, is used within the text and RLD to refer to an item. It is used instead of the symbolic name in order to save space. Since entry points are never referred to within the module by their symbolic names, they are not given ESDIDs.

The items themselves are differentiated by column 9 of the item, as seen in Figure 17.10.

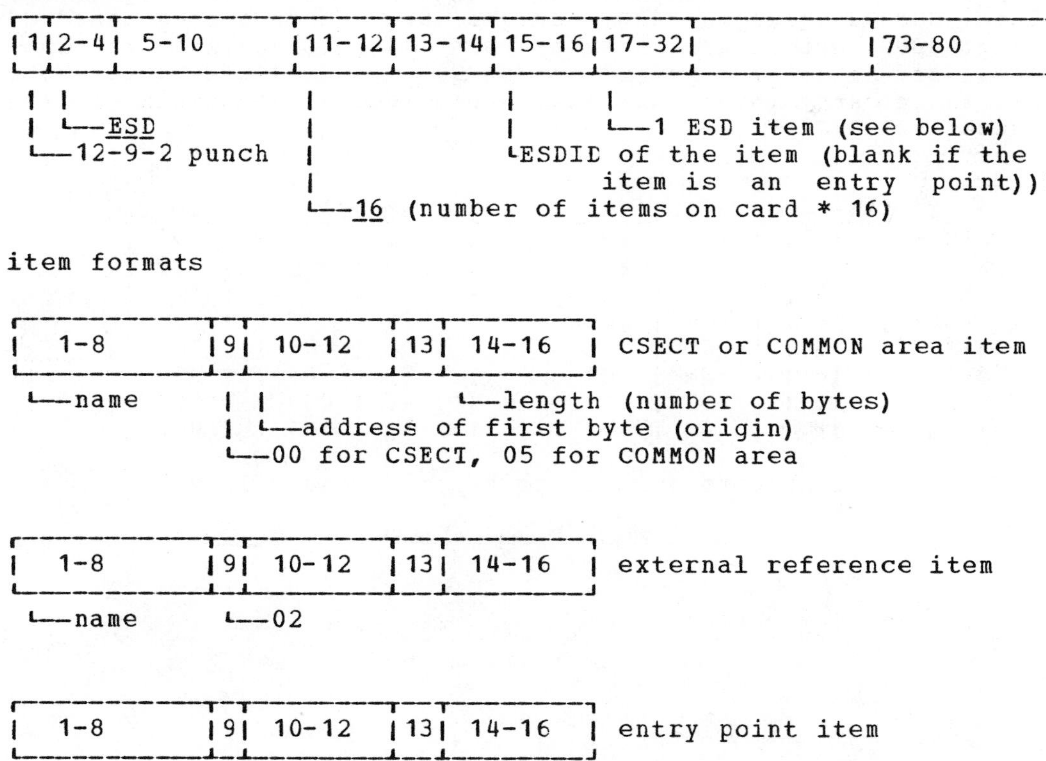


**FIGURE 17.10. External Symbol Dictionary Card Format.**

What other information is needed? For a CSECT or COMMON area we must indicate its length -- how many bytes are allocated to it. This is given in columns 14-16 of the item. We must also specify the beginning address, called the <u>origin</u>, of the first byte of the area, in columns 10-12. All addresses (offsets) of text within the area are given relative to this origin. Thus, if it is 500, the offset 500 refers to the first byte, 501 to the second, and so on. The origin may be 0.

For external references no other information can be given, since nothing else is known about it -- the CSECT referred to by the name is external to this module.

For entry points we need two pieces of information. First of all we need to know the CSECT in which it is located. This is done by putting the CSECT's ESDID in columns 14-16 of the item. Secondly, we need to know the offset of the entry point within the CSECT (with respect to the origin). This goes in columns 10-12.

Figure 17.11 gives an example of an ESD which describes a CSECT named A (length 100, origin 0), a CSECT named B (length 200, origin 501), external references to routines SIN and COS, blank COMMON (length 100, origin 0), a COMMON area named C1 (length 300, origin 0), an entry point A1 in CSECT A at the 20th byte, and an entry point B1 in CSECT B at the 100th byte. Note that these entry points are given relative to the origin of the respective CSECTs.

| 1 -4 | 11-12 | 15-16 | 17-24 | 25 | 26-28 | 30-32 |
|---|---|---|---|---|---|---|
| $ESD | 16 | 01 | A | 0 | 0 | 100 |
| $ESD | 16 | 02 | B | 0 | 501 | 200 |
| $ESD | 16 | 03 | SIN | 2 | | |
| $ESD | 16 | 04 | COS | 2 | | |
| $ESD | 16 | 05 | | 5 | 0 | 100 |
| $ESD | 16 | 06 | C1 | 5 | 0 | 300 |
| $ESD | 16 | 07 | A1 | 1 | 019 | 001 |
| $ESD | 16 | 08 | B1 | 1 | 601 | 002 |

(all numbers are in decimal for readability)

**FIGURE 17.11. Example of an ESD.**

**The Text Cards**

Each text card has the fcllowing format:

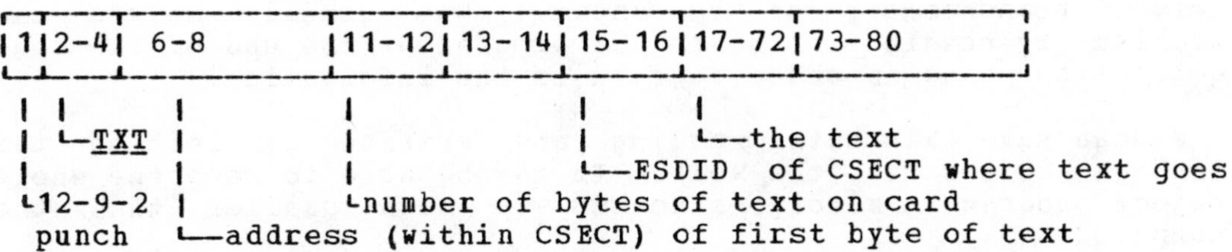


Note that each card contains the ESDID of the CSECT or COMMON area in which the text goes and the address within the CSECT of the text, relative to the origin specified in the item in the ESD. The first byte of text is put at the byte of text specified, the second immediately after it, and so on. If no text appears for all or part of a CSECT, the corresponding bytes are undefined when runtime begins.

The linkage editor will perform mcre efficiently if the text cards within a CSECT are in order of increasing offsets. This is nct a requirement, however, and one can sometimes save compile-time by putting text out in a different order. One can also have more than one card with text for the same address. When this happens, the <u>last</u> such text overrides all the previous ones. Figure 17.12 illustrates this. ("Patching" a deck used to be done frequently by programmers, in order to save the expense of reassembling a large program. When a programmer found an error, he would punch instructions to fix it onto cards in object module format. These cards were put at the end of the object module, and their contents would override and change the parts of the program in errcr.)

```
address-┐  nc. of bytes  ESDID  text
        |       |     ┌───┘  ┌───┘
0 -4| |6-8| |11-12| |15-16|17 - 72
$TXT| |000| |   56| |    1|A...A    (56 A's)
$TXT| |056| |   56| |    1|A...A    (56 A's)
$TXT| |112| |   56| |    1|A...A    (56 A's)
$TXT| |001| |    2| |    1|BB
$TXT| |010| |   10| |    1|CCCCCCCCCC
$TXT| |000| |    2| |    1|DD
$TXT| |167| |    1| |    1|E

    the above cards result in the data

000   DDBAAAAAAACCCCCCCCCCAAAAAAAAAAAAAAAAAAAAAAAAAAAAAAAAAAAA
056   AAAAAAAAAAAAAAAAAAAAAAAAAAAAAAAAAAAAAAAAAAAAAAAAAAAAAAAA
112   AAAAAAAAAAAAAAAAAAAAAAAAAAAAAAAAAAAAAAAAAAAAAAAAAAAAAAAE
```

**FIGURE 17.12. Example of Text Cards.**

A compiler has a fixed number of locations in which to store the object program it is generating. If this "buffer" fills up, the contents must be written on secondary storage. However, all the information may not be known yet. For example, addresses of forward branches may not be known. One usually solves the problem by reading in the object program at the end of the code generation phase in order to fill in the information.

We can save this extra reading and writing by letting the linkage editor do the work. It may be able to keep the whole object program in memory, since it is much smaller than the compiler.

When the object program buffer is filled, write out the TXT card images from it. Then, as the unknown information becomes available, write out extra TXT card images with the information to override the wrong text put out the first time. Again, this may give the linkage editor some trouble, but it saves compile-time.

Since each text card contains the ESDID to which it belongs, text cards for different CSECTs may be interspersed. We can also use this to advantage, particularly in one-pass compilers which generate code for the main program, procedures, and the constants used in the program, as the program is first parsed.

### The Relocation Dictionary

In a module, the address of any byte of text is specified in the form

(ESDID, offset)

where the ESDID is the number of the CSECT or COMMON area in which the byte goes, and the offset is its address within the area relative to the origin as defined in the ESD item. We already saw the use of such a pair in the definition of an entry point. During loading of the program, the CSECT or COMMON area will be allocated space in memory. The loader will then change this address pair to an absolute address

machine address of CSECT or COMMON area
+ (offset - origin as defined in the ESD)

For example, suppose that bytes 20-23 of CSECT 2 are to contain the address (2,100) -- the address of byte 100 in CSECT 2. Suppose further that the origin of CSECT 2 is 10, and that the CSECT is loaded beginning at location 1000. Then the machine address placed in bytes 20-23 will be

1000 + (100-10) = 1090

Please note the similarity between the compile-time addresses (data area, offset) of data in a data area as described in chapter 8, and these relocatable addresses.

The RLD (and the text itself in some cases) is used to describe all addresses to be relocated. What information is needed for an RLD item? We need to know the relocation address itself -- the address of the byte referenced -- and secondly where the relocated address is to be put -- its <u>position</u> in the text. This is also given in the form (ESDID, offset). Thirdly, we need to know the number of bytes the relocated address will occupy, its <u>position length</u>. Thus we need the following five numbers:

```
1.  relocation ESDID  ┐ relocatable
2.  relocation offset ┘ address
3.  position   ESDID  ┐
4.  position   offset | where the relocated
5.  position   length ┘ address goes
```

For example, suppose we have

```
1.  relocation ESDID  = 2
2.  relocation offset = 20
3.  position   ESDID  = 3
4.  position   offset = 50
5.  position   length = 3
```

Then, assuming the origin of both ESDIDs is 0, this specifies that bytes 50, 51, and 52 of CSECT 3 are to contain the machine address of byte 20 of CSECT 2.

Figure 17.13 shows the format of a card image of the RLD. Up to seven addresses, or RLD items, may be specified on each card. Actually, there are two different types of items. The first, the <u>internal</u> RLD item, is used when the position refers to a CSECT or COMMON area defined within the module. In this case, the relocation ESDID, and the position ESDID, offset and length are defined in the RLD item. Where does the relocation offset go? In order to save space <u>it is placed on a text (TXT) card at the position defined in the RLD item</u>.

The second type of RLD item is used when the relocation ESDID is an external reference. The position length must be 4 (one full word), and the relocation offset is automatically 0. This second type is needed because of problems with overlays, which we do not discuss here.

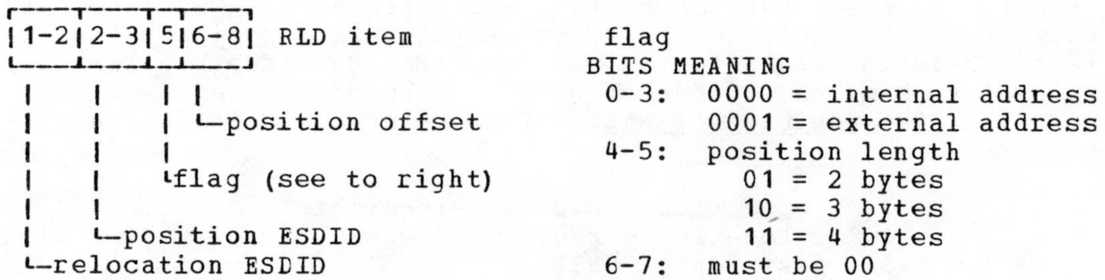


**FIGURE 17.13. RLD Card Format.**

### Summary

There are a number of points we have left out in the discussion. Up to three ESDID items may appear on one ESD card, and there are ways of reducing the space necessary for each RLD item. One CSECT in each module may have its length specified on the END card instead of in the ESD item; this may help, but it also places other restrictions on the order of the text cards.

We have not discussed the problem of overlays -- programs made up of several subprograms which get swapped in an out of core when necessary. Also, what does the linkage editor do when two different modules specify the same CSECT or COMMON area?

The OS/360 module format allows for two other types of ESD items, the "private code" (PC) and the "pseudo register". The latter is heavily used by the PL/I compiler. For more information see IBM(d) and Ehrman(68).

### EXERCISES FOR 17.6

1. Design and implement a linkage editor to link object modules as described here. Decide beforehand what should be done for duplicate COMMON areas, CSECTs, or entry points, etc.

2. Design and implement a loader. Assume the output of the linkage editor has the same format as the object module. However, external references should not be present, since all linking has been done by the linkage editor.

# Chapter 18.
# Code Optimization

Code optimization refers to the process of rearranging and changing operations in the program being compiled in order to produce a more efficient object program. The best code-optimizing compilers can produce object programs for complicated FORTRAN or ALGOL programs which will run as efficiently as a corresponding assembly language program coded by an expert -- and at far less expense.

We classify optimization techniques into two categories: those which are performed on the source program (its internal form) and which are therefore independent of the object language, and those which are performed at the object program level. The latter depend heavily on the object language, and we won't discuss them in detail. See section 18.4 for short discussions and references.

The first class of techniques is applicable to almost any algebraic language -- FORTRAN, ALGOL, PL/I, etc. The four main methods used are

1. Folding: performing operations whose operands are known at compile-time;
2. Eliminating redundant operations; (mostly factoring out some common subexpressions);
3. Moving operations whose operands do not change within a for-loop out of the loop; and
4. Reducing the strength of multiplications in loops (in effect, changing them to additions).

The amount of optimization performed by a compiler depends on many factors. Not all compilers should optimize as completely as possible. For example, the more sophisticated techniques should not be used in a compiler used extensively in checking out programs, since they radically alter the sequence of operations and thus make debugging difficult.

Hence, we will not illustrate one single, overall plan for full optimization. Instead, in section 18.1 we begin with two simple techniques, one of which <u>all</u> compilers should perform. In section 18.2 we discuss a moderately complex scheme for optimizing for-loops. However, it may still be implemented fairly efficiently. In section 18.3 we turn to more complex optimizations which require a more complete analysis of the source program structure. In this section, we give little detail about actual implementation; the reader desiring to implement the more complex methods should study the literature on the subject carefully in any case. Section 18.4 surveys the literature and briefly mentions other techniques which have not been discussed in preceding sections, including those dependent on the object language.

Throughout the chapter, we will use either triples or quadruples to illustrate an optimization technique, whichever is easiest at that point. It is difficult to say just which internal form is better, since no one has really studied the problem; all we have are educated opinions. In general, I favor triples or indirect triples, because quadruples always need a description of each temporary value. Triples, however, do cause more problems in processing, as we shall see. Often we shall write normal ALGOL statements instead of triples or quadruples, for readability purposes.

## 18.1 OPTIMIZATION WITHIN BASIC BLOCKS

As defined in section 11.5, a (basic) block is a sequence of operations to be executed in order, with only one entrance and exit -- the first and last operations respectively. The sequence of operations for assignment statements like

(18.1.1) I := 1+1; I := 3; B := 6.2+I;

forms such a block. Two types of optimization, folding and redundant operation elimination, are usually performed within a block.

### Folding

Folding is the process of executing at compile-time source program operations whose operand values are known, so that they need not be executed at runtime. Consider for example the program segment of Figure 18.1a, and its internal representation as triples in Figure 18.1b. Obviously, triple 1 can be executed at compile-time and replaced by the resulting constant. Less obviously, triple 4 can be executed, since the value of I is known to be 3, and this further allows the execution of triple 5. The final result of folding is illustrated in Figure 18.1c.

```
I := 1+1;          (1) +     1,1         (1) :=   2,I
I := 3;            (2) :=    (1),I       (2) :=   3,I
B := 6.2+I;        (3) :=    3,I         (3) :=   9.2,B
                   (4) CVIR  I
                   (5) +     6.2,(4)
                   (6) :=    (5),B

(a) Program segment  (b) Triples        (c) Optimized triples
```

**FIGURE 18.1. Illustration of Folding.**

Folding is applied mainly to the arithmetic operators +, -, *, and /, since these occur most often in source programs. It should also be applied to conversion operators, like CVIR (convert from integer to real) in Figure 18.1. This is simplified if the conversions actually appear in the internal form (as in Figure 18.1) rather than be implicitly realized.

The process of folding operators whose operands are constants is easy to understand and needs no further explanation. Folding operators whose operand values can be determined is a bit more difficult. It is usually implemented only within basic blocks, using a table T which is initially empty. During the folding process, T will contain pairs (A,K) of all simple variables A with known current value K. In addition, the folding process will replace folded triples by a new triple (C,K,0). C (for constant) is a new operator from which no code is to be produced, while K is the value resulting from folding the triple. The folding algorithm processes the triples in a basic block, in order of occurrence; each triple is processed as follows:

1. If an operand is a variable in T, replace it by the corresponding value K.
2. If an operand refers to a triple of the form (C,K,0), replace it by the constant K.
3. If all operands are constants and if the operation can be folded, then execute the triple and replace it by the triple (C,K,0), where K is the result of the execution.
4. If the triple is an assignment A := B to an unsubscripted variable A, then
   a) If B is a constant, add A with the value B to the table T (delete an old value of A from it, if necessary), or
   b) If B is not a constant, delete A with its known value from T, if present.

We illustrate this algorithm on the basic block of Figure 18.1 in Figure 18.2.

```
1 C  2         C  2          C  2          C  2          C  2          C  2
2 := (1),I     := 2,I        := 2,I        := 2,I        := 2,I        := 2,I
3 := 3,I       := 3,I        := 3,I        := 3,I        := 3,I        := 3,I
4 CVIR I       CVIR I        CVIR I        C  3.0        C  3.0        C  3.0
5 + 6.2,(4)    + 6.2,(4)     + 6.2,(4)     + 6.2,(4)     C  9.2        C  9.2
6 := (5),B     := (5),B      := (5),B      := (5),B      := (5),B      := 9.2,B

T:             (I,2)         (I,3)         (I,3)         (I,3)         (I,3)
                                                                       (B,9.2)
```

**FIGURE 18.2. Step by Step Execution of Folding.**

Care must be taken when processing triples which are calls on subroutines or functions. When compiling FORTRAN, one must delete all the actual parameters of the call and all COMMON variables from T, since the call may change their values. In ALGOL, T must be completely emptied, unless we know exactly the effects of the procedure call. Note also that input statements assign values to variables.

We must also make sure that folding does not produce a compile-time error of some sort. For example, if the programmer writes 1/0, the compiler must detect the zero denominator before dividing. Unfortunately, such an operation does not mean the object program will run incorrectly (although in most real programs it would). For example, if the source program contains the statement

```
IF FALSE THEN A := 1/0;
```

no runtime error will result. The best procedure to follow when folding an operation will produce a compile-time error is to print a warning message and leave it unfolded.

We have demonstrated folding in a separate pass over the internal source program in triple form. Indirect triples or quadruples could also have been used. Another possibility is to perform folding in the semantic routines which generate the internal form or machine language; no separate pass is necessary. For example, assuming a bottom-up parse, the routine for

$$E^1 ::= E^2 + T$$

need only check the semantics of $E^2$ and T. If both are constants, or if their values are known, the routine adds them together and associates the result with $E^1$. A table to hold variables with their known values can also be used; it must however be emptied at the parse of each label (or any place where code is generated that can be branched to).

### Eliminating Redundant Operations

The ith operation in a basic block is <u>redundant</u> if there exists an earlier identical operation j (say), and if none of the variables upon which the operation depends is changed by a third operation between the ith and jth. For example, consider the basic block for D := D+C*B; A := D+C*B; C := D+C*B;:

```
           (1) *  C,B        (4) *  C,B        (7) *  C,B
(18.1.2)   (2) +  D,(1)      (5) +  D,(4)      (8) +  D,(7)
           (3) := (2),D      (6) := (5),A      (9) := (8),C
```

The second and third occurrences of C*B are redundant, since neither C nor B change after triple (1). One might think that the second addition of D to C*B is redundant (triple 5), since C*B has not changed. This is not the case, since triple 3 changes the value of D after the first addition. The third addition of D to C*B is redundant, and can be replaced by a reference to triple 5.

Programmers are usually taught to program in a nonredundant manner, and the effectiveness of eliminating redundant operations might seem questionable. However, programming redundantly is often easier and makes a program easier to read. Moreover, there are some redundant operations, mostly arising from subscripted variables, over which the programmer has no control. Consider for example the assignment X[i,j]:=X[i,j+1] in triple form:

```
(1) *  i,d2      (3) *  i,d2       (5) +  (4),1
(2) +  (1),j     (4) +  (3),j      (6) := X[(2)],X[(5)]
```

Clearly, triples 3 and 4 are redundant and can be eliminated, yielding

```
(1) *  i,d2      (3) +  (2),1
(2) +  (1),j     (4) := X[(2)],X[(3)]
```

The algorithm for eliminating redundant operations scans the triples in order of occurrence. If triple i is redundant because of triple j, it is replaced by a triple (SAME,j,0). Here, SAME is a NO-OP; no code is generated for it. In order to keep track of the dependency relationship between variables and triples, we assign <u>dependency numbers</u> to them, as follows:

1. The initial dependency number dep(A) of a variable A is 0, since its initial value does not depend on any triple.
2. After processing triple i, if it assigns a value to a variable A, change dep(A) to i, since its new value depends on triple i.
3. When processing triple i, its dependency number dep(i) is

   1 + (maximum of the dependency number of its operands)

We use the dependency numbers as follows: if triple i is identical to triple j (j < i) then triple i is redundant if and only if dep(i) = dep(j).

We show this informally as follows. From the definition, we know that the dependency numbers of triple j's operands are less than j. Suppose that none of the variables on which triple i depends changes between triple j and i. Then triple i is redundant. Note that the dependency numbers of i's operands cannot change as triples j, ..., i-1 are processed. Hence dep(i) = dep(j).

Suppose, however, that some variable A on which i depends does change at triple k, $j \le k < i$. Then dep(A) is changed to k, where $k \ge j$. From the way in which dependencies are determined for triples, we see that dep(i) > dep(A) = $k \ge j \ge$ dep(j), and the dependency numbers are different.

The algorithm to eliminate redundant operations processes each triple, in order, as follows:

1. If an operand of the triple refers to a triple of the form (SAME j,0), replace the operand by (j).
2. Compute dep(i) := dependency number of triple i :=
   1 + (maximum dependency number of its operands).

3. If there exists an identical triple j, j < i with dep(i) = dep(j), then triple i is redundant; change triple i to (SAME, j,0). (Make this check by comparing against triples i-1, i-2, ..., 1. Hashing could be used to advantage here.)
4. If triple i assigns a value to an array element of an array B, or to a simple variable B, set dep(B) to i.

Figure 18.3 shows the step-by-step effect of the algorithm using the basic block (18.1.2). Each step shows the original triple, the dependency numbers for the variables <u>before</u> the step is executed, the calculated dependency number of the triple, and finally the resulting triple.

| Process triple i | dep(variable) A B C D | dep(i) | resulting triple |
|---|---|---|---|
| (1) * C,B | 0 0 0 0 | 1 | (1) * C,B |
| (2) + D,(1) | 0 0 0 0 | 2 | (2) + D,(1) |
| (3) := (2),D | 0 0 0 0 | 3 | (3) := (2),D |
| (4) * C,B | 0 0 0 3 | 1 | (4) SAME 1 |
| (5) + D,(4) | 0 0 0 3 | 4 | (5) + D,(1) |
| (6) := (5),A | 0 0 0 3 | 5 | (6) := (5),A |
| (7) * C,B | 6 0 0 3 | 1 | (7) SAME 1 |
| (8) + D,(7) | 6 0 0 3 | 4 | (8) SAME 5 |
| (9) := (8),C | 6 0 0 3 | 5 | (9) := (5),C |
| | 6 0 9 3 | | |

**FIGURE 18.3. Redundant Operation Elimination.**

For operands which are subscripted variables B[T], the triple's dependency number depends on the numbers for both B and T. Secondly, if an assignment is made to a subscripted variable B[T] at triple i, we change dep(B) to i. Thus, any future references to B depend on this triple.

The use of indirect triples instead of normal triples simplifies redundant operation elimination, since identical triples have already been detected. For example, the representation of block (18.1.2) would be

| OPER TABLE | | TRIPLE TABLE |
|---|---|---|
| 1. (1) | 6. (4) | (1) * C,B |
| 2. (2) | 7. (1) | (2) + D,(1) |
| 3. (3) | 8. (2) | (3) := (2),D |
| 4. (1) | 9. (5) | (4) := (2),A |
| 5. (2) | | (5) := (2),C |

We now associate dependency numbers with the triples instead of the operators in the OPER table. Before processing a block, dep(i) = 0 for each triple i; dep(i) will be changed each time an operation in OPER is processed which references triple i.

**Discussion of Folding and Eliminating**

The algorithms given are not optimal; we can do much better by taking advantage of the commutativity of some operations. For example, A*B and B*A should be considered identical. To do this systematically, we should order <u>all</u> the operands of an n-ary + (or n-ary *) canonically: first, terms which are not variables or constants, then subscripted variables in lexical order, then simple variables in lexical order, and finally constants. Any of the internal forms discussed in chapter 11 can be extended to include this. As an example, reordering the terms in

```
A := 1+B+C+2; B := B+C+6     to     A := B+C+1+2; B := B+C+6
```

allows us to fold 1+2 and eliminate the second occurrence of B+C. This does not, however, solve the whole problem; reordering the operands of

```
A := B+C+B+C     yields     A := B+B+C+C
```

which does not help us detect the fact that B+C need only be evaluated once. The problem of finding all common subexpressions is a difficult one to solve practically, because of the large number of factors possible in an expression. See section 18.4 for more discussion on this topic.

One could also propagate the unary operators ABS and - to the outsided at this time, instead of at code generation time as explained in section 17.4. This may not only save unary operators, but may also result in more redundant operations being detected. For example, if we indicate a unary minus by an apostrophe, the statements C := A-B; D := B-A; could be written in triples as

```
(1) +  A,B'                         (1) +  A,B'
(2) := (1),C      and then          (2) := (1),C
(3) +  B,A'       changed to        (3) +  A,B'
(4) := (3),D                        (4) := (3)',D
```

which allows the recognition of the identical operation. The use of a field to represent the negative of the operand is used often, even if elimination of redundant operations is not done, because it can be used to eliminate object code on some machines with "store negative" and "load negative" operations.

In the original triple form, each triple is referenced at most once. Similarly, when quadruples are used, each temporary variable T generated by the compiler is referenced only once as an operand. This happens naturally when normal assignment statements are translated into internal form. It is therefore easy to determine the range of a temporary. Note, however, that after this optimization process, a triple can be referenced several times. This makes it more difficult to determine the range of its result. See section 14.2 for details.

## 18.2 MODERATE LOOP OPTIMIZATION

An operation is invariant in a for-loop if none of the operands on which it depends change while the loop is being executed. An effective optimization is to move an invariant operation outside the loop. For example, if at compile-time we move a single multiplication out of a loop which will iterate 1000 times at runtime we have saved 999 runtime multiplications!

The second type of loop optimization we will describe is called reducing the strength of an operation, which in a sense replaces it by another operation which executes faster. We will be mainly interested in changing a multiplication like I*K, where I is the loop variable, to an addition. To illustrate strength reduction, consider the loop

```
For I := A STEP B UNTIL C DO
  BEGIN ... T1 := I*K ... END
```

where K is loop invariant. I is initially assigned the value A, and, within the loop, I is recursively defined; it is always defined in terms of itself. (The only assignement to I in the loop is the incrementation I:=I+B.) Now, every time I changes by the value B, the value of I*K (and T1) changes by B*K. That is,

```
(I+B)*K = I*K + B*K.
```

Hence, if T1 is not altered elsewhere within the loop, we can reduce the strength of the operation I*K by changing the loop as follows:

1. Insert the operations T1 := A*K; T2 := B*K before the loop, where T2 is a new temporary. This initializes T1 and calculates the increment B*K.
2. Delete the operation T1 := I*K from the loop statement.
3. Insert the operation T1 := T1+T2 at the end of the loop statement, yielding

```
T1 := A*K; T2 := B*K;
FOR I := A STEP B UNTIL C DO
  BEGIN ...              ... T1 := T1+T2; END
```

We have effectively replaced the multiplication within the loop by an addition. We assume, of course, that A and B are loop invariant, and I does not change within the loop except for the usual incrementation. (Actually, our implementation will reorder the operations a bit differently, so that it won't matter whether A is loop invariant or not.)

A word of caution here. We have assumed that B and K have type INTEGER. Never reduce the strength of a multiplication if K is REAL, because the addition which replaces it is not exact, due to the roundoff error involved when using floating point numbers. This roundoff error would tend to accumulate instead of cancel, as the loop is iterated. In general, I*K is much more accurate than K+K+...+K (I times).

Reducing the strength of multiplication can be helpful even if multiplication is just as fast as addition, because it allows us to identify and delete several occurrences of the same operation easily. Hence we are performing a limited form of redundant operation elimination within the loop. This is most useful for optimizing subscripted variable evaluation.

It should also be mentioned that strength reduction may not always optimize; in fact, it could make the program run much slower! Consider the program below on the left. During each execution of the loop statement, one multiplication will be performed. Strength reduction (and folding) changes the program to the one on the right. Now, no multiplications will be executed in the loop, but 10 additions will be executed!

Strength reduction almost always does make a program more efficient. It may not if a loop contains several subparts, very few of which are executed each time through the loop. For example, optimizing an interpreter like that of Figure 16.1 (the loop is implicit here) may very likely make the interpreter less efficient.

```
                                  T1:=1; T2:=2; ... T10:=10;
FOR I:=1 STEP 1 UNTIL 10 DO       FOR I:=1 STEP 1 UNTIL 10 DO
  CASE I OF                         BEGIN CASE I OF
     K := I*1;                              K := T1;
     K := I*2;                              K := T2;
       :                                      :
     K := I*10;                             K := T10;
  ENDCASE;                                ENDCASE;
                                     T1:=T1+1; ... T10:=T10+10;
                                    END;
```

### The Implementation Overview

We implement the optimization in three passes, placed between the usual analysis pass, which generates the internal source program, and the code generation pass (see Figure 18.4). The LOOP CHECKER checks for-loops for optimization suitability and generates information needed later. The next pass moves invariant operations out of each loop, while the third extra pass performs strength reduction.

We shall assume the source language is ALGOL; optimization in FORTRAN is actually easier because of the simpler do-loops. We will use the prototype

```
(18.2.1) FOR I := A STEP B UNTIL C DO <loop state>
```

where A, B, and C are arbitrary arithmetic expressions. We furthermore assume that the value of B is always positive and does not change while the loop is executing, for the sake of clarity. The extension to allowing a negative value for B is fairly easy.

We lastly assume that folding and redundant operation elimination in basic blocks is performed just before or during the invariant operation process.

We will be mainly interested in simple variables or formal parameters called by value; it will help to coin a term for them:

(18.2.2) DEFINITION. A SFVI (SFVR) is a simple variable or simple formal parameter called by value with type INTEGER (REAL).

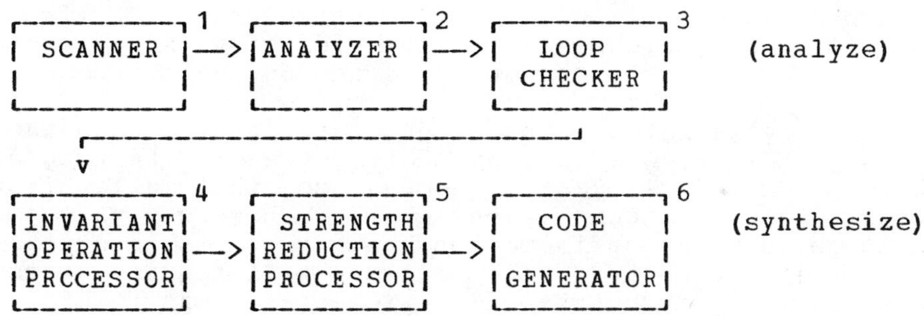


**FIGURE 18.4. Compiler for Moderate Loop Optimization.**

#### Internal Representation of Loops

We assume the operations appear in the order in which they are to be generated (if no optimization took place). The operations could be in the form of triples, quadruples, or what have you. We must only be able to recognize the different entities of the loop as they appear -- the beginning of the loop, I, A, B, C, the <loop state>, and the end of the loop. If no optimization took place we would generate code equivalent to the following for a loop:

```
          INIT: I := A;
          TEST: IF I > C THEN GO TO OVER;
(18.2.3)  LOOP: <loop state>;
          INCR: I := I+B; GO TO TEST;
          OVER:
```

Optimization transforms this into

```
         INIT: I := A; "initialization operations";
         TEST: IF I > C THEN GO TO OVER;
(18.2.4) LOOP: <altered loop state>;
         INCR: I := I+B; "increment operations";
               GO TO TEST;
         OVER:
```

That is, operations are inserted which will be executed just before the loop proper is executed, and others are inserted to be executed each time the loop variable is incremented. (If desired, one could insert another statement "IF I > C THEN GO TO OVER" immediately after I := A, so that the initialization operations would not be performed if the loop is not executed. This will not be necessary because, as we describe it, only temporaries used in the <loop state> will be changed by the initialization operations.)

The line labeled INIT is called the INIT (initialization) block; the line labeled INCR is called the INCR (increment) block. Both are basic blocks -- the operations are executed in order and there is only one entrance and one exit.

Since the optimization process generates new blocks and alters the <loop state>s, one is tempted to represent the program as a graph whose nodes are basic blocks, so that alteration and creation of blocks can be done easily. However, unless one is going to perform the optimizations described in section 18.3, this is not necessary, and indeed will require unnecessary bookkeeping. A more suitable representation is the following.

The source program operations are kept in sequence, be they quadruples, triples, Polish notation, or what have you. As the optimization passes are executed, three separate tables are built: a table which holds the operations in the INIT block for each loop, a table which holds the operations in the INCR block for each loop, and a loop table which contains information about each loop -- the loop variable, pointers to the INIT and INCR blocks for the loop, and so forth. Of course, the code generation pass must generate the code for the main internal source program and the INIT and INCR blocks in the correct order.

Note that the INIT block for a loop is not really part of that loop; it is executed only once. Therefore it can be optimized as if it belonged to the surrounding loop. This means that some operations can be moved step by step out of several loops, until they are outside all loops.

We shall not concern ourselves anymore with the representation of the INIT and INCR blocks; this is mainly a compiler organization problem and the solution will likely differ from machine to machine.

### Loop Restrictions

For moving invariant operations we need to know all the SFVIs and SFVRs which change within the loop. Reducing the strength of operators involving the loop variable I requires the following additional restrictions:

(18.2.5) I does not change within the <loop state>.

(18.2.6) None of the variables in the step expression B change within the <loop state>.

Note that we can move invariant operations, even if strength reduction is not possible. In our discussion, however, we will assume that both are performed or neither are performed.

In FORTRAN, conditions (18.2.5) and (18.2.6) always hold because of the simpler do-loops. Unfortunately, even in FORTRAN it is not possible to know exactly which variables change within the <loop state>, mainly because a procedure called within the <loop state> may change the values of variables. Our next step, therefore, is to impose stricter conditions which can be checked easily and rigorously, keeping in mind, of course, that we want to optimize as many loops as possible.

The following conditions must be satisfied in order to perform both types of optimization:

(18.2.7) The only calls allowed within I, B, C, and the <loop state> are those on procedures, functions, and formal parameters called by name for which the compiler knows which SFVIs and SFVRs are changed.

This allows calls on standard functions, input-output statements, and any other procedures which the compiler has itself analyzed carefully. In FORTRAN, all subroutine calls can be allowed if the compiler assumes that all SFVIs and SFVRs in COMMON and all actual parameters are changed by the subroutine.

The following three conditions must be met in order to perform strength reduction:

(18.2.8) The loop variable I must be a SFVI.

(18.2.9) The step expression B must have type INTEGER and cannot contain the loop variable I. Its operands must be constants, SFVIs and SFVRs.

(18.2.10) The loop may not contain an assignment (through an assignment statement, input statement, procedure call, or formal parameter call) to I or to a variable in the step expression B.

Conditions (18.2.7) through (18.2.10) must then be satisfied in order to perform the optimization described in this section.

### The Loop Table

The LOOP CHECKER will build a list of SFVIs and SFVRs changed in each loop. Three methods of structuring this list come to mind. The first is to have a list, emanating from the symbol table entry of each SFVI and SFVR of the loops in which it changes. This list should probably be chained, rather than sequential.

The second method is to assign a number to each SFVI and SFVR, and to have an n x m Boolean matrix C where n is the number of SFVIs and SFVRs and m is the number of loops. C[i,j] = 1 if the ith variable changes in loop j.

The third method, which we use here, is to have a loop structured table, much like a block-structured symbol table discussed in section 9.5. We need a table of loops which we call the LOOPTABLE; its ith element is a description of the ith loop in the program, counted in order of appearance of the word FOR. Along with this, we need a table SFV containing the actual list of SFVIs and SFVRs which change within each loop. Each element in LOOPTABLE contains the following five fields:

| LOOPVAR | SURRLOOP | FIRSTV | LASTV | BLIST |
|---|---|---|---|---|
| loop variable | surrounding loop number | index of first elem. in SFV list for loop | index of last elem. in SFV list for loop | pointer to list of step elem. SFVIs |

All variables in these tables can be represented by pointers to the corresponding symbol table entries. We can use the LOOPVAR field to indicate whether optimization is possible in the loop; just zero the field out when it is not optimizable. For reasons which will be obvious later, a 0th element will be in LOOPTABLE, with the value (0,0,0,0,0).

Fields FIRSTV and LASTV indicate the first and last elements in SFV for a loop, respectively. While this is similar to the block-structure case described in section 9.5, there is a major difference which makes things easier here. In the block-structure case, the tables for the different blocks had to be kept separate; here we can keep them nested, for if a variable changes within a loop, it changes within each surrounding loop also. Hence the SFV entries for a loop contain the SFV entries for all inner loops.

Figure 18.5 illustrates this, showing a program segment containing four loops, along with the corresponding tables.

The LOOPTABLE elements should also contain fields to describe the INCR and INIT blocks for each loop; we have omitted them to keep things simple.

```
FOR i := 1 STEP 1 UNTIL N DO
 BEGIN L1:= ...; ...
  FOR j:=1 STEP 1 UNTIL N DO
   BEGIN L2:= ...; ... END;

  FOR k:=1 STEP 1 UNTIL N DO
   BEGIN L3:=...; ... END;

  L4:=...;
 END;

FOR l := 1 STEP 1 UNTIL N DC
 BEGIN L5:=...; ... END;
```

(a) program segment

| | | | | | |
|---|---|---|---|---|---|
| (1) | i | 0 | 1 | 6 | 0 |
| (2) | j | 1 | 3 | 3 | 0 |
| (3) | k | 1 | 5 | 5 | 0 |
| (4) | l | 0 | 7 | 7 | 0 |

(b) LOOPTABLE

| | |
|---|---|
| (1) | L1 |
| (2) | j |
| (3) | L2 |
| (4) | k |
| (5) | L3 |
| (6) | L4 |
| (7) | L5 |

(c) SFV table

**FIGURE 18.5. Illustration of LOOPTABLE.**

### The Loop Checker

This pass processes the source program operations, in sequence, checking loops for optimization suitability. In addition, it builds the LOOPTABLE and SFV tables. It uses the following variables and routines.

1. OPENLOOP. An integer variable which contains the number of the innermost loop being processed. Initially 0.
2. LASTTLOOP. An integer variable containing the number of loops detected so far. Initially 0.
3. CPTLOOP. An integer variable containing the number of the innermost loop being processed which has not yet violated any of the optimization conditions.
4. CHECK(P). Argument P of the procedure is a pointer to a symbol table entry. CHECK(P) is called when an assignment is made to that variable. If the variable is a SFVR or SFVI, all loops still being processed (use OPTLOOP and the tables) are checked for violations of (18.2.10) and, if a violation is detected, that loop is made unoptimizable. The variable is then put into the SFV table for the loop CPTLOOP.
5. SURROUNDOPT. Whenever a loop becomes unoptimizable, it may be necessary to change OPTLOOP. This SURROUNDOPT does, by sequencing through the surrounding block chain beginning at loop OPTLOOP until a still-optimizable loop is found.

Note that OPENLOOP and LASTLOOP are the equivalent of CURRBL and LASTBL used in building block structured symbol tables in section 9.5.

We now give a brief description of the processing required for the different parts of the internal source program:

1. When FOR <variable> := A is processed: Call CHECK (<variable>), since an assignment is being made. Add an appropriate element to LOOPTABLE for the new loop. Move the operations for <variable> := A to the INIT block for the loop. If <variable> is a SFVI, change OPTLOOP to the new loop's number; otherwise set field LOOPVAR for the new loop to 0, indicating that the loop cannot be optimized.
2. When scanning the step expression B: Add each variable to BLIST for the loop. If a variable is the loop variable of this loop or is not a SFVI or SFVR, make the loop unoptimizable and call SURROUNDOPT. If the type of B is not INTEGER, make the loop unoptimizable and call SURROUNDOPT.
3. At an assignment <variable> :=, or READ(<variable>): Call CHECK(<variable>).
4. At the call of any nonstandard procedure or function, or a reference to a call by name parameter which is not an ARRAY: Make all loops currently being processed unoptimizable and call SURROUNDOPT.
5. At the end of a loop: If the loop being ended is still optimizable, check BLIST against the SFV list for the loop; if any variable is in both, make the loop unoptimizable. Fix OPENLOOP and OPTLOOP to point at the surrounding loop and call SURROUNDOPT.

Steps 2 through 4 need only by executed if an optimizable loop is being processed; that is, if OPTLOOP ≠ 0.

Note that we have broken the rather complex process of checking loops for optimization suitability into some very basic, simple steps. Step 4 should be checked in one routine only. This is probably easiest in the routine which scans the internal form of the source program and passes symbols to other parts of the pass. Any time it sees an identifier and an optimizable loop is being processed, if the identifier is a procedure, function, or formal parameter called by name, all loops currently being processed should be made unoptimizable.

### Invariant Operation Processor

An operation is invariant in a loop if its operands do not depend on any variables which change within the loop. Such operations can often be moved out of the loop into the INIT block. We will process only operations like +, -, *, ROUND, and CVRI (convert). Assignment operators will not be considered, since they require more program analysis than we are prepared to do. We assume that temporary variables Ti are only assigned values once (as is usually the case), and that they can be distinguished from source program variables.

This pass sequences through the internal source program operations, using the tables LOOPTABLE and SFV to detect invariant operations. Upon encountering an operation which can possibly be moved, the following occurs:

1. Suppose, for example, the operation is (*,A,B,T1). If either A or B is not invariant within the loop (check this by looking at the SFV table for the optimizable loop being processed), skip the remaining steps.
2. If an operation (*,A,B,T2) already exists in the INIT block, go to step 4; otherwise step 3.
3. Add the operation to the INIT block and go to step 5.
4. Change subsequent references to T1 within the loop to T2.
5. Delete the operation from the loop. Delete T1 from the list of variables which change within the loop (but not from the list for surrounding loops).

This is illustrated in Figure 18.6a and 18.6b. Note that we delete T1 from the list of variables which change within the loop; we are assuming, as is usually the case, that each temporary is changed only once within a loop. This allows subsequent operations involving T1 to be moved out also. Those variables that change more must be marked in some manner.

When a new optimizable loop is encountered, the statement T0 := B for a new temporary T0 can be inserted into the INIT block for the loop (if B is not a constant or simple variable). This can be done since, by virtue of the loop conditions, all operations in B are invariant. Any reference to B within the block is treated as a reference to T0.

Upon encountering the end of a loop, the pass may have moved several operations into the INIT block, as described below. The INIT block resides outside the loop just processed, and in the surrounding loop. So that operations may be moved further out, the pass processes this INIT block as part of the surrounding loop, before proceeding.

### The Strength Reduction Pass

This final optimization pass sequences through the operations of each loop. Whenever an operation of the form (* I,K,T1) or (* K,I,T1) where K is loop invariant is found, it makes it a NO-OP and performs the following:

1. If an operation (* I,K,T3) already exists in the INIT block, then we have already reduced the strength of an identical operation. Change every subsequent reference to T1 within the <loop state> to a reference to T3 and skip the rest of the steps.
2. Add the operation (* I,K,T1) to the INIT block.
3. If an operation (* B,K,T2) or (* K,B,T2) does not exist in INIT, generate a new temporary T2 and add the operation (* B,K,T2) to INIT (such an operation may have been put there by the INVARIANT OPERATION PROCESSOR).
4. Add the operation (+ T1,T2,T1) to the INCR block.

We have assumed that each temporary Ti is assigned a value only once. The temporary T1 is now assigned a value in two places -- in the INIT and INCR blocks. However, neither of these two assignments can be further optimized. The one in the INCR block will not be further optimized since we don't optimize this block. The operation (* I,K,T1) in the INIT block cannot be further optimized since I changes in the loop in which the assignment now occurs.

```
 INIT:I :=A               INIT:I :=A                 INIT:I :=A
                               T3:=J*d2                   T3:=J*d2
                                                          T1:=I*d2
                                                          TI:=1*d2
┌TEST:test I > N         ┌TEST:test I > N           ┌TEST:test I > N
|LOOP:T1:=I*d2           |LOOP:T1:=I*d2             |LOOP:
|     T2:=T1+J           |     T2:=T1+J             |     T2:=T1+J
|     T3:=J*d2           |                          |
|     T4:=T3+I           |     T4:=T3+I             |     T4:=T3+I
|     T5:=A[T2]+A[T4]|   |     T5:=A[T2]+A[T4] |    |     T5:=A[T2]+A[T4]
|     A[T2]:=T5          |     A[T2]:=T5            |     A[T2]:=T5
|INCR:I :=I+1            |INCR:I :=I+1              |INCR:I :=I+1
|                        |                          |     T1:=T1+TI
|     GOTO TEST          |     GOTO TEST            |     GOTO TEST
└>OVER:                  └>OVER:                    └>OVER:

(a)original program  (b)invariant process  (c)strength reduction

   FOR I:=1 STEP 1 UNTIL N DO BEGIN A[I,J]:=A[I,J]+A[J,I] END
```

**FIGURE 18.6. Illustration of Two Optimizations.**

### Discussion of the Two Techniques

Figure 18.6b illustrates the effect of moving invariant operations from the loops of Figure 18.6a. Figure 18.6c shows the next step of strength reduction. It is important that the invariant operation processor be applied first. Consider for example the expression (X+Y)*I where X and Y are invariant. Internally, this is represented by

(1) + X,Y,T1 (2) * T1,I,T2

The strength of the multiplication cannot be reduced since T1 is not loop invariant. However, if the first quadruple is moved to the INIT block by the invariant operation processor, then T1 becomes invariant.

It is also advantageous to work with n-ary + and *, instead of treating them as binary operations. Then we can put operands in a canonical order, such as

1. The loop variable of the loop in which the operation occurs;
2. Those operands which are loop invariant;
3. Those operands which are not loop invariant.

Within each classification, the operands should be ordered as discussed in the last section. Note that the ordering is different, depending on which loop the operation is in. As an example, consider the expression Y1*X1*I*X2*Y2 where Y1 and Y2 are not invariant and X1 and X2 are invariant. Representing this in quadruples yields

```
(1) * Y1,X1,T1          (3) * T2,X2,T3
(2) * T1,I,T2           (4) * T3,Y2,T4
```

for which no optimization is possible. However, suppose we consider it as * Y1,X1,I,X2,Y2,T1 (the result is to be put into T1). Now reorder to yield

```
* I,X1,X2,Y1,Y2,T1
```

We now remove the operation * X1,X2,T2 to get * I,T2,Y1,Y2,T1. Finally, we can reduce the strength of the multiplication I*T2.

One of the important "hidden" optimizations performed concerns subscripted variables. As discussed in section 8.4, the evaluation of a subscripted variable X[i,j,...,l,m] requires the evaluation of VARPART, which is given by

```
((...(((i*d2)+j)*d3)+...)+l)*dn + m.
```

If i is the loop variable, we can reduce the strength of i*d2. For optimization purposes, it is better to calculate VARPART using

```
i*d2*...*dn + j*d3*...*dn + ... + l*dn + m
```

since it reduces the calculation to n separate terms, each of which can be optimized independently.

When using triples, be careful about moving operations out of a basic block. A reference to a triple refers to the result of a particular execution of that triple. Within basic blocks, such a reference is always to the last execution of the triple. Suppose we have

```
(1) (+ A, B)            (2) (+ (1), C)
```

in a basic block and that we can move the first triple outside the loop. Then it is difficult to keep track of the fact that the reference (1) within the second triple is to the result of the triple removed. It is much better, when moving the first triple, to generate a new temporary T, to change the second triple to (2) (+ T,C), and to put the following operations into the INIT block:

```
(k) (+ A, B)            (k+1) (:= (k), T)
```

**Extending Strength Reduction**

The optimization methods do not work well on expressions like (I+K)*X where I is the loop variable and K and X are loop invariant. One method of improving the optimization is to recognize such subexpressions containing I, and to reform them, producing in this case I*X+K*X. Optimization is then more effective. Another solution is to extend strength in two directions, neither of which really adds much to complexity of optimization.

First of all, reduce the strength of an addition T1:=I+K as follows:

1. Put T1:=I+K into the INIT block.
2. Put T1:=T1+B into the INCR block (whenever I changes by B, so does T1).
3. Delete the operation T1:=I+K.

Secondly, allow other recursively defined variables to participate in strength reduction. The likely candidates, which require no extra source program analysis, are temporaries like T1 above, which were made recursive because of an earlier strength reduction.

We illustrate this below, showing the step by step process of optimizing quadruples for D:=(I*X+Y)*Z within a loop (only the INIT, INCR, and LOOP blocks are shown). The three operators are all optimized, with a new recursively defined variable being generated at each step.

```
INIT:I :=A         INIT:I :=A         INIT:I :=A         INIT:I :=A
                        T1:=I*X            T1:=I*X            T1:=I*X
                        T4:=B*X            T4:=B*X            T4:=B*X
                                           T2:=T1+Y           T2:=T1+Y
                                                              T3:=T2*Z
                                                              T5:=T4*Z

LOOP:T1:=I*X       LOOP:              LOOP:              LOOP:
     T2:=T1+Y           T2:=T1+Y
     T3:=T2*Z           T3:=T2*Z           T3:=T2*Z
     D :=T3             D :=T3             D :=T3             D :=T3

INCR:I :=I+B       INCR:I :=I+B       INCR:I :=I+B       INCR:I :=I+B
                        T1:=T1+T4          T1:=T1+T4          T1:=T1+T4
                                           T2:=T2+T4          T2:=T2+T4
                                                              T3:=T3+T5

(a) reduce I*X  (b) reduce T1+Y  (c) reduce T2*Z    (d) result
```

Note that many of the quadruples in the INCR block become useless as optimization progresses, and should be deleted. In the result column (d) above, T1 and T2 are never referenced in the loop, and T1:=T1+T4 and T2:=T2+B can be deleted.

### Performing the Optimization in Fewer Passes

Figure 18.4 shows how optimization can be performed using three additional passes. It is usually possible to merge the LOOP CHECKER with the semantic routines which generate the original internal form. It is also sometimes possible to merge all the optimization with the code generation pass. Thus we can omit much of the bookkeeping details and the corresponding compile-time involved in having the three extra passes. We wish to briefly describe how optimization can be merged with code generation.

However, the INIT block as described in (18.2.4) appears before the rest of the loop, but it is not completely constructed until *after* the loop is processed. To overcome this problem, we generate instead the following equivalent code:

```
                GO TO INIT;
          TEST: IF I > C THEN GO TO OVER;
(18.2.11) LOOP: <altered statement>;
          INCR: I := I+B; "increment operations"; GO TO TEST;
          INIT: I := A; "initialization operations"; GO TO TEST;
          OVER:
```

Although this program has two extra branches, it allows us to optimize the <loop state> and generate code for it at the same time; and later generate the code for the INIT and INCR blocks.

The internal source program from which code will be generated comes from three different input streams -- the main internal source program table, the INIT blocks, and the INCR blocks. It is only a matter of keeping track of which one is being currently used. We also must have the ability to turn the optimization on and off at will by setting some global variable.

The code generator begins with optimization off (except for folding and redundant operation elimination), and with the main internal source program table being processed. The operations are processed in order of occurrence, according to the type of operation, as shown below. The classes of operations are shown in order of preference.

1. Foldable operation: Fold it.
2. Redundant operation: Remove it, as discussed earlier.
3. Invariant optimizable operation: Perform the optimization -- move the operation to the INIT block for the current loop.
4. Strength reduction optimizable operation: Perform strength reduction.
5. Beginning of loop operation: Do bookkeeping to open a new loop. Put I:=A; T0:=B; into the INIT block. Put I:=I+T0 into the INCR block. Create a label INIT and generate a transfer to it. Create a label TEST and a label OVER and generate the code for

```
TEST: IF I > C GO TO OVER
```

Create and generate the label LOOP. Reset the "next operation pointer" to point to the first operation of the <loop state>. Turn optimization on if loop is optimizable.

6. End of <loop state>: Turn off optimization. Make the INCR block for that loop the current input stream.
7. End of an INCR block: Generate a GO TO TEST. Delete the INCR block for the current loop; code has been generated for it. Generate the label INIT. Make the surrounding loop the current one, and turn optimization on if it is optimizable (thus the INIT block gets optimized). Make the INIT block for the loop just ended the current input stream.
8. End of an INIT block: Generate a GO TO TEST. Generate label OVER. Delete the INIT block that just ended. Make the main internal source program the current input stream, and begin with the operation following the last one processed in that stream.
9. At any label or operation which is branched to: Clear tables used for folding and redundant operation elimination. A new basic block is beginning.
10. Any other operation: Generate code for it.

## 18.3 MORE EFFECTIVE OPTIMIZATION

The optimization procedures described here require the internal source program to be a directed graph whose nodes are basic blocks; the reader would do well to briefly glance at section 11.5 again at this point. The operations themselves could be quadruples, triples or indirect triples; only the details will change. We will use quadruples. We will not describe an implementation in detail, but will just describe the types of optimization used and the order in which they should be performed. The reader is referred to the excellent paper by Allen(69) (from which many of the ideas here have been taken), and to Lowry and Medlock(69).

We suppose first of all that loops have been translated into a more elementary sequence of assignment statements, tests, branches, and the like. For example, at the internal source program level there is absolutely no difference between the two program segments

```
                                           I := 1;
FOR I := 1                           LOOP: IF I > N THEN GO TO OVER;
  STEP 1 UNTIL N DO       and              A[I]:=A[I]+1;
   A[I] := A[I]+1;                         I := I+1, GO TO LOOP;
                                     OVER:
```

The first step in the optimization is to find certain subgraphs of the program graph called <u>regions</u> (to be defined later). The subgraphs for a conventional loop and for an equivalent loop written as above with branches and tests both form regions. However, the region concept allows us to find other subgraphs <u>within</u> for-loops which can be optimized to a certain extent.

The first four optimizations to be performed on a region are, in order,

1. Folding within basic blocks;
2. Redundant operation elimination within basic blocks.
3. Moving invariant operations out of a region; and
4. Strength reduction in a region.

The first two are performed exactly as described in section 18.1, and we will not discuss them further. The second two are applied to regions, you will notice, and not just for-loops. They are also more general than the two similar techniques described in the last section. After strength reduction, the region is further subjected to the following modifications:

5. Replacement of tests: replacing certain programmer tests with others allows us to delete other operations in a region; and
6. Elimination of "dead" variables and assignments, and the operations on which they depend.

We could also perform redundant operation elimination within a region (instead of within a basic block), but it is too time consuming relative to the operations saved.

### Regions and the Region List

A <u>strongly connected region</u> of a directed graph is a subgraph in which there is a path from any node of the set to every other node of the set. In Figure 18.7, there are five strongly connected regions: (6), (3,5), (2,3,5,6,7), (2,3,4,6,7,) and (2,3,4,5,6,7). The subgraph (3,5,6) is not a strongly connected region because there is no path from 6 to either 3 or 5. Similarly, no strongly connected region contains node 1 or 8.

Figure 18.8 shows the graph for a conventional loop, with a branch out of the loop. Note that the complete loop, except for the initialization statement I := 1, forms a region (blocks 2,3,4,5,6 in the figure).

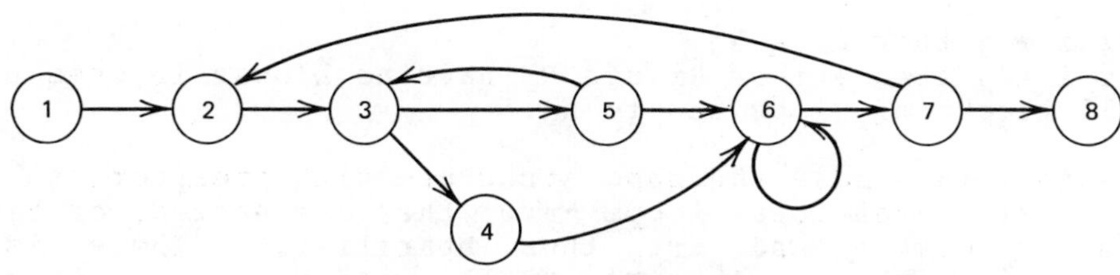


**FIGURE 18.7. A Directed Graph.**

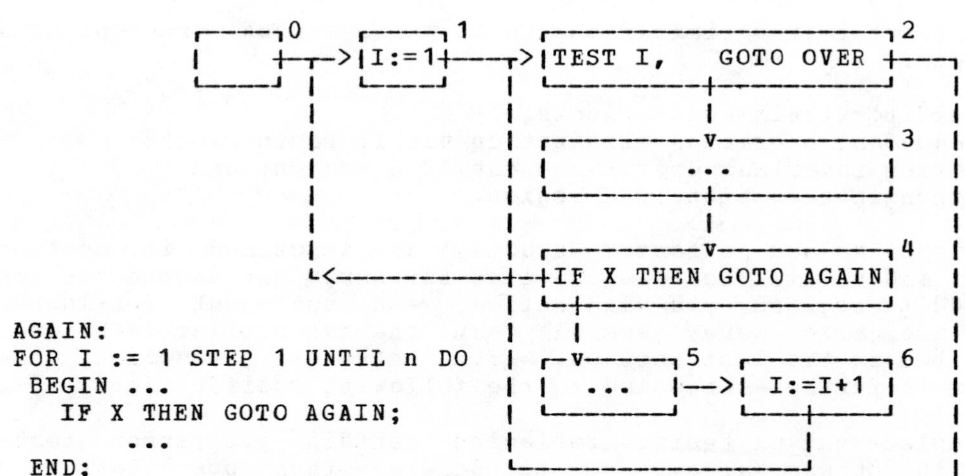


**FIGURE 18.8. A Loop with a Jump, and Its Program Graph.**

An entry block of a region is a block with an arc leading to it from a block outside the region. In Figure 18.7, region (6) has one entry block; itself. Region (3,5) has block 3 as an entry block.

A predecessor block of a region is a block outside the region with an arc leading from it to an entry block of the region. In Figure 18.7, (6) has two predecessor blocks: blocks 4 and 5. Region (3,5) has one predecessor block: block 2. Successor block is similarly defined.

An articulation block of a region is one which is on every path from a predecessor block, into the region, and to a successor. In Figure 18.7, 6 is an articulation block of (6), 3 is an articulation block of (3,5), while blocks 2,3,6 and 7 are articulation blocks of (2,3,4,5,6,7). Blocks 4 and 5 are not articulation blocks of the latter region.

Before optimization, the program, in the form of basic blocks and a program graph, must be analyzed in order to build a list R of strongly connected regions R1, R2, ..., Rn such that

1. If i ≠ j then Ri ≠ Rj
2. If i < j then either Ri and Rj have no blocks in common, or all blocks of Ri belong to Rj.

The regions in R have the same structure with respect to each other that conventional loops have; they are nested, or have no blocks in common and are thus "parallel." There is no overlapping. The regions R1, R2, ..., Rn will be optimized in that order. We must, of course, check to make sure that each region Ri is optimizable, as we checked each loop in section 18.2. We will not mention this again.

For the graph of Figure 18.7, the following region list could be developed: R1 = (6), R2 = (3,5), R3 = (2,3,5,6,7), and R4 = (2,3,4,5,6,7).

The program in Figure 18.8 has the two strongly connected regions (1,2,3,4) and (2,3,4,5,6). Both cannot be put on the region list, for this would violate condition 2. Which one should be put on the list? The most effective optimizations are removing and reducing operations from regions which are iterated often -- regions in which the program executes the most. From our knowledge of programming, we can estimate that conventional loops are iterated often, and it would seem reasonable to make sure they are on the region list.

How can we make sure the subgraphs for conventional loops are put in R? One way, of course, is to mark them in some manner in the internal source program. We may not want to do this, so let su derive another method for detecting them.

A region for a conventional loop has only one predecessor, the block containing the loop variable initialization; and one entry block, the single successor of the predecessor block. This characteristic will help us in determining which region to pick, for we can assert (without proof) that if two regions overlap but one doesn't cover the other, then at most one of them has both a single predecessor and single entry block. Hence, if two regions overlap, give preference to the one with one entry and one predecessor block.

Consider the graph of Figure 18.9. There are three regions: (1,2), (2,3) and (1,2,3). If we use the above rule we get the region list R1 = (2,3), R2 = (1,2,3).

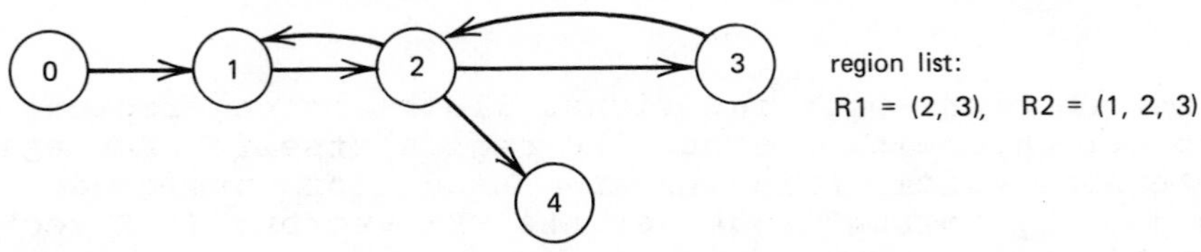


**FIGURE 18.9. Another Program Graph.**

**Data Dependencies**

For each block, we will need to know which variables are referenced in it, which are assigned values, and which are referenced before an assignment. To do this, we assign an integer to each source program variable and to each temporary Ti. For each basic block of the program three Boolean vectors are constructed:

1. REF[i] = 1 if the ith variable is referenced in the block;
2. ASS[i] = 1 if the ith variable is assigned a value in the block; and
3. RBA[i] = 1 if the ith variable is referenced in the block before an assignment to it.

A variable is <u>busy on exit</u> from a block if, at the end of the block, it contains a value which will later be referenced. In the program segment of Figure 18.10, D is busy on exit from block 1, but E is not. We similarly define busy on exit from a region. We could keep an extra vector to indicate the "busy-ness" of each variable; however this information can be obtained by examining the REF, ASS and RBA vectors of all successors (and their successors, etc.) of the block.

The vectors RBA are difficult to work with. They need only be used if the following two optimizations will be performed: moving assignments out of loops, and eliminating dead assignments.

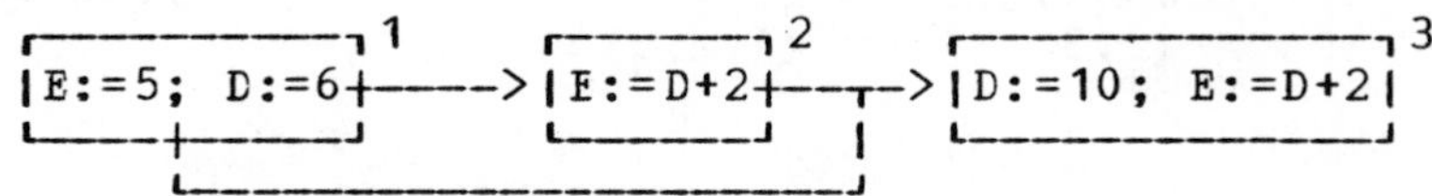


**FIGURE 18.10. Example of Busy on Exit Concept.**

The information about individual blocks in a region can be used to get information about the region itself. For example we can determine which variables are used (or assigned) in the region just by "oring" together the REF vectors (ASS vectors) of all the blocks.

For a large program, this is an awful lot of vectors to maintain. Since we will process one region at a time, it may be possible to keep vectors only for the blocks in the region being processed, as we now indicate.

### The General Optimization Plan

We optimize one region at a time, in the order R1, R2, ..., Rn. Hence we process innermost loops first. Optimization will create a new block, called the INIT (initialization) block, to be executed just before entry to the region. Consider the graph of Figure 18.11a, with region R1 = (4,5,6). Optimizing R1 results in the program graph of Figure 18.11b. Here, two copies of the INIT block are needed because there are two entry blocks. Since block 3 has only one successor, the operations of the INIT block could be stored at the end of block 3 itself, eliminating the need for the extra block.

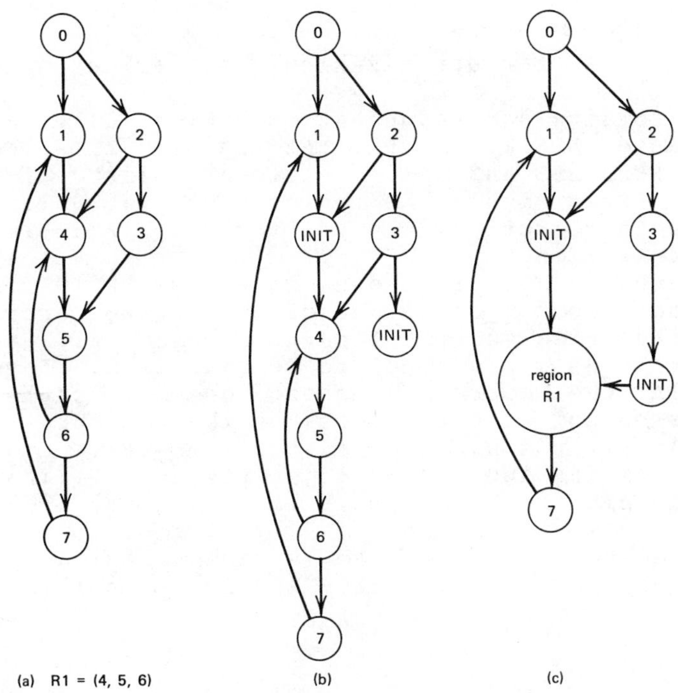


**FIGURE 18.11. Optimizing a Region R1.**

Once a region is optimized, it need not be optimized again. Hence, when optimizing the next outermost region we can consider the optimized one as a block (see Figure 18.11c). This block is marked as optimized, so it won't be processed again. The vectors REF, ASS and RBA for the region are obtained easily from those for the individual blocks in the region, as described above.

The INIT blocks, of course, belong to the surrounding region, and hence they will be optimized. This means that operations in the innermost region can be removed step by step from surrounding regions.

In general, we only need the three block vectors for those blocks in the region being optimized. The vectors can be constructed during folding and redundant operation elimination in basic blocks. Note, however, that as optimization progresses, these vectors change as operations get moved and changed. Moreover, new temporaries are created which must be assigned numbers and added to the three vectors for each block. (Equivalently, we can keep information about them in their symbol table entries; their exact method of use is known, so this can be done.) We will not mention this as we discuss the optimization procedures, but it must be done.

The complete process for a program is as follows:

1. Set i := 1;
2. Pick region Ri for optimization, set aside space for its INIT block.
3. Perform folding and redundant operation elimination within each basic block of Ri. At the same time, construct the vectors REF, ASS and RBA. Construct a list of recursively defined SFVIs within the region; such variables may be used in strength reduction, the way the loop variable was used in the last section.
4. Perform region optimizations, creating the INIT block. This may change block vectors and create new temporaries.
5. Create the three vectors for the region Ri; from now on consider it as a block not to be optimized. Insert the INIT block in the correct places (on all paths between a predecessor and an entry block of the region).
6. i := i+1. If i ≤ n, go to step 2; otherwise step 7.
7. Perform folding and redundant operation elimination within the basic blocks which appear in no region.

We now proceed to describe the various region optimizations (step 4 above), in the order they should be applied.

#### Moving Invariant Operations

We already discussed moving invariant operations out of a loop, for operations like +, *, CVRI, etc. The process is the same for moving operations out of a region. In addition, we now show when an assignment may be moved; the restrictions are (considering an assignment A := B or A := T where T is a temporary):

1. B (or T) must be invariant in the region;
2. The block in which the assignment occurs must be a region articulation block. This assures us that the assignment will be executed if the region is entered;
3. No other assignment to A occurs in the region; and
4. No use of A occurs on any path from an entry block to this assignment.

These restrictions can be checked using the REF, ASS, and RBA vectors for the basic blocks of the region. Consider Figure 18.12. The assignment B:=5 may be moved. The assignment E:=4 may not; it violates condition 3. The assignment A:=3 may not be moved; it violates condition 2. The assignment D:=B will be also moveable, once the assignment B:=5 is moved. The assignment C := E violates condition 1, while the assignment F := 5 violates condition 4.

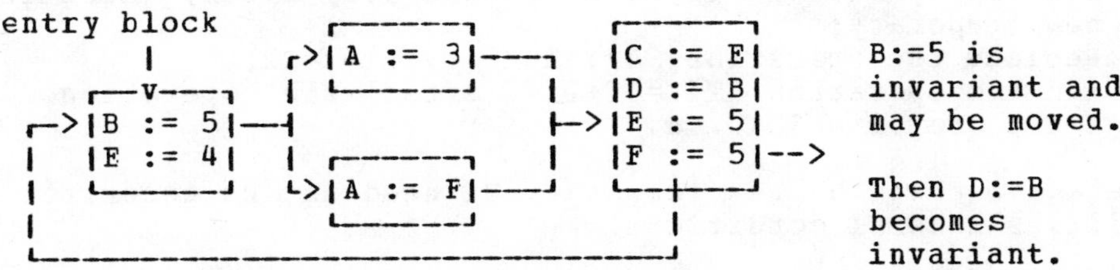


**FIGURE 18.12. Invariant Operation Illustration.**

### Strength Reduction

In order to reduce the strength of an operation involving a recursively defined variable I in a region, the following two conditions must hold.

1. I must be an integer simple variable or integer formal parameter called by value (SFVI);
2. Within the region all assignments to I must have the form I := I+D, where D is a signed integer expression which is invariant in the region.

Suppose I is recursively defined with the n assignments

I:=I+D1; I:=I+D2; ..., I:=I+Dn;

We reduce an operation T1:=I*K where K has type integer and is invariant in the region as follows:

1. Add the operation T2:=I*K to the INIT block, where T2 is a new temporary.
2. Generate n temporaries TINCRi and add the operations TINCRi := Di*K to the INIT block.
3. Replace the operation T1:=I*K in the region by T1:=T2.
4. Insert the operation T2:=T2+TINCRi after I:=I+Di, for i = 1,...,n.

Some improvements can be made. If Di=1, as is often the case, then TINCRi is not needed; just insert the operation T2:=T2+K instead of T2:=T2+TINCRi. Secondly, if both K and Di are constants, we can fold the operation and use the resulting value instead of TINCRi. Thirdly, under certain conditions we don't need a new temporary T2, in which case we use T1 instead of T2 everywhere and do not insert the operation T1 := T2. The conditions, which occur frequently, are that (1) T1 is not assigned another value in the loop; (2) all uses of T1 depend on this assignment; and (3) T1 is not busy on exit from the region.

We reduce the strength of an operation T1:=I+K as follows:

1. Add the operation T2:=I+K to the INIT block, where T2 is a new temporary;
2. Replace the operation T1:=I+K by T1:=T2;
3. Add the operation T2:=T2+Di after the operation I := I+Di, for i = 1,...,n.

Note again that the new temporary T2 need not be generated if T1 satisfies several conditions.

The increment operations T2:=T2+TINCRi and T2:=T2+Di which are inserted because of a strength reduction should be marked in some manner so that they themselves will not be further reduced. In the last section this was not necessary because the increment operations went into the INCR block, which was not further optimized. Here, we have no separate INCR block.

Note that T2 becomes recursively defined and can participate in strength reduction. The increment operations T2:=T2+INCRi should not, however, be reduced.

This optimization is essentially the same as the one performed in the last section. We now allow strength reduction with <u>all</u> recursively defined variables, and not just the loop variable.

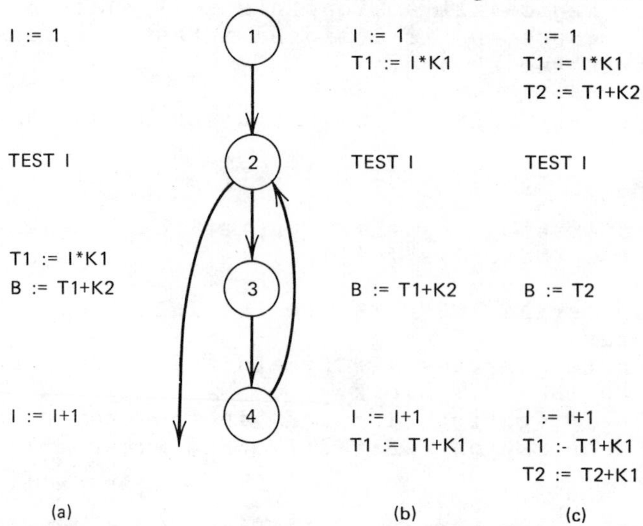


**FIGURE 18.13. Illustration of Strength Reduction.**

### Test Replacement

In Figure 18.13c the only uses of I are in its recursive definition and in the test on I. If we can transform the test into a test on some other variable, we can then eliminate the operation I:=I+1. In this example, we can replace it by a test on either T1 or T2; T2 would be the proper choice because the operation T1:=T1+K1 is already redundant and will be eliminated by the subsequent process.

We want to transform the test IF I > C ... into a test

```
IF T2 > C2 THEN GO TO OVER
```

Now, T2 is defined in terms of I by T2 := T1+K2 = I*K+K2. Therefore, if I > C then T2 > C*K+K2, so we insert the statement C2 := C*K+K2 into the INIT block to initialize C2. Note that we assume that C is region invariant. Note also that if the increments for I and T2 have different signs, the test should changed from ">" to "<".

Test replacement should be performed only under the following conditions.

1. The tests under consideration involve a variable I whose only other uses are in recursive definitions like I := I+K. I must not be busy on exit.
2. The tests must be simple enough (like, say, I > C) to be analyzed; C must be region invariant.
3. Another recursively defined variable T must exist, which arose ultimately through a strength reduction using I; that is, its definition must involve I.

The effectiveness of this optimization can be questioned. It may save an addition or two within a loop, but it is fairly time consuming at compile-time to find out whether I is busy on exit or not. Of course, in ALGOL or FORTRAN, the loop variable is never busy on exit, since its value is undefined after the loop.

### Eliminating Dead Assignments

An assignment operation is "dead" if the result of the assignment is never used, or if the assignment is recursive (like I := I+1) and the only uses are in such recursive definitions. Such assignments and the operations on which they depend can be eliminated.

Dead assignments often arise from strength reduction and test replacement, as Figure 18.13 indicates. Therefore this optimization should always be performed after test replacement. Obviously, all recursively defined variables should be tested for "deadness." It is, however, rather time-consuming to test all assignments within the region. The brute-force method of testing such an assignment A := T (say) is as follows:

1. Search through the subsequent operations in the block. If an assignment to A occurs, the definition is dead; if a use of A occurs, it is not dead. If no reference to A is found, continue with step 2.
2. Assuming the vectors REF, ASS and RBA are available for <u>every</u> block of the program, sequence through all paths leading from the one in which the assignment occured. If RBA for a block shows the use of A before an assignment, then A is not dead and the process can be stopped. If ASS indicates an assignment, then this path need not be further processed. If all paths lead to such an end or begin looping, then the variable is dead.

## 18.4 DISCUSSION AND HISTORICAL REFERENCES

### Folding, Redundant Expression Elimination

There are several early papers on translating arithmetic expressions into a particular machine language, performing limited optimization at the same time. Among these are Knuth(59) and Huskey(61). Floyd's(61a) algorithm reduces the number of store and load operations, performs folding, and does redundant operation elimination. It also recognizes equivalences involving the minus sign (eg. -b+a = -(b-a)). Gear(65) also discusses these techniques. Hopgood(68) discusses limited optimization of sequences of assignment statements using trees as the internal form.

More recently, Breuer(69) describes a method for factoring sequences of expressions and assignment statements, so that more common subexpressions can be detected. Thus

```
J := A+B+C+E; K := A+B+E+F; L := A+B+D+E+F;
```

would be changed to

```
T := A+B+E; J := T+C; K := T+F; L := K+D;
```

while

(18.4.1) A*B*C+A*B*D+A*E+F would yield A*(B*(C+D) + E) + F.

Once the factors are determined and the transformation made, the operations are rearranged to reduce the number of loads and stores (this is described later).

The method used for factoring is a heuristic procedure so that an optimum factorization may not be found. This is done to limit the possible different factors attempted in order to make the procedure practical.

As discussed by Fateman(69), factoring does not always give optimal code. For example, Breuer's method would change

$5+x+x^2+7x^4$ into 5+x*(1+x*(0+7*x*x)), while the following scheme uses one less addition and one less multiplication:

```
T1 := x*x; T2 := T1*T1; RESULT := 5+x+T1+7*T2.
```

Another important observation by Fateman is that the best code for serial computation is not always the best code for parallel computation. For example, evaluation of the right hand expression of (18.4.1) is a five step process, while on a computer capable of evaluating several independent arithmetic operations simultaneously, the expression could be evaluated in four steps, as follows, where each line is one step:

```
T1 := A*B        T2 := A*E
T3 := T1*C       T4 := T1*D
T3 := T3+T4      T2 := T2+F
RESULT := T3+T2
```

One must also realize that not all languages allow manipulation of expressions. Furthermore, the manipulation can (and usually does) lead to different results when floating point numbers are involved. What all this points up is that little is known about how and when to optimize assignment statements and expressions.

**Loop Optimization**

Gear(65) discusses the moderate loop optimizations of section 18.2 -- invariant operation processing and strength reduction involving the loop variable. He also discusses rearranging operands of the n-ary operations + and *.

Busam and Englund(69) have the same goals in mind: fairly good optimization and fast compile-time. They perform invariant operation movement out of loops, but do strength reduction only on subscripts (see below). An interesting feature used by them is the method of determining whether a variable (or expression) is assigned or referenced in a loop. For each such entity, a threaded list of assignment points and another list of reference points is maintained; These lists are kept in the internal source program itself, much the way forward references to labels were chained in section 13.3. As optimization progresses, the symbol table entry for a variable contains information indicating the assignment point ASS and reference point REF last processed. Thus, in Figure 18.14 we can easily tell from the definition chain that the operation I*5 is loop invariant (the braces indicate the linkage field of an operand in the internal form).

```
   :                        I's symbol table entry contains
10 I{50} =                  10 in the definition
20 DO 40 J = 1,N            chain field
   :
   K := I*5
   :
40 CONTINUE
50 I{0} =
```

**FIGURE 18.14. Forward Definition Chain.**

Several ALGOL compilers have implemented a scheme for moving the calculation of subscripted variable addresses out of loops, as do Busam and Englund. We have not discussed this in detail, because the optimizations described in section 18.2 automatically include it, with little or no increase in compile-time. See Hill et al(62), Huxtable(64), and Gries et al(65). This technique, called recursive address calculation, was first discussed by Samelson and Bauer(60).

The IBM FORTRAN IV level H compiler, described in Lowry and Medlock(69), and an experimental FORTRAN compiler designed by Allen(69) perform most of the more sophisticated optimization techniques described in section 18.3. Lowry and Medlock use quadruples, Allen uses indirect triples for the internal source program. Both use basic blocks and form the graph of the program. The Allen paper gives more details on the actual implementation method. Cocke and Schwartz(70) also contain a discussion of these and other techniques.

### Register Allocation

We have not discussed the optimization of the object program, because of the dependence on the computer. We will discuss this briefly here.

Assuming a machine with several fast registers which can be used to hold temporary results, one of the first optimizations that comes to mind is determining how to evaluate an arithmetic expression so that a minimum number of registers is needed. Anderson(64), Nakata(67), and Redziejowski(69) have treated this problem. The argument is as follows: If, in an operation like A*B, evaluation of A requires n registers and evaluation of B requires m (m > n) registers, then evaluation of A*B requires m+1 registers if we evaluate A first (one extra to hold the result A), and only m if we evaluate B first.

An expression is represented internally by a tree (see section 11.4). An extra pass then sequences through the tree, determining for each operator the number of registers needed for each operand, and marks each such node to indicate which operand should be evaluated first. Code is later generated accordingly.

Nakata also indicates some heuristic rules to determine which register to store in case there aren't enough registers. For example, since most computer operations for A-B or A/C require A to be in the accumulator, such a value A should not be stored if a register is needed. Redziejowski formulates the problem in terms of graph theory and develops a general algorithm which applies to the particular case of the minimum register problem.

The main drawback to the above schemes is that they don't tell which register to store in case there are not enough available. The problem we really want to solve is: given n fast registers, minimize the number of load and store instructions necessary to evaluate an expression. To begin our discussion of this, let us assume that we are not allowed to reorder the subexpressions, and that each value must be loaded into a fast register before it can be used.

Assume we have n registers R1, R2, ..., Rn. As an expression is evaluated, at some point the value of a variable V is needed. The following possibilities arise:

1. The value is already in a register Ri: the register is used.
2. No register is allocated to V yet, but an empty register is available (or one is available whose contents are not needed any more): load V into that register.
3. No register is allocated to V, and all registers are currently being used. Store the contents of one register (it will be reloaded later) and load V into that register.

The question is, of course, which register should be stored in step 3. The intuitive answer is to

(18.4.2) store that register whose use is furthest away in the sequence of operations.

This method of allocating registers is fairly well known, and has been used in several compilers. Belady proved that, under certain conditions, the register assignment is optimal -- it produces the fewest number of loads and stores.

Note that this algorithm requires us to know just where each temporary is used next; a threaded list of references through the object code may be the best way to do this.

Horwitz et al(66) have also solved the problem, with a slightly different set of ground rules. They assume a sequence of operations to be executed in order. An operation can reference a value (which must therefore be loaded into a fast register), and can change the contents of a register. The problem is still to minimize the number of load and store instructions. Their algorithm involves finding the shortest path from one node to another in a graph. Luccio(67) extends their result somewhat, in order to reduce the size of the graph, thereby making the algorithm more practical.

Sethi and Ullman(69) also present an algorithm for minimizing the number of loads and stores. The ground rules are also somewhat different: they consider arithmetic expressions using + and *, and operands which are all different, simple variables (no common subexpressions). Operations may be reordered.

### Optimization for Parallel Processors

The CDC 6600 computer has several independent arithmetic units, all of which can be executing in parallel. The problem is to generate code which takes advantage of this parallelism. Allard, Wolf and Zemlin(64) describe their attempts at this type of optimization of arithmetic statements. The major methods used are reordering the operations, elimination of redundant loads and stores, and assignment of registers. Hellerman(66) and Squire(63) also report on multipass algorithms for compiling arithmetic expressions for parallel processors. Stone(67) gives a one-pass algorithm which transforms, for example, A+B+C+D+E+F+G+H into an internal form of

((A+B)+(C+D))+((E+F)+(G+H))

instead of the usual

((((((A+B)+C)+D)+E)+F)+G)+H.

This allows parallel computation of A+B, C+D, E+F, and G+H. See also Baer and Bovet(68).

### Other Optimizations

McKeeman(65) describes "peephole" optimization: processing the object code after it has been generated, looking at only several instructions at a time. This allows one to recognize short sequences of instructions and to replace them by more efficient ones. For example, the IBM 7090 sequence

```
CIA A          can be
CHS            changed to        CLS A
```

One can also recognize redundant load register or load accumulator instructions within a small sequence of instructions in this manner.

Yershov(66) discusses a 24-pass compiler for ALPHA -- an extension of ALGOL -- written for the Russian M-20 computer (4096 45-bit words, three-address instructions). Besides the usual for-loop optimization and elimination of redundant operations, Yershov mentions the following:

1. Combining neighboring for-loops with identical <u>for</u> clauses, where possible (loop fusion);

2. Minimizing the number of words assigned to variables by determining which variables may occupy the same location;
3. If a procedure is called only once, then make a textual substitution for the call before optimizing and generating code.
4. If all calls to a procedure have the same actual parameter corresponding to a particular formal parameter, then make the substitution of the actual for the formal parameter at compile-time.

Wagner's thesis describes the optimization of expressions whose operands are arrays, in order to reduce the storage necessary for temporary arrays. He explains loop fusion, mentioned above, in detail. Busam and Englund describe when and how to merge <u>nested</u> loops into a single loop.

Besides these, we can mention the following:

1. Change division A/B to A*(1/B), in an attempt to take the operation 1/B out of a loop and have the faster multiplication inside.
2. Use multiplication for exponentiation to an integer constant. For example X**2 is X*X and Y**7 is (Y*Y)*(Y*Y)*(Y*Y)*Y.
3. On binary machines, integer multiplication or division by a power of two can be performed by a shift. Multiplication by 2.0 can become an addition.
4. Use in-line coding for ABS, ENTIER and other mathematical functions.
5. Combine moves of adjacent fields into a single instruction.
6. Eliminate unnecessary unconditional branches by changing the order in which code for basic blocks is generated.
7. Delete multiplications by 1 and additions by 0.
8. Delete unreachable code (this saves space, not time).

# Chapter 19.
# Implementing Macros

In this chapter we wish to explore the possibility of having a macro facility in a high-level language and to indicate how one might go about implementing such a facility. In section 19.1 we describe a simple macro scheme and show in detail how it can be implemented. Section 19.2 then describes the usual extensions to a macro scheme which provide more power and flexibility. The implementation of these extensions is sketched very briefly. In section 19.3 we describe a well known independent macro processor -- one which is not tied closely with any particular language but which can be used as a "preprocessor" for the compiler of many programming languages. Section 19.4 finally references the literature on the different aspects of macro processors.

## 19.1 A SIMPLE MACRO SCHEME

The basic idea of macros is text substitution or insertion: an identifier in the source program is replaced by a string of characters from some other character stream. This is illustrated in Figure 19.1. We assume that the name MAC has been associated with the string of characters "ST VW" in a <u>macro definition</u> (Figure 19.1a). As the source program is scanned, whenever the name MAC is encountered, it is replaced by the string "ST VW". Thus, while the programmer may write his program as in Figure 19.1b, the source program which is actually compiled looks like Figure 19.1c.

The string associated with a macro name is called the <u>macro body</u>. The name MAC, when it appears in the source program, is a <u>macro call</u>. The process of substituting a macro body for a macro call is generally referred to as a <u>macro expansion</u>.

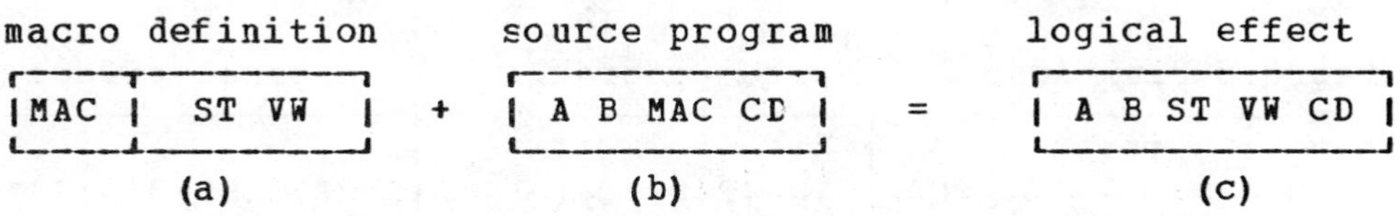


**FIGURE 19.1. Simple Macro Substitution.**

An additional feature which provides more flexibility is to allow the macros to have parameters. The string of characters which replaces a macro call varies with the parameters associated with that macro call. Figure 19.2 illustrates this. The string associated with the macro F has two so-called formal parameters in it -- &1 and &2 (Figure 19.2a). Correspondingly, the macro call F has two actual parameters -- XY and XZ (Figure 19.2b). When the body replaces the macro call, XY is substituted for the first formal parameter &1 and XZ is substituted for &2, yielding Figure 19.2c.

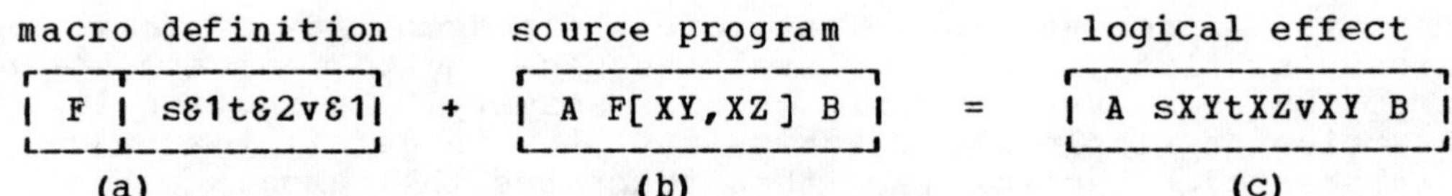


**FIGURE 19.2. Macro Expansion with Parameters.**

We have used the terms "formal parameter" and "actual parameter" in the above discussion, which usually refer to procedures or subroutines. This is because the macro calls closely resemble procedure calls. There is a big difference, however: the textual substitution occurring because of a macro call happens <u>before</u> the compiler proper ever parses the program. It could be done by a completely separate "macro processor" whose output is then passed on to the computer. We will actually show how to process macros in the scanner of the compiler.

### Nested Macro Calls and Definitions

Frequently, a macro call appears within a macro body or within an actual parameter. Figure 19.3 illustrates this using two macros named PI and ADD. The macro call PI appears both in the body of the macro ADD (Figure 19.3a) and in the second actual parameter of the macro call of ADD (Figure 19.3b). The effect of expanding all three macro calls is given in Figure 19.3c.

Macros like PI occur fairly often. The use of a mnemonic name for a constant makes a program more readable. Moreover, if the constant must be changed for some reason, one need only change it in one place -- in the macro definition.

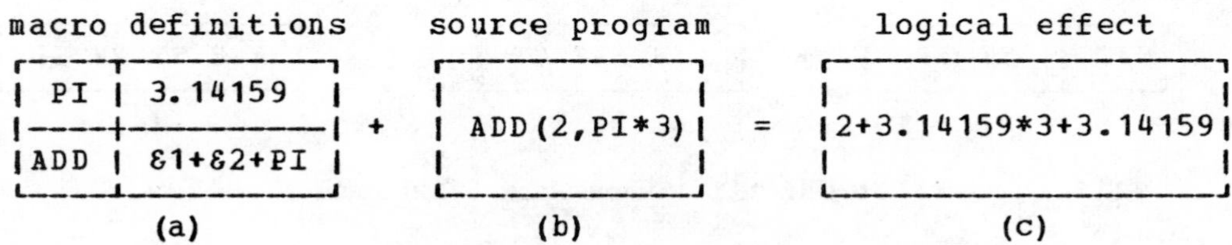


**FIGURE 19.3. Nested Macro Calls.**

It is convenient to use the concept of <u>level of nesting</u> of macro calls. We say that, when no macro expansion is occurring, we are on level 0. A macro call encountered during expansion of a macro call on level n has level n+1. In the example of Figure 19.3, the macro call ADD is on level 1, while each of the two macro calls PI have level 2.

macro definition

| A | MACRO B [XYZ] CBDBE |
|---|---|

**FIGURE 19.4. Nested Macro Definition.**

Nested macro definitions are less frequent but may be useful at times. Figure 19.4 illustrates a macro A whose body contains a macro definition for B. (We have not defined yet the exact form of a macro definition. In Figure 19.4, the definition MACRO B [XYZ] associates B with the body XYZ.) The effect of a nested macro definition is much like that of a variable declared local to a procedure. Within the macro A, the B refers to the macro B with associated string XYZ. Outside the macro A, this definition of B has no effect. B does not even appear in the "macro table" as a macro name with associated string unless a macro call for A is being expanded. Upon finishing the macro expansion, B will be deleted from the macro table.

Macro definitions occurring in an actual parameter are processed in essentially the same way. They are in effect only when that particular parameter is being evaluated and inserted into the source program.

One should note that, the way we have defined them, macro definitions and calls may appear anywhere in the source program. They are completely independent of the block structure or statement structure of the source language, since they are processed <u>before</u> the program is compiled. The only restriction is, of course, that the result of the macro processing be a syntactically and semantically correct source program.

### Format of Macro Definitions and Calls

Macro definitions and calls use the special symbols &, [ and ], which we assume are not symbols of the source language. This restriction allows us to separate distinctly the macro expansion process from the compilation process. The symbol "," is also used in macro calls, but this may be a source language symbol.

A <u>macro definition</u> has the form

(19.1.1) MACRO <macro id> [ <string> ]

where the <macro id> is a normal identifier in the programming language and <string> is any sequence of characters. Note that <u>all</u> characters between the two brackets, including blanks, are part of the <string>. We make a further restriction that square brackets come in pairs within the <string>: a left bracket [ must have a matching right bracket ] following it somewhere, and vice versa. Finally, in <string>, each occurrence of the character & must be directly followed by a nonzero digit. &i is called the ith *formal parameter* of the macro. Its use will be explained in a moment.

The macro definition associates the name <macro id> with its *body* -- the <string>. When a macro definition is scanned, the name and body are stored in a table of macros and the definition is deleted from the source program.

A *macro call* has one of the forms

(19.1.2) <macro id>

(19.1.3) <macro id> [ <par> , <par> , ..., <par> ]

where the <macro id> has been previously defined in a macro definition. Each *actual parameter* <par> has one of the forms

(19.1.4) [ <string> ]

(19.1.5) any string of characters, excluding commas and brackets

If <par> has the form (19.1.4) the actual parameter is the <string>, which must conform to the specifications given earlier for a <string>. In the second case (19.1.5), the actual parameter begins with the first nonblank character and ends with the character preceding the comma or ] following it. Thus, if leading blanks are desired, form (19.1.4) must be used.

We make one other restriction, for two reasons. The first is that we want to keep the implementation below simple so that you see easily enough how things work. The second is that you should have a chance to work something out yourself. Exercises 1 and 2 lift the restriction.

The restriction is that no actual parameter may contain a formal parameter &i. This may seem unreasonable when one uses macro calls within macro definitions. As an example, if B is already defined as a macro, then in

```
MACRO A [ B[c&1d] ]
```

the &1 should refer to the first actual parameter of the call of macro *A*, not B. Our restriction prohibits such constructions.

A macro call is expanded as follows:

1. The actual parameters are scanned and copied to a separate place and the macro call is deleted from the source program.
2. The macro table (containing macro names and associated strings) is searched for the *latest* definition of the macro <macro id>.

3. The characters in the macro body are inserted, one by one, into the source program. Whenever a formal parameter &i is recognized, stop inserting symbols from the macro body, and begin inserting symbols from the ith actual parameter (which must be present). When finished with the parameter, any macro definitions added during the processing of the actual parameter are deleted. Return to processing the macro body.
4. As step 3 progresses, new macro definitions or macro calls may occur. When this happens, they are immediately processed. The macro call is therefore recursive.
5. When step 3 is done, any macros added to the list of macros during this macro call are deleted from the macro table.

### Implementing the Simple Macro Scheme

In the programs below we have left out much error and table overflow checking, in the interests of a clear presentation.

We use three arrays to store the macro definitions. The macro bodies will be stored in an array S, one character per array element, with the last character of each body followed by the special character #. It is assumed that # cannot appear as a source language symbol. An array MACNAME holds the names of defined macros, while an array MACBODY contains indexes of the associated bodies in the array S. Another array, CALLS, contains information about calls currently being expanded. Figure 19.5 gives a complete list of variables needed. Figure 19.6 shows the tables for the macros PI and ADD of Figure 19.3.

```
STRING   ARRAY MACNAME(1:100);  | Holds macro names.
INTEGER ARRAY MACBODY(1:100);   | Holds indexes in array S of
                                | corresponding macro bodies.
INTEGER NMAC;                   | Number of macros in MACNAME.
CHARACTER ARRAY S(1:1000);      | Holds macro bodies and macro
                                | call parameters, one character
                                | per element.
INTEGER NS;                     | Number of characters in S.
INTEGER ARRAY CALLS(1:50);      | Holds information about current
                                | macro calls (acts like a stack)
INTEGER N;                      | Number of elements in CALLS.
INTEGER INPUT;                  | If 0, input is from cards.
                                | If not 0, contains index in S
                                | of current input stream char.
INTEGER LBSIGN;                 | When scanning source program
                                | or moving a macro definition or
                                | actual parameter, this is 0.
CHARACTER CHAR;                 | Holds current input character
STRING ID;                      | Holds the last identifier.
```

Initially, NMAC, NS, N, INPUT and LBSIGN are all 0.

**FIGURE 19.5. Declarations Needed for Macros.**

```
| ADD |      |  9  |     ┌──┐     ┌──┐     ┌──────────────────────────
| PI  |      |  1  |     | 2|     |17|     |3.14159#&1+&2+PI#
└─────┘      └─────┘     └──┘     └──┘     └──────────────────────────
MACNAME      MACBODY     NMAC      NS      S(one character/element)
```

**FIGURE 19.6. Illustration of Tables for Macros PI and ADD.**

All parts of the macro implementation are performed by the scanner, so let us briefly explain what happens there. First of all, a global location INPUT will contain 0 when the normal source program is being scanned. However, when a macro body or actual parameter is being inserted into the source program, we have a different input stream. In these cases, INPUT contains the index in the array S of the next character to be scanned in the macrc body or actual parameter. The location CHAR always contains the next input character, whatever its source.

One procedure, GETCHAR, is used in all parts of the scanner. Its function is to scan the next input character and put it in CHAR. Depending on INPUT, the next character may come from the source program, a macro body, or an actual parameter. In the latter two cases, when the symbol # is detected, it means the macro body or actual parameter has been completely scanned. GETCHAR then calls a procedure SWITCHBACK which causes the scanner to resume processing characters from the previous input stream. We will take a look at this procedure much later in this section. If we are not actually scanning an actual parameter or macro body, the character # cannot appear. If it does, an error message is given. The value of the variable LBSIGN indicates whether # can appear (1) or not (0). A general flowchart for GETCHAR is in Figure 19.7.

As can be seen from Figure 19.7, GETCHAR also calls a routine FORMPAR to switch to a new input stream for an actual parameter when the character & is recognized.

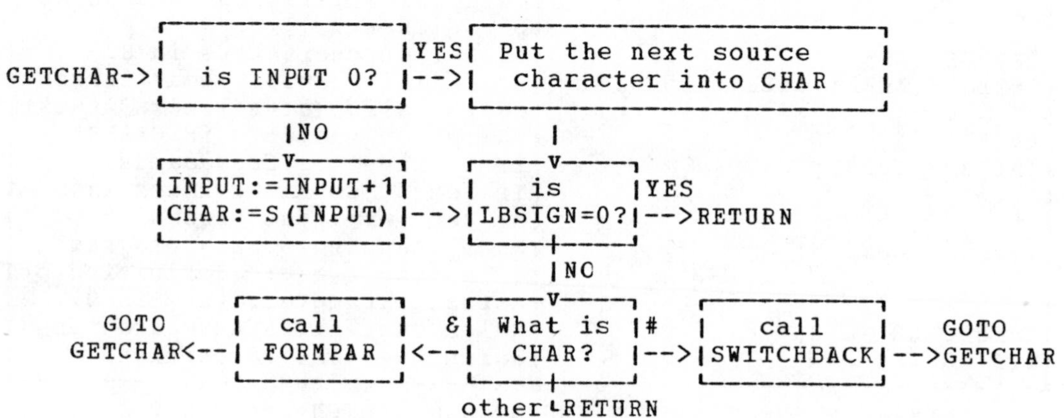


**FIGURE 19.7. Procedure GETCHAR.**

We need two other scanner procedures. The first, GETNONBLANK, checks to see if CHAR is blank. If so, GETCHAR is repeatedly called until a nonblank character is scanned.

The second procedure, BUILDID, is called when a letter beginning a reserved word or identifier is scanned. BUILDID scans the rest of the characters (using GETCHAR) making up the identifier, puts the identifier in a string location ID, scans the following character, and returns.

With this introduction we are ready to write the procedures which implement macros. The procedure MACRODEF is called when the scanner recognizes the reserved word MACRO. MACRODEF scans the macro name, stores it and the index (in S where the body will be) in the macro arrays MACNAME and MACBODY, and calls the procedure GETSTRING to actually move the body into array S. A special procedure is used here, because we must do essentially the same thing in another place for actual parameters. Note that the routine sets the variable LBSIGN to 0 so that "#" won't be scanned without producing an error message. The whole macro definition must come from the same input stream.

PROCEDURE MACRODEF

```
INTEGER LB;                 |Save the old LBSIGN indication and
LB := LBSIGN; LBSIGN=0;     |set to 0 so that # won't be scanned.
GETNONBLANK;  BUILDID;      |Get the macro name.
NMAC := NMAC+1;             |Push the macro name and the index
MACNAME(NMAC):= ID;         |in S where the body will be into the
MACBODY(NMAC):= NS+1;       |macro definition tables.
GETNONBLANK;                |Make sure we have a [ after the
IF CHAR ≠ "[" THEN ERROR;   |name and then call the routine to
GETSTRING;                  |move the body into S.
LBSIGN := LB;               |Reset the signal about # and scan
GETCHAR;                    |the next character.
```

The procedure GETSTRING moves characters one by one from the current input string to the array S. Upon entering, CHAR contains the opening bracket preceding the string. Note that initial blanks are copied. GETSTRING must keep a count of bracket pairs so that it knows when to stop. This is the purpose of the local variable C.

PROCEDURE GETSTRING

```
INTEGER C; C := 1;          |Set the bracket pair counter.
WHILE C ≠ 0 DO              |We keep scanning characters and
BEGIN GETCHAR;              |adding them to array S until the
 NS:=NS+1; S(NS) := CHAR;   |bracket pair count is 0.
 IF CHAR="[" THEN C:=C+1;   |
 IF CHAR="]" THEN C:=C-1;   |
END;                        |When done, we have put the last ] in
S(NS):="#"                  |already, so overwrite it with #.
```

The next step is to illustrate how a macro call begins. What we have to do is save information abcut the current input stream, the macro tables and the array S. This information will be restored at the end of the macro call. Because a macro call can occur while another is being expanded, we will use a stack to hold the information. For each call we use a number of elements of the stack CALLS (implemented as an array -- see Figure 19.5). The format for each call is given in Figure 19.8a.

```
|        old LBSIGN          |
|        old INPUT           |
|        old NMAC            |
|        old NS              |
|k (number of parameters)    |
|  index of par. k in S      |
|   :   :   :   :  :  :      |
|  index of par. 2 in S      |
|  index of par. 1 in S      |
L____________________________J
```

(a) FOR MACRO CALLS

```
|        old LBSIGN          |
|        old INPUT           |
|        old NMAC            |
|        old NS              |
|          -1                |
L____________________________J
```

(b) FOR PARAMETER CALLS

**FIGURE 19.8. Elements of the CALLS Stack.**

When the scanner finds an identifier, it looks for it in table MACNAME, starting from the top entry and proceeding down towards the first. If found, its index in MACNAME is passed as the actual parameter to the procedure MACROCALL. MACROCALL is straightforward. Aside from the CALLS stack manipulations, it just moves the actual parameters into S and begins scanning the macro body. Again, LBSIGN is set to zero because the whole macro call must appear in the same input stream. MACROCALL(I) assumes that the macro being called is the Ith one in MACNAME.

```
PROCEDURE MACROCALL(I); INTEGER I;
r-----------------------------------------------------------------------------1
|INTEGER LB,TEMP;               |Save the pointer to the current top |
|TEMP := NS;                    |of S so we can delete things later. |
|LB:=LBSIGN; LBSIGN:=0;         |# should not be scanned in the call.|
|N:=N+1; CALLS(N):=0;           |Initialize number of parameters to 0|
|GETNONBLANK;                   |and scan first nonblank character.  |
|IF CHAR = "["                  |If the call has actual parameters,  |
|THEN WHILE CHAR ≠ "]"          |then keep calling GETPARAM to move  |
|     DO GETPARAM;              |them to S until they are all there. |
|N:=N+1; CALLS(N):=TEMP;        |Stack the old indexes to top of S   |
|N:=N+1; CALLS(N):=NMAC;        |and MACDEF. When call is finished   |
|                               |we'll restore them. Then stack the  |
|N:=N+1; CALLS(N):=INPUT;       |current input stream pointer.       |
|N:=N+1; CALLS(N):=LB;          |Stack the termination (#) switch.   |
|LBSIGN:=1;                     |Since we begin scanning the macro   |
|INPUT :=MACBODY(I);            |body, we can have the #. Switch to  |
|CHAR := S(INPUT);              |macro body and get first character. |
L-----------------------------------------------------------------------------J
```

The following routine is called by the procedure MACROCALL to transfer a parameter from the current input stream to the array S. It calls the routine GETSTRING if the parameter begins with "["; otherwise it transfers the parameter itself. We use a procedure here just to make MACROCALL seem a bit simpler to follcw. Since GETPARAM is called only from one place it need not be a procedure.

PROCEDURE GETPARAM

```
|CALLS(N) := CALLS(N)+1;           |Add 1 to the parameter count,   |
|N:=N+1; CALLS(N):=CALLS(N-1);     |make room in stack for address  |
|CALLS(N-1) := NS+1;               |of parameter, insert address    |
|GETNONBLANK;                      |and scan the first character.   |
|IF CHAR = "[" THEN                |If parameter begins with [ then |
| BEGIN GETSTRING; GETCHAR;        |call routine to move a <string>|
|  GETNONBLANK;                    |and then get the next nonblank  |
|  IF CHAR ≠ "," OR CHAR ≠ "]"     |character. It must be a comma   |
|  THEN ERROR                      |or ] which ends the parameter.  |
| END                              |                                |
|ELSE                              |Here we move actual parameters  |
| BEGIN                            |containing no commas or         |
|  WHILE CHAR ≠ ","AND CHAR≠"]"    |brackets. Move the characters   |
|  DO BEGIN NS:=NS+1;              |one by one into S until the end|
|      S(NS):=CHAR; GETCHAR;       |of the actual parameter is      |
|     END;                         |detected.                       |
|  NS := NS+1; S(NS) := #          |Put in the termination symbol.  |
| END                              |                                |
```

PROCEDURE FORMPAR

```
|INTEGER TEMP; GETCHAR;    |We get the parameter number in CHAR.|
|IF N=0 OR CALLS(N-4)<0 OR|We must be expanding a macro but    |
|   CHAR is not a digit CR|not an actual parameter. CHAR must  |
|   CHAR = "0" OR          |be an integer referring to an actual|
|   CHAR > CALLS(N-4)      |parameter in the macro call.        |
|THEN ERROR;               |                                    |
|TEMP := CALLS(N-4);       |Get into TEMP the index in CALLS of |
|TEMP := N-5-TEMP+CHAR;    |the element which indexes the param.|
|N:=N+1; CALLS(N):=-1;     |specified by CHAR. Then stack the   |
|N:=N+1; CALLS(N):=NS;     |five elements necessary for an      |
|N:=N+1; CALLS(N):=NMAC;   |actual parameter call (see Figure   |
|N:=N+1; CALLS(N):=INPUT;  |19.8).                              |
|N:=N+1; CALLS(N):=LBSIGN; |                                    |
|LBSIGN := 1;              |We can see a # when scanning actpar.|
|INPUT:= CALLS(TEMP)-1;    |Now change input stream to the      |
|                          |actual parameter and return.        |
```

Routine FORMPAR is called by GETCHAR to process a formal parameter &i. Note that a formal parameter is in a sense a macro call without parameters and we treat it as such. We add an element of the form given in Figure 19.8b to the CALLS stack. Upon entrance to FORMPAR, & has been scanned. The only difference is that a formal parameter cannot appear in an actual parameter. Thus the use of "-1" as the first element in CALLS (see Figure 19.8b) to distinguish it from a real macro call. FORMPAR gets the digit following &, does some error checking, fixes the CALLS stack, switches the input stream to the actual parameter and puts its first character into CHAR.

The final task is to program the termination of scanning a macro body or actual parameter. They both are handled by the same routine, since they are similar. When GETCHAR recognizes the symbol "#" (which was put at the end of each macro body and actual parameter in S), it calls the procedure SWITCHBACK. SWITCHBACK just restores the information saved at the beginning of the call specified by the top stack elements.

```
PROCEDURE SWITCHBACK
┌──────────────────────────────────────────────────────────────────────┐
|LBSIGN:= CALLS(N)            |Restore the old termination signal.  |
|INPUT := CALLS(N-1);         |Restore the input stream pointer.    |
|NMAC  := CALLS(N-2);         |These assignments to NMAC and        |
|NS    := CALLS(N-3);         |NS effectively delete any macros and|
|                             |actual parameters added during this |
|N:= N-5;                     |call. Get rid of stack elements used|
|IF CALLS(N+1) >0             |during this call.  If CALLS(N+1)>0  |
|THEN N:=N-CALLS(N+1);        |we have to pop up actual parameters.|
└──────────────────────────────────────────────────────────────────────┘
```

### EXERCISES FOR 19.1

1. The restriction was made that no formal parameter &i appear in an actual parameter. If the restriction is not made, explain the use of such a formal parameter. To which actual parameter of which call does it refer?

2. Change the implementation described in this section to get rid of the restriction mentioned in Exercise 1.

## 19.2 OTHER MACRO FEATURES

### Line Oriented and Fixed Field Systems

The particular macro scheme we outlined is character-oriented; the source program was treated simply as a continuous sequence of characters. Many languages, including assembly languages and FORTRAN, are card oriented; one statement or instruction is permitted per card. A macro definition in an assembly language might look like

```
MACRO
PLUS          &1,&2,&3
FETCH         &1
ADD           &2
STORE         &3
END
```

where the macro name is PLUS, the body is cards 3 through 5, and the END signifies the end of the macro body. A macro call

```
PLUS          X,Y,Z
```

would then produce

```
FETCH         X
ADD           Y
STORE         Z
```

Such a macro system may be simpler to implement than the one we described because macro calls can only appear in one place, in the instruction field. The general idea of implementation is the same. Macro definitions are stored in a separate area and, when a macro call occurs, it is replaced by the macro body, with the actual parameters substituted for the formal parameters.

### Internal Forms of Macros

If macros are defined in a suitable manner, it is much more efficient to store a macro body in an internal form than in its original character form. When the macro definition is first scanned, it is translated once and for all into its internal form. Thereafter, for a macro call, the expansion process is much faster and simpler. The internal form for the above macro definition of PLUS might lock like

macro body table

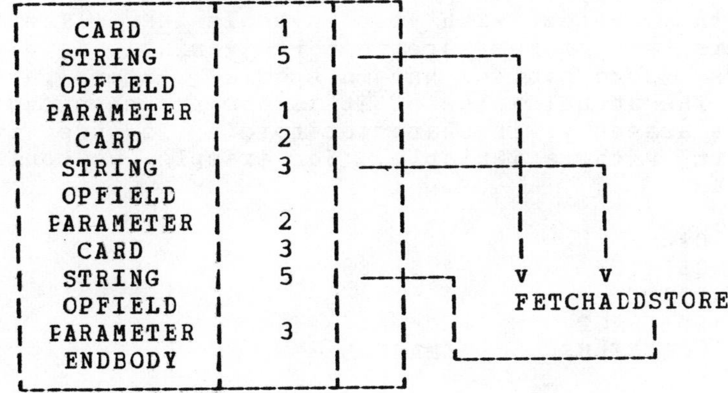

Here, the first column of the macro body table contains numbers meaning "begin new card", "a string of characters with no formal parameters in it", "begin the operand field", "formal parameter", and "macro call". The second column contains information like the card number, number of characters in the string, or the formal parameter number. The third column, used in case of strings, points to the actual string of characters in a separate table.

Such an internal form is much easier and faster to scan since blanks have been deleted, and since all the different possibilities have been already detected and sorted out. The process of expanding a macro call is an interpretive process, much like the one discussed in chapter 16. One has an internal form, the macro body, which must be interpreted.

We now briefly discuss the conventional macro features, which require the use of "macro time" variables, temporaries, and so forth. This makes the macrc expansion process even more like the interpretative process of chapter 16.

#### Created Symbols

The use of labels within a macro body is awkward in cases like

```
              MACRO
              GREATER       &1,&2,&3
              FETCH         &1
              SUBTRACT      &2
              GOIFMINUS     Z
              &3
     Z:       END
```

Every time we call the macro, we generate the label Z, and this produces multiple definitions of Z. Most assembly language macro facilities can generate variables in some way to alleviate the problem. One way is to precede any variable to be created uniquely by the system with two symbols &&. The system recognizes this and makes sure that the variable is different from all others. Some systems have a special system parameter, say &MACNUM. The actual value of it is the number of the macro call during the assembly, in character form. To use it, one concatenates it with a variable. For example, we could write GREATER above as

```
              MACRO
              GREATER       &1,&2,&3
              FETCH         &1
              SUBTRACT      &2
              GOIFMINUS     Z&MACNUM
              &3
     Z&MACNUM: END
```

```
If              GREATER        A,B,"STORE B"
                GREATER        B,A,"STORE A"
```

were the first two macro calls encountered in the source program, they would produce

```
                FETCH          A
                SUBTRACT       B
                GOIFMINUS      Z1
                STORE          B
     Z1:        FETCH          B
                SUBTRACT       A
                GOIFMINUS      Z2
                STORE          A
     Z2:
```

**Macro-Time Variables**

It is often useful to do some calculations at macro processing time. This usually requires the use of variables to store the results of the calculations. OS 360 assembly language allows, within macros, statements like

```
                LCLA           &X
                LCLC           &Y
```

which define &X and &Y to be variables local to the macro, of types arithmetic and character respectively. A later instruction like

```
     &X         SETA           &X+1
```

adds one to &X whenever the instruction is scanned and executed. We shall see later on how PL/I allows such facilities.

**Conditional Macros**

It is often convenient to prohibit the output of some statements during macro processing time, or to output different statements depending upon actual parameters. For example, we might want to have a macro PLUS which would produce

```
                FETCH          A
                ADD            B
                STORE          C
```

for a call

```
                PLUS           A,B,C
```

but would produce

```
                ADD1           A
```

for the call

```
                PLUS           A,1,A
```

where the ADD1 instruction is a special one used to add 1 to a location. What we need is some way of telling the preprocessor to jump over some instruction to be outputted. Some systems put a special sign in front of an instruction to indicate it is to be executed by the preprocessor. For example, one might write the above macro PLUS as

```
             MACRO                              (1)
             PLUS          &1,&2,&3             (2)
             LCLB          &X                   (3)
&X           SETB          (&1 NE &3)           (4)
             %GOIF         &X,%Z                (5)
&X           SETB          (&2 NE "1")          (6)
             %GOIF         &X,%Z                (7)
             ADD1          &1                   (8)
             %GO           %Y                   (9)
%Z           %NULL                              (10)
             FETCH         &1                   (11)
             ADD           &2                   (12)
             STORE         &3                   (13)
%Y           %NULL                              (14)
             END
```

Suppose the macro is called. Upon scanning the macro body, in line 3 the macro variable &X of type Boolean is declared (LCLB means *local Boolean*). Line 4 then compares the string of characters making up the first actual parameter with the string making up the third. If they are not the same, the local variable &X is set to TRUE, otherwise to FALSE. Line 5 then tests &X and jumps to %Z if it is TRUE. At %Z, the null statement is executed, after which lines 11-13 are outputted. If &X at line 5 is FALSE, the interpreter goes on to interpret line 6 through 9.

### PL/I Compile Time Facilities

PL/I has some so called "compile time facilities" (see IBM(c)) most of which one has in a macro processor. We will briefly look at these facilities here. A complete detailed account is not possible here.

In the PL/I compiler, the source program is first scanned by a *preprocessor* which does all the macro processing. We refer to this as *preprocessor time*. As the program is preprocessed, parts of it are put in an output buffer to be passed on to the compiler proper. If no macro processing is specified, the whole program is just copied over.

There is no real macro definition in PL/I. However, by putting a percent sign (%) in front of a statement, one indicates that the statement is to be executed at *preprocessor time* -- not runtime. Only certain statements may be preceded by a % -- among them are DECLARE, DO, END, GOTO, IF, PROCEDURE, and NULL (the empty statement). A procedure preceded by a % is the closest one comes to a macro. Whenever the name of such a procedure is scanned, the procedure is executed at preprocessor time, and the resulting string of characters replaces the call.

A short example will indicate the general idea of the preprocessor. Suppose we have

```
DECLARE I FIXED;
DO I = 1 TO 5;
A(I) = B(I) * C(I);
END;
```

This is a normal PL/I program segment, and it is just copied. When compiled, it produces a loop. On the other hand,

```
%DECLARE I FIXED;
%DO I = 1 TO 5;
A(I) = B(I)*C(I);
%END;
```

produces a completely different program. First of all, I is a preprocessor variable because its declaration is preceded by %, and it will never appear in the output of the preprocessor. Secondly, the loop is executed at preprocessor time. Each execution of the loop causes the statement A(I) = B(I)*C(I) to be scanned and outputted, with I replaced by its current value. Thus the actual program that will be compiled is

```
A(1) = B(1) * C(1);
A(2) = B(2) * C(2);
A(3) = B(3) * C(3);
A(4) = B(4) * C(4);
A(5) = B(5) * C(5);
```

Thus the loop has been expanded by the preprocessor. In this example, I is a kind of macro name, whose body is always the current value of I.

A second type of macro definition is the reserved word PROCEDURE preceded by %. It specifies that, whenever the preprocessor sees a call on this procedure, it is to be executed immediately. The result of the procedure call, a sequence of characters, replaces the call. This could be a good system. However, normal statements to be copied over (like A(I) = B(I)*C(I) above) are not allowed in a preprocessor procedure, just preprocessor statements to be executed immediately. Thus the only output possible is some string which was completely built up at preprocessor time.

The preprocessor is an interpreter. Its first phase is to scan the source program, translating the preprocessor statements into an internal form. The normal PL/I statements can be left in their original form. The second phase then interprets the output of the first phase, much as described in chapter 16. Whenever a normal PL/I statement is scanned during the interpretation, it is outputted; any preprocessor variables in it are replaced by their current values.

## 19.3 THE GENERAL PURPOSE MACRO GENERATOR (GPM)

GPM is a macro system devised by Strachey(65) for the purpose of helping to write a compiler for CPL -- an ALGOL-like language implemented at the Cambridge University Mathematical Laboratory in England. GPM is more sophisticated than the system of section 19.1; indeed, one can do some rather startling things with it. We will not show how to implement it, but we will indicate some of the difficult points. Its implementation should be an interesting project for the reader (exercise 1).

### The Macro Call

A macro call in GPM has the form

#<macro name>;

or

#<macro name>,<par>,<par>,...,<par>;

where the <par>s are the actual parameters. We would write the macro calls on PI and ADD in Figure 19.3 as

#ADD,2,#PI;*3;

As in the system of section 19.1, the macro name must first have been associated with the macro body in a macro definition. This macro body will in general contain some formal parameters &1, &2, ..., &9 which will be replaced upon macro expansion by the actual parameters. In addition, &0 is a formal parameter which is replaced by the macro name itself. Suppose the macro name PLUS is associated with the body

A:=&1+&2+&0

Then the macro call #PLUS,2*X,5; produces

A:=2*X+5+PLUS

Enclosing any string in string quotes < and > has the effect of preventing the evaluation of that string -- it just gets copied over. In place of evaluation, the string quotes are removed. This makes it possible to include any symbol in the output stream except an unmatched open or closing string quote. For example, the effect of the macro call

#PLUS,B(1<,>2),5;     is     A:=B(1,2)+5+PLUS

while

#PLUS,B(1,2),5;     produces     A:=B(1+2)+PLUS

In the second case parameter 5 was not used in the evaluation.

When a macro call is completed, all its actual parameters and any macro definitions evaluated during the call are eliminated. Thus we can have local macro definitions, as in the macro scheme discussed earlier.

### Macro Definition

The macro definition capability is implemented by providing a special system macro DEF. The two actual parameters which must be present in a call on DEF are the macro name and the corresponding body. Thus, we would define the macros PI and ADD of Figure 19.3 by

```
#DEF,PI,<3.14159>;      and      #DEF,ADD,<&1+&2+#PI;>;
```

Note again that a macro definition is just a call on another macro; we shall see later on how this can be used to our advantage.

### Macro Expansion

At first sight GPM looks like the simple macro scheme of section 19.1, with just a change of notation. This, to a certain extent, is true in that the usual, simple macro calls produced by an average programmer will usually produce the same result in both systems. The main difference, however, lies in what we haven't really talked about yet: how macro calls get expanded and what actual parameters can be. The generality allowed by GPM makes it a much more sophisticated and powerful system. Let us therefore look at the macro expansion algorithm. The algorithm may look innocent enough, unless one reads it very carefully. Following it, we will point out some of the features which one is bound to miss.

The input stream is scanned from left to right and copied into the output stream until a macro call is encountered (remember, macro definitions are just macro calls on a special macro DEF). The call is evaluated. The result of the call is copied into the output in place of the macro call itself. The scanning of the previous input stream is resumed. A macro call is evaluated as follows.

1. The macro name and the actual parameters are evaluated, in order of their appearance, the results being stored away somewhere. (If any macro call occurs while evaluating the name or a parameter, then <u>that</u> call is also immediately evaluated. The macro call process is thus recursive).

2. The macro definition table is searched, beginning with the most recent entry entered and proceeding down towards the first (which is the system macro DEF), for one whose name is the name of the macro called. If none is found, an error message is printed.

3. The body of the macro found in step 2 is now scanned in the same manner as the original input stream. That is, any macro calls detected will be expanded immediately. If a formal parameter &i where i = 0,1,2,...,9 is detected, it is replaced by an exact copy of the result of evaluating the ith actual parameter of the call in step 1. Note that &0 is replaced by the macro name. If i is greater than the number of parameters provided, an error results. Please note that the actual parameter is not evaluated again; it is just copied without any macro calls in it being processed. The result of the macro call is the output of this scan.

4. The complete macro call, the evaluated actual parameters, and any macro definitions added during steps 1 through 3 are completely deleted.

5. Scanning of the previous input stream is resumed at the character following the final semicolon of the macro call.

For the system macro DEF, step 3 is changed. There is no macro body to scan; instead, the first two evaluated actual parameters of the call to DEF are assumed to be the macro name and body, respectively, and are stored in a macro definition table.

#### Notes on the Macro Expansion Algorithm

First of all, since the macro definition is just a macro call on DEF, the macro name need not be a simple identifier but can be any string -- with preceding and succeeding blanks. In this system a blank is essentially like any other character.

Secondly, both the macro name and the actual parameters get evaluated before any scanning of a macro body is done -- even <u>before</u> the macro definition table is searched. Hence they correspond to value parameters in ALGOL procedures; in the system of section 19.1, parameters were similar to name parameters. To see what strange effects this can have, suppose we have a macro call

```
#A,X,Y,#DEF,A,B;;
```

That is, we call a macro A with actual parameters X, Y and #DEF,A,B;. Since actual parameters get evaluated before we do anything else, we begin by evaluating X (yielding X), Y (yielding Y), and the macro definition #DEF,A,B;. The latter results in the macro A with body B being added to the macro definition table. Next we search the macro definition table for the <u>last</u> macro named A. This yields the one we just added! The result of the call is just the character B. Note that any previous macro definition of A is ignored.

This technique of defining the macro to call in an actual parameter can be used to effect a kind of conditional expression; we can write macros which are equivalent to

```
IF x = y THEN w ELSE v
```

where x, y, v and w are strings. We write this in GPM as

```
#x,#DEF,x,<v>;#DEF,y,<w>;;
```

Evaluation of this call yields first of all two macros x and y with bodies v and w respectively (the evaluation of <v> and <w> is just the deletion of the quotes and the copying of the strings v and w). Next the macro definition table is searched for a macro with name x. If x is equal to y, then the resulting body is w, otherwise it is v. Note that this example involved the use of a macro name x which was not defined at the beginning of the call. Note also that the actual parameter for x is never called by a formal parameter; its only purpose is to define the local macros x and y.

While this may seem useless, we will show how it can be used later on.

Another interesting feature is that the macro name itself can contain formal parameters and/or macro calls. Suppose we have our macro PI with body 3.141520. Then the macro call

```
#DEF,#PI;+1,4.14159;
```

yields a macro with name 3.14159+1 and body 4.14159 .

One of the examples given by Strachey is the macro

```
#DEF,SUC,<#1,2,3,4,5,6,7,8,9,10,#DEF,1,<&>&1;;>;
```

This defines a macro SUC with body

```
#1,2,3,4,5,6,7,8,9,10,#DEF,1,<&>&1;;
```

Suppose we have a macro call #SUC,2;. When we begin scanning the macro body we immediately have a call of the macro 1 with parameters 2,3,4,5,6,7,8,9,10 and #DEF,1,<&>&1; This results first of all in the <u>definition</u> of macro 1 with body &2. (Note that the quotes around & have been deleted and &1 has been replaced by the first actual parameter of SUC, to produce &2.) We then call 1. Its body being &2, the result is just the second parameter 3. The complete result of #SUC,2; is therefore 3.

In general #SUC,r; produces r+1 for r = 0, 1, ..., 9; SUC is the successor macro for digits.

The use of the conditional statement technique can now be used to develop a macro SUCCESSOR which gives the successor of a two digit number. For example, #SUCCESSOR,2,3; is 2,4 and #SUCCESSOR,2,9; is 3,0. The macro body for SUCCESSOR is

```
#&2,#DEF,&2,&1<<,>#SUC,>&2<;>;#DEF,9,<#SUC,>&1<;<,>0>;;
```

Let us expand a call #SUCCESSOR,i,j; where i and j are digits. The evaluation of the actual parameters i and j produces no macro calls. Scanning the macro body yields a call on a macro j (the second actual parameter). Evaluating its single actual parameter yields first of all a macro

```
j      with body      i<,>#SUC,j;
```

and secondly a macro

```
9      with body      #SUC,i;<,>0
```

This is where the conditional statement technique is used. We now look for the macro j which we are calling. If j is not 9, we use the macro j with body i<,>#SUC,j;. Scanning this yields the result

```
i,k    where    k = j+1.
```

If j is 9, then the macro 9 with body #SUC,i;<,>0 is used, yielding

```
n,0    where    n = i+1.
```

Thus #SUCCESSOR,2,3; is 2,4, while #SUCCESSOR,2,9; is 3,0 and #SUCCESSOR,9,9; is 10,0.

This last example illustrates almost all the possibilities in GPM; a macro name which is a formal parameter, the use of string quotes to prevent evaluation until desired, the use of local macro definitions, the use of a call on a macro which is not defined when the call begins, and the use of conditional statements.

#### Discussion

As long as the pound sign, semicolon, comma, and & have no meaning in a programming language, GPM can be used as a preprocessor for that language. This in fact was the case of the assembly language of the Titan (Atlas 2) computer on which GPM was first implemented. (The symbols used there were not the same as ours.) The syntax is rather limited, but this does allow a rather simple implementation which is discussed by Strachey.

One might well question the worth of the examples SUC and SUCCESSOR given previously. I doubt that they would ever be used in a program, but they do cleverly illustrate what can be done. The practicality of a GPM-like system is illustrated by its actual use in writing a compiler in assembly language. The actual macro processor itself executes fairly slowly, but this is so of any sophisticated character-oriented macro processor. It takes time to make character by character substitutions.

### EXERCISES FOR 19.3

1. Draw flow charts for implementing GPM.

2. Implement GPM.

## 19.4 HISTORICAL REFERENCES

Macros were first implemented as part of assembly languages back in the late 50's. Greenwald(59) explains briefly how macros could be implemented for the SHARE 709 system on the IBM 709 (see also Greenwald and Kane(59). The system is line-oriented, as most assembly languages are. McIlroy(60) did much to spread the use of macros. The paper talks about conditional macros, created symbols, the use of sublists of actual parameters, and nested definitions and calls. He talks about implementation briefly. Kent(69) is a good tutorial on the use of macros.

The use of macros imbedded in a high level programming language to help extend the language was first discussed by McIlroy(60). The idea has therefore been around a long time. B5500 ALGOL permits pure text replacement without parameters. FORTRAN II had a special type of macro with parameters. One could declare, say,

```
FUNCTION F(A,B) = A*B*SIN(A)
```

Then, if one wrote

```
Q := F(2*G,H)
```

this would actually compile like the statement

```
Q := 2*G*H*SIN(2*G) .
```

Section 19.2 showed how a macro facility of some sort could be imbedded in PL/I. The compile time statements and PL/I statements look exactly the same except for the percent sign. Thus, the macro facility and the language are very closely related and dependent. One can also have a macro facility which is completely independent of the language in which it is used, like Strachey's GPM. McIlroy(60) attributes this idea to Perlis. The first paper which documents such a macro processor is Strachey(65). Since then, there have been several independent macro processors designed: TRAC (Mooers and Deutsch(65)), Waite's(67) LIMP, and the ML/1 macro processor by Brown(67). ML/1 works essentially by a keyword which begins a macro call, but it lets the user define the actual parameter separators and the terminator of the call. In Waite's system a keyword is not necessary (but can be used). It uses a general pattern matching scheme to detect macro calls.

Halpern(64,67a,67b) advocates using a sophisticated assembly language macro system as a base for a high-level language. Each source program in the high level language is actually an assembly language program. That is, each source language statement is a macro call of a macro defined in the assembly language. For example,

DO 10 I = 1, N

is a call on a macro DO with parameters I, 1, and N. := and , are actual parameter separators.

While this may be a good technique to use to implement some languages, the system is usually line-oriented, because the assembly language is. It is also difficult to achieve ALGOL-like nesting of blocks, conditional statements, and the like.

A more detailed account and survey of macro processors can be found in Brown(69).

# Chapter 20.
# Translator Writing Systems

## 20.1 INTRODUCTION

A translator writing system (TWS) is any program or set of programs which aids in writing translators -- compilers, interpreters, assemblers, and the like. Under this definition, a Production Language compiler (see chapter 7), or a constructor for an automatic parsing algorithm is a TWS. The purpose of a TWS is, of course, to simplify the implementation of translators, and to this end a TWS will contain primitives for the types of operations most translators must perform.

Much of the work in TWS has been specifically directed towards the problem of writing compilers, and the term compiler-compiler (CC) has been coined for this type (see Brooker, Morris, and Rohl(62) and Brooker et al(63)). The term arose because a TWS designed for writing compilers is a program which compiles other compilers. Similarly, we should call an assembler for an assembly language in which a compiler is written a compiler-assembler, but we don't.

We shall briefly describe what most TWS look like, and outline the usual classification of TWS. We will then direct our attention to two CC's, and describe in more detail how they work. This is not meant to be a survey of TWS, but a brief introduction to them. The reader is referred to Feldman and Gries(68) for a survey and for more references on the subject.

A compiler written in a TWS will most certainly use more memory and compile programs more slowly than an equivalent compiler written in assembly language. For example, Brooker, Morris, and Rohl(67) were able in a year to reduce the space requirement by a factor of 1.6 and the time by 1.7 by rewriting a compiler in assembly language. Nevertheless, in the long run, high-level languages and TWS will certainly replace assembly languages as the tools for writing compilers, just as high-level languages have replaced assembly languages for most scientific applications. It is easier, in a high-level language, to focus attention on what a compiler should do, since one doesn't have to worry about so many messy programming details. As an example of this, Lowry and Medlock(69) doubt they could have implemented all the code optimization features in the IBM FORTRAN IV H-level compiler, if it had been written in assembly language instead of FORTRAN.

### The Big Idea Behind TWS

Most TWS have at least the following two components:

1. A language for describing the syntax of the data (the source programs) to be translated.
2. A language in which semantic routines (as we have described them) are written. This is a procedural language, like assembly language, FORTRAN, ALGOL, and so on.

A translator consists of a syntax description, and a set of semantic routines. As depicted in Figure 20.1, these two are first compiled by the TWS into machine language or into some internal form. This process occurs at metacompile time. The resulting translator can then be executed; this occurs at the usual compile-time. Its execution is controlled by the syntax description and by the source program it is translating; semantic routines are executed as the syntactic constructs with which they are associated are recognized.

A large part of a TWS is a set of basic subroutines, which any translator will automatically use (see Figure 20.1). This is the equivalent of the usual library of I/O, mathematical, and other standard routines used in an algebraic language. However, there are more of them here, and, again, they perform functions which translators need.

That part of a TWS which compiles the syntax description is a constructor, as we have defined the term in the chapters on syntax. The input is usually BNF-like, and the constructor produces either a parsing algorithm in the form of a program to be executed or interpreted, or else a set of tables which are used by a basic routine in the library to perform the parse.

Note that Figure 20.1 uses the term "semantics of the source language L." This is quite misleading (although a number of TWS descriptions use the term), since it is not a semantic description in the same sense as the syntactic description; it is not a description which a user can look at to understand the semantics of L. Instead, it is just a set of semantic routines written in a procedural language, which, when executed, effect the analysis of the semantics of a source program and translate the source program into another form. The semantic language usually has the conventional constructs one has in other procedural languages:

1. Data types REAL, INTEGER, BOOLEAN, STRING
2. Simple variables, arrays, tables, perhaps structures (records)
3. Assignment, conditional, and iterative statements
4. I/O statements

In addition, it may have other constructs to help in writing compilers: pointer variables, stacks, primitives for entering and searching tables, primitives for generating code, and so forth.

Most TWS allow only single pass compilers. This is not a restriction inherent in the idea of a TWS; it is just that most of them have been implemented as short term projects designed to test out certain ideas and concepts. There are several multipass ones; see for example Cheatham(65), and the AED sytem (see Ross(67) and Ross(68)).

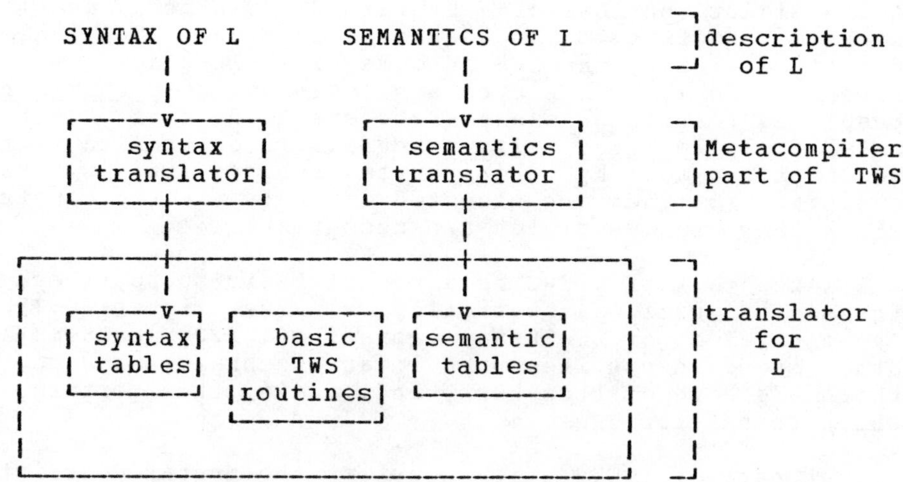


**FIGURE 20.1. Structure of a TWS.**

### Classification of TWS

CCs form one category of TWS. They are directed towards implementing compilers and thus contain primitives to help in code optimization, storage allocation, and so forth.

A second group of TWS is the syntax-oriented symbol processors. These are more general and have been used in such tasks as symbolic simplification of expressions, symbolic differentiation, translating from one high level language to another, and converting data from one format to another. They have been used in compiler writing, but the output is usually symbolic assembly language which must subsequently be assembled. Generally they are useful when the <u>structure</u> of the input contains a large part of the content, and when this structure can be described in BNF-like terms.

A third category is the set of extendible languages. In these, a programmer can define new data types and new statements in terms of existing ones. This in effect allows the programmer to extend or change the language to fit his needs. Several languages have existed for some time which allow restricted extensions. For example, MAD allows you to define new infix operators. A truly extendible language allows you to add a new statement or operation with almost any syntax. Such extensions are tied in with the idea of macros in high-level languages, which we discussed briefly in chapter 19. The Brooker and Morris compiler described briefly in the next section can be used as an extendible compiler as well as a CC.

## 20.2 A LOOK AT TWO COMPILER-COMPILERS

### FSL-Like Languages

Feldman's(66) FSL (Formal Semantic Language) is a compiler writing system which has been implemented on the G-20 at Carnegie Mellon University and on the TX-2 computer at Lincoln Laboratory. FSL uses a scanner definition facility, much like that of section 3.4, together with production language (PL, see chapter 7) for defining the syntax of the source language.

At compile-time, the syntax analyzer in the form of a PL program uses a stack S to hold symbols. A second parallel semantic stack can be used by the programmer to hold the semantics of the syntax symbols in S. A semantic routine called by a production references the semantic stack as follows: L1, L2, ..., L5 refer to the top, second, ..., fifth semantic stack elements, respectively, considering the stack configuration after matching the production but before the stack transformation has been made. R1, R2, ..., R5 refer to the semantic stack elements, considering the stack configuration <u>after</u> the stack transformation has been made.

An example will make this clear. If the production

```
E1 + T ANY  ->  E2 ANY    EXEC 5
```

matches, then in semantic routine 5, L2 and L4 refer to the semantics of T and E1 respectively, while R2 refers to the semantics of E2.

The main contribution of FSL is in the code generation mechanism used in the semantic language, which we will now discuss. The reader is reminded that we will not discuss FSL exactly; we change the notation and some of the unimportant features to arrive at a semantic language consistent with bastard ALGOL.

A new data type in the semantic language is the DESCRIPTOR (semantic word), which is used to describe runtime variables <u>in terms of the machine</u> for which code is being generated. Each compiler written in FSL uses a set of general code generation routines which use DESCRIPTORs to describe runtime variables. These code generation routines are not too much different from corresponding routines implemented in a normal compiler; they must just be somewhat more general.

A value of type DESCRIPTOR consists of several components. The first two, which we give names to below, are usually filled in by the compiler writer to initially describe a variable. The rest, which we won't name since we won't reference them, are changed and referenced mainly by the code generation system itself, and not by the compiler writer. The components of a DESCRIPTOR include:

1. ADDRESS: An integer giving the runtime address of the variable.
2. TYPE: An integer giving the type of the variable <u>in terms of the machine</u> for which code is being generated (for example, 1 = FIXED = fixed point word, 2 = FLOAT = floating point word, 3 = BITS = one word of bits or an unsigned integer).
3. A field which specifies indirect addressing.
4. Fields which indicate whether the variable is subscripted or not, and if so, what the subscript is (more on this later).
5. A field which indicates whether or not the negative of the runtime variable is desired (this is used to help produce locally good code).
6. Fields which indicate whether the value described is currently in an accumulator or register, and if so, which register, etc.

All except the first two fields help describe the "state" of the runtime machine as code is being generated. Their exact description depends on the machine for which code is being generated, and also the particular code generation system implemented.

In order to show how DESCRIPTORs are used in generating code, we illustrate semantic routines for processing a declaration, an identifier, and a multiplication in a conventional language with no block structure. The rules we are interested in are

```
         dec    ::= REAL idlist
(20.2.1) idlist ::= I | idlist , I
         F      ::= I
         T      ::= T * F
```

The corresponding productions in PL would be

```
         LDEC: REAL          ->         EXEC 1 SCAN GO LID
         LID:  idlist , I    -> idlist EXEC 2 SCAN SCAN GO LID
(20.2.2)       I             -> idlist EXEC 2 SCAN SCAN GO LID
                             :
         LF:   I ANY         -> F ANY  EXEC 3 GO LT
                             :
         LT:   T * F ANY     -> T ANY EXEC 4 GO LT1
```

Semantic routine 1 is called at production LDEC. Its sole function is to set a global variable T to the type of the identifiers in the following identifier list. Similar routines would exist for INTEGER, BOOLEAN, and so forth.

| 1:T := FLOAT; | FLOAT is a variable whose value means FLOATING POINT NUMBER |
|---|---|

Semantic routine 2 is called when a declared identifier is at the top of the stack. It thus references that identifier by L1. We suppose a symbol table SYMB is used in the compiler. Routine

2 looks up the identifier and make sure it isn't in yet (For the sake of simplicity, we assume a declaration must precede the use of an identifier). The identifier must then be entered in SYMB with its attributes.

One of the fields of an entry of SYMB is a DESCRIPTOR DESCR, which describes the <u>runtime</u> characteristics of the variable. We use the TYPE field of DESCR to also give the source program type of the variable: FIXED means INTEGER and FLOAT means REAL. In some cases it will be necessary to have an extra field of the symbol table entry to describe the source program type. For example, if integer and real values are all implemented in floating point, the compiler must still know the type of each identifier and expression so that it can perform or generate conversion operations at the proper times.

Routine 2 builds the DESCRIPTOR with type FLOAT or FIXED, depending on the value of the global variable T. STORLOC is a compiler variable used in assigning addresses to runtime variables; it is initially 0. When building a DESCRIPTOR, the system automatically fills in unreferenced fields with the proper initial value; they are not undefined.

```
2:LOOKUP(L1,P);                       |Look up the identifier --
  IF P ≠ 0 THEN ERROR(1);             |it shouldn't be there.
  INSERT(L1,P);                       |Put it in.  P.STRUC=1 means
  P.STRUC := 1;                       |it's a simple variable.
  D:=DESCRIPTOR(ADDRESS=STORLOC,      |Now make up a DESCRIPTOR of
                TYPE=T);              |the runtime variable and
  P.DESCR := D;                       |put it in the symbol table.
  STORLOC := STORLOC+1;               |Increase the runtime
                                      |address counter.
```

Routine 3 is called when an identifier I is being reduced to a factor F. It looks up the identifier in the table and puts the associated DESCRIPTOR on the semantic stack as the semantics of F. Note the check for P.STRUC=1, to make sure it's a simple variable. Array names, procedure names, and so forth, would have a different value in P.STRUC.

```
3:LOOKUP(L2,P);                       |Look up the identifier - it
  IF P = 0 THEN ERROR(2);             |must be in the table.
  IF P.STRUC ≠ 1 THEN ERROR(3);       |It must be simple variable.
  R2 := P.DESCR;                      |Put the DESCRIPTOR on stack
```

In most compilers, to generate code for a multiplication one would call a code generator MULT(D1, D2, D3) (say), where D1 and D2 describe the runtime operands of the multiplication and D3 would be used to store a description of the result. In FSL, such a code generation statement locks like

```
D3 := CODE(D1 * D2);
```

In semantic routine 4, code is generated for the rule T::=T*F. L2 and L4 are references to the semantic stack elements for E and T, respectively, and are DESCRIPTORs of those operands. The DESCRIPTOR resulting from generating the code is stored in R2 -- on the semantic stack corresponding to the left part nonterminal E.

```
|4: R2 := CODE(L4 * L2);          |                              |
```

In FSL, almost any sequence of statements or expressions can appear within code brackets "CODE(" and ")". When such a code bracketed sequence is executed at compile-time, code is generated for that sequence. The main restriction is that operands within code brackets must be DESCRIPTORs or constants. For example, suppose A, B, C and I are runtime variables, described by compile-time DESCRIPTORs DA, DB, DC, and DI. Execution of

```
(20.2.3) CODE(DI := DA+DB*DC)
```

causes code to be generated which, when executed at runtime, will perform the assignment I:=A+B*C.

In case the code brackets surround an expression, the result of executing the code statement is not only the code generated, but also a DESCRIPTOR of the result. This DESCRIPTOR is usually stored somewhere (as we did in semantic routine 4) for later use. As another example, executing

```
DI := CODE(DA+DB*DC);
```

causes code to be generated for evaluating A+B*C. The result is left (at runtime) in an accumulator or register. The compile-time DESCRIPTOR describing the result is stored in variable DI.

The notation used in code generation in FSL is much more elegant and readable than the usual code generation notation. Instead of a sequence of calls on code generation routines, we have a single statement which looks like a conventional statement, except it is surrounded by code brackets.

FSL provides a neat notation for describing runtime subscripting. Suppose we wish to write semantic routine 5 for the production

```
I ( E ) -> F   EXEC 5
```

where I is an array name (its DESCRIPTOR is in L4) and E is an expression (its DESCRIPTOR is in L2). Let us suppose that the ADDRESS field of I's DESCRIPTOR (L4.ADDRESS) is actually the address of the dope vector for the array, and that at runtime the first word of the dope vector contains the value CONSPART (see section 8.4). Then we want to generate a DESCRIPTOR which specifies that the address of the runtime variable is CONSPART + (current value of E). We do this in two steps:

D1 := *L4; L4 is a DESCRIPTOR. This statement says to generate and store into D1 a DESCRIPTOR whose components are the same as L4's except that indirect addressing is specified. Thus its runtime address is the value CONSPART.

R1 := D1(L2); Generate and store in R1 a DESCRIPTOR whose components are the same as those of D1, except that the address of the variable described is the runtime address described in DESCRIPTOR D1 + (the runtime value described by DESCRIPTOR L2).

The DESCRIPTOR in R1 then describes the subscripted variable. It is up to the code generation system to generate code to address the array element correctly. Note that the subscripting process looks much like normal subscripting; only DESCRIPTORs are involved instead of normal compile-time variables. We could actually have written the two statements above as the single statement R2 := *L4(L2).

The code generation statements in an FSL compiler will be translated by the metacompiler into a series of machine language calls on conventional code generation routines. For example, the statement (20.2.3) will be translated into the machine language equivalent of

```
MULT(DB,DC,DT1)
ADD(DA,DT1,DT2)
STORE(DT2,DI)
```

where MULT, ADD, and STORE are the code generation routines for multiplication, addition, and assignment, respectively.

The reader should not assume that code must be generated in the original semantic routines called by the parsing algorithm. In a flexible system, the semantic routines could generate an internal form in the conventional manner, and code could be later generated from the internal form using code brackets.

### BMCC

BMCC stands for the Brooker-Morris Compiler-Compiler (see Brooker and Morris(62), Brooker et al(63), and Rosen(64)), one of the oldest TWS. It is also one of the few TWS which are being used in a productive manner.

For syntax analysis, BMCC uses a standard system scanner (which the compiler writer may replace by his own) and a top-down parsing algorithm. To replace left recursion, which is not allowed in top-down parsing, the syntax description allows optional symbols and iteration. One need not associate a semantic routine with every rule of the grammar, and one usually doesn't. Consider for example the following (incomplete) syntax description for assignment statements, where the expression on the right is a sequence of arithmetic sums:

```
1.  FORMAT[SS]        ::= <var> := <sum>
2.  PHRASE <sum>      ::= [<sign>] <term> <terms>
3.  PHRASE <term>     ::= <var> | ( <sum> )
4.  PHRASE <terms>    ::= <sign> <term> <terms> | <empty>
5.  PHRASE <sign>     ::= + | -
```

The word PHRASE preceding a syntax rule indicates there is no semantic routine associated with it. The term FORMAT[SS] preceding the first rule indicates that Source program Statements can have the format <var> := <sum>, and that there is an associated semantic routine to be executed whenever a statement of that format is parsed.

At compile-time, as a source program is being parsed, a syntax tree of the program is formed. (Thus the top-down parser produces an internal form of the source program.) Whenever a subtree is formed whose root branch corresponds to a syntax rule preceded by FORMAT[SS] (e.g. the rule <var> := <sum> above), a corresponding semantic routine is called. The subtree parsed is passed as a parameter to the semantic routine. The purpose of the routine, as always, is to process the construct formed, semantically. In this case, the routine is supposed to "walk" around the subtree and generate code for it. A possible routine to process subtrees formed using the above rules, which we will discuss in a moment, is given below.

```
1.  ROUTINE[SS] ::= <var> := <sum>
2.      LET <sum> = [<sign>] <term> <terms>
3.      AC := [<sign>] <term>
4.  L1:GOTO L2 UNLESS <term> = <sign> <term> <terms>
5.      AC := AC <sign> <term>
6.      GOTO L1
7.  L2:STORE AC IN <var>
8.  END
```

The semantic language has several statements for performing pattern, or tree, matching. Any nonterminal of the syntax description can be used as a variable whose value can be a subtree whose root has that name. Consider for example the first line of the above routine, and remember that the syntax tree passed to the routine has its root branch corresponding to

```
FORMAT[SS] ::= <var> := <sum>
```

Aside from labeling the semantic routine, the first line says to assign to <var> the subtree emanating from the node <var> of the root branch and to assign to <sum> the subtree emanating from the node <sum>. Thus, if the assignment statement parsed was I:=A+B, <sum> would contain the leftmost tree of Figure 20.2.

Now, the root branch of the subtree <sum> corresponds to an application of the rule

<sum> ::= [<sign>] <term> <terms>

as depicted in Figure 20.2. Execution of line 2 of the routine assigns tree (b) to <term> and tree (c) to <terms>. <sign> is set to <empty>, since it doesn't appear and is optional. Statement 3 then generates object code to put the first <term> in the accumulator (AC). The code generated depends on the subtree currently assigned to <term>. We shall say more about this statement later.

Statement 4 then looks at the subtree in variable <terms> to see if it has the form <sign> <term> <terms> (the other possibility is <empty>); if so the variables <sign>, <term> and <terms> are given the new values and the next statement is executed. If not, control jumps to statement 7. Both statements 5 and 7 generate the obvious code based on the values of the subtrees currently in <sign>, <term>, and <terms>.

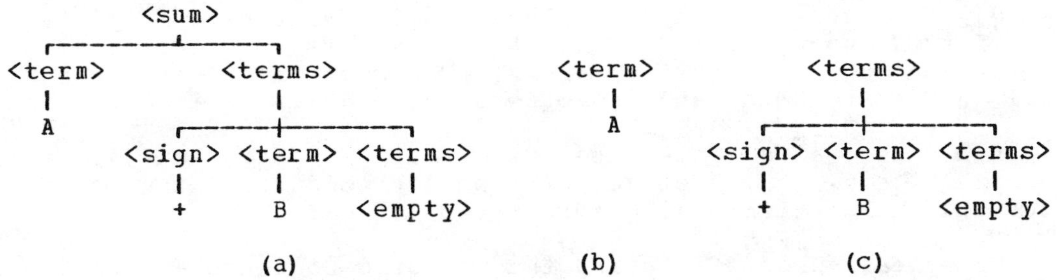


**FIGURE 20.2. Illustration of the LET Statement.**

In general, a syntactic nonterminal in the syntax description can be used as a variable to hold only a subtree whose root has that name. Since a tree walk may be quite complex and may require several subtrees with the same root name to be processed at the same time, the system allows an array of variables for each nonterminal. For the syntactic entity <term>, these would be referenced by <term/1>, <term/2>, <term/3>, ..., and <term/A> where A is an integer variable. We didn't need this facility in our example.

BMCC has some nice extendibility features. To a certain extent, a compiler written in BMCC is really an extention of BMCC itself. Because of its extendibility, execution can be quite slow; the system is continually building syntax trees and walking around them, not only for source language statements but for others as well.

The first step in writing a compiler might be to design some new statements to be used in implementing the compiler. For example, we could add some code generation statements like those on lines 3, 5, and 7 of the above semantic routine. These three were not really part of BMCC, but were added to make writing the compiler easier.

A new set of basic statements are added to BMCC to form an extended version BMCC1 of BMCC, as follows. Write a syntax description for each new statement, but use

FORMAT[BS] instead of FORMAT[SS]

to describe a rule which has an associated semantic routine. BS means basic statement, SS source program statement. Similarly write a semantic routine, which will be executed whenever a basic statement with that format is to be executed. Use

ROUTINE[BS] instead of ROUTINE[SS]

in the first line of the semantic routine. For example, the routine for AC := AC <sign> <term> would output code to add or subtract the <term> from the accumulator. If the <term> is a single variable, this would be a single instruction; if it has the form (<sum>), this would be a series of instructions, depending on the subtree <sum>. The semantic routine can use all BMCC statements, and any others added during this extension.

In a sense, at compile-time, execution of a statement AC := AC <sign> <term> is just a call on a procedure -- the semantic routine -- but with a nice format for the call.

The syntax descriptions and the semantic routines are then fed into BMCC and translated into an internal form. This internal form is coupled with a copy of BMCC itself to produce the new metacompiler BMCC1. BMCC1 accepts normal BMCC statements and the new basic statements just added.

The next step is to write the syntax descriptions and semantic routines for the source language statements; these are described using SS instead of BS in the FORMAT and ROUTINE statements. When these are fed into BMCC1, a third compiler BMCC2 is produced, which accepts normal BMCC statements, basic statements added during the extension to BMCC1, and the newly defined source language statements. At this point, BMCC2 is still an extendible compiler, and may be extended any number of times. To transform it into a compiler for just the source language statements, a switch is set which indicates that only statements declared as SS are to be allowed in the normal input stream. One then gets a compiler for only those statements.

# Chapter 21.

# Hints to the Compiler Writer

This chapter contains miscellaneous comments on subjects which are either too small to warrant a separate section or chapter, too important to be hidden away where they might be missed, or just don't belong anywhere. The comments are brief and point the reader to the literature for more details. I suggest the reader glance through the chapter from time to time and read any points touching on the subject he is currently studying.

The points covered are, in order:



### A General Philosophy

NEVER PUT OFF TILL RUNTIME, WHAT YOU CAN DO AT COMPILE-TIME

An operation performed at compile-time is only performed once; if left till runtime it may be performed hundreds of times. In this context, we refer mainly to conversion of constants, type checking, operations involving only constants or values known at compile-time, and so forth. Every compiler should perform a limited amount of reasonable optimization. The amount performed depends of course on the goals of the project, but a little thought on the subject will produce a better compiler.

### What Language Should the Compiler Be Written In?

The trend is away from assembly languages and towards higher level languages, as it should be. The reasons are obvious: easier programming, less debugging, less cost, more time spent on making a good compiler, and less time spent on fiddling with registers and bits.

Just which high-level language should be used depends very often on what is available and what the compiler writer is used to. The IBM FORTRAN IV level H compiler was written in FORTRAN, the Burroughs extended ALGOL compiler in extended ALGOL. I believe we will see the development of more "systems programming" languages, which are high-level but oriented towards a particular machine. This should allow the compiler writer more insight into the code generated for his compiler, and thus allow him to program more efficiently. The other alternative is to use a general purpose language like PL/I. This makes the compiler fairly mobile, but efficiency is lost.

### The Scanner Can Help the Parser

The syntax analyzer can be made simpler and easier to work with by performing some extra tasks in the scanner. For example, constants can be converted in the scanner, so that their syntax doesn't clutter up the syntax description. The scanner can also perform some error checking and recovery (or correction); examples are errors in constants, spaces between characters of double-character symbols like **, and missing end quotes on a string constant. These extra tasks should not, however, get too involved; the scanner should remain simple and efficient.

Often, several symbols appear in the same context in the syntax description. For example, + and - are used in the same way, and in ALGOL, the symbols REAL and INTEGER can appear in the same place. A common trick is to let the scanner return a single syntax symbol for all terminals which fall in such a class, and let the semantic routines worry about which symbol it actually is. (This can be done in PL (chapter 7) with CLASS declarations.) For example, to the user the grammar might contain

```
<type> ::= REAL | INTEGER | BOOLEAN
<dec>  ::= <type> <idlist>
<E>    ::= <T> | <E> + <T> | <E> - <T>
```

but in the internal parser these are replaced by

```
<dec>  ::= TYPE<idlist>
<E>    ::= <T> | <E> PM <T>
```

Note that the scanner already performs this service for identifiers; the syntax symbol I stands for the class of all identifiers, and the semantic routines distinguish between the different identifiers.

When a grammar isn't suitable for a particular parsing algorithm, it is often easier to let the scanner handle the problem, rather than try to change the grammar drastically. For example, one problem that comes up in ALGOL when using simple precedence is the violations concerning the comma because of its different uses as a separator of actual parameters and as a separator of bounds in an array declaration. It is a simple matter for the scanner to know whether an array declaration is being scanned, and to change commas separating bounds to an entirely different symbol.

Another example, in FORTRAN, is when DO10I is scanned at the beginning of a statement; it could be an assignment statement or a do-loop. The scanner can look ahead and make the decision much easier than a formal parsing algorithm can.

### Discussion of Parsing Algorithms

Various top-down and bottom-up parsing algorithms have been compared by Griffiths and Petrick (65), but these comparisons don't really help us from the standpoint of knowing which method will work faster in a compiler. Too much depends on exactly how the algorithm is implemented and how semantics fits in. I doubt that one would measure a significant difference in compile-time between two compilers which were similar except for the parsing algorithms, unless of course one of them was implemented in a very unreasonable manner.

Much more important is the flexibility of use of the parsing algorithm, the ease in which changes can be made and semantic routines can be incorporated, and the time it takes to get the compiler programmed and checked out. From this standpoint, as explained in section 5.5, simple precedence is the worst method to use. The only reason a whole chapter has been devoted to it is because it is the simplest one and therefore the easiest to use to get across the idea of bottom-up parsing.

If the compiler is being written in a language which allows recursive procedures, the method of recursive descent described in section 4.3 should certainly be considered. While there is nothing formal or automatic about it, if the procedures are written following the grammar, the technique is simple, clear, and fairly easy to debug.

The most widely used bottom-up method is operator precedence using precedence functions. Most implementations which use it do it in an intuitive fashion, instead of mechanically generating the functions from the grammar. They usually use two stacks, as discussed in section 6.1; one for the operators involved in the precedence relations and the other for the identifiers, constants, and other operands. Operator precedence is often used just for parsing expressions and, in fact, was first designed for this purpose. It is efficient and flexible.

A formal parsing algorithm should not always be used. Note that the previous two methods emphasized are usually programmed in an intuitive manner. The reason for spending one third of the book on syntax theory is that, once these formal methods are understood, programming a compiler and even talking about compilers becomes easier and more systematic. FORTRAN is a good example of a language which is easier to parse using ad hoc techniques. It is difficult to give a syntax description which fits any of the automatic techniques, and yet the structure of the language is fairly simple. There is no block structure, no nested conditionals, no case statements, and so forth. FORTRAN is line-oriented, and the type of statement on a line can almost always be determined from just the first symbol or two.

It is often advantageous to use different parsing techniques for different parts of the source language. Although it hasn't been done, people have discussed designing a constructor which would analyze a grammar, break it up mechanically into several parts, and create the most efficient parsing algorithm for each part. These parsing algorithms would call each other when necessary.

Conway(63) talks about a "separable transition diagram" compiler for COBOL, in which the language is separated into several such sections, each of which is parsed by a finite state automaton; these automata call each other recursively. Tixier(67) independently formalized the technique, but his formalization has not been used in a practical compiler.

Several compilers separate analysis into two parts. For example, FORTRAN H (see IBM(a)) uses ad hoc techniques to parse all declarations and statements, but all expressions are parsed by a single subroutine, using operator precedence (as described above).

### A Hint on Semantic Routines

A common practice in programming is to make everything that may be an input to a subroutine a formal parameter of that routine. While this produces general, independent subroutines, in compiler writing it is often better to make more use of global parameters (COMMON in FORTRAN). We illustrate this with one of the better examples in compiler writing.

Every semantic routine which processes an identifier or expression probably calls at least one other routine, to check for type compatability, to print error messages, to check for optimization possibilities, and so on. Each of these subroutines will have as a parameter a pointer to a description of the identifier or expression. Note, however, that at any point in compilation, at most one or two such operands are being processed. For example, a semantic routine which processes a binary operation has two operands to process. A semantic routine which processes an actual parameter has two: the actual parameter itself and the formal parameter with which it must be compared.

Let us therefore adopt the convention that each semantic routine which processes an operand (or two) move that operand (or a pointer to its description) into a global location P (P1 for the second one). Then, any routine which processes operands will reference them through the global locations P and P1. Just before the semantic routine returns to the parsing algorithm, it puts the pointer P (and possibly P1) in its proper place on the stack, or whatever.

This simplifies the calls to subroutines, makes compile-time more efficient from both a time and space standpoint, and in general leads to a "cleaner" compiler.

### Compiler Structure

We have discussed compilation as a four step process: scanning, analysis, preparation for code generation, and code generation. Cheatham(65) thinks of it as a six step process, by splitting syntax and semantic analysis into two steps, and by splitting code generation into two parts -- first code generation and secondly fixing up the code and outputting it.

While these models are good for the purpose of teaching about compiler writing, they can not always be used exactly in a real compiler. Too much depends upon the computer used, the source language, and the goals of the implementation. The compiler writer should feel free to structure his compiler as he wishes, but at the same time he should have valid reasons for changing the structure drastically from the models presented; these models have not been designed without serious thought being given to the problem.

A multi-pass compiler usually first produces an internal form of the source program (quadruples, triples, etc.). Then, for each operator in the internal form, it produces the machine language instructions. It should be clear that the original semantic routines could just as well produce machine language directly, if a few restrictions are placed on the language. The main restriction is that declarations or specifications of a variable precede all uses of that variable. Of course, the semantic routines are bound to be more complicated, and the code produced won't be as good, but these drawbacks are often worth the extra compile-time speed gained.

Keep the number of passes in a compiler to a minimum, taking into account the size of the machine and the goals of the project. Each extra pass means more overhead and bookkeeping, and probably more time spent in implementation.

### Table Organization Within a Compiler

Use as few different tables and stacks whose sizes depend on the source program, as possible. This reduces the number of tables which may overflow, and increases the size of the source programs that may be compiled. To do this, make use of the compile-time stacks (in a bottom-up compiler), and the object code table as much as possible. For example, we kept the addresses of forward conditional branches for an if-statement in the semantic stack element corresponding to <if-clause> (section 13.2), and forward branches were linked together through the internal source program (section 13.3). The same ideas can be used when compiling for-loops, case statements, and the like.

When adding an element to a table at compile-time, <u>always</u> check for overflow. Many hours have been lost tracking down errors caused by unchecked tables overflowing, months or years after a compiler was "debugged."

In some systems, the programmer can specify how much memory his job should use. In such systems, when a compiler begins, it should ask for the maximum amount of memory it can have, and then portion it out to the tables whose sizes depend on the source program begin compiled. This includes the symbol table, stacks, the table containing the internal source program, and so forth. This allows small programs to be compiled in small regions, and penalizes only the large ones.

If one really wants to have many tables or stacks of unrestricted size, then the compiler should be written in a language which permits this in a systematic fashion. That is, at compile-time, the system should have a general list structured storage allocation scheme, with primitives for adding to tables and deleting elements from them. Such an implementation is bound to be slower because of the increased bookkeeping.

Use secondary storage to store tables as little as possible. Don't penalize small programs by always writing out a table; do it only if overflow occurs. Don't write out a table which is accessed in a random fashion (e.g. the symbol table). The internal source program is the most likely candidate for secondary storage, since it is built and accessed in a sequential manner, and I/O and the compiler itself can overlap to a certain extent. Naur(65) is a good description of an elaborate compiler running on a very small machine.

If secondary storage must be used, design the compiler so that I/O can overlap with the CPU. For example, if the internal source program must be written onto a disk, fill up one buffer with the first part of it. Then, while this buffer is being written out, the compiler can continue processing and generating the next part of the internal source program into a second buffer.

In the analysis part of a compiler, the two main data structures to be manipulated are the symbol table and the semantic stack. In compilers written in assembly language, one often starts the symbol table at one end of a large section of core, and the stack at the other end (see below). These tables grow together, and no overflow occurs unless they overlap.

```
+----------+--------+------------------------------------+
| COMPILER | TABLES | STACK ->         <- SYMBOL TABLE   |
+----------+--------+------------------------------------+
```

In interpreters which use hash coding for the symbol table, much space is often wasted because of the large number of unoccupied entries. This space can be utilized by storing parts of the internal source program to be interpreted there (with extra branches inserted at the obvious places). This slows down interpretation somewhat, but not enough to matter. The space could also be used for constants and static variables.

### Reentrant Code

A program or procedure is reentrant if, while it is being executed, anybody else may also begin executing it (by interrupting the present execution for a while). This is most useful in a multiprogramming or time-sharing environment, where several programs may call, say, a SIN routine which is reentrant. Only one copy of the routine need be kept in memory, no matter how many people are executing it.

If possible, a compiler should produce reentrant code. Just as important, or even more important, is for the compiler to be reentrant. If it is, no matter how many people are compiling at the same time, only <u>one</u> copy of the compiler need be present.

A program must satisfy the following conditions to be reentrant:

1. It doesn't modify itself. That is, the instructions of the program are never changed.
2. Any variables used in the program which are changed by it are allocated space in data areas which belong to the particular <u>execution</u> of the program. Thus, when the program is first invoked, it must either receive from the calling program or get for itself by calling a system subroutine, storage for its data areas. Note that the ALGOL runtime administration scheme discussed in section 8.9 followed these conventions.
3. The computer should have a fixed set of fast registers. In one or more of these are placed the address(es) of some of the programs data areas. Any reference to a variable in memory is always made using a (base) address in one of these registers. When any program is interrupted, the system must save the contents of these registers; when the program is again resumed, these registers are restored by the system.

### Debugging the Compiler

Tools for debugging the compiler should be implemented at an early stage. Routines should be written to output the following, in symbolic form (not just in octal or hexadecimal):

1. The syntax and semantic stacks
2. The symbol table entries
3. The internal source program
4. The final code, in symbolic and internal form
5. A trace of the syntax rules used in parsing
6. A trace of the semantic routines called

Spend some time designing these routines so that the output is compact and readable; this will make debugging easier. For example, if the final code in symbolic form uses only 20 characters per instruction, then output it 3 or 4 columns per page, instead of one.

You should be able to turn these debugging facilities on and off independently by, say, control cards interspersed throughout the source program being compiled. The scanner can recognize these cards and set the proper switches. Try to make it easy to get debugging output for only parts of a source program, so that it won't be necessary to get output for a whole program just to see how one statement compiled.

In general, the different parts of the compiler will be programmed and checked out in their logical order: scanner, syntax, semantics, program preparation, and code generation. Runtime organization can influence the compiler design quite a bit, so this should be designed early in the game.

Have other people prepare test data for your compiler (many commercial installations do this for all new programs). You yourself are quite likely to unintentionally write programs which only check out certain parts of it.

Each compiler should print out on the first page of each source program listing the version of the compiler being used, the date of the run, and any other information which will help in identification when people come with problems.

Don't take the debugging facilities out of the compiler when you think the compiler is debugged; it definitely isn't.

### Compile-Time Error Messages

These should be sufficiently clear so that the user need not refer to a special list of error messages and their meaning. Provide concise but meaningful messages.

An often used technique is to split each message into phrases, and to have each message represented by a sequence of pointers to phrases. Not only can this save memory (certain phrases will be used very often), but it allows more complex, sophisticated messages. To illustrate this, suppose messages are printed after the source program has been analyzed, and that each element of the "message list" contains four values:

1. The error message number
2. Card number on which the error occurred (if applicable)
3. Identifier which was used incorrectly (0 if not applicable)
4. Incoming symbol when the error occurred.

The error message number would be used to reference a list of instructions which indicate how the message is to be printed. For example, let us suppose the instruction list for message number 1 is

1. Print phrase 1
2. Print card number
3. Print phrase 2
4. Print identifier
5. Print phrase 3
6. Print incoming symbol
7. Print phrase 4

where the phrases are

1. "On card"
2. "identifier"
3. "occurring before"
4. "is declared twice"

Execution of the message containing (1, 20, ABC, ;) would cause the following message to be printed:

On card 20 identifier ABC occurring before ";" is declared twice

The program which prints the message is just a simple interpreter. Among the compilers using such a technique are PUFFT (see Rosen et al(65)) and the ALCOR ILLINOIS 7090 (Gries et al(65)).

### Runtime Error Checking and Messages

A compiler used extensively for debugging should generate numerous runtime checks to help the programmer. In most languages, the following should be checked:

1. Subscripts of a subscripted variable out of range
2. Division by zero and other arithmetic checks
3. References to a variable before it has been assigned a value

Such checks serve two purposes; runtime errors are detected for the programmer at the earliest possible moment, and the system itself is safeguarded from programmer errors. These checks should be made optional, so that once a program is debugged and running, they can be turned off. It would also be useful to turn them off selectively -- for parts of the source program.

Implementation of these runtime checks is fairly simple; the compiler generates the code to perform them. Determining whether a variable is undefined is perhaps the hardest to check. Some machines have some "type" bits attached to each word, and a word with type "instruction" cannot be used as an operand of an arithmetic instruction. Hence, if the compiler initializes all variables with type "instruction", an attempt to reference the variable before an assignment to it causes a hardware interrupt.

Some computers allow one to set the "parity bit" of each word of memory, so that a reference to that word causes a hardware interrupt.

In machines with no such features, there are two possibilities; first have a template with each variable to indicate whether it has a value or not (this wastes space). Secondly, initialize each variable to a valid value, but one which will rarely occur, and check at each reference for this value. /360 WATFOR initializes each one to X'808080...80' (see

Cress et al(69)). This means, of course, that if that value actually gets generated by a program in a valid way, an erroneous message will be printed.

In a block structured language, each time a block or procedure is entered all local variables must be set to the undefined value.

Any error messages printed during runtime should include the card number on which the error occurred. This can be done as indicated in chapter 16 on interpreters; insert a NO-OP with the card number just before the code generated for statements on that card. When an error occurrs, just sequence through the machine language instructions beginning at the error point until a NO-OP is found.

Another method, used in PL/I, is to number the _statements_ on the listing of the source program. The object code for each statement is preceded by instructions which move the statement number into a global location E. Upon detecting a runtime error, E contains the statement number which was being executed.

The best runtime debugging facility is a symbolic dump -- a list of all referencable variables at the error point, together with their current values, in a _readable_ form (not in octal or hexadecimal). Chapter 16 outlined this dump procedure for interpreters. In compilers, such a dump is harder to provide, since the symbol table and map of the different data areas is not around at runtime.

Bayer et al(67) describe how to produce such a dump in a compiler; we explain it briefly here, assuming a block structured language. The main point is that the compiler produces a _second_ object program, called the L-list, of the same length as the normal machine language object program. For each instruction of the object program, the corresponding L-list entry contains the following information:

1. The corresponding card number in the source deck
2. The block number of the block for which the instruction was generated
3. Information about the part of statement being executed -- procedure call, subscript calculation, IF-THEN test, etc.
4. The source program operator
5. The entry number in the symbol table of the operand with which the instruction is concerned (if applicable)

When a source program is compiled, the compiler puts the L-list, the symbol table, and the block list onto secondary storage. This information is not used unless a runtime error occurs or the programmer specifically asks for a dump. Hence, execution is not slowed down because of the dump facility.

When a runtime error occurs, a DUMP procedure is invoked, which looks at the memory map (list of subprograms loaded and where they are) to find out the subprogram in which the error occurred. Then if the L-list is available for that subprogram, it, the symbol table, and the block list are read into memory. From the L-list entry corresponding to the instruction which caused the runtime error, the block number, card number and other information is used to produce the symbolic dump described in chapter 16.

It may not be necessary to make up an L-list if enough information can be kept in the object program itself. The symbol table and block list must, however, be available.

In the few systems where such a facility was available, the programmers learned quite early in the game to explicitly divide by zero at the end of execution, just to get a dump.

### Bootstrapping

Suppose we want to implement a compiler for a source language L on a computer M. The compiler is to be written in L itself. L might be a compiler implementation language, or just a high-level language like FORTAN or ALGOL. The reason we want to implement it in itself is that there is no other good language to write it in, except possibly assembly language. There are two possible ways of proceeding.

Write a compiler in assembly language for a small subset L0 of L. This subset should be small, so that it is easy to implement, but large enough to be used in the next step. The next step is to rewrite the compiler for L0 in itself and check it out. Now, we try to "bootstrap" our way up to L in a series of steps, as follows. At each step i, i = 1, ..., n, extend the compiler for L[i-1] to a compiler for a language Li, by implementing other features of the desired language L. At each step, old parts of the current compiler can be rewritten in the new language Li to take advantage of these new features. The main reason for extending the compiler for L0 to a compiler for Ln = L in a series of steps instead of one big step is because, at each step we have a more powerful language Li in which to write the extension, thus making the job easier.

The second approach is to use an existing compiler for a language L' on a different machine M'. If L' = L (a compiler for the language already exists on the other machine), then just write the compiler in L to produce code for machine M. If L ≠ L', then proceed as follows. Write in L' a compiler for L0 (as before), which will produce code for machine M. Compiling this compiler on machine M' produces a machine language version of a compiler for L0 to run on machine M. Now proceed as in the first method of bootstrapping.

# Appendix:
# The Programming Language Used in the Book

The programming language is an extension and variation of ALGOL. The purpose of describing the language here is only to describe to the reader how the programs in this book are to be executed. The description is as brief as possible, and assumes a knowledge of ALGOL. It is not as precise as could be in many cases; we rely on the reader's knowledge of programming languages to fill in the obvious or unimportant (for our purposes) details. The two points where we give more explanation and examples are the use of pointers and the use of structured values.

### Identifiers

An <identifier> has the format

<identifier> ::= <letter> {<letter> | <digit>}

where a <digit> is one of the characters 0, 1, ..., 9 and a <letter> is one of the characters $, A, B, ..., Z, a, b, ..., z. <Identifier>s are used as names of variables, procedure names, and labels. Certain identifiers are "reserved" and are not to be used in this way. They are: ARRAY, BEGIN, BOOLEAN, CASE, CAT, CHARACTER, CONTENTS, DO, ELSE, END, ENDCASE, FALSE, FOR, GOTO, GO TO, IF, INTEGER, POINTER, REAL, RETURN, STEP, STRING, THEN, TRUE, UNTIL, and WHILE.

### Constants

A sequence of one or more <digit>s 0, 1, ..., 9 is an INTEGER constant, as usual. An INTEGER constant may also be given in hexadecimal form. For example, the hexadecimal constant X'A' is equivalent to the constant 10, while X'3B' is equivalent to 59.

The constants of type BOOLEAN are TRUE and FALSE.

If $C^1$, $C^2$, ..., Cn are EBCDIC characters, then '$C^1C^2$...Cn' and "$C^1C^2$...Cn" are equivalent STRING constants consisting of the string of characters $C^1$, $C^2$, ..., Cn.

The constant 0 is also a POINTER constant; assigned to a POINTER variable, it means that the variable points at, or refers to, no other value.

### Data Types and Declaration of Variables

The basic data types in the language are INTEGER (any signed integer), REAL (any real number), BOOLEAN (TRUE or FALSE), CHARACTER (any EBCDIC character), STRING (zero, one, or more CHARACTERs), and POINTER (the address of, or a reference to, some other value).

If <type> is one of the basic types or a programmer-defined structured type (see below), then a declaration D has the format

```
D ::= <type> <identifier>, <identifier>, ..., <identifier>
```

and indicates that the <identifier>s are names of variables which can be assigned values of the given <type> (e.g. REAL A, B, C5).

Besides values with basic data types, a program can create, reference, and change two kinds of "composite" values. A declaration

```
D ::= <type> ARRAY <identifier> {, <identifier>}
              [ L1 : U1 ... , In : Un ]
```

declares the <identifier>s to be names of n-dimensional arrays with type <type>. As in ALGOL, the INTEGER expressions Li and Ui give the lower and upper bounds of the ith dimension of the array. The <type> can be a basic data type or a programmer-defined structured value type. The brackets [ and ] above are <u>not</u> metasymbols.

A <u>structured value</u> consists of a sequence of n other values (n > 0) called <u>components</u> or <u>fields</u>. Each of the components has a name and a <type>, and can be assigned values of that <type>. For example, the diagram below indicates that B is a structured value consisting of three components named N, M, and Q, with types REAL, INTEGER, and POINTER, respectively:

```
B  N (REAL)      M (INTEGER)  Q(POINTER)
 ----------------------------------------
| value of N | value of M | value of Q |
 ----------------------------------------
```

The declaration

```
STRUCTURE ST (REAL N, INTEGER M, POINTER Q)
```

could be used to declare ST to be a new structured value <type>. Any value with this <type> consists of three components as indicated. We could then declare variables to have this type. For example, to declare B to have this type, so that B has the form shown in the diagram above, use the declaration

```
ST B
```

Note that one can declare arrays of structured values.

Actually, we will not need to declare structured values and variables formally. Rather, we indicate by diagrams and English sentences, which variables can be assigned structured values, and what the names and types of the components are. The reader is referred to section 8.6 for a brief discussion of the use of structured values in three different languages.

### Scope of Identifiers

ALGOL-like block structure is used in this language to define the scope and allocation of variables. We will often talk about a variable A being "global" to several program fragments. This means that A is declared in a block surrounding all of the program fragments. In FORTRAN, A would be in COMMON.

### Procedure Declarations

Procedures are declared as in ALGOL. The syntax of a procedure declaration is

```
D              ::=  PROCEDURE <heading> ; {<specification> ;} <body>
<heading>      ::= [<type>] <identifier> [ ( <par> {, <par>} ) ]
<body>         ::= S (any statement)
<specification>
               ::= <type> [ARRAY] <identifier> {, <identifier>}
```

Each <par> is an identifier, and is called a *formal parameter*. If <type> appears in the <heading>, the procedure is a function which returns a value of that type. During execution of the procedure, an assignment to the function name should be executed to indicate the value to be returned. The specifications describe the types of the formal parameters; they need not be included if the types are obvious from the context and the surrounding discussion. The specifications may sometimes appear within the parameter list itself (this is not shown in the syntax description above). For example,

```
PROCEDURE X (INTEGER A, B; POINTER P); ...
```

indicates that the formal parameters A, B, and P have types INTEGER, INTEGER, and POINTER, respectively.

All actual parameters are called by reference unless otherwise specified (see page 188). When the procedure body is finished executing, or when a RETURN is executed, control returns to the point following the point of call.

### Variables and Values: Using Pointers

1. Identifiers. If an identifier has been declared to be a variable name, then that identifier references the <variable>:

```
<variable> ::= <identifier>
```

2. Subscripted variables. Let A be an n-dimensional array. As in ALGOL, the subscripted variable A[$e^1$, $e^2$, ..., en] references the appropriate array element. The expressions ei must be of type INTEGER. We also allow the syntax

```
<identifier> ( e¹, e², ..., en)
```

3. Components of structured values. Suppose B is any <variable> with a structured type. Let B's components be M, N, ..., Q. Then B.M, B.N, ..., B.Q reference <variable>s which are the components. Thus we can change the value of the component M to 5 (say) by executing B.M:=5. Other notations used in other languages for referencing component M are "M OF B" and "M(B)". The reader is referred to section 8.6 for brief discussions of these concepts.

4. Substrings. Let X be any STRING variable. Then

```
SUBSTR(X,e¹,e²)
```

(where the ei are INTEGER expressions) is a STRING variable whose value is the characters $e^1$, $e^1+1$, ..., $e^1+e^2-1$ of X. Please note that the characters of X are counted beginning at 0. Thus, if X = 'ABCD', we can change X to 'A1XD' by executing

```
SUBSTR(X,1,2) := '1X'
```

5. Indirect addressing. Let P be a POINTER variable and E be any expression. Then executing either

```
P := @E        or        P := ADDRESS(E)
```

assigns to P the address of a location which contains the result of evaluating E. If E is a <variable> then P will be a reference to that <variable>. We can now reference E by using

```
CONTENTS(P)
```

If E is a variable, we can change its value;

```
CONTENTS(P) := 3      is equivalent to      E := 3.
```

Thus we have indirect addressing as one finds in many computers.

Suppose P refers to a structured variable B, and that B has a component named M. Then we may use

```
P.M        as an abbreviation for        CONTENTS(P).M
```

Let us give a few examples of this. Suppose P is a pointer, and that B and C are structured variables with components N, M, and Q, as indicated below:

```
 P         B  N    M    Q      C  N    M    Q
┌───┐     ┌──────────────┐    ┌──────────────┐
│ 0 │     │ 3 │ 0  │ 0  │    │ 6 │ 0  │ 0  │
└───┘     └──────────────┘    └──────────────┘
```

Executing P:=@B; B.Q:=@C changes the diagram to

```
P         B  N    M    Q     C  N    M    Q
┌───┐     ┌──────────────┐   ┌──────────────┐
| ──┼──>| 3 | 0 |  ─┼──>| 6 | 0 | 0 |
└───┘     └──────────────┘   └──────────────┘
```

where the arrows indicate the values of pointer variables P and B.Q. Executing P.M:=5 changes the diagram to

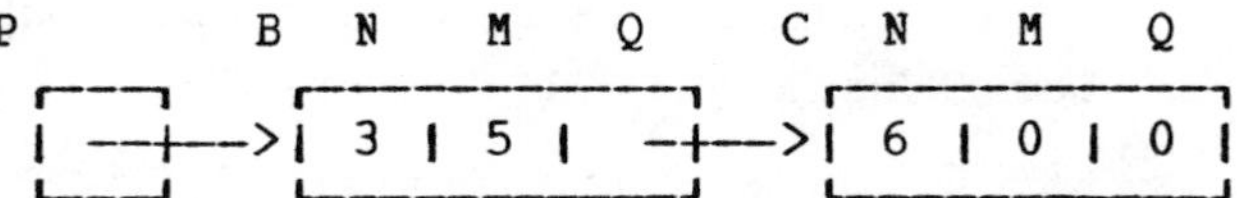

Executing P.Q.M:=4 changes the diagram to

```
P         B  N    M    Q     C  N    M    Q
┌───┐     ┌──────────────┐   ┌──────────────┐
| ──┼──>| 3 | 5 |  ─┼──>| 6 | 4 | 0 |
└───┘     └──────────────┘   └──────────────┘
```

P.Q references the variable consisting of component Q of B; its value is the address of C. Thus P.Q.M refers to component M of C. P.Q.M is equivalent to CONTENTS(CONTENTS(P).Q).M.

#### Expressions

Operations in an expression are evaluated from left to right, taking into account the use of parentheses and the priorities of the operators, as usual. These are given in the following table (the operator on the first line has highest priority):

```
**
- (unary) @
* / //
+ - (binary)
= ≠ < ≤ > ≥
NOT
AND
OR
CAT
```

Any variable or constant is an expression. If $e^1$ is an expression, then so is ( $e^1$ ) .

1. Arithmetic expressions. Let $e^1$ and $e^2$ be arithmetic (REAL or INTEGER) expressions. Then so are $e^1+e^2$, $e^1-e^2$, $-e^1$, $e^1*e^2$, $e^1/e^2$, $e^1//e^2$, and $e^1**e^2$. $e^1//e^2$ yields the largest integer not greater than $e^1/e^2$. Thus 3//2=1, 4//2=2, and (-3)//2=-2.

2. Boolean expressions. If $e^1$ and $e^2$ are Boolean expressions, then so are

$e^1$ AND $e^2$, $e^1$ OR $e^2$, and NOT $e^1$.

The three operators have the usual meanings.

The relational operators are =, ≠ >, ≥, <, and ≤. If $e^1$ and $e^2$ are expressions and R is a relational operator, then the relation $e^1$ R $e^2$ is an expression with obvious value TRUE or FALSE. If $e^1$ is arithmetic, then so must be $e^2$.

If $e^1$ is Boolean, then $e^2$ must be also. In this case R must be = or ≠. If $e^1$ is a CHARACTER or STRING, then so must $e^2$ be. In this case, the shortest of $e^1$ and $e^2$ is padded with blanks at the end until they are the same length, and the comparison is made according to the EBCDIC representation of the characters.

If $e^1$ is a POINTER, then $e^2$ must be. R must be either = or ≠.

4. Pointer expressions. Let $e^1$ be any expression or variable. Then @$e^1$ and ADDRESS($e^1$) both yield a POINTER value which is the address of or a reference to the value of the expression or variable. The constant 0 is also a POINTER value, which refers to no other value.

5. Structured expressions. Let ST be some structured type consisting of components N1, N2, ..., Nn with types R1, R2, ..., Rn, respectively. Let $e^1$, $e^2$, ..., en be expressions of types R1, R2, ... Rn, respectively. Then

($e^1$, $e^2$, ..., en)

is an expression of type ST. ei is the value of the ith component of the expression.

### Statements

Statements are executed in order of occurrence, unless changed by a branch statement. In the brief descriptions of the kinds of statements that follows, "S" is a nonterminal meaning "statement".

1. Labeled statement. S ::= <label> : S

   Any statement may be labeled. The <label> must be an <identifier> or unsigned integer.

2. Empty statement. S ::=

   This allows flexibiltiy in writing programs and keeps the syntax description simple.

3. Assignment statement. S ::= <variable> := <expr>

   This is executed as in ALGOL, with the usual conversion of types being performed automatically. The address of the variable is evaluated, the expression is evaluated, and the result of the expression is assigned to the variable.

4. Branch statement. S ::= GOTO <label> | GO TO <label>

   Execution continues at the statement labeled <label>.

5. Conditional statement. S ::= IF <expr> THEN $S^1$ [ELSE $S^2$]

   The expression is evaluated to yield a Boolean result TRUE or FALSE. If TRUE, $S^1$ is executed; if FALSE, and if $S^2$ is present, $S^2$ is executed. An ELSE belongs with the closest possible preceding THEN.

6. Compound statement. S ::= BEGIN S {; S} END

   The statements S are executed in order. Compound statements are used to group several statements together as a unit.

7. Block. S ::= BEGIN D ; {D ;} S {; S} END

   This is the ALGOL block. There must be at least one declaration D. Upon entry to the block, storage is allocated to the variables declared in the declarations. The statements are then executed in order. When an exit occurs from the block, storage allocated previously to the variables in the block is released. This exit may occur because of a branch statement, a RETURN statement, or because execution of the last statement S is finished.

8. WHILE statment. S ::= WHILE <expr> DO $S^1$

   This is equivalent to the statement

   ```
   AGAIN: IF <expr> THEN BEGIN S¹; GOTO AGAIN END
   ```

9. FOR statement. S ::= FOR <variable> ::= <expr> STEP <expr> UNTIL <expr> DO $S^1$

   This is executed as in ALGOL.

10. CASE statement. S ::= CASE <expr> OF S {; S} ENDCASE | CASE <expr> OF BEGIN S {; S} END

    As can be seen, there are two equivalent forms of the case statement. A case statement is executed as follows: the <expr> is evaluated to yield an integer i. The ith statement in the list of statements is executed. Control then passes to the point just beyond the case statement. If a branch occurs from anywhere into one of the substatements S, then when execution of S is finished, control passes to the point just beyond the case statement.

11. Procedure or function call.

```
S ::= <identifier> [ ( <par> , <par>, ... , <par> ) ]
```

The parameters can be any expression or array name. They are called by reference (see page 188) unless otherwise specified. The call is executed as in FORTRAN or ALGOL, with the usual correspondence between actual and formal parameters. Procedures may be recursive. Two standard functions and their definitions, which are used in the programs, are:

```
SIGN(X) = IF X < 0 THEN -1 ELSE IF X = 0 THEN 0 ELSE +1
MAXIMUM(X,Y) = IF X < Y THEN Y ELSE X
```

12. RETURN statement.    S ::= RETURN

Return to the calling pcint. May only occur in a procedure body.

# References

The following abbreviations are used:

| | |
|---|---|
| CACM | Communications of the ACM |
| JACM | Journal of the ACM |
| NACM | Proceedings of the National ACM Conference |
| SJCC | Proceedings of the Spring Joint Computer Conference |
| FJCC | Proceedings of the Fall Joint Computer Conference |
| EJCC | Proceedings of the Eastern Joint Computer Conference |
| WJCC | Proceedings of the Western Joint Computer Conference |
| AnnR | Annual Review in Automatic Programming, Pergammon Press |
| Comp J | Computer Journal |
| IFIP | Proceedings of the IFIP Congress |

The name of an author with more than one publication is followed by the year in parentheses; if more than one publication in one year, the year is followed by a, b, ....

Allard, R. W., Wolf, K. A., and Zemlin, R. A. Some effects of the 6600 Computer on language structures. CACM 7 (Feb. 1964), 112-127.

Allen, F. E. Program optimization. In AnnR 5 (1969), 239-307.

Anderson, J. P. A note on compiling algorithms. CACM 7 (March 1964), 149-150.

Arden, B. W., Galler, B. A. and Graham, R. M. (61) An algorithm for equivalence declarations. CACM 4 (July 1961), 310-314.

___, ___, and ___. (62) An algorithm for translating Boolean expressions. JACM 9 (April 1962), 222-239.

Backus, J. W. The syntax and semantics of the proposed international algebraic language of the Zurich ACM-GAMM Conference. Proc. International Conf. on Information Processing, UNESCO (1959), 125-132.

___, et al. The FORTRAN automatic coding system. WJCC (1957), 188-198.

Baer, J. L., and Bovet, D. P. Compilation of arithmetic expressions for parallel computations. IFIP 68, B4-B10.

Batson, A. The organization of symbol tables. CACM 8 (Feb 1965), 111-112.

Bauer, H., Becker, S., and Graham, S. ALGOL W implementation. CS 98, Computer Science Dept., Stanford Univ., 1968.

Bayer, R., Gries, D., Paul, M., and Wiehle, H. R. The ALCOR ILLINOIS 7090/7094 post mortem dump. CACM 10 (Dec 1967), 804-808.

Belady, L. A. A study of replacement algorithms for a virtual-storage computer. IBM Systems Journal 5 (1966), 78-82.

Bell, J. R. (69) A new method for determining linear precedence functions for precedence grammars. CACM 12 (Oct 1969), 567-569.

___. (70) Quadratic quotient method: a hash code eliminating secondary clustering. CACM 13 (Feb 1970), 107-109.

Berman, R., Sharp, J., and Sturges, L. Syntactical charts of COBOL 61. CACM 5 (May 1962), 260.

Berns, G. M. Description of FORMAT, a text-processing program. CACM 12 (March 1969), 141-146.

Breuer, M. A. Generation of optimal code for expressions via factorization. CACM 12 (June 1969), 333-340.

Brooker, R. and Morris, D. A general translation program for phrase structure languages. JACM 9 (Jan 1962), 1-10.

Brooker, R. et al. The compiler-compiler. AnnR 3 (1963), 229-275.

___, Morris, D., and Rohl, J. S. (62) Trees and routines. Comp J 5 (April 1962), 33.

___, ___, and ___. (67) Experience with the compiler compiler. Comp J 9 (1967), 345-349.

Brown, P.J. (67) The ML/1 macro processor. CACM 10 (Oct 1967), 618-623.

___. (69) A survey of macro processors. AnnR 6 (1969), 37-88.

Busam, V. and Englund, D. Optimization of expressions in FORTRAN. CACM 12 (Dec 1969), 666-674.

Cheatham, T. E. The TGS-II translator-generator system. IFIP 1965, 592-593.

___, and Sattley, K. Syntax directed compiling. SJCC 1964, 31-57.

Chomsky, N. (56) Three models for the description of language. IREE Trans. Inform. Theory, vol. IT2, (1956), 113-124.

___. (59) On certain formal properties of grammars. Information and Control 2, (1959), 137-167.

___. (63) Formal Properties of Grammars. In _Handbook of Mathematical Psychology, Vol. 2_, Luce, Bush and Galanter (Eds.) John Wiley and Sons, Inc., New York, 1963, 323-418.

Cocke, J. and Schwartz, J. T. Programming languages and their compilers. Preliminary notes. Courant Inst. of Math. sciences. New York Univ., 1970.

Cohen, D. J., and Gotlieb, C. C. A list structure form of grammars for syntactic analysis. Computing Surveys 2 (March 1970), 65-81.

Colmerauer, A. Total precedence relations. JACM 17 (Jan 1970), 14-30.

Conway, M. E. Design of a separable transition diagram compiler. CACM 6 (July 1963), 396-408.

Conway, R. W. and Maxwell, W. L. CORC - the Cornell computing language. CACM 6 (June 1963), 317-321.

___, et al. PL/C. A high performance subset of PL/I. TR 70-55, Computer Science Dept. Cornell Univ., 1970.

Cress, P. H. et al. Description of /360 WATFOR. Dept. of Applied Analysis and Computer Science, Univ. of Waterloo. Report No. CSTR-1000.

Dantzig, G. B. and Reynolds, G. Optimal assignment of computer storage by chain decomposition of partially ordered sets. Univ. of Calif., Berkeley. Operations research center Rpt. No. ORC-66-6, March 1966.

DeRemer, F. Simple LR(k) grammars. Computer Science Dept., Univ. of Calif at Santa Cruz, May 1970.

Dijkstra, E. W. An ALGOL 60 translator for the X1. AnnR 3 (1963), 329-356.

Domolki, B. An algorithm for syntactic analysis. Computational Linguist. 3 (1964), 29-46. (Hungarian Journal).

Earley, J. Generating a recognizer for a BNF grammar. Technical Report, Carnegie Inst. of Tech., Pittsburgh, Penn. June 1965.

Ehrman, J. Q-type address constants, dummy external symbols, and pseudo registers. CGTM 66, Stanford Linear Accelerator Center. April 1969.

Eickel, J. Generation of parsing algorithms for Chomsky 2-type languages. Report No. 6401. Math. Inst. der Tech. Hochschule, Munich, 1964.

___, Paul, M., Bauer, F. L., and Samelson, K. A syntax controlled generator of formal language processors. CACM 6 (Aug 1963), 451-455.

Evans, A. An Algol 60 Compiler. AnnR 4 (1964), 87-124.

Fateman, R. J. Optimal code for serial and parallel computation. CACM 12 (Dec 1969), 694-695.

Feldman, J. A. A formal semantics for computer languages and its application in a compiler-compiler. CACM 9 (Jan 1966), 3-9.

___, and Gries, D. Translator writing systems. CACM 11 (Feb 1968), 77-113.

Fischer, M. J. Some properties of precedence languages. Proceedings ACM symposium on theory of computing (May 1969), 181-188.

Flores, I. Computer Sorting. Prentice-Hall, Inc. Englewood Cliffs. 1969.

Floyd, R. W. (61a) An algorithm for coding efficient arithmetic operations. CACM 4 (Jan 1961), 42-51.

___. (61b) A descriptive language for symbol manipulation. JACM 8 (Oct 1961), 579-584.

___. (63) Syntactic analysis and operator precedence. JACM 10 (July 1963), 316-333.

___. (64a) Bounded context syntactic analysis. CACM 7 (Feb 1964), 62-67.

___. (64b) The syntax of programming languages -- a survey. IEEE Trans. EC13, 4 (Aug 1964), 346-353.

Freeman, D. Error correction in CORC: the Cornell computing language. Thesis, Cornell Univ., 1963.

Galler, B., and Perlis, A. J. A proposal for definitions in ALGOL. CACM 10 (April 1967), 204-219.

Garwick, J. V. GARGOYLE, a language for compiler writing. CACM 7 (Jan 1964), 16-20.

Gear, C. W. (64) Optimization of the address field computation in the ILLIAC II assembler. Comp J 6 (Jan 1964), 332.

___. (65) High speed compilation of efficient object code. CACM 8 (Aug 1965), 483-488.

Gilbert, P. On the syntax of algorithmic languages. JACM 13 (Jan 1966), 90-107.

Gill, A. Introduction to the Theory of Finite-State Machine. McGraw-Hill Book Co., New York, 1962.

Ginsburg, S. (62) An Introduction to Mathematical Machine Theory. Addison-Wesley, Reading, Mass., (1962).

___. (66) <u>The Mathematical Theory of Context-Free Languages</u>. McGraw-Hill Book Company, N. Y., 1966.

Glennie, A. E. On the syntax machine and the construction of a universal compiler. Techn. Rpt. No. 2, Computation Center, Carnegie Inst. of Tech. (1960).

Gorn, S. Specification languages for mechanical languages and their processors, a baker's dozen. CACM 4 (Dec 1961), 532-542.

Gower, J. C. The handling of multiway tables on computers. Comp J 4, (Jan 1962), 280-286.

Grau, A. A. Recursive processes and ALGOL translation. CACM 4 (Jan 1961), 10-15.

Greenwald, I. A technique for handling macro instructions. CACM 2 (Nov 1959), 21-22.

___, and Kane, M. The SHARE 709 system: programming and modification. JACM 6 (1959), 396.

Gries, D. The use of transition matrices in compiling. CACM 11 (Jan 1968), 26-34.

___, Paul, M., and Wiehle, H. R. Some techniques used in the ALCOR ILLINOIS 7090. CACM 8 (Aug 1965), 496-500.

Griffiths, T. V., and Petrick, S. R. On the relative efficiencies of context-free grammar recognizers. CACM 8 (May 1965), 289-299.

Halstead, M. H. <u>Machine-Independent Computer Programming</u>. Spartan Books, Washington D. C. 1962.

Halpern, M. (64) XPOP: a metalanguage without metaphysics. FJCC 1964, 57-68.

___. (67) A manual of the XPOP programming system. Electronic Sciences Lab., Lockheed Missiles and Space Company, Palo Alto, California, March 1967.

___. (68) Toward a general processor for programming languages. CACM 11 (Jan 1968), 15-25.

Hellerman, H. (62) Addressing multidimensional arrays. CACM 5 (April 1962), 205-207.

___. (66) Parallel processing of algebraic expressions. IEEE Trans. EC-15 (Feb 1966), 82-91.

Hext, J., and Roberts, P. Syntax analysis by Domolki's algorithm. Comp J 13 (Aug 1970), 263-271.

Hill, V., Langmaack, H., Schwarz, H. R., and Seegmuller, G. Efficient handling of subscripted variables in ALGOL 60 compilers. Proc. Symbolic Languages in Data Processing, Gordon and Breach, New York, 1962, 331-340.

Hoare, C. A. R. Record handling. In Programming Languages. Academic Press, 1968, pages 291-347.

Hopcroft, J. and Ullman, J. Formal languages and their Relation to Automata. Addison-Wesley, New York, 1969.

Hopgood, F. R. A. Compiling Techniques. American Elsevier, Inc., New York 1969.

Horning, J. J. Empirical comparison of LR(k) and precedence parsers. Memorandum. Computer research Group, Univ. of Toronto. Aug 1970.

Horwitz, I. P. et al. Index register allocation. JACM 13 (Jan 1966), 43-61.

Huskey, H. D. Compiling techniques for algebraic expressions. Comp J 4 (1961), 10-19.

___, Love, R., and Wirth, N. A syntactic description of BC NELIAC. CACM 6 (July 1963), 367-375.

Huxtable, D. H. R. On writing an optimizing translator for ALGOL 60. In Introduction to System Programming. Academic Press Inc., New York, 1964.

IBM. (a) FORTRAN (H) Compiler, Programming Logic Manual. Form Y28-6642.

IBM. (b) PL/I (F) Compiler, Programming Logic Manual. Form Y28-6800.

IBM. (c) An Introduction to the Compile-Time Facilities of PL/I. Technical Publication C20-1689. IBM Corporation. August, 1968.

IBM. (d) Operating System /360 Assembler Language. IBM Form C28-6514.

Ichbiah, J. D. and Morse, S. P. A technique for generating almost optimal Floyd-Evans productions for precedence grammars. CACM 13 (Aug 1970), 501-508.

Ingerman, P. Z. (61a) Thunks. CACM 4 (Jan 1961), 55-58.

___. (61b) Dynamic declarations. CACM 4 (Jan 1961), 59-60.

___. (66) A Syntax Oriented Translator. Academic Press, New York, 1966.

Irons, E. T. (61a) A syntax directed compiler for ALGOL 60. CACM 4 (Jan 1961), 51-55.

___. (63a) The structure and use of the syntax-directed compiler. AnnR 3 (1963), 207-227.

___. (63b) An error correcting parse algorithm. CACM 6 (Nov 1963), 669-673.

___. (64) "Structural connections" in formal languages. CACM 7 (Feb 1964), 67-72.

___, and Feurzeig, W. Comments on the implementation of recursive procedures and blocks in ALGOL 60. CACM 4 (Jan 1961), 65-69.

Johnson, L. R. Indirect chaining method for addressing on secondary keys. CACM 4 (May 1961), 218-222.

Johnson, W. L., Porter, J. H., Ackley, S. I., and Ross, D. T. Automatic generation of efficient lexical processors using finite state techniques. CACM 11 (Dec 1968), 805-813.

Kanner, H. An algebraic translator. CACM 2 (Oct 1959), 19-22.

Kent, W. Assembler-language programming. Computing Surveys 1 (Dec 1969), 183-196.

Kleene, S. C. Representation of events in nerve-sets, in Automata Studies pp. 3-42. Princeton Univ. Press, Princeton, N.J. 1956.

Knuth, D. E. (59) Runcible - algebraic translation on a limited computer. CACM 2 (Jan 1959), 18-21.

___. (65) On the translation of languages from left to right. Inf. Contr. 8 (Oct 1965), 607-639.

___. (68) The Art of Computer Programming. Vol 1. Addison-Wesley Publishing Company, Inc. Reading, Mass., 1968.

___. (70) The Art of Computer Programming. Vol. 3. Addison-Wesley Publishing Company, Inc. Reading, Mass., 1970.

Kuno, S. and Oettinger, A. G. Multiple-path syntactic analyzer. Information Processing 62 (IFIP Congress), Popplewell (Ed.), North Holland Publishing Co., Amsterdam, 1962, 306-311.

Leavenwirth, B. M. (64) FORTRAN IV as a syntax language. CACM 7 (Feb 1964), 72-80.

___. (66) Syntax macros and extended translation. CACM (Nov 1966), 790-793.

Lewis, P. M. II and Stearns, R. E. Syntax-directed transductions. JACM 15 (July 1968), 465-488.

Loeckx, J. An algorithm for the construction of bounded-context parsers. Report R99. Manufacture Belge de Lampes et de Materiel Electronique. March 1969.

Lowry, E. and Medlock, C. Object code optimization. CACM 12 (Jan 1969), 13-22.

Luccio, F. A comment on index register allocation. CACM 10 (Sept 1967), 572-574.

Lynch, W. C. A high-speed parsing algorithm for ICOR grammars. Report No. 1097, Andrew Jennings Computing Center, Case Western Reserve Univ., 1968.

Martin, D. F. Boolean matrix methods for the detection of simple precedence grammars. CACM 11 (Oct 1968), 685-687.

Maurer, W. D. An improved hash code for scatter storage. CACM 11 (Jan 1968), 35-38.

McCarthy, J. Recursive functions of symbolic expressions and their computation by machine. CACM 4 (April 1960), 184-195.

McClure, R. M. TMG -- a syntax-directed compiler. NACM 20 (1965), 262-274.

McCulloch, W. S. and Pitts, W. A logical calculus of the ideas immanent in nervous activity. Bull. Math. Biophysics 5, 115-333.

McIlroy, M. D. (60) Macro instruction extensions of compiler languages. CACM 3 (April 1960), 214-220.

___. (63) A variant method of file searching. CACM 6 (March 63), 101.

McKeeman, W. M. (65) Peephole optimization. CACM 8 (July 1965), 443-444.

___. (66) An approach to language design. CS 48, Computer Science Dept., Stanford Univ., 1966.

___, Horning, J. J., and Wortman, D. B. _A Compiler Generator implemented for the IBM System/360_. Prentice Hall, 1970.

Mendicino, S. and Zwackenberg, R. A FORTRAN code optimizer for the CDC 6600. UCRL-14162, Lawrence Radiation Lab, April 1965.

Mooers, C., and Deutsch, L. P. TRAC, a text handling language. NACM 20 (1965), 229-246.

Moore, E. F. Gedanken experiments on sequential machines. Automata Studies, pp 129-153. Princeton Univ. Press, Princeton, 1956.

Morgan, H. L. Spelling correction in system programs. CACM 13 (Feb 1970), 90-94.

Morris, R. Scatter storage techniques. CACM 11 (Jan 1968), 38-44.

Nakata, I. A note on compiling algorithms for arithmetic expressions. CACM 10 (Aug 1967), 492-494.

Naur, P. (63a) (Ed.). Revised report on the algorithmic language ALGOL 60. CACM 6, (Jan 1963), 1-17.

___. (63b) The design of the GIER ALGOL compiler. BIT 3 (1963), 124-140, 145-166.

___. (65) The design of the GIER ALGOL compiler. AnnR 4 (1965), 49-85.

Parikh, R. J. Language generating devices. M.I.T. Research Lab. Electron. Quart. Prog. Report. 60, 1961, 199-212. (Also in JACM 13 (Oct 1966), 570-581, under the title: On context free languages.)

Paul, M. ALGOL 60 processors and a processor generator. Proc. IFIP Congress, Munich, 1962, 493-497.

Peterson, W. W. Addressing for random-access storage. IBM Journal of Research and Development 1 (1957), 130.

Plaskow, J. and Schumann, S. The TRANGEN system on the M460 computer. AFCRL-66-516 (July 1966).

Post, E. L. A variant of a recursively unsolvable problem. Bull. Am. Math. Soc., 52 (1946), 264-268.

Purdon, P. W. A transitive closure algorithm. Computer Sciences Technical Report # 33, July 1968. Univ. of Wisconsin.

Radke, C. E. The use of quadratic residue search. CACM 13 (Feb 1970), 103-105.

Randell, B. and Russell, D .J. ALGOL 60 Implementation. Academic Press, London, 1964.

Redziejowski, R. R. On arithmetic expressions and trees. CACM 12 (Feb 1969), 81-84.

Reynolds, J. C. An introduction to the COGENT Programming System. NACM 20 (1965), 422-436.

Rishel, W. J. Incremental compilers. Datamation. Also in Software for Computer Systems, College Readings, Inc. Arlington, Va. 1970.

Rosen, S. A compiler-building system developed by Brooker and Morris. CACM 7 (July 1964), 403-414.

___, Spurgeon, R. A., and Donnelly, J. K. PUFFT - the Purdue University fast FORTRAN translator. CACM 8 (Nov 1965), 661-666.

Rosenkrantz, D. S. and Stearns, R. E. Properties of deterministic top down grammars. ACM Symposium on Theory of Computing (May 1969), 165-180.

Ross, D. (66) AED bibliography. Memo MAC-M-278-2, Project MAC, M.I.T., Cambridge, Mass., Sept. 1966.

___. (67a) The AED approach to generalized computer-aided design. NACM 1967, 367-385.

___. (67b) The AED free storage package. CACM 10 (Aug 1967), 481-492.

Rutishauser, H. Automatische Rechenplanfertigung bei programm-gesteuerten Rechenmaschinen. Mitt. Inst. fur Angew. Math. der ETH Zurich, Nr. 3, 1952.

Samelson, K., and Bauer, F. L. Sequential formula translation. CACM 3 (Feb 1960), 76-83.

Sattley, K. Allocation of storage for arrays in ALGOL 60. CACM 4 (Jan 1961), 60-65.

Schay, G. and Spruth, W. G. Analysis of a file addressing method. CACM 5 (Aug 1962), 459-462.

Schneider, F. W. and Johnson, G. D. Meta-3; A syntax-directed compiler writing compiler to generate efficient code. NACM 19 (1964).

Schorre, D. V. META II: A syntax-oriented compiler writing language. NACM 19 (1964), page D1.3.

Shaw, A. Lecture notes on a course in systems programming. CS 52, Computer Science Dept., Stanford Univ., 1966.

Shaw, C. J. A specification of Jovial. CACM 6 (Dec 1963), 721-735.

Sethi, R. and Ullman, J. D. The generation of optimal code for arithmetic expressions. JACM 17 (Oct 1970), 715-728.

Sheridan, P. B. The FORTRAN arithmetic-compiler of the IBM FORTRAN automatic coding system. CACM 2 (Feb 1959), 9.

Sibley, R. A. The SLANG system. CACM 4 (Jan 1961), 75-84.

Squire, J. S. A translation algorithm for a multiple processor computer. NACM 1963.

Standish, T. A. A data definition facility for programming languages. Computer Science Rpt., Carnegie Inst. of Tech., May 1967.

Stearns, R. E. and Lewis II, P. M. Property grammars and table machines. IEEE Conference record of the 1968 annual symp. on switching and automata theory, 106-119.

Stone, H. S. One-pass compilation of arithmetic expressions for a parallel processor. CACM 10 (April 1967), 220-223.

Strachey, C. A general purpose macrogenerator. Comp J 8 (1965-1966), 225-241.

Taylor, W., Turner, L., and Waychoff, R. A syntactical chart of ALGOL 60. CACM 4 (Sept 1961), 393.

Tixier, V. Recursive functions of regular expressions in language analysis. CS 58. Computer Science Dept., Stanford Univ., March 1967.

Unger, S. A global parser for context-free phrase structure grammars. CACM 11 (April 1968), 240-247.

Van der Poel, L. W. The construction of an ALGOL translator for a small computer. In Prog. Lang. in Data Processing, 229-236. Gordon and Breach, 1963.

Wagner, R. A. Some techniques for algebraic optimization with application to matrix arithmetic expressions. Thesis. Carneqie-Mellon Univ., June 1968.

Waite, W. A language-independent macro processor. CACM 10 (July 1967), 433-440.

Warshall, S. (61) A syntax directed generator. EJCC 1961, 295-305.

___. (62) A theorem on Boolean matrices. JACM 9 (Jan 1962), 11-12.

___, and Shapiro, R. M. A general-purpose table-driven compiler. SJCC 1964, 59-65.

Wegner, P. (68a) *Programming Languages, Information Structures, and Machine Organization*. McGraw-Hill, New York, 1968.

Whitney, G. An extended BNF for specifying the syntax of declarations. SJCC 1969, 801-812.

Wirth, N. and Weber, H. Euler -- a generalization of ALGOL and its definition. Part I, Part II. CACM 9 (Jan, Feb 1966), 13-25, 89-99.

___, and Hoare, C. A. R. A contribution to the development of ALGOL. CACM 9 (June 1966), 413-432.

Yershov, A. L. (58) On programming of arithmetic operations. CACM 1 (Aug 1958), 3-6.

___. (66) ALPHA - an automatic programming system of high efficiency. JACM 13 (Jan 1966), 17-24.

Zimmer, R. Weak precedence. Proc. of the International Computing Symposium 1970 / ACM Europe, Part II (May 1970), 576-587.

# Index

Under the heading "Variables" the reader will find a list of variables used throughout several sections or chapters, together with the page numbers where they are defined or explained. Similarly, under "Procedures" appears a list of many of the procedures and functions used. A list of compilers and the places where they are used as examples of the use of compiler techniques appears under the heading "Compilers".